LABOURING CANADA

LABOURING CANADA

Class, Gender, and Race in Canadian Working-Class History

Edited by
Bryan D. Palmer & Joan Sangster

OXFORD
UNIVERSITY PRESS

OXFORD
UNIVERSITY PRESS

8 Sampson Mews, Suite 204, Don Mills, Ontario M3C 0H5

www.oupcanada.com

Oxford University Press is a department of the University of Oxford.
It furthers the University's objective of excellence in research, scholarship,
and education by publishing worldwide in

Oxford New York
Auckland Cape Town Dar es Salaam Hong Kong Karachi
Kuala Lumpur Madrid Melbourne Mexico City Nairobi
New Delhi Shanghai Taipei Toronto

With offices in
Argentina Austria Brazil Chile Czech Republic France Greece
Guatemala Hungary Italy Japan Poland Portugal Singapore
South Korea Switzerland Thailand Turkey Ukraine Vietnam

Oxford is a trade mark of Oxford University Press
in the UK and in certain other countries

Published in Canada
by Oxford University Press

Library and Archives Canada Cataloguing in Publication

Labouring Canada : class, gender, and race in Canadian
working-class history / edited by Bryan D. Palmer and Joan Sangster.

Includes bibliographical references.
ISBN 978-0-19-542533-8

1. Working class—Canada—History. 2. Social history—Canada.
I. Palmer, Bryan D., 1951–   II. Sangster, Joan, 1952–

HD8104.L34 2008   305.5'620971   C2007-906267-9

3 4 5 - 15 14 13 12
This book is printed on permanent (acid-free) paper ∞.
Printed in Canada

CONTENTS

Introduction

The study of Canadian workers has a long history. Indeed, serious examination of labour in Canada began in the late nineteenth century, as organized workers made their presence felt in a series of economic and political challenges to established elites. Advocates of labour reform charted these beginnings. With the recognition on the part of scholars and researchers—many of whom first found themselves employed in the emerging bureaucracies of the twentieth-century state—that workers, their organizations, and their movements were a force to reckon with in industrial Canada, the academic study of labour took on increasing importance from the 1920s through the 1950s. Political economists such as Harold Adams Innis played a pioneering role, but by the 1940s it was the field of labour economics, in which the major figure was Harold A. Logan, where the study of trade unions was most developed. Maverick figures such as H. Clare Pentland, the Marxist historian Stanley Ryerson, the social-democrat and constitutional authority, Eugene Forsey, and a pioneering scholar of proletarian ideas and writing, Frank Watt, worked on important studies in the 1940s, 1950s, and early 1960s, as did various historians and political scientists.

By the 1960s, a new generation of historians, many of them trained at the University of Toronto by the social-democratic biographer of J.S. Woodsworth, Kenneth McNaught, had made labour history a central subject of study. Scholars such as David J. Bercuson and Irving Martin Abella exemplified a new professional historical interest in the events and institutions that were critically important in the rise of twentieth-century Canadian labour, among them the Winnipeg General Strike and the explosive development of mass production unionism in the 1930s and 1940s. In Quebec the historical study of labour was understandably less politically-tied to the cause of the Co-operative Commonwealth Federation (CCF) and its successor, the New Democratic Party (NDP). The study of working-class life and organizations in French Canada owed more to scholarship in France, then heavily concerned with material conditions of life, social structures, and consequent mobilizations of labour movements. Much of this work was associated with Jean Hamelin of Laval University. The 1960s that saw the refinement of such scholarship was, however, itself a decade of great change. With the radicalization of student youth and the emergence of new interest in Marxism and feminism in the late 1960s, workers came to be seen as potential agents of social change, class formation was appreciated as a foundation of capitalist inequality, and the different experiences of men, women, and children within the working class were understood as centrally important in the study of labouring life. This field of study was conceived as extending well beyond labour organizations and political parties affiliated officially with trade unions, such as the CCF or NDP. All of this changed the direction of working-class history in Canada.

New concerns with aspects of workers' everyday lives and cultural experiences were brought to light, sharpening the attention paid to the labour process in settings such as factories and mines. More empathetic approaches to minority movements of revolutionaries, and a growing understanding of how so much of the history of work and labour politics was gendered as masculine and feminine produced an outpouring of new scholarship in the 1970s and 1980s. Working-class history, in its modern guise, had arrived. Historians of women were central to this development as Veronica Strong-Boag, Andrée Levesque, Linda Kealey, Joan Sangster, Bettina Bradbury, and Joy Parr produced important gendered refinements on the originally male-centred research of Gregory S. Kealey, Bryan D. Palmer, Craig Heron, Fernand Harvey, Jacques Rouillard and others. Families, neighbourhoods, parades, and taverns were studied, as well as unions and political parties. The state was scrutinized, as were employers, whose approach to workers might run the gamut from violent repression to enticing paternalisms. Situating workers' initiatives within the determining context of specific socio-economic formations, in which regional particularity, occupational structures, and the period and place of capitalist development, figured forcefully proved decisive in much of the new writing. Increasingly, this published research took on sophisticated theoretical trappings as studies grappled with the complexities of working-class life.

Solidarities of labouring Canadians loomed large, especially in moments of economic and political upheaval, but so too did fragmentations, as the divisions among workers came to be appreciated. Among these divisions the social construc-tions of 'race' were appreciated by the 1990s as especially significant. Workers came to be seen as being constructed into oppositional 'racialized' categories of settlers/Native peoples; linguistic groups (French/English); ethno-religious contingents (Irish Protes-tants/Irish Catholics); 'non-white' immigrants, such as Italians, Jews, and Ukrainians versus 'native-born' Canadians and those from the United Kingdom and northern Europe; peoples of colour, be they Asians, African Canadians, or West Indians and those workers who embraced a 'white' identity. Much scholarship in the last two decades of labour history's Canadian development has addressed the importance of 'race' and ethnicity, as the writings of Donald Avery, Franca Iacovetta, Ruth A. Frager, Adele Perry, and others indicate. A range of interdisciplinary writings rooted in sociology and political science but reaching broadly across historicized terrain, has also been particularly influential.

Our selection of articles for this volume was guided by an appreciation of the importance of class formation in Canadian society. This broad focus on class allows us to include articles on all periods of Canadian history from the late eighteenth century to the present, just as it encourages the examination of workers' lives in ways that address other identities and historicized experiences, among the most important being race, gender, family, and place (neighbourhood/community).

Class is a designation of people's place in a hierarchically-ordered society, in which the critically important defining elements are one's structural relationship to the means of production and one's ability to decide the pace, nature, and products of their daily work. Where any given Canadian is located in this relationship is measured by whether they sustain themselves through wages or modest salaries, without owning or directing the businesses and institutions in which they labour or, in contrast, manage or live off of profits generated by productive enterprises, in which a significant portion of the value created accrues to those who have managed to secure these corporations as their legal and private property. Class is thus not only an identity, though it may involve a sense of distinct identity: it entails a set of social relations shaped by political economy and power.

How this class relation manifests itself in society is an ever-changing, historical process, but it is always rooted in differential power that produces, in different periods of Canada's development, distinct outcomes. Thus in the early nineteenth century trade unions were not central institutions of labouring life precisely because a clearly-defined working class was not readily separable from other social strata. Furthermore, an array of legal and ideological baggage prohibited those who toiled in various settings from identifying themselves as a class and forming institutions like trade unions to defend their economic interests. Their social relations of class might be bounded by paternal ties to 'masters' or they might erupt in riotous confrontation on work sites like canals. A century and a half later, the trade union has arrived as a major vehicle of working-class self-activity while at the same time it exhibits strains as it is embattled from many directions. If the high-water mark of trade union accomplishment in Canada lay in the immediate post-World War II period, then as we proceed into the second decade of the twenty-first century the labouring people and their institutions seem increasingly under attack.

Understanding the many transformations in the history of work and society in Canada thus entails grappling with the complexities of class formation, and doing so in ways that come to grips with how that experience of class intersected with many other features of day-to-day life. These include leisure activities and family strategies that co-joined the production of goods and services with the reproduction of human labour and the multifaceted sides of its social and cultural being. They entail looking at changing technologies, from the introduction of sewing machines into various trades in the mid-nineteenth century to the rise of the assembly line in the interwar years of the twentieth century to late capitalism's increasing dependency on advanced systems of communication associated with the computer. As the nineteenth century gave way to the twentieth, much of the changing relations of class came to be mediated, and then decisively ordered, by the state, which evolved into a many-headed hydra whose long reach into varied quarters of everyday life paralleled the long reach of the job into families, neighbourhoods, sexualities, churches, and ethnic and racial organizations. The history of labour, as we have conceived it in *Labouring Canada*, is a class history of complex change grounded in the complicated continuity of inequality, subordination, resilience, and resistance.

This volume brings together 28 articles that chart the nature of working-class life in Canada from the fur trade era of the eighteenth and early nineteenth century to the epoch of globalization in the first years of the twenty-first century. All of the included readings have been edited and abridged so as to be accessible to an undergraduate audience. Chosen to convey the diversity of the working-class experience as well as its ongoing continuities of struggle, organization, and combativity, the collected essays are also organized chronologically and thematically. Each section is introduced by short, but fairly detailed, summaries of the issues and periods with which the articles deal and in which they can be located historically. Taken together, this body of writing introduces the changing nature of Canadian capitalism and its class relations, illuminating how men, women, and children have negotiated the fruits—bitter and sweet— of working, both for wages and in the unpaid setting of the home. In the long and changing history of labouring Canada, the people who produce the goods and services on which we all depend come alive as architects of a nation as well as members of workplaces, communities, kinship networks, unions, circles of sociability, and political organizations. If there remains much to be discussed, detailed, and debated about the working class in Canada, past and present, the articles that follow indicate how the scholarly development of the historical study of labour has established definitively for our times that it is never possible to lose sight of the ways in which class, gender, and race have framed the lives of the vast majority of the population.

Further Reading

Irving Martin Abella, *Nationalism, Communism, and Canadian Labour: The CIO, the Communist Party, and the Canadian Congress of Labour, 1935–1956* (Toronto: University of Toronto Press, 1973).

Irving Martin Abella and David Millar, eds, *The Canadian Worker in the Twentieth Century* (Toronto: Oxford University Press, 1978).

Janice Acton, et al., eds, *Women at Work: Ontario, 1850–1930* (Toronto: Women's Press, 1974).

Donald Avery, *'Dangerous Foreigners': European Immigrant Workers and Labour Radicalism in Canada, 1896–1932* (Toronto: McClelland and Stewart, 1979).

Robert Babcock, *Gompers in Canada: A Study in American Continentalism Before the First World War* (Toronto: University of Toronto Press, 1974).

David Jay Bercuson, *Confrontation at Winnipeg: Labour, Industrial Relations, and the General Strike* (Montreal and Kingston: McGill-Queen's University Press, 1974).

David J. Bercuson and David Bright, eds, *Canadian Labour History: Selected Readings* (Toronto: Copp Clark Longman, 1994).

Paul Craven, ed., *Labouring Lives: Work and Workers in 19th-Century Ontario* (Toronto: University of Toronto Press, 1995).

Michael S. Cross, *The Workingman in the Nineteenth Century* (Toronto: Oxford University Press, 1974).

Cecilia Danysk, *Hired Hands: Labour and the Development of Prairie Agriculture, 1880–1930* (Toronto: Oxford University Press, 1995).

James Doyle, *Progressive Heritage: The Evolution of a Politically Radical Literary Tradition in Canada* (Waterloo: Wilfrid Laurier University Press, 2002).

Eugene Forsey, *Trade Unions in Canada, 1812–1902* (Toronto: University of Toronto Press, 1982).

Ruth A. Frager, *Sweatshop Strife: Class, Ethnicity, and Gender in the Jewish Labour Movement in Toronto, 1900–1930* (Toronto: University of Toronto Press, 1992).

Ruth A. Frager and Carmella Patrias, *Discounted Labour: Women Workers in Canada, 1870–1939* (Toronto: University of Toronto Press, 2005).

Judy Fudge and Eric Tucker, *Labour Before the Law: The Regulation of Workers' Collective Action in Canada, 1900–1948* (Toronto: Oxford University Press, 2001).

Jean Hamelin, et al., *Les Travailleurs Québécois, 1850–1896* (Montréal: Presses de l'Université du Québec, 1974).

Jean Hamelin, et al., *Les Travailleurs Québécois, 1941–1971* (Québec: Institut supérieur de sciences humaines, 1976).

Fernand Harvey, *Révolution industrielle et travailleurs: Une enquête sur les rapports entre le capital et le travail au Québec à la fin du 19e siècle* (Montréal: Boreal Express, 1978).

Fernand Harvey, *Le mouvement ouvrier au Québec* (Montréal: Boreal Express, 1980).

Craig Heron and Robert Storey, eds, *On the Job: Confronting the Labour Process in Canada* (Montreal and Kingston: McGill-Queen's University Press, 1986).

Craig Heron, *The Canadian Labour Movement: A Short History* (Toronto: Lorimer, 1996).

Craig Heron and Steve Penfold, *The Workers' Festival: A History of Labour Day in Canada* (Toronto: University of Toronto Press, 2005).

Franca Iacovetta, et al., eds, *A Nation of Immigrants: Women, Workers, and Communities in Canadian History, 1840s–1960s* (Toronto: University of Toronto Press, 1998).

Franca Iacovetta and Mariana Valverde, eds, *Gender Conflicts: New Essays in Women's History* (Toronto: University of Toronto Press, 1992).

H.A. Innis, ed., *Labor in Canadian–American Relations* (Toronto: Ryerson Press, 1937).

Stuart Marshall Jamieson, *Times of Trouble: Labour Unrest and Industrial Conflict in Canada, 1900–1966* (Ottawa: Task Force on Labour Relations, 1972).

Michael B. Katz, Michael J. Doucet, and Mark J. Stern, *The Social Organization of Industrial Capitalism* (Cambridge, Massachusetts: Harvard University Press, 1982).

Gregory S. Kealey and Peter Warrian, eds, *Essays in Canadian Working-Class History* (Toronto: McClelland and Stewart, 1976).

Gregory S. Kealey, *Toronto Workers Respond to Industrial Capitalism, 1867–1892* (Toronto: University of Toronto Press, 1980).

Gregory S. Kealey, *Workers and Canadian History* (Montreal and Kingston: McGill-Queen's University Press, 1993).

Linda Kealey, *Enlisting Women for the Cause: Women, Labour, and the Left in Canada, 1890–1920* (Toronto: University of Toronto Press, 1998).

Mark Leier, *Red Flags and Red Tape: The Making of a Labour Bureaucracy* (Toronto: University of Toronto Press, 1995).

Mark Leier, *Rebel Life: The Life and Times of Robert Gosden—Revolutionary, Mystic, Labour Spy* (Vancouver: New Star, 1999).

Andrée Levesque, *Making and Breaking the Rules: Women in Quebec, 1919–1939* (Toronto: McClelland and Stewart, 1994).

Andrée Levesque, *Red Travellers: Jeanne Corbin and Her Comrades* (Kingston and Montreal: McGill-Queen's University Press, 2006).

H.A. Logan, *Trade Unions in Canada: Their Development and Functioning* (Toronto: Macmillan, 1948).

Laurel Sefton MacDowell, *'Remember Kirkland Lake': The Gold Miners' Strike of 1941–1942* (Toronto: University of Toronto Press, 1983).

A. Ross McCormack, *Reformers, Rebels, and Revolutionaries: The Western Canadian Radical Movement, 1899–1919* (Toronto: University of Toronto Press, 1977).

Ian McKay, ed., *For a Working-Class Culture in Canada: A Selection of Colin McKay's Writings on Sociology and Political Economy, 1897–1939* (St John's, Newfoundland: CCLH Publications, 1996).

Kenneth McNaught, 'E.P. Thompson vs Harold Logan: Writing About Labour and the Left in the 1970s', *Canadian Historical Review* 62 (June 1981): 141–68.

Kathryn McPherson, *Bedside Matters: The Transformation of Canadian Nursing, 1900–1990* (Toronto: Oxford University Press, 1996).

Desmond Morton, *Working People: An Illustrated History of the Canadian Labour Movement* (Montreal and Kingston: McGill-Queen's University Press, 1998).

Bryan D. Palmer, *A Culture in Conflict: Skilled Workers and Industrial Capitalism in Hamilton, Ontario, 1860–1914* (Montreal and Kingston: McGill-Queen's University Press, 1979).

Bryan D. Palmer, *Working-Class Experience: Rethinking the History of Canadian Labour, 1800–1991* (Toronto: McClelland and Stewart, 1992).

Joy Parr, *Labouring Children: British Immigrant Apprentices to Canada, 1869–1924* (Montreal and Kingston: McGill-Queen's University Press, 1980).

Joy Parr, *The Gender of Breadwinners: Women, Men, and Change in Two Industrial Towns, 1880–1950* (Toronto: University of Toronto Press, 1990).

H. Clare Pentland, *Labour and Capital in Canada, 1650–1860* (Toronto: Lorimer, 1981).

Adele Perry, *On the Edge of Empire: Gender, Race, and the Making of British Columbia, 1849–1871* (Toronto: University of Toronto Press, 2001).

Michael J. Piva, *The Condition of the Working Class in Toronto—1900–1921* (Ottawa: University of Ottawa Press, 1979).

Ian Radforth, *Bushworkers and Bosses: Logging in Northern Ontario* (Toronto: University of Toronto Press, 1987).

James W. Rinehart, *The Tyranny of Work: Alienation and the Labour Process* (Toronto: Harcourt, Brace, Jovanovitch, 1987).

Jacques Rouillard, *Histoire du syndicalisme du québécois* (Montreal: Boréal, 1988).

Stanley B. Ryerson, *Unequal Union: Roots of Crisis in the Canadas, 1815–1873* (Toronto: Progress, 1968).

Joan Sangster, *Dreams of Equality: Women on the Canadian Left, 1920–1950* (Toronto: McClelland and Stewart, 1989).

Joan Sangster, *Earning Respect: The Lives of Working Women in Small-Town Ontario, 1920–1960* (Toronto: University of Toronto Press, 1995).

Mercedes Steedman, *Angels of the Workplace: Women and the Construction of Gender Relations in the Canadian Clothing Industry, 1890–1940* (Toronto: Oxford University Press, 1997).

Veronica Strong-Boag, *The New Day Recalled: Lives of Girls and Women in English Canada, 1919–1939* (Toronto: Copp Clark Pitman, 1988).

Eric Tucker, *Administering Danger in the Workplace: The Law and Politics of Occupational Health and Safety Regulation in Ontario, 1850–1914* (Toronto: University of Toronto Press, 1990).

Frank Watt, 'The National Policy, the Workingman, and Proletarian Ideas in Victorian Canada', *Canadian Historical Review* 40 (March 1959): 1–26.

Labour/Le Travail 46 (Fall 2000). A special Millennium issue.

Selected Websites

Canadian Committee on Labour History and *Labour/Le Travail*: www.mun.cclh.ca

Workers Arts and Heritage Centre, Hamilton: www.wahc-museum.ca/index/html (preserves and celebrates the arts, culture and heritage of working people)

Union Learning, Athabasca University: http://unionlearning.athabascau.ca (includes information on videos and some audio clips)

Centre for the Study of Education and Work, OISE: http://www.learningwork.ca/csew

Canadian Museum of Civilization: http://www.civilization.ca/hist/labour/lab01e.html

McMaster University Labour Studies Programme, Learning Centre, Resources: http://socserv.mcmaster.ca/labourstudies/LearningCentre/index.php/ (archived articles from *The Labour Gazette*, published by the Government of Canada, dating from its inception in 1900 to the end of the 1940s)

Labor and Working Class History Association (US organization): http://www.lawcha.org/

Labour Start: www.labourstart.org (international news)

H-Labor: www.h-net.org/~labor/ (US-based discussion network, with international information)

PART I

Aboriginal Peoples and Class Formation, 1750–1900

Social and political ferment generated new academic interest in the lives of workers, immigrants, racial minorities, women and children, and Native peoples in the mid-to-late 1970s. The result was that a more complex social history began to be written, one that increasingly addressed the ways in which Canada as a developing capitalist nation state depended on the work, paid as well as unpaid, of a wide array of peoples.

A critically important subject, especially in understanding Canada's emergence out of its colonized past into its standing as a twentieth-century capitalist nation, was the formative contact experience of indigenous Aboriginal peoples and white colonizers and settlers from the British Isles, France, and elsewhere in Europe. This set the stage on which the development of capitalist markets in land, labour, and commodities could take place. The fur trade, an eighteenth and nineteenth century commercial endeavour that flourished on the basis of a seemingly insatiable European demand for animal pelts (especially beaver, used to make fashionable hats) from North America, brought white merchants and traders into close working relations with Native peoples, who trapped and prepared the furs for exchange. The fur trade was thus one of Canada's earliest examples of structured labour relations, and Native people were central to its functioning.

It is not surprising, therefore, that before the revival of working-class history in the 1970s, fur trade studies were a well-established part of Canadian academic inquiry. Harold Adams Innis's *The Fur Trade in Canada: An Introduction to Canadian Economic History* (1930) was not only a founding text of Canadian political economy. It also had a profound impact within historical and anthropological circles. But Innis concentrated almost entirely on the fur trade as a producer of wealth destined to be accumulated in its European metropolitan centres. He knew well that Native peoples had been the bedrock on which the trade rested, but he studied them barely at all.

Fur trade studies, like working-class history, changed dramatically in the mid-to-late 1970s as they began to address what Innis had failed to consider. Especially influential were the emergence of a radical, late 1960s, Native rights movement in Canada and the growing interest of historians in documenting the responses of Aboriginal peoples to colonialism.

In the past decade, Native history and working-class history have moved closer together. Historians of Aboriginal experience are using the conceptual tools and perspectives of working-class historians to explore aspects of Native history, especially as they relate to material everyday life, in which work figures centrally. At the same time, debates within Native history, and insights of historians of Canada's indigenous peoples, are redefining understandings of work and social life in the late eighteenth and nineteenth centuries. Both trends are evident in the following two articles, which illuminate ways of understanding work and workers' lives in early Canada.

Carolyn Podruchny uses sources ranging from Hudson's Bay Company records to travellers' accounts and court records, to study the fur trade as a working environment. Rather than see those labouring in the trade as merely cogs in a wheel of exchange set in motion by those who profited from the transatlantic commerce in pelts, Podruchny focuses on the actions, decisions, and needs of those whose labour was pivotal in generating wealth out of the harvests of Canada's streams and forests. Drawing on the insights of E.P. Thompson, a historian of the English working class whose insistence on the need to study the self-activity of the labouring poor was highly influential in the United States and Canada, Podruchny recasts our understanding of how rigidly controlled the workforce of the Montreal-organized section of fur trade voyageurs and clerks actually was. To be sure, Podruchny demonstrates the importance of elite-orchestrated systems of paternalism and servitude. These systems could limit decisively what it was possible for early fur trade labour to do. Yet she also details the many ways in which such workers shaped their daily work lives, sometimes rebelling against the harsh disciplines characteristic of fur trade labour, which has often been seen as narrowly and legally defined as a master–servant relation. In the complex tug of war and 'theatre of performance' that governed work relations in the fur trade, Podruchny conveys effectively that this was a labour relation of power imbalances, but it was not one in which the subordinated workers were entirely at the mercy of their masters. Finally, drawing on insights from gender history and feminism, Podruchny also shows that fur trade labour was not only shaped by class difference, but also by prevailing notions of masculinity, which could both encourage labour accommodation *and* spawn rebelliousness and resistance.

John Lutz's article moves us ahead in time, exploring forms of Aboriginal labour in British Columbia outside of the fur trade. Earlier interpretations of Native history, published in the 1970s and 1980s, had sometimes inadvertently implied that Native peoples did not, for the most part, participate in waged work as industrial capitalism sank its late-nineteenth-century roots in British Columbia. The suggestion was that as First Nations people were pushed from the workforce by an influx of white settlers and wage labourers, they chose to pursue traditional means of subsistence largely outside of the developing capitalist economy.

Though this could well have happened to some extent, it was by no means the entire story. Lutz points out that Aboriginal peoples were engaged in a variety of wage labour pursuits in the period from the establishment of the Colony of Vancouver Island in 1849 to 1890, after which BC was incorporated as a province of Canada. Indeed, as late as 1871, Native peoples were the majority of the west coast population and the majority of its wage-earning workforce, with jobs in mining, lumbering, and agriculture predominating. Given the centrality of Native workers in nineteenth century British Columbia, Lutz draws on insights from working-class history to offer an explanation of why it was critically important for the ascendant capitalist state to ban the potlatch, a ceremony of deep cultural, social, and economic significance to many Native peoples in BC. In addition, he pushes labour historians to reconsider the centrality of Aboriginal experience in the early working-class history of Canada's west coast.

As the Podruchny and Lutz articles indicate, then, the histories of Native peoples and workers are neither separable nor able to be rewritten without understanding the extent to which they are deeply entwined. An important undertaking in future writings on work and workers will necessarily be to bring Native peoples into the picture of how the Canadian working class came into being and has been transformed over time.

Further Reading

Ron G. Bourgeault, 'Aboriginal Labour in the North-West', *Prairie Forum* 31, 2 (Fall 2006): 273–304.

Jennifer Brown, *Strangers in Blood: Fur-Trade Company Families in Indian Country* (Vancouver: University of British Columbia Press, 1980).

Edith Burley, *Servants of the Honourable Company: Work, Discipline, and Conflict in the Hudson's Bay Company* (Toronto: Oxford University Press, 1997).

Paige Raibmon, 'The Practice of Everyday Colonialism: Indigenous Women at Work in the Hop Fields and Tourist Industry of Puget Sound', *Labor: Studies in Working-Class History of the Americas* 3 (Fall 2006): 23–56.

Sylvia Van Kirk, *Many Tender Ties: Women in Fur-Trade Society in Western Canada, 1670–1870* (Winnipeg: Watson & Dwyer, 1980).

Visual Resources

National Film Board [NFB]: *Women in the Shadows* (1993), dir. Norma Bailey, 55 minutes (a woman probes her Métis roots, examining the Native and Métis women who were an integral part of fur trade society).

CHAPTER 1

Unfair Masters and Rascally Servants? Labour Relations Among Bourgeois, Clerks, and Voyageurs in the Montreal Fur Trade, 1780–1821

Carolyn Podruchny

The history of working peoples in the fur trade has recently become a subject of concentrated interest.[1] The publication of Edith Burley's *Servants of the Honourable Company*, which explores the master and servant relationship between Orkney workers and Hudson's Bay Company (HBC) officers stands as an important development in focusing attention squarely on the workers themselves, and demonstrates the extent of their power through insubordination and resistance.[2] A general pattern of master and servant relations existed among most fur trade companies and their labour forces which was similar to other eighteenth-century labour contexts. Servants signed a contract for several years, agreeing to be obedient and loyal to their master in exchange for food, shelter, and wages.[3] However, labour relations were highly influenced by local conditions. The personality of individual masters, the availability of food resources, the difficulty of work, and the cultural conventions of the labour force all affected the nature of the master–servant relationship. As many fur trade scholars have contended, there was never just one fur trade: it varied tremendously in different contexts (Francis and Morantz, 1983: 167). The same can be said of labour relations in the fur trade. Process and flexibility were dominant characteristics in the relationships between masters and servants. . . .

After the 1763 conquest of New France, the fur trade operating out of Montreal reorganized under the direction of Scottish, English, American, and a few French Canadian managers who called themselves *bourgeois*.[4] These companies, which eventually merged into the [North West Company] NWC, hired French Canadian men mainly from parishes around Montreal and Trois Rivières to transport goods and furs from Montreal to the North American interior during the summer months. They were also hired to work year-round at the company posts and handled trading with Native peoples. There is no question that the job of voyageurs was difficult. They performed near miraculous feats of transporting goods and furs over immense distances and undertook challenging canoe routes. Work at the interior posts was easier than that on the summer canoe brigades, but voyageurs were responsible for a tremendous range of duties, which included construction, artisan crafts, hunting, fishing, and trading. Threats to voyageurs' well-being, including starvation and physically debilitating overwork, came mostly from the harsh environment, but hostile Native peoples and cruel masters could contribute to the misery. Despite the harsh working and living conditions, voyageurs developed a reputation as strong, capable, and cheerful, although sometimes unreliable, servants. The writings of the bourgeois and clerks working in the trade reveal a deep admiration for their skill and effectiveness as workers, and a tolerance for petty theft and minor insolence.[5] This article concerns itself with two questions: why did voyageurs put up with their tough lot without overt revolt, and what was the substance of the relationship between voyageurs and their masters? Because voyageurs were primarily non-literate and left little record of their experiences, we must rely on the writings of a diverse group of literate outsiders, including the powerful fur trade partners, lowly clerks, and assorted travellers to the north-west interior. A close and extensive examination reveals a complex network of accommodation and resistance in the master and servant relationship. This article maps out some patterns in the period from 1780 to 1821, which was the height of competition between trade companies and the expansion into the interior.

The Montreal fur trade labour system was organized around indentured servitude, paternalism, and cultural hegemony. The fur trade managers and clerks acted as paternal masters directing the labour of voyageurs. Voyageurs signed a legal contract, or *engagement*, which established the framework for the paternal relationship. The principal tenet of the contract dictated that servants obey their masters in exchange for board and wages. Voyageurs and their masters, however, interpreted the contract differently in particular contexts. Their diverging and situational 'reading' of the legal contract led to the emergence of a 'social contract' which constituted the actual working relationship between the two groups. The 'social contract' was expressed in the customs which came to characterize the fur trade workplace and the dialogue between servants and masters over acceptable working conditions. Masters tried to enforce obedience, loyalty, and hard work among voyageurs, while the voyageurs struggled to ensure that their working conditions were fair and comfortable, and that masters fully met their paternal obligations. Voyageurs exercised relative cultural autonomy on the job, and often controlled the workpace and scope of their duties. Their

masters, however, maintained ultimate authority by exercising their right to hire and fire voyageurs and by successfully profiting in the trade.

Although masters and servants can be understood as constituting two loose but distinct 'classes' within the fur trade, it is important to be aware of the ranges within each class in terms of power, authority, and duty. Some masters were junior clerks, bound in a paternal relationship with senior clerks and partners. These clerks were paid a smaller annual salary than senior bourgeois, and did not hold shares in the partnerships that made up the Montreal fur trading companies. Partners were granted voting privileges in business meetings, in addition to their company shares and higher salaries.[6] *Engagés* also had varying status. At the bottom were seasonally employed summer men, referred to as *mangeurs du lard*, or Porkeaters, who paddled between Montreal and the Great Lakes. Wintering *engagés*, or *homes du nord*, who paddled canoes to and worked at the interior posts, scorned these greenhorns. Within the canoe, paddlers called middlemen or *milieu*, were subject to the authority of the foreman and steersman, or *devant* and *gouvernail*, who usually acted as canoe and brigade leaders. Some estimates suggest that these *bouts* could earn from one third to five times as much as paddlers.[7] Interpreters and guides, paid usually twice or three times as much as other *engagés*, also assumed more authority by their greater wealth and knowledge.[8]

Although the ethnic divisions did not entirely follow occupational lines, the Montreal bourgeois became more and more British after the 1763 Conquest, while the voyageurs were primarily French Canadians. British discrimination against French Canadians, and fellow-feeling among voyageurs contributed to the social distance between masters and servants. Voyageurs lived within a different cultural ethos than that of the bourgeois, one which emphasized independence, strength, courage, and cultural adaptation rather than profit, obedience, and cultural supremacy. These different frames of reference distanced voyageurs from their masters, and frequently impeded harmonious workplace relations. Despite the range of roles within each group, the division between bourgeois and voyageur, or master and servant, served as a basic social organization of the fur trade (Brown, 1980).[9] Class, ethnic, and cultural differences operated in conjunction to create a paternalistic and hegemonic labour system.

Masters and servants accepted their positions as rulers and ruled. Voyageurs could challenge the substance and boundaries of their jobs and loyalty to their masters without contesting the fundamental power dynamics. Voyageurs' acceptance of their masters' domination was based on a deeply held belief in the legitimacy of paternalism. Voyageurs certainly became discontented, resisted their masters' authority, and sometimes revolted, but it was outside of their conception of the world to challenge the hegemonic culture.[10] Thus, the structure of cultural hegemony was not inconsistent with the presence of labour strife. . . . Hegemony offered, in the words of E.P. Thompson, writing of the eighteenth-century English plebians, a 'bare architecture of a structure of relations of domination and subordination, but within that architectural tracery many different scenes could be set and different dramas enacted' (Thompson, 1993: 85–6).

What 'scenes of rule' were enacted in the north-west fur trade? The mutuality intrinsic to paternalism and hegemony governed social relations and made up the substance of the 'social contract' between the bourgeois and voyageurs in the northwest. Each party accepted their roles and responsibilities in the master and servant relationship, but they pressed the boundaries, and tried to shape the relationships to best suit their desires

and needs. The difficulty masters encountered in enforcing authority, and the precariousness of survival meant they had to be particularly responsive to their servants. Part of hegemony involved appearances (Thompson, 1993: 45–6). Masters often engaged in self-consciousness public theatre, while voyageurs offered their own form of counter-theatre. . . .

The labour contracts of all partnerships, both within and outside of the NWC were remarkably similar. Contracts reveal voyageurs' names, parishes of origin, destination in the northwest, job positions, lengths of term, and salaries. The language of most contracts underscored the paternal nature of the relationship, requiring voyageurs to obey their masters, to work responsibly and carefully, to be honest and well-behaved, to aid the bourgeois in making a profit, and to remain in the service. . . .

Masters were bound to pay the voyageurs' wages and provide them with equipment. The substance of the equipment, and the provision of food and welfare for the *engagé*, were rarely specified in contracts, and thus provided one of the few places for obvious negotiation between the masters and servants.[11] Custom came to dictate that equipment consisted of one blanket, one shirt, and one pair of trousers (Mackenzie, 101: 34).

In order to enforce the terms of the legal contracts, bourgeois tried to regulate their servants through legal and state sanctions. In January 1778, an official of the NWC sent a memorandum to Governor Guy Carleton asking him 'that it be published before the Traders and their Servants that the latter must strictly conform to their agreements, which should absolutely be in writing or printed, and before witnesses if possible, as many disputes arise from want of order in this particular.' . . .

Bourgeois on occasion turned to the law to enforce the terms of the contract. Voyageurs were charged with breaking contracts, mainly for deserting, rather than for insolence or disobedi-ence.[12] The files of the court of Quarter Sessions in the District of Montreal reveal a range of cases: voyageurs accepted wages from one employer while already working for another, they obtained advance wages without appearing for the job, and they deserted the service.[13] Cases of voya-geur desertion and theft can also be found in the records of the Montreal civil court. In 1803, the British government passed the Canada Jurisdiction Act by which criminal offences committed in the 'Indian territories' could be tried in Lower Canada, and the five JPs named were all prominent fur trade bourgeois, although the court's power remained limited.[14] It is difficult to determine the effective-ness of court action to control workers, especially since prosecution rates have not survived in most of the records. Presumably the bourgeois would not continue to press charges if their efforts did not pay off. Yet pressing charges against voyageurs did not seem to deter them from continuing to desert, cheat contract terms, and steal from their employers.

Other efforts to control workers included cooperation between companies to limit contract-jumping and blacklisting deserters. In 1800 NWC officer William McGillivray wrote to Thomas Forsyth of Forsyth, Ogilvy, and McKenzie:

> I agree with you that protecting Deserters would be a dangerous Practice and very perni-cious to the Trade and fully sensible of this when any Man belonging to People opposed to The North West Company have happened to come to our Forts, we have told the Master of such to come for them and that they should not be in any way wise prevented from taking them back.

. . . Voyageurs occasionally took their employing masters to court, most often to sue for wages.[15] Cases of this kind were widespread in all sorts of labour contracts in New France and Lower Canada, so it is not surprising that voyageurs followed suit. However, servants were not usually successful in claiming wages for jobs which they had deserted, or where they had disobeyed their masters (Hogg and Shulman, 1993). The colonial government and legal system supported fur trade labour contracts, but the contracts were difficult to enforce because of the limits of the policing and justice systems in the northwest. Masters thus relied more on the 'social contract' which they were constantly negotiating with their servants.

Masters and voyageurs had different views of their 'social contract', which frequently resulted in rocky negotiations. They agreed that servants were supposed to obey their masters' requirements to trade successfully in exchange for fair board and wages. Their divergent readings of 'the deal' were based on different ideas of what was fair. Estab-lishing a mutual understanding of obligations was easier if servants respected their masters. Servants respected those masters who they regarded as tough but evenhanded.

How did the masters command and maintain their authority? In many historic circumstances, masters turned to physical might or the law as a principal vehicle for hegemony. But at the height of fur trade competition, the arm of the law was short and the high value of labour discour-aged masters from physically intimidating their workers. Masters relied on paternalistic authority as an accepted ideology to justify and bolster their might. The ideology was expressed in the 'theatre of daily rule' (Thompson, 1993: 43, 45–6). . . . They ensured their access to more and better food, fancier clothing, and better sleeping conditions than voyageurs (Vibert, 1997: 110–12). Further in the interior, away from the larger fur trade admin-istrative centres, bourgeois and clerks had to rely on inexpensive symbols and actions to enforce their authority. Carefully maintained social isolation, differential work roles, control over scarce resources, reputation, and ability all symbolized master's authority (Hamilton, 1990).

Differentiation in work roles was very apparent in travel. Bourgeois were usually passengers aboard canoes, and only helped their men paddle and portage in cases of extreme jeopardy. At times the rituals of travel situated bourgeois at the head of a great procession. . . . At posts, bourgeois and clerks did not participate in the vigorous round of activities which kept the post functioning smoothly, such as constructing and maintaining houses, building furniture, sleighs and canoes, gathering firewood, hunting, and preparing food. Rather, these masters kept accounts, managed the wares and provisions, and initiated trade with Native peoples. . . .

Probably the greatest challenges the bourgeois and clerks faced in asserting authority and controlling workers came from the circumstance of the fur trade itself—the great distances along fur trade routes between posts, and the difficulties of transportation and communication. The arduous job of traversing an unfamiliar and inhospitable terrain led to frequent accidents. The incomplete nature of the sources obscure any measurement of mortality rates, but the writings of the bourgeois are filled with literally hundreds of cases of trading parties losing their way along routes, injuring themselves or perishing in canoeing accidents, being attacked by bears, and starving, to name a few of the mishaps.[16]

Masters and voyageurs dealt with the danger which infused the fur trade in a particular way. Both social groups idealized strength, toughness, and fortitude. Voyageurs competed with each other to perform awesome feats of dexterity and endurance.[17] They played rough and risk-taking games and tried to push themselves beyond their limits. In doing so, they tried to distract themselves from, and desensitize themselves to the risks inherent in fur trading and the deaths, accidents, and illnesses around them. Rather than being overwhelmed by the danger and tragedy, they made a virtue of necessity and flaunted their indifference. By incorporating manly violence and aggression into daily life, in their competitions and brawling, men could toughen themselves for the challenges of their jobs.[18] . . . Bourgeois encouraged the 'rugged' ethos of the voyageurs, which conveniently suited their agenda for quick, efficient, and profitable fur trade operations.[19] In some instances, bourgeois had to remind voyageurs of their manly pride in skill and endurance. . . .

Accommodation among voyageurs, clerks, and bourgeois made up part of the master and servant relationship. They worked closely for long periods of time, often shared living quarters, and faced many calamities and adventures together. As many disputes were caused by shortages of provisions, the surest way in which bourgeois and clerks could ensure loyalty was to provide plenty of good food for their men. Bourgeois and clerks fostered accommodation by meeting other paternal duties, such as attempting to protect their men from dangers in the workplace, providing medicines, and treating men with respect. Masters also solidified their hegemony through generosity and kindness, reminiscent of a kind of feudal largesse. Extra rations of alcohol and food, known as *regales*, were provided on significant occasions, such as settling accounts and signing new engagements. Routine 'rewards', such as the customary provision of drams at portages, were also incorporated into the more tedious aspects of fur trade work. Sometimes masters' generosity was self-interested. When McKay gave his men moose skin to make themselves shoes, mittens, and blankets to last them through the winter, he warned them that 'we have a strong opposition to contend with this year' and that they must be ready to go at a moment's notice.[20] His gifts no doubt consolidated his authority, but they also helped the voyageurs to perform their duties more effectively.

Despite these points of accommodation, harmony in the workplace was continually under stress as voyageur resistance to master authority characterized labour relations in the fur trade. Voyageurs' discontents focused on such unsuitable working and living conditions as poor rations, or unreasonable demands by masters. Voyageurs turned to strategies such as complaining to their bourgeois and attempting to bargain for better working conditions to highlight their concerns and initiate change. Like the Orcadians working for the HBC, individual action was a more common form of worker resistance than was organized collective protest (Burley, 1997: 118–20).

Complaining by the voyageurs became a form of 'counter-theatre', which contested bourgeois hegemonic prerogatives. Just as the bourgeois often asserted their hegemony in a theatrical style, especially with canoe processions, the voyageurs also asserted their presence by 'a theatre of threat and sedition' (Thompson, 1993: 67). . . . Voyageurs sometimes chose to limit the theatre of resistance to a small, and perhaps more effective scale by complaining to their bourgeois in private, so that they would not appear weak in front of the other men. . . . Often voyageurs restricted their complaining in front of the bourgeois to avoid losing favour. If they approached the bourgeois or clerk individually with strategic concerns, their demands were more likely to be met than if they openly abused their masters for unspecified grievances.

When labour was scarce, men often bargained for better wages, both individually and in groups. In a large and organized show of resistance in the summer of 1803, men at Kaministiquia refused to work unless they received a higher salary.[21] However, these types of group efforts to increase wages were more rare than the relatively common occurrence of men trying to individually bargain for better remuneration or conditions. . . . Voyageurs could refuse to do tasks outside the normal range of their duties without extra pay as a means of increasing their wages.[22] They also frequently demanded better working conditions. Most often their concerns centred on safety, and they could refuse to take unreasonable risks.[23] Men with valued skills and knowledge, such as interpreters and guides, were in the best position to bargain for better working conditions and more pay.[24] Because fur trade labour was frequently scarce, and the mortality rate was high, skilled men were valued. Masters often overlooked servant transgressions and met servant demands in an effort to maintain their services.

Voyageurs also attempted to deceive their masters by pretending to be ill, or by lying about resources and Native peoples in the area to evade work. It is difficult to judge the extent to which voyageurs tried to trick their masters, especially when they were successful. However, hints of this practice, and suspicions of bourgeois and clerks emerge frequently in fur trade journals, suggesting that the practice was widespread. In December 1818, stationed near the Dauphin River, George Nelson became frustrated with one of his men, Welles, who frequently sneaked in 'holiday' time by travelling slowly or claiming to be lost.[25] Less suspecting bourgeois probably did not catch the 'dirty tricks' more careful voyageurs played on them regularly. Some masters, however, questioned their men's dubious actions and sent out 'spies' to ensure that voyageurs were working honestly.[26] Other deceptions were of a more serious nature. Alexander Mackenzie was suspicious that his interpreters were not telling prospective Native trading partners what Mackenzie intended, which could have serious repercussions for the trade.[27]

When efforts to deceive their masters were frustrated, voyageurs could become sullen and indolent, working slowly and ineffectively, and even openly defying bourgeois orders. In one case in the fall of 1800, while trying to set out from Fort Chipewyan, James Porter had to threaten to seize the wages of a man who refused to embark. When the voyageur reluctantly complied he swore that the devil should take him for submitting to the bourgeois.[28] More serious breaches of the master and servant contract included stealing provisions from cargo. Though Edward Umfreville kept up a constant watch over the merchandise in his canoes, a father and son managed to steal a nine gallon keg of mixed liquor.[29] George Nelson described the pilfering of provisions as routine.[30] Men also sometimes stole provisions to give extra food to their girlfriends or wives (Coues, 1897: 25). For the Orcadians working in the HBC service, Burley characterizes this type of counter-theatre—working ineffectively and deceiving masters—as both a neglect of duty and as an attempt to control the work process (Burley, 1997: 139–44). The same applies to the voyageurs.

One area of particular unease between voyageurs and masters was the issue of voyageurs freetrading with Native peoples. Unlike the HBC, the Montreal fur trading companies did not prohibit voyageurs from trading with Native peoples on the side to augment their income; some masters even expected them to do so as long as they did not abuse the privilege (Mackenzie, 1801: 34).[31] However, masters were often upset to find their men trading with Native peoples because they wanted to concentrate the profit into their company's hands, and considered freetrading as 'contrary to the established rules of the trade and the general practice among the natives' (Ross, 1855: 159). . . .

Voyageurs sometimes moved out of the 'counter-theatre of daily resistance' to engage in 'swift, direct action' against their masters' rule. Deserting the service was an outright breach of the master and servant contract.[32] Desertion should not be viewed as the single and straightforward phenomenon of voyageurs quitting their jobs. Rather, voyageurs deserted for a variety of purposes. Temporary desertions could provide a means of shopping for a better job. Men deserted when they were ill and needed time to recuperate.[33] Men also deserted when they thought their lives might be in danger, as was the case in March 1805, when servants of . . . the NWC . . . ran off from the fishery at Lac La Pluie because they feared the Native people there wanted to kill them (Gates, 1965: 233–4). Voyageurs felt they could desert because they had a clear notion of their rights as workers which was instilled by the reciprocal obligations of paternalism. This may be one of the more significant differences between Orcadians working for the HBC and the voyageurs. Orcadians did not desert very often because of the lack of 'desirable places to go'. Orcadians would most often desert to NWC posts, while voyageurs more often became freemen, joined Native families, or returned to the St Lawrence valley (Burley, 1997: 153–4).

As part of the continual negotiation of the master and servant 'social contract', bourgeois and clerks responded to voyageurs' counter-theatre with intense performances of authority. They disciplined their men for transgressions of the master and servant contract, and sought to encourage voyageur obedience. Servant privileges, such as the provision of *regales* or sale of liquor might be curtailed or denied.[34] Bourgeois and clerks also frequently humiliated and intimidated their men. . . . This kind of ritualized public shaming reinforced masculine ideals of effectiveness and skill. On an expedition to the Missouri in 1805, one of Larocque's men wished to remain with Charles McKenzie's party. Larocque became angry and told the man his courage failed him like an old woman, which threw the man into a violent fit of anger.[35] On occasion, a voyageur could be whipped for delinquency,[36] and bourgeois and clerks sometimes used the fear of starvation as a means of asserting authority over their men.[37]

In cases of severe dereliction, bourgeois could take the liberty of firing their employees.[38] In some cases, voyageurs were happy to be let go because they desired to become freemen. Nelson fired Joseph Constant, for example, for his 'fits of ill humour without cause and Constant went on to become a prosperous independent trader'.[39] However, it was a very serious matter when voyageurs decided to quit. Bourgeois and clerks made efforts to recoup deserters, and could punish them with confinement.

The usual difficulties of the weather, accidents, and the constant challenge of the strenuous work could lead to high levels of stress and to anxieties among bourgeois, clerks, and voyageurs. Voyageurs' blunders, lost and broken equipment, and voyageur insolence often exacerbated tensions (Coues, 1800: 114). . . . On rare occasions violence punctuated the generalized tension of master–servant relations in the fur trade. Mutual resentments could lead to brawls between the masters and servants. More typically tensions in the master and servant relationship were expressed in nastiness and unfairness, rather than violence. Motivated by the desire to save money and gain the maximum benefit from their workers, bourgeois pushed their men to work hard, which could result in ill will. Most serious cases of ill will and injustice concerned bourgeois selling goods to voyageurs at inflated prices and encouraging voyageurs to go into debt as soon as they entered fur trade service. It is difficult to find many instances of 'bad faith' in bourgeois writings, as they would not likely dwell on their cruelty as masters, nor reveal their unfair tricks. However, travellers, critics of fur trade companies, and disgruntled employees provide

clues. . . . Lord Selkirk, certainly no fan of the NWC, criticized the bourgeois . . . for exploiting their men, pointing out that *engagés* often left their French Canadian families in distress, and were unable to provide for them because the cost of goods in the interior was double or triple the price in Lower Canada, and men were usually paid in goods rather than cash. The NWC saved further costs on men's wages by encouraging addiction to alcohol, and then paying wages in rum at inflated prices. The Company placed no ceiling on its men's credit, so that many of them fell deeply into debt (Selkirk, 1816). . . .

Voyageur responses to the cruelty of bourgeois and clerks could reach intense heights in the ongoing counter-theatre of resistance. Ill will between servants and masters could impede work. Sometimes the tensions were so strong that voyageurs refused to share the fruits of their hunting and fishing with their masters.[40] The more outrageous instances of masters abusing servants could lead to collective resistance among the voyageurs in the form of strikes or mass desertion. When a voyageur named Joseph Leveillé was condemned by the Montreal Quarter Sessions to the pillory for having accepted the wages of two rival fur-trading firms in 1794, a riot ensued. A group made up largely of voyageurs hurled the pillory into the St Lawrence River and threatened to storm the prison. The prisoner was eventually released and no one was punished for the incident.[41] . . .

On occasion voyageurs deserted *en masse* during cargo transports or exploration missions. In these cases men worked closely in large groups doing essentially the same difficult and dangerous tasks. Communication, the development of a common attitude to work, and camaraderie fostered a collective consciousness and encouraged collective action. In the summer of 1794 a Montreal brigade at Lac La Pluie attempted to strike for higher wages. . . . When they arrived at Lac La Pluie, the brigade demanded higher wages and threatened to return to Montreal without the cargo. The bourgeois initially prevailed upon a few of the men to abandon the strike. Soon after most of the men went back to work, and the ringleaders were sent to Montreal in disgrace (Morton, 1929: 6–7).

Efforts at collective action in the northwest did not always end in failure. In his third expedition to the Missouri Country in fall 1805 and winter 1806, Charles McKenzie's crew of four men deserted. They had been lodged with Black Cat, a chief in a Mandan Village, who summoned McKenzie to his tent to inform McKenzie of their desertion. The men had traded away all of their property to Native people and intended to do the same with McKenzie's property, but Black Cat secured it. When McKenzie declared he would punish his men, Black Cat warned that the Native people would defend the voyageurs. When McKenzie tried to persuade the men to return to service, they would not yield (Wood and Thiessen, 1985). . . .

Despite the occasions of mass actions, voyageurs more often acted individually than collectively. Their most powerful bargaining tool in labour relations was the option of desertion. The decision to desert could be caused by any number of poor working conditions, such as bad food, an unfair master, and difficult journeys. Voyageurs used desertion often as a means of improving their working conditions rather than quitting their jobs. Although bourgeois took voyageurs to court for deserting their contracts, the measure had little effect as voyageurs continued to desert anyway. The option to desert acted as a safety valve, relieving pressure from the master and servant relationship. If voyageurs were very unhappy with their master, they could leave to work for another company, return to Lower Canada, or become freemen. This safety valve worked against a collective voyageur consciousness. Collective action was also hindered

because voyageurs valued independence (Ross, 1855). They left farms where feudal relationships prevailed to enter into contracted servitude, but part of their pull to the northwest may have been the promise of a more independent way of life than that on the Lower Canadian farm. Voyageurs idealized freemen and many chose this path, becoming independent hunters and petty traders, living primarily off the land with their Native families.[42]

Some permanent deserters maintained a casual relationship with fur trading companies, serving the occasional limited contract, or selling furs and provisions. One man, Brunet, was forced to desert because his Native wife insisted on it. He rejoined the company under a freer contract. His wife began again to pressure him to desert the company and live with her Native relatives.[43] Another man named Vivier decided to quit his contract in November 1798 because he could not stand living with Native people, as he was ordered to do by his bourgeois, John Thomson. . . . Voyageurs may have returned to work for fur trader companies because they could not find enough to eat, or desired the protection that a post provided. Fear of starvation and the dangers of the northwest may have discouraged voyageurs from deserting in the first place. In one case, Alexander Henry the Younger came across a pond where André Garreau, a NWC deserter, had been killed in 1801 with five Mandans by a Swiss party.[44]

Although it is difficult to quantify the occurrence of turbulence and accommodation in the relations between masters and servants, negotiations over acceptable labour conditions dominated the northwest fur trade. Masters controlled the workforce by ensuring that all men immediately became indebted to their company, and by being the sole providers of European goods in the interior. Masters also capitalized on the risk-taking and tough masculine ethos to encourage a profitable work pace. However, their best way to maintain order was to impress their men with their personal authority which was garnered by a strong manner, bravery, and effectiveness. Formal symbols, such as dress, ritual celebrations, access to better provisions, and a lighter workload reminded voyageurs of the superior status and power of their bourgeois. This 'theatre of daily rule' helped to lay out the substance of the hegemonic structure of paternal authority. Masters also turned to the courts to prosecute their men for breaches of contract, and attempted to cooperate with other companies to regulate the workforce, but these methods were far from successful in controlling their voyageurs. The 'social contract' overshadowed the legal contract between masters and servants, establishing an effective working relationship that was key to ensuring a well-functioning trade and high profits.

In turn, voyageurs asserted their cultural autonomy and resisted master authority. Their 'counter-theatre' shaped the working environment. Voyageurs generally had very high performance standards for work, which were bolstered by masculine ideals of strength, endurance, and risk-taking. Nonetheless, voyageurs created a space to continually challenge the expectations of their masters, in part through their complaining. They also set their own pace, demanded adequate and even generous diets, refused to work in bad weather, and frequently worked to rule. When masters made unreasonable demands or failed to provide adequate provisions, voyageurs responded by working more slowly, becoming insolent, and occasionally freetrading and stealing provisions.

More extreme expressions of discontent included turning to the Lower Canadian courts for justice, but, like the bourgeois and clerks, voyageurs found that their demands were better met by challenging the social, rather than the legal, contract. Their strongest bargaining tool proved to be deserting the service, which they sometimes did *en masse*. Overall, voyageurs acted more individually than collectively, as the option to desert the service acted more as a safety valve against the development of a collective voyageur consciousness.

The master and servant relationship was thus a fragile balance, constantly being negotiated. Ruling-class domination was an on-going process where the degree of legitimation was always uneven and the creation of counter-hegemonies remained a live option. E.P. Thompson's emphasis on theatre and the symbolic expression of hegemony ring true for the voyageurs and bourgeois, whose power struggles were as often about respect and authority as about decent wages and provisions (Thompson, 1993: 74–5). The difficult working conditions, regular fear of starvation, and absence of a police force positioned labour mediation in the forefront of the trade and strengthened the symbolic power of the 'theatre of daily rule'. The 'social contract' between the masters and servants overshadowed their legal contract, and determined the day-to-day relations between the two groups. Frequently, accommodation allowed the fur trade to run smoothly, and voyageurs and bosses cooperated, especially in the face of external threats. Yet just as often, labour disputes and power struggles characterized the trade.

Notes

1. Some broader studies of labour and capital in early Canadian history briefly mention fur trade workers, such as H. Clare Pentland, *Labour and Capital in Canada, 1650–1860* (Toronto: James Lorimer & Co., 1981), 30–3; and Bryan D. Palmer, *Working-Class Experience: Rethinking the History of Canadian Labour, 1800–1991* (Toronto: McClelland and Stewart, 1992), 35–6. European labourers first received significant examination by Jennifer S.H. Brown, *Strangers in Blood: Fur Trade Families in Indian Country*

(Vancouver, UBC Press, 1980). Native labourers have been subject to some examination by Carol M. Judd, 'Native Labour and Social Stratification in the Hudson's Bay Company's Northern Department, 1770–1870', *Canadian Review of Sociology and Anthropology* 17, 4 (November 1980): 305–14.

2. Edith I. Burley, *Servants of the Honourable Company: Work, Discipline, and Conflict in the Hudson's Bay Company, 1770–1879* (Toronto, New York, and Oxford: Oxford University Press, 1997); Philip Goldring first began to compile information on labourers in *Papers on the Labour System of the Hudson's Bay Company, 1821–1900*, Volume I, Manuscript Report Series, no. 362, Parks Canada (Ottawa: Ministry of Supply and Services, 1979). Also see Ron C. Bourgeault, 'The Indian, the Métis and the Fur Trade: Class, Sexism and Racism in the Transition from "Communism" to Capitalism', *Studies in Political Economy: A Social Review* 12 (Fall 1983): 45–80, and Glen Makahonuk, 'Wage-Labour in the Northwest Fur Trade Economy, 1760–1849', *Saskatchewan History* 41 (Winter 1988): 1–17.

3. For a brief report of master and servant law in a colonial setting see Douglas Hay and Paul Craven, 'Master and Servant in England and the Empire: A Comparative Study', *Labour/Le Travail* 31 (Spring 1993): 175–84.

4. The term 'bourgeois' was used in eighteenth- and nineteenth-century Canada to refer to the Montreal fur trade merchants and managers, which included company partners and all but the most junior clerks.

5. For a representative example see W. Kaye Lamb, ed., *Sixteen Years in Indian Country: The Journal of Daniel Williams Harmon, 1800–1816* (Toronto: Macmillan Company of Canada, 1957), 197–8.

6. See Toronto, Ontario Archives (hereafter OA), North West Company Collection (hereafter NWCC), MU 2199, Box 4, No. 1 (Photostat of original), 'An Account of the Athabasca Indians by a Partner of the North West Company, 1795', revised 4 May 1840 (Forms part of the manuscript entitled 'Some Account of the North West Company', by Roderick Mackenzie, director of the North West Company. Original at McGill Rare Books (hereafter MRB), Masson Collection (hereafter MC), C18, Microfilm reel #22. Photostat can also be found at Library and Archives of Canada (hereafter LAC), MC, MG19 C1, vol. 55, Microfilm reel #C-15640), 51.

7. See George Heriot, *Travels Through the Canadas, Containing a Description of the Picturesque Scenery on Some of the Rivers and Lakes; with an Account of the Productions, Commerce, and Inhabitants of those Provinces* (Philadelphia: M. Carey, 1813), 254; and MRB, MC, C27, Microfilm reel #13, Roderick Mackenzie, Letters Inward [all the letters are from W. Ferdinand Wentzel, Forks, Mackenzie River], 1807–1824, pp. 3, 23.

8. See 'An Account of the Athabasca Indians by a Partner of the North West Company, 1795', 51; and Alexander Mackenzie, Esq., 'A General History of the Fur Trade from Canada to the North-West', *Voyages from Montreal on the River St Laurence through the Continent of North American to the Frozen and Pacific Oceans in the years 1789 and 1793 with a Preliminary Account of the Rise, Progress, and Present State of the Fur Trade of that Country* (London: R. Noble, Old Bailey, 1801), 34.

9. Also see E.P. Thompson's discussion of 'patricians' and 'plebs' in *Customs in Common: Studies in Traditional Popular Culture* (New York: The New Press, 1993), 16–17.

10. For a discussion on cultural hegemony and the consent of the masses to be ruled, see T.J. Jackson Lears, 'The Concept of Cultural Hegemony: Problems and Possibilities', *American Historical Review* 90 (June 1985): 567–93.

11. For examples see Joseph Defont's 1809 contract with the North West Company, Winnipeg, Provincial Archives of Manitoba (hereafter PAM), Fort William Collection (hereafter FWC), MG1 C1, fo. 32-1 and the contract of Louis Santier of St Eustache with Parker, Gerrard, Ogilvy, & Co. as a *milieu* to transport goods between Montreal and Michilimackinac, 21 Avril [sic] 1802, LAC, MG19 A51.

12. For one example see Montreal, McCord Museum of Canadian History, North West Company Papers, M17607, M17614, Deposition of Basil Dubois, 21 June 1798, and Complaint of Camuel Gerrard, of the firm of Parker Gerrard and Ogilvy against Basil Dubois.

13. Montreal, Archives nationals de Québec, dèpot de Montréal (hereafter ANQM), Court of Quarter Sessions of the District of Montreal, TL32 S1 SS1, Robert Aird vs Joseph Boucher, 1 April 1785, JP Pierre Foretier; Atkinson Patterson vs Jean-Baptiste Desloriers dit Laplante, 21 April 1798, JP Thomas Forsyth; and Angus Sharrest for McGillivray & Co. vs Joseph Papin of St Sulpice, 14 June 1810, JP J-M Mondelet. These cases were compiled by Don Fyson as part of a one in five sample of the whole series.

14. The JPs were William McGillivray, Duncan McGillivray, Sir Alexander Mackenzie, Roderick Mackenzie, and John Ogilvy. Marjorie Wilkins Campbell, *The North West Company* (Toronto: Macmillan Company of Canada, 1957), 136–7.

15. ANQM, CPCM, Cour du Vendredi (Matières civiles inferieurs), TL16 S3/00001, pp. 41, 314-25, 3 juillet 1770 and 3 juillet 1778, JPs Hertelle De Rouville and Edward Southouse; and TL16 S3/00008, no page numbers, 13 janvier 1786, JPs Hertelle De Rouville and Edward Southouse, 6 octobre 1786 (followed by several other entries later in the month), JPs John Fraser, Edward Southouse, and Hertelle De Rouville, and 27 octobre 1786, JPs Edward Southouse and Hertelle De Rouville; and Eliot Coues, ed., *New Light on the Early History of the Greater Northwest: The Manuscript Journals of Alexander Henry* (Minneapolis: Ross and Haines, 1897), vol. 2, 860–1, Sunday, 27 March 1814.

16. For a few examples of becoming lost see MRB, MC, C8, Microfilm reel #14, Alexander Mackenzie, Journal of Great Bear Lake, 18–26 June 1806, p. 20; MRB, MC, Journal of John Macdonell, Assiniboines-Rivière qu'Appelle, 1793–95, Thursday, 13 March 1794 and Monday, 8 December 1794, pp. 11, 22; and OA, Company of Temiscamingue, Microfilm #MS65, Donald McKay, Journal from January 1805 to June 1806, Thursday, 12 September 1805, p. 32 (page numbers added).

17. Coues, ed., *New Light*, 1:11 August 1800, pp. 30–1; MRL BR, S13, George Nelson's diary of events on a journey from Cumberland House to Fort William, part in code, 3 June–11 July 1822 (notes taken from a transcription made by Sylvia Van Kirk); Tuesday, 9 July 1822; *ibid.*, Nelson's diary of events on a journey from Fort William to Cumberland House, 21 July–22 August 1822 (notes taken from a transcript made by Sylvia Van Kirk); Monday, 19 August 1822; and Alexander Ross, *Fur Hunters of the Far West: A Narrative of Adventures in Oregon and the Rocky Mountains* (London: Smith, Elder and Co., 1855), II: 236–7.

18. Elliot J. Gorn describes this pattern as well in 'Gouge and Bite, Pull Hair and Scratch: The Social Significance of Fighting in the Southern Backcountry', *American Historical Review* 90 (February 1985): 18–43.

19. In a different case, Gunther Peck found that middle class commentators condemned Miners' penchant for risk-taking in late-nineteenth-century Nevada. Gunther Peck, 'Manly Gambles: The Politics of Risk on the Comstock Lode, 1860–1880', *Journal of Social History* 26 (Summer 1993): 701–23.

20. Approximately 20 June 1807, described in Toronto Metropolitan Reference Library (hereafter TMRL), Baldwin Room (hereafter BR), S13, p. 186, George Nelson's Journal 'No. 5', June 1807–October 1809, written as a reminiscence, dated 7 February 1851.

21. See Coues, ed., *New Light*, 1:247, 1 July 1804.

22. For one example of men demanding their pay be doubled for extra duties see Chabiollez, 'Journal for the Year 1797', 49, Tuesday, 20 March 1798.

23. See MRB, MC, C27, Microfilm reel #13, p. 2, Athabasca Department, Great Slave Lake, W.F. Wentzel to Roderick Mackenzie, Letters Inward, 1807–1824, 5 April 1819.

24. See LAC, MC, MG19 C1, vol. 3, Microfilm reel #C-15638, pp. 8–15, François-Antoine Larocque, 'Missouri Journal, Winter 1804–5'; and Nelson, 'A Daily Memoranda', pp. 30–2, Saturday, 8 April 1815.

25. See entries Monday, 2 November 1818, and from Tuesday, 1 December 1818 to Wednesday, 30 December 1818, OA, MU 842, pp. 10–11, 18–23, Diary of George Nelson, in the service of the North West Company at Tête au Brochet, 1818–19.

26. See LAC, MC, MG19 C1, vol. 15, Microfilm reel #C-15638, p. 7, Fragment of a journal, attributed to W. Ferdinand Wentzel, kept during an expedition from 13 June to 20 August 1800, Friday, 26 June 1800.

27. See MRB, MC, C8, Microfilm reel #14, p. 125, Alexander Mackenzie, Journal of Great Bear Lake, March 1806.

28. On trip from Athabasca to the Mackenzie River, LAC, MC, MG19 C1, vol. 6, Microfilm reel #C15638, p. 50, James Porter, Journal kept at Slave Lake, 18 February 1800 to 14 February 1801, 29 September 1800. Porter quotes the man as saying 'Si Je avait Point des gages que le Diable ma aport si vous ma Soucier Embarker.'

29. See OA, MWCC, MU 2199, p. 8, photostat of original, Edward Umfreville, 'Journal of a Passage in a Canoe from Pais Plat in Lake Superior to Portage de L'Isle in Rivière Ouinipique', June to July 1784, Wednesday, 23 June 1784.

30. See TMRL, BR, S13, p. 9, George Nelson's Journal 'No. 1', written as a reminiscence, describing a journey from Montreal to Grand Portage, and at Folle Avoine, 27 April 1802–April 1803 (a typescript can also be found in the George Nelson Papers of the TMRL, BR).

31. On the HBC prohibition of private trading see Burley, *Servants of the Honourable Company*, 24–5. However, Burley suggests that the lack of reporting on this offence may indicate that the officers tacitly allowed their men to do so (144–52).

32. For an example see MRB, MC, C7, Microfilm reel #4, p. 4, Journal of John Macdonell, Assiniboines-Rivière qu'Appelle, 1793–95, (typescript copy in LAC, MC, MG19 C1, vol. 54, Microfilm reel #C15640), 5 December 1793 to 6 December 1793.

33. McLeod, Journal kept at Alexandria, p. 40, Saturday, 30 May 1801; and 'The Diary of John Macdonell', in

Charles M. Gates, ed., *Five Fur Traders of the Northwest* (St Paul: Minnesota Historical Society, 1965), 72, 1 June 1793.

34. For example, see McLeod, Journal kept at Alexandria, 15, 2 January 1801.

35. See MRB, MC, C12, Microfilm reel #6, p. 41, Charles McKenzie, 'Some Account of the Missouri Indians in the years 1804, 5, 6, & 7', addressed to Roderick Mackenzie, 1809. Photostat and typescript copies can be found in LAC, MC, MG19 C1, vol. 59, Microfilm reel #C15640 and OA, NWCC, MU2204, vol. 3 and MU2200 Box 5-4(a), and the account is published by W. Raymond Wood and Thomas D. Thiessen, eds, *Early Fur Trade on the Northern Plains: Canadian Traders Among the Mandan and Hidatsa Indians, 1738–1818: The Narratives of John Macdonell, David Thompson, François-Antoine Larocque, and Charles McKenzie* (Norman: University of Oklahoma Press, 1985).

36. For one example see McLeod, Journal kept at Alexandria, Saturday, 22 November 1800.

37. See Nelson, Journal No. 1, p. 43, Saturday, 17 November 1809.

38. See Nelson, 'A Daily Memoranda', 8, Friday, 10 February 1815; and 'The Diary of Hugh Faries', p. 235, Tuesday, 2 April 1805.

39. TMRL, BR, S13, pp. 14–15, George Nelson's Coded Journal, 17 April–20 October 1821, entitled 'A Continuation of My Journal at Moose Lake', (notes made by Sylvia Van Kirk), Thursday, 10 May 1821. Constant had been threatening to desert the service for years, and he did make arrangements with another bourgeois, William Connolly, to leave the service. *Ibid.*, Thursdays, 10 and 24 May 1821, pp. 14–15, 20.

40. Nelson, 'A Daily Memoranda', pp. 17–18, 40–1, Thursday, 9 March 1815, Tuesday, 23 May 1815, and Wednesday, 24 May 1815.

41. LAC, 'Civil Secretary's Letter Books, 1788–1829', RG7, G15C, col. 2, CO42, vol. 100, Sheriff Edward Gray to Attorney General James Monk, 9 June 1794; J. Reid to same, 12 June 1794; T.A. Coffin to James McGill, 21 July 1794; cited by F. Murray Greenwood, *Legacies of Fear: Law and Politics in Quebec in the Era of the French Revolution* (Toronto: University of Toronto Press, 1993), 80, 285.

42. See TMRL, BR, S13; George Nelson, Tête au Brochet, to his parents, 8 December 1811, pp. 9–11; and Ross, *Fur Hunters of the Far West*, 1: 291–3.

43. Nelson, Journal, 13 July 1803–25 June 1804, pp. 22–3, Monday, 31 January 1804, Monday, 14 February 1804, Tuesday, 15 February 1804, and Thursday, 17 February 1804.

44. MRB, MC, C5, Microfilm reel #5, abridged version on Microfilm reel #6, p. 50, Alexander Henry the Younger, travels in the Red River Department, 1806, Wednesday, 23 July 1806.

References

Brown, Jennifer S.H. 1980. *Strangers in Blood: Fur Trade Families in Indian Country*. Vancouver: UBC Press.

Burley, Edith I. 1997. *Servants of the Honourable Company: Work, Discipline, and Conflict in the Hudson's Bay Company, 1770–1879*. Toronto, New York, and Oxford: Oxford University Press.

Coues, Eliot, ed. 1897. *New Light on the Early History of the Greater Northwest: The Manuscript Journals of Alexander Henry*. Minneapolis: Ross and Haines.

Francis, Daniel, and Toby Morantz. 1983. *Partners in Furs: A History of the Fur Trade in Eastern James Bay, 1600–1870*. Montreal and Kingston: McGill-Queen's University Press.

Gates, Charles M., ed. 1965. *Five Fur Traders of the Northwest*. St Paul: Minnesota Historical Society.

Hamilton, James Scott. 1990. 'Fur Trade Social Inequality and the Role of Non-Verbal Communication'. PhD thesis, Simon Fraser University.

Hogg, Grace Laing, and Gwen Shulman. 1993. 'Wage Disputes and the Courts in Montreal, 1816–1835', in Donald Fyson, Colin M. Coates, and Kathryn Harvey, eds, *Class, Gender and the Law in Eighteenth and Nineteenth Century Quebec: Sources and Perspectives*. Montreal: Montreal History Group.

Mackenzie, Alexander. 1801. 'A General History of the Fur Trade from Canada to the North-West', *Voyages from Montreal on the River St Laurence through the Continent of North America to the Frozen and Pacific Oceans in the Years 1789 and 1793 with a Preliminary Account of the Rise, Progress, and Present State of the Fur Trade of that Country*. London: R. Noble, Old Bailey.

Morton, Arthur S., ed. 1929. *The Journal of Duncan McGillivray of the North West Company at Fort George on the Saskatchewan, 1794–5*. Toronto: Macmillan Company of Canada.

Ross, Alexander, 1855. *Fur Hunters of the Far West; A Narrative of Adventures in Oregon and the Rocky Mountains*. London: Smith, Elder and Co.

Selkirk, Earl of (Thomas Douglas). 1816. *A Sketch of the British Fur Trade in North America; with Observations*

Relative to the North-West Company of Montreal, 2nd ed. London: James Ridgway.

Thompson, E.P. 1993. *Customs in Common: Studies in Traditional Popular Culture*. New York: The New Press.

Vibert, Elizabeth. 1997. *Traders' Tales: Narratives of Cultural Encounters in the Columbian Plateau, 1807–1846.*

Norman and London: University of Oklahoma Press.

Wood, W. Raymond, and Thomas D. Thiessen, eds. 1985. *Early Fur Trade on the Northern Plains: Canadian Traders Among the Mandan and Hidatsa Indians, 1738–1818: The Narratives of John Macdonell, David Thompson, François-Antoine Larocque, and Charles McKenzie*. Norman: University of Oklahoma Press.

CHAPTER 2

After the Fur Trade: The Aboriginal Labouring Class of British Columbia, 1849–1890

John Lutz

Aboriginal history is usually considered in isolation from mainstream Canadian history as though it were about aboriginal people and nobody else. But the major issues of native studies—such as the appropriation of aboriginal land and resources, the denial of citizenship rights to a large segment of the Canadian population, the conditions under which aboriginal people would agree to trap, hunt, or do wage-work for a capitalist economy—are major issues of national development and central to Canadian history.

This paper takes up questions about aboriginal wage labour and applies them to a 40-year period on the west coast of North America from the creation of the Colony of Vancouver Island in 1849, through the gold rushes, the founding of the giant export sawmills, Confederation, the development and spread of the salmon canning industry, to just past the completion of the Canadian Pacific Railway in 1885, an event which tied the province of British Columbia to the North American continental economy. Throughout this period aboriginal people in British Columbia comprised the majority of the population. Despite introduced diseases

which reduced the aboriginal population by approximately two-thirds, when British Columbia entered Confederation in 1871 it was in many important respects an 'aboriginal province'—there were three times as many aboriginal people as all the non-aboriginals taken together.

Although one might suppose historians would have turned their attention to the majority before beginning to examine minority groups, in British Columbia historiography the reverse has happened: only a few historians, notably Robin Fisher (1977) and Rolf Knight (1978), have given their attention to the majority population in this era. Most general accounts follow Fisher's pioneering work on aboriginal–non-aboriginal relations which argued that aboriginal peoples retained control of their lives during the fur trade, and had considerable influence over the trade itself. Fisher states that, with the gold-rush, the colonies which comprise modern British Columbia changed from 'colonies of exploitation, which made use of indigenous manpower, to colonies of settlement, where the Indians became at best, irrelevant' (Fisher, 1977: 96, 109, 111).[1] By contrast, this paper argues that aboriginal people were not made irrelevant by the coming of settlement. In fact, they were the main labour force of the early settlement era, essential to the capitalist development of British Columbia. . . .

Even in the 1860s opinion among white notables was divided about the usefulness and importance of aboriginal people to the British Columbia economy. While Charles Forbes's 1862 guide to Vancouver Island argued resolutely that 'their labour cannot be depended on, and with one or two slight exceptions at present forms no point of consideration in the labour market,' (Forbes, 1862: 25) and A.A. Harvey described aboriginal people as 'valueless in the labour market' (Harvey, 1867: 9), in his 1871 report on British Columbia the federal minister of public works observed that 'the Indians have been, and still are, and will long continue an important population for [British] Columbia, in the capacity of guides, porters and labourers' (Langevin, 1872: 28; see also Anderson, 1872: 80).

Who was right? Were aboriginal people 'valueless in the labour market' or 'an important population of . . . labourers'? How important was their labour to British Columbia's nineteenth century economy? How important was wage and contract labour to the aboriginal economy? What motivated aboriginal people to join the early paid labour force?[2] Who, and how many, were recruited? Based on a varied sample of aboriginal voices captured in biographies, ethnographies, and in letters to government and church officials, as well as the correspondence of colonial officials, fur traders, missionaries, and travellers, together with the records of the Department of Indian Affairs, this paper not only attempts to answer these questions, but in doing so provides a fresh perspective from which to view the early years of capitalist development in British Columbia.

Labourers of the Aboriginal Province

Of the 34,600 or so inhabitants of the Colony of Vancouver Island and its adjacent islands and shores in 1855, all but 774 were aboriginal. Outside the colony there were probably an additional 25,000–30,000 aboriginal people living in the remainder of what became British Columbia. This vast population was extremely heterogeneous, both culturally and historically. It was comprised of ten distinct nations or ethnic groups, speaking twenty-six distinct, and largely mutually unintelligible, languages. Each nation had its own customary laws that defined property rights, social and gender relations, and by 1849 each village had its own history of relationships with non-aboriginal people or their trade goods.[3]

Victoria, the west-coast headquarters for the Hudson's Bay Company (HBC) became the capital when the colony was established in 1849. As the largest community of non-aboriginal people north of Oregon, it became 'the great emporium' for aboriginal people from all over the Pacific Northwest, from Russian America (Alaska) down. The mass migrations to Victoria began in the summer of 1853, when Governor Douglas reported a gathering of 3,000 'Indians' at a potlatch hosted by the local Songhees people living across the harbour.[4] The next year aboriginal people from 'all parts of the mainland coast south of Cape Spencer, in north latitude 59 degrees' dropped in on Victoria itself. Annually, from 1853 through the 1880s, 2,000–4,000 aboriginal people canoed their way to Victoria to trade or spend part of the year, travelling as far as 800 miles to do so.

Why did thousands of aboriginal people, between 5 and 10 per cent of the whole aboriginal population north of Puget Sound, paddle so far to visit a community that in 1855 numbered only 232?[5] Trading was undoubtedly a major attraction—the variety in Victoria was greater, alcohol was more easily available, and the prices of goods were perhaps better than at closer trading posts; and in the beginning at least curiosity to see this alien community was, no doubt, another factor.

There was nevertheless a third and key reason why aboriginal people returned year after year. As Governor Douglas explained in his dispatches to the Colonial Office, he was not unduly alarmed about being out-numbered ten-to-one during these seasonal visits by 'ignorant and barbarous people. . . . For the object of the Indians in visiting this place is not to make War upon the White man, but to benefit by his presence, by selling their Furs and other commodities.'[6]

One of the commodities aboriginal people sold was labour, a practice well established as early as 1853, when Douglas had reported that 'a great part of the agricultural labour of the colony, is at present performed by means of the Natives, who though less skilled and industrious than the white men, work at a comparatively much cheaper rate, so that on the whole, they are exceedingly useful to the colonists.'[7] Indeed, nearly all early accounts mention the hiring of aboriginal labour. The first *bona fide* colonist, W.C. Grant, hired aboriginal people on his farm and reported in 1853 that 'with the proper superintendence [they] are capable of being made very useful. They all live by fishing but take kindly to any kind of rough agricultural employment, though their labour is not to be depended on for any continuous period.' . . . The Puget Sound Agricultural Company also hired aboriginal labour on their farms, and by 1857 missionary William Duncan observed that around Victoria 'most of the Farm Servants employed here . . . are Chimsyan (Tsimshian) Indians—and they all give them a good character.'[8]

The issue of wage labour was raised formally when, at the start of his 1856 seasonal visit, Douglas called the chiefs together and 'spoke to them seriously on the subject of their relations with the whites, and their duties to the public, and after exacting a pledge for the good behaviour of their respective Tribes, *I gave them permission to hire themselves out as labourers to the white settlers, and for the public works in progress.*' He reported at the end of August that 'the greater number of those people have lately departed *with their earnings* to their distant homes, and will not return to Vancouver's Island, before the spring of 1856; those who still remain about the settlements will spend the winter here. . . .'[9]

Although the economies of the aboriginal peoples varied from the coast to the interior and even within these divisions, generally they were based on a seasonal migration cycle from permanent winter villages to harvesting sites for fishing in the fall, hunting and trapping in winter, and harvesting roots and berries in the summer. From 1853 onwards, however, a spring and summer visit to Victoria became a part of the seasonal cycle, and those who could not find work in Victoria often continued south into the American territory of Puget Sound. John Fornsby, a Coast Salish living in Puget Sound first saw these 'Northern Indians' when 40–50 of them came to work at a Puget Sound sawmill around 1858, while James Swan wrote from Port Townsend that the Northern Indians 'yearly come to Victoria and whenever they get a chance, come over here to work—the men at our mills or among the farmers, where they prove themselves faithful and efficient; and the women, by their cleanly habits, their bright dresses and hoop skirts . . . winning the hearts or purses of the bachelors' (Collins, 1949: 301).[10] Others, who did not join the migration, found work closer to their own villages in the expanding activities of the Hudson's Bay Company posts, cutting shingles, spars, picking cranberries, harvesting ice, as well as gardening, fishing, preserving food, and doing general construction (Mackie, 1985).

While the summer migrants from the north worked on the farms and public works, some of the local Songhees people became established in year-round employment in the homes of the better-off colonists as servants and cooks. Reverend Staines wrote in 1852 that his Indian servant procured meat each day by trading with other Indians, and that he was teaching his Indian cook how to prepare beef, mutton, and venison. Other aboriginal people supplied venison, partridges, salmon, potatoes, and berries to the colonists, as well as shingles, lathes, mats, and baskets.[11]

With the 1858 gold rush and the consequent growth of Victoria came even more opportunities for work, and by 1860 whole villages might be deserted for the capital. Making for the Queen Charlotte islands in the *Alert*, James Cooper met the entire population of Masset heading for Victoria. At Skidegate, meanwhile, Chief 'Estercana' asked the officials to 'tell Mr Doouglas [sic] and the man-of-war to send my people home; I wanted to build a house this summer [but] nearly all my people are away at Victoria.'[12] That summer, the governor reported over 4,000 visiting Indians at Victoria, double the number of non-aboriginal inhabitants in the town.[13] Despite the large gold-induced increase in the non-aboriginal population, Douglas was still not concerned about its relations with the majority. 'When not under the influence of intoxication,' he told the Colonial Office in 1860, '[the aboriginal people] are quiet and well conducted, make good servants and by them is executed a large proportion of the menial, agricultural, and shipping labour of the Colony. Besides their value as labourers they are of value commercially as consumers of food and clothing. . . .'[14] He was not alone in his view. The San Francisco *Times*, for example, described the Indians around gold-rush Victoria as 'industrious', which 'alone establishes their superiority to the California aborigines'.[15] . . .

Despite claims by historians, aboriginal people were not made redundant by the influx of non-aboriginals to the gold fields, just less visible in the increasingly polyglot society of the colonies. Nor had they been bystanders as gold and coal became focal points of the economy of the Pacific Northwest between the 1840s and 1880s: in both cases, aboriginal people were the discoverers and the first miners, and they continued to work the mines throughout the century.

Coal was first discovered by aboriginal people on northern Vancouver Island. In 1846 the Royal Navy vessel *Cormorant* stopped there and 'with the assistance of the Indians they collected about 60 tons' (Bowsfield, 1974: 4). The Kwakwaka'wakw (Kwakiutl) at this site told the HBC that 'they would not permit us to work the coal as they were valuable to them, but that they would labor in the mines themselves and sell to us the produce of their exertions' (Rich, 1941: 335). Between 1849, when the HBC established Fort Rupert at the coal mines, and 1851 when the seam was exhausted, the Kwakwaka'wakw people mined 3,650 tons of coal for which they were paid the handsome price of 'one blanket 2½ pt.s or equivalent in Grey Cotton for every two tons delivered at the Fort.'[16]

Starting in 1852, the Fort Rupert experience was repeated in Nanaimo after trader Joe McKay, and then Governor Douglas, were led to various seams of coal by the local people. Douglas sent the HBC's *Cadboro* to the spot 'and succeeded in procuring, with the assistance of Indians, about 50 tons of coal in one day'. 'The natives,' he reported, 'who are now indefatigable in their researches for Coal, lately discovered a magnificent seam over six feet in depth. . . . Such places are left entirely to the Indians, who work with a surprising degree of industry, and dispose of the coal to the Agents of the Hudson's Bay Company for clothing and other articles of European manufacture.'[17]

With the removal of the surface coal and the need to dig shafts and use pumps, the Hudson's Bay Company brought skilled miners from Great Britain. However, as Douglas noted in 1857, aboriginal people remained crucial to the underground operations:

> The want of Indian labor is certainly a great inconvenience for the miners but really they must learn to be independent of Indians for our work will otherwise be subject to continual stoppage. (Douglas to Stuart, cited in Burrill, 1987: 54)

In the 1850s the coal mines regularly stopped production when the local people went to their seasonal fisheries, potlatched, or were attacked by illness. Although partly displaced by Chinese labour in the various coal mines that subsequently sunk shafts around Nanaimo, in 1877 it was noted that 'the Nanaimo Indians. . . have hitherto been chiefly employed about the coal mines as labourers.' In 1882 the Indian Agent overseeing Nanaimo noted that the aboriginal people there 'find constant employment at the coal mines and wharves' and in 1888 'many Indians are again working at the coal mines at Nanaimo, taking the place of the Chinese; the fear of accident by explosions deterred them for some time, but now the high wages paid has attracted them again to the mines.'[18]

Gold, meanwhile, was first offered to the HBC in trade by the Haidas of the Queen Charlotte Islands in 1851, and in the mid-1850s by the Interior Salish of the Fraser and Thompson Valleys. In both cases white men were 'obstructed by the natives in all their attempts to search for gold'

and 'when [the whites] did succeed in removing the surface and excavating to the depth of the auriferous stratum, they were quietly hustled and crowded by the natives who . . . proceeded to reap the fruits of their labours.'[19] In 1858, however, some 30,000 non-aboriginals surged into the Fraser Valley and up the Thompson, completely overwhelming the few thousand aboriginal inhabitants, who continued to work alongside them. In 1858 James Moore reported that the 'whole tribe of Yale Indians moved down from Yale and camped on Hill's bar, about three hundred men, women and children, and they also commenced to wash for gold' and Governor Douglas reported that 'it is impossible to get Indian labor at present, as they are all busy mining, and make between two and three dollars a day each man' (Douglas, cited in Rickard, 1938: 13).[20]

Within the decade the gold rushes had passed and while most of the aliens had abandoned the diggings, aboriginal people continued to include gold mining as part of their modified seasonal cycle. In 1871 Alfred Selwyn of the Geological Survey of Canada remarked that 'nearly all the Indians of the Fraser above Yale have now become gold washers. They return to the same spot on the river year after year, at the season of lowest water, to wash the sands, and, it is asserted, can almost always earn for a day's labour from one to two dollar's worth of gold.' . . . In addition to mining, many bands along the Fraser, Thompson, and Nicola rivers took up packing supplies as a vocation. Chief Justice Begbie, who travelled this circuit, recalled that 'no supplies were taken in [to the gold districts] except by Indians . . . Without them . . . the country could not have been entered or supplied in 1858–1860' (Langevin, 1872: 27).

Besides mining and packing, the aboriginal people of the southern Interior took up farming on their own behalf and worked as farm labour for others. In 1874 the Catholic missionary C.J. Grandidier wrote from Kamloops that 'The Indians in this part of the country are now quite awake to the necessity of working, of following the examples of the whites, they look to the future and are afraid for their children's sake if they do not work.' Acting on behalf of the people of the Fraser Valley Alexis, chief of Cheam, asked the Indian agent for advance warning if he visited 'in order to unite our people who are now a little dispersed as they are working for the whites.'[21] . . .

Did they also engage in more industrial pursuits? Martin Robin has argued that 'it was not merely the shrinking numbers . . . which accounted for the low participation of the Indians in the new industrial system. By inclination and habit, the Indian did not fit the industrial mould. His customary and casual and seasonal work schedule hardly prepared him for the discipline, pace and rhythm of industrial employment' (Robin, 1972: 30). Yet, the evidence shows aboriginal people were among the region's first factory workers.

The 'modern' factory arrived on Vancouver Island in 1861 when Captain Stamp commenced operation of the largest sawmill on the west coast of North America, a steam-powered facility that cost $120,000 to build and was eventually capable of cutting 100,000 feet of lumber a day. For the Tseshaht people of the Alberni Inlet, where the mill was located, the industrial revolution arrived at the end of a cannon. When the white labourers arrived to set up the mill they chose the site where the local people were camped. The mill's operators were satisfied that they had 'bought' the site from the local people for 'Some 50 blankets, muskets, molasses and food, trinkets etc. . . .' but the Tseshaht clearly had a different view of the transaction than the mill owners—they refused to leave. They were introduced to capitalist property relations when the mill managers trained their

cannons on them.[22] Ultimately they agreed to move, and when they returned to the mill site it was as workers. The mill manager subsequently recorded that when he 'first employed Indians at Alberni, the price of their labour was two blankets and rations of bisquits and molasses for a month's work for each man, if he worked the whole time'. One source reports that over its operation, the mill paid out close to $30,000 in wages, and a considerable portion of that was likely paid to the local Tseshaht people (Sproat, 1868: 40; Taylor, 1975: 23).

Two more giant export sawmills were established on Burrard Inlet between 1863 and 1867. Both rivalled the Alberni mill in size, but unlike their predecessor, they continued to operate into the next century. Together, these mills were the largest industrial operations in the colonies, each employing between 75–100 mill hands, exclusive of loggers and longshoremen (Taylor, 1975; Morton, 1977). As with other settlements around the colonies, whole aboriginal communities relocated to the sawmills, and in Burrard Inlet, most of the workers inside and outside the factory were aboriginal. . . .

Inquiring into the income of the Musqueem band that worked in the Burrard Inlet the Indian Reserve Commission reported in 1877 that from the 'saw mills and other concomitant interests . . . a sum variously computed at from $80,000 to $100,000 finds its way annually into the hands of the natives. The mill owners, too, and the shipping frequenting the mills, are benefitting by a corresponding degree, by having a local source of labour constantly available.' The Indian Commissioner remarked that in 1881 aboriginal sawmill workers were preferred to whites, and workers of both races earned up to $2.50 per day.[23] . . .

At the same time sawmills in Puget Sound, Washington Territory, employed hundreds of

British Columbia aboriginal people. William Pierce, a Tsimshian from Port Simpson, remarked that in the mid-1870s his co-workers in a Puget Sound sawmill included Haida from the Queen Charlottes, Tsimshian from the north coast, Nass and Skeena Rivers, as well as Bella Bella, Bella Coola, Kitamaat and Kwakwaka'wakw from the central coast and Tlingit from Alaska (Hicks, 1933: 15).[24] . . .

Some aboriginal people moved into skilled jobs but the majority of the aboriginal workers, like the non-aboriginals, were unskilled. Many aboriginal people, including the entire male population of the Sechelt band on the Sunshine Coast north of Burrard Inlet, cut wood for the mills. In addition to working for the big export mills, aboriginal people worked and ran several smaller sawmills that were scattered throughout the province, many of them first established by missionaries in order to encourage aboriginal people to adopt capitalist-Christian ethics. Not only was sawmill labour predominantly aboriginal but so were the longshore-men and -women.[25]

While the sawmills of Burrard Inlet were getting into full swing, the second major factory-based industry—salmon-canning—was in its infancy. First attempted in 1867, it was not until 1870 that continuous production started. Within a decade, however, the canneries were large, modern factories employing hundreds of people and using steam boilers and retorts to heat and cook the salmon and to seal the cans (Stacey, 1982). The early canneries relied almost exclusively on aboriginal men to do the fishing and a workforce comprised of aboriginal women and Chinese men to do most of the canning. Like the big export sawmills, they were frequently located in coastal inlets, remote from white settlement but in, or close to, aboriginal communities. One estimate suggested that the eleven canneries operating on

the Fraser River in 1883 employed 1,000–1,200 aboriginal fisherman plus hundreds of aboriginal women to process the fish.[26]

By 1885 a crude estimate based on the reports of the Indian Agents suggests that of the 28,000 aboriginal people in British Columbia in 1885, over 85 per cent belonged to bands that earned substantial incomes through paid labour. The remaining 15 per cent, although not wage labourers, participated to a lesser degree in the economy as fur traders.[27] More telling than the numbers are the accounts of whole villages being emptied by aboriginal people engaged in paid work. . . . One of the most interesting accounts is by Sayach'apis, a Nuu-cha-nulth, whose invitations to a potlatch in the mid-1880s were spurned by the Songhees, the Saanich, the Cowichan, and the Hikwihltaah: 'You are too late,' they told him; 'we are going to the hop fields,' to harvest the crop.[28]

Twenty-five years after the gold rush, aboriginal people had not been marginalized—rather they remained at the centre of the transformed, capitalist, economic activity. . . .

'The stranger coming for the first time to Victoria is startled by the great number of Indians living in this town,' wrote ethnologist Franz Boas in 1886. 'We meet them everywhere. They dress mostly in European fashion. The men are dock workers, craftsmen or fish vendors; the women are washerwomen or working women. . . . Certain Indian tribes have already become indispensable on the labour market and without them the province would suffer great economic damage (Rohner, 1969; Jacobsen, 1977; von Hesse-Wartegg, 1981). Moreover, Chinook, the *lingua franca* of the fur trade, and not English, was the language of the canneries, the docks, the sawmills, the hop-fields, and many other sites where large amounts of labour were performed.[29] At no time since have aboriginal people been so central to the province-wide capitalist economy than in the early 1880s, though they continued to be vital to specific industries long after.

Recruitment and Composition of the Aboriginal Workforce

There is virtually no information on how aboriginal people were recruited into the pre-industrial labour force for agriculture and public works, or the manifold handicraft industries sponsored by the Hudson's Bay Company and others. It seems clear, however, that with aboriginal labour abundant in and around the settlements of British Columbia, recruitment was not difficult. Moreover, in addition to the nearby bands, often whole communities moved to white settlements, some seasonally and others permanently to trade and work. The slim evidence available suggests that, in this period, chiefs acted as labour brokers for their local groups. . . .

Recruitment became more of an issue with the advent of large sawmills and canneries—the factories—because they demanded an unfamiliar work discipline. For one thing, it was critically important to have a large, regular workforce gathered at a single site for extended, and in the case of the salmon canneries, very precise periods; for another, everyone had to start and end work at the same time. In retrospect, however, it should come as no surprise that aboriginal people were recruited and employed in these factories in large numbers. They dominated the population and either lived close to the new industrial sites (since the canneries, especially, located specifically to take advantage of aboriginal labour) or had their own means of transport to and from them. In addition, aboriginal people, under some circumstances, could be paid less than 'White' labour. . . .

Evidence from the early twentieth century shows that canneries employed 'Indian bosses' who would be given cash advances for themselves and others, and who would be responsible for getting a specified number of fishermen and inside workers, particularly women, to come to individual canneries. Employers also used Indian Agents as informal recruiters, and large hop growers would send agents to visit bands and sign up workers in advance of the season.[30] However, it would seem . . . that as the number of industrial sites increased, local groups tended less to act as units; instead, individuals began to take control of their own labour and sell it independent of 'Indian Bosses' (Ford, 1968: 134). By the late 1880s, it was common for aboriginal women to be hired by Chinese labour contractors in the canneries on the Fraser and Skeena Rivers.[31] . . .

The incorporation of aboriginal people into the capitalist labour force was a spatially discontinuous process that did not affect all aboriginal groups simultaneously or in the same way. Industry did not spread out gradually from the central settlements of Victoria, New Westminster, and Nanaimo; rather it arrived suddenly on inlets far removed from settlement. Moreover, many aboriginal groups opted to travel long distances to obtain employment while their neighbours did not. Those aboriginal groups that had previous exposure to working with or for non-aboriginal people were the first to take up the long migrations to find wage labour in the south.[32]

Participation also varied across generations and gender. Overall, the industrial workplace favoured younger people; agriculture, on the other hand, did not discriminate between young and old or between men and women (Jacobsen, 1977: 13). The contrast was captured by William Lomas, the Cowichan Indian Agent: 'All the younger men can find employment on farms or at the sawmills and canneries, and many families are about to leave for the hop fields of Washington Territory. . . .' The elderly he saw were not faring so well:

The very old people who formerly lived entirely on fish, berries and roots, suffer a great deal through the settling up of the country. . . . With the younger men, the loss of these kinds of foods is more than compensated by the good wages that they earn, which supplement what they produce on their allotments; but this mode of life does away with their old customs of laying in a supply of dried meat, fish and berries for winter use, and thus the old people again suffer, for Indians are often generous with the food they have taken in the chase, but begrudge what they have paid money for.[33]

The British Columbia aboriginal societies had their own gender-based divisions of labour which were largely appropriated into the canneries (Fiske, 1988; Littlefield, 1988; Mitchell and Franklin, 1989). Although, generally speaking, native men would fish and women would mend nets and work in the canneries, some women also fished with their husbands (the boats required a puller and a fisher)[34] and some, particularly older, men would mend nets and work inside. The infirm would look after the infants, while even young children had work in the canneries cleaning cans. In peak cannery periods, every possible person would be brought in to work and infants were placed in a corner where they could be watched (Carmichael, *c.* 1885).

The traditional division of labour between male hunters and female processors of the catch was generally carried over into the capitalist economy of the sealing industry as well. When the local seals were hunted-out and schooners called at west coast villages to pick up crews, as many as 870 aboriginal people were hired, most of them men, although women were sometimes employed as boat-handlers. On the other hand, 'the Indian women and children are always the most eager to go to the hop fields, where they always earn considerable sums of money, and, among these Indians, the wife's purse is generally entirely separate from the husband's.'[35]

In some cases, however, aboriginal gender divisions of labour could not be grafted directly onto the capitalist economy. Were women or men better suited to work on steamships, in sawmills, or to sell food in the street markets? In the era 1849–90, both men and women worked at non-industrial occupations such as gold mining, farming, agricultural labour, rendering oil, and loading coal. With regard to the service trades, men are more often mentioned as cutting and selling firewood while women are commonly recorded as bringing fish and game to urban markets. In urban areas women did domestic work such as washing clothes, taking in ironing, and cleaning house,[36] and they were also employed to make fishnets.[37] Prostitution was an additional source of income for hundreds of aboriginal women from the late-1850s through the 1880s.[38] But in keeping with the gender divisions of labour prevalent in capitalist society, I have found no mention of aboriginal women being employed in the sawmills, coal mines, and on railroad crews. . . .

Why did Aboriginal People Work for Wages?

It is noteworthy in itself that aboriginal people in British Columbia chose, in large numbers, to work for pay. . . . Certainly in the 1840s and 1850s there was no pressure on the traditional resource base or subsistence economy which had sustained them for eons (McDonald, 1984: 49). Even by the 1870s and the beginning of truly industrial labour, only a few of the aboriginal groups on southern Vancouver Island and in the Fraser and Thompson valleys were finding their traditional resource-base eroded to the point that they could not have reverted to a totally subsistence economy if such was their preference. Nor did evangelism have a significant impact until the 1860s and then only in a few locations, by which time church representatives were merely reinforcing an existing desire to participate in wage labour.

Prior to the wide-scale opportunities for wage labour most of the peoples of the west coast participated in the fur trade for reasons which, according to the 'enrichment thesis', were broadly based in their own culture's traditions. Moreover, the new wealth generated by the fur trade, the relocation of bands to common sites around forts, population decimation from disease and firearms led to an enrichment of cultural activities, including, on the west coast, the potlatch (Drucker, 1965: 129; Fisher, 1977: 47–8). . . .

Potlatch is a word in the Chinook jargon that refers to the different ceremonies among many nations of the Pacific Northwest that included feasting, dancing, and the giving of gifts to all in attendance. The potlatch was a central feature of the lives and economy of, especially, the coastal Indians. It was only through potlatches that one's hereditary status and rights to resources, property (including songs and dances), and names could be claimed and maintained. The more guests and the more gifts, the higher the relative status of the person giving the potlatch. High-status recipients of potlatch gifts were expected to reciprocate with potlatches in order to maintain their own relative position, and to protect their claims to traditional prerogatives.[39] All the evidence suggests that the fur trade intensified potlatching, and along with it the carving of totems and masks, the weaving of blankets, and all the other arts that were associated with the ceremony.[40]

Because of the cultural necessity to periodically distribute valuable gifts in a potlatch, the west coast people were a natural trading market. They had uses for property, possessions, and wealth, which, while very different from those of

the traders themselves, were nevertheless complementary. The traditional potlatch goods were valuable precisely because they were rare, or because they took much time and laborious effort to make. 'On the other hand, the intrusive white civilization offered its goods for things that were relatively abundant': fur, fish, and unskilled labour (Drucker and Heizer, 1976: 15). Manufactured blankets and other mass-produced goods were substituted as potlatch goods for locally made, hand-produced items. . . .

It appears that the same cultural forces that drew aboriginal people into the fur trade continued to operate and draw them into the wage and industrial labour force. Aboriginal people permitted, if not welcomed, initial non-aboriginal expansion into their territories to take advantage of the wealth-generating potential that the aliens offered. In 1843 the Songhees people helped the HBC build Fort Victoria (Lowe, 1897; Kane, 1968). In the 1850s the Haida and the Cowichan both appealed to Governor Douglas to establish a settlement among them that they might find work.[41] When he first visited them in 1881, although their village was still suffering from an unprovoked attack by the Royal Navy, the Kitamaats asked Indian Commissioner Powell if he would establish a sawmill in their community.[42] . . .

Aboriginal people apparently found that these new forms of work could be used like the fur trade, to enhance their position in their own society. In 1853, for example, using the wealth they had accumulated from working around Victoria, the Songhees people hosted a potlatch. Three thousand aboriginal people, perhaps a tenth of the population of the entire coastal area, attended this feast.[43] . . . Wage work became another adaptation of the seasonal subsistence round that had already been modified to include an extended trapping season, when furs were the easiest route to accumulation.

White employers, government officials and missionaries noticed that aboriginal people worked to be able to potlatch. But the non-aboriginal immigrants could not reconcile their own work ethic with the motivations that led aboriginal people into the work force. . . . George Grant, who accompanied Sanford Fleming on his cross-country inspection of possible routes for the CPR, exhibited his puzzlement in describing the aboriginal work force at the Moodyville sawmill on Burrard Inlet in 1872:

> The aborigines work well till they save enough money to live on for some time, and then they go up to the boss and frankly say that they are lazy and do not want to work longer. . . . Another habit of the richer ones, which to the Anglo-saxon mind borders on insanity, is that of giving universal backshish or gifts to the whole tribe, without expecting any return save an increased popularity that may lead to their election as Tyhees or chiefs when vacancies occur.

Of particular interest was the story of 'big George', who had

> worked industriously at the mill for years until he had saved $2,000. Instead of putting this in a Savings Bank, he had spent it all on stores for a grand 'Potlatch'. . . Nearly a thousand assembled; the festivities lasted a week; and everyone got something, either a blanket, musket, bag of flour, box of apples, or tea and sugar. When the fun was over, 'big George', now penniless, returned to the mill to carry slabs at $20 a month.

Similar comments can be found scattered throughout the accounts of missionaries, government agents and travellers (Grant, 1873: 319–20).[44] . . .

In addition to accumulating wealth for potlatching, many aboriginal groups had other traditional uses for wealth. James Sewid, a Kwakwaka'wakw, told the story of his great-grandfather who trapped for several winters in order to hold a potlatch needed to recruit a war party to revenge his son's life. Northern men especially paid a substantial bride price to the families of their future wives. Shamans were paid to cure illness, and compensation was often demanded as restitution for intentional or unintentional killing or wounding of another (Wyatt, 1987; Sewid, 1989).

Helen Codere, who has made an intensive study of the Kwakwaka'wakw, has noted that while fur-trade wealth increased the frequency of potlatches, wage labour increased the number of guests and the wealth distributed to an even greater extent, and to her the years between 1849 and 1921 could justifiably be called 'the potlatch period'.[45] Her conclusions are borne out by Kwawkewlth (Kwakwaka'wakw) district Indian agent George Blenkinsop's 1881 observation that potlatches, 'of late years, increased to a very great extent'. He explained that among the Kwakwaka'wakw 'the custom was formerly almost entirely confined to the recognized chiefs, but that of late years it has extended to the people generally, and become very much commoner than before. . . . [The potlatch] has spread to all classes of the community and became the recognized mode of attaining social rank and respect' (Blenkinsop and Hall, cited in Dawson, 1887: 17). . . .

The same phenomena appeared to be drawing other aboriginal groups into the paid labour force. In 1881 Cowichan Indian agent Lomas predicted that a significant proportion of the $15,000 earned by the Cowichan people at the canneries that season would be given away at potlatches. Similarly, in 1884 a delegation of Nuu-chah-nulth chiefs explained that they worked for their money 'and like to spend it as we please, in gathering our friends together; now whenever we travel we find friends; the "potlatch" does that.' Among the Haida the number of new totems being raised with the accompanying ceremonies reached its peak in the period 1860–1876. . . .

However, the fact that aboriginal people had their own reasons for working for wages and chose when they would both enter and leave the labour force was a source of constant frustration to white employers. Indeed, the fact that aboriginal peoples had their own agendas probably accounts for the schizophrenic comments of white employers who spoke about them as 'indispensable' while condemning their 'unreliability' and 'laziness'.

Like most other groups outside the urban area, the Kwakwaka'wakw, for example, 'continued to earn their own subsistence, which meant that earnings could go to the purchase of manufactured goods. Since they required only a limited amount of manufactured goods for consumption needs and since they did not hoard, any surplus could be and was used in potlatching' (Codere, 1966: 126). Because of their subsistence cycle, winter was the main ceremonial season—and few aboriginal people were willing to work year-round and miss the winter festivities. In the beginning this was not a problem in labour-intensive activities like fishing, canning, harvesting, and logging, which were not conducted in the winter. Increasingly, however, the sawmills, the railways, the steamboats, and other large employers were anxious to have a year-round and stable labour force so that seasonal labour, the choice of large numbers of aboriginal people, was becoming less compatible with the demands of capitalism.

It is no coincidence, then, that the federal government passed a law banning potlatch in 1884, just as aboriginal peoples reached their peak importance in the economy. Although the potlatch had drawn many aboriginal people into paid labour, by the mid-1880s it was inconsistent with

the 'stable' habits of industry that both missionaries and government agents saw as essential to the development of a Christian capitalist society. Seeing the potlatch as a bulwark which enabled the aboriginal people to resist acculturation since the seasonal cycle kept them mobile and away from schools and churches, missionaries and the Indian agents argued that it kept aboriginal people poor and mitigated against the accumulation of individual dwellings, land holdings, and private property.

Although the law proved ineffectual, and was not successfully enforced until 1908, it did provide government agents and missionaries with powerful suasion against potlatching (Cole and Chaikin, 1990: 19–20). Some of the bands responded to government pressure, others that had been christianized gave up the institution at the insistence of their ministers.[46] Some bands in urban areas seemed to be slowly adopting the more individualistic and acquisitive ideals of the new majority. So, despite the ineffective laws, the 1880s were also the climax years of the potlatch along the coast generally.[47] Ironically, the very cultural imperative that had brought aboriginal people into the workforce was outlawed because, due to changing circumstances, it was no longer sufficiently compatible with the requirements of capitalism.

Conclusion

In the period 1849–1890 the connections to the capitalist economy varied widely among the many nations and linguistic groups that comprised the aboriginal people of present-day British Columbia. Depending on particular circumstances, integration into the paid labour force also had different effects on the social relations between men and women, youth and elderly, and nobles and commoners. . . .

Aboriginal people were central, not marginal, to the development of new industries and the spread of capitalism in the province-to-be. Coal would not have been mined in British Columbia in the 1840s and 50s, export sawmills would not have been able to function in the 1860s and 70s, canneries would not have had a fishing fleet, or the necessary processors in the 1870s and 80s, without the widespread participation of aboriginal people. The gold rush may have diverted the attention of historians, but it did not divert aboriginal people from the economy. It was the aboriginal workforce that allowed the creation of a capitalist regional economy based on fur trade, then coal mining, sawmilling, and salmon canning. This was the regional economy that kept the Hudson's Bay Company on the Pacific coast, persuaded Britain that the establishment of colonies could be profitable as well as strategic, and ultimately ensured that British Columbia would be *British* Columbia.

While the capitalist economy needed the vast pool of aboriginal labour, aboriginal people used the capitalist economy for their own cultural purposes. Wage labour was one juncture where the potlatch system and capitalism were curiously complementary. Aboriginal people fitted seasonal paid work into their own economic cycle and, in the era described, were able to maintain a level of control over their participation in both. However, the compatibility of capitalism and the aboriginal economy was breaking down by 1884, when the anti-potlatch laws were passed by the federal government: eager to participate in seasonal wage activities from spring to fall, aboriginal people were less interested in participating in the year-round employment that the economy was increasingly demanding.

By the taking of the census of 1891, British Columbia was no longer an 'aboriginal province'. Aboriginal populations had nearly reached their nadir and alternative pools of labour were becoming available. Since then, although aboriginal people have not comprised the majority of the labour force, they have been consistently important in key sectors, namely fishing, canning, and agricultural sectors. In this way, as well as others, the aboriginal and non-aboriginal histories of British Columbia are still inextricably linked.

Notes

1. For other statements along these lines see David McNally, 'Political Economy Without a Working Class', *Labour/Le Travail* 25 (Spring 1990): 220n; Paul Phillips, 'Confederation and the Economy of British Columbia', in W. George Shelton, ed., *British Columbia and Confederation* (Victoria: Morriss Printing Co. Ltd., 1967), 59; Martin Robin, *The Rush for the Spoils: The Company Province 1871–1933* (Toronto: McClelland and Stewart, 1972), 30.

2. For simplicity's sake, I have combined in the term 'paid labour': wage work, (whether paid in kind, scrip, or cash), piecework, and independent commodity production (hand logging for example), although each system produced its own set of social relations.

3. For an introduction see William C. Sturtuvant, *Handbook of North American Indians* (Washington, DC: Smithsonian Institute: 1978), vols 4, 6, 7.

4. The Songhees, a band of the Coast Salish, were an amalgamation of several nearby villages that relocated to a site across the harbour from Fort Victoria after the latter was founded in 1843.

5. Great Britain. Colonial Office, Original Correspondence, Vancouver Island, 1846–1867, CO 305/6, 10048, Governor James Douglas to Russell, 21 August 1855. Colonial Office correspondence (with a CO number) cited here was made available to me by James Hendrickson from his unpublished manuscript 'Vancouver Island: Colonial Correspondence Dispatches'.

6. See CO 305/14, 9267, Douglas to Colonial Office, 8 August 1860.

7. See CO 305/4, 9499, Douglas to Newcastle, 28 July 1853.

8. The Tsimshian were from the Skeena River area around Fort Simpson; William Duncan, 'Journal',

11 July 1857, cited in Jean Usher, *William Duncan of Metlakatla: A Victorian Missionary in British Columbia* (Ottawa: National Museum of Man, 1974), 40; W.C. Grant in William Grew Hazlitt, *British Columbia and Vancouver Island* (London: S.R. Publishers, 1858), 179; Dorothy B. Smith, *The Reminiscences of Doctor John Sebastian Helmcken* (Vancouver: UBC Press, 1975), 134.

9. See CO 305/6, 10048, Douglas to Lord Russell, 21 August 1855; CO 305/4, 12345, Douglas to Newcastle, 24 October 1853, emphasis mine.

10. See also 'Northern Indians,' San Francisco *Evening Bulletin*, 4 October 1860, reprinted in James Swan, *Almost Out of This World* (Tacoma: Washington State Historical Society, 1971), 99; CO 305/7, 3963, Douglas to Sir George Grey, 1 March 1856; and CO 305/7 5814, 10 April 1856.

11. See CO 305/3, Rev. R.J. Staines to Thomas Boys, 6 July 1852; Smith, *Reminiscences*, 134; CO 305/3 Douglas to Earl Grey, 31 October 1851.

12. British Columbia Archives and Record Services (BCARS), Colonial Correspondence, F347/26a; James Cooper, 'Report by the Harbor Master at Esquimalt to the Acting Colonial Secretary'; Usher, *William Duncan of Metlakatla*, 58.

13. See CO 305/14, 9267, Douglas to Colonial Office, 8 August 1860.

14. See CO 305/14, 8319, Douglas to Colonial Office, 7 July 1860. One major change during the gold rush was that aboriginal labour was increasingly being paid in cash instead of goods. Previously the goods most sought after as pay were blankets, which were commonly used as 'potlatch' gifts.

15. San Francisco *Times* (27 August 1858) in Hazlitt, *British Columbia*, 208, 215. See also Robin Fisher, 'Joseph Trutch and the Indian Land Policy', in W.P. Ward and R.A.J. McDonald, eds, *British Columbia: Historical Readings* (Vancouver: Douglas & McIntyre, 1981), 155; Sophia Cracroft, *Lady Franklin Visits the Pacific Northwest: February to April 1861 and April to July 1870* (Victoria: Provincial Archives of British Columbia, 1974), 79.

16. The reference is to a blanket of 2½ points specifying a particular quality of blanket. Douglas to the Governor and Committee, 3 September 1849, 3 April and 16 November 1850 in Bowsfield, *Fort Victoria Letters, 1845–1851* (Winnipeg: Hudson's Bay Record Society), 46, 84, 132: William Burrill, 'Class Conflict and Colonialism: The Coal Miners of Vancouver Island During the Hudson's Bay Company Era, 1848–1862', MA thesis, University of Victoria, 1987, 54.

17. See CO 305/3, 10199, Douglas to Pakington, 28 August 1852; also CO 305/3, 933, 11 November 1852.

18. Canada. Parliament, House of Commons, *Sessional Papers*, (hereafter Canada, *SP*) 1878, 8, lx; 1883, 54: 1889, 13, 100–2. The 1877 annual report of the BC Minister of Mines records 51 Indians working as coal-miners in Nanaimo plus an unrecorded number working as miners' helpers. These annual reports show some Aboriginal people working in the coal mines into the twentieth-century. British Columbia, Legislative Assembly, *Sessional Papers* (hereafter BC, *SP*) 1877, 617.

19. Quote from CO 305/3, 3742, Douglas to Earl Grey, 29 January 1852; CO 305/3, 9263, Staines to Boys, 6 July 1852; CO 305/3, Douglas to Earl Grey, 31 October 1851; CO 305/3, 8866, Captain A.L. Kuper to Admiralty, 20 July 1852; CO 305/9, 5180, Douglas to Labouchere, 6 April 1858.

20. There are other estimates of between 200 and 500 aboriginal people mining at Hill's Bar compared to 50–60 white miners in Hazlitt, *British Columbia and Vancouver Island*, 137.

21. Canada. National Archives (NA), RG10, Department of Indian Affairs, Vol. 1001, items 82, 186. C.J. Grandidier to W. Powell, 2 July 1874 and Alexis to James Lenihan, 5 September 1875.

22. BCARS, Colonial Correspondence, File 107/5, W.E. Banfield to the Colonial Secretary, 6 September 1860, from Lorne Hammond, unpublished manuscript on W.E. Banfield; James Morton, *The Enterprising Mr Moody and the Bumptious Captain Stamp* (Vancouver: J.J. Douglas, 1977), 22–3; H.G. Langley, *Pacific Coast Directory for 1867* (San Francisco: H.G. Langley, 1867), 158.

23. Canada, *SP* 1877, 8, 'Report of the Indian Reserve Commissioners', lii; Powell in Canada, *SP* 1884, 107.

24. In 1876 'Hundreds and sometimes thousands of northern Indians congregate every spring' to trade and work at Puget Sound mills, according to J.G. Swan, 'The Haida Indians of Queen Charlotte's Islands, British Columbia', *Smithsonian Contributions to Knowledge* XXI (1876): 2, 8.

25. In 1876 the 55 men of the Sechelt band cut 1,300,000 cubic feet of saw logs for the mills for which they received $3 per thousand, the same rate paid to white loggers; Canada, *SP* 1878, 8 'Report of the Indian Reserve Commissioners', lix; Knight, *Indians at Work: An Informal History of Native Indian Labour in British Columbia, 1858–1930*, (Vancouver: New Star Books, 1978), 114, 123–4. Missionary William Duncan established a sawmill and a soap

factory at Metlakatla by 1871. Other mission-mills followed at Alert Bay, Glen Vowell, Hartley Bay, and Kispiox. A description of the latter can be found in Hicks, *From Potlatch to Pulpit* (Vancouver: Vancouver Bindery, 1933), 69–70.

26. 'Salmon Pack for 1883, Fraser River Canneries', *Resources of British Columbia* 1 (1883): 4; aboriginal cannery labour has been considered in some detail by Muszynski and Knight.

27. This estimate subtracts the population figures of the Indian Affairs census for the bands listed as living primarily or exclusively on trapping, hunting and fishing, from the total aboriginal population. The bands subtracted are: 239 people in Chilcotin, 600 on the coast, 300 of Kootenays and 2,000 for tribes not visited. See Wilson Duff, *The Indian History of British Columbia: The Impact of the White Man* (Victoria: Royal British Columbia Museum, 1965), 35–40 for estimates of tribes not visited.

28. J.A. Jacobsen, *Alaskan Voyage, 1881–83: An Expedition to the Northwest Coast of America*, translated from the German text of Adrian Woldt by Erna Gunther (Chicago: University of Chicago Press, 1977), 13 and passim; Canada, *SP* 1888, 13, 109, 157–8; Edward Sapir, *Nootka Texts* (Philadelphia, Linguistic Society of America, 1939).

29. Chinook was made up of words from aboriginal languages, French, and English. A provincial business directory for 1877–78 published a Chinook–English, English–Chinook dictionary for the benefit of its readers: see T.N. Hibben, *Guide to the Province of British Columbia for 1877–78* (Victoria, T.N. Hibben, 1877), 222–49. Franz Boas noted in 1889 that it was impossible for someone to get around British Columbia outside the major cities without knowledge of the language. See Rohner, *Ethnography* 9 and BCARS. Add. Mss. 2305, Alfred Carmichael, 'Account of a season's work at a Salmon Cannery, Windsor Cannery, Aberdeen, Skeena' *c*. 1885, which records the widespread use of Chinook in the Skeena canneries in the mid-1880s.

30. See NA, RG10, vol. 1349, items 85, 255, 290, 483, 501.

31. Canner F.L. Lord told the BC Fishery Commission in 1892 that Chinese contractors hired the native women and 'of course these Chinamen pay the klootchmen' in BC, *SP* 1893, 178; 'When the fishing commences the boss chinaman hires Indians to clean the fish mid their squaws to fill the cans,' according to Carmichael, 'Account of a Seasons Work'.

32. The Tsimshian that lived around the HBC post at Fort Simpson went to Victoria before other Tsimshian groups not living at the fort. Similarly it was

the Fort Rupert Kwakwaka'wakw, and the southern Haida around Skidegate (who had exposure to white miners and whalers in addition to itinerant seaborne fur-traders) that were the first of their respective 'nations' to begin labour migration. For the Fort Rupert people see Philip Drucker and R.F. Heizer, *To Make My Name Good: A Re-examination of the Southern Kwakiutl Potlatch* (Berkeley: University of California Press, 1976), 215. For the Haida see J.H. Van Den Brink, *The Haida Indians: Cultural Change Mainly Between 1876–1970* (Leiden: Brill, 1974), 51.

33. Lomas in Canada, *SP* 1888, 13, 105.

34. Canada. *SP* 1883, 60, records an aboriginal husband and wife fishing team, the wife pulling the boat and the husband handling the net and making $240 in 14 days.

35. Canada, *SP* 1887, 5, 92; 1888, 13, 105. In 1913 Indian Agent Charles Cox reported that Nuu-chah-nulth men and women keep their incomes separate, in Royal Commission on Pelagic Sealing, Victoria, Indian Claims, December 1913, vol. 8. 135, in Crockford, 'Changing Economic Activities of Nuu-chah-nulth of Vancouver Island, 1840–1920', Hon. thesis, University of Victoria, 1991, 43. The Department of Fisheries Annual Reports in Canada, *Sessional Papers*, record the number of aboriginal people involved in pelagic sealing, 1882–1910.

36. Canada, *SP*, 1888, 13, 106; Cracroft. *Lady Franklin*, 79. W.F. Tolmie wrote in 1883 that the aboriginal women in Victoria worked 'as washerwomen, seamstresses and laundresses, earn much and spend it all in the city', BCARS A/E/Or3/C15.

37. Canada, *SP* 1884, 106; Carmichael, 'Account of a Seasons Work'; Indian women 'knit' nets that 'will average from 120–150 fathoms (long and 16 and a half feet deep), at the cost of one dollar per fathom', *Resources of British Columbia* 1 (1 December 1883).

38. By 1865 the Victoria police were writing the Colonial Secretary that some 200 Indian prostitutes lived 'in filthy shanties owned by Chinese and rented . . . at four to five dollars a month', in Peter Baskerville, *Beyond the Island: An Illustrated History of Victoria* (Burlington, ON: Windsor Publications, 1986), 39–44. For the 1880s see John A. Macdonald, Canada, *SP* 1885, lix. For an aboriginal account of prostitution, see Franz Boas, *Contributions to the Ethnography of the Kwakiutl* (New York: Columbia University Press, 1925), 93–4.

39. There is an enormous ethnographic literature on the potlatch; a good bibliography can be found in D. Cole and I. Chaikin, *An Iron Hand Upon the People* (Vancouver: Douglas & McIntyre, 1990), 213–23.

40. Fisher, *Contact and Conflict*; Duff, *Indian History of B.C.*; Cole and Chaikin, *An Iron Hand*; Helen Codere, *Fighting With Property: A Study of Kwakiutl Potlatching and Warfare, 1792–1930* (Seattle: AMS Press, 1966).
41. See CO 305/4, 12345, Douglas to Colonial Secretary, 24 October 1853; Margaret Ormsby states that when the Haidas were unable to mine gold on the Queen Charlotte Islands for lack of tools they offered to sell their rights if the HBC would form an establishment, Bowsfield, *Fort Victoria Letters*, xci.
42. Canada. *SP* 1881, 5, 143. This was also the wish of the Kincolith people of the Nass River, NA, RG10, Vol. 11007, W.H. Collinson to the Reserve Commissioner, 10 October 1887.
43. See CO 305/4,12345, Douglas to Newcastle, 24 October 1853.
44. Knight has a similar story from a completely different source that seems to describe a response to big George's Potlatch by a rival. *Indians at Work,*

114; Capt. C.E. Barrett-Lennard, *Travels in British Columbia With the Narrative of A Yacht Voyage Round Vancouver's Island* (London: Hurst and Blackett, 1862), 60.
45. 'The Kwakiutl had a potential demand for European goods in excess of any practical utility the goods might have possessed. This can be seen both as a stimulus to the Kwakiutl Integration in their new economy and as a direct stimulus to the potlatch,' Codere, *Fighting With Property*, 126.
46. With the acceptance of Christianity 'modified potlatching' continued in some places, but the new Christians also had new imperatives to work. New houses built with milled lumber, nails, and glass windows, as well as new standards for clothing, contributions to build a church or purchase musical instruments etc., all demanded cash incomes.
47. Although the Kwakwaka'wakw proved an exception in this regard.

References

Anderson, A.C. 1872. *The Dominion at the West; a Brief Description of the Province of British Columbia.* Victoria: R. Wolfenden, government printer.

Bowsfield, Hartwell. 1979. *Fort Victoria Letters 1846–1851.* Winnipeg: Hudson's Bay Record Society.

Burrill, William. 1987. 'Class Conflict and Colonialism: The Coal Miners of Vancouver Island During the Hudson's Bay Company Era, 1848–1862', MA thesis, University of Victoria.

Carmichael, Alfred. *c.* 1885. 'Account of a Season's Work at a Salmon Canner, Windsor Cannery, Aberdeen, Skeena'.

Codere, Helen. 1966. *Fighting With Property: A Study of Kwakiutl Potlatching and Warfare, 1792–1930.* Seattle: AMS Press.

Cole, D., and I. Chaikin. 1990. *An Iron Hand Upon the People.* Vancouver: Douglas & McIntyre.

Collins, June. 1949. 'John Fornsby: The Personal Document of A Coast Salish Indian', in Marian Smith, ed., *Indians of the Urban Northwest.* New York: Columbia University Press.

Cox, Bruce Alden, ed. *Native People, Native Lands: Canadian Indians, Inuit and Métis.* Ottawa: Carleton University Press.

Dawson, G.M. 1887. 'Notes and Observations on the Kwakiool People of Vancouver Island and Adjacent Coasts made during the Summer of 1885', *Transactions of the Royal Society of Canada*, section 2.

Douglas, James, and T.A. Rickard. 1938. 'Indian Participation in the Gold Discoveries', *British Columbia Historical Quarterly* 2.

Drucker, Philip. 1965. *Cultures of the North Pacific Coast.* New York: Addison-Wesley.

Drucker, Philip, and R.F. Heizer. 1976. *To Make My Name Good: A Re-examination of the Southern Kwakiutl Potlatch.* Berkeley, CA: University of California Press.

Fisher, Robin. 1977. *Contact and Conflict: Indian European Relations in British Columbia, 1774–1890.* Vancouver: University of British Columbia Press.

Fiske, Jo-Anne. 1988. 'Fishing is Women's Business: Changing Economic Roles of Carrier Women and Men', in Bruce Alden Cox, ed., *Native People, Native Lands: Canadian Indians, Inuit and Métis.* Ottawa: Carleton University Press.

Forbes, Charles. 1862. *Vancouver Island, its Resources and Capabilities as a Colony.* Victoria: The Colonial Government.

Ford, Chellan. 1968. *Smoke from their Fires: The Life of a Kwakiutl Chief.* Hamdon, CN: Yale University Press.

Grant, George M. 1873. *Ocean to Ocean: Sir Sanford Fleming's Expedition through Canada in 1872.* Toronto: J. Campbell.

Harvey, A.A. 1867. *A Statistical Account of British Columbia.* Ottawa: G.E. Desbartes

Hicks, J.P., ed. 1933. *From Potlatch to Pulpit: The Autobiography of W.H. Pierce.* Vancouver: Vancouver Bindery.

Jacobsen, J.A. 1877. *Alaskan Voyage, 1881–83: An Expedition to the Northwest Coast of America*, trans. from the German text of Adrian Woldt by Erna Gunther. Chicago: University of Chicago Press.

Kane, Paul. 1968. *Wanderings of an Artist Among the Indians of North America*. Edmonton: M.G. Hurtig.

Knight, Rolf. 1978. *Indians at Work: An Informal History of Native Indian Labour in British Columbia, 1858–1930*. Vancouver: University of British Columbia Press.

Langevin, H.L. 1872. *British Columbia: Report of the Hon. H.L. Langevin*. Ottawa: I.B. Taylor.

Littlefield, Lorraine. 1988. 'Women Traders in the Fur Trade', in Bruce Alden Cox, ed., *Native People, Native Lands: Canadian Indians, Inuit and Métis*. Ottawa: Carelton University Press.

Lowe, Thomas. 1897. Victoria *Colonist*, 29 October.

McDonald, J.A. 1984. 'Images of the Nineteenth-Century Economy of the Tsimshian', in M. Seguin, ed., *The Tsimshian: Images of the Past, Views for the Present*. Vancouver: UBC Press.

Mackie, Richard. 1985. 'Colonial Land, Indian Labour and Company Capital: The Economy of Vancouver Island, 1849–1858', MA thesis, University of Victoria.

Mitchell, Marjorie, and Anna Franklin. 1989. 'When You Don't Know the Language, Listen to the Silence: An Historical Overview of Native Women in B.C.', in P.E. Roy, ed., *A History of British Columbia: Selected Readings*. Toronto: Copp Clark Pitman.

Morton, James. 1977. *The Enterprising Mr Moody and the Bumptious Captain Stamp*. Vancouver: J.J. Douglas.

Rich, E.E., ed. 1941. *The Letters of John McLoughlin from Fort Vancouver, 1825–1838*. Toronto: Champlain Society for the Hudson's Bay Record Society.

Robin, Martin. 1972. *The Rush for the Spoils: The Company Province 1871–1933*. Toronto: McClelland and Stewart.

Rohner, R.P. 1969. *The Ethnography of Franz Boas*. Chicago: University of Chicago Press.

Sewid, James. 1989. *Guests Never Leave Hungry: The Autobiography of a Kwakiutl Indian*, James Spradley, ed. New Haven, CT: Yale University Press.

Sproat, G.M. 1868 [rpt. 1989]. *Scenes and Studies of Savage Life*. London: Smith, Elder/Victoria: Sono Nis Press.

Stacey, Duncan. 1982. *Sockeye & Tinplate: Technological Change in the Fraser Canning Industry, 1871–1912*. Victoria: British Columbia Provincial Museum.

Taylor, G.W. 1975. *Timber: History of the Forest Industry in B.C.* Vancouver: J.J. Douglas.

von Hesse-Wartegg, Ernst. 1981. 'A Visit to the Anglo-Saxon Antipodes (Chapter XVIII of *Curiosa aus der Neuen Welt*, 1893, John Maass, trans.)', *BC Studies* 50.

Wyatt, Victoria. 1987. 'Alaskan Indian Wage Earners in the 19th Century', *Pacific Northwest Quarterly* 78, 1/2.

PART II   Immigrant Settlers and the Tensions of Class Formation

The working class of nineteenth-century Canada is often regarded as insignificant, largely because the huge, mechanized factories and urban concentrations of labouring people that would come to be commonly associated with twentieth-century capitalism showed almost no signs of coming into being until after Confederation in 1867. Nevertheless, as the previous account of aboriginal peoples and class formation indicates, Canada's emergence as a nation over the course of the nineteenth century was never separable from the work that governed the everyday lives of its residents. That work was a persistent feature of life in rural economies where subsistence was eked out of an always challenging attempt to grow crops or harvest timber from the abundant forests. It also characterized ports such as Halifax and Saint John, dependent as they were on transatlantic commerce and the seafaring trades that provided many in the British Isles with employments that ultimately brought them to British North America. And in the developing cities of this early Canadian society, apprentices and craftsmen toiled in the small artisan shops where the products needed to sustain a growing population were fashioned out of leather, cloth, and iron. Building tradesmen, carters, and others congregated at job sites in and adjacent to the muddy streets of York or Old Montreal.

If, as we will see below, this experience of work, and the discontents associated with it, resulted in early eruptions of class struggle, the dominant tensions of pre-Confederation class formation often registered in more subtle ways. This was the case because the institutions of class identification and the consciousness of class place were as undeveloped as were the differentiations of workers from their social superiors. Society seemed, compared to later historical periods, more open to the possibility of upward mobility: newly arrived poor immigrants might, in a generation, rise to positions of social prominence and relatively high status; the young apprentice could, decades later, own his own tailoring or shoemaking establishment. In this context, various forms of paternalism thrived, as older, male authority figures guided their younger counterparts in the ways of social, economic, and political advancement. Identifications of religion, ethnicity, gender, and age blurred the ways in which work itself was becoming more and more associated with the impersonal features of a developing market in which commodity production and wage labour were forces of transformation that left some people dependent and others in positions of ownership and power.

As Bonnie Huskins shows, while early nineteenth-century Canadians were not necessarily what they ate, how they did eat and drink was very much a measure of their class place. Her discussion of celebratory feasting and drinking in Atlantic Canada raises important questions about social distance in urban settings, outlining how specific locales and built environments became associated with particular classes. Types of food and drink reinforced understandings of social station. The centrality of place was both a geographical and a social expression of class and status: the banquet— held indoors and involving seated guests and convivial toasts—was an expression of the rich and their superiority, while the out-of-door ox roasts and picnic feasts so often associated with paternalistic authority's caring command over its subordinates were primarily peopled by the labouring poor. If specific events—a Queen's birthday, a Prince's marriage, a Royal visit—might be celebrated by all, the ways in which these festivities were ordered proved fundamental in establishing class inequality as a matter of course in everyday life. But the provisioning for the poor always carried with it the possibility that the plebeian masses would extend the democracy of the moment, and demand more than the share they were charitably offered by their social superiors.

This, indeed, was what happened as a fragmented working-class began to organize and challenge employers in the pre-1860 years. Trade unionism in these years was weak, most often being a local undertaking; its successes registered almost entirely with the skilled, male, craft workers whose intimate connections to one another were sealed in the small workshops of the pre-industrial capitalist order. Conventional understandings of the law often suggested that combinations of workmen were illegal conspiracies in restraint of trade, and mechanics who formed associations of printers, tailors, shoemakers, shipwrights, bakers, or early metalworkers, might well find themselves hauled into the courts if an employing master decided he needed to resist their irksome solidarity. Strikes and unions were understandably few, then, and preliminary research reveals that prior to mid-century less than 50 local unions had been formed in the Canadian colonies; in a half century there had only been 59 formal strikes.

As Ruth Bleasdale reveals, however, unskilled labour raised the voice of class struggle in this period, often in ways that indicated how workers who had no unions were driven to revolt, the most vehement expression of which was the riot. Canal labourers were arguably one of the most volatile elements of the pre-Confederation Canadian working class. They struck worksites with more force in the pre-1850 years than any other occupation, the simple reason being that they had little alternative: the contractors who employed them subjected the largely Irish and French canal labour workforce to abominable conditions, paid them miserable wages, and often shut down work on canal construction without paying the full wage bill owing. If craft workers in the cities, organized in small, local unions, were the respectable segment of early nineteenth-century Canadian labour, the canallers were their rough counterpart. Often these newly-arrived immigrant workers had no recourse but to riot in order to secure their jobs or their pay. They battled not only their bosses, but also farmers whose fencing they pillaged to warm their makeshift domiciles, and magistrates and militias who did their utmost to keep their unruly behaviour in line. Sometimes the canallers fought among themselves, Irish Protestants battling Irish Catholics, each looking to control the local job market; French versus Irish wars along the canals were not uncommon, as they were, as well, in the timber trade of the Ottawa Valley. All told, canallers rioted at least 68 times in the 55 years from 1820–1875, this number representing fully 20 per cent of the occupationally-identified 139 riots that took place in these years. The tensions of early class formation were perhaps nowhere as clearly visible.

Further Reading

Michael S. Cross, 'The Shiners' War: Social Violence in the Ottawa Valley in the 1830s', *Canadian Historical Review* 54 (March 1973): 1–26.

Judith Fingard, 'The Winters' Tale: The Seasonal Contours of Pre-Industrial Poverty in British North America, 1815–1860', Canadian Historical Association, *Papers* (1974): 65–94.

Judith Fingard, *Jack in Port: Sailortowns of Eastern Canada* (Toronto: University of Toronto Press, 1982).

Eugene Forsey, *Trade Unions in Canada, 1812–1902* (Toronto: University of Toronto Press, 1982).

Bryan D. Palmer, 'Discordant Music: Charivaris and Whitecapping in Nineteenth-Century North America', *Labour/Le Travailleur* 3 (1978): 5–62.

Bryan D. Palmer, 'Labour Protest and Organization in Nineteenth-Century Canada, 1820–1890', *Labour/Le Travail* 20 (Fall 1987): 61–84.

H. Clare Pentland, *Labour and Capital in Canada, 1650–1850* (Toronto: James Lorimer, 1982).

Eric Tucker, '"That Indefinite Area of Toleration": Criminal Conspiracy and Trade Unions in Ontario, 1837–1877', *Labour/Le Travail* 27 (Spring 1991): 15–54.

Peter Way, *Common Labour: Workers and the Digging of North American Canals, 1780–1860* (New York: Cambridge University Press, 1993).

CHAPTER 3

From *Haute Cuisine* to Ox Roasts: Public Feasting and the Negotiation of Class in Mid-Nineteenth-Century Saint John and Halifax

Bonnie Huskins

Introduction

. . . . One of the most popular and universal forms of celebration is feasting and drinking. Despite its popularity and universality, the public feast has not received sufficient scholarly attention from historians. . . . Thus, the primary objective of this paper is to delineate a typology or hierarchy of public feasts in mid-nineteenth-century Saint John and Halifax, which will provide us with an alternate lens through which to view class and culture. Joseph Gusfield has commented that 'what is eaten and how it is eaten constitute a mode of communication and can be read as a cultural object, embodying attributes of social organization or general culture'[1] (1987: 76). In the popular bestseller, *Much Depends on Dinner*, Margaret Visser similarly notes: 'Food—what is chosen from the possibilities available, how it is presented, how it is eaten, with whom and when, and how much time is allotted to cooking and eating it—is one of the means by which a society creates itself and acts out its aims and fantasies' (1986: 12). While an analysis of feasting and drinking can provide many insights into the nature of society, this paper will focus on how we can use food and drink as markers of class and as instruments in the process of class formation. This emphasis on food, drink, and social relations is borrowed from structuralists like anthropologist Mary Douglas and sociologist Pierre Bourdieu, who argue that 'food categories encode social events, as . . . they express

hierarchy, inclusion and exclusion, boundaries, and transactions across boundaries'[2] (Mennell, 1985: 11). Mary Douglas has noted that 'we need to stop thinking of food as something that people desire and use apart from social relations. . . . It is disingenuous to pretend that food is not one of the media of social exclusion' (1984: 36). Did feasting and drinking in mid-nineteenth-century Saint John and Halifax help to define the boundaries of inclusion and exclusion, as suggested by these social scientists?

In order to answer this question, it will be necessary to explore the various meanings and uses of public feasts. Why did people in different classes partake of 'victuals' and 'spirits'? How does this reflect their different priorities and social practises at mid-century? Mary Douglas argues that '. . . the ordinary consuming public in modern industrial society works hard to invest its food with moral, social, and aesthetic meanings.' If we do not seek out these meanings, 'festivities [will be] treated as illegitimate demands on the world's productive system, the source of social inequalities and ultimately responsible for the maldistribution of food,' clearly an incomplete and misleading understanding of such events (1984: 5–6). In this paper I will systematically explore the meanings of the public feast for the middle-class and working-class inhabitants of mid-Victorian Saint John and Halifax. Emphasis will be placed on public secular feasts—that is, the banquet, ox roast, institutional repast, and tea and coffee soirée—which were held to commemorate royal and patriotic anniversaries. The most notable celebrations in this analysis include the observance of Queen Victoria's coronation in 1838 and her marriage in 1840, the birth of the Prince of Wales in 1841, and the celebration of his visit in 1860 and his marriage in 1863. . . .

Context

Saint John and Halifax were both commercial entrepôts in the nineteenth century. Saint John processed timber from its hinterland—the Saint John River Valley—and competed in an international timber trade and shipbuilding industry (Wynn, 1981; Acheson, 1985). Halifax relied on a salt fish trade, particularly with the West Indies, and a general import trade.

By mid-century, urbanization had created rather complex urban landscapes in Saint John and Halifax. Initially the ward had been the basis of civic government, with the alderman functioning as a *paterfamilias*, creating an intricate network of relationships operating on the foundation of blood, service, and patronage. By mid-century, however, ward politics was being supplanted by a professionalized civic administration, which was 'more comprehensive, less personal, better organized, less arbitrary but more capable of imposing its will on a broader front' (Acheson, 1985: 195).

Increasing class differentiation also accompanied the growth of these urban centres. Irish Roman-Catholic immigrants swelled the ranks of the working class in the 1840s. Poverty was further accentuated by the susceptibility of the colonial economy to the vagaries of external and internal trends and erratic business depressions (Whalen, 1972: 60; Fingard, 1975: 33). Many 'respectable' middle-class citizens distanced themselves as much as possible from the working-class poor in order to avoid the social problems associated with poverty, such as the outbreaks of cholera which infested the cities at mid-century (Bilson, 1974). This desire for social distance is most effectively illustrated by the residential make up of the two cities. In Halifax, suburbanization of the rural Northwest Arm began when middle-class businessmen, politicians, and lawyers moved there and built lavish estates in the 1840s and 1850s. By the 1860s, the south end of the city had become known as the 'court end of town', because of the existence of the residences of major merchants and government officials. A black community called Africville established itself by 1850 on the shores of the Bedford Basin and the Harbour, and the presence of the railway in the north end of the city encouraged the creation of a working-class community called Richmond. Halifax's major British garrison and naval station also reinforced residential segregation as a sailortown emerged along the waterfront and a soldiertown around the base of Citadel Hill.[3] In Saint John, the southernmost ward of Sydney was comprised largely of working-class inhabitants who provided services for the resident garrison. The adjacent Dukes ward boasted a mixed neighbourhood of 'artisans, merchants, and mechanics'. Queens ward, a little further north, housed the largest proportion of merchants and other 'businesspeople'. A 'Protestant' artisan population resided in the eastern part of Kings ward, and an Irish Roman-Catholic neighbourhood in the western end, called York Point. By the early nineteenth century African-New Brunswick residents had settled in a segregated community in the vicinity of Loch Lomand (Acheson, 1985; See, 1993).

The garrisons in both cities reinforced the distinction between 'rough' and 'respectable' in more ways than one. Rank and file soldiers supported networks of taverns, brothels, and similar industries, while the officers entered the ranks of the local elite. This effect was particularly magnified in Halifax due to the large size of the garrison. Regular soldiers, numbering 2,000 to 4,000, comprised close to 25 per cent of the resident male population of Halifax in the nineteenth century (Fingard, 1983–4: 3; 1989: 15).

What role did drinking and feasting play in the creation and dramatization of class distinctions in mid-Victorian Saint John and Halifax? All classes dined and imbibed at mid-century; it was a 'heavy-eating, hard-drinking age' (Beck, 1985: 903). Residents could choose from a wide variety of taverns and saloons. In 1830, Saint John issued 206 tavern licenses and 29 retail licenses, which meant that 1 citizen in 50 held a liquor seller's license. Halifax contained between 200–300 drinking houses and shops by the 1860s, approximately 1 drinking establishment for every 100 inhabitants, including women and children (Acheson, 1985; Fingard, 1988). Many working-class recreations 'centred on the tavern', and liquor had also become an 'integral part of the work culture'. Respectable men and women largely confined their drinking to the home or to more exclusive venues. Eliza Donkin, a young Victorian woman from Saint John, noted the 'habitual use of liquor in the family circles'[4] (Acheson, 1985: 142). National societies often celebrated their anniversaries with annual banquets.[5] Celebrants also dined in observance of certain *rites de passage*, Christmas, and other high days and holy days, as well as during commemorative celebrations. Although all classes drank and feasted, did they do so in the same way and for the same purpose? Indeed, it is the argument of this paper that different forms of feasting reflected and reinforced contemporary class divisions. Middle-class and elite residents, for example, drew their social circles tighter by partaking of exclusive indoor banquets.

Banquet

The banquet, a frequent accompaniment to the grand ball, was one of the most long-standing

and popular elite entertainments. Judith Fingard mentions the ball (and banquet) as one of the leisure activities which united the 'well-to-do' in the winter months in pre-industrial Canada (Fingard, 1985). Private citizens, provincial and civic officials, and voluntary organizations usually orchestrated the entertainments. . . .

Balls and banquets promoted exclusivity by restricting attendance to a clique of local, provincial, imperial, and military dignitaries, and by charging a relatively high subscription or admission price for everyone else. A perusal of the guest list for Saint John's 'corporation' banquet in 1838 shows that it mainly consisted of civic and provincial officials, military and militia officers, and commercial and mercantile elites. . . . Organizers of the ball and banquet held for the Prince of Wales in Halifax in 1860 restricted admission to 250 invitations and 1,000 tickets, priced at a restrictive two sovereigns for a man and one sovereign for a woman. According to the *Evening Express*, these prices kept the attraction 'a rather more aristocratic affair than it otherwise would have been'.[6]

Such events provided an opportunity for the display of respectability, breeding, and refinement. Thorstein Veblen has remarked that 'conspicuous consumption' is *primae facie* evidence of one's 'pecuniary success' and 'social worth' (Veblen, 1934: 127). 'A Bluenose' described the typical ball and banquet as an event at which

> Tom, Dick, and Harry, tag, rag, and bobtail, might have an opportunity of displaying their breeding before the wives and daughters of the big wigs; and the wives and daughters of the little wigs an opportunity of being laughed at by Tom, Dick, and Harry, by Lord Somebody, and the honble [sic] Mr Nobody, or the red-coat and blue-coat schools. No such thing Mr Editor—by the powers!—this is not the way the Coronation of Her Majesty should be

observed in any of her dominions—at home or beyond the seas. (Halifax *Times*, 22 May 1838)

The dinners served at these events were notable for the 'strict rules' governing the 'presentation of food, the varieties permitted at a given occasion, and rules of precedence and combination' (Douglas, 1987: 15). The menu for the Prince of Wales's marriage feast at the Halifax Hotel in 1863 is an example of nineteenth-century *haute cuisine*. Many of the dishes featured in the bill of fare are French in origin. Indeed, culinary respectability has been associated with French (and Italian) cooking since the exchange of cooks and recipes among the 'courtly strata' in the Middle Ages (Mennell, 1984: 60, 102). However, the nineteenth century witnessed the 'full establishment of a French international culinary hegemony', not only in Europe, but in North America as well, as the great French chefs fled from their aristocratic employers after the Revolution, and set up their own restaurants, and wrote cooking manuals, which disseminated their culinary arts (Mennell, 1984: 135–6). . . .

The courses served at the Prince of Wales's marriage feast resemble those associated with 'service à la française'. 'Service à la française' was a tradition of serving dinner dating back to the Middle Ages, and was characterized by three set courses and dessert. . . . The Prince of Wales's marriage feast in Halifax also reflects 'service à la russe' in that menus were evidently printed, and courses listed as sets of alternatives in the bill of fare. However, it is not known whether or not the dishes were served this way by the servants; also, the courses themselves still reflect 'service à la française'. Regardless, Haligonians evidently found it important to structure their banquets according to typical middle-class rules of etiquette. This structure undoubtedly helped to define the banquet as

'one of the weapons in the social armory' of respectability and exclusivity (Levenstein, 1988: 16).

The nature of the wines served at such events also expressed class identity. Mary Douglas reminds us: 'We must take note of the exclusionary potential represented by the serried ranks of vintage and lesser wines. . .' (1987: 9). For the banquet held in Halifax in 1860 in celebration of the visit of the Prince of Wales, the organizing committee selected 12 dozen sherries, 31 dozen high quality champagnes, including 23 dozen of 'Mumm's', and 28 dozen of the cheaper wines.[7]

Banquets also reinforced middle-class masculinity. Although the ball was one of the only celebratory activities in the mid-Victorian period in which middle-class women could actively participate (Halifax *Morning Sun*, 27 July 1860), they usually retired from the banquet table before the toasts began because public drinking was primarily a male ritual. The men often raised their glasses in honour of the women, but such 'accolades' were only 'minor and perfunctory exercises' (Halifax *Sun*, 11 June 1845; Halifax *Novascotian*, 20 August 1860).[8] According to Levenstein, women were also expected to show greater 'gastronomic restraint' (1988: 12).

The list of toasts at such affairs acknowledged the hierarchy of colonial society. Royal occasions particularly paid tribute to the lieutenant governor, as the Queen's representative. At Saint John's corporation dinner in 1838, those present acknowledged Lieutenant-Governor Sir John Harvey and his actions in the recent border war with the United States (*New Brunswick Courier*, 30 June 1838). Toasts were also customarily extended to Queen Victoria and the royal family, the colonial secretary, the governor general, the British officers and the army and navy, the provincial administration, the sister colonies, the lieutenant governor's wife and the 'fair daughters' of the colonies, and other special guests.[9]

Thus, the balls and banquets held during public celebrations in the early-to-mid nineteenth century promoted exclusivity and respectability by restricting attendance, encouraging displays of opulence and finery, serving *haute cuisine* and fine wines, and toasting and thereby reinforcing the *status quo*, including the inequalities of class and gender.

Ox Roast

Celebratory regalement was not confined to the middle and upper classes. The general public also partook of 'great outdoor feasts where massive quantities of meat, game, and liquor were consumed' (Karsky, 1985: 61). The Nova Scotia Philanthropic Society inaugurated the custom of having an annual picnic to celebrate the founding of Halifax (Harvey, 1939: 292).[10] The first natal day picnic at the Prince's Lodge in 1839 consisted of an 'abundance of viands and lots of good liquor to moisten them'. Similarly, approximately 300 people enjoyed a feast of 'fish, flesh, and fowl' during the 1845 picnic.[11]

Larger outdoor feasts were also held in the public squares and commons. It is significant that the feasts provided for the general public and the poor took place out of doors. One reason was pure logistics. Organizers did not have the facilities sufficient to accommodate large crowds. But the 'out of doors' also conveyed images of democracy and freedom which suited the mass demonstration. . . .

In eighteenth- and early ninteenth-century England, public outdoor feasts functioned as instruments of paternalism organized by the British gentry, well-to-do farmers, and members of the local government, on such occasions as the completion of the harvest, and historical and patriotic anniversaries.[12] In mid-Victorian New Bruns-wick, ruling merchants in single industry towns provided similar feasts, as in Chatham, where Joseph Cunard provided free food and drink for the working-class inhabitants dependent on his sawmills and mercantile enterprises (Wynn, 1981: 135–7, 167).

Providers of outdoor feasts in the more complex urban centres of Saint John and Halifax also wished to gratify the masses and ensure their own popularity. In Saint John, the onus for such meals lay primarily with the mayor, aldermen, and assistants who were primarily artisanal in make-up (Acheson, 1985). Most of the common council's appropriation for Queen Victoria's coronation and marriage festivities in 1838 and 1840 went toward the provision of outdoor feasts for the public. . . . Since Halifax was not incorporated until 1841, private citizens and provincial and imperial officials organized and financed the events in 1838 and 1840. In addition, the Nova Scotia Philanthropic Society sponsored outdoor feasts for the Mi'kmaqs in 1840 and during the Halifax centenary in 1849. During its first year, the new Halifax city council conformed to the Saint John practice by superintending a spread for the poor.

The provision of these feasts was based on the premise that a full stomach ensured favourable and loyal sentiments. 'A Looker On' observed that Carleton's coronation feast in 1838 produced 'an effect on the people, calculated to call forth the best feelings toward the parent state and our youthful and maiden Queen'. . . .

Gratuitous feasts can also be understood as an expression of philanthropy. The well-to-do were 'goaded by tender consciences and insistent churches' to provide for the poor as a 'christian duty'. Many believed the maxim that the rich man's 'wealth is a talent, for the employment of which he must hereafter render an account' (Fingard, 1975).[13] Providers also responded to popular demand; the public expected good deeds during such occasions, just as the English gentry were 'obliged by custom to make disbursements for recreations' (Malcolmson, 1973:56, 66). . . .

The public feast also had great ritual significance. The selection of the ox as the favoured entrée for these public feasts can partially be explained by its capacity to feed a large number of people, but also by its symbolism. Feasts were based on 'mythical or historical events' which were 're-enacted . . . through symbols and allegories' (Metraux, 1976: 7). According to Hugh Cunningham, roast beef, plum pudding, and ale revived images of John Bull and Merrie England, and were considered part of the English 'birthright'. In the latter half of the nineteenth century, Victorians adopted these staples as 'sacraments' in a 'continuing mythology of national superiority and class identity' (Cunningham, 1981). Ritual significance also accompanied the practice of roasting the ox. In proposing an ox roast for the poor on the Grand Parade in Halifax in 1838, a correspondent referred to it as 'an imitation of good old English hospitality' (Halifax *Times*, 29 May 1838).[14] The ox roast also had pagan roots and, as such, exhibited ritualistic behaviours and traits developed through custom and precedents (Metraux, 1976: 8). Before the barbecue, participants adorned the ox with ribbons in imitation of 'sacrificial garlands', and processed with the animal as during pagan sacrificial rituals (Saint John *Daily Telegraph*, 21 April 1883). In Saint John in 1838, the ox was led on its cortege by a black man named Jim Brown, probably a butcher, for later he carved the ox after it had been slaughtered and roasted. Butchers often marched with oxen during trades processions, afterwards slaughtering them and distributing the meat as alms.[15]

The class makeup of those who attended these events is difficult to determine. It is clear that the providers were primarily artisanal (in the case of Saint John), and middle class (in the case of Halifax). It is also clear that these providers intended the repasts primarily for the working class and the poor. While the 'rich' could 'partake [of public feasts] if they pleased', Alderman John Porter of Saint John contended, the 'poor should be especially invited' (*New Brunswick Courier*, 25 May 1840). Some middle-class feasters did attend, often distancing themselves from the crowds in private marquees and tents. . . .

What did outdoor repasts mean to the working-class participants who partook of them? First and foremost, the public feast was a source of free food and drink. As in eighteenth-century America, ceremonial occasions and holidays determined the type of meal to be eaten by the 'lower orders' (Karsky, 1985: 59). Not only did the public dine on ox meat, but other foodstuffs as well. In 1838, Saint John's common council provided barrels of bread baked into small half-pound loaves, plum pudding, and two hogsheads of ale. . . . The prevalence of large fatty joints and sweets, and the paucity of vegetables and fruits, reflects the general nature of the working-class diet in nineteenth-century America (Levenstein, 1988: 4–5).

Although a Saint John newspaper congratulated the citizens in 1840 for 'not having outraged *all* decency', a little 'irregularity' was observed, which suggests that some tried to commandeer more than their fair share, a reflection of the tendency of the poor in pre-industrial Canada to 'feast and be merry' during seasons of plenty.[16] . . .

Homeless children also enjoyed the feast organized in honour of Queen Victoria's marriage in 1840:

Ragged urchins about the streets were upon the alert much earlier than usual, and strained their treble pipes more outrageously than ever to testify their joyful anticipation of roast beef and cake. (Saint John *Morning News*, 25 May 1984)

Roast beef and cake were also anticipated by those who found themselves in poor houses and public carceral facilities during public celebrations.

Institutional Repast

. . . Public feasts not only served to differentiate working-class recipients from respectable artisans and middle-class providers and participants, but also to distinguish the 'deserving' from the 'undeserving' poor. Victorian middle-class philanthropists portrayed the 'deserving' poor as honest and enterprising citizens victimized by illness or misfortune, while the 'undeserving' poor were characterized as lazy, profligate, and even criminal (Fingard, 1975: 38–9). Organizers of public feasts wished to ensure that only the 'deserving' poor received victuals, but at public distributions it was difficult to identify the deserving recipients (Andrews, 1974: 4). During a public meeting to consider the celebration of the birth of the Prince of Wales in Halifax in 1841, Samuel G.W. Archibald, the attorney general of Nova Scotia, referred to the disorder of the coronation feast in 1838 which interfered with the orderly distribution of the food (Halifax *Novascotian*, 16 December 1841).[17] A correspondent of the *New Brunswick Courier* believed that very few poor deserved a feast in honour of the Queen's marriage in 1840 because in Saint John he perceived 'very little suffering from poverty, unless it be where poverty and vice are united' (*New Brunswick Courier*, 18 April 1840).

The distribution of food could be more readily monitored by institutionalizing the public feast. The fragmentation of public feasts into individual dinners for the poor in penal and charitable institutions made them much easier to control than outdoor ox roasts.[18] Thus, provisions for

the poor and unfortunate during special occasions frequently took the form of 'repasts' in the poor asylums and public carceral facilities. Halifax's committee for the celebration of Queen Victoria's coronation in 1838 organized special dinners for inmates of the poor house, the city jail, and the Bridewell. Similarly, the Saint John common council organized a dinner in the gaol and, in 1840, distributed provisions to the almshouse, hospital, asylum, gaol, and workhouse in commemoration of Victoria's marriage. . . .

Who attended the feasts in these institutions and what functions did they play? The institutions catered to a wide spectrum of working-class inhabitants, ranging from the 'under-class' recidivists described by Judith Fingard, to the elderly poor, homeless children, and otherwise well-established artisans who had fallen on hard times. Indeed, poor asylums have been described as 'catch-all' institutions (Whalen, 1972: 60).[19] A reporter described the different categories of recipients who sat down to a repast in the Saint John asylum in 1863:

> . . . such inmates as were able to move sat down to the sumptuous repast provided for them. The sight was truly interesting. At one table might be seen the poor, decrepid old man, at another the child of misfortune; at one table the emaciated youth, at another, the enfeebled woman. (*New Brunswick Courier*, 14 March 1863)

Judith Fingard has discovered that some poor inhabitants arranged to enter the poor house and the prison in order to take advantage of special dinners, as well as for protection and security (1989: 52–7). The poor debtors in the gaols who did not have the resources to buy bread, and had to rely on rations from other prisoners, undoubtedly welcomed these celebratory meals.[20] . . .

Regardless of need, inmates expected to be treated 'properly' during these dinners in the institutions (Fingard, 1989: 51). The gaol commissioners in Saint John prepared a special meal for the prisoners during the Prince of Wales's visit in 1860, consisting of salmon, roast beef, vegetables, plum pudding, and a keg of ale. However, two or three 'turbulent spirits' led by an elderly debtor named Barney O'Brien, managed to convince the other prisoners in the upper hall *not* to attend the dinner because they were not being treated like *gentlemen*. They contended that it would not be 'dignified' to sit down to a feast unless one of the gaol committee or at least the high sheriff presided at the table as chairman. Participation would also be considered if they were provided with the 'proper appendage'—a gallon of whiskey. Unfortunately, their protest came to naught, and the next day their share was fed to the prisoners in the lower hall.[21]

Thus, the organization of special feasts for the inmates of the poor relief and penal institutions can be understood as a more rational and controlled means of providing for the poor during public celebrations. Inmates utilized these feasts as sources of much-needed 'victuals', and Barney O'Brien and his conspirators even attempted to use the repast as a vehicle for the attainment of working-class respectability.

Tea and Coffee Soirée

For another segment of the population, none of these forms of feasting sufficed. They provided an alternative—the tea and coffee soirée.

Why would people turn away from the customary feast and search for an alternative? Changing palates may have led to a gradual shift in eating patterns and preferences. Among the articulate, the popularity of roast beef and plum pudding waned by the late 1840s. . . .

The changing palates of the residents was accompanied by a growing concern over the manner in which the ox was cooked, primarily the waste involved in roasting the whole animal, and the aesthetics of the practice.[22] In 1838, the *Novascotian* thought that the 'days of ox-roasting may as well go after the days of chivalry' (5 July 1838). As ox roasts became more sporadic, the knowledge of how to cook the animals properly gradually disappeared. The Charitable Irish Society tried to roast an ox in Halifax during the coronation in 1838, but it was eventually disposed of, probably due to over-cooking (Halifax *Times*, 3 July 1838).

The effects of urbanization also help to explain the erosion of public feasts. Ox roasts were initially a product of pre-Victorian times, when Saint John (and Halifax) resembled a 'collection of small market villages' (Acheson, 1985: 5).[23] But the 'village atmosphere' which had generated communal feasts was changing in the nineteenth century. . . . Communal ward activities like ox roasts were being superseded by city-wide spectacles organized by a more impersonal civic administration.

Public feasting also suffered from the effects of nineteenth-century moral reformism. Beginning in the 1820s, Halifax and Saint John experienced the emergence of evangelical, temperance, and rational recreation movements. While these causes found support at all social levels, abstinence and prohibition were taken up in force by the evangelical elements of the lower middle and respectable working classes. Besides an array of temperance organizations, a reformist clique called the 'puritan liberals' emerged on the Saint John common council who were committed to temperance and purity in public life. The Halifax city council also demonstrated a growing commitment to the bourgeois ideals of efficiency and progress.[24]

Reformers displayed a variety of responses to public feasting and drinking. Some reformers had no use at all for public festivities, particularly when they functioned as gratuitous charities. The emerging bourgeoisie in Victorian England experienced considerable tension between work and leisure, accentuated for those with the evangelical convictions of the 'Protestant work ethic'. Public entertainments such as feasts were considered to be frivolous and irreconcilable with the 'dignity of labour'. Indeed, a familiar maxim advised that the 'truest charity is to find employment that will give food; and not food without employment.' The feast tended to induce idleness, drinking, and other slothful qualities.[25]. . .

The arrival in the 1840s of the American fraternal temperance organization called the Sons of Temperance facilitated the movement toward abstinence as a form of social control. These abstainers thought that public celebrations should be changed into more rational and orderly events by prohibiting the use of alcohol. . . .

Alderman Salter, a puritan liberal on Saint John's common council, objected to the availability of intoxicating beverages at the marriage celebration in Saint John in 1840. He believed that the common council would not be setting a good example for their constituents by encouraging intemperance in this way. He saw drunkenness at the ox roast in Carleton in 1838 and had no doubt that again many would go away 'gloriously drunk'. He advocated a more 'rational and consistent' celebration which avoided unnecessary noise, confusion, and intemperance: 'Englishmen might not get drunk on ale, because they were accustomed to it; but Bluenoses might, and the temptation might be very dangerous.' He did not approve of the loyalty of the bottle, but preferred 'sober, honest' loyalty.[26] However, fellow puritan liberals Aldermen Porter and John Humbert, and 'populist conservatives' such as Gregory Vanhorne, Thomas Harding, and Assistant Aldermen William Hagarty and Ewan Cameron spoke out in favour of the feast.[27] Alderman Porter saw little drunkenness at

the coronation. He 'would let the poor have a good glass of ale if they wished it', and did not think it would do them any harm. Indeed, the majority of the aldermen voted in favour of a conventional feast for the celebration of Queen Victoria's marriage in 1840.[28]

Other proponents of temperance and abstinence suggested offering more rational alternative events, such as temperance soirées. These attractions did not merely offer free food and entertainment, but also instruction and thereby respectability (Bailey, 1978: 39, 42; Acheson, 1985: 159). Offended by the drunkenness during public celebrations, the St John Temperance Society organized a tea and coffee soirée during Queen's Victoria's coronation celebration in Saint John in 1838, as did the Provincial Temperance Society and the St John Auxiliary to the New Brunswick Foreign Temperance Society in 1840 to celebrate the Queen's nuptials.[29] The programs were pseudo-religious and instructive, incorporating hymns, band music, and discourses on themes ranging from temperance to 'Our Laws' and the 'British Constitution'. The messages of many of these speeches reinforced middle-class family values and separate spheres of ideology. During the soirée in celebration of the Queen's marriage, Captain O'Halloran delivered an oration on 'Matrimony' in which he urged those who had not yet been 'tyed by Hymen' to follow the illustrious example of their Queen and Prince Consort (Saint John *Morning News*, 27 May 1840). . . .

Moral reformers in the temperance and abstinence camps were not entirely successful in regulating popular behaviour during celebrations. The inherent class bias of their organizations posed one of the most serious problems. While reformers condemned the nature of public feasts and tried to change them in an effort to contribute to the improvement and elevation of the general public, their efforts at individual reformation, and the provision of alternative forms of celebrating, catered more to people of their 'own kind', that is, the middle class and particularly the respectable working class. William Baird contended that the 'more important work for the members of the Division [Sons of Temperance] seemed to be the reformation of talented and influential men, whose example was producing a most damaging effect' (Baird, 1890: 162). The restriction of attendance at the soirées reflected this class bias, as tickets were first offered to members of the temperance societies and then to the general public.[30] An 'insistence upon certain prerequisites of conduct and appearance' at the events further excluded 'the unscrubbed'. At a time of heightened social extremes, attempts to ameliorate and elevate the lower orders were jeopardized by many middle-class citizens who were more concerned with reinforcing not reducing social distance.[31]

Conclusion

Public feasting and drinking in Saint John and Halifax obviously reflected and reinforced the more general pattern of mid-Victorian diversity and class differentiation. In the first place, each type of feasting supported a very different class of recipient: the banquet was attended largely by the middle class, the ox roast by the general public (particularly the working class), the institutional repast by the 'institutionalized poor' (representing a wide spectrum of working-class citizens), and the temperance soirée by the lower middle and upper working classes.

The food, drink, and attendant ritualism of these different types of public feasts also expressed hierarchy and defined the boundaries of inclusion and exclusion. The structure and content of French *haute cuisine* and the drinking and toasting rituals at middle-class banquets symbolized the respectability and exclusivity of the dinners. The ox roast, on the other hand, revived images of Merrie England and John Bull paternalism. There is evidence, however, that the working-class recipients interpreted the ox roast in a more pragmatic utilitarian fashion: as a source of free food and drink, and as a vehicle of respectability. Finally, the soirée's juxtaposition of tea, coffee, and instruction against the alcohol, heavier fare, and drunkenness of the banquet, ox roast, and institutional repast permitted respectable working-class temperance advocates to separate themselves from the gluttony of the 'gentry' and the vulgarity of the 'masses'.

Social distance was also reinforced by accessibility; middle-class participants could attend just about any form of festivity they wished (indeed, they organized most of the ox roasts and institutional repasts). The lower classes, however, were blocked from attending the balls and banquets, the temperance soirées, and institutional repasts, as organizers instituted various forms of 'screening', such as high ticket prices and availability, codes of dress and etiquette, and evidence of deservedness.

This desire for social distance intensified by the 1860s, as middle-class and respectable working-class organizers began appropriating more of the celebration budgets for their own exclusive banquets. In other words, they transformed 'feasts of participation' into 'feasts of representation' (Metraux, 1976: 8–9). . . . The *St John Globe* of 1863 commented on the changing priorities of celebration committees:

> A provision to give a good dinner to the poor was voted down, that two or three hundred of the elite, including the Common Council, may be able to enjoy a dance. Was there ever anything more heartless or cruel? (St John *Globe*, 7 March 1863)

The end result of this 'gentrification' of public celebrations was that, by the late nineteenth century, few alternatives save private picnics and treats remained for the general public and poor who 'measured improvement' by the 'bellyful' (Bailey, 1978: 89).

Notes

1. This comment is an explanation of the structuralist perspective.
2. Mennell is discussing the contributions of the structuralists; Mary Douglas, 'A distinctive anthropological perspective,' in Douglas, *Constructive Drinking*, 8.
3. Description based on Janet Guildford, 'Halifax, 1850–1870', unpublished paper, 18–23; Susan Buggey, 'Building Halifax, 1841–1871', *Acadiensis* 10 (Autumn 1980): 90–112. For discussions of sailor-town and soldiertown, see Judith Fingard, *The Dark Side of Life Victorian Halifax* (Porters Lake: Potterfield Press, 1989) and Fingard, *Jack in Port: Sailortowns of East Canada* (Toronto: University of Toronto Press, 1982).
4. Reminiscences of Eliza Donkin were collected and compiled by Morley, Scott, 33, New Brunswick Museum (NBM).
5. See I. Allen Jack, *History of St Andrew's Society of St John New Brunswick, 1798–1903* (Saint John 1903); D.C. Harvey, 'N.S. Philanthropic Society', *Dalhousie Review* 19 (October 1939): 287–95; Robert P. Harvey, 'Black Beans, Banners and Banquets: The Charitable Irish Society of Halifax at Two Hundred', *Nova Scotia Historical Review* 6 (1986): 16–35.
6. Meeting of the Acting Committee, 21 June 1860, in Minutes of the Meetings of the Committee for the Reception of HRH the Prince of Wales, 1860, MG I, 312A, Public Archives of Nova Scotia (PANS); Halifax *Evening Express*, 3 August 1860.
7. Meeting of the Acting Committee, 10 July 1860, in Minutes of the Meetings of the Committee for the Reception of HRH the Prince of Wales, 1860, MG1, 312A, PANS.
8. In San Francisco in 1855, women were invited to observe the elaborate preparations for a banquet, but were then expected to leave 'demurely'. See Mary P. Ryan, *Women in Public: Between Banners and Ballots, 1825–1880* (Baltimore: The Johns Hopkins Symposia in Comparative History, 1990), 18; men raising their glasses, see Ryan, *Women in Public*, 135. In court circles, Queen Victoria tried to avert excessive drunkenness by insisting that gentlemen not be left on their own for too long, see Alan Delago, *Victorian Entertainments* (New York: American Heritage Press, 1971), 12. Cheryl Krasnick Warsh notes that the drinking woman in Victorian Canada was viewed as a form of 'bastardized masculinity', see Warsh, '"Oh Lord, Pour a Cordial in Her Wounded Heart"', 89.
9. For a customary list of toasts, see Halifax *Times*, 3 July 1838, 28 April 1840.
10. The Charitable Irish Society had their first picnic in 1846; see Harvey, 'Black Beans, Banners, and Banquets,' 22–3.
11. See *Nova Scotian*, 12 June 1839; *Halifax Sun*, 6 and 11 June 1845.
12. Robert W. Malcolmson, *Popular Recreations in English Society, 1700–1850* (Cambridge: Cambridge University Press, 1973), 59–65; G.S. Metraux, 'Of Feasts and Carnivals,' *Cultures* 3 (1976), 8. For a description of a harvest supper in rural England in the early nineteenth century, see Thomas Hardy, *Far From the Madding Crowd* (London: Penguin, 1967), 240–6.
13. See also Judith Fingard, 'Attitudes Towards the Education of the Poor in Colonial Halifax', *Acadiensis* 2 (Spring 1973): 19; Gwenyth Andrews, 'The Establishment of Institutional Care in the Mid-Nineteenth Century', Honours essay, Dalhousie University, 1974, 2.
14. The Halifax *Times*, 28 April 1840 commented re: a dinner and dance given by the St George's Society: 'For once John Bull forgot to grumble, and did his best to honour his Patron by proving the strength and tension of his digestive faculties, qualities in the composition of Englishmen, which, where roast beef and plum pudding are concerned, are said to be of no mean order.'
15. Excerpt in Saint John *Daily Sun*, 18 June 1887; Susan G. Davis, *Parades and Power: Street Theatre in Nineteenth Century Philadelphia* (Berkeley: University of California Press, 1986), 121. I am unsure whether or not the meat was distributed cooked or uncooked.
16. Saint John *Morning News*, 25 May 1840 (emphasis is mine); Fingard, 'The Poor in Winter', 76.
17. Also recall the 'irregularities' during the marriage feast in Saint John. See Saint John *Morning News*, 25 May 1840. In 1897 the Halifax *Herald* described a feast for the poor as an 'indiscriminate and unintelligent' form of almsgiving. See *Herald*, 5 July 1897.
18. Institutional repasts were also a function of the 'discovery of the asylum' as an accepted mode of dealing with poverty and other social problems. See

Andrews, 'The Establishment', 2, 89; Whalen, 'Social Welfare', 55–6. However, Francis does not think that the Lunatic Asylum was a humane method. See Daniel Francis, 'The Development of the Lunatic Asylum in the Maritime Provinces', *Acadiensis* 6 (Spring 1977): 23–38.

19. Judith Fingard defends her use of the term 'under class' in the introduction to *The Dark Side of Life*.

20. See John Smith to Mayor Robert Hazen, 17 April 1838, in Robert F. Hazen papers, Box 1, Shelf 36, Packet 2, #15, NBM.

21. See the Report of Justice Balloch to a meeting of the sessions in Saint John *Morning News,* 5 September 1860; Saint John *Freeman,* 6 September 1860.

22. See the mayor's comments in *New Brunswick Courier,* 28 March 1840, and Alderman Porter's remarks in 23 May 1840. There was also concern about the waste and excess of festivals in early modern Europe. See, Burke, *Popular Culture,* 213.

23. An ox was roasted in many pre-Victorian celebrations in Saint John, including the defeat of Napoleon in May 1814, the coronation of George IV in October 1821, and the ascension of William IV. See J.V. Saunders, 'Early New Brunswick Celebrations', *New Brunswick Historical Society Newsletter* 24 (November 1987), 3–4; *New Brunswick Courier,* 13 October 1821. In this sense they resembled the roasts held during village fairs and festivals. See Malcolmson, *Popular Recreations,* 59–64.

24. For puritan liberals, see Acheson, *Saint John,* 181–2; for Halifax city council, see Janet Guildford, 'Public School Reform and the Halifax Middle Class, 1850–1870', PhD thesis, Dalhousie University, 1990.

25. For Protestant work ethic, see Bailey, *Leisure and Class,* 5; Fingard, 'The Relief of the Unemployed Poor', 36. A correspondent of the Halifax *Herald* opposed holding a feast for the poor during Queen Victoria's diamond jubilee celebration in 1897 because it undermined the 'pride and spirit of self-reliance' of the deserving poor. See *Herald,* 5 July 1897.

26. This connection between drunkenness and loyalty can be traced back to at least 1809, when the press commented regarding King George III's jubilee: 'It is not amidst intoxication . . . that we are to look for that steady or enthusiastic loyalty which is at once the pledge and test of popular allegiance.' See Colley, 'The Apotheosis of George III', 117.

27. For a discussion of these aldermen, see Acheson, *Saint John,* 181–2.

28. For debate, see *New Brunswick Courier,* 23 May 1840.

29. Although there were no soirées in Halifax for the public celebrations in question, they were becoming popular events there as well. The *Novascotian,* 9 December 1841, recommended a soirée as an event for the celebration of the birth of the Prince of Wales.

30. *New Brunswick Courier,* 23 June 1838, 18 April 1840, 22 and 25 May 1840.

31. For prerequisites, see Bailey, *Leisure and Class,* 105; Because of 'mischievous conduct', no youths were permitted at the temperance meetings in Halifax in 1843 unless accompanied by a parent or guardian, or signed in by a member. See Halifax *Morning Herald,* 31 May 1843; for social distance, see Malcolmson, *Popular Recreations,* 164.

References

Acheson, T.W. 1985. *Saint John: The Making of a Colonial Urban Community.* Toronto: University of Toronto Press

Andrews, Gwenyth. 1974. 'The Establishment of Institutional Care in the Mid-Nineteenth Century', Honours essay, Dalhousie University.

Bailey, Peter. 1978. *Leisure and Class in Victorian England: Rational Recreation and the Contest for Control, 1830–1885.* Toronto: University of Toronto Press.

Baird, William I. 1890. *Seventy Years of New Brunswick Life.* Saint John: Geo. E. Day.

Beck, J. Murray. 1985. 'James Boyle Uniacke', *Dictionary of Canadian Biography* VIII: 903.

Bilson, Geoffrey. 1974. 'The Cholera Epidemic in St John, New Brunswick, 1854', *Acadiensis* 4 (Autumn): 85–99.

Cunningham, Hugh. 1981. 'The Language of Patriotism, 1750–1914', *History Workshop* 11.

Douglas, Mary. 1984. 'Standard Social Uses of Food: Introduction', in Mary Douglas, ed., *Food in the Social Order: Studies of Food and Festivities in Three American Communities.* New York: Routledge.

———. 1987. 'A Distinctive and Anthropological Perspective', in Mary Douglas, ed., *Constructive Drinking: Perspectives on Drink from Anthropology.* Cambridge: Cambridge University Press.

Fingard, Judith. 1975. 'The Relief of the Unemployed Poor in Saint John, Halifax, and St. John's, 1815–1860', *Acadiensis* 5 (Autumn): 32–53.

———. 1983–4. 'Beyond the Halifax Barracks: Social context of Late Victorian Army Life'. The MacNutt Memorial Lecture, University of New Brunswick.

————. 1985. 'The Poor in Winter: Seasonality and Society in Pre-Industrial Canada', in Michael S. Cross and Gregory S. Kealey, eds, *Pre-Industrial Canada, 1760–1849*. Toronto: McClelland and Stewart.

————. 1988. '"A Great Big Rum Shop": The Drink Trade in Victorian Halifax', in James H. Morrison and James Moreira, eds, *Tempered By Rum: Rum in the History of the Maritime Provinces*. Porters Lake: Pottersfield Press.

————. 1989. *The Dark Side of Life in Victorian Halifax*. Porters Lake: Pottersfield Press.

Gusfield, Joseph. 1987. 'Passage to Play: Rituals of Drinking Time in American Society', in Mary Douglas, ed., *Constructive Drinking: Perspectives on Drink from Anthropology*. Cambridge: Cambridge University Press.

Halifax *Acadian Recorder*. 1838. 2 June.

Halifax *Morning Sun*. 1860. 27 July.

Halifax *Novascotian*. 1838. 5 July.

Halifax *Novascotian*. 1841. 16 December.

Halifax *Novascotian*. 1860. 20 August.

Halifax *Sun*. 1845. 11 June.

Halifax *Times*. 1838. 'A Bluenose', 22 May.

Halifax *Times*. 1838. 29 May.

Halifax *Times*. 1838. 3 July.

Harvey, D.C. 1939. 'N.S. Philanthropic Society', *Dalhousie Review* 19 (October): 287–95.

Harvey, Robert P. 1986. 'Black Beans, Banners and Banquets: The Charitable Irish Society of Halifax at Two Hundred', *Nova Scotia Historical Review* 6: 16–35.

Karsky, Barbara. 1985. 'Sustenance and Sociability: Eating Habits in Eighteenth-century America', *Annales* 40 (September–October).

Levenstein, Harvey A. 1988. *Revolution at the Table*.

The Transformation of the American Diet. New York: Oxford University Press.

Malcolmson, Robert W. 1973. *Popular Recreations in English Society, 1700–1850*. Cambridge: Cambridge University Press.

Mennell, Stephen. 1985. *All Manners of Food*. Oxford: Blackwell.

Metraux, G.S. 1976. 'Of Feasts and Carnivals', *Cultures* 3: 7–12.

New Brunswick Courier. 1838. 30 June.

New Brunswick Courier. 1840. 'Letter to the editor'. 18 April.

New Brunswick Courier. 1840. 23 May.

New Brunswick Courier. 1863. 14 March.

Saint John *Daily Telegraph*. 1883. 21 April.

Saint John *Morning News*. 1840. 25 May.

Saint John *Morning News*. 1840. 27 May.

Saint John *Weekly Chronicle*. 1838. 'Corporation Dinner, alias Humbug!', 22 June.

See, Scott W. 1993. *Riots in New Brunswick: Orange Nativism and Social Violence in the 1840s*. Toronto: University of Toronto Press.

St John Globe. 1863. 7 March.

Veblen, Thorstein. 1934. *The Theory of the Leisure Class*. New York: Penguin.

Visser, Margaret. 1986. *Much Depends on Dinner: The Extraordinary History and Mythology, Allure and Obsessions, Perils and Taboos, of an Ordinary Meal*. Toronto: McClelland and Stewart.

Whalen, James M. 1972. 'Social Welfare in New Brunswick, 1784–1900', *Acadiensis* 2 (Autumn): 54–64.

Wynn, Graeme. 1981. *Timber Colony: A Historical Geography of Early Nineteenth-century New Brunswick*. Toronto: University of Toronto Press.

Chapter 4

Class Conflict on the Canals of Upper Canada in the 1840s
Ruth Bleasdale

Irish labourers on the St Lawrence canal system in the 1840s appeared to confirm the stereotype of the Irish Celt—irrational, emotionally unstable, and lacking in self-control. Clustered around construction sites in almost exclusively Irish communities, they engaged in violent confrontations with each other, local inhabitants, employers, and law enforcement agencies. Observers of these confrontations accepted as axiomatic the stereotype of violent Paddy, irreconcilable to Anglo-Saxon norms of rational behaviour, and government reports, private letters, and newspaper articles characterized the canallers as 'persons predisposed to tumult even without cause'.[1] . . .

Yet men attempting to control the disturbances along the canals perceived an economic basis to these disturbances which directly challenged ethnocentric interpretations of the canallers' behaviour. In the letters and reports of government officials and law enforcement agents on the canal works in Upper Canada the violence of the labourers appears not as the excesses of an unruly nationality clinging to old behaviour patterns, but as a rational response to economic conditions in the new world. The Irish labourers' common ethnoculture did play a part in shaping their response to these conditions, defining acceptable standards of behaviour, and providing shared traditions and experiences which facilitated united protest. But the objective basis of the social disorder along the canals was, primarily, class conflict. With important exceptions, the canallers' collective action constituted a bitter resistance to the position which they were forced to assume in the society of British North America.

Southern Irish immigrants flooding into the Canadas during the 1840s became part of a developing capitalist labour market, a reserve pool of unskilled labourers who had little choice but to enter and remain in the labour force (Pentland, 1959). Most southern Irish arrived in the new world destitute. . . . The only option open to most southern Irish was to accept whatever wage labour they could find.

Many found work in the lumbering, shipping, and shipbuilding industries, and in the developing urban centres, where they clustered in casual and manual occupations. But the British North American economy could not absorb the massive immigration of unskilled Irish (Naylor, 1972). Although the cholera epidemics of 1832 and 1834 and the commercial crisis of 1837 had led to a decline in immigration and a shortage of labour by 1838, a labour surplus rapidly developed in the opening years of the 1840s, as southern Irish arrived in record numbers (Pentland, 1960).[2] Added to this influx of labourers from across the Atlantic was a migration of Irish labourers north across the American border. . . .

The public works in progress along the Welland Canal and the St Lawrence River attracted a large proportion of the unemployed Irish throughout the decade. The Emigration Committee for the Niagara District Council complained that construction sites along the Welland operated 'as beacon lights to the whole redundant and transient population of not only British America, but of the United States' (Niagara Chronicle, 4 August 1847). From the St Lawrence Canals came similar reports of great numbers of 'strange labourers' constantly descending on the canals. . . .

Many did secure work for a season or a few years. The massive canal construction programme undertaken by the government of the Canadas during the 1840s created a demand for as many as 10,000 unskilled labourers at one time in Upper Canada alone. The work was labour intensive, relying on the manpower of gangs of labourers. While mechanical inventions such as the steam-excavator in the Welland's Deep Cut played a small role in the construction process, unskilled labourers executed most aspects of the work, digging, puddling, hauling, and quarrying (Merritt, 1875: 310). . . .

Despite this heavy demand, there were never enough jobs for the numbers who flocked to canal construction sites. Winter brought unemployment of desperate proportions. While some work continued on the Cornwall and Williamsburg Canals and on the Welland to a greater extent, the number of labourers who could be employed profitably was severely limited. Of the 5,000 along the Welland in January 1844, over 3,000 could not find jobs, and those at work could put in but few days out of the month because of the weather.[3] . . .

Only a small number of those unable to get work on the canals appear to have found jobs on farms in the area. Despite the pressing demand for farm labourers and servants during the 1840s, the peasant background of the southern Irish had not equipped them to meet this demand, and many farmers in Upper Canada consequently professed reluctance to employ Irish immigrants (Duncan, 1965: 25–6).[4] The Niagara District Council's 1843 enquiry into emigration and the labour needs of the district noted that farmers were not employing the labourers along the canal because they did not know 'the improved system of British agriculture'. In the last half of the decade, fear that famine immigrants carried disease acted as a further barrier to employment of the Irish on farms (Duncan, 1965: 26).

Despite their inability to find work the unemployed congregated along the canal banks. As construction commenced on the Welland, canal Superintendant Samuel Power endeavoured to explain why the surplus labourers would not move on: 'the majority are so destitute that they are unable to go. The remainder are unwilling as there is not elsewhere any hope of employment.'. . .

These shanties of the unemployed became a part of all construction sites. Their occupants maintained themselves by stealing from local merchants, farmers, and townspeople. According to government and newspaper reports, pilfering became the order of the day along public works projects, the unemployed stealing any portable commodity—food, fence rails, firewood, money, and livestock.[5] While reports deplored this criminal activity, observers agreed that it was their extreme poverty which 'impelled these poor, unfortunate beings to criminal acts' (*Niagara Chronicle*, 4 August 1847) . . .

Upper Canada lacked a system of public relief which might have mitigated the suffering of the unemployed and their families. Only gradually

between 1792 and 1867 was there a 'piecemeal assumption of public responsibility for those in need' and not until the mid-1840s did the province begin to operate on the principle of public support (Splane, 1965). Even had the principle of public relief been operative, the Niagara, Johnston, and Eastern Districts lacked the resources to provide a relief programme such as that offered by Montreal to unemployed labourers on the Lachine Canal (*St Catharines Journal*, 26 January 1844). Nor was private charity a solution to the endemic poverty of the unemployed. When thousands of destitute immigrants first arrived in St Catharines seeking employment on the Welland Canal in the spring of 1842, many citizens in the area came to their aid. But as the *St Catharines Journal* pointed out in similar circumstances two years later: 'Those living in the vicinity of the Canal [had] not the means of supporting the famishing scores who [were] hourly thronging their dwellings, begging for a morsel to save the life of a starving child' (*St Catharines Journal*, 16 February 1844).

The suffering of the unemployed shocked private individuals and government officials such as William Merritt who led a fund-raising campaign for the starving and charged the Board of Works that it was 'bound to provide provisions, in some way' (Harris, 1895: 255).[6] The crime of the unemployed became an even greater concern as desperate men violated private property in their attempts to stay alive. But for the Board of Works and its contractors the surplus labourers around the canals provided a readily exploitable pool of unskilled labour. . . .

Contractors offered temporary relief from the threat of starvation; but they offered little more. The typical contractor paid wages which were consistently higher than those of farm labourers in the area of construction sites. But for their back-breaking, dangerous labour and a summer work day of 14 hours, navvies received only the average or slightly above average daily wage for unskilled labour in the Canadas. Since individual contractors set wage rates, wages varied from canal to canal and from section to section on the same canal: however, they usually hovered around the 2s6d which Pentland suggests was the average rate for unskilled labour during the decade. . . .

These wage levels were barely adequate to sustain life, according to an 1842 government investigation into riots on the Beauharnois Canal. Many of those who testified at the hearings— foremen, engineers, magistrates, and clergymen— maintained that along the St Lawrence labourers could not live on 2s6d per day. A conservative estimate gave the cost of food alone for a single labourer for one day at 1s3d, suggesting that at the going rate a labourer could only feed himself and his wife, not to mention children, and then only on days when he was employed.[7] . . . Inadequate as his wages were, the labourer could not even be certain of receiving them. After a few months in a contractor's employ, labourers might discover that they had worked for nothing, the contractor running out of funds before he could pay his men. Other contractors, living under the threat of bankruptcy, forced labourers to wait months on end for their wages. These long intervals between pay days reduced labourers to desperate circumstances. Simply to stay alive, they entered into transactions with cutthroat speculators, running up long accounts at stores or 'selling their time at a sacrifice', handing over the title to their wages in return for ready cash or credit. Such practices cost labourers as much as 13 per cent interest, pushing them steadily downward in a spiral of debt and dependency.[8] . . .

The combination of low wages, payment in truck, and long waits between pay days kept canallers in poverty and insecurity, barely able to secure necessities during seasons of steady employment, unable to fortify themselves against seasons of sporadic work and the inevitable long periods when there was no work at all. Government commissions and individual reports detailed the misery of the labourers' existence. Drummond, a member of the Legislature for Quebec, had served on the Commission investigating conditions along the Beauharnois. During debate in the House, his anger at the 'grinding oppression' which he had witnessed flared into a bitter denunciation of 'sleek' contractors who had 'risen into a state of great wealth by the labour, the sweat, the want and woe' of their labourers (Nish, 1970). . . . Conditions were equally bad on canals further up the St Lawrence system. Work did not guarantee adequate food even on the Welland, which offered the highest wages.[9] David Thorburn, Magistrate for the Niagara District, wondered how the labourers could survive, as he watched them hit by a drop in wages and a simultaneous increase in food prices, struggling to feed their families, unable to provide 'a sufficiency of food—even of potatoes.'[10]

Work did not guarantee adequate housing either. A few contractors lived up to the commitment to provide reasonable and 'suitable accommodation', constructing barrack-like shanties along the works for the labourers and their families.[11] But as Pentland has pointed out, the bunkhouse, 'a sign of some responsibility of the employer for his men', was a development of the latter half of the nineteenth century (Pentland, 1948: 259). The typical contractor of the 1840s left his employees to find whatever housing they could. Since only a very small percentage of canallers found room and board among the local inhabitants, most built their own temporary accommodation, borrowing and stealing materials in the neighbourhood to construct huts and shacks, similar to the shanties thrown up by the unemployed (Bleasdale, 1975: 36–7). A caneller usually shared accommodation with other canallers either in the barrack-like structures provided by contractors or in the huts they erected themselves. Of the 163 shanties built by labourers at Broad Creek on the Welland, only 29 were single-family dwellings. The rest were occupied by one, two, or three families with their various numbers of boarders. These dwellings formed a congested shanty town typical of the shanty towns which sprang up along the canals, and reminiscent of squalid Corktown, home of labourers on the Rideau Canal in the 1820s and 1830s.[12]

For the brief period of their existence, these shantytowns along the canals became close-knit, homogeneous working-class communities, in which the bonds of living together reinforced and overlapped with bonds formed in the workplace. Canallers shared day-to-day social interaction and leisure activities, drinking together at the 'grog' shops which sprang up to service the labourers and lying out on the hillsides on summer nights.[13] And they shared the daily struggle to subsist, the material poverty and insecurity, the wretched conditions, and the threat of starvation.

Bound together by their experiences along the canals, the Irish labourers were also united by what they brought from Ireland—a common culture shaped by ethnicity. Canaller communities were not simply homogeneous working-class communities, but Irish working-class communities, ethnic enclaves, in which the values, norms, traditions, and practices of the southern Irish ethno-culture thrived. Central to this culture was a communal organization which emphasized mutuality and fraternity, primarily within family and kinship networks (Arensberg, 1950). While the persistence of kinship relationships amongst the canallers cannot be measured, many labourers lived with women and children in family units. . . .

Given the Irish pattern of migrating and emigrating in extended families, kinship networks may also have been reproduced on the canals.

The fact that both newly-arrived immigrants and labourers from the United States were from the limited region of Munster and Connaught increases the probability that canallers were bound together by strong, persisting kinship ties. But whether or not the labourers were bound by blood they brought to the construction sites traditions of co-operation and mutual aid in the workplace. As peasants in Munster and Connaught, they had held land individually, but had worked it co-operatively. . . .

The clearest evidence of cultural unity and continuity along the canals was the labourers' commitment to the Roman Catholic faith. In contrast with the Irish Catholic labourers in the Ottawa Valley lumbering industry whom Cross found to be irreligious, canal labourers took their religion seriously enough to build shanty chapels for worship along the canals and to contribute to the construction of a new cathedral in St Catharines. . . .

Canallers were prepared to defend their faith in active conflict with Orangemen. Each July 12th brought violent clashes between Orangemen commemorating the Battle of the Boyne, and Roman Catholic labourers infuriated at the celebration of an event which had produced the hated penal code. The entire canaller community rallied to participate in anti-Orange demonstrations. In 1844 all the canallers along the Welland, organized under leaders and joined by friends from public works projects in Buffalo, marched to confront Toronto Orangemen and their families on an excursion to Niagara Falls.[14]

The canallers also demonstrated a continued identification with the cause of Irish nationalism and the struggle for repeal of the legislative union of Britain and Ireland. They participated in the agitation for repeal which spread throughout the British Isles and North America in 1843 (Adams, 1932: 89). Lachine Canal labourers joined

Irishmen in Montreal to call for an end to Ireland's colonial status; and labourers on the Welland met at Thorold to offer 'their sympathy and assistance to their brethren at home in their struggle for the attainment of their just rights' (*St Catharines Journal*, 24 August 1843). . . .

Strong, persisting ethno-cultural bonds united the canallers, at times in active conflict with the dominant Protestant Anglo-Saxon culture. But their ethno-culture was also a source of bitter division. A long-standing feud between natives of Munster County and those from Connaught County divided the labourers into two hostile factions. The origin of the feud is obscure. It may have developed during confrontations in the eighteenth and nineteenth centuries between striking agricultural labourers of one county and black leg labourers transported across county lines. Or possibly it dated as far back as the rivalries of the old kingdoms of mediaeval Ireland (Williams, 1973: 31). Whatever its origin, the feud had become an integral part of the culture which southern Irish labourers carried to construction projects throughout Britain and North America (Thompson, 1972).

The feud did not simply flare up now and then over an insult or dispute between men who otherwise mingled freely. Feuding was part of the way in which canallers organized their lives, membership in a faction dictating both working and living arrangements. Men of one faction usually worked with members of the same faction. At times Cork and Connaught did work together under one contractor on the same section of the work, particularly during the first few seasons of construction on the Welland when contractors hired labourers regardless of faction. But contractors quickly learned to honour the workers' preference to work with members of their faction, if only for the peace of the work.[15] Members of the same faction usually lived together also, cut off from the

other faction in their separate Cork or Connaught community. Members of these communities offered each other material assistance in weathering difficult times. . . .

The other side of this communal help and support, however, was suspicion of outsiders and intense hostility towards members of the rival faction. Hostility frequently erupted into violent confrontations between the factions. These confrontations were not a ritualized reminder of past skirmishes, but battles in deadly earnest, involving severe beatings and loss of life. The brutality of the encounters between Cork and Connaught led the *St Catharines Journal* to denounce the participants as 'strange and mad belligerent factions—brothers and countrymen, thirsting like savages for each other's blood—horribly infatuated' (*St Catharines Journal*, 7 July 1842). Most participants in these skirmishes were heavily armed with 'guns, pistols, swords, pikes, or poles, pitch forks, scyths', many of which were procured from local inhabitants or the militia stores. In preparation for their revenge on the Corkmen, in one of their more spectacular thefts, Connaughtmen on the Welland actually took possession of blacksmith shops and materials to manufacture pikes and halberds! Usually they simply accosted citizens in the streets or raided them at night.

Armed conflict between the factions could reduce the canal areas to virtual war zones for weeks on end, 'parties of armed men, 200 or 300 in number constantly assembling and parading', planning attack and counter-attack, at times fighting it out on the streets of St Catharines and smaller centres around the Williamsburg Canals.[16] As Power explained to military authorities in the Niagara District: 'one riot is the parent of many others, for after one of their factional fights the friends of the worsted party rally from all quarters to avenge the defeat.'[17]

. . . These observers appreciated the fact that the feud was a deep-seated hostility rooted in the southern Irish culture. They also believed that the Irish were given to letting their hostilities erupt into open conflict. Nonetheless, they were convinced that the problems associated with the feud, the open conflict and disruption of the work, would disappear if the problem of unemployment were solved.

This was the argument put forward by the labourers themselves at a meeting called by James Buchanan, ex-consul at New York and a respected member of the Irish community in North America. Buchanan posted notices along the Welland asking the 'Sons of Erin' to meet with him to 'reconcile and heal the divisions of [his] countrymen in Canada'.[18] Corkmen refused to attend since the Connaughtmen's priest was helping to organize the meeting. But the Connaughtmen sent delegates to meet privately with Buchanan and assembled for a public meeting at Thorold. After listening to patriotic speeches and admonitions to peace and order, the Connaughtmen laid down their terms for an end to factional fights: 'give us work to earn a living, we cannot starve, the Corkmen have all the work, give us a share of it.'[19]

Thus, along the canals the feud of Cork and Connaught became the vehicle through which an excess of labourers fought for a limited number of jobs. In this respect, the feud was similar to other conflicts between hostile subgroups of workers competing in an over-stocked labour market. In the unskilled labour market of the Canadas, competition was frequently between French Canadians and Irish labourers. Along the canals, in the dockyards, and particularly in the Ottawa Valley lumbering industry, the two ethnic groups engaged in a violent conflict for work, at times as intense and brutal as the conflict of Cork and Connaught.[20] . . .

Yet the feud and the bitter fight for work did not preclude united action in pursuit of common economic goals. In a few instances the factions joined together to demand the creation of jobs. During the first summer of construction on the Welland thousands of labourers and their families repeatedly paraded the streets of St Catharines with placards demanding 'Bread or Work', at one point breaking into stores, mills, and a schooner. In a petition to the people of Upper Canada, they warned that they would not 'fall sacrifice to starvation': 'we were encouraged by contractors to build cantees [sic] on said work; now can't even afford 1 meals victuals . . . we all Irishmen; employment or devastation' (cited in Harris, 1895: 255). Setting aside their sectional differences and uniting as 'Irish labourers', Cork and Connaught co-operated to ensure that no one took the few hundred jobs offered by the Board of Works. Posters along the canal threatened 'death and vengeance to any who should dare to work until employment was given to the whole'. Bands of labourers patrolled the works driving off any who tried to take a job (*St Catharines Journal*, 11 August 1842). By bringing all construction to a halt the labourers forced the Superintendent of the Welland to create more work. Going beyond the limits of his authority, Power immediately let the contract for locks three to six to George Barnett, and began pressuring contractors to increase their manpower.[21] But as construction expanded the canallers began a scramble for the available jobs until the struggle for work was no longer a conflict between labourers and the Board of Works, but a conflict between Cork and Connaught, each faction attempting to secure employment for its members (*St Catharines Journal*, 11 August 1842).[22]

. . . In general, Cork and Connaught appear to have united to demand jobs only during periods when there was virtually no work available, and consequently no advantage to competing amongst themselves. It was in their attempts to secure adequate wages that the canallers most clearly demonstrated their ability to unite around economic issues. During frequent strikes along the canals the antagonistic relationship between the two factions was subordinated to the labourers' common hostility towards their employers, so that in relation to the contractors the canallers stood united.

. . . Unity may have been fragile, but the overriding pattern that emerges during strikes is one of co-operation between the factions.[23] Not only did the factions unite in large strikes, but during a small strike involving only members of one faction, the other faction usually did not act as strike-breakers, taking the jobs abandoned by the strikers. What little information there is on strike-breaking concerns striking labourers confronting members of their own faction who tried to continue work, suggesting that the decision to work during a strike was not based on factional loyalties or hostilities.[24] Thus, most strikers did not become extensions of the bitter conflict for work. Rather strikes brought labourers together to pursue common economic interests. The instances in which Cork and Connaught united provide dramatic evidence of the ability of these economic interests to overcome an antipathy deeply-rooted in the canallers' culture.

Canallers frequently combined in work stoppages demanding the payment of overdue wages. More often their strikes centred on the issue of wage rates. In a report concerning labour unrest on the canals of Upper and Lower Canada, Captain Wetherall concluded: 'the question of what constitutes a fair wage is the chief cause from which all the bitter fruit comes.'[25]

Since officials often reported 'many' or 'a few' strikes without indicating how many, the level of strike activity can only be suggested. Contractors expected, and usually faced, strikes in the late fall when they tried to impose the seasonal reduction in wage rates.[26] Strikes demanding an increase in wages were harder to predict, but more frequent.

Each spring and summer on the Cornwall, Welland, and Williamsburg Canals work stoppages disrupted construction. Even in winter those labourers fortunate enough to continue working attempted to push up wages through strikes.[27] The degree of success which canallers enjoyed in their strikes cannot be determined from the fragmentary and scattered references to work stoppages. It is clear, however, that they forced contractors to pay wages above the level for unskilled, manual labour in general, and above the 2s or 2s6d which the Board of Works considered the most labourers on public works could expect.[28]

How did the canallers, a fluid labour force engaged in casual, seasonal labour, achieve the solidarity and commitment necessary to successful strike action during a period of massive unemployment? Work stoppages protesting non-payment of wages may have been simply spontaneous reactions to a highly visible injustice, requiring little formal organization, more in the nature of protests than organized strikes. But the strikes through which canallers aggressively forced up wages or prevented contractors from lowering wages required a greater degree of organization and long-term commitment. Labourers might be on strike for weeks, during which time they would become desperate for food.

In a variety of ways, the canallers' shared ethno-culture contributed to their successful strike action. Strikers found unity in the fact that they were 'all Irishmen', in the same way that the unemployed identified with each other as 'Irishmen' in their united demands for work. In the only well-documented strike by canallers, the Lachine strike of 1843, the labourers themselves stated this clearly. Corkmen and Connaughtmen issued joint petitions warning employers and would-be strike-breakers that they were not simply all canallers, they were 'all Irishmen' whose purpose and solidarity would not be subverted.[29] Membership in a common ethnic community provided concrete aid in organizing united action. At least in summer 1844 on the Welland, leadership in anti-Orange demonstrations overlapped with leadership in labour organization. . . . The situation on one canal during one season cannot support generalizations concerning organization on all canals throughout the 1840s. It does, however, suggest one way in which unity around ethno-cultural issues facilitated unity in economic struggles, by providing an established leadership.

Of more significance to the canallers' strike activity was the vehicle of organization provided by their ethno-culture. Like other groups of Irish labourers, most notably the Molly Maguires of the Pennsylvania coal fields, canallers found that the secret societies which flourished in nineteenth-century Ireland were well-adapted to labour organization in the new world.[30] At a time when those most active in strikes were subject to prosecution and immediate dismissal, oath-bound societies offered protection from the law and the reprisals of employers. The government investigation into disturbances on the Beauharnois found sufficient evidence to conclude that secret societies were the means by which the canallers organized their strikes. . . .

The oaths which swore labourers to secrecy also bound them to be faithful to each other, ensuring solidarity and commitment in united action, and enforcing sanctions against any who betrayed his fellows. In addition, societies operated through an efficient chain of communication and command which allowed for tactics to be carefully formulated and executed (Williams, 1973: 31). Navvies did not develop a formal trade union. Consequently, in comparison with the activities of workers in the few trade unions of the 1820s, 1830s, and 1840s in British North America, the direct action of the Irish labourers appears 'ad hoc' (Langdon, 1973: 3–4). But the fact that the navvies' organization

was impenetrable to authorities and remains invisible to historians should not lead to the error of an 'ad hoc' categorization. Although clandestine, secret societies were noted for the efficiency, even sophistication, of their organization (Williams, 1973: 31), and although not institutionalized within the formal, structured labour movement, they were the means of organizing sustained resistance, not spontaneous outbreaks of protest. Organization within secret societies, rather than within a formal trade union also meant that canallers did not reach out to establish formal ties with other segments of the working class. As a result, they have left no concrete evidence of having identified the interests of their group with the interests of the larger working class, no clear demonstration that they perceived of themselves as participating in a broader working-class struggle. But while their method of organization ruled out formal linking and expression of solidarity with the protest of other groups of workers, secret societies testified to the Irish labourers' link with a long tradition of militant opposition to employers in the old world. . . .

Irish labourers also brought to the new world a willingness to defy the law and, if necessary, use force to achieve their ends. Years of repression and discrimination had fostered what Kenneth Duncan has characterized as 'a tradition of violence and terrorism, outside the law and in defiance of all authority' (Duncan, 1965). In Britain the Irish labourers' willingness to challenge the law and the authorities had earned them a reputation for militance in the union movements, at the same time that it had infused a revolutionary impulse into Chartism (O'Higgins, 1961). In the Canadas, this same willingness marked their strike activity.

Newspapers and government officials usually reported the strikes along the canals as 'rioting' or 'riotous conduct', the uncontrollable excesses of an ethnic group addicted to senseless violence (*St*

Catharines Journal, 31 August 1843).[31] Yet far from being excessive and indiscriminate, the canallers' use of violence was restrained and calculated. Force or the threat of force was a legitimate tactic to be used if necessary. Some strikes involved little, if any, violence. Although he claimed to have looked very hard, Dr Jarrow could find no instances of 'outrage' during the first week of the Marshville strike, a strike involving 1,500 labourers along the Welland. In another large strike on the Welland the following summer, the *St Catharines Journal* reported that there were no riotous disturbances.[32] When strikers did use force it was calculated to achieve a specific end. Organized hands of strikers patrolling the canal with bludgeons were effective in keeping strike-breakers at home.[33] Similarly, when labourers turned their violence on contractors and foremen, the result was not only the winning of a strike but also a remarkable degree of job control.[34] . . .

The canallers' willingness to resort to violence and defy authority antagonized large segments of the population who lamented the transplanting to the new world of outrages 'characteristic only of Tipperary' (*Cornwall Observer*, 9 January 1845). But despite the protestations of newspapers and private individuals that the canallers' use of force was inappropriate to the new world, the Irish labourers' militant tradition was well-suited to labour relations and power relations in the Canadas. The canallers' experience with the government and law enforcement agencies could only have reinforced what the past had taught—that the laws and the authorities did not operate in the interests of workers, particularly Irish Catholic workers. In their strikes, canallers confronted not just their employers, but the united opposition of the government, courts, and state law enforcement officers.

The government's opposition to strikes was based on the conviction that labourers should not

attempt to influence wage rates. To government officials such as J.B. Mills of the Williamsburg Canal, the repeated strikes along the canals added up to a general 'state of insubordination among the labourers', an 'evil' which jeopardized the entire Public Works programme. Reports of the Board of Works condemned strikers for throwing construction schedules and cost estimates into chaos, and applauded contractors for their 'indefatigable and praiseworthy exertions' in meeting turnouts and other difficulties with their labourers.[35] Leaving no doubt as to its attitude toward demands for higher wages, the Board worked closely with contractors in their attempts to prevent and break strikes. On their own initiative, contractors met together to determine joint strategies for handling turnouts and holding the line against wage increases.[36] The Board of Works went one step further, bringing contractors and law enforcement officers together to devise stratagems for labour control, and assuming the responsibility for co-ordinating and funding these stratagems.[37] Contractors and the Board joined forces in a comprehensive system of blacklisting which threatened participants in strikes. Operating on the assumption that the majority of the 'well-disposed' were being provoked by a few rabble-rousers, contractors immediately dismissed ringleaders. Even during a peaceful strike such as the one at Marshville, in winter 1843, contractors discharged 'those most active'.[38] For its part the Board of Works collected and circulated along the canals descriptions of men like 'Patrick Mitchell, a troublesome character' who 'created insubordination amongst labourers' wherever he went.[39] Once blacklisted, men like Mitchell had little hope of employment on the public works in Canada.

Many labourers thus barred from public works projects also spent time in jail as part of the Board's attempt to suppress disturbances. Although British law gave workers the right to combine to withdraw their services in disputes over wages and hours, employers and the courts did not always honour this right. When the Board of Works' chief advisor on labour unrest argued that the Board should suppress the 'illegal' combinations on the Welland and Williamsburg Canals, he was expressing an opinion widely-held in British North America and an opinion shared by many officials involved in controlling labour unrest on the Public Works.[40] While opinion was divided over the rights of workers, there was general agreement that employers had the right to continue their operations during a strike, the course of action usually chosen by contractors, who seldom opted to negotiate with strikers. Workers who interfered with this right, by intimidating strike-breakers or contractors or generally obstructing the work, invited criminal charges. Since the charge of intimidation and obstruction was capable of broad interpretation, including anything from bludgeoning a contractor to talking to strike-breakers, this provision of the law gave contractors and the Board considerable scope for prosecuting strikers.[41]

To supplement existing labour laws, the Board of Works secured passage of the 1845 Act for the Preservation of the Peace near Public Works, the first in a long series of regulatory acts directed solely at controlling canal and railway labourers throughout the nineteenth century.[42] The Act provided for the registration of all firearms on branches of the Public Works specified by the Executive. The Board of Works had already failed in earlier attempts to disarm labourers on projects under its supervision. . . .

Most members of the Assembly accepted the registration of firearms along the canals as unavoidable under circumstances which 'the existing law was not sufficient to meet'.[43] A few members joined Aylwin of Quebec City in denouncing the measure as a dangerous over-reaction to a situation of the government's own making, 'an Act of proscription,

an Act which brought back the violent times of the word Annals of Ireland'.[44] A more sizeable group shared Lafontaine's reservations that the bill might be used as a general disarming measure against any citizen residing near the canals. But the Attorney General's assurances that the disarming clause would apply 'only to actual labourers on the public works', secured for the Bill an easy passage.[45]

In addition to disarming the labourers, the Public Works Act empowered the Executive to station mounted police forces on the public works. Under the Act, Captain Wetherall secured an armed constabulary of 22 officers to preserve order among the labourers on the Williamsburg Canals. The Board of Works had already established its own constabulary on the Welland, two years prior to the legislation of 1845. Throughout 1843 and 1844 the Welland force fluctuated between 10 and 20, diminishing after 1845 as the number of labourers on the canals decreased. At a time when even the larger communities in Upper Canada, along with most communities in North America, still relied on only a few constables working under the direction of a magistrate, the size of these police forces testifies to the Board's commitment to labour control.[46] While the forces fulfilled various functions, in the eyes of the Board of Works their primary purpose was to ensure completion of the works within the scheduled time. . . .

Canal police forces worked closely with existing law enforcement agencies, since the common law required the magistrates to give direction in matters 'relating to the arrest of suspected or guilty persons', and generally to ensure that the police acted within the law (Radzinowicz, 1948: 284). But Wetherall's investigation into the conduct of the Welland Canal force revealed that magistrates did not always keep constables from abusing their powers: 'The constables oft exceed their authority, cause irritation, and receive violent opposition, by their illegal and ill-judged manner of attempting to make arrests.' In one instance, the constables' behaviour had resulted in a member of the force being wounded. In another, an action had been commenced for false imprisonment. Wetherall also drew attention to complaints that the police force was composed of Orangemen, at least one of whom had acted improperly in 'publicly abusing the Roman Catholic Religion—damning the Pope—etc., etc.'[47] . . .

Of invaluable assistance to the constables and magistrates were the Roman Catholic priests, hired by the Board of Works as part of the police establishment, and stationed amongst canallers. Referred to as 'moral' or 'spiritual' agents, they were in reality police agents, paid out of the Board's police budget, and commissioned to preserve 'peace and order' by employing the ultimate threat—hell.[48] They were of limited value in controlling Orange/Green confrontations. They were actually suspected of encouraging them.[49] Their effectiveness in stopping factional fights was also limited, at least on the Welland where the Reverend McDonagh was suspected of harbouring sectional sentiments.[50] Their most important function was to prevent or break strikes. Intimate involvement in the canallers' daily lives equipped them as informers concerning possible labour unrest.[51] When canallers struck, authorities could rely on priests to admonish labourers to give up their 'illegal' combinations and return to work, to show 'that the Gospel has a more salutory effect than bayonets.'[52] Priests were not insensitive to the suffering of their charges, and to its immediate cause. McDonagh repeatedly argued the canallers' case with government officials, contractors, and civil and military authorities.[53] On the Williamsburg Canals, the Reverend Clarke's criticism of the treatment of labourers became such an embarrassment to the government that he was shipped back to Ireland, supposedly for health reasons.[54] But at the same time that priests were protesting

conditions along the canals, they were devoting most of their energy to subverting the protest of their parishioners. McDonagh fulfilled this function so successfully that the Superintendent on the Welland Canal told the Board he knew of 'no one whose services could have been so efficient'.[55]

By supplementing existing laws and enforcement agencies, the government was able to bring an extraordinary degree of civil power against the canal labourers. Even an expanded civil power, however, was inadequate to control the canallers and the military became the real defenders of the peace in the canal areas. As early as the first summer of contraction on the Welland, the Governor-General asked the Commander of the Forces to station the Royal Canadian Rifles in three locations along the Welland, 60 men at St Catharines, 60 at Thorold, and 30 at Port Maitland. In addition, a detachment of the coloured Incorporated Militia attached to the Fifth Lincoln militia was stationed at Port Robinson. . . .

With a long tradition of military intervention in civil disturbances both in Great Britain and British North America, the use of troops was a natural response to the inadequacies of the civil powers (Radzinowicz, 1948). Troops were important for quickly ending disturbances and stopping the escalation of dangerous situations such as an Orange/Green clash or a confrontation between labourers and contractors.[56] . . . On the canals of Upper Canada, however, the military does not appear to have charged or opened fire on canallers. No matter how great their numbers or how well they were armed, canallers usually disbanded with the arrival of troops and the reading of the Riot Act.

Detachments were valuable as a preventive force. Before special detachments were posted along the Welland, the Governor-General explicitly instructed magistrates to use the troops in a preventive capacity, calling them out if 'there should be any reason to fear a breach of the Peace, with which the civil power would be inadequate to deal'.[57] Magistrates gave the broadest possible interpretation to the phrase 'any reason to fear' and repeatedly called in the military when there had been merely verbal threats of trouble. When a large number of unemployed labourers appeared 'ripe for mischief', when strikers seemed likely to harass the strike-breakers, magistrates requisitioned troops.[58]

Magistrates used the troops to such an extent that they provoked the only real opposition to military intervention in civil affairs—opposition from the military itself. Both on-the-spot commanders and high-ranking military officials complained that troops were being 'harassed' by the magistrates, that the requisitions for aid were 'extremely irregular', and that the troops were marching about the frontier on the whim of alarmists.[59]

This dispute was the only disharmony in the co-operation between civil and military authorities and even it had little effect on the actual operation of the system of control. At the height of the dispute, commanding officers still answered virtually all requisitions, although in a few instances they withdrew their men immediately if they felt their services were not required.[60] After the Provincial Secretary ruled that commanders must respond to all requisitions, whatever the circumstances, even the grumbling stopped.[61]

Particularly on the Welland, regular troops were kept constantly patrolling the canal areas in apprehension of disturbances, 'looking for trouble', as Colonel Elliott put it.[62]

With special laws, special police forces, and a military willing, if not eager to help, the government of the Canadas marshalled the coercive power of the state against labourers on the public works. Yet the government failed to suppress labour unrest and to prevent successful strike action. Many officials and contractors accepted this failure as proof of the Celt's ungovernable disposition. Invoking the Irish stereotype to explain the disorder along the canals, they ignored their own role in promoting unrest and obscured the class dimension of the canallers' behaviour. They also misinterpreted the nature of the relationship between the canallers' ethno-culture and their collective action. What the southern Irish brought to the new world was not a propensity for violence and rioting, but a culture shaped by class relations in the old world. Class tensions, inseparably interwoven with racial hatred and discrimination, had created in the southern Irish suspicion and hatred of employers, distrust of the laws and the authorities, and a willingness to violate the law to achieve their ends. This bitter cultural legacy shaped the Irish labourers' resistance to conditions in the Canadas and gave a distinctive form to class conflict on the canals.

Notes

1. Public Archives of Canada, Record Group 11, Department of Public Works: 5, Canals (hereafter cited RG11-5), Welland Canal Letterbook, Samuel Power to Thomas Begly, Chairman of Board of Works (hereafter cited WCLB), Power to Begly, 12 August 1842.
2. In the fall of 1840, contractors in the Chambly Canal could not procure labourers even at what the government considered 'most extravagant rates'. Canada, *Journals of the Legislative Assembly,* 1841, Appendix D; W.F. Adams, *Ireland and the Irish Emigration to the New World* (New York: Russell and Russell, 1932); and Helen I. Cowen, *British Emigration to British North America: The First Hundred Years* (Toronto: University of Toronto Press, 1961).
3. See RG11-5, Vol. 407, file 113, Thorburn to Daly, 10 January 1844.
4. For a discussion of the application of the improved system of British agriculture to Upper Canada, see Kenneth Kelly, 'The Transfer of British Ideas

on Improved Farming to Ontario During the First Half of the Nineteenth Century', *Ontario History* 63 (1971): 103–11.

5. See RG11-5, Vol. 390, file 93, Public Notice of Board of Works, 26 February 1844; *Legislative Journals*, 1844–5, Appendix Y, Report of Mills, 20 January 1845; Mills to Begly, 21 January 1845; Jarvis to Daly, 28 October 1845.

6. See RG11-5, Vol. 388, file 87, Correspondence of General Killaly, 1841–55, Welland Canal, Merritt to Killaly, 12 August 1842.

7. Given that labourers at Beauharnois used company stores and received store pay as did many canallers in Upper Canada, and considering the fairly constant price of foodstuffs along the St Lawrence system, the findings of the Beauharnois Commission can be applied to labourers on the Cornwall, Welland, and Williamsburg Canals. *Legislative Journals*, 1843, Appendix T; RG5-B21, Information to Immigrants, April 1843.

8. WCLB, Power to Begly, April 1842.

9. The cost of living does not appear to have fluctuated significantly from canal to canal.

10. See RG11-5, Vol. 407, file 113, Thorburn to Daly, 19 January 1844.

11. See RG11-5, Vol. 388, file 87, Articles of Agreement between the Board of Works and Lewis Schiclaw, 1 April 1845. See Ruth Bleasdale, 'Irish Labourers on the Canals of Upper Canada in the 1840s', MA thesis, University of Western Ontario, 1975, 34–7.

12. See RG11-5, Vol. 407, file 104, Memorandum of Dr Jarrow, 1 October 1842. A.H. Ross, *Ottawa, Past and Present* (Toronto: Musson Book Company, 1927), 109.

13. WCLB, Power to Begly, 17 January 1845; RG11-5, Vol. 390, file 93, Mills to Begly, 26 June 1845; RG11-5, Vol. 389, file 90, Miscellaneous, 1842–51, Keefer to Robinson, 1 March 1842.

14. C. Series, Vol. 60, Merritt to Daly, 21 September 1844; C. Series, Vol. 60, Elliott to Young, 23 July 1844.

15. By commencement of the second season of construction, employers followed William Hamilton Merritt's suggestion to employ only Corkmen on the upper section and only Connaughtmen on the lower section of the Welland Canal. On the Williamsburg Canals also the factions laboured on different sections of the work.

16. Appendix Y, Killaly to Daly, 5 November 1844; RG11-5, Vol. 389, file 89, Power to Begly, 17 January 1845; Vol. 407, file 113, Thorburn to Daly, 10 January 1844; *St Catharines Journal*, 7 July 1843; *Brockville Recorder*, 8 August 1844.

17. WCLB, Power to Elliott, 28 December 1843.

18. See RG11-5, Vol. 407, file 113, Public Notice to the Sons of Erin, Engaged on the Welland Canal, who are known as Corkmen and Connaughtmen, 12 January 1844.

19. WCC-6, Thorburn to Daly, 19 January 1844.

20. Pentland, 'The Lachine Strike of 1843', *Canadian Historical Review* 29 (1948): 255–77.; J.I. Cooper, 'The Quebec Ship Labourers' Benevolent Society', *Canadian Historical Review* 30 (1949): 338–43; Michael Cross, 'The Dark Druidicial Groves', PhD thesis, University of Toronto, 1968; Michael Cross, 'The Shiners' War: Social Violence in the Ottawa Valley in the 1830s', *Canadian Historical Review* 54 (1973): 1–26.

21. WCLB, Power to Begly, 12 August 1842.

22. WCLB, Power to Begly, 15 August 1842.

23. Pentland, in 'The Lachine Strike', describes the betrayal of one faction by the other in one of the large strikes on the Lachine.

24. For example: RG11-5, Vol. 407, file 104, Cotton and Row to Wheeler, 26 August 1846.

25. C. Series, Vol. 60, Memorandum of Wetherall to the Board of Works, 3 April 1843; Vol. 90, file 94, Clarke to Killaly, 6 March 1845; RG11-5, Vol. 407, file 113, Thorburn to Daly, 10 January 1844.

26. See for example: *Legislative Journals*, 1844–5, Appendix Y, Jarvis to Begly, RG11-5, Vol. 390, file 93, Mills to Killaly, November 1844; Mills to Killaly, 29 November 1845.

27. *Legislative Journals*, 1843, Appendix Q; *Legislative Journals*, 1844–5, Appendix AA; RG11-5, Vol. 381, file 56 Godfrey to Begly, 26 March 1844; Vol. 390, file 94, Wetherall to Killaly, 2 March 1844; Vol. 389, file 89, Power to Begly, 4 March 1845.

28. *Legislative Journals*, 1843, Appendix Q; *Legislative Journals*, 1844–5, Appendix AA.

29. *Montreal Transcript*, 28 March 1843, cited in Pentland, 'The Lachine Strike', 266.

30. For an analysis of secret societies in Ireland see Williams, *Secret Societies in Ireland* (Dublin: Gill and Macmillan). For a study of the Molly Maguires see Anthony Bimba, *The Molly Maguires* (New York: International Publishers, 1932).

31. See also: *Niagara Chronicle*, 10 July 1844. For further examples of the sensational manner in which newspapers reported labour disturbances see: *St Catharines Journal*, 16 November 1843, 14 December 1843, 21 December 1843, 17 May 1844, 2 August 1844, 16 August 1844, 20 September 1844; *Niagara Chronicle*, 20 February 1845; *Brockville Recorder*, 7 September 1843, 21 December 1843, 21 March 1844, 8 August 1844; *Cornwall Observer*, 8 December 1842, 9 January 1845.

32. See RG11-5, Vol. 407, file 104, Jarrow to Merritt, 6 January 1843; *St Catharines Journal*, 28 June 1844.

33. See RG11-5, Vol. 407, file 113, Thorburn to Daly, 10 January 1844; C. Series, Vol. 60, testimony of James McCloud, sworn before Justices Kerr and Turney, 14 September 1844.

34. *Legislative Journals*, Jarvis to Daly, 28 October 1844; WCLB, Power to Begly, 3 January 1844.

35. See RG11-5, Vol. 390, file 93, Mills to Killaly, 29 November 1845; *Legislative Journals*, 1845, Appendix AA.

36. See RG11-5, Vol. 407, file 113, Thorburn to Daly, 10 January 1844; Vol. 407, file 113, Thorburn to Daly, 17 January 1844.

37. See RG11-5, Vol. 407, file 113, Thorburn to Daly, 10 January 1844.

38. See RG11-5, Vol. 407, file 104, Jarrow to Merritt, 6 January 1843.

39. WCC-7, Power to Begly, 10 February 1843; Begly to Power, 8 April 1843; WCC-8, Begly to Power, 3 September 1845.

40. A.W.R. Carrothers, *Collective Bargaining Law in Canada* (Toronto: Butterworths, 1965), 13–15. C. Series, Vol. 60, Wetherall to Board of Works, 3 April 1843; *Legislative Journals*, 1843, Appendix T.

41. Carrothers, *Collective Bargaining Law*, 14; Henry Pelling, *A History of British Trade Unions* (Oxford: Clarendon Press, 1973), 31–2.

42. Act for the better preservation of the Peace and the prevention of riots and violent outrages at and near public works while in progress of construction, 8 Vix.c.6.

43. *Legislative Debates*, 1844–5, Attorney General James Smith, 1443.

44. *Ibid.*, Thomas Aylwin, 1459.

45. *Ibid.*, Louis Hippolyte Lafontaine, 1505; *Ibid.*, Attorney General James Smith, 1515–17.

46. WCLB, Bonnalie to Begly, 12 March 1844; RG11-5, Vol. 388, file 89, Power to Begly, 11 February 1846, Power to Begly, 17 January 1847; RG-8, C. Series, Vol. 60, Daly to Taylor, 17 May 1845; RG11-5, Vol. 390, file 94, Hill to Begly, 16 February 1847, Hill to Begly, 21 June 1847. Both forces continued until the great bulk of the work on their respective canals was finished, the Welland Canal constabulary until 31 December 1849, that on the Williamsburg Canals until 31 October 1847, the month that the last of the canals was opened.

47. See RG11-5, Vol. 407, file 104, Wetherall to Killaly, 26 March 1844.

48. Report of a Committee of the Executive council, 31 July 1844, cited in Pentland, 'Labour and the Development of Industrial Capitalism in Canada', PhD thesis, University of Toronto, 1960, 432. The Board of Works also employed moral agents on the Beauharnois and Lachine Canals in Lower Canada. Pentland, 'Labour and Industrial Capitalism', 414, Reverend McDonagh received £200 per annum for his services on the Welland Canal.

49. C. Series, Vol. 317, MacDonald to Begly, 14 July 1849.

50. See RG11-5, Vol. 407, file 104, Wetherall to Killaly, 26 March 1844.

51. *Ibid.*, Vol. 279, #2, 195, Extract from Report of the Committee of the Executive Council, 25 October 1849; Vol. 407, file 114, McDonagh to Killaly, 2 May 1843; Vol. 407, file 104, Hobson to Daly, 20 January 1844.

52. See RG11-5, Vol. 407, file 114, McDonagh to Killaly, 2 March 1843; Vol. 90, file 94, Clarke to Killaly, 6 March 1845; Vol. 90, file 94, Wetherall to Killaly, 2 March 1844; Vol. 388, file 87, McDonagh to Killaly, 25 January 1843; Vol. 407, file 113, Thorburn to Daly, 10 January 1844; Vol. 407, file 104, Killaly to Begly, 10 October 1849.

53. *Ibid.*, McDonagh to Killaly, 25 January 1843; Vol. 407, file 114, McDonagh to Killaly, 2 May 1843; Vol. 407, file 104, Wetherall to Killaly, 26 March 1844.

54. PSO CW, Vol. 164, #11, 611, MacDonald to Daly, 12 September 1845.

55. See RG11-5, Vol. 407, file 104, Killaly to Begly, 10 October 1849.

56. See, for example, WCLB, Power to Begly, 3 January 1844; Vol. 407, file 104, Hobson to Daly, 20 January 1844.

57. See RG11-5, Vol. 407, file 113, Thornburn to Murdock, 18 August 1842.

58. WCLB, Power to Elliott, 3 January 1844; C. Series, MacDonald to Col. Elliott, 2 April 1844, Merritt to Daly, 21 September 1844; PSO CW, Vol. 100, #4956, Milne to Bagot, 21 December 1842.

59. C. Series, Vol. 60, Armstrong to Browning, Military Secretary, 11 January 1844, Temporary Commander of Canada West to Elliott, 16 July 1844.

60. See RG11-5, Vol. 379, file 44, Tuscore to Killaly, 5 September 1842; WCLB, Power to Elliott, 3 January 1844, Power to Elliott, 28 December 1843.

61. C. Series, Vol. 60, Elliott to Cox and Gaele, 30 September 1844.

62. *Ibid.*, Temporary Commander of Canada West to Elliott, 16 July 1844.

References

Adams, W.F. 1961. *Ireland and the Irish Emigration to the New World*. New York: Russell and Russell.

Arensberg, Conrad. 1950. *The Irish Countryman*. New York: P. Smith.

Bleasdale, Ruth. 1975. 'Irish Labourers on the Canals of Upper Canada in the 1840s', MA thesis, University of Western Ontario.

Cornwall Observer. 1845. 9 January.

Duncan, Kenneth. 1965. 'Irish Famine Immigration and the Social Structure of Canada West', *Canadian Review of Sociology and Anthropology* 12: 19–40.

Harris, Dean. 1895. *The Catholic Church in the Niagara Peninsula*. Toronto: W. Briggs.

Langdon, Stephen. 1975. *The Emergence of the Canadian Working Class Movement, 1845–75*. Toronto: New Hogtown Press.

Merritt, J.P. 1875. *Biography of the Hon. W.H. Merritt*. St Catharines: E.S. Leavenworth.

Naylor, R.T. 1972. 'The Rise and Fall of the Third Commercial Empire of the St Lawrence', in Gary Teeple, ed., *Capitalism and the National Question in Canada*. Toronto: University of Toronto Press.

Niagara Chronicle. 1847. 'Report of the Niagara District Council'. 4 August.

Nish, Elizabeth, ed. 1970. *Debates of the Legislative Assembly of United Canada, Volume IV, 1844–5*. Quebec: Presses de l'École des Hautes études commerciales.

O'Higgins, Rachel. 1961. 'The Irish Influence in the Chartist Movement', *Past and Present* 20: 83–96.

Pentland, H.C. 1948. 'The Lachine Strike of 1843', *Canadian Historical Review* 29: 255–77.

———. 1959. 'Development of a Capitalistic Labour Market in Canada', *Canadian Journal of Economics and Political Science* 25: 450–61.

———. 1960. 'Labour and the Development of Industrial Capitalism in Canada', PhD thesis, University of Toronto.

Radzinowicz, Leon. 1948. *A History of the Criminal Law and Its Administration from 1750*, Volume III. London: Stevens.

Splane, Richard. 1965. *Social Welfare in Ontario, 1791–1893*. Toronto: University of Toronto Press.

St Catharines Journal. 1842. 7 July.

St Catharines Journal. 1842. 11 August.

St Catharines Journal. 1843. 24 August.

St Catharines Journal. 1843. 31 August.

St Catharines Journal. 1844. 16 February.

Thompson, E.P. 1972. *The Making of the English Working Class*. Harmondsworth: Penguin.

Williams, T.D. 1973. *Secret Societies in Ireland*. Dublin: Gill and Macmillan.

PART III

Industrializing Canada: Waged Work, Everyday Life, and Class Mobilization, 1860–1900

In the latter half of the nineteenth century industrial capitalism transformed the lives of Canadians. The 1850s and 1860s marked a transition away from the older dominance of the fur and timber trades as factories employing hundreds, even thousands, began to appear. The city began the climb to prominence that would, by the early twentieth century, see most Canadians living, not on farms and in small villages, but in urban centres. In 1851, barely 135,000 people lived in Ontario cities; 30 years later that number had almost tripled, exceeding 375,000.

Technological developments introduced machinery into traditional crafts such as shoemaking and tailoring, but it was railways, with their steam-powered locomotives, that became the revolutionizing symbol of a new age. From a mere 72 miles of track in 1850, Canadian railways expanded to over 2,000 miles in 1865. The railway knit a disparate group of colonies together, providing the material mesh of the nation-building experiment that would culminate in Confederation in 1867. It called into being huge factories in cities like Montreal, Toronto, and Hamilton, where the rails and their rolling stock were produced. In the politics of industrialism, railways also loomed large: no economic sector was so central to the close connections of capitalist development and state formation, and the vision of a transcontinental railroad was a pivotal plank in the 1879 National Policy that promised to settle the west and protect native Canadian industry, establishing a British Dominion that reached from the Atlantic to the Pacific.

The replacement of an earlier age of wood, wind, and sail with an industrializing epoch of iron and fire was not without its downsides. Late nineteenth-century Canadian industrial capitalism consolidated the regional dominance of urban, south-central Canada, especially in Ontario and Anglo-Montreal, where the advanced production methods of the new era were most evident. Other regions—the Maritimes and the West, for instance—often seemed to be developing in the shadow of central Canadian interests. Nor was social and economic advance uninterrupted in its buoyancy. Periodic depressions, most markedly in 1857–60, 1873–77, and 1893–96 caused businesses to curtail their activities or shut down entirely. Workers often faced reduced hours and pay, or were thrown out of work entirely. These economic downturns all affected the beginnings of Canadian labour organization dramatically.

The new industrial age thus presented opportunities and threats for a working class that was expanding in numbers and facing new challenges and rapidly changing circumstances. This registered in the proliferation of working-class organizations and the escalating numbers of strikes. Local unions, largely of craft workers but supplemented by the organization of ship labourers and teamsters in ports and large cities, remained an important mechanism of defence as late as the 1850s. With capitalism's growth and obvious expansion outside the narrow confines of small-scale production, however, workers began to affiliate with the large, international unions whose roots in the more developed capitalist economies of Britain and the United States provided them with a widening perspective and important linkages that proved critical to surviving in the new epoch. Not surprisingly, skilled workers associated with the railways led the way, establishing 22 locals of engineers and machinists from the 1850s to 1880. Iron moulders, carpenters and joiners, printers, cigarmakers, and other craftsmen founded dozens of internationally-affiliated trade union brotherhoods in the same period. A United States-based shoeworkers' organization, the Knights of St Crispin, chartered 26 lodges from Saint John, New Brunswick to Petrolia, Ontario in the late 1860s and early 1870s.

The expanding number of local and international craft unions led an upturn in class struggle that commenced in the early 1850s. Central Canadian newspapers identified an 1853–54 'insurrection of labour' that involved unskilled canal and railway labourers, as well as craftsmen and mechanics. Over the course of the 1860s, more and more of the decade's 72 strikes were waged by skilled workers, but it was in the 1870s, when central Canadian workers launched the first coordinated mobilization for the nine-hour day, that the tempo of class struggle really picked up. That decade saw unprecedented ferment in working-class circles. Nine Hour Leagues were formed, and there was an attempted general strike to secure the shorter workday. The creation of the country's first working-class political organization, the Canadian Labor Union, signalled a new sense of purpose, and as the class struggles of the nine-hour agitation wound down, workingmen were put forward for political office for the first time in both provincial and federal elections. Growing labour conflict followed as employers tightened the screws during the mid-1870s depression. Viewing the 1870s as a whole, strikes climbed to new highs, tripling previous levels with 204 work stoppages taking place over the course of the decade.

All of this set the stage for the culmination of nineteenth-century working-class developments, what historians have referred to as 'The Great Upheaval' of the 1880s. As an entirely new player on the scene of working-class life, the Noble and Holy Order of the Knights of Labor combined with the Provincial Workmen's Association (PWA) in the Maritimes and international craft unions and local bodies of workers to chart the first serious country-wide mobilization of Canada's working class. Over the course of the 1880s almost 440 local assemblies of the Knights of Labor, 220 local unions, 110 international unions, and 35 lodges of the PWA had been created in Canada. Together these labour organizations led the bulk of the 425 strikes that erupted between 1880–90, fully 25 per cent of them in the momentous years of greatest class conflict, 1886–87. The 1880s also witnessed the founding of the Trades and Labor Congress of Canada, which first met in 1883.

Bettina Bradbury poses a series of vital questions about how industrial capitalism reconfigured not only the public working lives of Canadians, but also dimensions of private life. The family was perhaps the most important setting in which workers negotiated the vast changes of the late nineteenth century. Men, women, and children all contributed to the domestic economies that working-class people created out of the possibilities on offer in a society where waged employment opportunities, conditions of housing, and the nature of unpaid work in the household were all structured around understandings of what was appropriate for males and females, the young and the old, to do. As Bradbury shows, gender was a significant factor in industrializing Canada, and how gender 'worked' in families influenced how work in factories was performed and assigned. Other historians, such as Peter DeLottinville and Lynne Marks, have revealed that this gendering of class was operative in a variety of other settings, from the tavern to the church.

In a chapter of her book, *Spreading the Light: Work and Labour Reform in Late Nineteenth-Century Toronto* (1999), Christina Burr takes as background one of the central moments of class struggle in the immediate post-Confederation period, the Toronto–Hamilton led campaign to secure the nine-hour day in 1872. This mobilization produced one of the first tangible institutionalizations of labour-reform thought in Canada. As early writings have suggested, the 1872 shorter-hours parades, organizational initiatives, and strikes gave rise to a layer of working-class spokesmen whose ideas and oppositional challenge to the disciplines of the emerging capitalist order were espoused in labour newspapers such as the *Ontario Workman*. Burr explores this discourse with particular attention to its articulation in a working-class novel, written by the President of the Coopers International Union, Martin Foran, and later published in the United States under the title *The Other Side* (1886). Particularly attentive to this labour rhetoric's capacity to construct working-class identity in ways that both gendered and racialized respectable producers as male and white, Burr points to the ironic ways in which reformers of the 1870s promoted the interests of a select group of workers, thereby fragmenting working-class experience as much as they consolidated it.

Such processes of fragmentation would continue to haunt workers and their organizations from the late nineteenth century to the present. As Kealey and Palmer show, during the Great Upheaval the Knights of Labor did much to overcome past legacies of exclusion, struggling to unite the skilled and unskilled, allowing women an important place in the workers' movement of the 1880s, arguably for the first time, and breaking down some, albeit not all, of the stigmatization of people of colour in the ranks of labour organizations. The culmination of nineteenth-century working-class agitation, the Knights of Labor made huge strides forward in building a movement culture of opposition to the now irreversible industrial-capitalist transformation. Breaking new ground in leading workers at the workplace and in the political arena, in creatively offering Canadian labour a sense of independence, and in espousing a sense of working-class entitlement, dignity, and worth, the Noble and Holy Order of the Knights of Labor was the architect of an eclectic radicalism. In its strengths and weaknesses lay lessons for future working-class mobilization.

Further Reading

Peter Baskerville and Eric Sager, *Unwilling Idlers: The Urban Unemployed and Their Families in Late Victorian Canada* (Toronto: University of Toronto Press, 1988).

John Battye, 'The Nine Hour Pioneers: The Genesis of the Canadian Labour Movement', *Labour/Le Travailleur* 4 (1979): 25–56.

Bettina Bradbury, *Working Families: Age, Gender, and Daily Survival in Industrializing Montreal* (Toronto: McClelland and Stewart, 1993).

Peter DeLottinville, 'Joe Beef of Montreal: Working-Class Culture and the Tavern, 1869–1889', *Labour/Le Travail* 8/9 (1981/1982): 9–40.

Russell G. Hann, 'Brainworkers and the Knights of Labor: E.E. Sheppard, Phillips Thompson, and the Toronto *News*, 1883–1887', in Gregory S. Kealey and Peter Warrian, eds, *Essays in Canadian Working-Class History* (Toronto: McClelland and Stewart, 1976), 35–57.

Craig Heron, 'Factory Workers', in Paul Craven, ed., *Labouring Lives: Work and Workers in Nineteenth-Century Ontario* (Toronto: University of Toronto Press, 1995), 479–590.

Gregory S. Kealey and Bryan D. Palmer, *Dreaming of What Might Be: The Knights of Labor in Ontario, 1880–1900* (New York: Cambridge University Press, 1982).

Robert McIntosh, *Boys in the Pits: Child Labour in Coal Mines* (Montreal and Kingston: McGill-Queen's University Press, 2000).

Ian McKay, '"By Wisdom, Wile, or War": The Provincial Workmen's Association and the Struggle for Working-Class Independence in Nova Scotia, 1879–1897', *Labour/Le Travail* 18 (Fall 1986): 13–62.

Lynne Marks, *Revivals and Roller Rinks: Religion, Leisure, and Identity in Small-Town Ontario* (Toronto: University of Toronto Press, 1996).

Frank W. Watt, 'The National Policy, the Workingman, and Proletarian Ideas in Victorian Canada', *Canadian Historical Review* 40 (March 1959), 1–26.

CHAPTER 5

Gender at Work at Home: Family Decisions, the Labour Market, and Girls' Contributions to the Family Economy

Bettina Bradbury

Introduction

'Gender at work' can be read in two ways. In the first work is a noun, and the central question is 'How do definitions of skill, of appropriate work for men and women, get negotiated within the workplace by men and women, workers and capital?'. Recent discussions of the sexual division of labour in diverse industries, of 'gender at work', the social construction of skill and of the role of unions in perpetuating women's unequal position in the workforce have made major contributions to our understanding of the complexities of the relationships between gender and class, between patriarchy and capitalism. Historical research in this field is rich and fascinating, and is reshaping both women's history and working class history in Canada as elsewhere (Hartman, 1976; Lown, 1983; Rose, 1986).[1]

'Gender at work' can also be read, if my grammar is correct, as a verb. Here the question posed would be 'How does gender work as a process in society which means that men and women end up with different work and life experiences?' To answer this question involves consideration of factors other than those found in the workplace. In this paper I would like to argue that while workplace-centred approaches go a long way toward explaining sex segregation within specific trades, they ignore different levels of decision making and other institutions which have already gendered the workforce before it arrives at the factory gate.[2] Equally, while approaches stressing the strength of patriarchal ideology or the importance of domestic labour help explain why married women remained out of the workplace they fail to grasp the complex interactions between patriarchy and capitalism. Furthermore they are more difficult to apply when dealing with the work of daughters rather than their mothers.

Within families decisions were made about who should stay home to look after children and do housework and who should earn wages which had wide reaching impact on the composition of the workforce. Such decisions were never made in an ideological or economic vacuum; they represented a complex and often unconscious balance between basic need, existing ideology, and practise regarding gender roles, the structure of the economy, and the particular economic conjuncture. Schools taught specific skills and implanted tenacious ideas about future roles. At its broadest level this paper represents a simple plea to those looking at divisions of labour in the workplace to also consider the work done by historians of the family and education. In Canada such work offers some clues about this broader process, although little research systematically examines the question (Parr, 1987).[3] To the extent that historians interested in how gender is worked out within the workplace and in the unions ignore what happens prior to men and women's arrival at work, their explanations will fail to consider the wider and deeper sexual division of labour, which not only relegated women to jobs defined as less skilled in workplaces shared with men and to feminine ghettos, but also determined that large numbers would simply not enter the workforce or would do so only sporadically.

More specifically the paper focuses on one aspect of the question, namely how family decisions in interaction with the nature of local labour markets influenced sons' and in particular daughters' contribution to the family economy. The paper concentrates on the micro-level, examining what I have been able to deduce about family decision making processes regarding which family members should seek wage labour in two Montreal working-class wards between the 1860s and 1890s. A brief description of the major sectors employing males in Montreal is followed by an assessment of the importance of additional wage earners to working class families. The respective work of sons and daughters within the family economy is evaluated.

The sexual division of labour within the family, and the need for additional domestic workers as well as extra wage labourers, I argue, meant that the context, timing, and contours of boys' and girls' participation in wage labour were different. By looking at the role of girls in the family economy and not just in the labour market,[4] we can better see how the major changes accompanying the emergence of industrial capitalism in Montreal did not modify the dominant sexual division of labour.

Montreal Families and Wage Labour, 1860–1890

The years 1860 to 1890 were characterized by the growing dominance of industrial capital in the economic structure of Montreal, the increasing dependence on wage labour of a major proportion of its population. Canada's first and largest industrial city, 'the workshop' of Canada, had a wide and complex array of industries. Most important were those relating to rail and water transportation, shoemaking, clothing, and food and beverages. The metallurgy sector, dominated by production for the railroads, provided jobs for skilled immigrants from Great Britain, and some French Canadians with a long tradition of working in metal. In shoemaking and dressmaking, as in numerous other smaller trades, artisanal production was rapidly, if unevenly giving way to production in large factories. Minute divisions of labour accompanied the utilization of new types of machinery throughout the period, drawing immigrants and French Canadians new to the city into the myriad of largely unskilled jobs that were being created. Broadly speaking, the male workforce was divided into four groups. Best paid and most secure were the relatively skilled workers involved in the new trades that emerged with the industrial revolution—the engineers, machinists, moulders, and others who worked in the foundries and new factories. More subject to seasonal and conjunctural unemployment were skilled workers in the construction trades. A third group comprised those workers in trades undergoing rapid deskilling and re-organization: most important amongst these were the shoemakers. General unskilled labourers made up the other major sub-group within the working class. About twenty-five cents a day separated the average wage of each of these groups, setting the stage for potential differences in their standard of living, and their family economy.[5] Women and girls worked largely in separate sectors of the economy, particularly as domestic servants, dressmakers, and in specific kinds of factory work. In virtually every sector, their wages were half those of males or less.[6]

The Importance of Additional Earners in the Family Wage Economy

These disparities of approximately twenty-five cents a day had the potential to separate the working class into identifiable fractions each capable of achieving a different standard of living in good times, each vulnerable in diverse ways to the impact of winter, cyclical depressions, and job restructuring. Throughout most of the period the most skilled had more flexibility in their budget and a greater chance of affording to eat and live at a level which may also have helped to ward off the diseases which spread only too quickly through the poorly constructed sewers and houses of the city. This greater margin of maneouvre which higher daily wages, greater job security, and the possession of skills that were scarce and usually in demand gave to the skilled was not constant. It was particularly likely to be eroded in times of economic depression or of rapid transformations in the organization of work.

While some skilled workers organized successfully during this period, the major element of flexibility in the family income, for skilled and unskilled alike, lay not so much in the gains that organization could offer, but in the ability to call on additional family members to earn wages, to gain or save money in other ways, or to limit the necessity of spending cash. Decisions about who additional family workers would be, were therefore crucial in determining the contours of the family economy and of the labour force. An examination of the importance of secondary wage earners, and of who they were in terms of their age and sex allows a better grasp of the interaction between family labour deployment decisions, the 'gendering' of the workforce and the structure of the economy. This section therefore assesses the importance of additional wage earners in families headed by men in different types of occupations.[7] The following section then attempts to determine who such workers were.

The average number of workers reported by the families of the two working class areas studied here, Ste Anne and St Jacques wards, fluctuated over the family life cycle. Amongst young couples who had not yet borne children, the wife would occasionally report an occupation, sometimes another relative lived with the couple, contributing to the number of workers in the household, so that until 1881 families averaged just over one worker at this first stage of a couple's married life. Most families then passed through a long period of relative deprivation as children were born, grew, and required more food, clothing, and larger living premises. Between the time when the first baby was born and some children reached 12 or 13 the families of Ste Anne and St Jacques continued to have only slightly more than one worker. Then children's contribution began to make up for the difficult years. In 1861 families where half the children were still under 15 averaged 1.34 workers; once half were 15 or more they averaged 1.97. In subsequent decades the expansion of wage labour made children's contribution even more important. Whereas in 1861 the average family with children over the age of eleven had only .48 of them at work, in 1881 it had 1.16. By 1871 the average family with offspring aged 15 or more had nearly as many children living at home and working as there had been total number of workers a decade earlier. From .85 children at work, the number reported increased to 1.85. The total number of family workers increased from an average of under two at this stage in 1861 to nearly three a decade later. Children's wages became more and more important as children came to constitute a wage-earning family's major source of security.

The prosperity that this number of workers could have secured was temporary. It depended largely on the ability of parents to keep their wage-earning children in the household. As older sons or daughters began to leave home to work or marry the average dropped down again. If both members of a couple survived they would find themselves struggling again in their old age on a single wage, or no wage at all. For aged working-class widows and widowers the situation was particularly bleak if there were no children able to help.[8]

Over these years the patterns of the working class and non working class families diverged. In 1861 the non-working class, particularly in St Jacques, included a high proportion of artisans and shopkeepers, men whose family economy required not the wages, but the work of wives and children. As a result the average number of workers and of children at work in their families was higher than in all other groups except the unskilled. Over the next two decades artisans became less and less common. Family labour was increasingly limited to enterprises like small corner groceries. Professionals and some white-collar workers became more important among the non-working class populations. After 1871, the reporting of jobs by children was least likely amongst this group.

It was within the working class family economy that the most dramatic changes occurred over this period, although there were significant and changing differences between the skilled, the unskilled, and those in the injured trades. The inadequacy of the $1.00 a day or less that a labourer could earn remained a constant throughout this period. As a result unskilled

families consistently relied on additional workers when they were able to. In 1861 they averaged 1.45 workers, compared to 1.27 among the skilled. Over the next two decades the growing number of jobs available allowed them to increase the average number of family workers to 1.62 then 1.66. . . .

For these unskilled workers the period before children were old enough to work was the most difficult. It is worth examining how some such families managed at the critical stage of the family life cycle and later as children matured. Olive Godaire, wife of labourer Pierre, worked, probably at home as a dressmaker in 1861, to help support their three children aged two to eight. Ten years later, it was her 18-year-old daughter who was taking in sewing, while a ten-year-old boy was apprenticed to be a tinsmith.[9] In the case of labourer John Harrington's family, the period when the father was the only earner within the nuclear family lasted for at least eighteen years. When John and Sarah's children were under ten they took in boarders and had John's 50-year-old father, also a labourer living in the household. Whatever money these extra family and household members contributed would have helped compensate for John's low wages or irregular work and they continued to take in boarders over the next ten years. Their oldest son, Timothy, was still going to school in 1871 and the family was cramped in a rear dwelling where rent was minimal. Somewhere between 1871 and 1881 the boys joined their father in seeking general labouring jobs. For the first time the family lived alone, without additional household members, and with three wage earners, even three labourers, must have enjoyed a standard of living that was relatively high compared to the previous year.

The degradation of work conditions and lower wages that typified trades like shoemaking appear to have been counteracted by sending growing numbers of family members to seek steady work.

In 1861 such families had only 1.08 workers— fewer than any other group. By 1881 they averaged 1.62 workers. Most dramatic was the increased importance of the contribution of children resident at home. The average number of children reporting a job amongst those families with children of working age nearly tripled over the two decades from .55 to 1.51. At that date a few families like that of Angeline and Alexis Lariviere had four workers. Their two daughters, 22-year-old Josephine and 16-year-old Marie-Louise worked as general labourers. Their 20-year-old son Charles was a stone-cutter (Mss Census St Jacques, 1881: 110).

The relative superiority of the wages of skilled workers seems clear in 1861 when they appear to have been able to manage with fewer workers than other groups—averaging only 1.27. A decade later, with 1.5 workers, they still needed fewer than the rest of the working class. The depression which hit in 1874, however, appears to have eroded much of the superiority of the skilled workers. In 1881 after seven years of major depression, which was only just lifting and which must have left many a family heavily indebted, the pattern of family labour deployment was similar to that of the unskilled and those in the injured trades.

This convergence of experiences within the working class over this period is not surprising, given the impact of the depression, combined with the degeneration of work conditions in some skilled trades. In the metal working trades, for example, trade was said to be dead in the winter of 1878. Half the local unionized workers were said to be 'working at any kind of labouring work'. Two years earlier, a moulder drew attention to the desperate condition of Montreal mechanics, 'working on a canal at 60 cents per day, men who have served years in securing a trade, the wages they receive being only a mockery of their misery'.[10]

Families clearly attempted to shape their own economies by adjusting the numbers of wage earners to fit their expenses when they were able to do so. Additional wage earners were not only needed, but were used by all fractions of the working class, with differences stemming from the economic conjuncture, the nature of the labour market, their own life cycle, and earning power. In so doing they influenced the city's labour pool and enhanced their own survival. The increasing availability of wage labour in the factories, workshops, and construction sites of Montreal meant that even in times of depression more and more sons and daughters could and did find work. The reliance of employers in certain sectors on women and youths resident at home depressed male wages generally, while offering families the opportunity to counter a father's low earnings.

Economic transformation thus interacted dialectically with family needs reshaping the labour market, the family economy, and the life course of children. This interaction is clearest in the case of workers in those sectors undergoing the most dramatic transformation. The continued re-organization of production in trades like shoemaking was reflected not only in the greater increase in the number of their children seeking waged work over the period but also in a tendency to delay marriage and reduce family size. In the labour market in general, children living at home became a much more significant proportion of workers.[11] In the sewing trades, for example, one quarter of the workers had been co-resident children in 1861, by 1881 55 per cent were.

Age, Gender, and Additional Family Earners

To try to grasp the decision making processes behind these patterns of change in the average numbers of family members reporting work over this period, it is necessary to determine who the family workers were in terms of age and gender and to examine the families from which they came.

Older sons still living at home were the most usual second earners in a family. The number of really young children or married women reporting a job was insignificant beside the importance of children in their late teens or twenties, despite the attention focused on such young workers by contemporaries.[12] Once sons in particular reached 15 or 16 they were expected to work. 'In our culture', reported Alice Lacasse, the daughter of a French Canadian immigrant to New Hampshire, 'the oldest children always went to work' (Hareven and Langenbach, 1978: 262). Wage labour for boys over 15 became the norm in this period as more and more were drawn into the labour force. Growing numbers of girls did report a job, but the proportion of boys at work remained consistently higher than that for girls in all age groups. And, the pattern of involvement over a girl's life course continued to be completely different from a boy's.

By the age of fifteen or sixteen, 30 per cent of the boys who lived at home in these two wards were reporting a job in 1861. Others no doubt sought casual labour on the streets, working from time to time, at other times roaming together in the gangs of youths which dismayed middle class contemporaries and filled up the local police courts. In 1871, when times were good, and industrial capitalism more entrenched, nearly 46 per cent of boys this age could find a job, while in the depression of the 70s and early 80s the percentage dropped back to 37 per cent. After the age of 16, and increasingly over the period, boys' involvement with wage labour or other work would grow steadily as they aged. At ages 17 to 18, 50 per cent reported a job in 1861, nearly 68 per cent two decades later. By age 21 nearly 90 per cent of boys listed a job at the end of the period.

Among the girls of Ste Anne and St Jacques wards, the work found and the pattern of job reporting over their lives was very different from that of the boys. Once boys passed their early teens they found work in a wide variety of jobs in all sectors and workplaces of Montreal. Girls, in contrast, remained concentrated within specific jobs and sectors. For girls as for boys, the chances of finding work clearly expanded with the growth of Montreal industry. At ages 15 to 16, for instance, only 13 per cent reported a job in 1861 compared to 30 per cent in 1881. At the peak age at which girls reported working, 19–20, 25 per cent worked in 1861, nearly 38 per cent did so in 1871, then 35 per cent in 1881. Even then, however, the visible participation rate of girls was only half that of boys.[13] After age 20, the experiences of boys and girls diverged quickly and dramatically, as most, but never all women, withdrew from the formal labour market while most men found themselves obliged to seek work for the rest of their lives.

For those girls who did earn wages, then, paid labour was apparently undertaken for a brief period of their lives prior to marriage. At any one time, most girls aged 15 or more who remained at home with their parents in these wards reported no job at all. Joan Scott and Louise Tilly have suggested that within the 'industrial mode of production' 'single women are best able to work, since they have few other claims on their time' (Scott and Tilly, 1979: 231). The discrepancy in the formal wage labour participation rates for boys and girls in these two Montreal wards suggests to me that single women did, in fact, have other claims on their time. In particular, the heavy and time consuming nature of nineteenth century housework, the prevalence of disease, the wide age spread amongst children in most families, and the myriad of other largely invisible pursuits and strategies necessary to survival for the working class family, meant that many of these girls were needed by their mothers to help with work at home. Their role in the division of labour within the family is highlighted on one census return where members' roles were explicitly described. Louis Coutur, a carter who was 50 in 1861, reported that his 21-year-old son was a shoemaker, his wife's job was 'housework', and the 17-year-old daughter's job was 'helping with the housework' (Mss Census St Jacques, 1961: 7750). It seems fair to assume, making allowance for the under-enumeration of steady labour and casual work among daughters, that most of the girls who listed no job or school attendance, worked periodically, if not continually, at domestic labour as mother's helpers in and around the home. It is thus in the light of family decisions about the allocation of labour power at home, as well as in the structure of jobs available in the market place, that the patterns of children's wage labour as well as of their schooling must be interpreted.

At home girls served an apprenticeship in the reproduction of labour power—in babysitting, cleaning, mending, sewing, cooking, and shopping, and by the end of the century in nursing and hygiene.[14] Religious leaders were explicit about the need for mothers to educate their daughters in their future roles. 'Apply yourselves especially to the task of training your daughters in the functions they will have to perform for a husband and family, without neglecting your other children', wrote Pere Mailloux in a manual for Christian parents which was republished several times between the middle and end of the nineteenth century (cited in Dion, 1984). When girls attended school, the subjects learned were not very different. Education for females, except in a few expensive academies, out of reach of the working class, taught only the most basic and general of subjects and housekeeping-type skills. Whereas boys' schools offered bookkeeping and geography, girls' schools offered music, needlework, and sewing (Huguet-Latour,

1877). Curriculums aimed to prepare girls for their future role as housekeeper, wife, and mother (Malouin, 1983: 90). The Minister of Education was explicit. He feared that too many young women were being educated above their station in life and suggested that bookkeeping and domestic economy constituted the best basis of female education.[15] In separate schools, with curriculum that moulded life roles based on gender distinctions, girls were not going to reshape their futures dramatically by slightly increasing the average number of years which they spent at school and in the workplace over this period.

Girls then, did become secondary wage earners within the working class family economy, were increasingly likely to do so over this period, but remained less likely to report a job than were boys. The importance of their contribution to domestic labour, the lower wages they could make in the formal labour market, or an ideological repulsion to girls' labour either within the working class or amongst capitalists constitute partial explanations for their lower rate of participation. In the absence of interviews or written memoirs, it is important to examine the work patterns of specific families more closely to see what reasons can be deduced from the evidence.

Even among the families apparently in greatest need, sons seem to have been sent out to work in preference to daughters. If any families needed to draw on as many workers as possible it should have been those headed by the labourers or shoemakers of these wards. In such families food costs alone for a family with several growing children rapidly outstripped a man's incoming wages. Yet even these families appear to have avoided sending girls out to work, if possible. Among labourer's families in Ste Anne in 1881, for example, 66 per cent of those who had boys over 10 reported having a son at work, while only 28 per cent of those with girls the same age did so. If older brothers were working, girls generally did not. Girls of 20 or more would stay at home while a teenage son worked. Their respective roles seem clearly defined. Twenty-six-year-old Ellen Mullin, for example, reported no occupation. Two brothers aged 19 and 23 worked as carters. Ellen's role was to help her mother with the domestic labour for the three wage earners and her 14-year-old younger brother (Mss Census, Ste Anne, 1881: 1).

In Ste Anne, even families without sons, or with young sons only, seem to have been either unwilling to send girls to work or unable to find work that was seen as suitable in the neighbourhood. Forty-two-year-old Octave Ethier must surely have had trouble supporting his four daughters aged one to seventeen and his wife on his labourer's wages. Yet neither 17-year-old Philomène, nor 15-year-old Emma reported having a job (Mss Census, Ste Anne, 1881: 1).

The girls in labourer's families who did report an occupation fell into two categories. Half were the oldest child, either with no brothers or only brothers who were much younger than they were. Nineteen-year-old Sarah Anne Labor, for instance, was the oldest in a family of six children. The closest brother was only seven. She worked as a soap maker. Her wages and the fact that the family shared the household with several other families must have helped make ends meet (Mss Census, Ste Anne, 1881: 208).

The second group of girl workers in Ste Anne and St Jacques came from labourer's families which sent almost all their children to work regardless of gender. Catherine Harrigan, for instance, was 14. She worked as a servant. Her two brothers aged 15 and 20 were labourers like their father. In the family of St Jacques labourer, Damase Racette, four girls aged 17 to 25 were all dressmakers, as was his wife, Rachel. A 27-year-old son was a cigar maker (Mss Census, St Jacques, 1881: 340). This latter group of families appears the most desperate,

perhaps because of recurrent illness, or the habitual drunkeness of a parent. When Commissioners Lukas and Blackeby were examining the work of children in Canadian mills and factories in 1882 they reported finding too many cases in the cities and factory districts where parents with 'idle habits' lived 'on the earnings of the children, this being confirmed' in their eyes by one instance where three children were at work having a father as above described.[16] Yet, such a family could simply have been taking advantage of the fact of having more children of working age to make up for years of deprivation on the inadequate wages most family heads could make. . . . When a father was chronically ill, or a habitual drunkard, the wages of several children would indeed have been necessary to support a family. The use of daughters and of children aged 10 to 12 to earn wages in this minority of labourer's families contrasts with the absence of such workers in other labourers' families, highlighting the relative infrequency of daughter's work even among those in greatest need.

Was it in part working class ideology that kept girls at home if at all possible, seeing the workplace as unfit for them, or was it rather a pragmatic response to the fact that boys' wages rapidly outstripped those of girls? Pragmatism, made necessary by the exigencies of daily existence, must certainly have played an important part. It made good sense to have boys earn wages rather than girls, for while young children of each sex might earn a similar wage, once they reached fifteen or sixteen girls' wages were generally half those of a young man. On the other hand, when there was work available that girls could do, more were likely to report a job. Thus the labourers of St Jacques were more likely to have daughters at work than those of Ste Anne. An equal percentage of those with children eleven or over had girls at work as had boys. The fact that nearly 80 per cent of these girls worked in some branch of the sewing industry shows how advantage was taken of the availability of this kind of work in the neighbourhood.

Family labour deployment decisions, then, were forged in the context of their own needs, invariably arising partly from the size, age, and gender configurations of the family, as well as from the kind of work the family head could find. They were realized in relationship with the structure of the local labour market, of job possibilities and local wage rates for men and women, boys and girls. And they were influenced by perceptions, ideologies, and gut reactions about what was appropriate for sons and daughters. Thus, it was not just the fact that sewing was available in St Jacques ward that made this such a popular choice for daughters living in that ward, for putting out could theoretically operate anywhere in the city or the surrounding countryside. It was, I suspect, the very fact that it could be done at home which was crucial. For, while domestic service no doubt took some young women from families in these wards away from their own families and into the homes of others, sewing usually kept daughters working at home.[17]

Home-work offered parents, and mothers in particular, several advantages. Firstly they could oversee their daughters' work and behaviour, avoiding the individualism that working in a factory might encourage, and skirting the dangers and moral pitfalls which at least some contemporaries associated with factory work for young, unmarried women.[18] More importantly, girls sewing at home, like their mothers, could combine stitching and housework, could take care of younger children, run odd errands, or carry water as needed because they were right there and were always paid by the piece.

The clustering of two to five family members, all seamstresses, commonly found in the census returns for St Jacques ward suggests very strongly

that here was a centre of the homework that was crucial to Montreal's sewing and shoe-making industries during this period. It was not uncommon to find three to four sisters, ranging in age from 11 to 28 all working, presumably together, as sewing girls. In the Moisan family of St Jacques ward, for instance, four daughters worked as seamstresses in 1871. The father was a labourer, and although the wife reported no occupation, she probably also did some sewing at home at times (Mss Census, St Jacques, 1871: 137). In 1881, the family of Marie and Michel Guigère had reached a relatively secure stage in their family life cycle. With nine children at home aged two to 23, this joiner's family reported seven workers. Four of the girls, aged 13 to 23 were seamstresses, one son worked as a labourer, and the 13-year-old son was an apprentice. The girls could combine sewing with helping their mother keep house for other workers, caring for the younger children, shopping, cooking, cleaning, and also looking after her husband's 70-year-old father who lived with them. Marie too probably helped sporadically with sewing (Mss Census, St Jacques, 1881: 101).

Some parents with the liberty to choose must have been reluctant to expose their daughters to the long hours, continual supervision, exhausting work, and brutal forms of discipline which existed in some of Montreal's workshops and factories. Work at home could counteract such factors of 'repulsion' (Pollard, 1965: 162) in some of the sectors employing girls. Cigar-making factories provided jobs for girls and boys in Ste Anne and St Jacques alike. While some manufacturers appear to have been decent men, neither fining nor beating their employees, others, in an apparently desperate attempt to control their youthful workforce resorted to physical violence, heavy fines, even locking up children as they strove to mould this young generation of workers to industrial work. Children, like adults in these factories, worked from six or seven in the morning until six at night, and sometimes later.[19] Unlike adult males, they were subject to a vast array of disciplinary measures aimed at making them more productive and more responsible as workers. One child reported:

> If a child did anything, that is, if he looked on one side or other, or spoke, he would say: I'm going to make you pay 10 cents fine, and if the same were repeated three or four times, he would seize a stick or a plank, and beat him with it.[20]

Mr Fortier's cigar-making factory was described as a 'theatre of lewdness'. There was said to be 'no such infamous factory as M. Fortier's . . . nowhere else as bad in Montreal'. There, one cigar-maker described apprentices as being 'treated more or less as slaves'.[21] It was the evidence of the treatment of one 18-year-old girl that really shocked both the public and the commissioners examining the relations between labour and capital in 1888. Georgina Loiselle described how Mr Fortier beat her with a mould cover because she would not make the 100 cigars as he demanded.

> I was sitting, and he took hold of me by the arm, and tried to throw me on the ground. He did throw me on the ground and beat me with the mould cover.
> Q. Did he beat you when you were down?
> A. Yes, I tried to rise and he kept me down on the floor.[22]

The case of Mr Fortier's cigar factory was not typical. It created a sensation when the evidence was heard. At least some of the mothers of girls working there got together, perhaps encouraged by Mr Fortier, to give evidence to counteract the impact of such bad publicity. 'I am the mother of a family and if I had seen anything improper I would not have stayed there,' explained a Mrs Levoise. 'I have my girl working there.'[23]

While conditions in other Montreal factories were not as extreme, there was sufficient evidence of beatings, other draconian forms of discipline, and heavy fines to explain why many girls and their parents may have wished to avoid factory labour. In cotton factories there was some evidence of boys and girls being beaten. Furthermore fines in at least one Montreal cotton factory could reduce pay packages by between $1.00 and $12.00 in two weeks. Work there began at 6:25 a.m. and finished at 6:15 p.m. When extra work was required, employees had to stay until 9 p.m., often without time off for supper.[24] There were some perks to work in the textile industry. Nineteen-year-old Adèle Lavoie explained that the girls were accustomed to 'take cotton to make our aprons'. Apparently this was usually allowed, but on at least one occasion she was accused by the foreman of having taken 40–50 yards. When a search of her house produced no results, she reported that the foreman returned to the factory to insult and harass her sister. When she did not produce the cotton, 'he stooped at this time and raising the skirt of my sister's dress, he said she had it under her skirt.'[25]

Airless, hot, dusty factories, such sexual abuse by foremen, work conditions, and the long hours, were all factors which may have discouraged parents from sending girls into factory work. More significant were the wages they earned. For children under 14 or so, wages varied little by sex. After that male and female differentials hardened. Girl apprentices in dressmaking, mantle-making, and millinery sometimes earned nothing for several years until they learned the trade; then they received around $4.00 a week only. 'Girls' in shoe manufactories received $3.00 to $4.00 compared to the $7.00 or $8.00 earned by men. A girl bookbinder made between $1.50 and $6.00

weekly, compared to an average of $11.00 for male journeymen. Even on piecework girls and women generally received less than men. In general wage rates for women were approximately half those of men.[26]

Duties at home and low wages whether they worked in or outside the home meant that whereas over this period more and more working class boys would have reached manhood accustomed to wage labour, their sisters were much more likely to move backwards and forwards between paid work and housework in response to the family's economic needs and their position in the household. Once boys, and particularly those who had been fortunate enough to acquire a skill in demand in the marketplace, reached their late teens, their earning power might rival that of their father. Wage labour offered such children potential freedom from their family in a way that had not been possible in family economies based on shared work and the inheritance of property. Such freedom was seldom possible for girls unless they were willing to complement wage labour with prostitution.[27] _— discussed in the homeless article too_

Age, Gender, and Changing Patterns of Residence, Schooling, and Domestic Labour

Yet, boys in general do not appear to have taken dramatic advantage of such potential freedom. Nor did girls.[27] In 1861 living with others was still an important stage in the lives of some young people of both sexes. Amongst the 17-year-old girls residing in Ste Anne and St Jacques 35 per cent were boarding with other families, living with relatives, or working and living in as a servant. Twenty years later only 12 per cent of girls that age were not living with their parents, and half of these were already married. Amongst boys aged eighteen, 34 per cent were not living with their parents in 1861

compared to only 17 per cent two decades later. Living longer at home with their parents was a fundamental change in the life cycle of boys and girls alike during this period of industrial expansion.[28]

Behind the percentages of children living with their parents or elsewhere lies a complex history of tension between family needs and individual desires, of children balancing off the advantages of the services offered at home against the relative independence that living with strangers, or even relatives might offer.[29] For all families who had passed through at least 15 years of budget-stretching, house-sharing, and debt-building while their children were young, the relative prosperity that several workers could offer was to be jealously guarded. It was precisely 'because young adults could find jobs' that it 'was in the interest of parents to keep their children at home as long as possible' (Spagnoli, 1983: 238). The patterns of residence of children suggest that, whatever conflicts there were overall, in these two wards of Montreal between 1861 and 1881 it was increasingly the parents who were the winners.

The motives behind individual decisions, the weight of traditions of family work, are difficult to grasp in the absence of written records. The factors constraining or encouraging one choice or another are clearer. Most children would have left home once they had a job only if their wages were adequate to pay for lodgings and they felt no commitment to contributing to the family income. Clearly more older boys earned enough to pay for room and board than did girls. Thus, in 1871, when work was readily available 29 per cent of the 23-year-old males living in these wards were boarding or with relatives; 39 per cent were living with their parents, and 32 per cent had married. Amongst girls the same age the low wages they could make severely limited their options. Only 15 per cent were boarding; 41 per cent were still with their parents, and 44 per cent were already married. The contraction of work and lower wages that accompanied the Great Depression which hit in 1874 limited the possibility of leaving home to lodge with others or to marry. In 1881, the percentage of 23-year-old boys married had dropped to 25 per cent; only 10 per cent were boarding or living with relatives. Sixty-five per cent remained at home with their parents, presumably pooling resources to survive the difficult times. The depression appears to have hastened the decline of this stage of semi-autonomy. What occurred in subsequent years remains to be determined.

The different roles of boys and girls in the family economy are confirmed in the different patterns of school attendance by age and sex. In general school and work appear to have been complementary rather than in competition. Some children began school at four years old. By age seven approximately 60 per cent of boys and girls were receiving some education. In 1881 this percentage rose to a peak of 78 per cent for eight- and nine-year-old boys and of around 80 per cent for girls aged nine to 12 then fell off rapidly once both sexes reached 13. The proportion of children receiving some schooling increased, but not dramatically between 1861 and 1881. Age, gender, and the economic conjuncture created variations within this overall trend. Most important was the more erratic pattern in the attendance of boys, which hints at relationships between age, gender, schooling, and wage labour which require further investigation. Overall the percentage of 10–14-year-old girls at school increased slowly but steadily from 57 per cent in 1861 to 68 per cent in 1881.[30] The increase was greater in St Jacques than Ste Anne, but the pattern was similar. Amongst boys in each ward, in contrast, the proportion at school was lower in 1871 than any other year, and the proportion of 10–19-year-olds at work increased. In Ste Anne, in particular, the factories, workshops, and general

labouring jobs attracted growing numbers of these youth. The percentage of 15–19-year-old boys reporting working in that ward increased from 38 in 1861 to 64 a decade later. While a certain number of families appear to have taken advantage of boom periods to draw their sons, in particular, out of school, the majority of families appear to have got the best of both worlds. Most working class boys went to school for varying lengths of time before they reached thirteen or so, and then sought wage labour.

These figures confirm the greater importance of sons' wage contribution to the family economy. Girls' role is clear in the high proportion that continued to report neither a job, nor school attendance. Transformations of the economy and the passage of time were slow to modify this gender difference in the relationship between girls' and boys' schooling and their roles in the family economy. A study conducted in Quebec in 1942, just before schooling was finally made compulsory in that province, found that among children quitting school before the age of 16, 61 per cent of girls gave as their reason 'Maman avait besoin de moi,' while 50 per cent of boys stated 'Ma famille avait besoin d'argent.' Only 10 per cent of girls gave that reason (cited in Jean, 1988). The centrality of girls domestic labour in a different Canadian city, Toronto, is corroborated by evidence showing that potential foster parents in that city at the turn of the century were four times more likely to seek girls than boys, specifically for their usefulness as domestics and nursemaids (cited in Bullen, 1988).

Conclusion

Gender was clearly at work in both senses of the word in nineteenth-century Montreal. On the one hand the labour market was characterized by a sexual division of labour which, despite the rapid and dramatic changes occurring in the period, limited the numbers of jobs where capitalists considered employing women. This was not immutable, as the cases where 'girls' were used as strikebreakers made clear. Montreal's labour market included major sectors, particularly sewing and shoemaking, which employed large numbers of girls and women. Yet, the figures of labour-force participation rates for the two wards studied here, suggest strongly that girls and women seldom entered the workforce in proportions equivalent to their brothers or boys the same age, and that over their life courses their participation was totally different.

The reasons why lie at least partially within the workings of the family wage economy. Working class families in Montreal clearly both needed and used additional family workers to counteract low wages and to improve their standard of living. The number of extra workers varied with the skill of the family head and the worth of that skill in the labour market. Thus, while in good times, skilled workers managed with fewer family workers than the unskilled or those in injured trades, economic depression eroded such superiority. Yet in whatever complex and probably tension loaded decisions were made about who would seek what kind of work, boys were much more likely to be the auxiliary wage earners than girls.

To explain why brings us, in a sense, to the heart of the debate about the relative importance of patriarchy and capitalism in explaining women's oppression. That the domestic labour of wives has been crucial both to family survival and to women's inequality has long been recognized both empirically and theoretically. But where do daughters fit in? Fathers, one could argue, by keeping girls at home along with their mothers to serve their daily need for replenishment ensured that the work of all women was viewed as intermittent and secondary to that of the major wage earners.[31]

Alternatively, the accent can be put on the nature of specific industries or more generally on the capitalist labour market, which, by setting women's wage rates at half those of men, made it logical to send boys to work rather than girls.[32] Unequal access to work on the same terms of men thus not only perpetuated women's position in the home, but tragically disadvantaged those single women and widows who alone or supporting children or elderly parents had to live on such wages.

Clearly a dialectic is at work here. Neither empirically nor theoretically can the workings of patriarchy, or of capitalism, be neatly separated from each other.[33] The nature of the interaction between the two and the weight of one over the other will vary historically and geographically. Among Montreal families, decisions were made in part in relation to existing jobs and wage rates and such decisions perpetuated, reified the idea that women's work was temporary, performed before marriage or in moments of family crisis. Admitting the dialectic adds complexity to the explanation but remains, I suspect, insufficient. It does so, because the emphasis remains on the formal, wage earning labour market. Domestic labour in the nineteenth century was fundamental to family survival, to the transformation of wages into a reasonable standard of living, and to the reproduction of the working class. Historians have recognized the importance of this job for the working class wife and mother; the role of daughters has been examined less explicitly. Yet, for nineteenth century mothers whose children were widely spaced in age, in whose homes technology had made virtually no inroads to lighten their labour, the help of daughters was invaluable. Housewives had no control over the amount of wages the husband earned, and little over how much was turned over to them. Housework was labour intensive and time consuming. One of the only ways in which wives could control the content and intensity of their work was to get children to help. Wherever possible once girls reached an age where they could be of use to the mother they were used to baby-sit, to run errands, to clean, sew, and cook. If this could be combined with wage earning activities, as in the case of home-work in the sewing industry, then such girls did work more formally. If there were no brothers of an age to earn, daughters might work in factories, offices, shops, or as domestics. But the need of mothers for at least one helper at home would mean that the rate of formal labour force participation for girls would generally be lower than that for boys. Patriarchal ideas within the working class, elements of male

pride and self interest, economic pragmatism, and the daily needs of mothers and housewives thus interacted, creating a situation in which most girls served an apprenticeship in domestic labour prior to or in conjunction with entering the workforce.[34] In cities and towns where the labour market was completely different, where whole families or women were explicitly sought by employers, this division of labour, indeed the very institutions of marriage and the family, could be modified. The question of how to ensure that the necessary domestic labour was performed, however, would remain fundamental. The working out of roles by gender at home would continue to influence the configurations of gender at work.

Notes

1. For Canadian articles touching the question see: Gail Cuthbert Brandt, 'The Transformation of Women's Work in the Quebec Cotton Industry, 1920–1950', in Bryan D. Palmer, ed., *The Character of Class Struggle: Essays in Canadian Working Class History, 1840–1985* (Toronto: McClelland and Stewart, 1986); Mercedes Steedman, 'Skill and Gender in the Canadian Clothing Industry, 1890–1940', in Craig Heron and Robert Storey, eds, *On the Job: Confronting the Labour Process in Canada* (Montreal and Kingston: McGill-Queen's Press, 1986), 152–76; Jacque Ferland, 'Syndicalisme "parcellaire" et syndicalisme "collectif": Une interpretation socio-technique des conflits ouvriers dans deux industries québécoises, 1880–1914', *Labour/Le Travail* 19 (Spring 1987): 49–88.

2. This argument is obviously not mine alone. It is fundamental to much of the discussion of the workings of patriarchy and to the domestic labour debate, where too often it remains at an abstract theoretical level or based on cursory historical data.

3. Mark Rosenfeld's article '"It was a hard life": Class and Gender in the Work and Family Rhythms of a Railway Town, 1920–1950', *Historical Papers* (1988) carefully unravels how the rhythms of work in the running trades structured the family economy and gender roles in Barrie, Ontario, a railway town.

4. Marjorie Cohen makes a similar argument without elaborating on its implications for daughters in

stating that 'the supply of female labour was limited by the labour requirements of the home.' *Women's Work, Markets and Economic Development in Nineteenth Century Ontario* (Toronto: University of Toronto Press, 1988), 139.

5. On the average, in the early 1880s, for example, a labourer earned around $1.00 a day, a shoemaker $1.25, a carpenter $1.50, and various more highly skilled workers anything from $1.75 (blacksmith) up. See Bettina Bradbury, 'The Working-Class Family Economy, Montreal, 1861–1881', PhD, Concordia University, 1984, 18; *Canada*, Parliament, Sessional Papers, 1882, Paper No. 4, Appendix 3, Annual Report of the Immigration Agent', 110–11, lists the wages in a variety of trades.

6. In this, Montreal and Canada were little different from other cities and countries, nor has much of the discrepancy been eliminated today.

7. The figures used in this paper are derived from research done for my PhD thesis, currently under revision for publication. A ten per cent random sample was taken of households enumerated by the census takes in Ste Anne and St Jacques in 1861, 1871, and 1881. This resulted in a total sample of 10,967 people over the three decades. They resided in 1,851 households and 2,278 families as defined by the census takers.

8. For a brief and preliminary examination of how widows of all ages survived see my 'Surviving as

a Widow in Nineteenth Century Montreal', *Urban History Review* 17, 3 (1989): 148–60.

9. These life histories were recreated by tracing families between the censuses of 1861, 1871, and 1881.

10. See *Iron Moulders Journal*, January and June, 1878, Report of Local 21; *Iron Moulders Journal*, January 1876, Report of Local 21 and open letter from Local 21 to the editor, cited in Peter Bischoff, 'La formation des traditions de solidarité ouvriere chez les mouleurs Montréalais: la longue marche vers le syndicalisme, 1859–1881', *Labour/Le Travail* 21 (Spring 1988): 22. Bischoff suggests, sensibly, that amongst moulders the homogenizing experience of these years of depression left them more open to the idea of including less skilled workers in their union in the 1880s. The widespread appeal of the Knights of Labor could be seen in the same light.

11. In 1861, for example, only 16 per cent of those reporting jobs in these two wards were children residing at home; 20 years later nearly one-third of all reported workers were offspring living with their parents.

12. There is no doubt that the wage labour of both young children and married women was under-enumerated. However, as no labour laws existed in Quebec until 1885, and education was not compulsory until 1943, it is unlikely that fear of repercussions would have inhibited parents from responding as it might have elsewhere.

13. Caution has to be exercised when using reported jobs for women and children. . . . While I am sure that some under-enumeration of women's work occurred in Montreal, as elsewhere, I don't think that under-enumeration can explain away the differential. Nor is the phenomenon easy to measure. More regularity, its more informal nature, was less likely to be reported. On the problem of under-reporting see, in particular, Sally Alexander, 'Women's Work in Nineteenth Century London: A Study of the Years 1820–1850', in Juliett Mitchell and Ann Oakley, eds, *The Rights and Wrongs of Women* (London: Penguin, 1976), 63–6.

14. By the end of the century the need for this kind of education of daughters was being explicitly preached by Montreal doctors and by church representatives and was formalized in Quebec with the creation of écoles menageres after the 1880s. Carole Dion, 'La femme et la santé de la famille au Québec, 1890–1940', MA thesis, Université de Montréal, 1984).

15. See *Québec, Documents de la Session*, 1874, 'Rapport du minister de l'instruction publique', vii.

16. 'Report of the Commissioners Appointed to Enquire into the Working of the Mills and Factories of the Dominion and the Labour Employed therein', Canada, Parliament, *Sessional Papers*, 1882, Paper No. 42, p. 2.

17. The fact that domestic service was Montreal's leading employment for girls and that it usually involved living in, complicates this analysis of the work of children. Girls could work away from home as a domestic and contribute their pay to their parents; they would not, however, figure among the average number of workers found in census families, nor would their experience be captured in the proportion of girls having a job.

18. On the commissioners' concerns about this see Susan Mann Trofimenkoff, 'One hundred and one muffled voices', in Susan Mann Trofimenkoff and Alison Prentice, *The Neglected Majority: Essays in Canadian Women's History* (Toronto: McClelland and Stewart, 1977).

19. See RCRLC. *Quebec Evidence*, evidence of Wm. C. McDonald, Tobacco manufacturer, p. 529.

20. See RCRLC. *Quebec Evidence*, anonymous evidence, p. 42.

21. See RCRLC. *Quebec Evidence*, pp. 44–7.

22. See RCRLC. *Quebec Evidence*, p. 91.

23. See RCRLC. *Quebec Evidence*, evidence of Mrs Levoise.

24. See RCRLC. *Quebec Evidence*, evidence of a machinist, Hudon factory, Hochelaga, pp. 273–4.

25. See RCRLC. *Quebec Evidence*, evidence of Adèle Lavoie, pp. 280–2.

26. See RCRLC. *Quebec Evidence*, evidence of Patrick Ryan, cigarmaker, p. 37; machinist Hudon Mills, p. 271; Samuel Carsley, dry goods merchant, p. 15; Oliver Benoit, boot and shoemaker, p. 365; Henry Morton, printer, p. 297; F. Stanley, foreman at the *Star*, p. 331.

27. Here I am referring to the percentage of children at home as opposed to boarding, living with relatives or living in someone else's house as a servant. The samples taken in each census do not allow me to follow children over time and identify those who actually left home.

28. The same process occurred in Hamilton, and in other cities that have been studied. See Michael Katz, *The People of Hamilton, Canada West*, 257, 261; Mary P. Ryan, *The Cradle of the Middle Class: The Family in Oneida County, New York, 1790–1865* (New York: Cambridge University Press, 1981), 168–9; Richard Wall, 'The Age at Leaving Home', *Journal of Family History* 8 (Fall 1983): 238.

29. For a careful analysis of the relationship between women's wages, costs of board, and decisions about where to live see Gary Cross and Peter Shegold, 'The Family Economy and the Market: Wages and

Residence of Pennsylvania Women in the 1890s', *Journal of Family History* 11, 3 (1986): 245–66.

30. A similar, but greater increase in girls' school attendance is described for Hamilton by Michael B. Katz and Ian E. Davey, in 'Youth and Early Industrialization', in John Demos and Sarane Spence Boocock, eds, *Turning Points: Historical and Sociological Essays on the Family*, p. S94.

31. One of the great advantages of the domestic labour debate was its recognition of the importance of housework and reproduction of labour power to capitalism. Less clear in much of the writing was the failure of most writers to acknowledge the interest of men in the perpetuation of domestic labour. For an elaboration of this critique see Sylvia Walby, *Patriarchy at Work: Patriarchal and Capitalist Relations in Employment* (Minneapolis: University of Minnesota Press, 1986), pp. 18–19.

32. Ruth Milkman criticizes labour-segmentation theory, early Marxist feminist writing as well as Hartman's description of patriarchy for paying insufficient attention to the effect of industrial structure on the sexual division of labour and struggles over 'woman's place' in the labour market. Looking much more concretely than theorists have done at specific industries she argues that 'an industry's pattern of employment by sex reflects the economic, political, and social constraints that are operative when that industry's labor market initially forms'. Ruth Milkman, *Gender at Work: The Dynamics of Job Segregation by Sex during World War II* (Urbana and Chicago: University of Illinois Press, 1987), p. 7.

33. Herein lies the problem of the 'dual systems' approach of Hartman and others. Heidi Hartman, 'Capitalism, Patriarchy and Job Segregation by Sex', *Signs*, 1 (Spring 1976): pp. 137–69; Varda Burstyn, 'Masculine Dominance and the State', in Varda Burstyn and Dorothy Smith, *Women, Class, Family and the State* (Toronto: Garamond Press, 1985).

34. Psychological, Freudian theories about gender identity seem less important here than the practical day to day experience in the home and the role model of the mother. Nancy Chodorow, *The Reproduction of Mothering* (1978).

References

Bullen, John. 1988. 'J.J. Kelso and the "New" Child-Savers: The Genesis of the Children's Aid Movement in Ontario'. Paper presented to the CHA Annual Meeting, Windsor, Ontario, June.

Dion, Carole. 1984. 'La femme et la santé de la famille au Québec, 1890–1940', MA thesis, Université de Montréal.

Hareven, Tamara K., and Randolph Langenbach. 1978. *Amoskeag: Life and Work in an American Factory City*. New York: Pantheon Books.

Hartman, Heidi. 1976. 'Capitalism, Patriarchy, and Job Segregation by Sex', *Signs* 1 (Spring): 137–69.

Huguet-Latour, L.A. 1877. *L'Annuaire de Ville Marie. Origine, utilité et progrès des institutions catholiques de Montréal*. Montréal: Senecal.

Jean, Dominque. 1988. 'Les familles québécoises et trois politiques socials touchant les enfants, de 1940 à 1960: Obligation scolaire, allocations familiales et loi controlant le travail juvenile'. Thèse de doctorat, Université de Montréal.

Lowan, Judy. 1983. 'Not so much a Factory, More a Form of Patriarchy: Gender and Class During Industrialisation', in E. Gamarnikow, et al., *Gender, Class and Work*. London: Heinemann.

Malouin, Marie-Paule. 1983. 'Les rapports entre l'école privée et l'école publique: l'Academie Marie-Rose au 19e siècle', in Nadia Fahmy-Eid and Micheline Dumont, *Maîtresses de maison, maîtresses d'école*. Montreal: Boreal Express.

Mss Census, St Jacques. 1861. 11, p. 7750.

Mss Census, St Jacques. 1871. 6, p. 137.

Mss Census, St Jacques. 1881. 17, p. 110.

Mss Census, St Jacques. 1881. 17, p. 340.

Mss Census, Ste Anne. 1881. 5, p. 1.

Mss Census, Ste Anne. 1881. 9, p. 208.

Mss Census, St Jacques. 1881. 12, p. 101.

Parr, Joy. 1987. 'Rethinking Work and Kinship in a Canadian Hosiery Town, 1910–1950', *Feminist Studies* 13, 1 (Spring): 137–62.

Pollard, Sydney. 1965. *The Genesis of Modern Management: A Study of the Industrial Revolution*. London: Edward Arnold.

Rose, Sonya O. 1986. 'Gender at Work: Sex, Class and Industrial Capitalism', *History Workshop Journal* 21 (Spring): 113–31.

Scott, Joan, and Louise Tilly. 1979. *Women, Work, and Family*. New York: Holt, Rinehart, and Winston.

Spagnoli, Paul. 1983. 'Industrialization, Proletarianization and Marriage', *Journal of Family History* 8 (Fall): 230–47.

CHAPTER 6

'The Other Side': The Rhetoric of Labour Reform
Christina Burr

During the early 1870s, in a period of economic growth and industrialization in Ontario, trade-union membership increased, new unions were organized, the important struggle for shorter hours occurred, and the institutional framework for the labour movement was put into place. . . .

In response to the rhetoric of employers—most notably that of George Brown, editor of the *Globe* and Grit politician—which negatively defined working men as a class to be feared, labour reformers were confronted with the task of building a positive working-class identity. The language of labour reformers during the early 1870s created a positive image of working-class manhood for purposes of mobilizing working-class support and combatting the opponents of the nascent labour movement. Labour reformers presented a distinctive masculine subject organized around the honest, skilled, Anglo-Saxon working man who struggles against the evils of capitalist exploitation. The masculinity of the working man was not completely autonomous, however, and its content was influenced by the dominant middle-class culture.

The role of the nineteenth-century labour reformer was to educate working-class men, and to transform them into concerned citizens, workers, trade unionists, husbands, and fathers. A handful of intellectuals and reform-oriented journalists attempted to create an alternative 'serious' working-class fiction and labour press that was unlike the 'penny dreadfuls' or dime novels favoured by workers during their leisure hours.

The representations of male workers in working-class fiction was counter to the images of working men presented in the writings of middle-class reformers (Watt, 1957; Vicinus, 1974; Grimes, 1986; Denning, 1987; Clark, 1992). In response to the subjection of workers in the factory and the workshop, working-class narratives reversed bourgeois discourses that disparaged workers, and trade unionism in particular. This portrayal opened up a space for counter-identification that empowered rather than victimized male workers.

Melodrama was used to educate workmen in the cause of labour reform. A novel entitled *The Other Side*, by American labour reformer Martin Foran, was published in the *Ontario Workman* in weekly installments between 27 June 1872 and 27 February 1873. The working man subject was partially constituted by the discourses of the state, the trade union, the workplace, and the family, but that subject was also less formally, perhaps, but no less effectively, constructed through literature.

Rethinking Labour Reform in Toronto during the Early 1870s

During the spring of 1872, George Brown, editor and owner of the *Globe*, played a prominent role in mobilizing employer resistance to the nine-hours movement through his editorials in that newspaper. He spearheaded the organization of an employers' association, named the Master Printers' Association. Brown also had the striking printers in his employ prosecuted for conspiracy to combine (Careless,

1989). A follower of Manchester liberalism, Brown reduced the issue to one of the simple operation of the economic law of supply and demand. 'It is a question of profit and loss as between the employer and the employed,' he argued. '[I]t is one that may well be discussed on social and moral grounds; but there is no law in morals or philosophy that makes eight or nine hours' labour right, and ten hours' wrong.' In his editorials, Brown suggested that workers had a right to bargain with employers for shorter hours and higher wages, but he further indicated that if employers decided to make a bargain for a ten-hour workday, there was no injustice in their position.[1]

Brown denounced the arguments in favour of a reduction in working hours made by labour reformers at nine-hour rallies held throughout southwestern Ontario in the spring of 1872. He classified the speakers who addressed the crowds gathered at these rallies as 'foreign agitators' or 'the agents of English trades' unions who make money out of labour agitation'. Another even more dangerous class, Brown further suggested, were those men 'of dreamy, imaginative character, who form exaggerated notions of the evils of manual labour and vague aspirations after a different and what they consider a much higher life.' . . .

Following a nine-hour demonstration held in the Music Hall on 15 March 1872, which was addressed by Richard Trevellick, president of the National Labor Union, Brown accused Trevellick of being 'profoundly ignorant of how the social fabric of Ontario is constituted'. In his editorial, Brown claimed a position of authority as an 'insider', and utilized the consensual 'we' pronoun in order to claim that he spoke for 'the people' (Fowler, 1991). 'We all work,' he wrote. 'We all began with nothing. We have all got by hard work all we own—and the richest among us work on still, and like to do it' (*Globe*, 23 March 1972). These 'agitators' were ignorant of conditions in Canada, where, according to Brown, no class distinctions existed.

. . . In Brown's view, any man who refused to work ten hours a day was a 'loafer', and did not properly carry out his 'manly' obligations in the public realm or provide adequately for his family. Brown did not agree that a reduction in working hours would necessarily be used for purposes of self-help, education, or a healthier home life. He further asserted that an increase in leisure time would only heighten the moral degeneration among the working class by giving them more time to frequent the tavern and the billiard hall (*Globe*, 16 February 1872, 23 March 1872). Thus, Brown transformed the issue of a reduction in working hours into a problem of lack of moral fibre among working-class men.

During the early 1870s, Toronto labour reformers confronted the task of constructing a positive working-class masculine identity. In doing so, they emphasized that their efforts were not isolated, but were instead, as John Hewitt stated at the 15 February rally, 'on the heels of the noble working men of Great Britain and those in the United States' (*Globe*, 15 February 1872). . . .

Canada's colonial relationship with Britain was incorporated into labour-reform discourse, and was used to define a community that included Canadian working men. Rather than the 'foreign agitators' depicted by George Brown, Toronto labour reformers indicated that the nine-hours movement was derived from the 'Mother Country', and as members of the 'great Anglo-Saxon race' working men should endeavour to align themselves with their 'brethren at home'. Toronto labour reformers promoted identification with the nine-hours movement as a 'duty' owed by workers to the Mother Country. . . .

Poetry was also used by articulate workers to construct a working-class variant of patriotism. In the first issue of the *Ontario Workman* a poem entitled 'Canada' was published. Written especially for the *Ontario Workman*, it was signed 'Canadian'. In the opening stanza the anonymous bard expressed the patriotic and political ideals of Anglo-Canadian labour reformers:

> Canadian hearts, let us be loyal,
> And remain 'neath England's wing
> Till she can no longer guard us
>> Then to Canada e'er cling.
> Patriot's love and heal inspire us
>> To maintain our country's rights;
> Yield—no, never, to our formen,
>> Though we come to bloody fights. . . .

Patriotism, which embraced the notions of duty, obligation, and sacrifice for Canada and the 'Mother Country', was expected of male workers, but as the above verse suggests, working men also had rights as citizens and as 'freemen'. Contrary to the rhetoric of employers, notably George Brown, which excluded or 'otherized' working-class men, Toronto labour reformers constructed their own variant of national identity using a discourse that emphasized working men's obligations to the British empire and their role as 'the mainstay of the country'.

This construction of working men as vital to the project of nation-building applied to 'white' workers only. In 1874, when the Mackenzie Liberal government announced that Chinese labourers were being considered to complete the Canadian Pacific Railway, this particular group of workers was targeted for exclusion by the [Toronto Trades Assembly] TTA. The editor of the *Ontario Workman* stated outright that the government should not use 'cheap Chinese labor', and that a 'great injustice would be done to the white population of the country'. Racist metaphors, such as 'pig tail', were used to define Chinese labourers as undesirable immigrant workers (*Ontario Workman*, 22 January 1874).

During the early 1870s labour reformers united working men around the demand for universal manhood suffrage so that they might eventually win their full rights as citizens. They drew both on the tradition of British constitutionalism and Painite egalitarianism, and spoke of 'the universal rights of man'. J.S. Williams indicated that in politics the motto of labour reformers was 'first, Man, and then Property' (*Ontario Workman*, 18 April 1872). The existing franchise based on property qualification was targeted as a relic of the feudal age, and independence became a powerful masculine ideal. Labour reformers rejected the rhetoric of liberal political economy that compared them to 'serfs'. In rejecting the qualification for the vote based on property, labour reformers spoke of themselves as 'free men' with a 'natural right' to the vote. . . .

Toronto labour reformers also confronted the employer–worker relationship. Their critique of the new industrial order was based on the labour theory of value (Palmer, 1979; Kealy, 1991). 'Labor is both superior and prior to capital, and alone originally produces capital,' editor J.S. Williams stated in the *Ontario Workman* (22 August 1872). Elements of the older pre-industrial ideology of the mutuality of interests between worker and employer, and the skilled working man's property of skill and control over his labour, were retained, however. 'The interests of both classes are bound together,' Williams concluded. 'If either one is harmed, the other must ultimately suffer.' Toronto trade unionists stated at nine-hours rallies and in the *Ontario Workman* that they believed in 'a fair day's work for a fair day's pay.'[2]

Toronto labour reformers referred to the 'nobility of labour' and the 'dignity of labour', in contradistinction to employers' efforts to 'master' the labour force. In pre-industrial social relations, the term 'master' meant a 'master of the craft', who had also perhaps acquired his own shop. With industrial capitalism, the term 'master' was redefined to mean a 'master of men'. In a letter-to-the-editor of the *Ontario Workman*, journalist John McCormick ridiculed 'money-grubbers' who believed that 'We, the employers of labor, are your masters, you are our servants, and we have the right to dictate to you the terms upon which you shall labor and live or exist.' For McCormick the very term 'master' was an abomination, as man was systematically robbed and held cheap by current social relations of production, and by laws that placed property first and man afterwards (*Ontario Workman*, 23 May 1872).[3] . . .

During the early 1870s, the 'body politic' emerged as a site of political intervention for Toronto labour reformers.[4] In addition to investing power in the body through their articulation of labour as the source of all capital, labour reformers constructed a whole series of codes of discipline over the individual. Among nineteenth-century labour reformers few words enjoyed more popularity than 'manly', with its connotations of dignity in labour, respectablility, and defiant egalitarianism. 'Self-help' and 'self-elevation' were consistently cited as crucial to the objectives of the labour movement. This ideal of manliness was reinforced in workers' poetry.[5] A stanza of 'A True Mechanic', written for the *Ontario Workman*, suggests that

The man who polishes heart and mind,
While he frames the window and shapes the blind,
And utters his thoughts with an honest tongue,
That is set as true as his hinges are hung,
He is the nobleman among
    The noble band of mechanics.
                (*Ontario Workman*, 4 July 1872)

. . . Although the notion of 'self-help' articulated by labour reformers in the editorials, letters, poetry, and improving literature published in the *Ontario Workman* embraced many aspects of dominant middle-class constructions, including a Christian belief in the building of a moral character, humility, honour, and a commitment to honest hard work, there were important discrepancies between the classes. Labour reformers criticized the measurement of success as represented by the boy who rises from poverty to become a millionaire like American Jacob Astor. The fallacy of the middle-class ideal was in the manner of acquiring success. Labour reformers argued that under the prevailing social system wealth could not be acquired without chicanery in bargaining and disregard for workers. 'The standard of success is a false one,' Williams wrote. 'It is impossible for one man to get rich without causing others to suffer. It is proverbial that just and generous men do not get rich' (*Ontario Workman*, 29 January 1874). . . .

Labour reformers were confronted with how to reconcile self-elevation with the collective objectives of labour organization. They suggested that the growth of intelligence among workmen was needed to promote understanding of the importance of cooperation to the workers' cause. Cooperation among working-class men could only be furthered through the progress of intelligence. The short-lived Canadian Labor Protection and Mutual Improvement Association, organized by the leaders of the Nine-Hours League in April 1872, provided the institutional framework for the discourse of self-elevation. The intent of the organization was to elevate the intelligence of workmen, and to promote workers' common interests across local and trade boundaries (*Ontario Workman*, 9 May 1872, 26 September 1872). Intelligent, sober, industrious, and, consequently, independent, mechanics would ultimately combine and save the country from monopolies and corrupt politicians.

The cooperative goals of Toronto labour reformers did not easily incorporate unskilled labourers, however. An 'Ex-Labourer' wrote that 'while the artisans and tradesmen of all classes are asserting the rights of labor and manhood, the laborers *par excellence*—the men of the pick and shovel, of the crowbar and hod—are, I regret to say, lying in a state of lethargy and supineness.' The 'Ex-Labourer' attributed the situation to a lack of organization (*Ontario Workman*, 23 May 1872). . . .

Among labour reformers individual elevation and self-education included a commitment to domesticity and sobriety. Opponents of a reduction in working hours argued that if workers were given more leisure time they would only spend it drinking and gambling. They targeted those male workers who spent their time away from home and in the pub. 'If the laborer thus released applies his leisure hour to his own domestic business, to his garden or his shop, to his needed rest or the education of his children . . . to almost anything except dissipation, idleness and debauchery—it will prove a blessing,' J.S Williams remarked.[6] In a subsequent editorial, Williams attributed the propensity to drink among workingmen to the monotony and drudgery of incessant labour, and for this reason he concluded that moral suasion could never succeed, and that a strict prohibitory law was necessary (*Ontario Workman*, 8 January 1874). The rhetoric of domesticity was used to defend the morality of male workers in the larger political context, and was integral to the positive masculine identity for working men constructed by labour reformers.[7]

The nine-hours campaign of 1872 politicized the wives of working men, and a 'militant domesticity' evolved that differed from middle-class ideals of female domesticity. In a letter to the editor of the *Ontario Workman*, 'A Printer's Wife' responded to comments made by George Brown in the *Globe*. On 23 March, Brown wrote that 'the man who thinks ten hours hurtful or oppressive, is too lazy to earn his bread; and in the name of all the women of Canada, we protest against sending home such

a fellow to pester his wife, loafing around for another hour daily.' The printer's wife indicated that she became indignant upon reading the 'lies' in the *Globe,* but that she thought it prudent to wait until the strike was over before commenting. No doubt she feared that her husband would lose his job had she responded before the strike was settled. In her letter the woman remarked: 'The extra hour is spent at home, 'tis true, but it is in the shape of gardening, fixing up things generally, or reading and writing, and miserable fellow—playing with the children.' She also urged the wives of working men to support trade unionism and not to 'rat it'. 'Don't let your men "go back" on the Union,' she advised; 'the extra will do good to all concerned, and will not, as some have said, be spent in the tavern or in idleness' (*Globe*, 23 March 1872; *Ontario Workman*, 9 May 1872). . . .

'The Other Side': Melodrama and Labour Reform

On 23 May 1872, editor Williams announced that Coopers International Union president Martin Foran had consented to the publication of his novel entitled *The Other Side* in serial installments in the *Ontario Workman*. . . . In the introduction to *The Other Side*, Foran provided two reasons for writing the novel. First, he shared with other labour reformers the belief 'that if the laboring class could be made a *reading* class, their social and political advancement and amelioration would be rapid and certain.' He pointed to the 'popular taste among the masses' for fiction, especially those whose education was limited and did not include 'a classical training'. Rather than disparage the love of fiction and dime novels among the working class, Foran used the novel to encourage workmen to develop their intellectual side. For nineteenth-century labour reformers intellectual development was essential to the attainment of complete manhood (*Ontario Workman*, 27 June 1872).

Foran's second objective was to counter the anti-trade-union rhetoric used by the popular British novelist Charles Reade in a melodrama entitled 'Put Yourself in His Place', which was published serially in *Cornhill Magazine*, in 17 installments beginning in March 1869.[8] . . . Reade characterizes trade unionists as blackguards and ruffians— 'skilled workmen at violence.' . . . Trade unionism, however, was given a dramatically different representation in Foran's novel. In his introductory remarks Foran admitted that many of the measures and means employed by workmen to redress grievances were 'neither born of justice nor wisdom'. Before these men were condemned, however, he urged that their side of the story be told. Foran criticized Reade for 'not delineating both sides of the subject, in not putting himself in the places of all the characters in his story'. *The Other Side*, therefore, was both instructional and defensive in its intent (*Ontario Workman*, 27 June 1872).

The conventions of melodrama were followed quite closely by Foran in the novel. Melodrama was the dominant modality in the nineteenth century. As Martha Vicinus has argued, 'it was important as a psychological touchstone for the powerless, for those who perceived themselves as "the helpless and unfriended".' . . .

In their fiction, labour reformers departed somewhat from the stereotypical characterization and plotting of melodrama, and emphasized the political implications of the situation. Working-class audiences identified with the tragedies suffered by the honest-hearted mechanic hero. This departure from the conventions of melodrama reinforced perceptions of working-class oppression. These writings, which focused on the manly and virtuous mechanic hero and his many misfortunes, were intended to mobilize workers to support the collective goals of the labour movement (Vicinus, 1974; Denning, 1987).

Each literary genre employs certain textual strategies, which cue readers to expect a particular kind of discursive experience. Melodrama denotes the indulgence of excessive emotionalism, inflated rhetoric, overt villainy, persecution of the good and the final reward of virtue, exaggerated expressions of right and wrong, remarkable and improbable coincidences, dark plottings, suspense, and numerous plot twists (Grimsted, 1971; Brooks, 1976; Vicinus, 1981). Nineteenth-century melodrama was organized around a binary world of good and bad, rich and poor, male and female, and was bounded by faith in a universe ruled by morality. Evil drives the plot by unleashing a betrayal of the moral order. The hand of Providence ensures the triumph of good, but only after the virtuous hero or heroine was sorely tried. Romance and sexual desire were integral to this drama of persecuted innocence and virtue triumphant. Villains were always destroyed, thus providing the reader with catharsis and, finally, solace. A potent dogma of democracy assured equality among all men, but only if they retained a pure heart.

Domesticity was the cardinal virtue of nineteenth-century melodrama. The family was the setting for passion, sacrifice, and sympathy. Within the home women were both a symbol of purity and the focus of emotional tension and self-sacrifice. Home, with its cornerstone of feminine purity, was the most potent symbol of good. The focus on the family gave melodrama its power. In industrializing nineteenth-century society, melodrama provided a resolution of conflicts between home and the outside world through happy endings (Vicinus, 1981).

Foran created a facsimile of himself in his manly worker hero, Richard Arbyght, a young farm-bred cooper.[9] As in all melodramas, a series of tragedies befall the young hero. Richard's father is robbed and murdered on a roadside as he journeys homeward. Completely devastated by the death of her husband, Irene Arbyght dies of a broken heart soon afterward. Orphaned at the age of nine, Richard is separated from his younger sister, Bertha, when a wealthy woman visiting a neighbour adopts the girl, and pledges to raise her respectably, give her an education, and make her a lady. A year later, Richard receives a letter from the woman informing him that Bertha has died from a severe attack of the croup.

Squire Stanly takes in the orphaned boy and raises him. The Squire is Foran's ideal of the sturdy, honest, intelligent farmer who existed before widespread urban and industrial development. Foran indicates that the Squire is of the 'old school of political economists', who believe 'that our laws should be so framed and administered that they would tend to better advancement of the toiling masses, and the greater glory of the nation'. The Squire and the pure country life are associated with good, in contrast to the evils and dangers of the city for workmen and their families.

Richard excels in the village school, but he is quick to recognize that the teacher treats the children from socially prominent backgrounds with considerable deference. Foran's political message was clearly delineated for his audience: the educational system privileges one class, not necessarily the more intelligent one, while another class is kept in hopeless ignorance. The perceptive young hero concludes that, '[t]o preserve a republic like ours free and intact, it requires a grand national education.' Nineteenth-century labour reformers' broader demand for a national system of state-funded education to ensure that working-class children are educated about their duties as citizens was injected into the plot of the melodrama.

Deprived of the inheritance that would have allowed him to continue his education, Richard must learn a trade. He is apprenticed to a local cooper. Artisanal pride in craftsmanship is reinforced in the narrative. Richard 'was especially fond of excelling in skilled and superior workmanship'. At age 20 the hero is fully six feet tall, sinewy and strong, with 'a quick, elastic movement, and fiery, dark eye'. His countenance is 'open and expressive, his demeanor dignified and grave, his mind inquisitive, his heart brave and sympathetic'. His every look and movement 'gave assurance of the greatness and goodness of that noblest attribute of man—SOUL'. While Foran's worker hero was inflicted with some of the same signifiers as the hero of bourgeois fiction, specifically courage and a sympathetic heart, the 'mechanic accents' are different (Denning, 1987).[10] Manliness for the worker hero in Foran's melodrama incorporated craft skill and trade-union membership. The upper-case type of the word 'SOUL' in the copy published in the *Ontario Workman* reinforces the idea that for labour reformers manliness was not based on wealth.

Following a period of service in the army during the Civil War, which in true heroic fashion is marked by bravery, Richard relocates to Chicago. The villain, a tyrannous employer named Alvan Relvason, who was described by Foran as 'the typical employer', is introduced. . . . Richard secures a position in Relvason's shop. A few days later, employer and worker confront one another in the shop. Annoyed by what he interprets as Richard's impudence, Relvason reminds him, 'You are the employed and I the employer.' Richard in turn responds, 'I would have you remember that I, too, am a MAN as well as you.' Richard tells Relvason that they are 'equals', who meet as buyer and seller: 'I have a commodity which you desire to purchase and which I am willing to sell for a consideration which you are disposed to give in exchange for it.' In opposition to the dominant political economy, Foran uses a labour theory of value.

With the aid of two trusted workmen, Richard secretly organizes the journeymen coopers into a union. The villain, Relvason, discovers that a union has been organized, and he schemes to destroy it. He threatens to dismiss any worker who refuses to sign an ironclad agreement. In the binary world of melodrama, and consistent with the politics of labour reform, Relvason is the antithesis of virtue. He is an example of 'abnormal humanity', and is described metaphorically as 'ghoulish', a 'leviathan', 'knavishly cunning', and a 'monster'.

The workers, of course, refuse to abandon their union. In contrast to the representation of trade unionists presented by Reade, the mechanics who support the union in Foran's novel are classified as 'manly'. They also have a distinctive physical appearance from years of hardship and toil, 'a young old look', Foran writes, 'a dull, oppressive, heavy expression, seen only on those who toil ten hours or more per day.' Commitment to family and nation are integral to Foran's construction of the manly and honest working man: 'the honest man who married and brought up a large family did more service than he who continued single and only talked of population.' Trade unionists were depicted by Foran as men who love their children, and for this reason they willingly, even cheerfully, endure lives of never-ending toil.

Relvason issues an ultimatum that Richard must abandon the union or else be fired. Concerned with the plight of his union brothers, and consistent with the heroic ideal of self-sacrifice typical of melodrama, Richard decides to leave the trade. 'He did not regard it good unionism for one man to throw a hundred men out of employment, and stop their children's supply of bread.' The hero's hardships mount. He is blacklisted by the employers, and is thus unable to secure another position. . . .

Frustrated by the unwillingness of any employer to hire him, Richard returns to his boarding house, where he finds Alexander Fargood waiting for him. Fargood agrees to give Richard a job. Foran presents his conceptualization of the ideal employer in the character of Fargood: 'The bearing of the employer was never that of a *master*. In a word the relations existing between these two men were pre-eminently those that should ever exist between all employers and employees: MUTUAL OR RECIPROCAL INDEPENDENCE AND DEPENDENCE' (*Ontario Workman*, 22 August 1872, emphasis in Labour Press reprint). Like other nineteenth-century writers of working-class fiction, Foran recreated a world of artisanal independence rather than developing a critique of proletarianization under industrial-capitalist social relations (Vicinus, 1981).

A series of improbable plot twists occur, most of which are attributed by the author to 'Fate', or an act of God. The worker hero undergoes more hardships, which elevates the emotional intensity for the novel's readers. Working-class readers would easily have identified with the hardships suffered by the hero.

In another incident that the author attributes to 'Fate', a young woman, Grace, is driven from the home of her benefactor. She wanders the city until a woman, 'showily attired, middle-aged, with a forbidding, libidinous look', tries to tempt her into prostitution. Once again, 'Fate' intervenes, and Richard, who happens to be walking along the street intuitively senses that something is amiss. He rescues the woman, and discovers that Grace is actually his sister Bertha, whom he had long believed to be dead. Foran's construction of working-class womanhood differs from middle-class representations of working-class femininity. For much of the nineteenth century the bourgeois class associated the single working woman with prostitution (Strange, 1995). In Bertha, Foran creates a pure and virtuous working-class girl, whom he describes as 'slight, graceful, *spirituelle*'. Bertha earns her own living by giving music lessons and taking in sewing at home. Foran, however, never mentions the issue of the sexual morality of women who worked in factories.

While the political objectives of labour reform were at the forefront of Foran's narrative, the plot of *The Other Side* centres around the unresolved tragedy of the Arbyght family and the romance between Richard and Vida Geldamo—the daughter of a banker. In Vida, Foran presents what he suggests is the 'true woman'. Vida is described as having all of woman's spiritualized nature: 'She was all goodness, all loveliness—an angel.' This ideal of femininity is analogous to middle-class constructions of womanhood. Foran articulated an ideal of womanhood that values feminine purity above wealth. Vida in all her goodness of heart could never believe 'that the possession of money made the heart warmer . . . or the soul purer'. In the conflict between marriage based on property and romantic love, Mr Geldamo favours property. He orders Vida to marry Mr Allsound, who, although not as morally worthy as Richard, is a man of property. In the spirit of heroic self-sacrifice characteristic of melodrama, Richard resolves not to see Vida again in view of the barrier erected between them 'by caste and wealth'. Vida becomes despondent, and then seriously ill from a broken heart. Her father relents and agrees to let her marry Richard, but the young hero must first prove himself capable of building a home.

As in all melodramas, moral virtue triumphs in *The Other Side*. The villain, Relvason, is destroyed. The hero, Richard, discovers that it was Relvason who murdered his father. He also wins the hand of Vida Geldamo. While it appears that romantic love has triumphed over the traditional idea of marriage based on property, their union is sanctioned only after her father loses all of his money in a business downturn. While sexuality based on heterosexual desire triumphs over property, Foran, in his narrative, was unable to overcome the class tensions emerging from the marriage of a working-class man to a woman from a wealthy family.[11] Arbyght and Geldamo establish their own business, and employ several men who are treated as 'social equals'. The novel concludes with trade unionism flourishing in the city. 'Through its agency,' Foran writes, 'workingmen are fast becoming more thoughtful, more industrious, more temperate, and are making fearful strides in mental and moral worth and social elevation.'

The Other Side thus becomes caught up in the central paradox of melodrama. While the domestic ideal is defended in Foran's melodrama against the evils of industrial-capitalist society under the belief that a universal moral order would prevail, the moral order championed in the melodrama is in fact a reflection of dominant middle-class gender and class values. Foran never proposed that the existing social order be overthrown, and for Foran the home remains the symbol of moral permanence and feminine purity. Also, the relationship between this literature and working-class and middle-class cultures remains ambiguous. In trying to create a work that measured up to the criteria of the bourgeois literary community, Foran neglected the ethnic variables in working-class culture. For instance, dialect was a major vehicle for literary expression among working-class writers in Britain during the nineteenth century, and was used to join older folk traditions with emerging industrial and urban values. Foran, however, rejects any ethnic identification and indicates that he cannot understand 'how our language is to be made purer or purged of crudities and become universally classical, by spreading before the rising generation our ideas and thoughts, clad in the garb of broken French or German, Irish idioms, broad Yorkshire cockneyisms or backwoods Yankeeisms' (*Ontario Workman*, 27 June 1872).

By August 1872 the nine-hours movement had been defeated, and by the end of the decade labour reform's initial upsurge in Toronto had been crushed by a combination of economic recession, stifled militancy, trade-union isolation, and Tory domination (Battye, 1979; Palmer, 1992). During the early 1870s, however, Toronto labour reformers defined the social subjectivity of the honest working-class mechanic, which encompassed their own distinct class-based representation of manliness. While employers, most notably George Brown, sought deference from workers, the nascent labour movement through its central institution, the Toronto Trades Assembly, and its organ *The Ontario Workman*, constructed a counter-discourse that emphasized worker independence and the collective goals of trade unionism.

The masculine rhetoric of labour reformers, with its emphasis on progress, citizenship, and self-culture, was not entirely unlike that of the late Victorian middle class, but it was inscribed with a distinctively working-class politic. It sustained a radical critique of employer–worker relations under the prevailing social relations of production. To define their status as citizens, and make the case for universal male suffrage, Toronto labour reformers maintained that they held property in their labour. In this way, Toronto labour reformers, like their British counterparts, articulated a notion of class that excluded women and children.[12] Toronto labour reformers also drew on their colonial relationship with Britain to shape their notion of class. Patriotism, which embraced a sense of 'Britishness' stemming from Canada's colonial status, was incorporated into their discourse of working-class manhood.

Alongside the institutions of labour reform, working-class fiction, poetry, and improving literature guided workers in the collective goals of the labour movement, and provided instructions on how to be a 'good' trade unionist, worker, citizen, husband, and father. This rhetoric was an important part of the cultural world of Toronto workers, and the strategy used to challenge employers' incursions upon the long-established rights of skilled mechanics.

. . . The ideal of domesticity, as found at the conclusion of working-class melodramas, never translated into a resolution of the problems created for working-class families by the growth of industrial capitalism. For most working-class families domesticity was an illusion, as few families were able to survive on the wage of a single male breadwinner. During the 1870s, furthermore, the plight of women workers was rarely mentioned. It was only in the 1880s, with the rise of the Knights of Labor in Toronto, that women workers were put onto the political agenda of the labour movement.

Although labour reformers constructed a national identity that outlined an imagined community incorporating all workers, unskilled and Chinese labourers were effectively excluded. The labour-reform movement of the early 1870s functioned to promote the social and political interests of one segment of the working class, namely, skilled, Anglo-Saxon working men, and ultimately fragmented, as much as it consolidated, the working class.

Notes

1. See *Globe*, 16 February 1872, 27 February 1872, 23 March 1872, and 20 May 1872.
2. See *Globe*, 15 February 1872; *Ontario Workman*, 15 August 1872, 10 April 1872, and 4 September 1873.
3. During the early 1870s, McCormick, an Irish Catholic, was a correspondent for Patrick Boyle's *Irish Canadian*. In 1880 he published a pamphlet entitled *Conditions of Labour and Modern Civilization*, much of it consisting of reprints of columns for the *Irish*

Canadian. The articles contain an extensive critique of Malthusianism and liberal political economy. John McCormick, *Conditions of Labour and Modern Civilization* (Toronto: Bell, 1880).

4. Michel Foucault has argued that during the late nineteenth century the body became directly involved as a political field. See Foucault, *Discipline and Punish: The Birth of the Prison*, trans Alan Sheridan (New York: Vintage, 1979; originally 1975), 25–6.

5. See also Vicinus, *The Industrial Muse: A Study of Nineteenth Century British Working-Class Literature* (New York: Barnes and Noble, 1974), 95.

6. Peter Bailey has argued that working-class culture was more additive than substitutive, and that workers engaged in the concurrent pursuit of 'thinking and drinking'. While I agree with Bailey's argument, my intent here is to illustrate how labour reformers used the rhetoric of working-class respectability and sobriety for political purposes. See Peter Bailey, "'Will the Real Bill Banks Please Stand Up?" Towards a Role Analysis of Mid-Victorian Working-Class Respectability', *Journal of Social History* 12, 3 (Spring 1979): 336–53.

7. For a similar argument concerning Chartist domesticity, see Clark, 'The Rhetoric of Chartist Domesticity', *Journal of British Studies* 31, 1 (1992): 62–88.

8. Charles Reade, *Put Yourself in His Place* (New York, Adamant: 2001; reprint from the 1896 edition). According to Reade's original agreement with his publisher George Smith, the novel was to be completed in thirteen installments. Smith was to pay outright £2000, with a right of purchasing the copyright for £2000 more four months before completion. Reade was to have the exclusive right of sending early sheets to American publishers for publication after the completion of the series. On 28 May 1870, Reade presented a dramatic version of his novel under the title 'Free Labour'. Malcom Elwin, *Charles Reade* (New York: Bookman, 1931, reissued 1969), 201–2; Elton E. Smith, *Charles Reade* (Boston: Twayne, 1976), 20.

9. Born in 1840, Martin Foran grew up in rural Pennsylvania, where his father owned a farm and a cooper shop. After a brief stint in the cavalry, Foran taught school briefly and worked as an oilfield hand. In 1868 he moved to Cleveland, where he found work as a journeyman cooper. Foran helped to organize the International Coopers Union and the Industrial Congress while simultaneously attending law school. In 1882, Foran, a Democrat, was elected to Congress. He was re-elected twice before retiring to private law practice in 1899. David Montgomery, *Beyond Equality: Labor and the Radical Republicans 1862–1872* (New York: Knopf, 1967), 214–15.

10. Denning borrows the term 'accents' from Voloshinov, a Soviet-language theorist associated with the circle of Mikhail Bakhtin. These theorists argue that the ambiguity of ideological signs comes not only from their rhetorical character, but from the different class accents with which they are inflected.

11. Foucault described this power relationship as the 'deployment of sexuality'. See Michel Foucault, *The History of Sexuality, Vol. I: An Introduction*, trans Robert Hurley (New York: Vintage, 1978, 1990), 106–8.

12. For a discussion of the British context see Anna Clark, 'Manhood, Womanhood, and the Politics of Class in Britain, 1790–1845', in Laura L. Frader and Sonya O. Rose, eds, *Gender and Class in Modern Europe* (Ithaca and London: Cornell University Press, 1996), 263–79.

References

Battye, John. 1979. 'The Nine Hour Pioneers: The Genesis of the Canadian Labour Movement', *Labour/Le Travailleur* 4: 25–56.

Brooks, Peter. 1976. *The Melodramatic Imagination: Balzac, Henry James, Melodrama, and the Mode of Excess*. New Haven and London: Yale University Press.

Careless, J.M.S. 1989. *Brown of the Globe: Statesman of Confederation 1860–1880, Volume Two*. Toronto and Oxford: Oxford University Press.

Clark, Anna. 1992. 'The Rhetoric of Chartist Domesticity: Gender, Language, and Class in the 1830s and 1840s', *Journal of British Studies* 31 (January): 62–88.

Denning, Michael. 1987. *Mechanic Accents: Dime Novels and Working-Class Culture in America*. London: Verso.

Fowler, George. 1991. *Language in the News: Discourse and Ideology in the Press*. London and New York: Routledge.

Globe. 1872. 15 February.

Globe. 1872. 16 February.

Globe. 1872. 23 March.

Grimes, Mary. 1986. *The Knights in Fiction: Two Labor Novels of the 1880s*. Urbana and Chicago: University of Illinois.

Grimsted, David. 1971. 'Melodrama as Echo of the Historically Voiceless', in Tamara K. Hareven, ed., *Anonymous*

Americans: Explorations in Nineteenth-Century Social History. Englewood Cliffs, NJ: Prentice Hall.

Kealey, G.S. 1991. *Toronto Workers Respond to Industrial Capitalism, 1867–1892*. Toronto: University of Toronto Press.

Ontario Workman. 1872. 18 April.

Ontario Workman. 1872. 9 May.

Ontario Workman. 1872. 23 May.

Ontario Workman. 1872. 27 June.

Ontario Workman. 1872. 4 July.

Ontario Workman. 1872. 15 August.

Ontario Workman. 1872. 22 August.

Ontario Workman. 1872. 26 September.

Ontario Workman. 1873. 23 January.

Ontario Workman. 1873. 10 April.

Ontario Workman. 1873. 4 September.

Ontario Workman. 1874. 8 January.

Ontario Workman. 1874. 22 January.

Ontario Workman. 1874. 29 January.

Palmer, B. 1979. *A Culture in Conflict: Skilled Workers and Industrial Capitalism in Hamilton, Ontario, 1860–1914*. Montreal and Kingston: McGill-Queen's University Press.

———. 1992. *Working-Class Experience: Rethinking the History of Canadian Labour, 1800–1991*, 2nd ed. Toronto: McClelland and Stewart.

Strange, Carolyn. 1995. *Toronto's Girl Problem: The Perils and Pleasures of the City, 1880–1930*. Toronto: University of Toronto Press.

Vicinus, Martha. 1974. *The Industrial Muse: A Study of Nineteenth Century British Working-Class Literature*. New York: Barnes and Noble.

———. 1981. "Helpless and Unfriended": Nineteenth-Century Domestic Melo-drama', *New Literary History* 1 (Autumn).

Watt, Frank William. 1957. 'Radicalism in English-Canadian Literature since Confederation'. PhD dissertation, University of Toronto.

CHAPTER 7

The Bonds of Unity: The Knights of Labor in Ontario, 1880–1900

Gregory S. Kealey and Bryan D. Palmer

There has historically been no moment in the experience of North American labour that weighed so heavily on the collective mind of the working-class movement in the years 1900–30 as that of the Knights of Labor upsurge of the 1880s. . . .

'Never since the palmiest days of the Knights of Labor', declared Toronto's *Citizen and Country* in the midst of the craft union boom of 1898–1904, 'have trade unions taken such a firm hold of the toilers as today' (*Citizen and Country*, 4 May 1900). . . . When the One Big Union in Canada sought a glorious past to contrast with the dismal realities of AFL-TLC trade unionism in the 1920s, it was the fires of the Knights of Labor it chose to rekindle. 'One of the great land-marks in the history of class struggle,' the Knights were regarded as 'a mass organization grouped in Geographical units' that prefigured the industrial unionism of the One Big Union. The Order, claimed these dissident workers, had been the very same 'one big union' that they were trying to build and sustain.[1] . . . By 1929, the radical challenge of the post-war reconstruction years had been at least partially undermined, and in this context of 'normalcy' the AFL met in Toronto in October. With southern textile workers urging the organization of their mill towns, observers at the convention reported 'a pitch of enthusiasm not seen in labor gatherings since the spring tide of the Knights of Labor' (Bernstein, 1960: 34). For these, and many other, reasons, Norman J. Ware, perhaps the most perceptive student of the Knights of Labor, saw the

Order as just that 'sort of One Big Union of which Karl Marx would have approved, if—and this is a large "if"—it could have been transformed into a political organization under socialist leadership' (Ware, 1968: 258). . . .

By examining the structural situation of the Order, where and when it organized in Ontario, and how many (in rough terms) it drew to its ranks, we believe that we can establish the class character and importance of the Knights of Labor. We shall argue that the Noble and Holy Order of the Knights of Labor represented a dramatic shift away from past practices within the history of Ontario workers. Although the Knights built very much on the accumulated experience of the working class, they channelled that experience in new directions. . . . In the breadth of their vision, the scope of their organization, and the unique refusal to collapse the cause of workers into this reform or that amelioration or restrict entry to the movement to this stratum or that group, the Knights of Labor hinted at the potential and possibility that are at the foundation of the making of a class. Politically, the Order's efforts in the federal, provincial, and municipal fields testified to the movement's willingness and ability to transcend the economistic concerns of the workplace. At the same time, the Order's important place in the class struggles and confrontations of the last two decades of the nineteenth century points to problems inherent in viewing the Knights of Labor from the perspective of its leaders' anti-strike rhetoric. To be sure, both in the political sphere and at the workplace, the Knights found themselves caught in many ambiguities and contradictions, among the most important being their political relationship to the established Grit and Tory parties, and their capacity to defend the interests of their membership in the face of fierce employer resistance and a post-1886 trade-union opposition. Some, but not all, of these difficulties were of the

Order's own making. But as the first expression of the social, cultural, and political emergence of a class, the Knights of Labor understandably groped for answers more than they marched forcefully towards solutions. The Order was itself inhibited by the context of late nineteenth-century Ontario which, aside from its own peculiar 'regional' divisions, stood poised between an economy of competitive capitalism, but recently arrived, and the monopoly capitalism which stood literally around the corner with the Laurier boom years of the twentieth century. The Knights, in many ways, straddled each epoch, looking simultaneously forward and backward, longing for the rights they knew to be justly theirs, attacking the monopolists they saw controlling the business, politics, and culture of their society.[2] . . .

Economic Background: Labour and Industrial Capitalism to 1890

The nineteenth century was the crucible from which Canada would emerge as a capitalist economy and society. . . . All this, to be sure, developed in the context of a social order wracked by major depressions and frequent recessionary downturns. Nevertheless, as early as the 1860s the transforming power of capital had become visible in the rise of the factory, the increasing use of steam-power, and the mechanization of important industries such as tailoring and boot and shoe production. For the *People's Journal* these were the hallmarks of momentous change, factors which had 'set agoing an industrial revolution' (cited in Langdon, 1975: 3).[3]

Between 1870 and 1890 the industrial sector tasted the fruits, both bitter and sweet, of this great transformation: establishments capitalized at $50,000 and over increased by about 50 per cent; employment in manufacturing rose by 76 per cent and output in constant dollar terms by

Table 7.1 Aggregate Ontario Data, 1871–1911

Year	Capital Invested ($)	Hands Employed	Yearly Wages ($)
1871	37,874,010	87,281	21,415,710
1881	80,950,847	118,308	30,604,031
1891	175,972,021	166,326	49,733,359
1901	214,972,275	151,081	44,656,032
1911	595,394,608	216,362	95,674,743
Year	Value Raw Material($)	Value Product ($)	Value Added ($)
1871	65,114,804	114,706,799	49,591,995
1881	91,164,156	157,889,870	66,825,714
1891	128,142,371	231,781,926	111,639,555
1901	138,230,400	241,533,486	103,303,086
1911	207,580,125	579,810,225	282,230,100

Source: Canada, *Census*, 1871–1891. Note that the 1901 and 1911 figures are unadjusted in light of the changing criterion employed by the census in enumerating manufacturing establishments. All firms were considered for 1871–91, while only those firms employing five or more hands were considered in 1901 and 1911. The capital invested figures for 1901 and 1911 are computed by adding together the figures for fixed and working capital. There had been no distinction between these realms in the earlier period.

138 per cent; railway mileage jumped from 3,000 in 1873 to over 16,000 in 1896; manufacturing's place, in terms of value-added, rose from 19 per cent of the Gross National Product in 1870 to 23.5 per cent in 1890; the rate of real manufacturing output climbed from 4.4 per cent in the decade 1870–80 to 4.8 per cent in the 1880–90 period, slipping to 3.2 per cent in the 1890s, thus establishing the 1880s as an extremely significant moment in the historical rate of growth, surpassed only by the boom years 1900–10 and 1926–29. Indeed, it is the growth of manufacturing facilities in many industries during the cresting fortunes of the National Policy that is most striking. Between 1880 and 1890, for instance, the value of cotton cloth output rose by 125 per cent, but even this dramatic increase understated the gains of the decade's first five years: the number of mills, spindles, looms, and capital investment tripled in that short period (Bertram, 1962; Warrian, 1971; Acheson, 1972; Bland, 1974). Such developments took place, moreover, within the context of a general decline of prices which, using Michell's index, plummeted from roughly 100 in 1873 to a low of about 75 in 1886 (Bertram, 1962).[4]

Ontario stood at the very centre of this process of capitalist development. Aggregate data begin to tell the story. Capital invested more than doubled in each decade between 1870 and 1890, while the number of hands employed increased 90 per cent over the 20-year period. These aggregate data can give us an imprecise measure of the character of social and productive relations, the setting within which the Knights of Labor operated, and one which it must have influenced.

There is no mistaking the tremendous expansion in the manufacturing sector. An analysis of county data shows impressive quantitative gains in workers employed in manufacturing between 1871 and 1891. This growth displayed tangible regional patterns—the dominance of Toronto–Hamilton, the underdeveloped but nevertheless significant economic activity along the St Lawrence and Ottawa Rivers, the manufacturing importance of various small towns. More than 50 per cent of the manufacturing of the 1880s was located in small Canadian communities, where the population never climbed above 10,000 (Acheson, 1972).[5] The regional economy of Ontario, then, was a far from homogenous entity, even as late as the 1880s. The closing years of the century were something of a struggle for industrial hegemony, in which the small manufacturing unit servicing a local market gave way to the larger productive concern, often contributing towards the decline of the small town and a shift in the location of industry to the population centre of a larger city. Thus the value added in all manufacturing activity in York County (Toronto) rose from 27.44 per cent in 1870 to 32 per cent in 1890. Toronto and Hamilton each accounted for 20 per cent of industrial employment in southern Ontario in 1881, although they contained only 6.5 per cent of the region's population. But even given this increasing specialization, localization, and gross expansion in the manufacturing sector the 1880s were still a decade of contrasts: handicraft forms of production still co-existed with thoroughly mechanized processes; the large factory still occupied minority status given the number of small shops (Chambers and Bertram, 1966; Spelt, 1972; Bland, 1974).[6]

➔ How did this process of advancing but uneven development stamp itself upon the character of specific Ontario locales, where the Knights of Labor would come to prominence in the later years of the nineteenth century? As we have already seen, the industrial cities of Toronto and Hamilton led the way. (We have commented briefly on the experience of these major centres in other works.[7]) Beyond the boundaries of these reasonably well-studied industrial cities lies a virtual no man's land, where our knowledge of economic activity is severely restricted. Yet it is clear that in countless

Ontario communities capitalist development touched the lives of many workers and employers. Linked closely to this process was the importance of railways, which served as a connecting link, integrating a developing home market. This revolution in transportation was perhaps the key element in the shifting location and expansion of manufacturing in these years from 1870–90.[8]

Most of the railways built in southern Ontario after 1881 radiated out from Toronto, further contributing to that city's metropolitan dominance. Of great significance was the increasing importance of the old established lines in western Ontario— the Grand Trunk, Great Western and Canada Southern—which received great stimulus as the CPR and GTR battled for control of the country's rail lines. . . . Centres such as St Thomas and Stratford became links in a chain of economic development, and their wage-earning class was often tied directly to the shops that served the railways or the rail systems themselves. St Thomas, for instance, grew rapidly in the 1870s, being transformed from a modest pre-industrial service town to a dynamic railway centre linked to the major Ontario metropolitan markets. Major shops of the American-owned Canada Southern Railway located there, employing about 700 men by the mid-1880s, and the Great Western established a repair shop in the city. By 1885 the New York Central had also commenced similar operations. Because of this rapid growth the city's class boundaries were rigid and geographically specific (Glazebrook, 1964; Clark, 1976).

The railways, through declining freight rates and economies of scale, helped to concentrate economic activity in a number of diversified manufacturing centres, whose growth took place at the expense of the smaller towns where factories were insufficiently developed to capitalize on transport costs compared to their larger, better situated rivals. London was just such a place. Its strength seemed to reside disproportionately in the food-processing sector, with concentrations of capital in bakeries, breweries, and tobacco-related works. But this city also gained prominence as a marketing and distributing centre for the dairy belt of western Ontario's Middlesex, Oxford, Elgin, Lambton, Perth, and Huron counties. In the textile sphere, the city's garment industry grew on the basis of its proximity to the Niagara Peninsula's cotton mills. Finally, in the wood-processing sector concerns like the London Furniture Company employed 50 men, while in metal fabricating the city's McClary Manufacturing Company, Ontario Car Works, and E. Leonard & Sons produced stoves, engines, and other goods. These latter firms employed between 80 and 450 hands throughout the decade of the 1880s (Scott, 1930; Grimwood, 1934; Trumper, 1937).

Other western Ontario towns also exhibited indications of the importance of industrial activity. Brantford's economic place in late nineteenth-century Ontario was dominated by the Harris, Wisner, and Cockshutt agricultural implements companies, and a hosiery factory. Harris & Son, taken together with the Massey works of Toronto (and with which it would merge in 1891), accounted for 60 per cent of all agricultural implements sales in the Dominion by the mid-1880s. Guelph, Galt, Berlin, Hespeler, and even Collingwood to the north all housed similar, if much smaller, manufacturing concerns, producing for local, even regional, markets. . . .

Further to the north and to the east industrial production was less well established, particularly in the area of secondary manufacturing. By the 1880s the Ottawa-Hull and Muskoka regions had established hegemony over the production of wood products, and a number of mills engaged in the preparation of sawn lumber, shingles, and matches. The dominance of lumber was even more pronounced in the Ottawa Valley, where the five largest producers in Canada had congregated by 1874. Over 2,500 men were employed in the production of lumber in 1891 in the city of Ottawa alone, and the industry found market outlets in both Britain and the United States.

East of Toronto, along the St Lawrence River and Lake Ontario, small-scale processing industries and metal-fabricating plants attempted to capture a share of a largely local market. In the larger regional towns, however, there was room for some consolidation. Gananoque, Brockville, Cobourg, Belleville, Smiths Falls, Oshawa, and Kingston all had the ubiquitous foundries, machine shops, and agricultural implements works of the period. . . .

But the most dramatic expression of industrial growth in Ontario was Cornwall's cotton mills. Here was one city where the National Policy tariff of 30–35 per cent was never challenged. Cornwall's Canada Company cotton mills were the largest in the nation with the value of the plant hovering near the half-million dollar mark, the annual product valued at $400,000. Approximately 350 workers (100 males and 250 females) toiled over 20,000 spindles to earn yearly wages of $75,000. Five years later, protected by the newly-revised tariff and stimulated by the return to prosperity, Cornwall's three cotton mills—one was a relatively small firm—employed 133 men, 277 women, 186 boys, and 190 girls. Their yearly wages totalled $179,900, and $456,000 worth of material was used to produce cotton goods and cloth valued at $833,000. By the time another half-decade had passed, Cornwall's two major textile producers—the Canada Company and the Stormont—had made impressive expansionary strides.[9]

Across the province, then, in spite of the increasing dominance of Toronto and Hamilton, of underdevelopment, uneven growth, and reliance upon primary production of the old timber staple in some areas, capitalist production was a force to reckon with by the 1880s. It transformed social and productive relations in the large cities as well as in the tiny rural hamlets. In this changed context class came to the fore as a clearly perceived reality; a culture premised upon this historic relationship of antagonism emerged more forcefully than it had in the past, and old distinctions appeared to fade in the face of a common experience and a recognition of the unity of life and work within a generalized system of appropriation. . . .

Warp, Woof, and Web: The Structural Context of the Knights of Labor in Ontario

'To write the history of the Knights of Labor is an impossibility,' warned Terence V. Powderly. 'Its history was the history of the day in which it moved and did its work.' The much-maligned leader of the Order was aware that 'some young men fresh from college have tried to write the history of the organization,' but he argued that they had failed: 'They applied logic and scientific research; they divided the emotions, the passions, and feelings of the members into groups, they dissected and vivisected the groups; they used logarithms, algebraic formulas, and everything known to the young ambitious graduate of a university.' Given this, Powderly felt that it was not advisable to take 'the historian too seriously; at best he but weaves the warp of fancy into the woof of fact and gives us the web called history.' Powderly's words of warning are worth remembering. Yet, in spite of our recognition of the importance of his skeptical assessment of a history premised on impersonal data and mere quantities, we commence with plenty of numbers. They, too, were part of the day in which the Noble and Holy Order moved and did its work (Powderly, 1940: 3–4, 120).

Organizationally, the Knights drew workers into their ranks through a relatively simple procedure and institutional apparatus. Individual members joined local assemblies, either in mixed (diverse occupational affiliations) or trade (adhering more rigidly to specific craft categories) assemblies. Normally those who were part of a specific trade assembly followed a particular skilled calling, but occasionally the trade assembly was merely an organization of all workers employed in the same plant, shop, or factory. For a local assembly to be organized formally a minimum of 10 members was required, and once established local assemblies were known to swell in membership to over 1,000. If a specific geographical region or trade contained five or more assemblies a district assembly could be formed. District assemblies were of two types: the national trade district, representing the interests of all assemblies of a specific craft, such as the window glass workers or the telegraph operatives; or the mixed district assembly, in which diverse interests of many mixed and trade assemblies were represented. In Canada it was this latter mixed district assembly that was pre-eminent, and in Ontario the various district assemblies were always mixed in form and representative of specific geographical/territorial units. Local assemblies were allowed one delegate in the district assembly for each 100 members they had enrolled, and one for each additional 100 or fraction thereof. Presiding over all these bodies were a series of leading elected officials: the master workman of the local assembly; the district master workman; and many lesser figures. Each district elected delegates to the annual convention of the Order, the general assembly, and at this gathering, in turn, were elected the national officers and the general executive board. The Order, then, was a highly centralized body, with a well-defined hierarchy and structure; yet it was also egalitarian,

Map 7.1 Number of Knights of Labor Local Assemblies in Southern Ontario, 1880–1902

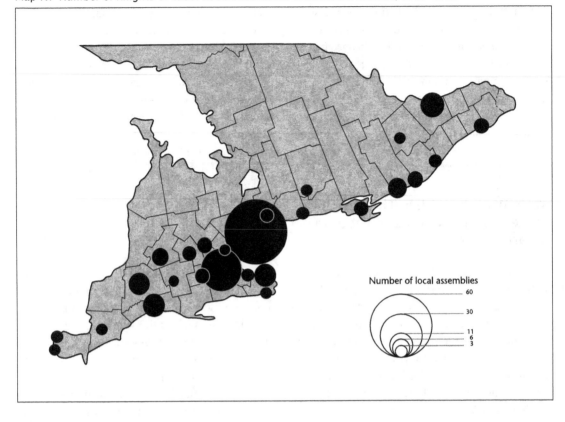

Number of local assemblies

and the local assemblies had a large measure of autonomy, with their own courts to prosecute those who transgressed the discipline and regulations of knighthood.

How many of these local assemblies were there, where were they, and what type of assembly prevailed in specific places?[10] Although strongest in Ontario's rapidly expanding industrial cities like Toronto and Hamilton, the Knights also penetrated the province's towns, villages, and tiny hamlets. In its approximately 30-year lifespan (1875–1907), the Order organized locals in 82 towns from Amherstburg in the west to Cornwall in the east, and from Port Colborne in the south to Sudbury in the north. These 82 towns contained a total of at least 249 local assemblies, which in turn formed 10 district assemblies. Toronto, Hamilton, and Ottawa led the way with 58, 30, and 12 local assemblies respectively, but the Knights were also active in eight communities of less than 1,000 people, and there were 31 local assemblies in places with populations of under 3,000. Ontario's five largest cities in the 1880s (Toronto, Hamilton, Ottawa, London, and Kingston) contained 46 per cent of all Knights of Labor assemblies, but it was the range and dispersal of the Order that was perhaps most significant: of the 47 Ontario towns with a population of at least 3,000 in the 1880s, fully 38, or 81 per cent, witnessed the formation of a local assembly. . . . Map 7.1 portrays graphically the relative strength of the Order in specific locales which contained two or more local assemblies.

In Ontario there was an almost even division between trade and mixed locals, but if we consider the size of the town where the assembly was located a discernible pattern emerges. Mixed assemblies were far more popular in smaller places while trade assemblies were most often found in the cities. . . . Thus in towns under 5,000 the mixed assembly was dominant with 58 per cent of all local assemblies, while trade assemblies and locals of unknown character each provided 21 per cent of all local assemblies. Cities with a population in excess of 30,000, however, were the more likely home of the trade assembly; 57 per cent of all local assemblies were of this type and 30 per cent were mixed, with 13 per cent of unknown character.

How many members were drawn into the ranks of the Knights of Labor? This is a difficult question. In the United States, at their peak, the Knights were said to have enrolled between 700,000 and 1,000,000 members, but this is a static count taken in the spring months of 1886. The data are questionable and tend to underestimate the membership. Moreover, the central problem is the timing of influx into the Order, for the Knights peaked at different moments in different regions. . . . As in the United States, the Ontario Knights did not peak until 1886, a year that saw the founding of 99 local assemblies, and even then the dating of the upsurge varied from region to region within Ontario. Thus, across south-central Ontario the Knights of Labor climbed to their highest membership point in 1886 and then deteriorated, rapidly in some places, more slowly in others. Towns close to the American border (Brockville and Hamilton, for instance) experienced the Order's impact earliest. But in the northwest, in the timber country of the Muskoka region, the Order achieved prominence later, as it did in some eastern Ontario towns like Kingston, where the Knights had 1,500 supporters

in 1887. In Ottawa the Order's successes came, not in the 1880s, but in 1891. . . .

We can, nevertheless, start with peak official membership at single points in time for some specific locales. Toronto DA 125's 41 local assemblies had 5,000 members in 1886, while Hamilton DA 61's 2,200 workers were organized in 30 local assemblies. District Assembly 6, of Ottawa, had 2,000 affiliated in 1892. The London–St Thomas DA 138 reported a membership of 4,435 in 1886–87, enrolled in 36 assemblies in western Ontario towns like Aylmer, Ingersoll, Listowell, and Wyoming. St Catharines DA 207 encompassed some 2,000 advocates in 22 local assemblies. Other district assembly peaks were Windsor DA 174's 616, Belleville DA 235's 1,548, Uxbridge DA 236's 523, and Berlin DA 241's 348. Perhaps more striking still are some of the individual town reports: Brockville's Franklin LA 2311 with 430 members in November 1883; Gananoque's 700–800 members in 1887; Gravenhurst LA 10669's 300 lumber workers in June 1888; the 500 cotton workers in Merritton's Maple Leaf LA 5933 in 1886; Petrolia's Reliable LA 4570 with 500 members in 1886; LA 6722's 200 workers at the Frost and Woods agricultural implements works in Smiths Falls in August 1887; and the 500 workers of Woodstock's Unity and Concord LA's 3151 and 4922 in 1886. If we recall our earlier discussion of the localized nature of manufacturing activity in various Ontario cities and towns, in fact, we see that the Knights were strong wherever a particular industrial activity predominated: among Cornwall's cotton workers, Hamilton's iron and steel workers, or St Thomas's railway workers the Order had many advocates.

. . . If we take the total peak memberships (at specific points in time with no account taken of volatility) across the province and add them together we see that over the course of their history the Knights organized a minimum of

21,800 members. (A figure double this might not overstate the numbers actually enrolled.) This represented 18.4 per cent of the hands employed in manufacturing in 1881 and 13.1 per cent of those so employed in 1891. If we add to these figures the percentages of workers enrolled in trade unions but not members of the Knights of Labor (and we have no accurate statistics on this phenomenon, although it is estimated that in the United States approximately one-half of the Knights' members were trade unionists) it is apparent that at a very minimum the 1880s saw 20–25 per cent of the total non-agricultural work-force drawn to the ranks of organized labour. This, we need remember, is a higher percentage than any period prior to the post-World War II upsurge, and it is only with the increasing unionization of the public sector in recent decades that we have seen the figure climb to 35 per cent and over. For much of the early twentieth century, especially prior to World War I, no more than 10 per cent of the work-force was organized (Pentland, 1968: 70–1; Smucker, 1980: 209). . . .

What all this means, we would argue, is that the Knights of Labor represented a critical moment in the history of Ontario labour. . . . More workers were drawn to the cause of the Order in more Ontario communities and in greater numbers than most of us can actually believe. Across the province between 10 and 80 per cent of all workers in particular cities, and we stress once more that these are minimum estimates, became Knights of Labor. That structural context was a large part of the warp, woof, and web of the history of the 1880s. We have, against Powderly's advice, divided this out from the passions, emotions, and feelings of the membership, and it is now time to turn to another aspect of the history of the Order. For if the Knights of Labor represented a quantitative breakthrough for Ontario's workers, they also represented a crucial qualitative shift in the orientation of the working class. The Order took the raw material of a class culture—ambiguous, fragmented, and unfocused—and moulded it into a movement culture of opposition and alternative.

Spreading the Light: The Emergence of a Movement Culture

There is no such historical phenomenon as an alternative hegemony attained. At the moment that it is realized, an alternative hegemony passes into hegemony and assumes its place as arbitrator of social, economic, political, and cultural values, expressed through the control of state power, the majesty of the law, and a wide range of formal institutions and informal sanctions. A subordinate class can thus only reach towards an alternative hegemony but it cannot 'dominate the ethos of a society' (Thompson, 1978). Alternative hegemonies can, historically, pass into new hegemonic cultures, although this necessarily involves the rise to power of new classes and the dissolution of old ways of life. The revolutions of 1789 and 1917 were just such epoch-shaking moments of transformation, although it is questionable if North America has ever witnessed upheavals of such magnitude: certainly Canada has not.

In the Ontario of the 1880s, however, there was an alternative hegemony in formation. It did not win the day, although it raised a series of challenges and oppositions that remain with us yet; its lifespan was indeed short, although the issues it addressed seem timeless. We refer to this creative moment as a movement culture, a recognition that the Knights of Labor built upon a culture of class experience that had little direction and unity to consolidate a class effort that sought to transform the very nature of the society in which workers found themselves.

The movement culture was formed in the process of daily life, both on and off the job, and it was tempered in the political and workplace struggles that we will examine shortly. It began with the worker's initiation into the Knights of Labor assembly, where a whole series of symbolic and ritualistic practices rooted the member in the movement, reinforcing traditions of collectivity and solidarity in an age of hostile, individual- istic pieties. Each new initiate vowed to defend the interest and reputation of all true members of the Order, be they employed or unemployed, fortunate or distressed, and was instructed that 'Labor is noble and holy.' . . . Upon admission to the Order, the recently christened Knight was informed that 'open and public associations have failed, after a struggle of centuries, to protect or advance the interest of labor,' and that the Knights of Labor merely imitated 'the example of capital', endeavouring 'to secure the just rewards of our toil'. 'In all of the multifarious branches of trade,' the convert was told, 'capital has its combinations, and whether intended or not, it crushes the manly hopes of labor and tramples poor humanity in the dust.' To counteract this distressing tendency of the modern age, the Order asserted: 'We mean to uphold the dignity of labor, to affirm the nobility of all who earn their bread by the sweat of their brow.' In these ritualized incantations, which resounded in local assembly halls across south- central Canada, lay much of the promise and potential of the Knights of Labor (Cook, 1886; Wright, 1887: 142–3; Powderly, 1940: 434–5).[11]

That promise and potential reared its head in many cultural events: in the many picnics, parades, demonstrations, dances, hops, and balls that the Knights organized across the province in the heady days of the upheaval of the 1880s. These occasions were no doubt moments of recreation, diversions which moved people away from the everyday concerns of the next day's work, the next week's groceries, and the next month's rent—the range of insecurities the next year could bring. But they

were also exhilarating reminders of self-worth and class strength. They were prominent in Toronto and Hamilton, as we would expect, but places like London, Woodstock, Ingersoll, Chatham, Thorold, Gananoque, and Belleville were also the sites of such cultural activities, and the Order was capable of drawing anywhere from 1,000 to 5,000 people to these 'monster' gatherings. After an 1887 Gananoque Knights of Labor picnic, the local newspaper commented: 'Probably no gath- ering anywhere near the size ever took place here, where there was such good order . . . They have shown that they are a power in the community, able to command respect' (*Gananoque Reporter*, 25 August 1887).

. . . Thousands of Ontario workers took Richard Trevellick's words to heart when he promised that the Knights of Labor would 'make Labor respect- able by having men and women respect them- selves, and while courteous and kind, refuse to bow and cringe to others because they possess wealth and social position.' Certainly Thomas J. O'Neill, of Napanee's Courage Assembly (LA 9216), regarded such proclamations with appro- priate seriousness, writing to Powderly that, 'this section of the country is sadly in need of organiza- tion, but fear of the money kings [The Rathbuns] keep the working class in slavery.' Railroad men, organized in Headlight Assembly (LA 4069) of St Thomas, acted upon Trevellick's words in 1885. They conducted their own statistical survey of their town of 11,000 with the intention of using 'all lawful means of obtaining their rights, also to educate those of our members who hereto- fore have permitted others to do their thinking, thereby allowing themselves to be used as mere machines in the hands of unscrupulous men'. The *Labor Union* proclaimed its mission in mid-January 1883: 'To Spread the Light; to expose the inequali- ties of distribution by which the few are enriched at the expense of the many. To call things by their right names, and to point out to workingmen how these inequities could be redressed and the workingman secure the full reward of his toil.' Employers found much to dislike in the words of Trevellick, O'Neill, LA 4069, and the *Labor Union*. Their actions throughout the 1880s spoke loudly of their antagonisms. They regarded the increasing consciousness of class, and threat of active opposition, as a dangerous development. By 1891 the business community was convinced that 'the spirit of trades unionism is strangling honest endeavour, and the hard-working, fearless thorough artisan of ten years ago is degenerating into the shiftless, lazy, half-hearted fellow who, with unconscious irony, styles himself a knight of labor.' The culture had, as well as advocates, staunch opponents.[12]

It was in the midst of a virtual war between these contending forces (in which battles were both practical and intellectual) that the labour reform cause gained hard-won adherents. And it was in this context that the 'educational' thrust so prominent in the Order's own priorities consolidated. Local assemblies became, in the parlance of the 1880s, 'schools of instruction' in which the lessons learned turned on the principles of labour reform, reaching a mass audience in literally hundreds of reading rooms, Knights of Labor libraries, and assembly halls. In the words of Trevellick, it was in the 'schoolroom' of the local assembly where members first learned 'their duties and their rights' (Ontario Bureau of Industry, 1885; *St Thomas Times*, 21 April 1886). . . . This was an important component of what Frank Watt has referred to as the 'freely germinating' radicalism in the 1880s, a phenomenon spawned by the presence of the Knights of Labor (Wrigley, 1901; Watt, 1959).

This radicalism was popularized by a group of brainworkers and local advocates: men like Toronto's Phillips Thompson, as well as more obscure, but highly talented and committed local figures. Among these were Joseph Marks of London, who

began as a Knight, organized the Industrial Brotherhood in the 1890s, and edited the *Industrial Banner* well into the century; Galt's J.L. Blain, a lecturer who described himself to Powderly as a well-educated 'rat from the sinking ship of aristocracy'; a Hamilton coppersmith, George Collis, who boomed the Order under the nickname 'Sandy the Tinker', travelling to Oshawa, London, and other southern Ontario towns; poets like the carpenter Thomas Towers and Listowell's blind and deaf Walter A. Ratcliffe; or anonymous supporters—St Thomas' 'Knight of the Brush' and 'True Reformer'; Brantford's 'Drawbar'; or 'Pete Rolea' from the oil-producing community of western Ontario. Individuals like these helped the Order to establish itself in countless communities, and made the cause of reform a popular and lasting one. 'Lignum Vitae' reported to the *Journal of United Labor* on the progress of Guelph LAs 2980 and 4703: 'The masses are beginning to believe us when we tell them this endless toil for a miserable existence was never intended by an all wise creator. I wish I had only more time that I could go out to these people and invite them into an Order whose object is the complete emancipation of all mankind, and lift from off their necks the yoke of subjection, and often tyranny of a few.' From virtually every corner of the province anonymous correspondents informed labour newspapers of the local state of reform agitation (*Journal of United Labor*, 25 March 1886). . . .

As Albert V. Cross reported to Powderly from Hamilton's LA 2481 in 1887:

> When we entered the Order we were taught that in the home of labor there would be no distinctions of Country, Creed & Color because all were of the Earth and with equal rights to Earth, when we understood this great truth that all men are brothers we rejoiced, and we solomly [*sic*] resolved that we would do all

in our power to strengthen the bonds of unity between the workers of the world.[13]

Perhaps the most significant aspect of this strengthening of the bonds of unity was the Order's role in overcoming past deficiencies of workers' organizations. Nowhere was this more visible than in the Knights of Labor effort to draw *all* workers into one large movement. Across the province skilled and unskilled workers, craftsmen, factory operatives, and labourers, united in local assemblies to oppose a common enemy and to cultivate common ties. Unlike virtually every previous chapter in the history of Ontario workers' rebellion, the Knights of Labor stamped these pages of the 1880s with concern for those whose status in the working-class community ill-suited them to wear the badge of respectability, a consensual cultural norm that the Order recast to express class antagonisms. Premised on the fundamental rejection of exclusion (tarnished certainly, by the Order's stand on the Chinese), the Knights of Labor, most often led by skilled workers, offered their ideals and their strengths as a force protecting and speaking for all of those 'below' them. As Leon Fink has argued in the case of the United States, masses of workers who had never experienced the fruits of full citizenship joined the skilled leadership sector of the Order, forging an alliance of the 'privileged' working class and a younger thoroughly proletarianized group, composed of male and female factory operatives and unskilled labourers.[14]

Indeed, the introduction of women into the mass struggles of the 1880s shattered decades of complacency and effected a fundamental shift in attitude. To be sure, the Knights acted out of chivalrous intent, and did not abandon age-old conceptions of hearth and home, domesticity and place. But they could turn all this to new purpose, and strike out at forces which they felt

to be undermining all that was good and proper in such traditional practices. Thus, at a London speech by the popular and well-travelled Knight, Richard Trevellick, members of the Order raised 'their hands to heaven and pledged themselves that wherever women were employed, they would demand equal pay for equal work without regard to sex whatsoever'. It is difficult to see in such action only a retrogressive glance over one's shoulder to a pre-industrial arcadia: the language is unmistakably that of an industrial society, and the problem has yet to be resolved. Finally, the Knights did not stop and settle comfortably in this economistic niche, but attacked those who would define women's rights in some circumscribed way. In Knights of Labor centres like Belleville, Brantford, London, Stratford, St Thomas, Thorold, Hamilton, and Toronto, where 'the ladies' joined the Order in assemblies named 'Advance' and 'Hope', and attended musical and literary entertainments as 'Goddesses of Liberty', the possibility forged in the 1880s was on many women workers' lips. With the passing of the Knights of Labor those lips were sealed for a time, but the possibility itself could not be written out of the past (*Brantford Expositor*, 16 July 1886; *London Advertiser*, 29–30 October 1886; Levine, 1978, 1979).

It is this notion of possibility, this movement towards alternative hegemony, that is central to an understanding of the Knights of Labor in the 1880s. . . . To explore both the strengths and weaknesses of this reform crusade we now turn to the political and workplace struggles in which the Knights of Labor both thrived and foundered.

The Knights in Politics

To those familiar with conventional Canadian political history, the role of the Order in the politics of the 1880s may come as a considerable surprise. Yet it was no secret to the political partisans of the day.

Not only in Toronto and Hamilton but throughout the southwestern Ontario manufacturing belt and even penetrating into eastern Ontario, the Knights created a political movement that demanded attention. John A. Macdonald in assessing the political climate in the summer of 1886 worried that the Conservative party was 'not in a flourishing state'. The 'rocks ahead' which threatened the Tory 'ship' were 'Riel, Home Rule, the Knights of Labor, and the Scott Act' (cited in Pope, 1921: 382). The Knights thus specifically merited 'the old chieftain's' close attention and two of the three other threatening reefs were movements intimately tied to the Order and its ideals, namely the Irish question and temperance.[15]

From the moment of their entrance into Canada the Knights actively engaged in politics. December 1882 saw the first stirrings of these activities when in Hamilton labour helped elect two aldermen[16] and meanwhile in Toronto the Labour Council played a prominent role in defeating a candidate identified as particularly anti-labour (Kealey, 1980: ch. 11). Those initial successes propelled labour reformers in both cities into independent campaigns in the 1883 provincial election. In Hamilton locomotive engineer and prominent Knight Ed Williams, an English immigrant and the epitome of the respectable working man, ran and won a solid 23.4 per cent of the vote in a three-way race.[17] In Toronto, where partisan politics had flared during the nominating process, the campaign results were more mixed. Painter John Carter, a labour leader of the 1870s and a member of Toronto's Excelsior LA 2305, ran in Toronto West and won 48 per cent of the vote. His candidacy, however, had gained the unstated support of the Reform Party which ran no candidate against him. In Toronto East, carpenter Samuel R. Heakes faced nominees from both old-line parties and finished a distant third with only seven per cent of the vote.[18]

Despite the relative success of these campaigns, partisan recriminations followed and were to re-emerge in subsequent campaigns. In both cities disgruntled Tory workingmen accused the Grits of double-dealing.[19] In Hamilton these charges died down, however, and labour reformers created the Hamilton Labor Political Association to continue the thrust for an independent working-class party. In subsequent municipal elections in 1883 and 1884, the association under the leadership of Knights' activist Robert Coulter enjoyed some success in electing Knights as aldermen. The best known of these figures was Irish carter Thomas Brick who provided Hamilton workers with a colourful and bombastic leader.[20]

In Toronto, Excelsior LA 2305's leadership core of old labour reformers led by Daniel J. O'Donoghue with the able support of Charles March and Alfred Jury, consolidated the position of the Knights of Labor first in the newly-created Trades and Labor Congress of Canada (which first met in 1883) and subsequently in the Toronto Trades and Labor Council (TTLC). Once entrenched there they proceeded to make good use of both bodies as effective lobbying agencies, especially against the federal Tory government (Kealey, 1980: ch. 11). Their success in attracting political attention was evident on T.V. Powderly's 1884 Toronto visit. The stage at his major address was graced by the presence of Edward Blake, Timothy Anglin, Toronto Tory Mayor Boswell, and numerous Tory aldermen (*Globe*, 14 October 1884). In the ensuing 1884 municipal election Toronto workers threw a considerable scare into the Tory machine although it held the mayoralty by a slim margin.[21] In 1885, however, this hold was broken with the sweeping victory of W.H. Howland who enjoyed the united support of the Toronto reform community, including the . . . Knights of Labor and TTLC.[22] His victory led to considerable soul-searching on the part of the Tories both in Toronto and in Ottawa

. . . and later influencing the creation of the Royal Commission on the Relations of Labor and Capital (Kealey, 1973; Harvey, 1991).

These quite considerable concessions to the political strength of the working-class movement did not prevent it from contesting the December 1886 Ontario provincial election and the February 1887 federal election. In December seven labour candidates took the field. One could be described as Lib-Lab, two as Tory-Labour, and the other four were independents who faced candidates from the other two parties. St Thomas brakeman and leading Knight Andy Ingram won West Elgin,[23] while in Lincoln Lib-Lab candidate William Garson succeeded.[24] . . .

Workers had entered politics with considerable skepticism and their failure to make a quick and decisive breakthrough led to much discouragement, especially since it appeared that their leaders were still intriguing in partisan politics. Nevertheless, throughout the late 1880s municipal politics continued to gain much attention from the Order and victories were recorded which ranged from Brantford and Chatham to Brockville and Ottawa.[25] In Cornwall, for example, the Knights helped defeat a municipal railroad bonus in the 1888 municipal election and two years later were reported to have elected nine of 13 aldermen and the mayor and reeve (*Brockville Recorder*, 4 January 1888; *Cornwall Freeholder*, 3, 10 January and 7 February 1890).[26] Moreover the Order was particularly prominent in lobbying activities in Ottawa after the creation of a Canadian Knights of Labor Legislative Committee (Kealey, 1980: ch. 12).

The Knights thus made significant political efforts and enjoyed some success, but they certainly did not overcome all the tensions in the working-class world. Partisan politics had established a deep hold on Canadian workers and the battle to create an independent working-class party was sharp and difficult. Yet on the local level tangible gains were made—early closing, union wages, and jobs in corporation work, just assessment rates, more responsible public transit. Nevertheless the Knights had never regarded the political arena as their major battlefield. It was only one campaign in a war on many fronts. This war was perhaps sharpest at the workplace.

The People's Strike

Much of the previous literature on the Knights of Labor has focused on their dislike of strikes. Frequent citation of major Knights' leaders such as T.V. Powderly and lengthy consideration of splits within the Order, such as the expulsion of the general executive board member T.B. Barry in 1888, lead to the image of an organization committed to class co-operation through the vehicle of arbitration. Like most long-propounded views, these arguments contain a kernel of truth but they also disguise much that is central to an understanding of the Knights of Labor. In Ontario the Knights either led or were involved in almost all the major strikes of the 1880s and early 1890s. This should not surprise us since, as we have already argued, the Order should not be viewed as one contending force within the working-class world, but rather as the embodiment of that class in these years. Thus in the period of the Order's growth in Ontario from 1882 to 1886, the Order came to represent a solid working-class presence united behind its eclectic but critical aims.

In the Order's earliest years in Canada it grew owing to its willingness to organize the larger class forces on behalf of localized trade or industrial struggles. Thus in Toronto the Order emerged from the coalition of forces knit together by experienced trade-union militants to support the striking female boot and shoe operatives in the spring of 1882 (Kealey, 1980: ch. 3, ch. 10). This was apparent again the following summer when

DA 45 (Brotherhood of Telegraphers) engaged in a continent-wide strike against the monopolistic telegraph companies. Although DA 45 had done little preparatory work within the Order before their epic struggle, as a bitter Powderly would argue again and again, it did appear to have established sufficient local contacts so that organized labour, and especially the Knights, rallied to its cause (Kealey, 1980: ch. 10; Palmer, 1979: ch. 6). In Hamilton and Toronto, for example, support came from union contributions to the strike fund, benefit concerts, lectures, and theatricals (Kealey, 1980: ch. 10; Palmer, 1979: ch. 6). Meanwhile the first wave of massive Labour Day demonstrations organized by the Knights, but involving all organized labour, took place in Toronto, Hamilton, and Oshawa (*Palladium of Labor*, 19 August 1883; *Iron Moulders Journal*, 31 August 1883). In each case, support for the telegraphers played a prominent role in the speeches and provided a compelling symbol for the necessity of labour solidarity. The ultimate failure of the telegraphers' strike and its bitter aftermath, which saw DA 45 withdraw from the Knights of Labor, appear to have been less important than the solidarity expressed in its course. As the *Palladium of Labor* declared: 'The telegraphers' strike is over. The People's Strike is now in order' (25 August 1883).

'The People's Strike' took many forms in the following few years. At its most dramatic it involved mass strikes that crippled whole industries or communities. Examples of struggles of this magnitude included the two Toronto Street Railway strikes of the spring and summer of 1886, a Chatham town-wide strike of December 1886, the cotton strikes in Merriton (1886 and 1889) and Cornwall (1887, 1888, and 1889), and the massive lumber strikes in Gravenhurst in 1888 and in Ottawa-Hull in 1891.[27] Each of these struggles rocked their communities with . . . unprecedented class conflict and involved workers previously untouched by trade-union organization. Yet the Knights of Labor also led or took part in conflicts far less riveting. In the early 1880s this often meant coming to the support of striking trades or labourers as with Toronto female shoe operatives in 1882 and their Hamilton sisters in 1884, or Toronto printers in 1884 (Kealey, 1980: ch. 10; Palmer, 1979: ch. 6). In these cases and in countless others, the Order proved its mettle by practising what it preached and aiding all workers' struggles. It was this type of activity that initially helped to break down entrenched conservative craft suspicions of the Order. Then, as craft unionists and craft unions flooded into the Order in 1885–86, the Order continued to fight their battles. . . .

Typical of these craft/Knights' strikes were those fought out in Oshawa, where there was an organized relationship between the Iron Molders International (IMIU) Local No. 36 and the Knights. The IMIU which dated from 1866 was joined in Oshawa by the Knights on 12 August 1882 when Aetna LA 2355 was organized by a Buffalo Knight.[28] This large assembly with nearly 300 members in 1883 was entrenched in the local iron and agricultural implements industry. Co-operating closely with the IMIU, the Oshawa Knights hosted nearly 2,000 workers at their August 1883 labour demonstration. IMIU Local 136 marched in a uniform of 'gray shirts, black hats, and black neckties' and were joined by their brother moulders from Toronto (Nos 28 and 140) and Cobourg (No. 189) and over 1,500 Knights of Labor. Local 136 provided the 'main feature of our procession', 'the moulding, melting, and casting of iron in the line of march', reported LA 2355 and IMIU No. 36 Recording Secretary Joseph Brockman. The commemorative coins that they struck during the procession were distributed to the participants. Two months later the labourers at the Malleable Iron Works, members of Aetna LA 2355, struck against a wage reduction. The moulders, out in support of the labourers and facing a similar wage cut, were warned that if they did not return, the shop would 'be permanently closed against them'. Six weeks into the strike the Oshawa Stove Works and the Masson Agricultural Implements Works locked out their moulders to create a solid employer block against the workers. Even then it was only after the Oshawa moulders' sister unions in Hamilton (No. 26) and Toronto (No. 28) accepted 10 per cent wage cuts in December without striking, that Oshawa No. 136 felt compelled to concede defeat. Earlier in December the labourers had returned on the advice of the LA 2355 executive which argued that 'it would have broke Jay Gould with his seventy-three millions of stolen money to have kept labourers and immigrants away from here.'[29]

By the next fall, however, the union had reasserted itself and another of its leaders (and a charter member of LA 2355), Lewis Allchin, wrote Powderly seeking his support for a profit-sharing plan at the Oshawa Stove Works. He also mentioned that they had 'affected every Reform obtained in the shop, one for instance, piece workers used to work almost all noonhour, and not later than last spring, we managed to institute a rigid observance of noonhour, we also limited the wages to $2.50 per day'.[30] The new success of the moulders probably made another struggle almost inevitable and it came two years later in late January 1886 when the Malleable Iron Works again tried to force the union out of its foundry. This time the issue was simply the question of a closed shop. John Cowan, the manager of the works, insisted on continuing to employ two non-union moulders; IMIU No. 36 and Tylers LA 4279 (Moulders) refused to work with them. After a bitter two-month strike in the depths of a severe winter which witnessed alleged incendiarism, a 'surprise party' (charivari?), sending the non-union moulders out of town, and considerable public

support for the men, the company finally caved in and recognized the closed shop. The concession came at the end of March when the union and LA 4279 began to call for a total boycott of the foundry's goods.[31]

Similar events involving moulders and Knights occurred in Lindsay in 1886,[32] in Kingston in 1887,[33] in London in 1882 and 1886,[34] and in Ayr, Galt, and Smiths Falls later in the decade.[35] Success varied dramatically, but in all these cases the principles of the Knights, of craft control and of labour reform were carried on. Lewis Allchin, Oshawa moulder-Knight and the author of 'Sketches of our Organization' (a serialized history of the IMIU from its founding to 1890 published in the *Iron Molders Journal*), summed up the close intertwining of these themes: 'The object, in brief, is the *complete emancipation of labor*, and the inauguration of a higher and nobler industrial system than this of the present, under which one human being is dependent upon another for the means of living.' Denying at the outset later historians' views of the Knights, he emphasized: 'We cannot turn back if we would; we cannot return to a primitive system of working, however much we might desire it.' Trusts and syndicates, he viewed as 'an inevitable phase' of 'an excessive and pernicious competitive system', but they would not 'be the *finale* of the whole question'. They 'contained within themselves the germs of their own dissolution', since 'selfishness and greed were but foundations of sand to build upon'. The future he would not predict, but he hazarded one final conclusion:

That no system which does not recognize the right of labor to a first and just share of its products, which refuses each and every toiler a voice in the business transactions of the enterprise, that does not establish a just and relative measure or standard of value for all services rendered, labor performed, products manufactured, and commodities exchanged, will ever be a just or permanent one. (*Iron Molders Journal*, 31 January 1891)

Here, quite clearly, we can see that the values and ideas of the late nineteenth-century working-class world were shared by its articulate leadership, be they Knights or craft unionists, and, as was so often the case, the very personnel overlapped. For our chosen group of skilled workers, the moulders, this unity demonstrated itself most clearly in the streets of London in the late summer of 1886 when the IMIU held its seventeenth convention. The city's first labour demonstration 'of 4000 unionists in line' was held to honour the assembled moulders and was witnessed by crowds estimated at between 8,000 and 10,000 (*Iron Molders Journal*, 31 October 1890, 31 July 1886; Palmer, 1976). Addressed by Captain Richard Trevellick, the Knights' chief itinerant lecturer, the convention also considered at length a motion to amalgamate the IMIU with the Knights of Labor. After a full day of debate the resolution was soundly defeated but it did win support from militant moulders' strongholds such as Albany and Troy, New York. In registering his opposition, the IMIU president made clear his support 'for always remaining on the most friendly terms with the Knights of Labor, and rendering them all the assistance that our organization can possibly give them in all legitimate undertakings in the interest of labour.'[36] This solidarity began to disintegrate the following year during the vicious war between the Founders Association and the moulders in the United States.[37]

The solidarity so evident in the London streets in July 1886 had also spread far beyond the moulders and their other skilled worker brethren. The Knights also successfully organized the unskilled—women factory workers, male operatives, and large numbers of labourers both in Ontario's cities and towns, and in her resource hinterland. These workers, organized for the first time under the banners of the Knights of Labor, also engaged in militant struggles in the 1880s and early 1890s. Strikes to gain either the right to organize or to win modest economic advances occurred in these sectors as opposed to the control struggles of the skilled workers. Ranging in size from minor affairs to massive, almost general, strikes which polarized single-industry communities, these struggles were most prominent in the mill towns of eastern and western Ontario.

Cotton mill struggles hit Merritton in 1886 and 1889 and Cornwall in three successive years, 1887, 1888, and 1889. The Merritton mill, which remained totally organized as late as 1892, witnessed numerous work stoppages led by the Knights in 1886 (Ontario Bureau of Industry, 1886, 1889, 1890). Three years later a week-long strike over a wage reduction won a compromise settlement (Ontario Bureau of Industry, 1886, 1889, 1890). None of these represented major victories but in an industry known for its exploitation and anti-unionism Maple Leaf LA 5933's 500 workers were more successful than most. Their achievement may well have been one of the factors that led Canadian Coloured Cottons to shut down the plant after the merger of 1892 (de Lottinville, 1979).

Cornwall's cotton workers joined the Knights of Labor in 1886 in LAs 6582 and 6583. The first test of the Order came in the summer of 1887 when 18 dyers demanded that their hours be reduced from 10 to nine. Although the Order provided $400 in financial assistance to its striking members, they still lost the strike (Ontario Bureau of Industry, 1887; *Brockville Recorder*, 12 July 1887). In February 1888 wage reductions at both the Canada and Stormont mills precipitated strikes involving from 1,300 to 1,500 employees. After a few weeks the workers returned with a compromise settlement. The wages were still cut but by an estimated 10 per cent instead of the alleged 20–23 per cent originally imposed. This settlement held at the Stormont mill, but the Canada mill was struck again when workers accused the company of not living up to the agreement. After another month these workers again returned (Ontario Bureau of Industry, 1888).[38] One year later in the spring of 1889 the Stormont mill workers struck once again. After five weeks the 600 operatives returned when the company agreed to honour the weavers' demands (Ontario Bureau of Industry, 1889; *Gananoque Reporter*, 16 March 1889).

The lumber industry, another long hold-out against trade unionism, also experienced two major strikes led by the Knights of Labor. Gravenhurst LA 10669 was organized in 1887 under the leadership of Uxbridge DA 236 after a short lumber strike in which the hours of work in the mills on Muskoka Bay had been reduced from 11 to ten-and-a-half with a promise that in 1888 they would be further shortened to 10. In 1888, however, a province-wide agreement was signed by the Muskoka, Georgian Bay, and Ottawa River lumber barons that prevented a further reduction of hours under pain of forfeiting a bond. The angry workers of LA 10669 consulted the DA 236 leadership which counselled caution and urged the assembly to strengthen its ranks. By June 300 of the 375 workers had joined the Order and they then appointed a committee to meet with the mill owners. This met with a blanket refusal from the employers and the workers again sought aid from DA 236. Although reluctant, the district assembly had no choice but to sanction a strike, which began on 3 July 1888. A few mills acceded but the majority held out. Aylesworth of the Knights' general executive board responded to an emergency call from DA 236, but his efforts were unsuccessful and by September the men had returned to work with no gains.[39] In the Chaudiere region of the Ottawa-Hull area, another lumber workers' strike erupted in September 1891.[40] . . .

As three years earlier in Gravenhurst, a particularly harsh winter created the situation that would lead to that fall's huge mill strike. Already late returning to work because of the weather, the workers were informed of a 50-cents-a-week wage cut. In return for the reduction, the owners offered the 10-hour day but soon violated their own concession. With hours again extended to 11 and 12 the workers sought the aid of the Knights of Labor in May. When the Order would not sanction a strike until they had been in the organization for at least six months, the workers remained on the job. By fall, however, their tempers had worn thin and on Saturday, 12 September 1891, the outside workers at Perley and Pattee demanded that their wages be reinstated to the 1890 rate. Denied this, the workers met on Sunday and agreed to repeat their demand the next day. Again rebuffed, they proceeded to march from mill to mill pulling all the workers out. Over 2,400 workers left their jobs and the Knights quickly took over the strike leadership. The mill workers were subsequently enrolled in Chaudiere LA 2966 and Hull's Canadienne LA 2676.

Over the next few weeks some of the smaller mills conceded to the workers' demands of the previous year's rate and a 10-hour day, but the larger mills stood firm. As community support for the workers stiffened, massive meetings of 3,000 to 10,000 people were held. Meanwhile incidents of violence occurred, the militia was mobilized, and workers responded with a charivari, and with their own security force. Over $1,500 was raised by the Order and an extensive relief system was established. By the end of September, however, strike leaders urged their followers to seek employment elsewhere and by early October the relief system began to break down. By 12 October the workers were back with their 1890 wage but with the same long hours of work. Two hundred of Bronson's workers promptly struck again on 14 October when they claimed he had reneged on his agreement. By the end of the month, however, work was back to normal. Although not an unmitigated success, the Order had won a limited victory and the millmen stayed with the Knights. The next year Ottawa DA 6 was created with an impressive 2,000 workers, largely from the lumber industry. These workers finally won the 10-hour day in 1895.

Turbulence, strikes, and class conflict thus played an important role in the history of the Knights of Labor in Ontario. The oft-invoked image of an organization interested in avoiding strikes at all cost and the implicit projection of a class-cooperative, if not collaborationist, body begins to dissipate under more careful scrutiny.

Conclusion

The 1880s were a critical decade in Canadian history—a decade which witnessed the fulfillment of the National Policy industrial strategy with a rapid expansion in Canadian manufacturing, especially in textiles. Yet these years also saw the breakdown of the previous consensus on industrial development as Canadian workers, especially in the country's industrial heartland, began to raise their voices in an unfamiliar, concerted fashion to join the growing debate about the nation's future. Ontario's mainly British and Canadian workers, many with previous trade-union and industrial experience, provided leadership to the emerging working-class movement which found its most articulate expression in the Knights of Labor.

The challenge which this movement mounted in all realms of Ontario society—the cultural, intellectual, and political as well as the economic—engendered in turn a class response from employers and from the state. The employers engaged in a virulent, open warfare with their worker-Knights, especially in the period of economic decline after 1886. In the 1890s, they began as well to turn to the ever-increasing concentration and centralization of capital and later to the modern management devices of a rampant Taylorism in their battle with labour. Meanwhile the state and the political parties responded in a more conciliatory fashion. Mowat and, to a lesser degree, Macdonald interceded to provide workers with many of the protections they demanded—factory acts, bureaux of labour statistics, arbitration measures, suffrage extension, employers' liability acts, and improved mechanics' lien acts. The political parties proved even more flexible and managed through patronage and promises to contain much of the oppositional sentiment that flared in the 1880s. Thus the Canadian political system functioned effectively to mediate the fiery class conflict of the 1880s.

In the following decade, with the exception of eastern Ontario, the Knights were moribund. Their precipitous decline was halted by a slight resurgence in the late 1890s. . . . Yet as we suggested earlier, the heritage of the Order lived on. Its major contributions to working-class memory centred on its oppositional success as a movement which for the first time provided *all* workers with an organizational vehicle and, further, which, for a moment at least, overcame many of the splintering forces which so often divided the working class.

Notes

1. See University of Toronto, Kenny Papers, *The Knights of Labor, the American Federation of Labor and the One Big Union*, One Big Union Leaflet No. 2 (Winnipeg, c. 1920).
2. Previous Canadian work on the Knights of Labor in Ontario includes Victor Oscar Chan, 'The Canadian Knights of Labor with special reference to the 1880s', MA thesis, McGill University, 1949; Douglas Kennedy, *The Knights of Labor in Canada* (London: University of Western Ontario, 1956); Eugene Forsey,

'The Telegraphers' Strike of 1883', *Transactions of the Royal Society of Canada*, Series 4, 9 (1971): 245–59; Bernard Ostry, 'Conservatives, Liberals, and Labour in the 1880s', *Canadian Journal of Economics and Political Science*, 27 (May 1961): 141–61; F.W. Watt, 'The National Policy, the Workingman and Proletarian Ideas in Victorian Canada', *Canadian Historical Review* 40 (March 1959): 1–26. Cf., given the above, Fred Landon, 'The Knights of Labor: Predecessors of the CIO', *Quarterly Review of Commerce*, 1 (Autumn 1937): 1–7. While all this work provides valuable empirical detail it has been dated by the availability of new sources and lacks a firm grounding in local contexts. Interpretatively, it presents us with few benchmarks in understanding the Knights of Labor. We have drawn upon Raymond Williams, 'Base and Superstructure in Marxist Cultural Theory', *New Left Review* 82 (November–December 1973): 1–16; Lawrence Goodwyn, *Democratic Promise: The Populist Movement in America* (New York: Oxford University Press, 1976).

3. See also *Journal of the Board of Arts and Manufactures for Upper Canada* 7 (1867): 220.

4. On the importance of this period of price deflation in the United States see Harold G. Vatter, *The Drive to Industrial Maturity: The U.S. Economy, 1860–1916* (Westport, Conn.: Greenwood, 1975), and on the twentieth century, Harry Braverman, *Labor and Monopoly Capital: The Degradation of Work in the Twentieth Century* (New York: Monthly Review, 1974).

5. See maps on 'Manufacturing Employment by County', in *Economic Atlas of Ontario*, W.G. Dean, ed., (Toronto: University of Toronto Press, 1969).

6. See the important statement in Raphael Samuel, 'The Workshop of the World: Steam Power and Hand Technology in Mid-Victorian Britain', *History Workshop Journal* 3 (Spring 1977): 6–72.

7. On Hamilton, see Palmer, *A Culture in Conflict: Skilled Workers and Industrial Capitalism in Hamilton, Ontario, 1860–1914* (Montreal: McGill-Queens University Press, 1979), pp. 3–31, and on Toronto, Kealey, *Toronto Workers Respond to Industrial Capitalism, 1867–1892* (Toronto: University of Toronto Press, 1980), pp. 1–34.

8. Note V.I. Lenin, *The Development of Capitalism in Russia* (Moscow: Progress, 1964), p. 551.

9. See *Report of the Select Committee on the Causes of the Present Depression of the Manufacturing, Mining, Commercial, Shipping, Lumber and Fishing Interests* (Ottawa, 1876), pp. 142–8; Kealey, *Canada Investigates Industrialism: The Royal Commission on the Relations of Labor and Capital, 1889* (Toronto: University of Toronto Press, 1973), pp. 179–92; Chambers

and Bertram, 'Urbanization and Manufacturing in Canada, 1870–1890', *Canadian Political Science Association Conference on Statistics, June 1964* (Toronto: University of Toronto Press), pp. 242–55.

10. All organizational data throughout are based on our own calculations. We should note, however, a debt of gratitude to two pieces of pioneering research on the Knights which were of inestimable value to us. Eugene Forsey's massive compilation of materials on organized labour in Canada before 1902 includes much on the Knights and a helpful attempt at a local-by-local reconstruction. See Eugene Forsey, *Trade Unions in Canada, 1812–1902* (Toronto: University of Toronto Press, 1982). Jonathan Garlock, *Knights of Labor Data Bank* (Ann Arbor, Mich.: Inter University Consortium, 1973), and 'A Structural Analysis of the Knights of Labor', (PhD disseration, University of Rochester, 1974) have been of considerable help. For a description of the data bank, see Jonathan Garlock, 'The Knights of Labor Data Bank', *Historical Methods Newsletter*, 6 (1973): 149–60. Our corrections to the data bank will be incorporated into the computer file at Ann Arbor. These corrections are based on the labour and local press of Ontario, on the Ontario Bureau of Industry, *Annual Reports*, on various trade-union minutes and proceedings, and on the extensive Ontario correspondence scattered throughout the Powderly Papers, recently indexed at the PAC by Russell Hann. The population data are from the 1881 and 1891 censuses.

11. See also Catholic University of America, Washington, DC, Powderly Papers (hereafter PP), 'The Great Seal of Knightwood' and 'Secret Circular: Explanation of the Signs and Symbols of the Order'; Carrol D. Wright, 'An Historical Sketch of the Knights of Labor', *Quarterly Journal of Economics* 1 (January 1887): 142–3; Powderly, *The Path I Trod: The Autobiography of Terence Vincent Powderly*, Harry Carman, Henry David, and Paul Gutherie, eds (New York: Columbia University Press, 1940), pp. 434–5.

12. See *Palladium of Labor* (Hamilton), 5 September 1885; PP, O'Neill to Powderly, 13 January 1885; *Statistics as Collected by Headlight Assembly no. 4069, Knights of Labour for Its Exclusive Use* (St Thomas, 1885), p. 3; *Journal of Commerce*, 13 March 1891, as cited in Bliss, *A Living Profit*, p. 78; *Labor Union* (Hamilton), 13 January 1883.

13. See PP, Cross to Powderly and G.E.B, 9 June 1887; *Gananoque Reporter*, 3 December 1887.

14. See, especially, Fink, 'Workingmen's Democracy: The Knights of Labor and American Politics', *The Working Class in American History* (Chicago: Urbana, 1983).

15. On the Knights and the Irish see Eric Foner, 'Class, Ethnicity, and Radicalism in the Gilded Age: The Land League and Irish America', *Marxist Perspectives* 1 (Summer 1978): 6–55; on Home Rule see Kealey, *Toronto Workers Respond to Industrial Capitalism, 1867–1892*, ch. 14.

16. See PP, George Havens to Powderly, 4 January 1883.

17. *Labor Union*, 3, 10 February, 3 March 1883; PP, Gibson to Powderly, 7 February 1883, and Powderly to Gibson, 9 February 1883.

18. See *Trade Union Advocate* (Toronto), 11, 18, 25 January, 1, 8, 15 February 1883; Public Archives of Canada (hereafter PAC), Toronto Trades and Labor Council, Minutes, 19 January, 2 February 1883; *Globe* (Toronto), 5, 8, February 1883.

19. See PP, D.B. Skelly to Powderly, 15 December 1884; PAC, Macdonald Papers, Small to Macdonald, 10 April 1883.

20. See *Palladium of Labor*, 25 August, 28 September, 13, 20 October, 24 November 1883; 12 January, 31 May, 5 December 1884; 8, 15 May, 4 July, 28 November, 5 December 1885.

21. PAC, Macdonald Papers, Boultbee to Macdonald, 12 September, 29, 30 December 1884; Macpherson to Macdonald, 27 December 1884.

22. PAC, Toronto Trades and Labor Council, Minutes, 4, 14, 18, 29 December 1885; *News* (Toronto), 4 January 1886; *Palladium of Labor*, 5 December 1885; PP, O'Donoghue to Powderly, 7 January 1886.

23. *St Thomas Daily Times*, February–December 1886; *Canada Labor Courier* (St Thomas), 29 July, 30 December 1886. See also Barbara A. McKenna, 'The Decline of the Liberal Party in Elgin County', unpublished paper presented to the Canadian Historical Association, London, 1978.

24. PP, William Garson to Powderly, 21 March 1884 and 22 October 1885.

25. *Courier* (Brantford), 4 January, 15 April, 28 December 1886; *Brantford Expositor*, 16 April, 20 August, 24 September, 17, 31 December 1886; *Canada Labor Courier*, 30 December 1886, 13 January 1887; *Brockville Recorder*, 1887–88; *Ottawa Citizen*, 1890–91.

26. These newspaper discussions are somewhat confusing as various candidates denied formal connections with the Order. Yet in the aftermath the *Cornwall Freeholder*, 7 February 1890, argued that one loser 'had arranged against him the workingmen, which is no mean factor in election contests in Cornwall these days'.

27. For Toronto see Kealey, *Toronto Workers Respond*

to *Industrial Capitalism, 1867–1892*, ch. 10; for Chatham see *Canada Labor Courier*, 30 December 1886, 13 January 1887.

28. PP, James R. Brown to Powderly, 29 September 1882.

29. See *Palladium of Labor*, 20 October, 8, 15, 22 December 1883; *Iron Molders Journal*, 31 August 1890.

30. See PP, Lewis Allchin to Powderly, 20, 25 October 1884.

31. See *News*, 23 February, 6, 9, 15 March 1886; *Iron Molders Journal*, 30 September 1890.

32. See *Labour Record* (Toronto), 14 May 1886; Trent University Archives, Gainey Collection, IMIU Local 191, Minutes, 1886.

33. *British Daily Whig* (Kingston), 13, 14, 16, 18, 19, 23 May 1887; *Gananoque Reporter*, 21 May 1887; and Ontario Bureau of Industry, *Annual Report* (Toronto, 1887), p. 42.

34. IMIU, *Proceedings*, 1882 and 1886; *Iron Molders Journal*, 31 May 1890.

35. IMIU, *Proceedings*, 1890 and 1895; *Iron Molders Journal*, August 1889.

36. IMIU, *Proceedings*, 1886; *Iron Molders Journal*, 31 October 1890.

37. IMIU, *Proceedings*, 1888; Richard Oestreicher, 'Solidarity and Fragmentation: Working People and Class Consciousness in Detroit, 1877–1895' (PhD dissertation, Michigan State University, 1979), ch. 7.

38. See also *Cornwall Standard*, 28 January, 2 February 1888; *Montreal Gazette*, 14 February 1888. Our thanks to Peter de Lottinville for these newspaper references. See also *Gananoque Reporter*, 4, 11, 18 February 1888.

39. This draws on: PP, R.R. Elliot to Powderly, 12, 19 July 1888; William Hogan to Powderly, 21 September, 5 November 1888; Archy Sloan to Powderly, 3 September 1888; Powderly to William Sloan, 10 September 1888; *Journal of United Labor*, 12 July 1888. See also PP, D.J. O'Donoghue to Powderly, 9 August 1888; *Globe*, 25 July, 10 August 1888.

40. The following draws on: Edward McKenna, 'Unorganized Labour versus Management: The Strike at the Chaudière Lumber Mills, 1891', *Histoire Sociale/Social History* 10 (1972): 186–211; Forsey, *Trade Unions in Canada, 1812–1902*, ch. 7; Peter Gillis, 'E.H. Bronson and Corporate Capitalism' (MA thesis, Queen's University, 1975), esp. pp. 72–81; Ontario Bureau of Industry, *Annual Report* (Toronto, 1892); and *Ottawa Citizen* and *Ottawa Journal*, September–October 1891.

References

Acheson, T.W. 1972. 'The Social Origins of the Canadian Industrial Elite, 1880–1885', in David S. Macmillan, ed., *Canadian Business History: Selected Studies, 1847–1971*. Toronto: McClelland and Stewart.

Bernstein, Irving. 1960. *The Lean Years: A History of the American Worker, 1920–1933*. Boston: Houghton Mifflin.

Bertram, G.W. 1962. 'Historical Statistics on Growth and Structure of Manufacturing in Canada, 1870–1957', *Canadian Political Science Association Conference on Statistics, June 1962*. Toronto: University of Toronto Press.

Bland, Warren. 1974. 'The Location of Manufacturing in Southern Ontario in 1881', *Ontario Geography* 8: 8–39.

Brantford Expositor. 1886. 16 July.

Brockville Recorder. 1887. 12 July.

Brockville Recorder. 1888. 4 January.

Chambers, Edward, J., and Gordon Bertram. 1966. 'Urbanization and Manufacturing in Central Canada, 1870–1890', in Sylvia Ostry, ed., *CPSA Conference on Statistics 1966*. Toronto: University of Toronto Press.

Citizen and Country. 1900. 4 May.

Clark, Kenneth Lloyd. 1976. 'Social Relations and Urban Change in a Late Nineteenth Century Southwestern Ontario Railroad City: St Thomas, 1868–1890'. MA thesis, York University, Toronto, ON.

Cook, Ezra, ed. 1886. *Knights of Labor Illustrated: Adelphon Kruptos: The Full Illustrated Ritual Including the 'Unwritten Work' and an Historical Sketch of the Order*. Chicago: n.p.

Cornwall Freeholder. 1890. 3, 10 January; 7 February.

De Lottinville, Peter. 1979. 'The St Croix Manufacturing Company and Its Influence on the St Croix Community, 1880–1892'. MA thesis, Dalhousie University, Halifax, NS.

Forsey, E. 1971. 'The Telegraphers' Strike of 1883', *Transactions of the Royal Society of Canada*, Series 4, 9: 245–59.

Gananoque Reporter. 1887. 25 August.

Gananoque Reporter. 1889. 16 March.

Glazebrook, G.P. de T. 1964. *A History of Transportation in Canada*, 2 vols (Toronto: McClelland and Stewart).

Globe. 1884. 14 October.

Grimwood, Carrol J. 1934. 'The Cigar Manufacturing Industry in London, Ontario'. MA thesis, University of Western Ontario, London, ON.

Harvey, F. 1991. *Révolution industrielle et travailleurs*. Montreal: Boréal.

Iron Molders Journal. 1883. 31 August.

Iron Molders Journal. 1886. 31 July.

Iron Molders Journal. 1890. 31 October.

Journal of United Labor. 1886. 25 March.

Kealey, G. 1973. *Canada Investigates Industrialism: The Royal Commission on the Relations of Labor and Capital, 1889*. Toronto: University of Toronto Press.

———. 1980. *Toronto Workers Respond to Industrial Capitalism, 1867–1892*. Toronto: University of Toronto Press.

Langdon, Steven. 1975. *The Emergence of the Canadian Working Class Movement*. Toronto: New Hogtown Press.

Levine, Susan. 1978. 'The Best Men in the Order: Women in the Knights of Labor'. Unpublished paper presented to the Canadian Historical Association, London, ON.

———. 1979. 'The Knights of Labor and Romantic Ideology'. Paper presented to the Centennial Conference, Newberry Library, Chicago, 17–19 May.

London Advertiser. 1886. 29–30 October.

Ontario Bureau of Industry. 1886. *Annual Report*.

Ontario Bureau of Industry. 1887. *Annual Report*.

Ontario Bureau of Industry. 1888. *Annual Report*.

Ontario Bureau of Industry. 1889. *Annual Report*.

Ontario Bureau of Industry. 1890. *Annual Report*.

Palladium of Labor. 1883. 18 August.

Palladium of Labor. 1883. 25 August.

Palladium of Labor. 1885. 21 February.

Palmer, Bryan. 1976. '"Give us the road and we will run it": The Social and Cultural Matrix of an Emerging Labour Movement', in G. Kealey and P. Warrian, eds, *Essays in Canadian Working Class History*. Toronto: McClelland and Stewart.

———. 1979. *A Culture in Conflict: Skilled Workers and Industrial Capitalism in Hamilton, Ontario, 1860–1914*. Montreal: McGill-Queens University Press.

Pentland, H.C. 1968. 'A Study of the Changing Social, Economic, and Political Background of the Canadian System of Industrial Relations'. Draft study for the Task Force on Labour Relations, Ottawa, ON.

Pope, Joseph, ed. 1921. *The Correspondence of Sir John A. Macdonald*. Toronto: Oxford University Press.

Powderly, Terence V. 1940. *The Path I Trod: The Autobiography of Terence V. Powderly*. New York: Columbia University Press.

Scott, Benjamin S. 1930. 'The Economic and Industrial History of the City of London, Canada from the Building of the First Railway, 1855 to the Present, 1930'. MA thesis, University of Western Ontario, London, ON.

Smucker, J. 1980. *Industrialization in Canada*. Scarborough: Prentice Hall.

Spelt, Jacob. 1972. *Urban Development in South-Central Ontario*. Toronto: McClelland and Stewart.

St Thomas Times. 1886. 21 April.

Thompson, E.P. 1978. 'The Peculiarities of the English', in *The Poverty of Theory and Other Essays*. London: Merlin Press.

Trumper, Richard A. 1937. 'The History of E. Leonard & Sons, Boilermakers and Ironfounders, London, Ontario'. MA thesis, University of Western Ontario, London, ON.

Ware, Norman J. 1968. *Labor in Modern Industrial Society*. New York: Russell and Russell.

Warrian, Peter. 1971. 'The Challenge of the One Big Union Movement in Canada, 1919–1921'. MA thesis, University of Waterloo, Waterloo, ON.

Watt, F.W. 1959. 'The National Policy, the Workingman and Proletarian Ideas in Victorian Canada', *Canadian Historical Review* 40, 1: 1–26.

Wrigley, G. Weston. 1901. 'Socialism in Canada', *International Socialist Review* 1 (May): 686.

PART IV

Radicals and Union Struggles in Industrializing Canada, 1900–1925

The era beginning with Wilfrid Laurier's federal Liberal victory in 1896 (based on the promise of reciprocity with the United States, or freer trade) to World War I saw Canada transformed socially and economically. Regional economies boomed, labour markets expanded with a massive influx of European peoples, and urban populations exploded in size and significance.

Early in the twentieth century it was apparent that Canadian industrial capitalism was developing into its monopolistic stage. Large, highly-centralized enterprises, sometimes connected to international firms, played an ever increasing role in Canada's burgeoning economy. Many of these sprawling factories were located in south-central Canada, and used new managerial strategies and technologies that substituted machines for workers to undermine the power of skilled labour. Unevenly developed across the country, the new industrial capitalism thrived on new products such as rubber and chemicals, as well as new production processes like the assembly line in the emerging automobile industry. Change was in the air. So too were new working-class discontents.

Craftsmen, who in the nineteenth century often had proud traditions of independence and long-years of apprentice training, as well as strong occupationally-based unions, found their bargaining power with employers weakened and their skills and status eroded. Newly-arrived immigrants and women played more and more of a role as machine-tenders in workplaces now often ruled by foremen and managers; differences of gender and ethnicity figured forcefully.

Influential Liberals, such as Minister of the Interior Clifford H. Sifton, hoped that newly-arrived immigrants would farm the vast prairies but many gravitated to large cities and to the resource-extractive mining and lumbering frontiers. The cities, however, were where they were most visible, and where they were identified as a social 'problem'. Immigrant neighbourhoods rested on a precarious family economy of low wages sustained by the paid and unpaid work of men, women, children, and the aged. Substandard living arrangements in working-class tenements caused middle-class reformers to fear that overcrowded immigrant districts were the breeding grounds for disease and rebellion.

Most immigrants were from the British Isles, but there were also southern and eastern Europeans, viewed with trepidation by both the Anglo elite and by many within the respectable English-speaking working class. Some thought these 'alien' labourers would turn to radical politics, or fail to assimilate into 'modern' Canada. In response to rising numbers of strikes and class altercations, both the federal government and many provincial counterparts became more interventionist. Laws regulating labour conflict were passed in legislatures; the courts were called upon to issue injunctions banning workers from walking picket lines. Posing as a 'neutral' umpire, the state was more often concerned with protecting industrial peace to the benefit of employers.

Only a very small percentage of all workers were organized in unions, but those that were organized worked to pressure municipal, provincial, and national governments. They demanded collective bargaining rights, health and safety protections, curbs on immigration, minimum wages and working hours for women and children, and ways of settling labour disputes that might end some of the chaos of industrial life.

Since the demise of the Knights of Labor, the Trades and Labour Congress of Canada (TLC)—an umbrella organization representing primarily skilled craft workers—was the main voice of labour. Many TLC unions were branches of the United States-based American Federation of Labor (AFL), which, under the leadership of Samuel Gompers, endorsed cautious 'bread and butter' or 'business' unionism. This kind of labour organization protected the most privileged sections of the working class, avoided organizing the unorganized, and stuck to the tried and true task of improving the economic lot of its members rather than challenging the capitalist order. This kind of trade unionism might organize strikes but it never preached revolution, and it ventured into the political arena rarely and timidly.

Some workers grew dissatisfied with the political and economic limitations of these craft unions. As the stark inequalities and ravages of the largely unregulated capitalist marketplace grew more and more apparent, alternative movements and oppositional labour voices emerged, challenging the dominance of the TLC. Socialist and labour parties developed, moving in different directions than the utopian and Christian forms of radical anti-capitalism that had predominated in the nineteenth century. Bodies like the Socialist Party of Canada (SPC) and the Social Democratic Party of Canada (SDP) used Marxist concepts to analyze capitalism and point out to workers that they lived in an exploitative and oppressive society. The SPC was arguably the more revolutionary of the two bodies, demanding an all-out struggle against capital and its political arm, the state. The Industrial Workers of the World (IWW/Wobblies), less interested in electoral campaigns than in winning power at the workplace, assimilated a rough-and-tumble language of class struggle that drew on similar ideas. In the case of the SDP, more concentrated in the immigrant urban communities and in central Canada than was the SPC, mobilizations often centred on specific reforms, including women's suffrage.

Mark Leier's essay on the Wobblies explains the economic conditions that gave rise to this boisterous and radical labour body. His reference to IWW songs, bellowed in the midst of key struggles in British Columbia's resource communities, shows us how economic struggles were connected to, and sustained, vibrant radical cultures of opposition. Craig Heron's wide-ranging discussion of the national contours of the labour revolt from 1917–25 situates the period's most momentous developments—the Winnipeg General Strike of 1919 and the rise of the radical One Big Union move-ment—within the pervasive upsurge of workers in the immediate aftermath of World War I. These were years that saw impressive radical gains and expressions of soli-darity, but as Heron shows, they were are also marked by fragmentations and divisions among workers, rooted in the structures of economic life, the ways in which power was organized, and the importance of differentiations of gender, ethnicity, and occupa-tion/skill in all aspects of working-class life.

Janice Newton's contribution addresses the issue of gender more explicitly, exploring the published writings of the SPC and the SDP about the urban 'working girl'. Too often male socialists believed, like their less political working-class counter-parts, that women's place was primarily in the home. There were, however, militant and articulate women who thought and argued otherwise. They stepped out of the confinements of conventional gender roles to give speeches on public platforms and called for an end to the exploitation of working-class women. The relationship of class, ethnicity, and gender was never a settled and easy one.

Perhaps no single event so rocked the world of Canadian workers as World War I. Many working-class men enlisted during the war, but even as this occurred there was recognition of class polarization in the country. War profiteering by a wealthy few, rampant war-induced inflation, and the subsequent decline of real wages and their purchasing power, as well as the sacrifice of young men from labouring families on the battlefields of Europe all combined, in conjunction with radical and socialist critique, to create dissatisfaction among workers, regardless of their regional place or ethnic background. When it appeared that the state and employers would simply return to 'business as usual' with the winding down of hostilities in 1918, class resentment boiled to the surface of Canada's domestic scene. The rhetoric of business and government reconstruction seemed to undermine the democracy Canadians had been fighting overseas to preserve: it seemed to provide little space for the right to organize unions or the need to bring consumer prices in line with wages. As 1918 gave way to 1919, country-wide campaigns, general and sympathetic strikes, and politically rebellious mobilizations marked the period as one of unprecedented class struggle. This, in turn, prompted employers and the state to dig in their heels and fight back. Ultimately, their resistance to radicalism and the trade union upsurge of the 1917–1925 years prevailed.

Further Reading

Donald Avery, *'Dangerous Foreigners': European Immigrant Workers and Labour Radicalism in Canada, 1896–1932* (Toronto: McClelland and Stewart, 1979).

David Bercuson, *Confrontation at Winnipeg: Labour, Industrial Relations, and the General Strike* (Montreal and Kingston: McGill–Queen's University Press, 1990).

Craig Heron, 'Labourism and the Canadian Working Class', *Labour/Le Travail* 13 (Spring 1984): 35–76.

Gregory S. Kealey, '1919: The Canadian Labour Revolt', *Labour/Le Travail* 13 (Spring 1984): 11–44.

Linda Kealey, *Enlisting Women for the Cause: Women, Labour, and the Left in Canada, 1890–1920* (Toronto: University of Toronto Press, 1998).

Mark Leier, *Red Flags and Red Tape: The Making of a Labour Bureaucracy* (Toronto: University of Toronto Press, 1995).

James Naylor, *The New Democracy: Challenging the Social Order in Industrial Ontario, 1914–1925* (Toronto: University of Toronto Press, 1991).

Visual Resources

Labour Café Productions, *The Notorious Mrs Armstrong* (2001), dir. Paula Kelly, 44 minutes (the story of Helen Armstrong, a socialist and tireless advocate for working women, as well as an activist in the Winnipeg General Strike).

Film West, *Prairie Fire: The Winnipeg General Strike of 1919* (1999), 72 minutes (the story of the Winnipeg General Strike).

National Film Board of Canada [NFB], *12,000 Men* (1978), dir. Martin Duckworth, 34 minutes (the struggle of unionists in Cape Breton's coal and steel industries, from the 1880s to the 1920s).

CHAPTER 8

Monopoly Capitalism and the Rise of Syndicalism: Rallying Round the Standard in British Columbia
Mark Leier

By the last years of the nineteenth century, many American and Canadian workers were keenly aware that the craft unions affiliated with the American Federation of Labor and the Trades and Labour Congress of Canada would not alter the basic relations between capital and labour. Unions could continue to carve out better wages for their members, but they would not help the mass of workers who were not organized. Nor would they work to abolish the unjust system of capitalism. At the same time, the socialist movement was isolated from the working class and its daily struggles. Prompted by the Western Federation of Miners and the left wing of the Socialist Party of America, unionists and radicals tried to create a new organization that would be able to unite all workers and work towards revolution as the only way to solve labour's problems once and for all. Late in 1904, workers from the American Labor Union, the United Railway Workers, the Amalgamated Society of Engineers, and the Brewery Workers met to begin the formation of 'a labor organization that would correspond to modern industrial conditions'. In January 1905, several delegates drew up a manifesto that would lay the foundation for a revolutionary industrial union. The manifesto decried the power of monopoly capitalism and outlined the fundamental changes in the labour process which accompanied it. As machines replaced skilled workers, the tradesman was 'sunk in the uniform mass of wage slaves. . . . Laborers are no longer classified by differences in trade skill, but the employer assorts them according to the machines to which they are attached.' Trade unions could not address this problem; at best, they could offer 'only a perpetual struggle for slight relief within wage slavery'. The manifesto ended with a call for unionists and radicals to assemble in Chicago that June to create a new labour organization (Brissenden, 1957; Dubofsky, 1969: 74–6).

By early morning on 27 June 1905, Brand's Hall in Chicago was filled with tobacco smoke and people. More than two hundred delegates had shown up in response to the January manifesto. . . .

At 10 a.m., William Dudley Haywood, secretary of the Western Federation of Miners, picked up a short board and pounded this makeshift gavel to silence the crowd. He chose his opening salutation with care, for this new organization did not want to be tainted by rituals and reminders of other radical groups. Haywood wanted to avoid the 'brothers and sisters' so redolent of the American Federation of Labor [AFL], while 'fellow citizens', the address of the French Communards, hardly fit the multilingual and multinational gathering. He brushed aside the 'comrades' that had been appropriated by the Socialist Party, and decided on his opening:

> Fellow workers! . . . This is the Continental Congress of the working class. We are here to confederate the workers of this country into a working class movement that shall have for its

purpose the emancipation of the working class from the slave bondage of capitalism. There is no organization, or there seems to be no labor organization, that has for its purpose the same object as that for which you are called together today. The aims and objects of this organization should be to put the working class in possession of the economic power, the means of life, in control of the machinery of production and distribution, without regard to capitalist masters. (Haywood, 1977: 181)[1]

With this speech the Industrial Workers of the World [IWW] came into being. It was created to do what the AFL could not, or would not, do: organize unskilled, immigrant workers to fight not just for 'more, more, more', but for a revolution that would destroy capitalism and the state.

The radicalism of the IWW was different from that of its contemporaries, the Socialist Party and the Socialist Labor Party. These parties had come to see the state as the potential liberator of the working class, and believed that the fundamental contradiction of capitalism was its inability to produce and distribute goods fairly and efficiently. Consequently, they believed that the task of the socialists was to take over the state in order to control production and distribution.

The IWW agreed that capitalism was a tyrannical, oppressive way to organize production and distribution. Capitalism meant a handful of people who did little real work reaped the rewards of great wealth, power, and prestige, while those who actually produced society's goods and services were often unable to provide themselves with even basic necessities.

The Wobblies' critique, however, went beyond the socialists' concern for a more equitable distribution of wealth. It was a broader attack on power and privilege as well. Their view, known as syndicalism, held that workers' control was the essential element of socialism, and that the state was as much the enemy as capitalism, for the two were inseparable allies.[2] Most syndicalists would agree with the anarchist Michael Bakunin, who held that the state would always be a tool of oppression, even if it ruled in the name of the workers. Instead of working for a socialist state, the IWW fought for a co-operative commonwealth that would eliminate 'such things as the State or States'. Rather, worker-controlled 'industries will take the place of what are now existing States'. . . .

The IWW played an important part in the BC labour movement. Within six months of its founding convention, the IWW had a local of miners at Phoenix; by the end of 1906, other locals were established in Greenwood, Victoria, Moyie, and Vancouver. By 1907, there were five locals in the Kootenay region, and at least three in Vancouver (*Industrial Union Bulletin* [hereafter *IUB*], 20 April, 10 October 1907; Phillips, 1967: 46; McCormack: 1979: 99). Following Big Bill Haywood's enjoinder that the IWW was 'going down in the gutter to get at the mass of workers and bring them up to a decent plane of living', Wobblies organized miners, loggers, farm workers, longshoremen, and road and railway construction workers. Unlike many AFL unions in BC, the IWW organized among all ethnic groups, including Asians. As one member put it, 'all this anti-Japanese talk comes from the employing class. Which is better: to have the Japanese in the Union with you, or to force him to scab on the outside?' The word 'Wobbly', a nickname for IWW members, humourously illustrates the union's efforts to combat racism. A Chinese restaurant keeper in Vancouver in 1911 supported the union and would extend credit to members. Unable to pronounce the letter 'w', he would ask if a man was in the 'I Wobble Wobble'. Local members jokingly referred to themselves as part of the 'I Wobbly Wobbly', and by the time of the Wheatland strike of 1913, 'Wobbly' had become a permanent moniker for workers who carried the red card. Mortimer Downing, a Wobbly who first explained the etymology, noted that the nickname 'hints of a fine, practical internationalism, a human brotherhood based on a community of interests and of understanding' (*Industrial Worker* [hereafter IW] 8 April 1909).[3]

The IWW actively organized women and did not exclude them from important positions in the union. Women such as Lucy Parsons and Elizabeth Gurley Flynn went on speaking tours of BC; Alice Marling and M. Gleason headed Local 44 in Victoria. Edith Frenette, a friend of Gurley Flynn, was an active organizer throughout the Pacific Northwest who took part in the first important IWW free speech fight, that of Missoula, Montana, in 1909. Some years later, she was a participant in the tragic events in Everett, Washington, where a number of Wobblies were murdered by vigilantes and deputies as they tried to leave a ferry and join a free speech fight. In June 1911, Frenette gave birth to a daughter, Stella Bonnie, in a desolate lumber camp in Holberg, BC, near the northern tip of Vancouver Island. The baby was given a red diaper baptism: at its regular business meeting, Local Union 380 of the IWW issued Stella union card number 11014. In November, Edith was working with her husband and brother-in-law to organize the loggers of Port Alberni. When company thugs and AFL supporters threatened to pull the brother-in-law off the soapbox he used to address a crowd of workers, she

butted in and got on the box myself. This was something they hadn't figured on as they were hardly prepared to beat up a woman. When I got my breath I sailed into them and they quieted like any other whipped cur, only a few snarls being heard from them. I called them a few choice names and appealed to their manhood if they had any.

After she quelled the mob, the camp resolutions and grievances were read out and adopted unanimously by the assembled workers. Frenette's courage and skill could not protect her, however, from personal tragedy. In March 1912, Stella Bonnie died as the result of a fall. The *Industrial Worker* was quick to 'join all other rebels in extending sympathy to our bereaved fellow workers in the hour of their affliction.'[4]

The union was active in the hinterlands of the province. John Riordan, a Canadian delegate to the founding convention, had insisted the union be named the Industrial Workers of the World instead of the proposed Industrial Workers of America. He continued to organize in the Boundary area and served on the General Executive Board of the IWW during its first year. Riordan, along with the secretary-treasurer, William Trautman, was instrumental in opposing the corrupt and conservative administration of the union's first and only president, C.O. Sherman. Sherman and his cronies were draining the union treasury by submitting inflated vouchers for travel expenses. With Trautman organizing for the union, Riordan was left alone to try to stem the flow of money. Outvoted and outmanoeuvred by Sherman and his supporters, 'Honest John' fought back by stamping 'for graft' on all the travel vouchers. Later, he joined with others to throw out Sherman, and ensure that the IWW would remain a revolutionary organization. . . .

Support for the IWW increased when other unions, such as the United Mine Workers of America, turned in more conservative directions. As early as 1907, BC miners organized into the UMWA's District 18 announced they were 'ready to start the propaganda for the IWW'. This agitation culminated in the attempt in 1912 to break away from the United Mine Workers. Led by Wobbly miners, this serious rank and file movement was defeated by an alliance of socialists and UMWA loyalists, but the IWW managed to exact some changes and concessions. In the dramatic coal miners' strikes on Vancouver Island in 1912–14, the Miners' Liberation League was influenced greatly by the IWW, and a Wobbly was elected president of the League in 1913. Wobblies helped guide the strikes, and IWW tactics such as parades and direct action were used, while the union's call for a general strike was greeted enthusiastically. Only the refusal of the Vancouver Trades and Labor Council to support such a strike prevented it from taking place (*IUB*, 23 November 1907; Phillips, 1967: 60; McCormack, 1979: 113–15).

The IWW's drives in the logging industry ran a parallel course to those in mining. By October 1907, Wobblies were active in Cranbrook, and late in 1909, IWW Lumber Workers' Local 45 was established in Vancouver. Its members went throughout the province organizing and working in the camps. Conditions in the lumber industry were uniformly dreadful, and one Wobbly's report described them with anger and humour:

> The Canadian Western Lumber Co., camp 7, Courtenay. The conditions of the camp: the oats are bum; plenty of slave drivers; in fact, the collar of your shirt is worn out in a few days, the stares from the drivers are so piercing. 'Whoop her up boys, or hike.' Bunk house fair. Monthly payment discount on checks; 50 cents for the use of stable for first month; wages from $3 to $6.50. Hospital fee $1.00. This entitles the slaves to the slaughter house and the services of a second-class butcher. For further information, I will refer you to a cock-eyed, caloused-brained stick of bobo, the bull cook second in command. Yours for Industrial Unionism, C. Nelson. (McCormack, 1979: 101)[5]

Wobbly organizing drives went from Port Alberni to the Lower Mainland to the Kootenays.

In Phoenix, John Riordan penned a poem for the timber beasts:

> When you chance to hit a strange burg,
> And you're absolutely broke,
> You're feeling rather hungry
> And there's nothing in your poke;
> You don't look up a preacher,
> And the police you're sure to shun,
> For no matter how you've rustled
> They will spot you for a bum.
>
> Your belt is getting very slack,
> And you're about all in;
> With the togs that you're arrayed in
> Your chance is mighty thin.
> For all to you are strangers,
> And you've travelled from afar,
> So in you drop to interview
> The man behind the bar.
>
> You take a glance around the room,
> Some familiar face to see;
> A gang of husky lumber jacks
> Are out upon a spree.
> They seem to understand your plight
> As you saunter from the street,
> And after asking you to drink,
> They invite you out to eat. . . .
>
> You make great resolutions
> When your labor there begins.
> Never again to taste or handle
> Whiskey, beer or gin.
> But labor all the winter long,
> Until the good old summer-time,
> Then hoist your bundle on your back
> And hike it down the line. (*IW*, 29 December 1910)

The loggers' union was small but militant. In Port Alberni, camp workers led by the Frenettes went on strike in 1911 to protest the trial of the McNamaras, two AFL activists who dynamited a Los Angeles newspaper building that was being built by non-union labour. In Vancouver, the local helped raise money for the New Bedford, Massachusetts textile strike and sent support to the McNamaras, whose case had become a *cause célèbre* for labour and the left (*IW*, 25 June 1910, 6 July, 26 October, 2 November, 1911; Hak, 1986: 172–3).

The local opposed attempts of employers to buy off workers with small reforms, and rejected measures that did not come from the working class. It bitterly denounced a provincial bill that called for health inspections of camps, pointing out that the bill was unopposed by bosses because they knew 'they could get more work out of the men if better sanitary conditions were had. If the master ever discovers that more work can be accomplished with dirt, the same reasoning will apply and a "BILL" will pass allowing lots of dirt.' The writer concluded that the workers should instead fight for the eight-hour day, for then they would have 'lots of time to keep nice and clean'. Similarly, the local railed against a proposal from the Pacific Coast Loggers' Association, an 'industrial union of slave drivers', to establish a government home for retired loggers. The union maintained that the welfare of the loggers should not depend on the state, for if the robbery by the bosses was ended, workers would 'not need to be an object of charity'. Instead, it reasoned, the Industrial Workers of the World would 'put overalls on every capitalist in the country. To hell with their gifts' (*IW*, 2 February, 13 July 1911).

But attempts to organize loggers were largely unsuccessful, as were all attempts, until the International Woodworkers of America, taking advantage of PC 1003, the Canadian government's war-time Order-in-Council which paved the way for large-scale organizing drives by unions, would win out in the 1940s. Accounts of the IWW obtaining the eight-hour day in the woods by simply blowing the whistle and heading back to camp after eight hours may be accurate in the United States, but there is no evidence to suggest that the tactic was used in BC. Organizing was difficult, for bosses could effectively keep agitators out of the camps. Alex Ferguson, Wobbly organizer in the 1920s, recalled that knapsacks and bindles were routinely searched as workers came to camp. Dedicated members often beat the searches, though, by picking up religious pamphlets in the city and hiding the union literature among their pages. Suspicious bosses 'wouldn't mind a religious nut in camp', and once past inspection, the pie in the sky pamphlets could be dumped (Ferguson, 1976). . . .

In cities and towns, where most BC workers lived, the IWW formed mixed locals of general labourers. In Vancouver, the Lumber Handlers' Local 526 and Mixed Local 322 had organized nearly two hundred workers by March 1907. The locals sent telegrams of support during the famous Moyer, Haywood, and Pettibone murder trial in Idaho, and condemned the 'proceeding of the capitalist class as perpetrating a worse condition than exists in barbarous Russia'. In April of the same year, the locals supported a Vancouver strike of AFL painters and carpenters, and resolved that no IWW member would work in the building trades industry. The locals went so far as to expel one member who refused to join the boycott (*IUB*, 23 March, 20, 27 April, 4 May 1907). Later in the year, two Wobbly organizers who would later figure importantly in the union came to Vancouver. Joseph Ettor, who would help organize the famous Lawrence textile strike of 1912, organized an Italian local and applied for a charter for a general teamsters' local. In the fall of 1907,

John H. Walsh helped organize a strike of lumber handlers in Vancouver. Walsh would later lead the famous 'overalls brigade' from Spokane to the 1908 IWW convention in Chicago to help orchestrate the purging of Daniel DeLeon and the political faction from the union. He was also the first to use songs as an organizing tool, and was the pioneer behind the Wobblies' little red song book. The local of lumber handlers was composed of men from eighteen nationalities, and had already won two small strikes, one a protest against the use of deepwater sailors on the docks, the other a fight to increase wages and decrease hours. On 1 October 1907, the local was locked out by stevedores in an attempt to cut wages from 40 cents an hour to 35 and increase the hours of work from nine to 10. The union held out for a month, but when police prevented picketing and helped scabs to cross, the members voted to return to work at 40 cents an hour and a 10-hour day. Though the strike was viewed as a loss, Walsh pointed out proudly that 'all our boys stood steadfast,' and that the decision to return to work and keep the union intact for a winter organizing drive was made by the entire local unanimously (*IUB*, 2, 9 November 1907; 2 May 1908). . . .

In 1910, Vancouver Wobblies helped lead a strike of Italian excavators for an eight-hour day and engineered a short strike of labourers who were constructing the city's race track. The city's Wobblies worked to put the union on a more solid footing by calling for a convention of all Pacific Coast locals. In order to produce and distribute more literature, fund and organize speaking tours, and promote better co-operation and solidarity, they reasoned, a tighter network had to be created. Even with the existing loose ties, the Vancouver locals managed to bring in speakers such as Lucy Parsons, William Haywood, Joe Ettor, and Elizabeth Gurley Flynn. The locals supported the AFL's

general strike in the building trades in 1911, and held meetings and raised money for the effort. Several Wobblies left town rather than add to the growing army of unemployed. One, George Drogowicz, had been a member for only eight days when he rode the rails to the United States. His body was found outside Seattle on 25 June, hit by a train on the North Pacific tracks. Meanwhile, AFL bricklayers refused to join the strike and kept working (*IW*, 21 May, 8, 15, 22, 29 June, 6, 13, 20, 30 July, 15 December 1991).

Victoria was home to a number of IWW locals. Number 44, with Alice Harling as secretary, was established by the summer of 1909. In May 1911, the union filled the Crystal Theatre to its capacity of 580 to call for a general strike to free the McNamaras. In the winter of that year, the IWW joined with the SPC to commemorate the anniversary of the murder of Spanish educator and radical José Ferrer. While the branch remained critical of the SPC and the AFL, it had friendly relations with them and often supported their rallies and strikes. In November 1911, Wobblies marched with AFL members to support union musicians who had been replaced by non-union ones at the Empress Hotel. While pointing out that the chairman of the parade was a union official who was also a 'noted heeler for the Conservative party', the IWW concluded that it was not 'wise to altogether knock on such occasions, but to march and strike with craft unions and endeavor to pave the way for the ONE BIG UNION idea, class organization, and solidarity of the working class' (*IW*, 26 August 1909; 25 May, 7 December 1911).

In April 1912, Victoria's IWW organizers were surprised to find three hundred 'Greeks, Italians, Americans, Canucks, and colored men' show up at the union hall and ask to join up. Employed by the Canadian Mineral Rubber Company to pave the city streets, the men were paid $2.75

a day—25 cents less than the city's minimum scale. A black man was elected chairman of the strike committee, and together with the IWW, the workers put forward a demand for a 25-cent raise, full-time work, and a ban on overtime. The spontaneous uprising was chaotic, for the workers had little idea how to picket. Several were arrested and sentenced to a month in jail; others were beaten. In a show of solidarity, the SPC, the Social Democratic Party, and the Victoria Trades and Labor Council held joint meetings to support and raise money for the IWW strikers. The strike was over by early May, with no reports of victory, but IWW members promised that 'the agitation still goes on' (*IW*, 18 April, 9 May 1912). . . .

The Prince Rupert labourers' local was the most successful. In April 1909, Patrick Daly, a former WFM member, helped organize railway construction workers into an IWW branch, and immediately launched a strike against the Grand Trunk Pacific railway. The strike did little to increase wages or better conditions, but over four hundred men joined the union and the IWW was established as a force to be reckoned with. In June, 123 men walked off a sewer construction site and appealed to the union for help. The contractor was forced out of business, and when the municipality took over the job it was compelled to pay the union rate. The IWW office became the hiring hall for most of Prince Rupert's labourers, and by October IWW longshoremen controlled the local waterfront (*IW*, 15 April, 20 May, 8, 15, 22, 24, 29 June, 6 July, 17 October 1909). In 1911, the local helped establish the Prince Rupert Industrial Association, a broadly-based union of construction workers. The association soon raised the going rate from $3.00 per eight-hour day to $3.60, but some private contractors refused to raise wages. On 1 March, the association voted to strike to win the higher rate for all workers. At first the strike was limited to private contractors, but as scabs were imported from Vancouver, city workers joined in. On 6 April, a parade of several hundred workers marched through Prince Rupert to Kelly's Cut. Special police hired by the contractors shot four of the strikers and ransacked the union hall. More than fifty workers were arrested on charges ranging from unlawful assembly to attempted murder, and craft union workers were hired to build a bull pen to hold the men. Fifteen men were later tried in Victoria: while some were acquitted, one was sentenced to three years, five to two years, three to one year, and one to six months, though all were released in less than a year. The members of the PRIA voted to join the Wobblies *en masse*, and over one thousand men were issued red cards. One union activist wrote 'The Battle of Kelly's Cut' to commemorate the strike:

> Come all you workers if you want to hear,
> I will tell you a story of a great pioneer.
> Prince Rupert is the pioneer's name;
> The way she started she won her fame.
>
> Her streets were of plank, her people of pluck,
> Who had gathered on the townsite
> To try their luck.
>
> The railroad was coming and that we knew.
> Our hopes were many, but our dollars few.
> A port was to open to world wide trade.
> A lot then held was a fortune made.
>
> Some had not lot, and had no coin;
> So a pick and shovel they had to join.
> Wages were small and the rain did pour;
> To feed our families we had to get more.
>
> In a little Church up on the hill,
> A union was formed that is remembered still.

Prince Rupert Industrial Association was the
   union's name:
At the Kelly Cut Battle it won its fame.

Some members were from Sweden and some
   came from Spain.
Others came from Serbia and the State of
   Maine;
Ireland had her quota, England had a few;
Scotland had her number and Italy too.

In that union we had some men,
Who could coin you a nickel from an old hair
   pin.
All went well that day
When from a parade a few did stray
To a Scabby Spot along the way.

Within a minute a battle did start
And as a union, all took part.
Some threw rocks, others had a gun;
Believe me or not, it was no fun.

All nations were at war; police came running
And arrested quite a few.
A bullpen was built; our boys placed inside.
A court then was held and many took a ride.
To the pen they were sentenced—up to seven
   years;
If you had a heart it would drive you to tears.

The result of that battle never will die,
In the hearts of Oldtimers it still does lie.
A wage scale was established and there did
   remain,
Until the workers moved and revised it again.
A boycott was established and soon put on
   the bum
Was the man who had the store and was
   handy with the gun.

So Boys, keep up your courage,
Though it is no fun;
You will never win the battle
If you turn and run. (*IW*, 6, 20, 27 April, 25
   May, 29 June 1911)

But the IWW's greatest successes were among the
upwards of 8,000 railway navvies who worked on
the Canadian Northern and Grand Trunk Pacific
lines and electrified the province with their strike.
The drives to organize the construction workers
meant that the Wobblies were able to move from
the periphery to the very heart of the province's
economy. Organizers were active on the western
end of the GTP in 1909, and reports came in from
other areas in the province. . . .

Organizing began in earnest in the summer of
1911. By August, Carl Berglund had put together a
'propaganda club' of 800 men at Spence's Bridge
on the CN line and reported that the men were waiting
for an IWW organizer so a union local could be
formally established. Organizers were busy at
Lytton, a few miles south, as well. J.S. Biscay was
sent from Vancouver to bring in the workers to the
IWW, and signed up over six hundred in his first
few weeks on the job. The organizer was excited by
the progress, and wrote that the 'bunch here are so
enthusiastic that they won't stand for a non-union
man around the camps. . . . I never saw a finer
example of solidarity than has been manifest here.
The boys simply won't stand for any foolishness.'
By October, Biscay had lined up over 1500 in the
union, and plans were made to build a headquarters in Lytton. Despite initial interference from the
police, regular meetings were held in the town and
the agitation continued (*IW*, 17, 31 August, 14, 25
September 1911).

Contractors were first skeptical about the
prospects for the union's success. But the efforts
of Biscay and others soon started them into

action. On 22 September, at a camp fifteen miles from Savona, police and company thugs beat and kidnapped Biscay. When his valise was later searched, a gun was found, and the Wobbly was charged with 'being a dangerous character and a menace to public safety'. Held in the Kamloops jail for over a month, Biscay was finally found not guilty by a jury and released. By this time, the union had grown to over 3,000 members (*IW*, 5, 12, 19 October, 2 November 1911).

The Wobbly penchant for poetry continued during the drive. An allegory entitled 'It Pays to Kick' was written by 'A Jobite on the Canadian Northern':

There lived two frogs, so I am told,
In a quiet wayside pool;
One of those frogs was a darn big frog;
The other frog was a fool.

Now a farmer man with a big milk can,
Was wont to pass that way;
And he used to stop and add a drop
Of the Agua, so they say.

It happened one morn in the early dawn,
When the farmer's sight was dim,
He scooped those frogs in the water he
    dipped,
Which same was a joke on him.

The fool frog sank in the swishing tank,
As the farmer bumped to town.
But the smart frog flew like a tugboat screw,
And swore he'd never go down.

So he kicked and splashed and spluttered and
    thrashed,
He kept on top through all.
And he churned that milk in first class shape,
Into a nice large butter ball.

Now when the farmer got into town
And opened the can, there lay
The fool frog drowned.
But hale and sound, the KICKER; he flopped
    away.

Moral:
Don't waste your life in endless strife,
But let this teaching stick.
You'll find, old man, in the world's big can
It sometimes pays to KICK. (*IW*, 4 January
    1912)

On 27 March 1912, the workers on the CN line did kick. IWW members at Nelson and Benson's camp number four, a few miles from Lytton, walked out to protest wages and sanitary conditions. A meeting was held in the town to draw up a list of demands and elect strike committees. Soon over 4,000 men from Hope and Kamloops were out on strike. The men built their own camps, started commissaries, and set up 'courts' to police the camps. Infractions of the rules were punished by sentences such as 'go and cut ten big armsful of firewood,' 'carry ten coal-oil cans full of water for the camp cooks,' or 'help the cooks for one day.' The men were restricted to two drinks of liquor a day, and local saloon keepers were warned that all liquor would be thrown out if the rule was broken. One newspaper reporter observed that the 'strike seems to have acted like a wave of reform,' and that the Yale camp resembled a 'miniature republic run on Socialistic lines, and it must be admitted that so far it has been run successfully' (*IW*, 4, 11 April 1912; *Vancouver Province*, 3 April 1912).

In May, the VTLC received an appeal for help from the workers, but before sending aid, the council had a member investigate the conditions. He reported that they were as bad as the Wobblies had alleged:

The men live in shacks without floor or windows. . . . Owing to the overcrowding and lack of ventilation, the air became so foul nights that it was not an uncommon occurrence for the men to arise in the morning too sick to work. . . . [I]n one camp, a toilet was placed so that the refuse was discharged in the river immediately upstream from the place where water was drawn for cooking purposes.

The report encouraged the VTLC to give some financial support to the strikers, and the council issued a call to its affiliates for money. In June, its paper, the *BC Federationist*, became the official strike bulletin for the tie-up (*IW*, 11 April 1912; *BC Federationist*, 22 June 1912; Phillips, 1967).

In the camps, the strike committees arranged talks on industrial unionism 'and other working class matters, not only from the view point of the immediate strike, but also as to the future' (*IW*, 18 April 1912). Joe Hill, the famous IWW songwriter and martyr, arrived in Yale ten days after the strike broke out and wrote several songs. The only one which has survived intact is 'Where the Fraser River Flows,' written to the tune of 'Where the River Shannon Flows':

> Fellow workers, pay attention to what I'm going to mention,
> For it is the fixed intention of the Workers of the World,
> And I hope you'll all be ready, true-hearted, brave and steady,
> To gather round our standard when the Red Flag is unfurled.

Chorus:
> Where the Fraser River flows, each fellow worker knows

> They have bullied and oppressed us, but still our union grows;
> And we're going to find a way boys, for shorter hours and better pay, boys,
> We're going to win the day boys, where the Fraser River flows.

> Now these gunny sack contractors have all been dirty actors;
> They're not our benefactors, each fellow workers knows.
> So we've got to stick together in fine or dirty weather,
> And we will show no white feather where the Fraser River flows.

> Now the boss the law is stretching, bulls and pimps he's fetching,
> And they are a fine collection, as Jesus only knows.
> But why their mother reared them, and why the devil spared them,
> Are questions we can't answer where the Fraser River flows. (*IW*, 9 May 1912; Smith [1969] 1984: 24–6)[6]

Louis Moreau, who had been a camp delegate during the strike, later remembered the effect the songs had:

> The Wobblies drove those contractors nuts. One day Martin [a contractor] came by our camp at Yale annex and started to talk to a bunch of Swedes that were sitting alongside of the road. When the groaning brigade, our singing sextet, started to sing the song Joe had made for him, Martin tore his hair and swore he'd get us. (Smith [1969] 1984: 24–6)

The IWW made Martin and other contractors do more than just pull their hair. By 2 April, they had met with Premier Richard McBride and asked for militia troops to end the strike; while the premier demurred on the question of military aid, he did dispatch special constables and allowed the companies to swear in and arm foremen as constables. The men were sent on the pretext that order needed to be restored, in spite of police reports that the level of violence and disorderly conduct had actually gone down during the strike. Provincial health inspectors were sent to close the workers' camps, even though they were cleaner than the CN camps. Strikers were harassed by police and company thugs: one man was shot in the leg by a company constable, while another was run down by a train.

During the third week of April, the police intensified their campaign against the strike. The men were ordered to return to work, and when they refused, armed constables entered the camps and ousted them at gunpoint. Several camps were destroyed and sweeping arrests were made. By June, nearly 300 men were imprisoned on charges ranging from vagrancy to inciting to murder, and many more were driven from the area. Immigration authorities kept IWW men from entering the area, but they eased restrictions for men willing to scab. Donald Mann, one of the magnates of the CN, used his influence to change immigration regulations to facilitate the importation of navvies from the United States, and it became more difficult to keep scabs out. The Wobblies' '1,000 mile picket line', which had union members picketing employment offices in Vancouver, Seattle, Tacoma, Minneapolis, and San Francisco to curtail the hiring of scabs, began to falter. An IWW request for arbitration under the Industrial Disputes Investigation Act was refused by the federal government and the railways, thus supporting the Wobbly contention that the state was not a friend to labour (*Vancouver Sun*, 16, 17 April 1912; *IW*, 25 April, 1 May, 1912; *Solidarity*, 4 May 1912).[7]

On 20 July, workers on the Grand Trunk Pacific line from Prince Rupert to Edmonton struck for demands similar to those of the CN workers. The strike bulletin published a grim joke that reflected the conditions:

> Undertaker: I've advertised for an assistant. Have you any experience at funerals?
> Applicant: I should say so! I was doctor in a railroad construction camp for three years. (*IW*, 25 July, 5 September 1912)

Though both strikes continued into the winter, work had resumed on the CN line by July and the GTP line by September. The CN strike was never officially called off, but in January 1913, the Prince Rupert local declared the GTP strike over. The local noted that the strikers had forced the federal government to promise to enforce sanitary regulations and that the strike 'really gained more than the strikers had hoped for' (*IW*, 23 January 1913; Phillips, 1967: 54; McCormack, 1979: 109).

Organizers continued their work on the railways. In February 1913, several men struck the Kettle Valley line near Naramata in a short-lived attempt to improve conditions. Workers struck again in April, and in May 400 navvies went out. But it was too difficult to feed and house the men, and the strike was called off a week later, though some concessions were granted (*IW*, 6 March, 24 April, 8 May 1913).

Railway contractors had learned from the earlier strikes and organizers found it increasingly difficult to agitate. Wobblies were run out of town, arrested, and beaten. Joseph Ettor was deported, and other IWW men were driven out of camps. One writer described the lengths to which contractors would go:

> To show how scared the thieving railroad contractors are, we mention the fact that a

crippled man, who was unable to work, went up to Tuohey's camp on the North Thompson to beg a few dimes and was run out of the place because the gunnysackers thought he was an IWW organizer in disguise. Just wait until we really get into action! (*IW*, 6, 13, 27 March, 3, April, 15 May 1913; *Solidarity*, 15 March 1913, 10 January 1914)

Despite this bold challenge, the IWW was unable to repeat the success of 1912. Indeed, the railway strikes remained the high-water mark of the union's activities in BC. Continued employer hostility, wartime repression, and the end of the railway boom all played a part in the decline of IWW, as they did in the decline of all left-wing groups at the time. . . .

Notes

1. See also *The Founding Convention of the Industrial Workers of the World, Proceedings.* 1905. Reprint. (New York: Merit Publishers, 1969), 1; Ray Ginger, *The Bending Cross: A Biography of Eugene V. Debs* (New Brunswick: Rutgers University Press, 1949), 238.

2. Larry Peterson, 'The One Big Union in International Perspective: Revolutionary Industrial Unionism, 1900–1925', *Labour/Le Travailleur* 7 (Spring 1981): 41–66, gives a helpful definition of syndicalism. Briefly, its tenets are an emphasis on decentralization; opposition to political parties and parliamentary politics; advocacy of the general strike as the means to the revolution; a vision of a new society as a federation of economic organizations based on the structure of craft and industry. See Dubofsky, 166–70, for a similar appraisal. See also Philip Foner, *The History of the Labor Movement in the United States*, volume 4, *The Industrial Workers of the World, 1905–1917* (New York: International Publishers, 1965), 20–3.

3. For the etymology of the word 'Wobbly', see *The Nation*, 5 September 1923, p. 242. Stewart Holbrook, in *American Mercury*, volume 7, January 1926, p. 62, claims the term was similarly coined in Saskatchewan in 1914 during the construction of the CNR. H.L. Mencken, in *The American Language*, suggests that this etymology is 'unlikely', but offers no other. In fact, no other explanation has ever been accepted. Fred Thompson, in the official IWW history, Frederick W. Thompson and Patrick Murfin, *The IWW: Its First Seventy Years, 1905–1975* (Chicago: Industrial Workers of the World, 1976), p. 67, suggests that the term may have come from the 'wobble saw', a circular saw mounted askew so that it cut a groove wider than the thickness of the blade—an interesting metaphor for the union.

   In a letter to the author, dated 31 January 1989, Craig M. Carver, managing editor of the *Dictionary of American Regional English*, states that the Chinese restaurateur version is not given 'much credence. . . because the story is simply unverifiable'. Those with a scientific bent must conclude that the etymology is unknown. . . .

4. See Star Rosenthal, 'Union Maids: Organized Women Workers in Vancouver, 1900–1915', *BC Studies* 41 (Spring 1979): 36–55, for the attitude of the IWW to women. Details on Edith Frenette may be found in Elizabeth Gurley Flynn, *The Rebel Girl: An Autobiography—My First Life (1906–26)* (New York: International Publishers, 1971), 104, 108, 221; and in Foner, *History of the Labor Movement*, volume 4, 525–29. The story of Stella Frenette and the organizing in Port Alberni is in *IW*, 3 August 1911, 2 November 1911, 18 April 1912. The names of women who headed to the Victoria local are in *IW* 16 August 1909 and 29 December 1910; I could find no other details about them.

5. See also *IUB*, 12 October 1907; *IW*, 30 April, 2 November 1910.

6. The *IW* of 9 September 1909 defined a 'gunnysack contractor' as 'an exploiter of the proletariat having very little capital'. In this case, it was a reference to the stationmen who often made little more than the navvies did.

7. See also *IW*, 9 May, 16 May, 23 May, 30 May 1912; Thompson and Murfin, *IWW: Its First Seventy Years*, 65–6; Donald Avery, *'Dangerous Foreigners': European Immigrant Workers and Labour Radicalism in Canada, 1896–1932* (Toronto: McClelland and Stewart, 1980), 55.

References

BC Federationist. 1912. 22 June.

Brissenden. [1919] 1957. *The IWW: A Study of American Syndicalism*. New York: Russell and Russell Inc.

Dubofsky, Melvyn. 1969. *We Shall Be All: A History of the Industrial Workers of the World*. New York: Quadrangle/The New York Times Book Company.

Ferguson, Alex. 1976. Interview with author.

Hak, Gordon. 1986. 'On the Fringes: Capital and Labour in the Forest Economies of the Port Alberni and Prince George Districts, British Columbia, 1910–1939'. PhD dissertation, Simon Fraser University.

Haywood, William D. [1929] 1977. *Bill Haywood's Book: The Autobiography of William D. Haywood*. New York: International Publishers.

Industrial Union Bulletin. 1907. 23 March
Industrial Union Bulletin. 1907. 20 April.
Industrial Union Bulletin. 1907. 27 April.
Industrial Union Bulletin. 1907. 4 May.
Industrial Union Bulletin. 1907. 10 August.
Industrial Union Bulletin. 1907. 10 October.
Industrial Union Bulletin. 1907. 12 October.
Industrial Union Bulletin. 1907. 2 November
Industrial Union Bulletin. 1907. 9 November.
Industrial Union Bulletin. 1907. 23 November.
Industrial Union Bulletin. 1908. 2 May.
Industrial Worker. 1909. 15 April.
Industrial Worker. 1909. 20 May.
Industrial Worker. 1909. 8 June.
Industrial Worker. 1909. 15 June.
Industrial Worker. 1909. 22 June.
Industrial Worker. 1909. 24 June.
Industrial Worker. 1909. 29 June.
Industrial Worker. 1909. 6 July.
Industrial Worker. 1909. 26 August.
Industrial Worker. 1909. 26 August.
Industrial Worker. 1909. 17 October.
Industrial Worker. 1910. 30 April.
Industrial Worker. 1910. 21 May.
Industrial Worker. 1910. 25 June.
Industrial Worker. 1910. 30 July.
Industrial Worker. 1910. 2 November.
Industrial Worker. 1910. 15 December.
Industrial Worker. 1910. 29 December.
Industrial Worker. 1911. 2 February
Industrial Worker. 1911. 6 April.
Industrial Worker. 1911. 20 April.
Industrial Worker. 1911. 27 April.
Industrial Worker. 1911. 25 May.
Industrial Worker. 1911. 8 June.
Industrial Worker. 1911. 15 June.

Industrial Worker. 1911. 22 June.
Industrial Worker. 1911. 29 June.
Industrial Worker. 1911. 6 July.
Industrial Worker. 1911. 13 July.
Industrial Worker. 1911. 20 July.
Industrial Worker. 1911. 17 August.
Industrial Worker. 1911. 31 August.
Industrial Worker. 1911. 14 September.
Industrial Worker. 1911. 28 September.
Industrial Worker. 1911. 5 October.
Industrial Worker. 1911. 12 October.
Industrial Worker. 1911. 19 October.
Industrial Worker. 1911. 26 October
Industrial Worker. 1911. 2 November.
Industrial Worker. 1911. 7 December.
Industrial Worker. 1912. 4 January.
Industrial Worker. 1912. 4 April.
Industrial Worker. 1912. 11 April.
Industrial Worker. 1912. 18 April.
Industrial Worker. 1912. 25 April.
Industrial Worker. 1912. 1 May.
Industrial Worker. 1912. 9 May.
Industrial Worker. 1912. 16 May.
Industrial Worker. 1912. 23 May.
Industrial Worker. 1912. 30 May.
Industrial Worker. 1912. 25 July.
Industrial Worker. 1912. 5 September.
Industrial Worker. 1913. 23 January.
Industrial Worker. 1913. 6 March.
Industrial Worker. 1913. 13 March.
Industrial Worker. 1913. 27 March.
Industrial Worker. 1913. 3 April.
Industrial Worker. 1913. 24 April.
Industrial Worker. 1913. 8 May.
Industrial Worker. 1913. 15 May.

McCormack, Ross. [1977] 1979. *Reformers, Rebels, and Revolutionaries: The Western Canadian Radical Movement, 1899–1919*. Toronto: University of Toronto Press.

Phillips, Paul. 1967. *No Power Greater: A Century of Labour in B.C.* Vancouver: Federation of Labour and the Boag Foundation.

Smith, Gibbs M. [1969] 1984. *Joe Hill*. Salt Lake City: Peregrine Smith Books.

Solidarity. 1912. 4 May.
Solidarity. 1913. 15 March.
Solidarity. 1914. 10 January.
Vancouver Province. 1912. 2 April.
Vancouver Province. 1912. 3 April.
Vancouver Sun. 1912. 3 April.
Vancouver Sun. 1912. 16 April.
Vancouver Sun. 1912. 17 April.

CHAPTER 9
The Workers' Revolt, 1917–1925
Craig Heron

. . . In the four years after 1916, workers in Canada developed a remarkably assertive sense of purpose and power—their society could be different and their actions could transform it. The war launched Canadian workers on a trajectory of escalating demands and expectations. By the mid-1920s, however, labour's upsurge had been snuffed out across the country. The rise and fall of the workers' revolt followed a distinctive rhythm in each region, but there were key features that emerged in all major industrial centres. . . .

The Worker's Challenge, 1917–1920

The most visible manifestation of the emerging workers' revolt was the wave of strikes that began after 1916—a clear indication that the more individualistic drifting and shifting of the preceding two years was moving towards more collective responses and longer-range concerns about post-war society. As the research of Douglas Cruikshank and Gregory Kealey (1987; Kealey, 1989) indicates,[1] the 218 strikes recorded for 1917 involved more than 50,000 workers, twice the previous year's total and far more than in any single year since the turn of the century. . . . The annual total of strikers had doubled by 1919, when nearly 150,000 workers marched out in 427 strikes. In 1920 the number of strikes peaked at 457, though the number of strikers dropped by half. Over the four-year period 350,000 wage earners participated in strikes in Canada, distributed remarkably evenly across the country. . . .

Workers were not simply striking; they were also rapidly banding together into unions. . . . At the end of 1915 union membership reported to the federal Department of Labour bottomed out at just over 140,000, and during the next year rose to only 160,000, still below the totals for 1913 and 1914. By the end of 1917, however, it was just shy of 205,000 and then leaped to almost 250,000 in 1918. Yet the most spectacular increase was recorded in 1919, when total reported union membership in Canada reached 378,000, the highest to that point in Canadian history (Canada, Department of Labour, 1917–20).[2] . . . A reasonable estimate is that at least one worker in five took out a union card. Probably well more than one in four passed through a union in these years, a level comparable to that of the mid-1940s. . . . Workers were not simply trying to win immediate demands; they were turning to unions to solidify wartime gains and to prevent a return to the insecurity and indignity of the pre-war era. 'If we don't do something we will get our heads taken off after this great war is over,' a Gananoque unionist warned (Heron and De Zwaan, 1985).

Initially, the growth in union membership primarily revived pre-war patterns of organization. The first to put their unions back on their feet were craft unionists, especially the metalworkers in munitions plants and shipbuilding yards, and coal miners in the East and West (Canada, Department of Labour, 1916–20; Siemiatycki, 1978; Frank, 1979; Seager, 1981). Union locals then began to appear among the less skilled workers who also had a record of organizing—street railwaymen, teamsters, longshoremen, and the like. By 1918, however, workers who had never before shown much interest in unions were signing up. Among the new union members were factory workers in resource processing plants in British Columbia and mass-production plants in southern Ontario, Quebec, and Nova Scotia; loggers in the West and northern Ontario; unskilled workers of various kinds; clerical workers in several cities; and public-sector workers at all three levels of government, including municipal labourers, policemen (in ten cities), firemen, teachers, and letter carriers (Montague, 1950; Schonning, 1955; Scott, 1977; Thomson, 1977; McLean, 1979; Kealey, 1984; Siemiatycki, 1986; Radforth, 1987; Heron, 1988; Marquis, 1898, 1990; Hak, 1989; Naylor, 1991; Doherty, 1991). In fact, public-sector strikes were often the most controversial and menacing to dominant social relations (Kealey, 1989). Wage earners in all parts of the country, in large cities and small towns, were entering the house of labour. Women were found in growing numbers among the unionized and even on union executives, although in a role subordinate to that of men (Campbell, 1980; Frager, 1983; Bernard, 1984; Horodyski, 1986; Kealey, 1989, 1991; Roome, 1989). There was also more ethnic diversity in many of these unions, especially those in the mass-production and resource industries, from Sydney steel mills to Thetford asbestos mines to Toronto meat-packing factories to Trail smelters. A number of unions were organized primarily along ethnic or racial lines—for example, the Chinese Shingle Weavers' Union and Japanese Camp and Mill Workers' Union in British Columbia, the Finnish loggers in northern Ontario, the Jewish clothing workers in Montreal and Toronto, the black sleeping-car porters on the CPR, and the Italian construction labourers in several cities (Avery, 1979; Rouillard,

1981–2; Martynowych and Kazymyia, 1982; Wickberg, 1982; Calliste, 1987; Radforth, 1987; Creese, 1988; Frager, 1992). Some of these workers were inspired by the Russian Revolution; many more rode a wave of ethnic self-consciousness and assertiveness as political change convulsed their homelands (Radeki, 1976; Harney, 1978: 20–2; Montgomery, 1984; Burnet, 1988; Zucchi, 1988). Whatever their inspirations, all these workers were eager to confront the oppression and exploitation they experienced as wage earners in Canada.

. . . 'At the foundation of all this agitation is the general restlessness and dissatisfaction,' the national government's security chief warned. 'The greater number of labour men, and probably the community as a whole, are in an uncertain, apprehensive, nervous and irritable temper. Perhaps these agitators are but the foam on the wave' (Kealey, 1984: 39). Montreal machinist J.O. Houston captured both the spirit and trajectory of working-class mobilization: 'More and more each worker is doing his own thinking, is becoming his own intellectual, and to the extent that this is so he is placing less and less trust in labour leaders. He is looking for neither a Moses nor a Saviour. All the Sammy Gompers are doomed. His new representative will be an instrument to perform a specific act decided upon by the rank and file of an industrial organization' (International Association of Machinists, 1918).

Rank-and-file activism and solidarity soon forged a qualitatively different labour movement. More than ever before, divisions between workers seemed to be giving way to a remarkable spirit of working-class unity and class consciousness. . . . Organizational structures became more flexible in devising imaginative experiments readily adapted to immediate needs and conditions. In addition to less exclusivist craft unionism and more widespread industrial unionism, there was an innovative, all-inclusive 'community unionism' that touched many centres with weak or non-existent union traditions, and in some cases, a small, diverse local workforce close to primary production. Across the country the objective was the same: to mobilize greater numbers in common cause. Before the middle of 1919, the great majority of these new unions were affiliated with international organizations headquartered in the United States. At the same time, Canadian branches everywhere found new ways to work together with other union locals while maintaining considerable independence from their American parents. District councils linked up locals of some of the larger unions, and many locals federated across occupational lines into more cooperative local, district, and provincial bodies. For the most part, it was the local trades and labour council or district miners' organization that played the active coordinating role of drawing together and speaking for the local wage-earning population. In many cities trades councils sponsored, directly or indirectly, local labour newspapers that were produced independently of the international union publications, and that grew in number from four in 1914 to 17 by 1919 and became important forums of information on local issues, international labour news, and debate about evolving strategies.[3] Some radicals even began to envisage the trades councils as the new base of the labour movement.[4] Whatever their political cast, the councils reflected the decentralized, community-based focus of most of the workers' movements in these years.

The new spirit of solidarity and working-class consciousness was evident in action as well as organization. The best-known example, the general sympathy strike, was widely discussed and began to appear in many parts of the country in 1918. It had mass popular support when it got its first major tests in Winnipeg and Amherst, Nova Scotia, in May 1919. As sympathy strikes spread

across the West in response to the repression of the Winnipeg strikers, the radical leadership could do no more than place itself at the head of a burst of solidarity and militancy that was largely beyond its control (Friesen, 1976; McCormack, 1977: 145–6; Reilly, 1980; Siemiatycki, 1986; Bercuson, 1990).

In this context of militancy and confrontation, the thousands of new unionists quickly grew impatient with some of their more cautious leaders.[5] Although most of the existing labour leaders held on to their old power bases, they had to face an emergent cadre of feistier, more radical leaders in the new union locals: Pictou County's Clifford Dane, Cape Breton's J.B. McLachlan, Montreal's Tom Cassidy, Gananoque's Gordon Bishop, Toronto's Jack MacDonald, Hamilton's Fred Flatman, Winnipeg's R.B. Russell, Regina's Joseph Sambrook, Calgary's R.J. Tallon, Edmonton's Joe Knight, the Crows Nest Pass's Phillip Christophers, and Vancouver's Jack Kavanagh (Bercuson, 1978; Frank, 1979; Angus, 1981; Heron, 1981; Heron and De Zwaan, 1985; Heron, 1987; Akers, 1992). Among the best-known female militants were Helena Gutteridge in Vancouver, Amelia Turner in Calgary, Sarah Johnston-Knight in Edmonton, Helen Armstrong in Winnipeg, Mary McNab in Hamilton, and Rose Henderson in Montreal (Wade, 1980; Heron, 1981; Horodyski, 1986; Kealey, 1989; Roome, 1989). . . . Many were local socialists who after years of conflict with the existing labour leadership had found a receptive ear among the increasingly militant workers. They were more popular partly because, as socialists, they had reassessed their long-standing reservations about industrial action and were undertaking, among themselves, an ideological renewal that reflected lessons learned from the massive militancy of Canadian workers in the period (Friesen, 1976; Angus, 1981; Peterson, 1984). . . .

The workers' movements that took shape in the 1917–20 period were rooted first and foremost in industrial action. They followed in the long Anglo-American tradition of struggling for their goals primarily (though not exclusively) in the workplace, as opposed to the European tradition of forging a broader assault on an illiberal, authoritarian state through some kind of socialist party. It was powerful unions and tough bargaining with employers that held out the most promise for shoring up the male breadwinner's family wage and guaranteeing his dignity and relative independence in the workplace. Many radicals in this period put special emphasis on organizing the working class for confrontations at the point of production. Yet, apart front some voices in the West Coast logging camps (Hak, 1989), few were espousing genuine 'syndicalism'—that European brand of radicalism that rejected radical social change through electoral politics in favour of the revolutionary potential of direct action on the picket line. . . .

In a period of great experimentation and fluidity of working-class organization, the precise form of independent working-class politics could have been an open question. . . . But . . . Anglophone and Francophone labour leaders of all stripes were thoroughly constitutionalist in their political orientation, and the vehicle chosen in working-class communities across the country was the independent labour party. Well before the Trades and Labor Congress of Canada put out its call for a Canadian Labor Party in the fall of 1917, many union leaders had taken the initiative in organizing such a party in their own communities. These local labour parties, which always remained completely separate from their union structures, soon began to federate into loosely structured provincial political organizations, though never into an official national labour party. . . .

The local labour parties became remarkably lively, relatively non-sectarian forums for discussion and debate about pressing concerns in working-class life and the most appropriate strategies for

organizing. Until the middle of 1919 a rare ideological openness, fluidity, and tolerance prevailed among the labourists, single-taxers, socialists, and sundry freethinkers who joined the parties. Each local branch tended to have a slightly different ideological emphasis that fell somewhere between the old pre-war working-class liberalism known as 'labourism' and unadulterated Marxist socialism.[6] Generally, these organizations had shifted considerably further to the left than their pre-war counterparts—a shift owing largely to the presence of committed socialists or a regular dialogue with members of the main socialist parties (especially the Social Democrats, who had now carved out a primarily educational role for themselves within the political wing of the workers' movements). Across the country the labourist–socialist alliance expressed itself through more visionary rhetoric and more ambitious programs aimed at, in the words of the Cape Breton ILP, 'the working class ownership and democratic management of all the social means of wealth distribution at the earliest possible date', or, at least, in the words of the Ontario and Quebec labour parties, 'the industrial freedom of those who toil and the political liberation of those who for so long have been denied justice' (qtd in Frank, 1979: 304–5).

. . . For some, these demands were part of a revolutionary project that would sweep away capitalist society and replace it with a democratically managed workers' republic; for others, they were the harbingers of social reforms that would democratize government and soften the impact of market forces. But the distinction between reform and revolution was frequently blurred in the millennial rhetoric of the period (how many hopes and dreams were hung on, for example, the oft-repeated slogans 'production for use' and 'New Democracy'?). Political distinctions were also blurred by the commitment of virtually all political factions to orderly social change through some combination of mass industrial action and parliamentarism.

At all points along the political continuum, the new vision was about workers' power. It was a revolt against the kind of subordination that workers had hitherto known in Canadian capitalist society, against the elitist, authoritarian, and paternalistic ways in which business and the state had grown accustomed to ruling in Canada. It was an affirmation of working-class pride in their role as producers and a deep sense of natural justice captured in the constitutional preamble of Toronto's Domestic Workers' Association (chartered as Local 599 of the Hotel and Restaurant Employees International Alliance), which proclaimed its belief in 'the natural right of those who toil to enjoy to the fullest extent the wealth created by their labor, realizing that under the changing conditions of our times it is impossible for us to obtain the full reward of our labor except by united action' (*Globe*, 20 March 1919). . . . Fundamentally, the workers' revolt was a movement rooted in notions of rank-and-file mobilization, autonomy, and democracy. In place of the traditional authority of bosses, politicians, and even union officials, working-class organization and action would be the surest safeguard of Canadian labour's interests.

In large part what was at stake was the contested meaning of democratic citizenship as workers strove to articulate their own sense of citizenship and nationhood within the British political and cultural heritage. As they invoked the traditions of British rights and justice, for which they believed the war had been fought and the peace treaty signed, they could more easily make common cause with returned soldiers and challenge both the undemocratic examples of 'Kaiserism' and the post-war capitalist efforts to define citizenship more narrowly as a matter of 'loyalism'. 'We, brought up under British laws, thought that the fight for political freedom had been fought and won . . . [but] the fight is on!' the *Western Labor News* announced in the midst of the Winnipeg General Strike. For these workers, democratic citizenship brought broad entitlements within the body politic. The Union Jack itself became a contested symbol. For Peterborough's Labour Day parade in 1919, the moulders decorated their float with 'a bull dog in a setting of Union Jacks' and a sign announcing, 'What We Have We'll Hold' (Naylor, 1991; Reimer, 1993: 231).

At the same time, the 'industrial democracy' so often demanded would mean much more working-class power on the job. Organized wage earners used their unions to confront their employers with demands not only for immediate changes in the terms of their employment (especially higher wages) but also for a formalization of the union-management relationship that would give them greater decision-making authority in the workplace.[7] A huge proportion of the strikes in the period that did not formally include the demand for union recognition resulted from employers' refusal to deal with union leaders and the demands they carried from their members. By the end of the war many union leaders, confident of workers' labour-market leverage, were turning to the state for support. . . . Union requests for boards of conciliation poured into the federal Department of Labour, as did demands for royal commissions to investigate various industries (Selekman, 1927: 168–78).[8] . . . Workers and their employers on the railways, in urban construction and printing, in Nova Scotia and Alberta coal mining, and in the Toronto and Montreal clothing industries devised more elaborate agreements, with signed contracts and grievance and arbitration structures (Brecher, 1958; Peitchinis, 1971; Seager, 1981; Zerker, 1982; McKay, 1983, 1985; Naylor, 1991). 'Industrial legality' became one concrete mechanism sought by many local union leaders in their campaign for 'industrial democracy'.

Determining the most appropriate negotiating structures provoked considerable debate and ideological disagreement. Many union leaders, including the Trades and Labor Congress executive, supported the single-enterprise industrial councils proposed by the British government's Whitley Committee—a model involving equal numbers of management and union representatives. This notion of collective bargaining was challenged on two fronts. Employers preferred the so-called Colorado Plan (developed for the Rockefellers by William Lyon Mackenzie King) because it involved no unions from outside the enterprise (McGregor, 1962; Scott, 1976; Levant, 1977; Naylor, 1991). Radicals, for their part advocated a soviet-style council, described by a Victoria printer as an agreement in which 'the employer does not appear, he is pitched overboard, and the people themselves take control of the industry' (Royal Commission on Industrial Relations, 1919). Cape Breton's workers had some of the country's most elaborate plans for workers' self-management presented to them in their local labour paper in the early 1920s (Frank, 1986). Visions of some kind of workers' control of production began to assume a mass resonance. . . . The mass general strike and the increasing interest in strikes as political weapons set this working-class upsurge dramatically apart from most of its predecessors in Canada.

The single demand that probably rolled up most of the aspirations of the workers' movements in this period was for a shorter workday. In 1919 a quarter of strikes incorporated this issue, far more than ever before or since (Kealey, 1989: 40). The One Big Union was prepared to launch a general strike across the West over the issue (Bercuson, 1978: 85). . . . Most often the demand was for an eight-hour day, though the western labour movement and radicals elsewhere in the country wanted only six hours. The demand for a shorter workday served many functions: it encapsulated the desire for greater independence from the rigours of intensified work in mines and mills of Canadian industry; it held out the promise of minimizing unemployment by spreading around available work; it raised the possibility of a fuller social, recreational, and political life for wage earners, a prospect first introduced in the shorter-hours campaigns of the 1870s and 1880s; and it could touch a responsive chord among middle-class sympathizers. By 1919 several groups of workers had convinced their employers to shorten their hours of work, though no legislature would yet touch the issue.[9]

. . . The democratizing vision behind all these demands nonetheless incorporated important distinctions within the working class itself. This imaginative vision was conceived primarily by white, English-speaking men (especially married men) whose manhood was deeply enmeshed in their status as breadwinners for their families. Throughout the language of the workers' revolt their notion of entitlement assumed male dominance of public life and the dependence of women and children on their men. Most working-class leaders continued to believe that the best place for women was tending the home fires while their menfolk earned the family's wages. Yet these same leaders gave more help to women who wanted to unionize than had ever been extended before, allowed a few into leadership roles, and welcomed small bands of committed working-class housewives into a special supportive relationship within the workers' movements with their own Women's Labor Leagues and Women's Independent Labor Parties. Female activists used this separate space provided for them, along with the greater public receptiveness to gender equality that had flowed from the granting of voting rights to women during the war, to push for a wider social and political role—one that recognized their participation in both the men's world of production and the domestic realm of reproduction. The main thrust of their activities nonetheless remained a working-class variant of what has become known as 'maternal feminism', in this case a central concern with family and community needs (Campbell, 1980; Lindstrom-Best and Seager, 1985; Kealey, 1989; Lindstrom-Best, 1988, 1989; Roome, 1989; Parr, 1990; Naylor, 1991; Penfold, 1994). Similarly, labour leaders carried an image of the typical worker as not only male but also white and English-speaking. Yet while they still suspected the European newcomers as a potential threat to their 'skilled' status in the workplace and to their expectations of a 'British' standard of living, they willingly gave them union membership cards (Scott, 1977; Seager, 1986; Heron, 1988). Distinctions and prejudices did not disappear during the workers' revolt, but they were certainly eroded.

By 1910 most Canadians of any class would have been aware that something profoundly different was afoot in working-class Canada. They could even see it from their windows. . . . Instead of keeping to the confined paths of their individual daily lives, workers used the public spaces of their towns and cities for parades, mass picnics and sporting events, huge educational forums featuring guest speakers, and spontaneous gatherings for particular protests. Since their towns and cities had few facilities built to hold large numbers, they took control of streets, parks, theatres, and churches. In reasonably compact urban centres where most workers still got around by foot or on streetcars, the working-class crowd was an aggressive force to be reckoned with. Strikes would become massive community events as working-class families extended their long-standing patterns of mutual support out of their neighbourhoods and into picket-line support, collective action against strike-breakers, or sympathy strikes. Workers thus became a much more publicly visible force in Canada's urban centres.

The Workers' Defeat, 1919–1925

The workers' revolt had emerged in full form by the spring of 1919, and maintained much of its momentum across the country for at least another year. (In the eastern and western coalfields, the buoyancy lasted through 1922.) Yet, as early as the spring of 1919, the severe limitations on the workers' movements were becoming evident. From that point onward, workers were on the defensive. By 1922 most of their gains had been lost almost everywhere outside the coalfields. Strikes were defeated, union locals lost members and often disintegrated, provincial federations collapsed, independent labour parties expired, and the spirit of hope and determination drained away. The decline and fall of such a major social force was a complex process. In part, as so many Canadian historians have argued, the momentum of the revolt was sapped by ideological disagreements between a right and a left that had serious consequences for the strategic direction of the movements. To a much greater extent, however, the workers' revolt foundered on the hard, inhospitable rocks of the Canadian economy, class formation, and state.

Workers never get to choose the terrain on which they confront capital or the state. By 1919 a variety of capitalists had already made some decisions about the location and structure of their enterprises and the kind of workforce they would need. At the same time, the larger market forces continued to set constraints on what kind of working-class resistance would be possible. In Canada the industrial capitalist economy was fragmented into a myriad of widely separated projects in capital accumulation that followed quite different rhythms of development and crisis. The many isolated parts of the resource economy struggled to secure a space in highly competitive markets, the manufacturers cowered behind their tariff walls, and the transportation industries tried to survive on the success of the others. After the war each of these sectors, and their many subsectors, faced its own agonizing readjustment. Every capitalist economy contains this diversity but Canada seemed to be an exaggerated version, not least because of the vast distances that separated industrial activity but even more because of the various sectors' disarticulated links to the larger international economy that were unconnected to each other. Here was a good part of the explanation for the regionalism that ran through the workers' movements, as it did through the rest of Canadian society. Yet none of the regions itself had a single industrial pattern. So, despite their efforts at solidarity, wage earners found themselves divided by the fragmented, uneven structure of the Canadian economy and drawn into the ideological framework of regional politicians and businessmen who had their own agendas for coping.

Reinforcing those divisions was the unevenness of working-class power within the production processes of the various industries. While this different leverage was partly a matter of the skill content of jobs and workplace independence of wage earners, skilled workers usually had the additional advantage of ethnic and sexual homogeneity. Once again, these were for the most part structural characteristics of particular occupations that emerged from that process of capitalist planning and organizing. But, by World War I, occupational identities of skilled, white, English-speaking (and many French-speaking) male wage earners bore the stamp of long-standing fights to preserve their shop-floor power, independence, and self-esteem. The occupational groups at the forefront

of the workers' revolt—coal miners, metal trades workers, and 'frontier labourers'—had each fashioned a version of the distinctive muscular, masculine working-class culture that was idealized in the visual arts of the period, whether art nouveau or socialist realism (Donegan, 1988–9).

. . . The white, anglophone and francophone male wage earners who marched in the front ranks of the workers' revolt remained ambivalent about the role of women in the workforce and labour movement. 'There is no doubt that the women are being exploited by the manufacturers,' wrote a machinists' union official in 1917, 'and their use in the munitions factories has been the cause of reducing the wages of men shell operators' (qtd in Heron, 1981: 388–9). Despite women's enhanced role in working-class organizing, the patriarchal mould of the working-class family had certainly not been broken. On the contrary, a central goal of the workers' revolt of 1917–25 was to defend the household economy that had been the bedrock of working-class life in Canada for more than half a century and of the husband–father's role as chief bread winner.[10] Working men took their families on labour picnics and welcomed them onto mass picket lines, yet the vast sea of men's faces that fill up photographs of labour meetings taken during the Winnipeg General Strike suggest how thoroughly male the public life of the workers' movements still was.[11] Even the radical left had a heavily male-centred, productionist focus that left little room on its agenda for the female half of the working class (Frager, 1989; 1992; MacKay and Morton, 1998).

Not all men were welcome, however. Anglo-Canadian wage earners had often been highly suspicious of capitalists' use of non-Anglo-Celtic and non-white immigrants as cheap labour in many industries and feared a direct threat to their status and earnings within the rapidly changing capitalist labour process. As a result,

Anglo-Canadian and other workers eyed each other cautiously and often resentfully in ways that suggested that the elements that employers had drawn together into a workforce had not yet congealed into a full community of working-class solidarity, especially considering the continuing transiency of so many of the non-Anglo-Celtic 'sojourners'. Three vigorous counterpoints to the workers' revolt stood out in the 1917–20 period: the French Canadians' blistering anger over their forced participation in the 'English' war; rising Anglo-Canadian hysteria about European 'enemy aliens', accompanied by demands (spearheaded by the veterans) for their expulsion from industry;[12] and the revival of anti-Asian agitation in British Columbia. The two exclusionary campaigns, which led to the immigration restrictions of 1920, must have sown deep bitterness in immigrant urban enclaves. Many labour leaders refused to be associated with such nativist activities and appealed for tolerance and working-class brotherhood. But the ethnic fissures did not disappear. The French kept their distance from the Jewish and English-Canadian radicals in Montreal (Ewen, 1998). Rarely were European immigrants as well integrated into the rising workers' movements as they would be in the CIO period. They were virtually never found within the ranks of the labour parties in this period (although left-wing elements in some eastern European communities maintained contact with radical socialists). The Asians, who were so numerous in West Coast industries, were completely shut out (Seager and Rother, 1998). Not until the 1930s and 1940s, when the endless waves of sojourners and newcomers stopped and the working-class communities stabilized somewhat, would the ethnic divides start to close. In the meantime, the wage-earning members of many ethnic groups were drawn into rising cross-class nationalism within their own communities in Canada, especially in Quebec and in many European immigrant

ghettoes in central and western Canada. These ethnic divisions had different dimensions in each region, and, aside from the West Coast anti-Asian animus, they may not have amounted to the same wall of hostility that rose up in the United States as hundreds of thousands of blacks moved north in this period.[13] But they did deflect some of the energy of the workers' revolt along paths that weakened class-conscious solidarity.

In addition to overcoming internal fragmentation and division, working classes in industrial capitalist societies sought to situate themselves within a larger configuration of classes. In most industrialized countries outside Britain, they found themselves in a minority, and the Canadian class structure was essentially no different. Unless the workers' movements opted for the Bolshevik model of seizing power and imposing the dictatorship of the proletariat, as few Canadian labour leaders suggested before 1920, they had to find political allies. In Canada labour leaders attracted, or maintained a friendly dialogue with, disaffected elements of the urban middle class whose influence could be great but whose numbers were not large. In fact, aside from such celebrated exceptions as J.S. Woodsworth, most of the middle class either stood uncomfortably aloof from the workers' revolt or participated in attempts to contain or repress it. The white-collar workers who organized their own unions, especially teachers and civil servants, generally kept their distance from the rest of the labour movement.[14] Even the country's most celebrated suffragist, Nellie McClung, nervously opposed the Winnipeg General Strike (Savage, 1979: 142–3). Most social gospellers began looking for some mechanisms for reconciling the warring camps of capital and labour (Allen, 1973).

. . . At the end of the war, farmers were still by far the largest and electorally most powerful element in Canada, at least east of the Rockies. . . . In their relationship with workers, farmers were, at best, ambivalent allies and, at worst, strong hindrances. They occasionally sniped at the militancy, showed limited concern about the mass working-class unemployment of the early 1920s, and refused to support labour's most prized legislative measures, most notably the eight-hour day (Yeo, 1986, 1989; Naylor, 1988).[15] But this rural population posed an even thornier problem. People in the rural world of early-twentieth-century Canada often shaded over from independent primary producer to wage earner, bringing far more uncertainty about their quasi-proletarian status and far less commitment to urban-based movements.[16] Much of the logging, fishing, and construction industries rested on their labour. Some undertook remarkable organizational campaigns on an unprecedented scale—the Fishermen's Protective Union of Newfoundland under William Coaker and the Lumber Workers' Industrial Union in British Columbia, in particular (MacDonald, 1987; Hak, 1989). But most rural workers remained outside the workers' revolt or were only tangentially connected. . . .

Beyond calling for unity and solidarity, the leaders of Canadian workers' movements rarely reflected on the structural constraints of economic, regional, sexual, and ethnic fragmentation and isolation of Canadian workers. Probably pondering such dilemmas was a luxury the immediate organizational exigencies did not allow them. Whatever theorizing they did drew not from the specifics of the Canadian social formation but rather from the thinking of labourists or Marxists elsewhere. In this sense they were clearly disadvantaged in the face of corporate capital and the state in Canada, whose existence rested on their ability to overcome that kind of fragmentation and to integrate diverse parts of the social formation. By the end of World War I, workers confronted highly centralized corporations with national or continental networks of organization and a national state with

a remarkably strong executive branch (much more aggressive as a result of its interventionist wartime experience). The workers' movements were thus overwhelmed by powerful forces that were better able to manoeuvre in the difficult Canadian setting. . . .

After the Armistice employers launched a concerted offensive of union-busting and wage-cutting in an effort to reclaim ground conceded to labour under extraordinary wartime circumstances. Workers in virtually all the 28 cities visited by the Royal Commission on Industrial Relations in the spring of 1919 complained of extensive firing and blacklisting of union supporters since the end of the war (Siemiatycki, 1986: 249). Many of the protracted (and ultimately defeated) strikes of the post-war era were marked as much by capitalist intransigence as by labour's militancy. In 1920 workers won less than one strike in five, and employers were clear winners in a third—a dramatic reversal of the strike outcomes in 1917–18. From 1921 to 1924 close to half these confrontations ended on employers' terms, to which could be added many of those strikes whose outcomes were classified as 'Indefinite' (27 per cent in 1920, 24 per cent in 1921, and 20 per cent in 1922) (Kealey, 1989: 241). The decisive defeats came at different points in each industry and region. The collapse of the Winnipeg General Strike and the various sympathy strikes marked the beginning of the end in urban centres across the West. The defeat of the prolonged metal trades strikes in several Canadian cities in 1919 was devastating, but for most manufacturing industries in Ontario, Quebec, and Nova Scotia the major symbolic defeats did not arrive until mid-1920. The shipyards strikes of that year were catastrophes for organized labour in several parts of central and eastern Canada. Even the solidly entrenched printers' unions were dealt a crippling blow in their unsuccessful struggle for the 44-hour week

(Allen, 1973; Zerker, 1982). Sydney steelworkers did not meet their Waterloo until 1923, and coal miners in Cape Breton and Alberta held on for two more years (Macgillivray, 1971; MacEwan, 1976; Frank, 1979; Seager, 1981; Heron, 1987; McKay and Morton, 1998). The final confrontation of Cape Breton's miners and corporate bosses in 1925 was as bitter, brutal, and devastating as any in the whole period under study.

As the many studies of strikes in the period have revealed, a common pattern emerged almost everywhere. Companies forced a strike by refusing to negotiate and then frequently hired strike-breakers, often from professional strike-breaking operations such as the Pinkerton or Thiel detective agencies. As defeated workers drifted back, employers blacklisted local union militants to drive them out of town; some even installed spies on the shop floor to watch for potential trouble-makers. Little of this activity was carried out under the defiant 'open shop' banner that American capitalists were unfurling at this time (Naylor, 1991), but the outcome was the same. Anti-union tactics became much easier to implement in the context of a rapidly declining economy. The 16.5 per cent unemployment rate among unionized workers in the spring of 1921 was destroying their leverage in the labour market (*Labour Gazette*, May 1921: 709; June 1921: 817). Nearly universal wage cuts of 10–20 per cent in the early months of that year met with little resistance. By the end of 1922 the Department of Labour's statistics showed over 100,000 fewer union members than at the 1919 peak—a loss of 27 per cent.[17] . . .

The Canadian state made no effort to curb the attacks on workers and their organizations. On the contrary, politicians and state officials moved decisively to repress and undermine working-class militancy and radicalism. They turned loose against radical leaders their secret-service spies, federal troops, and new criminal-law and immigration legislation, as well as their blandishments of more moderate leaders with a royal commission and a National Industrial Conference. The federal government offered no solid inducements or protection for working-class organization.

At this point the structure of Canadian federalism played its complicated role in mediating class relations. Workers' movements across the country had directed much of their political energy into provincial politics wherein resided many of the constitutional responsibilities for such worker concerns as the eight-hour day. That meant battling on nine different fronts. Provincial governments had been the first to respond to the general unrest in the population after 1916, and several administrations (especially those run by reform-minded Liberals) had used such measures as minimum-wage legislation and mothers' allowances to try to buy back some legitimacy for the social and political system (Oliver, 1975; Campbell, 1980; McCallum, 1986; Kealey, 1987). . . . Each of these moves by the provincial branches of the Canadian state reinforced the regional particularities in the timing and rhythms of the workers' revolt. Since no federal election was called until 1921, workers' movements were not able to confront the national Borden government directly on the hustings until after the revolt had lost most of its momentum.

It is against this agonizingly difficult backdrop of structural constraint and repressive counterattack that we must assess the splits that had opened up within the labour leadership by the spring of 1919. Once again, they hit each region at different moments. Yet this was fundamentally a divergence between left and right, not East and West. In every region of the country labour leaders were engaging in heated debate about the appropriate industrial and political working-class response to the new resistance that the revolt was facing. While the left urged escalation, the right called for a retreat. The major points of disagreement concerned the most appropriate form of union organization, the link with the international unions centred in the American Federation of Labor, and the willingness of the workers' movements to show more aggressiveness in pursuit of their goals. Since the middle of the war, labour leaders had argued over these issues with those who constituted the movements' national voice in the Trades and Labor Congress of Canada always advocating restraint. The confrontation came to a head at the 1918 Congress convention, where a minority report denouncing the executive's cozy relations with the government sparked a furious debate about the directions of the labour movement. A set of militant tactical resolutions was defeated and a more conservative slate, headed by carpenters' union organizer Tom Moore, was elected to the Congress executive. Moore had been a solid supporter of conscription and a central figure in the rapprochement with the Borden government in 1918. The defeat for the left at the 1918 convention was not simply a matter of the East overpowering the West (51 easterners joined 29 westerners on the losing side, against a majority of three from the West and 81 from the East). It was quite significant, however, that the Western delegates constructed the defeat in regional terms. They chose to minimize the evidence of support for their position East of the Lakehead and to use a Western Labour Conference as a springboard for reconstruction of the whole labour movement. Then, in the early spring of 1919, they moved decisively towards secession with the creation of the One Big Union (Robin, 1968; Frank, 1976; Bercuson, 1978; Siemiatycki, 1986).[18]

That spring well-established craft union leaders in most major cities began to consider the risks associated with the widening solidarity and political radicalism. In the Western conferences leading up to the formation of the One Big Union, there were dissenting voices. J.H. McVety in Vancouver, David Rees in Fernie, Alfred Farmilo in Edmonton, Alex Ross in Calgary, and Ernie Robinson in Winnipeg all opposed withdrawing from the international unions to form the One Big Union. The Calgary labour movement was lukewarm about this new experiment, while the Edmonton trades council stayed out altogether (Bercuson, 1978; Bright, 1990, 1992). In southern Ontario and Montreal the more entrenched craft union leaders were not prepared to see their organizations disrupted by surging notions of industrial unionism (Naylor, 1991; Ewen, 1998). All these men were still looking to the state and capital for the legitimacy and recognition they believed caution and moderation would bring. Their strategy was to raise the threat of labour unrest and to present themselves as the restraining force that would curb militancy and radicalism. In an address to the Canadian Manufacturers' Association in February 1919, Tom Moore was reported to have advised his audience that 'the responsible, intelligent trades unionist was the capitalist's strongest bulwark, if only a friendly co-operation were extended to him, since the trade unionist, and indeed, the worker fully realized that the downfall of the capitalist, and the cessation of the work in the factory spelled his own idleness and possible starvation' (Canadian Labor Press, 1 March 1919). . . .

By the end of 1919, the fluidity of the previous two years had evaporated, and positions on the right and left were hardening. In the wake of the OBU breakaway, the Canadian branches of the international unions threw themselves into a campaign to win back the West and to prevent any further secessions. The more conservative craft union leaders steadily withdrew their support for the more experimental organizational forms and practices that had blossomed alongside the normal channels of international union procedure. They insisted on the honouring of contracts negotiated with individual employers (this abiding faith in 'industrial legality' discouraged various groups of wage earners from joining larger struggles) (Ewen, 1998; Naylor, 1998). They used the disciplinary power of their organizations to curb unauthorized sympathy or general strikes. In many cases they seriously undermined local struggles by curtailing solidarity actions by their members. By rejecting cooperation and amalgamation of crafts and rigourously defending individual craft jurisdiction and rights, these union officials undoubtedly robbed less skilled workers of leadership, resources, and negotiating strength. Over the next two years the leading figures in the craft union movement distanced themselves from the main currents of the workers' revolt. They also opened a rhetorical barrage against the left in general, using some of the existing labour newspapers as well as the new *Canadian Labor News*, the *Edmonton Free Press*, and, from the end of 1919, *New Democracy*. By 1921 the leaders of the Trades and Labor Congress even refused to endorse the independent labour candidates who were running in that year's federal election. These craft unionists settled solidly into the cautious, complacent, apolitical mould that had been developed in the Gompersite American Federation of Labor and would not wander far from those moorings until World War II (Robin, 1968; Siemiatycki, 1986; Naylor, 1991).

Facing these men across the increasingly bitter political battlefield were a variety of militants and radicals who, as we have seen, were spread across the country. Region does not help explain their location as much as industry, occupation, ethnicity, and the recent history of industrial relations in their respective communities. Some were based in the older male occupations with long traditions of workplace pride and independence and recent success in confronting their employers, especially the coal miners and the highly skilled railway shopcraft workers (Frank, 1979; Seager, 1981; Bercuson, 1990). Others had a solid following in the newly organized unions of semi-skilled and unskilled workers, notably in mass production, resource processing, and water transport (Naylor, 1991; Heron, 1988; Ewen, 1998). Also providing some ginger were clusters of European-born socialists who were found in logging, mining, and clothing production (Hogan, 1975; Seager, 1981, 1986; Rouillard, 1981–2; Radforth, 1987; Frager, 1992). The radicals' success depended on the strength of the local unions in their respective industries and on the established power of the international craft union leadership in the local labour movement. AFL-style craft unions were much weaker in the Maritimes and the West, where they had never put down as deep roots and had always had to coexist with bumptious industrial unions, usually most solidly based in mining (MacEwan, 1976; Frank, 1979; McKay, 1985; Heron, 1987). They were also somewhat weaker in Quebec, where their insensitivity to francophones had limited their impact (the AFL finally appointed a bilingual organizer for the province in 1918) (Rouillard, 1989; Ewen, 1998). Southern Ontario was the heartland of this cautious brand of unionism and the headquarters of a solid cadre of full-time labour officials—business agents, organizers, Canadian vice-presidents, and the leading officials of the Trades and Labor Congress of Canada—who were committed to the link with the AFL and industrial legality in collective bargaining (Heron and Palmer, 1977; Heron, 1981; Naylor, 1991). . . .

The divisions in the labour leadership went beyond the right–left tensions. The radicals themselves were divided on the issue of staying with the international unions. The great majority of westerners voted to leave and form the One Big Union. In central and eastern Canada, this strategy had its supporters.[19] (Because unions in these regions generally refused to hold referendums on secession, it is impossible to gauge the precise amount of support for the OBU.) However, most militant leaders in central and eastern Canada opted to remain within the international union movement. The left within the workers' movement was therefore divided at a crucial moment. By the end of 1919 the radicals' secessionist project in the West had foundered. East of the Lakehead those who remained in the mainstream labour movement became increasingly isolated. Only in the Maritimes did they maintain a leadership role, which persisted until 1923.

Beset by failures and a heavily repressive environment, many socialist militants began to gravitate towards the emerging Communist movement. The old Social Democratic Party had disintegrated soon after the state's iron heel came down on it late in 1918. Socialists from the party's right wing (notably James Simpson in Toronto) settled into independent labour party work. At the same time, feistier members of its left wing joined forces with a handful of revolutionary socialists and radical members of some Eastern European immigrant groups, some of whom had already begun clandestine propaganda early in 1919. In the heat of state repression and the general Red Scare, this new pro-Bolshevik left had both an underground life for theorizing and strategizing and a public forum for revolutionary education and unbridled attacks on the dominant labour leadership. Many of the militant sparkplugs from the workers' revolt—including Jack MacDonald in Toronto, Fred Flatman in Hamilton, Annie Buller in Montreal, and J.B. McLachlan in Cape Breton—were drawn to this emerging movement, as were many European-born socialists. In May 1921, at a secret meeting in a barn outside Guelph, the underground Communist Party of Canada was founded, uniting all these revolutionary socialists east of Manitoba. Its public face, the Workers' Party of Canada, emerged in February 1922. In the West the aging Socialist Party of Canada eventually disintegrated as branches left to join the Workers' Party. Branches of a few local labour parties in such places as Halifax and Fernie followed suit. Ironically, shortly after its founding the Communist Party, in line with the new direction of the Third International in Moscow, began to favour the politics of coalition over sectarian attacks on the established labour institutions and their leaders. The Workers' Party affiliated with the Canadian Labor Party, and individual Communists directed their energies back into locals of international unions, the trades councils, and the Trades and Labor Congress. However, the craft union leadership was unwelcoming, and by the late 1920s most Communists had been expelled from unions for their agitation (Rodney, 1968; Vance, 1968; Avakumovic, 1975; Watson, 1976; Buck, 1977; Avery, 1979; Angus, 1981; Frank, 1990; Akers, 1992; Campbell, 1992; Heron, 1992; Manley, 1992). The left, then, had also been unable to meet the challenge of the crisis facing workers after 1919. At that critical moment, the radicals' flamboyant sectarianism may have sometimes been unrealistic, but it was the divisive issue of secession from the mainstream international labour movement, combined with the ideological hardening that had taken place in the context of the well-orchestrated Red Scare, that deprived the radicals of the credibility and effectiveness that would have allowed them to take a larger role. . . .

By the mid-1920s labour leaders from all these political camps must have looked back in sober dismay at the opportunities that had been lost. In the years between 1917 and 1920 a massive number of Canadian workers had become part of a great collective groping for a new kind of society.

With the limited resources available in working class neighbourhoods across the country, they had united in countless ways to show their determination to change the lot of workers in Canada. They had pursued their goals in a constitutionalist fashion through the existing institutions of society, especially unions and political parties, rather than armed insurrection, but their open-ended vision of working-class power had nonetheless carried radical dimensions and potential that did not escape the notice of bourgeois leaders. The workers had never been given the opportunity to carry their planning and dreaming far forward into the post-war era because Canadian capitalists would not consider the shift in power that even the mildest reforms implied, and because those in control of the state had shared this apprehension about a more powerful working class. When the crunch had come, the workers' revolt had failed to transcend the great diversity and structural weaknesses of the Canadian working class. Workers in every part of the country, in almost every occupational group, had participated in the revolt, but they had failed to coalesce (sometimes even at the local level) into an effective, coherent force able to withstand the crippling attacks of capital and the state and the enervating impact of unemployment. In this moment of crisis the leadership of the workers' movements had fragmented into three distinct currents according to their divergent readings of how to respond—cautious craft unionism, revolutionary Communism, and social democratic parliamentarism—none of which managed to capture the dynamism, mass mobilization, and ideological and strategic diversity of the early stages of the revolt. . . .

The long-term impact was devastating for the Canadian working class. For the next twenty years, despite some determined efforts in the 1930s, workers did not come close to regaining the collective power they had summoned up in 1917–20.

Although unions did not disappear (total union membership by the mid-1920s had not, in fact, tumbled to the pre-war lows), they were for the most part marginal to Canadian industrial life. Most industrial corporations could confidently expect to operate in a 'union-free' environment. Canadian political life would take some time to recover from the various post-war crises, but in working-class communities voter absenteeism or traditional Liberalism and resurgent Toryism were predominant by 1925. The moment when the Canadian capitalist system faced one of its most serious challenges in the country's history had clearly passed (Palmer, 1992). . . .

On a more positive note, the working class had undoubtedly carved out a somewhat larger place in Canadian public life. Canadian politicians could never again ignore the concerns of workers to the extent they had in the past. A small residue of social legislation remained on the statute books (Findlay, 1923), and a handful of labour parliamentarians at all three levels of the state would continue to voice workers' concerns. J.S. Woodsworth's success in extracting an old-age pension plan from Mackenzie King in 1926 was the most impressive example (McNaught, 1959). Moreover, in some parts of the country where the revolt was not buried beneath the suffocating blankets of Maritime Rights, francophone nationalism, or industrial protectionism, the struggles of 1917–20 were not forgotten and would be used to rally workers in future battles. It seems that the mass strikes (such as those in Winnipeg and Cape Breton) that had drawn workers into direct confrontation with the armed might of the state, rather than simply mobilization through the ballot box, had etched the deepest memories.

The working class in Canada would indeed rise up again a quarter-century later. The form of the new workers' movements would be as different as the workers' revolt had been from its predecessors in the 1880s, but workers' renewed aspirations for economic security, independence, and dignity would make clear that they were not prepared to remain on their knees forever.

Notes

1. Their statistics provide the basis for the following discussion.

2. A careful reading of these Labour Department reports makes clear that the totals were rough estimates and undoubtedly underestimated union membership. Tables that broke the statistics down by province reveal that generally about a third of the local failed to report their membership. The Department then filled in the holes 'from Dept. Records and other sources' (Canada, Department of Labour, *Labour Organization in Canada, 1914–20*).

3. In 1914 there were four labour papers: Vancouver's *BC Federationist*, Winnipeg's *Voice*, Hamilton's *Labor News*, and Toronto's *Industrial Banner*. By mid-1919 all but the *Voice* were flourishing and had been joined by the *Citizen* (Halifax), the *Eastern Federationist* (New Glasgow), *Worker's Weekly* (Stellarton), the *Union Worker* (Saint John), *Le Monde ouvrier* (Montreal), *l'Unioniste* (Quebec City), the *Canadian Labor Press* (Ottawa), the *Labor Leader* (Toronto), *New Democracy* (Hamilton), the *Herald* (London), the *Western Labor News* (Winnipeg), the *Confederate* (Brandon), the *Searchlight* (Calgary), and the *Edmonton Free Press*. Canada, Department of Labour, *Labour Organization in Canada*, 1919, 295.

4. At the famous 1918 convention of the Trades and Labor Congress of Canada, radicals failed to win majority support for their proposal that the officials at this level should be consulted by the government, not the officers of international unions. The One Big Union later made these bodies the centre of its organizational structure. Robin, *Radical Politics and Canadian Labour*, 161; Bercuson, *Fools and Wise Men*, 149.

5. Among the discredited or ignored were Nova Scotian miners' leader John Moffatt, the aging Quebec Lib-Lab MP Alphonse Verville, prominent Hamilton labour journalist Sam Landers, Winnipeg's venerable Arthur Puttee, Alberta miners' leader David Rees, and Vancouver's J.H. McVety and W.R. Trotter. MacEwan, *Miners and Steelworkers*, 46; Ewen, 'Quebec: Class and Ethnicity', 87–143; Heron, 'Working-Class Hamilton'; McCormack, *Reformers, Rebels, and Revolutionaries*, 137–64; Bercuson, *Fools and Wise Men*, 65–7.

6. Labourism was a brand of working-class liberalism that challenged political privilege, undemocratic practices, economic monopoly, and the exclusion of workers from social and political power, but stopped short of a full-scale assault on the capitalist system. Craig Heron, 'Labourism and the Canadian Working Class', *Labour/Le Travail* 13 (Spring 1984): 45–76.

7. Wages were an issue in 46 per cent of the strikes in 1917, 44 per cent in 1918, 39 per cent in 1919, and 45 per cent in 1920. Gregory Kealey, 'Parameters of Class Conflict', 420.

8. The device of the royal commission was used, for example, in the Toronto and Hamilton munitions industry and Cobalt silver mining in 1916, and the Nova Scotia coal and steel industries several times after 1916. Siemiatycki, 'Munitions and Labour Militancy'; Hogan, *Cobalt*; MacEwan, *Miners and Steelworkers*; Heron, 'Great War and Nova Scotia Steelworkers'.

9. See Bryan D. Palmer, *A Culture in Conflict: Skilled Workers and Industrial Capitalism in Hamilton, Ontario, 1860–1914* (Kingston and Montreal: McGill-Queen's University Press, 1979); Gregory Kealey and Palmer, *Dreaming of What Might Be: The Knights of Labor in Ontario, 1880–1900* (New York: Cambridge University Press, 1982). The issue of shorter hours within workers' movements has been the subject of much fascinating recent research. See David Roediger and Philip Foner, *Our Own Time: A History of American Labor and the Working Day* (New York: Verso, 1989); Gary Cross, *Quest for Time: The Reduction of Work in Britain and France* (Berkeley: University of California Press, 1989); Cross, ed., *Worktime and Industrialization: An International History* (Philadelphia: Temple University Press, 1988).

10. Joy Parr has appropriately dubbed this collective defence of the family wage 'social fathering' and 'breadwinner unionism'. Parr, *Gender of Breadwinners*, 149–50.

11. See photos in Norman Penner, ed., *Winnipeg 1919: The Strikers' Own History of the Winnipeg General Strike* (Toronto: James Lorimer, 1973), and Jack Bumsted, *The Winnipeg General Strike of 1919: An Illustrated History* (Winnipeg: Watson Dwyer, 1994). Even the large Central Strike Committee had only two female members.

12. The 'Reconstruction Policy' of the Greater Toronto Labor Party called on the government to 'tax all Aliens and enemy aliens very heavily; immigration

after the War to be of friendly Aliens only for a definite period'. *Canadian Annual Review* (Toronto), 1918, 343.

13. See, for example, William Tuttle, *Race Riot: Chicago in the Red Summer of 1919* (New York: Atheneum, 1970).

14. The BC Provincial Service Association affiliated with the Trades and Labor Congress but refused to join the Victoria Trades and Labor Council. McLean, *A Union amongst Government Employees'*, 5, 15. See also Thomson, 'The Large and Generous View'; and Glen Makahonuk, 'Masters and Servants: Labour Relations in the Saskatchewan Civil Service, 1905–1945', *Prairie Forum* 12, 2 (Fall 1987): 257–76.

15. On the general topic of rural workers, see Daniel Samson, ed., *Contested Countryside: Rural Workers and Modern Society in Atlantic Canada, 1800–1950* (Fredericton: Acadiensis Press, 1994).

16. This important feature of the Canadian social formation has had far too little attention from Canadian historians, especially in English Canada. For some discussion, see McKay and Morton and Ewen in Craig Heron, ed., *The Workers' Revolt in Canada, 1819–1925* (Toronto: University of Toronto Press, 1998); Séguin, 'L'économie agro-forestière: Genèse du développement au Saguenay au 19 siècle', in Normand Séguin, ed., *Agriculture et colonization au Quebec: Aspects historiques*, pp. 159–64 (Montreal: Boréal Express, 1980); Everett Hughes, *French Canada in Transition* (Chicago: University of Chicago Press, 1943); Bruno Ramirez, *On the Move: French-Canadian and Italian Migrants in the North Atlantic Economy, 1860–1914* (Toronto: McClelland and Stewart, 1991); José Igartua, 'Worker Persistence, Hiring Policies, and the Depression in the Aluminum Sector: The Saguenay Region, Quebec, 1925–1940', *Histoire sociale/Social History* 43 (May 1989): 9–34; Radforth, *Bushworkers and Bosses*; Jay Parr, 'Hired Men: Ontario Agricultural Wage Labour in Historical Perspective', *Labour/Le Travail* 15 (Spring 1985): 91–103; John Thompson, 'Bringing in the Sheaves: The Harvest Excursionists, 1890–1929', *Canadian*

Historical Review 59, 4 (December 1978): 467–89'; Donald Avery, 'Canadian Immigration Policy and the "Foreign" Navvy, 1896–1914', in Michael S. Cross and Gregory S. Kealey, eds, *The Consolidation of Canadian Capitalism, 1896–1929*, pp. 47–73 (Toronto: McClelland and Stewart); L. Anders Sandberg, 'Dependent Development, Labour, and the Trenton Steel Works, Nova Scotia, c. 1900–1943', *Labour/Le Travail* 27 (Spring 1991): 127–62; James Sacouman, 'Semi-Proletarianization and Rural Underdevelopment in the Maritimes', *Canadian Review of Sociology and Anthropology* 17 (1980): 232–45; Leo Johnson, 'Precapitalist Economic Formations and the Capitalist Labour Market in Canada, 1911–71', in James E. Curtis and William G. Scott, eds, *Social Stratification: Canada*, pp. 89–104 (Scarborough: Prentice Hall, 1979); Rolf Knight, *Stump Ranch Chronicles and Other Narratives* (Vancouver: New Star Books, 1977).

17. Two years later total reported union membership had fallen by a further 17,000 to 260,000. Canada, Department of Labour, *Labour Organization in Canada*, 1921, 257; and 1924, 10.

18. Gregory Kealey presents slightly different figures for the 1918 vote (a minority of 58 easterners and 32 westerners versus a majority of three westerners and 97 easterners) but notes that the pattern remains the same. The West sent only 45 of the 440 delegates to the 1918 convention, which was held in Quebec City. Kealey, '1919', 36.

19. In Amherst, Nova Scotia, the local labour movement affiliated with the OBU, as did its counterpart in Carleton Place, Ontario, and several northern Ontario miners' and loggers' organizations. In Montreal, Toronto, Hamilton, and a few smaller towns in southern Ontario, small groups of socialist militants set up local OBU units and set out to compete with the established local leadership for working-class support. Fred Flatman expanded the circulation of his Hamilton paper *New Democracy*, which became the eastern mouthpiece for the OBU. Reilly, 'General Strike in Amherst'; Bercuson, *Fools and Wise Men*; Naylor, *New Democracy*, 64–71.

References

Akers, David. 1992. 'Rebel or Revolutionary? Jack Kavanagh and the Early Years of the Communist Movement in Vancouver, 1920–1925', *Labour/Le Travail* 30 (Fall): 9–44.

Allen Richard. 1973. *The Social Passion: Religion and Social Reform in Canada, 1914–1928*. Toronto: University of Toronto Press.

Angus, Ian. 1981. *Canadian Bolsheviks: The Early Years of the Communist Party of Canada*. Montreal: Vanguard Press.

Avakumovic, Ivan. 1975. *The Communist Party in Canada: A History*. Toronto: McClelland and Stewart.

Avery, Donald. 1979. *'Dangerous Foreigners': European Immigrant Workers and Labour Radicalism in Canada, 1896–1932*. Toronto: McClelland and Stewart.

Bercuson, David J. 1978. *Fools and Wise Men: The Rise and Fall of the One Big Union*. Toronto: McGraw-Hill Ryerson.

———. 1990. *Confrontation at Winnipeg: Labour, Industrial Relations, and the General Strike*, 2nd edn. Montreal and Kingston: McGill-Queen's University Press.

Bernard, Elaine. 1984. 'Last Back: Folklore and the Telephone Operators in the 1919 Vancouver General Strike', in Barbara K. Latham and Roberta J. Pazdro, eds, *Not Just Pin Money: Selected Essays on the History of Women's Work in British Columbia*, pp. 279–86. Victoria: Camosun College.

Brecher, Michael. 1958. 'Patterns of Accommodation in the Men's Garment Industry in Quebec, 1914–1954', in H.D. Woods, ed., *Patterns of Dispute Settlements in Five Canadian Industries*, pp. 89–186. Montreal: Industrial Relations Centre, McGill University.

Bright, David. 1990. 'Bonds of Brotherhood? The Experiences of Labour in Calgary, 1903–1919'. MA thesis, University of Calgary.

———. 1992. '"We Are All Kin": Reconsidering Labour and Class in Calgary, 1919', *Labour/Le Travail* 29 (Spring): 59–80.

Buck, Tim. 1977. *Yours in the Struggle: Reminiscences of Tim Buck*, William Beeching and Phyllis Clarke, eds. Toronto: NC Press.

Burnet, Jean, with Howard Palmer. 1988. *'Coming Canadian': An Introduction to a History of Canada's Peoples*. Toronto: McClelland and Stewart.

Calliste, Agnes. 1987. 'Sleeping Car Porters in Canada: An Ethnically Submerged Split Labour Market', *Canadian Ethnic Studies* 19, 1: 1–20.

Campbell, Elizabeth Jane. 1980. '"The Balance Wheel of the Industrial System": Maximum Hours, Minimum Wage and Workmen's Compensation Legislation in Ontario, 1900–1939'. PhD dissertation, McMaster University.

Campbell, Marie. 1980. 'Sexism in British Columbia Trade Unions, 1900–1920', in Barbara Latham and Cathy Kess, eds, *In Her Own Right: Selected Essays on Women's History in B.C.*, pp. 167–86. Victoria: Camosun College.

Campbell, Peter. 1992. '"Making Socialists": Bill Pritchard, the Socialist Party of Canada, and the Third International', *Labour/Le Travail* 30 (Fall): 45–63.

Canada. Department of Labour. 1901–25. *Labour Organization in Canada*. Ottawa: King's Printer.

Creese, Gillian. 1988. 'Class, Ethnicity, and Conflict: The Case of Chinese and Japanese Immigrants, 1880–1923', in Rennie Warburton and David Coburn, eds, *Workers, Capital and the State in British Columbia: Selected Papers*, pp. 55–85. Vancouver: UBC Press.

Cruikshank, Douglas, and Gregory S. Kealey. 1987. 'Canadian Strike Statistics, 1891–1950', *Labour/Le Travail* 20 (Fall): 85–145.

Doherty, Bill. 1991. *Slaves of the Lamp: A History of the Federal Civil Service Organizations, 1865–1924*. Victoria: Orca Book Publishers.

Donegan, Rosemary. 1988–89. 'The Iconography of Labour: An Overview of Canadian Materials', *Archivaria* 27 (Winter): 35–56.

Ewen, Geoffrey. 1998. 'Quebec: Class and Ethnicity', in Craig Heron, ed., *The Workers' Revolt in Canada, 1917–1925*, pp. 87–143. Toronto: University of Toronto Press.

Findlay, Marion. 1923. 'Protection of Workers in Industry', in W.P.M. Kennedy, ed., *Social and Economic Conditions in the Dominion of Canada*, pp. 254–66. Philadelphia: American Academy of Political and Social Science.

Frager, Ruth. 1983. 'No Proper Deal: Women Workers and the Canadian Labour Movement, 1870–1940', in Linda Briskin and Lynda Yanz, eds, *Union Sisters: Women in the Labour Movement*, pp. 44–64. Toronto: Women's Press.

———. 1989. 'Class and Ethnic Barriers to Feminist Perspectives in Toronto's Jewish Labour Movement, 1919–1939', *Studies in Political Economy* 30 (Autumn): 143–66.

———. 1992. *Sweatshop Strife: Class, Ethnicity, and Gender in the Jewish Labour Movement of Toronto, 1900–1939*. Toronto: University of Toronto Press.

Frank, David. 1979. 'The Cape Breton Coal Miners, 1917–1926'. PhD dissertation, Dalhousie University.

———. 1986. 'Contested Terrain: Workers' Control in the Cape Breton Coal Mines in the 1920s', in Craig Heron and Roberts Storey, eds, *On the Job: Confronting the Labour Process in Canada*, pp. 102–23. Montreal and Kingston: McGill-Queen's University Press.

———. 1990. 'Working-Class Politics: The Election of J.B. McLachlan, 1916–1935', in Kenneth Donovan, ed., *The Island: New Perspectives on Cape Breton History, 1713–1990*, pp. 187–219. Fredericton: Acadiensis Press.

Friesen, Gerald. 1976. '"Yours in Revolt": Regionalism, Socialism, and the Western Canadian Labour Movement', *Labour/Le Travail* 1: 139–57.

Hak, Gordon. 1989. 'British Columbia Loggers and the Lumber Workers Industrial Union, 1919–1922', *Labour/Le Travail* 23 (Spring): 67–90.

Harney, Robert F. 1978. *Italians in Canada*. Toronto: Multicultural History Society of Ontario.

Heron, Craig. 1981. 'Working-Class Hamilton, 1895–1930'. PhD dissertation, Dalhousie University.

———. 1987. 'The Great War and Nova Scotia Steel-workers', *Acadiensis* 16, 2 (Spring): 2–34.

———. 1988. *Working in Steel: The Early Years in Canada, 1883–1935*. Toronto: McClelland and Stewart.

———. 1992. 'Frederick J. Flatman', in *Dictionary of Hamilton Biography, Vol. 3, 1925–1939*, pp. 52–7. Hamilton: Dictionary of Hamilton Biography.

Heron, Craig, and Bryan Palmer. 1977. 'Through the Prism of the Strike: Industrial Conflict in Southern Ontario, 1901–1914', *Canadian Historical Review* 58, 4 (December): 423–58.

Heron, Craig, and George De Zwaan. 1985. 'Industrial Unionism in Eastern Ontario: Gananoque, 1918–1921', *Ontario History* 77, 3 (September): 159–82.

Hogan, Brian F. 1978. *Cobalt: Year of the Strike, 1919*. Cobalt, ON: Highway Book Shop.

Horodyski, Mary. 1986. 'Women and the Winnipeg General Strike of 1919', *Manitoba History* 11 (Spring): 28–37.

Kealey, Gregory S. 1984. '1919: The Canadian Labour Revolt', *Labour/Le Travail* 13 (Spring): 11–44.

———. 1989. 'The Parameters of Class Conflict: Strikes in Canada, 1891–1930', in Deian R. Hopkin and Gregory S. Kealey, eds, *Class, Community, and the Labour Movement: Wales and Canada, 1850–1930*, pp. 213–48. Aberystwyth, Wales: Llafur and Canadian Committee on Labour History.

Kealey, Linda. 1987. 'Women and Labour during World War I: Women Workers and the Minimum Wage in Manitoba', in Mary Kinnear, ed., *First Days, Fighting Days: Women in Manitoba History*, pp. 76–99. Regina: Canadian Plains Research Centre.

———. 1989. '"No Special Protection—No Sympathy": Women's Activism in the Canadian Labour Revolt of 1919', in Deian R. Hopkin, and Gregory S. Kealey, eds, *Class, Community, and the Labor Movement: Wales and Canada, 1850–1930*, pp. 134–59. Aberystwyth, Wales: Llafur and Canadian Committee on Labour History.

———. 1991. 'Women's Labour Militancy in Canada, 1900–20'. Paper presented to the Canadian Historical Association, Kingston, ON.

Levant, Victor. 1977. *Capital and Labour: Partners? Two Classes—Two Views*. Toronto: Steel Rail Press.

Lindstrom-Best, Varpu. 1988. *Defiant Sisters: A Social History of Finnish Immigrant Women in Canada*. Toronto: Multicultural History Society of Ontario.

———. 1989. 'Finnish Socialist Women in Canada, 1890–1930', in Linda Kealey and Joan Sangster, eds, *Beyond the Vote: Canadian Women and Politics*, pp. 196–216. Toronto: University of Toronto Press.

Lindstrom-Best, Varpu, and Allen Seager. 1985. 'Tover-itar and Finnish Canadian Women, 1900–1930', in

Christiane Harzig and Dirk Hoerder, eds, *The Press of Labour Migrants in Europe and North America, 1880s to 1930s*, pp. 243–64. Bremen, Germany: Labor Migration Project, Labor Newspaper Preservation Project, Universität Bremen.

McCallum, Margaret. 1990. 'Keeping Women in Their Place: The Minimum Wage in Canada, 1910–1925', *Labour/Le Travail* 17 (Spring): 29–59.

McCormack, A. Ross. 1977. *Reformers, Rebels, and Revolutionaries: The Western Canadian Radical Movement, 1899–1919*. Toronto: University of Toronto Press.

McDonald, Ian D.H. 1987. *'To Each His Own': William Coaker and the Fishermen's Protective Union in Newfoundland Politics, 1908–1925*. St John's: ISER Books.

MacEwan, Paul. 1976. *Miners and Steelworkers: Labour in Cape Breton*. Toronto: Samuel Stevens Hakkert and Company.

Macgillivray, Don. 1971. 'Industrial Unrest in Cape Breton, 1919–1925'. MA thesis, University of New Brunswick.

McGregor, F.A. 1962. *The Fall and Rise of Mackenzie King, 1911–1919*. Toronto: Macmillan.

McKay, Ian. 1983. 'Industry, Work, and Community in the Cumberland Coalfields, 1848–1927', PhD dissertation, Dalhousie University.

———. 1985. *The Craft Transformed: An Essay on the Carpenters of Halifax, 1885–1985*. Halifax: Holdfast Press.

McKay, Ian, and Suzanne Morton. 1998. 'The Maritimes: Expanding the Circle of Resistance', in Craig Heron, ed., *The Workers' Revolt in Canada, 1817–1925*. Toronto: University of Toronto Press.

McLean, Bruce. 1979. *'A Union amongst Government Employees': A History of the B.C. Government Employees' Union, 1919–1979*. N.p.

McNaught, Kenneth. 1959. *A Prophet in Politics: A Biography of J.S. Woodsworth*. Toronto: University of Toronto Press.

Manley, John. 1992. 'Preaching the Red Stuff: J.B. McLachlan, Communism, and the Cape Breton Miners, 1922–1935', *Labour/Le Travail* 30 (Fall): 65–114.

Marquis, Greg. 1989. 'Police Unionism in Early-Twentieth-Century Toronto', *Ontario History* 81, 2 (June): 109–28.

———. 1990. 'The History of Policing in the Maritime Provinces: Themes and Perspectives', *Urban History Review* 19, 1 (October): 84–99.

Martynowych, Orest T., and Nadia Kazymyra. 1982. 'Political Activity in Western Canada, 1896–1923', in Manoly R. Lupul, ed., *A Heritage in Transition: Essays in the History of Ukrainians in Canada*, pp. 85–107. Toronto: McClelland and Stewart.

Montague, John Tait. 1950. 'Trade Unionism in the Canadian Meatpacking Industry'. PhD dissertation, University of Toronto.

————. 1984. 'Immigrants, Industrial Unions, and Social Reconstruction in the United States, 1916–1923', *Labour/Le Travail* 13 (Spring): 101–5.

Naylor, James. 1988. 'Ontario Workers and the Decline of Labourism', in Roger Hall, et al., eds, *Patterns of the Past: Intrepreting Ontario's History*, pp. 278–300. Toronto: Dundurn Press.

————. 1991. *The New Democracy: Challenging the Industrial Order in Industrial Ontario*. Toronto: University of Toronto Press.

————. 1998. 'Southern Ontario: Striking at the Ballot Box', in Craig Heron, ed., *The Workers' Revolt in Canada, 1917–1925*, pp. 144–75. Toronto: University of Toronto.

Oliver, Peter. 1975. 'Sir William Hearst and the Collapse of the Ontario Conservative Party', in Peter Oliver, ed., *Public and Private Persons: The Ontario Political Culture, 1914–1934*, pp. 16–43. Toronto: Clarke Irwin.

Palmer, Bryan D. 1992. *Working-Class Experience: Rethinking the History of Canadian Labour, 1800–1991*. Toronto: McClelland and Stewart.

Parr, Joy. 1990. *The Gender of Breadwinners: Women, Men, and Change in Two Industrial Towns, 1880–1950*. Toronto: University of Toronto Press.

Peitchinis, Stephen G. 1971. *Labour–Management Relations in the Railway Industry*. Ottawa: Queen's Printer.

Penfold, Steven. 1994. '"Have You No Manhood in You?": Gender and Class in the Cape Breton Coal Towns, 1920–1926', *Acadiensis* 23 (Spring): 21–44.

Peterson, Larry. 1984. 'Revolutionary Socialism and Industrial Unrest in the Era of the Winnipeg General Strike: The Origins of Communist Labour Unionism in Europe and North America', *Labour/Le Travail* 13 (Spring): 115–32.

Radeki, Henry, with Benedykt Heydenkorn. 1976. *A Member of a Distinguished Family: The Polish Group in Canada*. Toronto: McClelland and Stewart.

Radforth, Ian. 1987. *Bushworkers and Bosses: Logging in Northern Ontario, 1900–1980*. Toronto: University of Toronto.

Reilly, Nolan. 1980. 'The General Strike in Amherst, Nova Scotia, 1919', *Acadiensis* 9: 56–77.

Reimer, Chad. 1993. 'War, Nationhood, and Working-Class Entitlement: The Counter-hegemonic Challenge of the 1919 Winnipeg General Strike', *Prairie Forum* 18, 2 (Fall): 219–37.

Robin, Martin. 1968. *Radical Politics and Canadian Labour, 1880–1930*. Kingston: Industrial Relations Centre, Queen's University.

Rodney, Williams. 1968. *Soldiers of the International: A History of the Communist Party of Canada, 1919–1929*. Toronto: University of Toronto Press.

Roome, Patricia. 1989. 'Amelia Turner and Calgary Labour Women, 1919–1935', in Linda Kealey and Joan Sangster, eds, *Beyond the Vote: Canadian Women and Politics*, pp. 89–117. Toronto: University of Toronto Press.

Rouillard, Jacques. 1976. *Histoire du syndicalisme québécois: Des origines à nos jours*. Montreal: Boreal.

————. 1981–2. 'Les travailleurs juifs de la confection à Montreal (1910–1980)', *Labour/Le Travail* 8/9 (Autumn/Spring): 253–9.

Savage, Candace. 1979. *Our Nell: A Scrapbook Biography of Nellie McClung*. Saskatoon: Prairie Books.

Schonning, Gil. 1955. 'Union–Management Relations in the Pulp and Paper Industry in Ontario and Quebec, 1914–1950'. PhD dissertation, University of Toronto.

Scott, Bruce. 1976. '"A Place in the Sun": The Industrial Council at Massey-Harris, 1919–1929', *Labour/Le Travail* 1: 158–92.

Scott, Stanley. 1977. 'A Profusion of Issues: Immigrant Labour, the World War, and the Cominco Strike of 1917', *Labour/Le Travail* 2: 54–78.

Seager, Allen. 1981. 'A Proletariat in Wild Rose Country: The Alberta Coal Miners, 1905–1945'. PhD dissertation, York University.

————. 1981. 'Finnish Canadians and the Ontario Miners' Movement', *Polyphony* 3 (Fall): 35–45.

————. 1986. 'Class, Ethnicity, and Politics in the Alberta Coalfields, 1905–1945', in Dirk Hoerder, ed., *'Struggle a Hard Battle': Essays on Working-Class Immigrants*, pp. 304–24. De Kalb: Northern Illinois University Press.

Seager, Allen, and David Roth. 1998. 'British Columbia and the Mining West: A Ghost of a Chance', in Craig Heron, ed., *The Worker's Revolt in Canada, 1917–1925*, pp. 231–67. Toronto: University of Toronto Press.

Selekman, Ben M. 1927. *Postponing Strikes: A Study of the Industrial Disputes Investigation Act of Canada*. New York: Russell Sage Foundation.

Siemiatycki, Myer. 1978. 'Munitions and Labour Militancy: The 1916 Hamilton Machinists' Strike', *Labour/Le Travail* 3: 131–52.

————. 1986. 'Labour Contained: The Defeat of a Rank and File Workers' Movement in Canada, 1914–1921'. PhD dissertation, York University.

Thomson, Anthony. 1977. '"The Large and Generous View": The Debate on Labour Affiliation in the Canadian Civil Service, 1918–1928', *Labour/Le Travail* 2: 108–36.

Vance, Catherine. 1968. *Not by Gods, But by People: The Story of Bella Hall Gauld*. Toronto: Progress Books.

Wade, Susan. 1980. 'Helena Gutteridge: Votes for Women and Trade Unions', in Barbara Latham and Cathy Kess, eds, *In Her Own Right: Selected Essays on Women's History in B.C.*, pp. 187–204. Victoria: Camosun College.

Watson, Louise. 1976. *She Was Never Afraid: The Biography of Annie Buller*. Toronto: Progress Books.

Yeo, David Patrick. 1986. 'An Alliance Unrealized: Farmers, Labour, and the 1919 Winnipeg General Strike'. MA thesis, University of Calgary.

———. 1989. 'Rural Manitoba Views the Winnipeg General Strike', *Prairie Forum* 14, 1 (Spring): 23–36.

Zerker, Sally. 1982. *The Rise and Fall of the Toronto Typographical Union, 1832–1972: A Case Study of Foreign Domination*. Toronto: University of Toronto Press.

Zucchi, John E. 1988. *Italians in Toronto: Development of a National Identity, 1875–1935*. Montreal and Kingston: McGill-Queen's University Press.

CHAPTER 10
The Plight of the Working Girl
Janice Newton

Although socialists were reluctant to place domestic labour on their agenda, they were eager to wrestle with one of the more startling social changes of the century—the increasing number of women entering the paid labour force. A larger proportion of women were visible working in urban centres and industry, and the mounting concern about the impact of industrialization and urbanization often coalesced around images of women 'taking men's jobs' and abandoning their traditional place in the home.

In this context, it is important to remember that the vast majority of women were not engaged in paid labour outside the home. Across the country, roughly one in six women worked for wages and roughly one in seven workers were women. The women who worked tended to be employed in jobs that were thought suitable for their sex. The largest percentage were in the service sector (42 per cent), most as domestic servants. A significant number (31 per cent) did manual work, mainly in light manufacturing. Some 24 per cent of women in the paid labour force had white-collar jobs, more than half of which were in low-paying and racially segregated professions such as teaching and nursing. . . .

Immigrant women often occupied the lowest-paid sector of the female labour market, for race and ethnicity further divided the workforce.[1] Governments and private agencies actively encouraged women's immigration to fill jobs that Canadian women shunned, such as domestic service (Leslie, 1974; Barber, 1985, 1986a, 1986b, 1987; Lacelle, 1987). The female presence in the labour force was further characterized by its youth. In 1921 almost 70 per cent of wage-earning women were under 25 years of age and few women older than 35 worked for wages (Synge, 1975; Leacy, 1983). Women typically worked when they were young and single, often while they were still living at home, and most quit their jobs when they married. This pattern was imposed by employers, who refused to hire married women, and it was also expected by the wage-earning women, for they anticipated a life of unpaid domestic work once they married and had a family to raise. Both the inexperience and expectations of women hampered their ability to organize and fight for better working conditions. However, some wage-earning women defied these generalities, did not live with their parents, and had dependants to support. These women struggled to make ends meet in the face of employer discrimination, low wages, significant increases in the cost of living, and widespread discrimination against women as tenants. . . .

All workers at this time faced enormous difficulties maintaining acceptable working conditions and wages. The trade union movement was beleaguered by uncertain business cycles, dramatic increases in the cost of living, hostile employers, and pro-management governments. By 1911, only 5 per cent of the entire Canadian labour force was unionized, and by 1921 this had increased to only 10 per cent (White, 1980). Women workers faced additional barriers. Since they assumed that their employment in the labour force was temporary, and since they received low wages and had to endure long, arduous hours of labour both at work and at home, few women had the resources, energy, or will to devote to the improvement of their wages and working conditions. Yet women workers did unionize in a variety of sectors. Garment workers, textile workers, telephone operators, domestics, nurses, retail clerks, waitresses, laundry workers, and teachers tried to organize in a number of communities across Canada between 1900 and 1920, though some jobs, such as domestic labour, proved exceedingly difficult to unionize because of the isolated nature of the work.

. . . In 1889 the Trades and Labor Congress (TLC) voted to include in its platform the 'abolition of child labour' and 'female labour in all branches of industrial life such as mines, workshops, factories, etc.'. The clause was not removed until 1914 (Hobbs, 1988: 34). While some trade unions supported wage-earning women's right to equal pay or minimum wages, they seldom had

the inclination or power to enforce these claims consistently. Furthermore, the issue of equal pay was double-edged; many of the male trade unionists assumed that if employers were forced to pay equal wages, they would preferentially hire men. Even union support for a minimum wage for women was attenuated and was given far less support than wages for men. . . .

In short, women confronted powerful forces, both ideological and structural, in their efforts to defend their interests as workers. Representing less than 20 per cent of women, the female labour force was young, inexperienced, segregated into low-paying jobs, and often isolated in the workplace. All this served to inhibit these workers' ability to act collectively. The trade union movement, which might have offered some help, was in itself small and beleaguered, and when not actively hostile to employed women, it was at best ambivalent. The other potential ally of the employed woman, the women's movement, consistently failed to support employed women's interests, often speaking *for* working-class women rather than letting them represent their own interests. In this context, socialists were eager to claim the 'problem' of wage-earning women for the socialist agenda, but much of the structural and ideological ambivalence of the era was echoed by the Canadian left.

The left and the labour movement both drew upon the myth of the family wage. They harked back to an idealized bygone era when a man earned enough wages to support a wife and family.[2] This ideal of a family wage in fact obscured the reality of working-class life, for women (and children too, in many cases) had always worked and contributed to the economic survival of the working class, though much of their labour was unpaid. How did socialists reconcile the family-wage ideal with women's fight for rights as workers? . . .

The socialist movement offered different theoretical analyses of women in the labour force, but none resolved the contradictory interests of working-class women. The ideal of the family wage was used by some to attack women's presence in the labour force. One of these critics was the German Marxist, Karl Kautsky,[3] who pointed out that the economic development of capitalism, through the introduction of machinery, enabled employers to use weaker and unskilled workers, especially women and children. . . . The demand for the family wage did not necessarily prevent socialist women from demanding their rights as waged labourers. . . . Some socialists of the period argued that men ought to earn a family wage but that if they did not (or if a woman was not supported by a father or husband), women ought to have the right to work and have equal pay so that they could support themselves and their families.

The German socialist August Bebel was frequently cited for his study of women in Germany, where 30 per cent of women worked for pay.[4] Unlike some trade unionists and socialists, Bebel spoke out against the working-class antipathy to women in the labour force. The solution to the problem, he argued, lay in recognizing capitalism as the source of women's oppression. In seeking liberation, women must join male comrades, and socialists should accept women as fellow workers, fight for their rights, and educate them to the need for socialism (Bebel, 1904; *Western Clarion*, 1906: 3). While Bebel's ideas were progressive, he was encouraging women to integrate themselves into a struggle that was essentially defined by the experience of men.

Socialist women took an interest in theoretical works that offered an analysis of their position. In 1908 members of the [Social Party of Canada] SPC in Toronto started a women's study club and urged other women to follow suit. The group studied Engels's *Origin of the Family, Private Property and the State*, Rappaport's *Looking Forward*, Morgan's *Ancient Society*, and Bebel's *Woman in the Past,*

Present and Future (*Western Clarion*, 17 October 1908). American socialists and feminists, including several of the leading women socialists in the American left, further articulated and developed ideas on women and work, drawing on American experience and moulding socialist theory to the North American context. . . .

This literature provided Canadian socialists with a third perspective on working women, one that more closely focused on the problem of woman's dependence in the home and in the labour force. Charlotte Perkins Gilman was one such American feminist whose ideas gained currency in the Canadian socialist press, mainly through the women's columns.[5] Gilman acknowledged that women had unique natural and moral virtues, and argued that these had been stultified in modern society because of woman's economic dependence. She articulated the positive side of women taking part in waged labour—that work beyond the home had the potential to develop woman's independence and maturity to the full in areas other than the maternal and feminine realms. . . .

More revealing than this abstract theorizing were themes that emerged in specific discussions regarding different kinds of work. First, the left's astonishing ignorance about the actual nature of women's waged labour in Canada crippled its ability to develop a coherent response to the needs of women in the labour force. Second, different voices spoke to women's issues within the left, and those of wage-earning women were rarely publicized and were not well represented. Third, colouring discussions about different types of work were implicit assumptions about the kind of paid work that was appropriate to men and women; socialists did not universally endorse the family-wage ideal, but they consistently argued that certain kinds of paid work 'naturally' belonged to women.

. . . In both Britain and the United States, socialist movements served an important role in publicizing the working conditions of women in factories and shops. Specific analyses of real working conditions informed and enriched the theoretical analyses of women's work in both Britain and Germany. These accounts, which were often cited by Canadian socialists, were used to dramatize the exploitation of women workers under capitalism. Canadian socialists also exposed working conditions across Canada, but reports involving women workers were comparatively rare. The extent of coverage varied among the different socialist parties, tending to increase when the party paper had a women's column. Despite this, the left-wing press's coverage of the actual working conditions of women in Canada was sparse. . . .

In 1899 and 1900 the efforts of garment workers to unionize in Ontario did receive considerable attention. The most notorious firm was Eaton's. It paid its workers less than other stores and enforced rules which, according to the union, were unbearable 'to ordinary human nature'. In describing some of these rules, the *Citizen and Country* provided a rare published glimpse of the working conditions for women at Eaton's:

All operatives are locked out till noon if they are not at work fifteen minutes before eight o'clock in the morning—not a minute's grace is allowed although they all work by the piece. When they are in they are locked in, and are not allowed to leave the room, no matter what the cause may be, unless they procure a pass, written by one man and signed by another. If these worthies are not in the department the applicant must wait till noon or six o'clock . . . These are only a few of the rules which obtain in the T. Eaton Co's departmental store. (*Citizen and Country*, 29 July 1899: 2)

The paper sympathetically announced union meetings and condemned Eaton's for paying wages on which a woman could neither live nor dress properly. 'A firm that treats its work-people like The T. Eaton Co., Limited, ought not to get the patronage of decent people,' (*Citizen and Country*, 8 July 1899: 2) it concluded. Independent of Eaton's advertising revenue, the *Citizen and Country* published correspondence about labour disputes from the garment workers' organizer, Sam Landers.[6]

Socialist papers often relied on trade unionists for reports of working conditions, but the interests of women workers and racial minorities were poorly represented. One union committee investigating the use of Chinese labour in Vancouver shops noted that orientals outnumbered whites in the garment industry. The union report stated that 'a large amount of this trade is taken away from our white girls, who are thus left without a means of subsistence.'. . .

Because 70 per cent of women who earned wages were under the age of twenty-five, the union movement often linked the problem of women with the problem of child labour. After lengthy deliberation, the Toronto Dominion Labour Council of 1902 supported demands for equal pay, equal civil and political rights for men and women, and the abolition of child labour under the age of 15. However, the *Canadian Socialist* criticized this platform for not being socialist enough. Its socialist solution? The abolition of child labour under 18 years of age (*Canadian Socialist*, 12 July 1902: 3).

The early socialist press uncritically publicized reports by factory inspectors, who tended to focus narrowly on health and morality issues that did not necessarily reflect the concerns of women. One source claimed that factory women, who were frequently overworked in comparison with seamstresses and shop girls, were a threat to 'the mothers of the future workman' (*Western Socialist*, 6 December 1902: 3). More often, factory life was seen as a prelude to a life of immorality. The *Citizen and Country* reported the findings of Ontario's provincial inspector of prisons and public charities, Mr Noxon, who attributed the increase in drunkenness and vice among young women to their migration from the countryside to the city and the loss of the 'restraining influences of home life'. . . .

Socialists rarely conducted first-hand investigations of women's work. While travelling with her husband to establish a left-wing paper in British Columbia, Mrs G. Weston Wrigley took pains to observe the working conditions of women in Chicago, and she expressed surprise at finding married women, even middle-class women, engaged in business (*Western Socialist*, 24 January 1903: 3). Her surprise is a measure of how superficially even a prominent socialist woman appreciated the average woman's working conditions. A factory in British Columbia was visited by a representative of the *Western Socialist*, who applauded the 'great advance' the company had made 'by casting aside the old methods of Chinese sweatshop labor' and replacing them with 'the modern factory system of machine-made shirts and garments, the machines being operated exclusively by girls who belong to the garment workers' union'. . . .

The women's column edited by Bertha Merrill Burns provided a more coherent focus on the problems of women in the labour force. . . . Merrill Burns defended women in the labour force. To the argument that they drove down men's wages, she responded, 'Of course no woman goes into business life with the idea of remaining in it forever or securing sufficient salary to support a family. She expects someday to be a housewife. Her pay is small accordingly, and she becomes thus a leverage for the lowering of the salaries of her male competitors for employment.' With those who

argued that the solution lay in men's hands—'to marry them'—Burns disagreed. 'I do not believe if all women of the working world were instantly married and settled in homes it would solve the industrial problem for the men workers and until that problem is solved marriages and homes will continue to grow appallingly less.' . . .

Merrill Burns cited the American socialist Josephine Conger, who dismissed the idea that it was unnatural for women to work for wages: 'The capacities of the women of today are so broadened that it is impossible to relegate them to the narrow limits of household duties and expect these to fill their lives . . . Under Socialism the opportunity to work will be open to every man and woman' (*Western Clarion*, 22 October 1903: 3). Another writer, May Drummond, disagreed with Conger. In response to the question 'Will a wife be allowed to work for a lazy husband under socialism?' she argued that under socialism no man, unless physically or mentally incapacitated, would have his wife work: 'A man will not let a woman support him in these times . . . if he is able to use the powers with which he has been endowed'; but if he could not work, it would be 'a woman's privilege and joy' to supply 'whatever is necessary for his as well as for her own maintenance' (*Western Socialist*, 29 November 1902: 3). . . .

It was Merrill Burns's belief that in the absence of equal pay, women workers drove down wages of men, but she repeatedly contested the idea that the prohibition of female labour would solve this problem. It was the exigencies of poverty, not women, that she criticized. Women worked because they needed to support themselves and their families. Ideally, they should be able to stay at home when nursing and raising children, but this was not meant to preclude work for wages. Indeed, waged labour for women was discussed as a positive, enriching experience, of which a woman could be proud. Socialists should fight to include women workers as equals in their struggles.[7] Merrill Burns's views did not carry the day in the socialist movement prior to 1905. The early movement wrestled with the 'problem' of women in the labour force while missing a crucial piece of the puzzle: the voice of working women.

After the SPC gained ascendancy within the Canadian left, the coverage of women's issues changed. With the abolition of the women's column from the party paper, first-hand descriptions of women in the Canadian labour force all but disappeared. When the party covered the telephone strike of 1906, which included female operators, it addressed its remarks not to women workers but to male trade unionists. However, the poverty of women workers continued to be a favoured illustration of the brutality and decadence of capitalism. In 1905, for instance, the party's report of a laundry strike took particular note of the financial plight of the women strikers: 'Some of the female workers were so emphatically out of funds as to have nothing to carry them over Sunday, and were forced to accept the assistance at the hands of good Samaritans . . . A woman with three small children had been turned into the street by the landlord, and the only breakfast her little ones got on the morning of the strike was such as came from the lunch pails of the strikers' (*Western Clarion*, 24 June 1905: 2, 31 March 1906: 4; 19 May 1906: 4).

As the SPC imposed greater consistency in discussions of women in the labour force, naivety vanished. The party eagerly exposed the class bias of reformers, yet the party platform rejected any immediate demands, including equal pay for women, minimum wage legislation, and even women's right to work. Even while sections of the labour movement in Vancouver fought for women's right to work during the depression of 1913–14,

the SPC remained silent.[8] Instead of offering support, the party insisted that capitalism forced women to work—a weak footing from which to defend women in the labour force.

Individual party members often defied the SPC platform. In Vancouver, four socialist candidates running in the school board elections demanded better payment of teachers, equal pay for men and women, and the end of discrimination against married women. Frederick Urry, a candidate in Port Arthur, Ontario, was criticized by the SPC for making such demands and was told he should stand only for the abolition of the wage system. . . .

A central problem was the concern that work, especially factory work, violated a woman's modesty, threatened her moral purity, and led to prostitution: 'I have seen women scantily and improperly clad . . . hauling heavy wagons by chains, past rows of men to the ovens. The heat was stifling and it was almost impossible to breath because of the gases that filled the room. Because of this women had their arms bare to the shoulders, and in order to get every bit of refreshing air to their bodies their scanty garments were thrown back at the throats, so that [t]heir persons were exposed to the gaze of the men workers, especially when they stooped to lift the chains or to empty or fill the wagons.' This accusation was balanced by the claim that 'a glimpse into the hall room of the social elite would show women more improperly clad than would be found in any foundry in Massachusetts.'[9] Eaton's was censured for moral threats to its garment workers: 'Young girls on starvation wages have been subjected to gross insults and temptations from foremen and examiners' (*Western Clarion*, 20 April 1912: 1). Beyond the shelter of a home, the factory hand or shop girl was seen as especially vulnerable to sexual abuse or prostitution. Socialists dramatized this threat to the moral character of working-class women

in order to imply that women were unsafe in the public world of paid employment. . . .

While discussions of single women focused on their morality, the discussions of married women centred on their abandonment of maternal and domestic duties. According to the *Western Clarion* writer Gourock, 'Socialists don't believe in mothers working at all. They hold that under a sane industrial system wherein the worker would obtain the full value of his products, the man would earn sufficient to raise and maintain his family under proper conditions, and that the various exigencies which may arise, such as sickness and accident, be provided against by the community'. . . .

Working conditions that threatened woman's health were especially pernicious because they threatened maternal potential. Gourock echoed contemporary eugenists when he accused employed mothers of contributing to the 'deterioration of the race'. Moses Baritz reported Dr Helen MacMurchy's findings that the infant mortality rate had risen from 128.22 per thousand in 1898 to 162.54 per thousand in 1906, with an especially high rate of 196 per thousand in Toronto. . . . This ostensible concern for the health of working women needs close examination. First, it was directed at the effects that a woman's health had on her family, rather than concern for the woman herself.[10] Second, although domestic work, paid or unpaid, was physically demanding, it was only with regard to work outside the home that socialists decried the consequences for a woman's physical and moral well-being. Their fears about the immoral or strenuous nature of factory work were partly rooted in anxiety about women leaving their 'natural' sphere and being unable to guard the health of the working class family. . . .

In some respects, the Social Democratic Party of Canada (SDPC) approached the rights and interests of working women differently. Most important, it endorsed immediate demands, was more willing to discuss women's issues in the party press, and included them in its party platform. These distinctions were evident in *Cotton's Weekly* even before it became the official party paper of the SDPC. *Cotton's* carried on the early socialist tradition of reporting working conditions in Canada and sometimes providing sympathetic coverage of labour disputes involving women workers. A nurses' strike in Brantford in 1909 and in New Glasgow in 1910, a textile strike in Montreal in 1911, and a garment workers' strike in Montreal in 1913 were all briefly mentioned.[11] However, in comparison with the detailed coverage of labour disputes involving male workers, these brief references provided limited information about the cause, nature, or extent of women's strikes.

Like the SPC, *Cotton's* dramatized the desperate position of women. Census data highlighted the wage disparity between men and women. Women's wages were less than half that of men's; in Ontario, wages fell below subsistence level for female workers. As illustrated in C.P. Gilman's poem 'The Wolf at the Door', poverty drove women to accept such low wages. Weakened by unsafe and strenuous working conditions, women's maternal capacity declined, resulting in feeble and stunted children.[12] William U. Cotton, editor of *Cotton's Weekly*, blamed the growing infant death rate on the poverty that compelled mothers to enter the labour force and abandon their children: 'Bottle fed babies are the ones that die . . . The babies whose mothers are in an economic position to care for them do not die . . . Woman labour is responsible for the slaughter of the innocents. What woman labour? It is not the parasite wives of the parasite receivers of rent, interest and profit among whom the infant death rate is high. It is the labouring class who suffer the snatching away of their little ones' (*Cotton's Weekly*, 8 September 1910).[13] Dora F. Kerr questioned the assumption that work caused women injury: 'It is not the industrial work which injures women, but overwork whether in home or factory' (Kerr, 1909: 7). . . .

Although the SDPC had greater sympathy than the SPC for wage-earning women, it too sometimes blamed them: 'You may not be aware that every woman working outside of the home is in part responsible for the lower rate in wages. The girls go out of the home to earn something, and gladly accept anything that is offered to them.' As a result, the boss 'sends away the men whom he had to pay twice the wage for which the girls will work, and employs girls instead' (Malkiel, 1913: 3). The SDPC was unable to resolve the contradiction between the view that women worked because they had to, and that working women drove down men's wages—or worse, that they caused male unemployment. Many argued that socialism would solve the problem through the full employment of men who supported families. Under socialism, 'instead of thousands of female clerks working twelve and fourteen hours a day for wages upon which they cannot live, male clerks could be employed who would work four hours a day at a salary of a hundred dollars a week' (*Cotton's Weekly*, 2 September 1909: 1). Socialism would simply eliminate children and women from the labour force.

Through the women's columns in the SDPC press, women disputed this view and emphasized how important women's economic independence was to socialism. Mary Cotton Wisdom led the offensive. She was thankful that things had changed from the old days when 'marriage was considered a woman's only salvation,' she said. 'Girls today are not dependent on fathers and brothers for their support till some other comes along to do her the honour of choosing her; giving her bed and board together with the privilege of wearing his name . . . The fact of sex makes no difference; woman can, and does, and will earn her own living and live her own life independent of man' (Wisdom, 1909: 7) . . .

Anxious to avoid the charge that if women worked, socialism would destroy the home, some writers stressed the advantages that women's economic independence could bring to marriage: 'Socialism will guarantee to women as well as to men, an opportunity for employment, and at the same reward for an hour's labour. Women will thus be enabled to earn their own living, if they choose, and not be dependent on some close-fisted, autocratic lord of creation called man. Women being free can follow out their individuality, and being the equal of man, will be companions instead of mere housekeepers, playthings or sex slaves.' For this writer, the demand for women's economic independence did not contradict the claim that men should support families: 'Socialists believe that it is the father's business to provide for the family and since socialism will enable every man to easily do this, marriage and home life will be encouraged' (*Cotton's Weekly*, 11 February 1909: 7). . . . As is evident from these excerpts, the women's columns in the SDPC press provided a broader forum for feminist ideas about women's economic independence. What did this mean for the party's platform?

Party members endorsed the crucial but limited demand for equal pay, for this could reduce the fear that women would displace men and drive down overall wage rates. However, only a few articles in *Cotton's* also acknowledged that socialism had to go beyond equal pay, to challenge the waged-labour relationship itself and demand that a woman receive the 'full value of the wealth she creates' or of 'the labour she produces'. Rejecting the liberalism inherent in equal pay demands, these articles cast the discussion within a socialist theoretical framework.[14] In answer to the question 'Would women in the co-operative Commonwealth get the same pay as men?' one writer replied, 'In socialized industry each would be paid for his or her product, such value to be determined by the amount of human labour socially required for its production. . . . If the average woman would produce equal amount of a given product in the same time required by the average man, the result would be the same pay for the same work. If the woman would do more—produce more—than the man she would get more pay for it' (*Cotton's Weekly*, 26 May 1910: 3). . . .

Some articles favoured minimum-wage laws for women workers but . . . the SDPC was . . . discerning in its support of other immediate demands to help the woman worker. It criticized the government for being slow to introduce measures that employers opposed, such as early closing laws and minimum hours of labour for women and children. It attacked the hypocrisy of laws that forbade Chinese to employ white girls, thus reserving for 'white Christian gentlemen' the exclusive right to exploit. Shelters for working girls and consumer leagues did not provide the wages women needed, it maintained. Some specific suggestions to help employed mothers, such as creches, were discussed. Prohibiting the employment of women before and after childbirth was rejected because the three-week period of 'maternity leave' was too short: 'That this is not sufficient is readily appreciated by whoever knows that at least two months are required for the restoration of the organ, and as a rule much more for the restitution of a fair amount of health' (*Cotton's Weekly*, 4 March 1909: 3). Although the SDPC was prepared to support immediate demands, it remained skeptical about many of the reforms directed at working women.[15]

In 1911 a labour dispute inspired the SDPC to act. The garment workers' strike at Gordon Mackay's in Toronto involved 45 members of the International Ladies' Garment Workers Union. The dispute involved piece-work rates, which resulted in a wage cut of more than 20 per cent. Union members across Toronto contributed to the strike fund, 'men giving 50 cents a week and girls 25 cents'. But the company carried on with the help of female strike breakers, who were duly criticized in *Cotton's*:

> While it is very encouraging to see such unity among the union workers we are disgusted to find that our Canadian girls are not unwilling to slave 'faithfully' and 'diligently' at the very work our Jewish comrades who are in the overwhelming majority in this union would scorn to touch . . . CANADIAN GIRLS ARE HANDED WORK THAT JEWISH GIRLS REFUSE TO DO. They are so selfish that they have refused the union offers. This union realizes that as they are Jewish, racial and religious prejudices are animating the girls to take their places and to decline to go out on strike with Jews. In view of this fact, Jewish unionists made a very fair offer of five dollars per week to single workers who would go on strike with them and ten dollars a week to any having someone to support . . . OH TORONTO WORKING WOMEN, WHY BE SO BLIND, SO SELFISH, SO HEARTLESS? SHAME ON THE VAUNTED WARMTH OF WOMANLY HEARTS

> IF JEWISH WORKING MEN CAN BE REPLACED BY CHEAP FEMALE LABOUR. (*Cotton's Weekly*, 17 August 1911: 4)

The union's efforts to dissuade the scabs were unusual. In allocating strike pay, the union ignored sex and distinguished between single workers and those supporting others. This did not dissuade the women strike breakers, and the strike dragged on for months. Members of the Toronto Suffrage League approached the women to show them 'the injustice of their act in taking the places of these family men who cannot live on ten dollars per week, a wage that is considered exceptionally good by a single girl.' Although the union acknowledged that some women might support families, the suffragists did not make this distinction. Neither did the SDPC. In support of the strike, several thousand copies of this issue of *Cotton's* were distributed, and *Cotton's* coverage was credited with assisting the union's victory. After three months, the employer was forced to accept a closed shop, and the strikebreakers were laid off (*Cotton's Weekly*, 17 August 1911: 4).[16] In the context of this labour dispute, the needs of men to support their families quickly overshadowed any sympathy for the single working woman.

Two features of the left's positions on working women stand out. First, socialists spoke *about* working women, but the women themselves rarely spoke directly about their work experiences.[17] Second, arguments about women and work were often contradictory. An article which claimed that socialism would allow men to earn sufficient wages to support a family could at the same time claim that under socialism women would have economic independence and be free to work. Compared with the SPC, the SDPC was more supportive of claims for women's economic independence, but both parties unabashedly discriminated against women in their own hiring and advertising practices. None of the parties offered a coherent resolution of the contradictory claims about socialism and women's work. This reflected the low status of women's issues in the party and the relative silence of working women.

Notes

1. The importance of gender, class, ethnicity, and religion in the Nova Scotia labour force is discussed by D.A. Muise in 'Industrial Context of Inequality: Female Participation in Nova Scotia's Paid Labour Force, 1871–1921', *Acadiensis* 20 (Spring 1991): 3–31. Alicja Muszinski discusses gender and race in 'Race and Gender: Structural Determinants in the Formation of British Columbia's Salmon Cannery Labour Forces', in Gregory S. Kealey, ed., *Class, Gender and Region* (St John's: Committee on Canadian Labour History, 1988); Silvia Hamilton looks at aspects of black women's work in Nova Scotia, including the exclusion of black women from professions such as nursing until well into the twentieth century, in 'Our Mothers Grand and Great', *Canadian Women's Studies* 11 (Spring 1991): 45–53. Ruth Frager's 'Class and Ethnic Barriers to Feminist Perspectives in Toronto's Jewish Labour Movement, 1919–1939', *Studies in Political Economy* 30 (Autumn 1989): 143–65, and *Sweatshop Strife: Class, Ethnicity, and Gender in the Jewish Labour Movement of Toronto, 1900–39* (Toronto: University of Toronto Press, 1992) show that ethnicity served to undermine support for women's issues in the Jewish labour movement. Varpu Lindstrom-Best offers extensive research on women in the Finnish community. There are several useful sources on women from other ethnic or racial groups: Jean Burnet, *Looking into My Sister's Eyes: An Exploration in Women's History* (Toronto: Multicultural History Society, 1986); Doreen Marie Indra, 'The Invisible Mosaic: Women, Ethnicity and the Vancouver Press, 1905–1976', *Canadian Ethnic Studies* 13, 1 (1981): 63–74'; Anna B. Woywitka, 'A Pioneer Woman in the Labour Movement', *Alberta History* 26 (Winter 1978): 10–16; Joseph Pivato, 'Italian Canadian Women Writers Recall History', *Canadian Ethnic Studies* 18, 1 (1986): 79–88'; Tamara Adilman, 'A Preliminary Sketch of Chinese Women and Work in British Columbia, 1858–1950', in Barbara Latham and Roberta Pazdro, eds, *Not Just Pin Money* (Victoria: Camosun College, 1984), 53–78; Mahinder Kaur Doman, 'A Note on Asia Indian Women in British Columbia, 1900–1935', in Barbara Latham and Roberta Pazdro, eds, *Not*

Just Pin Money (Victoria: Camosun College, 1984), 99–104; and a special issue of *Polyphony* 8 (1986) devoted to women and ethnicity.

2. For a discussion of the family wage debate, see Jane Humphries, 'Class Struggle and the Persistence of the Working Class Family', *Cambridge Journal of Economics* 1 (September 1977): 241–58; 'The Working Class Family, Women's Liberation, and Class Struggle: The Case of Nineteenth Century British History', *Review of Radical Political Economics* 9 (Fall 1977): 25–41; and 'The Working Class Family: A Marxist Perspective', in Jean Berthke Elshtain, ed., *The Family in Political Thought* (Amherst: University of Massachusetts Press, 1982); Michelle Barrett, *Women's Oppression Today: Some Problems in Marxist Feminist Analysis* (London: Verso, 1980); and Hilary Land, 'The Family Wage', *Feminist Review* 6, 3 (1980): 55–77. For Canadian sources on the family wage, see Patricia Connelly, 'Women Workers and the Family Wage in Canada', in Anne Hoiberg, ed., *Women and the World of Work* (New York: Plenum Press, 1980), 223–37; Linda Kealey, 'Canadian Socialism and the Woman Question', *Journal of Canadian Labour Studies* 13 (Spring 1984): 77–100.

3. Kautsky's work was reprinted by both the SPC and the SDPC. See 'The Dissolution of the Proletarian Family', *Western Clarion*, 9 December 1911, 3, and the following articles in *Cotton's Weekly*: 'Breaking Up the Home', 10 April 1913, 3; 'A New Middle Class', 29 May 1913, 2; 'Wages', 13 November 1913, 3.

4. See *Cotton's Weekly*, 26 December 1912, 2; 'May Day', 1 May 1913, 1; 28 August 1913, 4; 'The Socialization of Society', 11 December 1913, 2. See also *Western Clarion*, 1 December 1906, 2, and 'Treat Them as Pariahs', 3; 'Women and Socialism', 8 December 1906, 4; letter to Eugene Debs, 6 July 1907, 2.

5. See *Cotton's Weekly* as follows: 'We, as Women', 18 February 1909, 7; 'The Poor Ye Have Always with You', 20 May 1909, 7; 'The Wolf at the Door', 27 May 1909, 7, and 21 July 1910, 2; 'A Hope', 10 June 1909, 7; 'To Labour', 28 July 1910, 2; and 7 November 1912, 4; see also *Canadian Forward* as follows: 'It Takes Strength', 27 December 1916,

7; 10 May 1917, 1; and excerpt from *Women and Economics*, 10 June 1918, 3; and see *Western Clarion* as follows: 'To the Workers', 27 October 1906, 4; and 8 December 1906, 4.

6. Landers sold subscriptions for the *Citizen and Country* (27 July 1900, 4).

7. Letter from L.G.C., *Canadian Socialist,* 13 September 1902, 3; A.M. Simon, 'Who are the Union Wreckers?', *Canadian Socialist*, 30 August 1902, 1.

8. Mainly through the efforts of Helena Gutteridge, a Women's Employment League was established in Vancouver to aid women who were unemployed and seeking work during this depression. According to one report, 882 women registered: 132 of them were married and were sent to the relief office; 150 were employed in doll making; 140 were engaged as domestics; which left 495 women who also needed help. See 'Work of the Women's Employment League', *Minutes*, Vancouver Trades and Labor Council, book 3, 23a, and Irene Howard, *The Struggle for Social Justice in British Columbia: Helena Gutteridge the Unknown Reformer* (Vancouver: University of British Columbia Press, 1992), ch. 6.

9. See *Western Clarion* as follows: 'Work Women Like Beasts in Iron Plant', 24 February 1912, 3; 23 June 1906, 1; 21 July l906, 1; and 29 June 1912, 1.

10. This point is made by Jane Lewis in '"Motherhood Issues" in the Late Nineteenth and Twentieth Centuries', in Katherine Arnup, Andrée Lévesque,

and Ruth Roach Pierson, eds, *Delivering Motherhood* (London: Routledge, 1990), 7.

11. See *Cotton's Weekly*, 2 December 1909, 1; 3 November 1910, 2; 30 November 1911, 1; 7 December 1911, 4; and 21 December 1911, 3.

12. See the following in *Cotton's Weekly*: 'Wolf at the Door', 27 May 1909, 7; 'The Toll of the System', 24 March 1910, 2; 'Girl Workers in Montreal', 25 February 1909, 1; 'Vicious Fining System in Factories', 26 March 1914, 1; 'The Dangers from Dust', 10 June 1909, 7; and 'Sacrificing Young Girls', 22 April 1909, 7.

13. See also *Cotton's Weekly*, 23 July 1914, 2.

14. See *Cotton's Weekly* as follows: 'Women's Rights', 5 December 1912, 1; William Shier, 'About Women', 9 September 1909, 7; 'Women Should be Socialists', 18 March 1909, 7; and 12 May 1910, 2.

15. See *Cotton's Weekly* as follows: 'Early Closing Laws', 29 July 1909, 1; 16 December 1909, 4; 7 April 1910, 1; 19 May 1910, 2; 28 July 1910, 2; 26 January 1911, 1; 'Why a Working Man Should Be a Socialist', 25 May 1911, 3; 13 April 1911, 1; 20 February 1913, 1; 10 April 1913, 1; 22 May 1913, 1; and 31 July 1913, 4.

16. See *Cotton's Weekly*, 17 August 1911, 4; and 14 September 1911, 1.

17. In one rare instance, *Cotton's* published a working woman's letter that explained she had little time to read because she worked so hard (5 February 1914, 4).

References

Barber, Marilyn. 1985. 'The Women Ontario Welcomed: Immigrant Domestics for Ontario Homes, 1870–1930', in Alison Prentice and Susan Trofimenkoff, eds, *Neglected Majority*, vol. 2. Toronto: McClelland and Stewart.

———. 1986a. 'In Search of a Better Life: A Scottish Domestic in Rural Ontario', *Polyphony* 8: 13–16.

———. 1986b. 'Sunny Ontario for British Girls, 1900–1930', in Jean Burnet, ed., *Looking into My Sister's Eyes*. Toronto: Multicultural History Society.

———. 1987. 'The Servant Problem in Manitoba, 1896–1930', in Mary Kinnear, ed., *First Days, Fighting Days*. Regina: Canadian Plains Research Centre.

Bebel, August. 1904. *Women under Socialism*. New York, n.p.

Canadian Socialist. 1902. 12 July.

Citizen and Country. 1899. 8 July.

Citizen and Country. 1899. 'Organization Committee', 29 July.

Cotton's Weekly. 1909. 'Women', 11 February.

Cotton's Weekly. 1909. 4 March.

Cotton's Weekly. 1910. 26 May.

Cotton's Weekly. 1910. 'Why Do Children Die?', 8 September.

Cotton's Weekly. 1911. 17 August.

Cotton's Weekly. 1911. 14 September.

Hobbs, Margaret, and Ruth Roach Pierson. 1988. '"A Kitchen that Wastes No Steps": Gender, Class and the Home Improvement Plan, 1936–40', *Histoire Sociale/Social History* 21 (May): 9–37.

Kerr, Dora F. 1909. 'Should Women Work?', *Cotton's Weekly*, 15 April.

Lacelle, Claudette. 1987. *Urban Domestic Servants in 19th Century Canada*. Studies in Archaeology, Architecture and History. Ottawa: Environmental Canada, National Historic Parks and Sites.

Leacy, F.H., ed. 1983. *Historical Statistics of Canada*, 2nd ed. Ottawa: Statistics Canada and the Social Science Research Federation, series D102-122.

Leslie, Genevieve. 1974. 'Domestic Service in Canada, 1880–1920', in Janice Acton, et al., eds, *Women at Work in Ontario, 1850–1930*. Toronto: Women's Press.

Malkiel, Theresa S. 1913. 'The to [sic] Working Women', *Cotton's Weekly*, 4 December.

Synge, J. 1975. 'Young Working Class Women in Early 20th Century Hamilton: Their Work and Family Lives', in A.H. Turritin, ed., *Proceedings*, Workshop Conference on Blue Collar Workers and Their Communities. York University, 10–11 April.

Western Clarion. 1903. 22 October.

Western Clarion. 1905. 24 June.

Western Clarion. 1906. 31 March.

Western Clarion. 1906. 19 May.

Western Clarion. 1906. 1 December.

Western Clarion. 1908. 17 October.

Western Clarion. 1912. 20 April.

Western Socialist. 1902. 29 November.

Western Socialist. 1902. 6 December.

Western Socialist. 1903. 'Made in B.C. by Organized Labour', 24 January.

White, Julie. 1980. *Women and Unions*. Ottawa: Canadian Advisory Council on the Status of Women.

Wisdom, M. 1909. 'Woman's Suffrage', *Cotton's Weekly*, 8 April.

PART V

Capitalist Canada Consolidated and the Weight of Special Oppression, 1880–1939

'Race' clearly matters to working-class history. As capitalism consolidated in Canada, it complicated the ways in which a working-class was being formed and reformed, layering the experience of labouring people with the special oppressions of designated markers of visible difference. Not only were workers subordinate to their employers and inferior to those whose social station was always going to be higher than theirs, but there were also segments of the working class marked as additionally oppressed because their skin was darker or other features of their physicality discernibly different than the supposedly more Canadian component of the population that had come from the British Isles, and was privileged in its 'whiteness'.

Recent scholarship in Canadian working-class history has increasingly addressed how 'race' and ethnicity have shaped the lives of workers and their families. It has drawn on recent writings on race and labour in the United States, where the legacies of chattel slavery, the influence of the civil rights movement, and the 1960s politics of black liberation shaped a set of writings in the 1980s and 1990s that are increasingly cognizant of the importance of 'whiteness' in the making of the American working class. This scholarship posed critical questions about the historical construction of white identity as a 'norm', superior to all other ethnic and racial identifications. In the process it exposed how certain groups, including African Americans, Asians, Latinos, and Aboriginal peoples, had been structured into particular social spaces, restricted to certain kinds of work, and excluded from other occupations sectors. As the working class was made and remade in the United States and Canada (albeit differently), its history was never far removed from general and wide-ranging processes of racialization.

'Race' itself is a historical category. In the nineteenth century, conventional scientific wisdom posited that specific population groups could be labelled in accordance with their physiological characteristics, which included skin colour, hair texture, and facial configuration, designated as 'races'. Because this was an epoch of social Darwinism and European dominance, these 'races', with their specific differences, were also ordered hierarchically, situated according to their supposedly innate intelligence and capabilities. Whites ranked highest; blacks lowest. With advancing scientific knowledge establishing conclusively in the twentieth century that humanity is not a racially ordered hierarchy, but rather a continuum, the racialization of the world's population that was developed in the nineteenth century has been proven to be a social construction. Each supposed 'race', rather than being a singular group, actually contains individuals who have more in common with other demographic groups than with their own supposed 'kind'. There is no serious scientific evidence to suggest that specific human populations are superior or inferior, more or less intelligent, or that particular physiological characteristics signify attributes. There is, however, abundant historical evidence that physical difference has been racialized; that this labelling has influenced state policy and popular culture; and that both individuals and institutions have espoused the powerful ideology of racism that has privileged whites and oppressed peoples of colour. Though race, as a scientific entity, does not exist, 'race' as a social construction has played a powerful role in the making of the modern world, and of the class forces within it.

In Canada, the history of racialization is deep and historically wide-ranging. It has also changed remarkably over time. French Canadians were, historically, designated a 'race' apart throughout much of the nineteenth and twentieth centuries; Canada as a country of 'two races' was a terminology that was employed as late as the mid-1960s. Jewish citizens of Canada were categorized as a 'race' throughout much of the same period. Today, designation of such linguistic and cultural groups as races appears anachronistic or worse. Yet African Canadians, Asians, Aboriginal peoples, and, increasingly, in the post 9/11 world of the War on Terror, those who appear to be Muslim, continue to be racialized with specific, often quite horrible, consequences.

The following articles address 'race' as a component of Canadian working-class history. For much of Canadian history, including in the years leading up to 1945, the racialization of particular groups was of fundamental importance in both capitalism's consolidation *and* the ways in which labour as a social class was recruited, reconfigured, and resisted by those who would secure its subordination. Important areas where racialization figured prominently include the immigration policies of the state, the growth of unions and the ways in which they opened or closed their doors to particular groups, scientific management and its understanding of how specific sectors of the workforce needed to be 'handled' so as to increase their productivity, and welfare capitalism and its appreciation of the need to 'Canadianize' labour to better integrate it into the broad project of sustaining a certain 'standard of living'.

Sarah-Jane Mathieu examines the recruitment of black labour as sleeping car porters for the growing and politically powerful railroad monopolies in the late nineteenth and early twentieth centuries. The railroads originally targeted men from impoverished urban enclaves such as Halifax's Africville, home to a community of Nova Scotia blacks, but they also turned increasingly to other black populations in the US and in the Caribbean. They imagined such locales ideal places from which to draw the malleable labour force that they considered suitable for the servile occupation of railroad porter.

The racialized nature of the porter's work culture figures prominently in Mathieu's account. So, too, do the ways that African Canadians strove to secure some measure of job security on the railroads, and the variety of political and organizational tactics that these workers used. The lengths that the railroad employers went to secure the labour they needed, including circumventing government immigration restrictions and facing an oppositional public outcry, remind us of how significant capitalist interests have been in fomenting the tensions associated with racialization.

As black workers struggled to create the kind of class solidarities necessary to combat this powerful interest, they unfortunately found that they could not count on the support of white workers employed in other railroad occupations, many of them in the pivotal skilled running trades that were essential to keeping trains moving on the transcontinental tracks. The Canadian Brotherhood of Railway Trainmen, like many craft unions of this period, clung to lily-white racist exclusionary practices, maintaining Jim Crow policies of segregation well into the twentieth century. Shunned by their white co-workers, black porters eventually had no option but to set up their own union, the Brotherhood of Sleeping Car Porters. Its history is outlined in a memoir by Stanley G. Grizzle, who worked on the railways for 20 years before becoming the first African Canadian judge in the Court of Canadian citizenship. As the history of railroad work reveals, the struggle to limit capital's capacity to exploit labour often faltered on the social wreckage of racism's divisive impact.

Andrew Parnaby's study of native longshoremen in British Columbia moves us forward in time, ending in the interwar period. He asks why Aboriginal men from the Squamish First Nation on Burrard Inlet worked in the longshoring trade on the Vancouver waterfront, exploring how Native workers' experiences changed over time. Like John Lutz, whose earlier article explored nineteenth-century Aboriginal peoples and waged labour, Parnaby demonstrates that Native workers managed to combine waged employment and the largely non-market economies of more traditional ways of life. They were enmeshed in a 'mixed' economy that saw them strategically enter wage labour to do particular jobs at specific times of the year, only to move out of such paid employment to engage in other activities as the seasons and the bounty of subsistence hunting and fishing dictated.

In the early twentieth century, Aboriginal men were able to have a foot in both Indigeneous and colonizing political economies. They used their communal solidarities and particular skills to carve out a place for themselves in the organization of longshoring. Able to adapt effectively to the distinct methods of hiring on the waterfront that prevailed in the early years of the industry, in which a casualized 'shape up' system suited Native interests, Aboriginal workers secured for themselves a niche in the demarcation of certain jobs and skills as being particularly associated with identifiable ethnic/cultural groups (with Native gangs allocated work associated with logs and lumbering). Aboriginal workers thus maintained their place in Vancouver's waterfront labour market up until World War I.

By the 1920s, however, the waterfront and its employment structures and workforces had been altered profoundly by a series of class struggles and employer innovations. Workers' attempts to unionize had been beaten back, and employers, feeling their strengths, had struck out at the informal mechanisms by which labour had flexed its muscles in terms of hiring processes. Employers determined that they needed to break the back of hiring casualization, which meant that they insisted on hiring non-union labour and ending the dominance of part-time, seasonally-orchestrated waterfront work. The carrot of welfare capitalism, more enticing to white workers than it was to Natives, was dangled in front of labouring noses. For the Squamish longshoremen these changes spelled the end of their integration into the wage labour market of Vancouver's waterfront.

Like Mathieu, Parnaby discusses the interconnections between political and union organizing on the part of racialized workers, as well as the changing relationship of Native men to the labour movement. At times, Aboriginal workers made common cause with trade unions; they also attempted, however, to create their own Native Brotherhood on the docks, a pattern of dual unionism that also developed in the British Columbia fishing industry. The relationship between white and Native workers within the labour movement did change over time, however. Depending on specific circumstances, as Gillian Creese has argued with respect to another racialized group in Vancouver, 'Oriental' labour, workers' organizations might in some periods reach toward and even develop racial integration and solidarity, while in other historical periods they could contribute to segregation, division, and white dominance.

Further Reading

Constance Backhouse, *Colour-Coded: A Legal History of Racism in Canada, 1900–1950* (Toronto: University of Toronto Press, 1999).

Gillian Creese, 'Exclusion or Solidarity? Vancouver Workers Confront the "Oriental" Problem', *BC Studies* 80 (Winter 1988–9): 24–51.

Ruth Frager, *Sweatshop Strife: Class, Ethnicity, and Gender in the Jewish Labour Movement in Toronto, 1900–1939* (Toronto: University of Toronto Press, 1992).

Stanley G. Grizzle, *My Name's Not George: The Story of the Brotherhood of Sleeping Car Porters in Canada—Personal Reminiscences of Stanley G. Grizzle* (Toronto: Umbrella Press, 1998).

Steven High, 'Native Wage Labour and Independent Commodity Production during the "Era of Irrelevance"', *Labour/Le Travail* 37 (Spring 1996): 243–64.

Franca Iacovetta with Paula Draper and Robert Ventresca, eds, *A Nation of Immigrants: Women, Workers, and Communities in Canadian History, 1840s–1960s* (Toronto: University of Toronto Press, 1998).

Rolf Knight, *Indians at Work: An Informal History of Native Labour in British Columbia, 1858–1930* (Vancouver: New Star Books, 1996).

John Marlyn, *Under the Ribs of Death* (Toronto: McClelland and Stewart, 1957).

Vic Satzewich, 'Whiteness Limited: Racialization and the Social Construction of "Peripheral Europeans"', *Histoire Sociale/Social History* 33 (November 2000): 271–89.

Visual Resources

NFB, *The Road Taken* (1996), dir. Selwyn Joseph, 52 minutes (on the Brotherhood of Sleeping Car Porters of Canada).

NFB, *Journey to Justice* (2000), dir. Roger McTair, 47 minutes (four pioneer activists against discrimination, including Stanley Grizzle, of the Brotherhood of Sleeping Car Porters).

Peripheral Visions Film and Video, *Continuous Journey* (2004), dir. Ali Kazemi, 87 minutes (in 1914, the *Komagata Maru*, with immigrants from India bound for British Columbia on board, became the first ship carrying migrants to Canada to be turned away by Canadians).

CHAPTER 11

North of the Colour Line: Sleeping Car Porters and the Battle Against Jim Crow on Canadian Rails, 1880–1920

Sarah-Jane (Saje) Mathieu

Canadian railways experienced unprecedented growth after the completion of the CPR trans-continental line in 1885. The Grand Trunk Railways (GTR), in conjunction with the Intercolonial Railway (ICR) and Canadian Northern Railway (CNRY), completed another transcontinental line and joined the rapacious competition for passenger traffic (Mika and Mika, 1986: 97, 208). Steam railway revenues soared at the turn of the century thanks to William Van Horne's and Charles M. Hays' enterprising expansion of railway service, especially in sleeping, dining, and parlour car departments.[1] A four hundred-pound bonvivant, Van Horne decided that he would make Canadian sleeping cars the most palatial liners in North America. The ambitious president tripled investments in the CPR's parlour and sleeping car department between 1885 and 1895.[2] He commissioned artists and interior designers who improved on Pullman's designs: they broadened berths to accommodate Van Horne's girth, installed bathrooms on first-class sleepers, and served generous portions in dining cars (Vaughn, 1920: 50–2, 141–3). . . .

Corporate enthusiasm over sleeping car service produced a prodigious demand for other symbols of Pullman's signature service—black railway workers. Soon after the Civil War, George Pullman singled-out newly emancipated African American men for his service, regarding them as seasoned service workers. Historian B.R. Brazeal contends that Pullman also solicited black porters because they were a 'plentiful source of labor [and] societal caste distinctions between Negro and white people

created a "social distance" which had become an accepted fact in the mores of American society' (Brazeal, 1946: 1–5). Canadian railway companies avidly sought black railroaders for their sleeping car service because the image of broad smiling, white-gloved, crisply uniformed black men proved a moneymaking triumph with Canada's wealthy white railway clientele. Initially, the CPR, GTR, and ICR culled early black railwaymen from Canadian cities with sizable African Canadian populations, namely Halifax, Montreal, and Toronto.[3] In later years, Canadian railway companies turned to the Southern United States and West Indies for other black railroaders.

The Intercolonial Railway found a ready supply of black transportation workers in Africville, Halifax's historically black neighbourhood. Bordered by railway tracks and Halifax Harbour, Africville became a black neighbourhood during the eighteenth century when thousands of African American Loyalists and West Indians migrated to Halifax (Winks, 1977; Walker, 1992). A vibrant port city and the railway capital of the Maritimes, Halifax teemed with black transportation workers (Fingard, 1995). . . .

Black Haligonians enthusiastically joined the rails during the ICR's heyday. The railroad promised steady employment and a respectable wage for those fortunate enough to land full-time employment, such as W.H. Blair, John Collins, Thomas Corbett, Joseph H. Daley, P. Driscoll, and P. Grannan, each of whom portered over 340 days during 1898 (*Auditor General's Report*, 1900:

R-242). In fact, black railroaders readily found work across Canada. Many African Canadians migrated westward for promotions or better opportunities with the Pullman Palace Car Company, the Canadian Pacific Railway, and the Grand Trunk Railways headquartered in Montreal. Payroll rosters indicate that 49 men in Montreal, 100 in Toronto, and 39 in London portered for the GTR in 1902.[4] Full-time porters drew monthly salaries ranging from $20–35 per month to $300–450 a year (*Auditor General's Report*, 1900: R-38). Experienced porters were rewarded with higher-waged runs on private government cars. David Hawes and John B. Cameron, who manned the sleepers *Cumberland*, *Montreal*, and *Ottawa* exclusively reserved for prominent members of Parliament, earned annual salaries of $420.[5] Even Winnipeg offered work for men willing to bear its harsh winters and long runs to the Pacific coast. . . .

Black railroaders in Canada enjoyed a broad range of employment options not available to black railwaymen in the United States at the turn of the century, where Jim Crow and the Big Four brotherhoods limited their occupational choices. Variable wages, uncertain demand, and exclusion from white unions taught these black railroaders the importance of diversifying their experience on the rails, as evidenced by employment patterns on the Intercolonial Railway. R.J. Murray was a brakeman for 51¾ days, worked as a baggagemaster for 2 days, and portered for 12¾ days, while L. Scothorn worked as a brakeman for 67 days, then as a shunter for 14 days, and finally portered for 5 days (*Auditor General's Report*, 1900: R-196-7). . . .

Working the rails in any capacity meant flirting with danger. Brakemen had the death-defying task of running on top of moving railway cars, made icy during winter months, and turning the brake wheel while also maintaining their balance. Those who failed met with sudden death along the tracks. The shunter's work proved no less perilous.

Switchmen, as they were also known, dropped a levy to stop the cars and switched often poorly lit tracks so that trains going in the opposite direction could gain safe passage. Less hazardous, though equally rare, were black nightwatchmen who moonlighted when on leave from the sleeping car service (*Auditor General's Report*, 1900: R-195-9). Other black railroaders like Peter Bushenpin and David Jones worked as coopers for the ICR after years of portering (Fingard, 1995: 54). Black men worked as waiters and cooks on the ICR, GTR, and CPR, higher paying positions otherwise solely reserved for white men working for other North American railway companies.[6]

Black railwaymen in Canada held a virtual monopoly over sleeping car service as early as the 1880s. Caring for passengers in first class sleeping cars remained the porter's primary function, though the company also expected that he render various other services without compensation. The porter was responsible for all aspects of the sleeping car ride, except for collecting tickets, which the conductor performed. Railway companies required that porters report to their cars two hours prior to a scheduled run in order to prepare their sleepers. Once assigned to a car, they ensured that it was clean and fully equipped; in case it was not, they hurriedly buffed and polished before passengers boarded. Canadian railway companies did not pay porters for this time consuming compulsory dead work.

Wood or coal burning ovens heated early sleepers not yet equipped with central heating at the turn of the century. Before leaving the station on a run, porters had to load their sleepers with enough fuel for the journey. They constantly struggled to keep soot from soiling the car or flying cinders from starting unruly fires. In the summer, huge blocks of ice cooled down the sleepers. Loading these slabs was clumsy, dangerous work as it required that porters crawl onto the sleeper's roof and drop the cube down into its cooling mechanism compartment. Controlling the temperature, an on-going annoyance to both passengers and workers, often made early sleeping cars unbearably hot or cold, depending on the season.

Once on the road, the sleeping car porter tended to his passengers' every whim. The porter greeted travellers, stowed luggage, pulled down berths in the evening, and hurriedly converted them back into seats in the morning. Responsible for remembering passengers' schedules, he was severely reprimanded when someone missed their stop. The porter, whom passengers condescendingly called 'George' or 'boy', served food, mixed drinks, shined shoes, cared for small children, sick passengers, and drunken ones too (Santino, 1983).[7] Herb Carvery, who portered during the 1950s, remembered 'we were babysitters, not only for little kids but for adults. . . . [S]omeone would get drunk on the train and many times you would have to stay up all night just to watch them so they wouldn't aggravate somebody else.' He added that when 'someone would get sick, you would have to attend to them' ('Good Morning. . .', 11 August 1998). Historians on wheels, passengers expected that the sleeping car porter know the landscape and history of areas along his trek. A confidante and armchair therapist, the porter feigned interest in travellers' tales and told a few of his own.

Sleeping car porters tended smoggy smoking cars, swept up cigarette and cigar ashes, washed out cuspidors, and inhaled stale, smoky air for hours on end. In the days before automated washrooms, they did their best to maintain sanitary conditions in crudely equipped lavatories. Porters frequently suffered chronic sleep deprivation since the company worked them on 72-hour shifts without providing any sleeping quarters. They endured other health hazards on the road as well. Derailments, common in the early days of rail travel, cost many railroaders their lives,

particularly when travelling through the Rockies' slippery slopes (Halliday, 1999). Policing gamblers, thieves, and rambunctious passengers also posed a constant danger for black railwaymen.

The consummate diplomat, the porter walked a social tight rope in Pullman's romanticized mobile time capsule. In 1930, journalist Murray Kempton reflected that for many white travellers, porters seemed like 'a domestic apparently unaltered by the passage of time or the Emancipation Proclamation'. Yet alluding to the film *The Emperor Jones* featuring Paul Robeson, Kempton proposed that '[t]here was a certain thrill to the notion that he might be a Communist or a murderer or even an emperor' (Kempton, 1935: 240). Sleeping car porters understood that these racialized fantasies were inseparable from their passengers' other expectations. They enabled white passengers to cling to an Antebellum racial ideal, while black workers understood that their livelihood—and at times their very lives—depended on acting out the part of this offensively racialized construction. Challenges to the charade and perceived social transgressions, especially against white women, carried heavy penalties: a porter could be fired or subjected to a worse fate—lynching. Required to smile and act submissively, they did so hiding their thoughts, their dreams, and sometimes their rage (Scott, 1990).

Though the work was certainly taxing, black Canadians embraced railway employment since other industrial jobs presented a different set of hazards without the reward of lasting employment. Likewise, working for Canadian railway companies afforded enterprising black transportation workers the freedom to pursue other professional interests. African Australian John D. Curl portered for a time before opening a cigar shop in Halifax (Fingard, 1995: 53). B.A. Husbands operated a West Indian import goods store with money obtained from seafaring and portering, while Jamaican-born Rufus Rockhead financed his famous Montreal jazz club with income earned on the rails (Gilmore, 1989: 163–7, 193–5; Fingard, 1995: 54). . . .

African Canadian railroaders hoped for a secure place on the rails but they did not find it. During periods of high unemployment or economic recession, Canadian railway companies discharged black workers, replacing them with inexperienced white labour. The *Halifax Herald* exposed this practice in the spring of 1898 when it headlined 'Colored Porters on the Intercolonial Railway Were All "Fired" and Without Cause' (28 March 1898: 2). J.S. Barbee, one of the dismissed ICR porters, told reporters '[o]ur places have been filled by white officials,' and accused railway managers with 'drawing the color line with a vengeance' (*Herald*, 28 March 1898: 2). William Dixon, another fired ICR sleeping car porter and brother of the celebrated pugilist George Dixon, informed Halifax journalists that 'the action of the government . . . is a shabby piece of business. Men with families have been turned out without notice or cause, and failing to find work in Halifax they must leave the city' (*Herald*, 28 March 1898: 2).

All of the fired Intercolonial Railway porters shared similar backgrounds. Experienced transportation workers, many had joined the ICR after careers at sea. A number of the men were West Indians, residing in Africville after marrying white or bi-racial women. All of the porters also belonged to Union Lodge, a black freemasons' temple popular with seafarers, sleeping car porters, and prosperous black Haligonian businessmen. Established in January 1856, Union Lodge members controlled commercial assets in Africville and served as guardians of their community's interests.[8] Hence, the federally-owned Intercolonial Railway's move against sleeping car porters roused black Haligonians who viewed these Union Lodge men as Africville's prominent denizens. Disillusioned, black Haligonians questioned whether the rails were indeed a wise investment in their future

when white supremacy—more than industriousness—determined their fate.

'Righteously indignant', black Haligonians gathered to 'consider the best means to be taken to remedy a most serious matter' (*Herald*, 25 March 1898: 3). Reverend Doctor J. Francis Robinson, an African American Baptist minister stationed in Halifax, led the charge. Speaking before his predominantly black congregation at the Cornwallis Street Baptist Church only days after the firings, Reverend Robinson did not mince words. 'The recent dismissal of the porters from the service of the ICR brings us face to face again with the race, which in the United States and here remains an unsettled question.' Robinson urged his congregation and all African Canadians to concede that race 'is no longer a sectional question: it is a national question' (*Herald*, 6 April 1898).

Reverend Robinson and other black Haligonian protesters insisted that in addition to race, the ICR's move against black workers underscored citizenship, right to work, and living wage issues of import to all Canadians. 'Don't drive the poor white or the poor black man out of your country. Give him work and give him good pay. . . . [A] policy which would arm the strong and cast down the defenceless is unwise . . . and one fraught with disastrous consequences.' Robinson admonished white supremacist employment practices, reminding the Canadian government that '[p]eace between the races is not to be secured by degrading one race and exalting another; by giving power and employment to one and withholding it from another.' . . .

For Reverend Robinson, the solution to black railwaymen's problems was a simple one. He insisted that if 'the Negro porters and the race [were] as strongly organized into labour protective unions, etc., like their white brothers, the ICR would not have succeeded so well and peaceably in displacing their colored labour and substituting white in their stead' (*Herald*, 6 April 1898:

2).[9] Without unionization, black railwaymen in Canada would never enjoy true job security and would continually be forced into unemployment or positions 'at starvation wages,' held Robinson (*Herald*, 6 April 1898: 2). He berated the Canadian government and ICR managers for subjecting black men and their families to a life of poverty and degradation. . . .

Black Haligonians called immediate attention to Jim Crow in railway employment policy by notifying the national press.[10] 'Have No Use For Them—Coloured Men on the Intercolonial Railway All Fired,' exclaimed the Tory newspaper *Chatham Planet*. The Ontario newspaper accused the Liberal government of betraying its African Canadian constituents. 'Liberal leaders at Ottawa seem to have completely lost their heads. . . . While Premier Laurier speaks in the most flattering manner of the African race, his officials strike them down in a most brutal way, no complaint, no investigation—just kick them out' (cited in *House of Commons Debates*, 6 April 1898: 3167).

Blacks in the Maritimes also contacted their federal members of Parliament Benjamin Russell and future Prime Minister Sir Robert Borden. Reverend Robinson emphasized that one thousand African Canadian voters in the Maritimes, 'a sufficient number to give them the balance of power' would 'get organized . . . so that their voices and vote would be respected' (*Herald*, 6 April 1898: 2). Conservative Parliament members took Robinson's warning to heart and laid the case of 'Coloured Intercolonial Porters' before the House of Commons' (*House of Commons Debates*, 31 March 1898: 2852). George Foster, the member from New Brunswick, inquired whether newspaper reports that 'all the porters on the Pullman cars had been dismissed from the service of the Intercolonial' were indeed true. If so, Foster demanded that the Minister of Railways and Canals explain 'whether they were dismissed for cause or whether the hon.

gentleman is drawing the colour line in that service' (*House of Commons Debates*, 31 March 1898: 2852).

Speaking for the Liberal government, Minister Blair rejected any notion that the colour line fueled employment practices on the government-owned ICR. 'I am quite sure that the colour line has not been drawn.' He assured the House that nothing had 'been done in view of discriminating against the colour line in that service'. Alphonse La Rivière of Quebec was not so easily persuaded, proposing instead '[p]erhaps the gentleman is colour-blind' (*House of Commons Debates*, 31 March 1898: 2852). Ironically, while Blair denied any governmental wrongdoing with respect to ICR porters, the Minister of Railways and Canals never actually disputed the existence of a colour line in Canadian industries. Over the next two weeks, federal legislators debated the application of discriminatory employment policies, worrying less about its existence than its gentlemanly exercise.

Representatives from Ontario and Nova Scotia resuscitated the 'colour line' debate again during question period in early April, this time in defence of ICR managers. Ontario member Archibald Campbell motioned that the House retract 'unfounded and unwarranted' charges of discrimination against black railroaders (*House of Commons Debates*, 6 April 1898: 368–9). In the end, the House resolved that '[t]he report that the Government would at once draw the colour line and dismiss all the men, ought to have been rejected by . . . common sense.' Mr Fraser hoped 'that hereafter those who publish those statements will understand what the country understands, that there must be a terrific dearth of any ground of attack upon the Government, when they are compelled to fall back upon an attempt to raise the prejudices of the coloured population of Canada' (*House of Commons Debates*, 6 April 1898: 3169).

Campbell's and Fraser's peculiar parade of circular reasoning branded African Canadians the racists for unveiling the spectre of Jim Crow in a federal corporation and in Canadian railway policy. Yet African Canadians' swift mobilization of national advocates demonstrated their political sophistication and understanding of local and national institutions. Reverend Robinson and other advocates shrewdly argued for black railwaymen's entitlement to positions in the most powerful industry of the era, likely preventing greater unemployment among black railroaders. They couched their protest in the language of citizenship, suffrage, and civil rights.

The problems faced by black railroaders on the ICR mirrored growing tensions between management and employees. White workers also protested unfair labour practices, with miners and textile workers most vocal about their grievances. To complicate matters, at least in employers' minds, unions mushroomed, particularly in Quebec and Ontario where their numbers doubled between 1899 and 1903. . . .

Intent on shaping a distinctly Canadian union movement, Aaron Mosher and other white railway unionists on the Intercolonial Railway created the Canadian Brotherhood of Railway Employees and Other Transport Workers (CBRE) in 1908. He pledged that his union would be a 'wholly-Canadian organization' for all railway workers (cited in Greening, 1961). Mosher's nationalist vision appealed to white railroaders who joined the CBRE *en masse*. Within its first two months, the CBRE recruited one thousand ICR running tradesmen, including freight and office clerks, freight handlers, car checkers, roundhousemen, station engineers, watchmen, day labourers, and 'all classes of the Sleeping, Parlour and Dining Car employees, except Sleeping Car Porters' (*Labour Gazette*, December 1908: 606; Greening, 1961: 9).

White supremacy formed the bedrock of Mosher's 'wholly Canadian organization'. The CBRE's exclusion of sleeping car porters clearly implied

black railroaders given that cooks, waiters, and other railwaymen who were black were likewise denied membership. By contrast, the CBRE welcomed white sleeping car porters, though they were extremely rare and often recent immigrants (Greening, 1961: 59–60). Evidently, Mosher perceived white members' grievances—long hours, hazardous working conditions, low wages, workmen's compensation, lack of job security, and bargaining rights—as distinct from those of black railroaders. By adopting a motion ostracizing black running tradesmen from its brotherhood at its inaugural meeting, the nationalist CBRE gave its assent to racism in Canadian railway unionism.[11]

Like American Railway Brotherhoods, Canadian unionized railroaders defined their movement along the lines of white manhood rights (Arnesen, 1994; Jacobson, 1998; Nelson, 1999). White unionists demanded that the most lucrative jobs on the rails be reserved for Anglo-Saxon Canadian men. . . . During negotiations with the Intercolonial Railway, Aaron Mosher's new union called for separate negotiating schedules for white and black workers. In December 1909, the ICR agreed to a new contract that secured segregated collective bargaining rights, wage increases, and improved working conditions for white running tradesmen (*Labour Gazette*, December 1909; Greening, 1961: 17–19). Black railwaymen on the ICR, however, gained nothing from the 1909 contract.

Emboldened by its agreement with the government-owned Intercolonial Railway, Mosher celebrated the CBRE's triumph for Canadian trade unionism. He now represented the largest class of previously non-unionized white running tradesmen and proclaimed the CBRE the forerunner of twentieth-century nationalist industrial unionism. Yet by shutting out black workers, Mosher revealed that pioneering Canadian industrial unionists valued Jim Crow and white manhood rights as much as their American neighbours.

White railwaymen extended their segregationist union vision westward throughout the 1910s. Mosher struck victory for Canadian segregationist railway unionism in April 1913 with a new ICR agreement (*Labour Gazette*, October 1913). The CBRE's newest contract promised its members protection from harassment or discrimination by Canadian railway companies. It established requisite due process for all dismissal claims, with back pay in the event of wrongful termination. The agreement recognized white railroaders' seniority rights after six months of permanent employment, secured two weeks paid vacations, and payment for statutory holidays (*Labour Gazette*, October 1913: 468–9). White running tradesmen won a 10-hour workday, with time and a half for overtime. . . .

Most importantly, the 1913 ICR contract instituted segregated contract negotiation schedules for black and white railway workers. All CBRE members' contracts were negotiated under Schedule 1, while separate terms set conditions of employment for black workers. The agreement between the federally-owned ICR and the CBRE mandated that promotions to conductorships could only come from the parlour car staff. Both parties knew that Canadian railway companies rarely employed black workers in that higher waged sector. Consequently, the ICR agreement of 1913 institutionalized separate and unequal promotion scales for railway workers, reserving well-remunerated supervisory positions exclusively for white men. Moreover, it permanently locked black railroaders into service positions. The Grand Trunk Railways, Canadian Northern Railway, and Canadian Pacific Railway also followed the federal government's railway lead, segregating their workforces by 1915. By the dawn of World War I, white supremacy dictated employment policy on all Canadian railway lines. Whereas Americans eventually desegregated their sleeping and parlour car departments in 1945, Canadian railway corporations did not seriously consider African Canadians for managerial positions until 1964 (Calliste, 1988: 44–7).

Canadian railway companies worried that with all other classes of white workers unionized and their benefits publicized, black railroaders would soon demand a contract of their own.[12] Without seniority, rights, paid holidays, or workmens' compensation, and in constant danger of harassment by company officials for vocalizing union ideals, black railwaymen had ample cause for dissatisfaction. Remembering the 1898 ICR affair yet expecting continued prosperity with their sleeping car service, Canadian railway companies could not chance that their latest rebuke would rekindle discontent among African Canadian railwaymen.

The decision to turn to Southern African American and West Indian railroaders by Canadian railway companies corresponds with the emergence of the CBRE. Soon after white running tradesmen organized into the CBRE and demanded segregated promotion schemes, Canadian companies began complaining that African Canadian railroaders were ill-suited for their sleeping car service. Experienced black railwaymen were in short supply in Canada; such workers, they argued, would have to come from abroad. Because the Canadian Pacific Railway company owned and operated 60 per cent of first class sleeping and dining cars in Canada during the 1910s, no other Canadian line matched its aggressive pursuit of African American and West Indian railroaders.[13] It therefore offers insight into railway corporations' approaches to foreign black labour.

Canadian railway companies dispatched recruitment agents to the United States. They combed American cities, black churches, and historically black colleges for prospective African American railwaymen. During such trips, S.A. Simpson,

Superintendent of the Canadian Pacific Railway sleeping car department, enlisted African American would-be porters in Harlem, Philadelphia, Washington, Detroit, Chicago, and Minneapolis.[14] CPR officials deliberately targeted American cities affected by recent Southern African American immigration, believing that having been raised in a Jim Crow South, Southern black railwaymen would make for a pliant class of workers (Arnesen, 1994; Foner, 1974). . . .

Employment scouts even drafted would-be porters as far south as the West Indies. West Indian workers were thought to suit Canadian railway companies, given that colonial rule and plantation economies had forced black workers into service positions for the white ruling class (Dookhan, 1975; Adelaide-Merlande, 1994; Palmer, 1995). Canadian corporate labour recruiters were particularly active in the Lesser Antilles, a string of archipelagoes stretching from the southeast of Puerto Rico to the northern tip of Trinidad. These little islands, too often reliant on single crop economies, faced labour surpluses just as Canadian industries needed more workers. . . .

Southern African Americans and West Indians who came to Canada reveal the breadth of black industrial labour migration at the turn of the century. Seasoned employment-driven intra-regional migrants, Southern African Americans willingly extended their journeys northward in search of better working conditions and fair wages. When hundreds of skilled black migrants bypassed Pittsburgh, New York, Chicago, and Detroit for Canadian railways, they affirmed that African Americans included Canada in their vision of a Great Migration (Grossman, 1989; Lemann, 1991). . . .

West Indian and African American sleeping car porters who crossed into Canada on short term contracts demonstrated that international migration did not depend on guaranteed long-term employment. Relief from segregationist politics compelled black migrant workers north, as much as the promise of better working and living standards. These early West Indian and African American shuttle industrial migrants followed the work when and where it became available, setting new roots in their host communities. They could not have known, however, the extent to which white supremacist employment policies circumscribed the lives of both white and black workers in Canada. If some returned to a South they knew and understood after a short sojourn in the Dominion, others dug their heels in determined to make their Canadian citizenship more meaningful than the one they had left behind.

Canadian corporations encouraged American and West Indian emigration by reinforcing their interests in the Caribbean, appealing to the notion of Empire, and downplaying Canada's hostility towards black migrants. . . . Canadian businesses like the Canadian Pacific Railway and Dominion Iron and Steel Company trusted that the Caribbean could supply Canada with cheap labour in ways that would not circumvent the Alien Labour Act, which outlawed enticing foreign workers. In 1913, a CPR agent lured nine Antiguans to Canada—including Charles Este, future Reverend of Montreal's influential Union United Church—with hollow promises of lucrative employment (Bentley, 1982).[15] DISCO, acquainted with Southern African American workers since the turn of the century, courted West Indian steelworkers for its Nova Scotian mills (Schultz, 1982). In 1915, DISCO executive A.W. Macdonald petitioned the Department of Immigration for permission to import 150 West Indian steelworkers. The federal government's longstanding resistance to black immigration forestalled Macdonald's plan. The Department of Immigration's chief administrator, William D. Scott, flatly denied DISCO's request, proposing instead that the company find suitable workers in Newfoundland.[16]

Frustrated by Ottawa's bureaucracies, Canadian industrialists resolved that if the government insisted on barring foreign black labour, then extending provincial status to a West Indian island would cancel out the immigration question. Likewise, incorporation would secure greater trading rights and secure a permanent harbour for Canada's navy (*Globe*, 8 April 1911, 12 April 1911: 9).[17] If the Department of Immigration insisted on sealing the border to West Indians, Canadian financiers would extend the frontier to the Caribbean. Chief among these corporate imperialists, and co-founders of the Canadian-West Indian League, were T.B. Macaulay, future president of Sun Life Insurance Company of Canada, and Thomas G. Shaughnessy, first President of the Canadian Pacific Railway.

Macaulay and Shaughnessy lobbied for political union with the West Indies, recommending provincial status for the Bahamas, Bermuda, Jamaica, Barbados, and other smaller islands and in the process rekindled alarm over the growth of Canada's black population (Mathieu, 2001). Advocates for West Indian appropriation argued that as guardians of the British Empire in the Americas, Canada was the logical and 'natural "big brother" of the British West Indies'. Speaking for Bahamian confederacy, Macaulay proclaimed '[w]hy should not Nassau become the Key West of Canada? I am an Imperialist. I am proud of our Empire, and jealous of its interests' (Winks, 1968: 35, 32).

Macaulay persistently courted Bahamian and Jamaican parliamentarians with promises of favourable trade agreements, bountiful Canadian markets, and bustling tourism. To Canadians, he pledged strategic access to the Panama Canal and glory for the Empire. Just as the United States held Cuba, Haiti, the Dominican Republic, and Puerto Rico in its grasp, so too should Canada possess its own 'great South,' claimed members of the Canadian–West Indian League. . . .

If Canadian industry readily envisioned gloriously upholding Anglo-Saxon imperialism in the Caribbean, the presence of blacks soiled their reverie. The colour question quickly soured Macaulay's negotiations with the House of Commons. White Canadians' jaundiced view of blacks sparked protest in Parliament and the press. Newspapers echoed admonitions that the presence of lascivious black men, whether from the West Indies or the United States, imperiled the morality of all white women in Canada. Robin Winks contends that for many white Canadians, 'West Indians were aggressive, invariably urban, thought to be morally loose, and sufficiently hard working to constitute a threat' (Winks, 1968: 7–9, 36, 12). . . .

By World War I, public debate over West Indian confederacy depicted blacks as not only a threat to white women's chastity but also to Canada's very democracy. With so many white Canadians certain of the inherent racial inferiority of blacks, nativists questioned their ability to assimilate complex democratic ideals. The *Manitoba Free Press* predicted that extending the franchise to a 'race of people . . . who have become indolent' would not only ensure the Dominion's demise, it might well sound the death knell of the British Empire's North American custodian (*Manitoba Free Press*, 5 April 1911: 13). The threat of blackening Canada with West Indian federation eradicated Canadian imperialist designs in the Caribbean, if not corporate interest in cheap black labour.

Canadian railway companies carried on their recruitment of African American and West Indian workers, continually displaying blatant disregard for federal immigration and labour laws. Section 1 of the Alien Labour Act of 1897 expressly forbade 'any person, company, partnership or corporation, in any manner to prepay the transportation, or in any way to assist or encourage the importation or immigration of any alien or foreigner into Canada, under contract or agreement . . . made previous to the importation or immigration of such alien or foreigner, to perform labour or service of any kind in Canada.'[18] . . . The revised Alien Labour Act of 1906 intensified limitations on foreign labour by barring persons and companies from importing immigrants 'by promise of employment through advertisements printed or published' in foreign countries.[19]

Canadian railway companies did not feel bound by the Alien Labour Act; neither were they concerned with restrictions under the Immigration Act. They intentionally wooed Southern African American and West Indian immigrant workers, despite widespread press coverage of public agitation over black immigration. The Immigration Act of 1906 made violation of the law a costly expenditure. 'All railway or transportation companies or other persons bringing immigrants from any country into Canada' were made responsible for deportation costs for 'a period of two years' after entry.[20] The Act's section 38 expressly outlawed the solicitation, 'either orally or by handbill or placard or in any other manner' of immigrants by unlicensed agents.

Yet Canadian Pacific Railway agents not only publicized their recruitment of black workers, Sleeping and Dining Car Department managers handed out company cards to American would-be porters. They informed new employees that border guards presented with the CPR's business cards would overlook restrictions on black migrants. . . .

Canadian Pacific Railway executives blamed their insatiate demand for African American and West Indian railroaders on the Great War. With white men ripped from the rails for military service abroad, Canadian companies argued that the war aggravated existing labour shortages, forcing them into 'bringing in colored help.' Since special troop trains hauled soldiers and implements of war to eastern ports, railway companies maintained that more sleeping and dining car personnel were urgently needed, especially on western lines. . . .

Canadian railway unionists filed several complaints with the Minister of Immigration and Minister of Labour over the introduction of foreign black railway workers on Canadian lines. In June 1918, tensions between unionized white railwaymen and the CPR landed both parties before Industrial Disputes Investigations Boards of Conciliation. It was the first of many disputes over foreign black railroaders taken to federal court over the next two decades. At issue was the CPR's 'alleged dismissal of certain employees who were union members and their replacement by negroes, the number affected being given as 205 directly and 500 indirectly' (*Labour Gazette*, June 1918: 396).

The Board, chaired by Justice W.A. Macdonald of Vancouver, heard evidence that 'white employees of the Dining Cars, between Vancouver and Calgary, were being discharged by the company and replaced by negroes imported from the United States' (*Labour Gazette*, August 1918). White workers claimed that they were 'being discriminated against because of their membership in the Canadian Brotherhood of Railway Employees' (*Labour Gazette*, August 1918). According to white railwaymen, the CPR added insult to injury by supplanting them with 'negroes'. George Hepburn of the CBRE averred that 'the men wanted better conditions, and they didn't like being replaced by black labor as Canadians and white men' (cited in *Labour Gazette*, August 1918: 603). . . .

Canadian Pacific Railway executives presented the Board of Conciliation with an alternative labour scenario on its western lines. Superintendents bemoaned the perennial workforce shortage occasioned by war and explained that 'a policy formulated in February 1918' envisioned 'introducing colored help' on Canadian rails. Superintendent Matthews, the CPR's advocate at the IDIA proceedings, could not supply any reliable evidence that his company's policy predated the CBRE's April union drive. . . .

The Board's majority report exposed a dizzying case of circular reasoning. Justice Macdonald argued that '[i]t was not, and could not be contended, that there was any right or agreement on the part of the employees for continuous employment or that the company could not, without notice, discharge any, or all, of such employees at any time.' Trade unionists certainly agreed. Lack of job security and due process in dismissals were long-standing union grievances. Justice Macdonald then argued that the CPR was justified in displacing white railroaders since 'dining car employees are migratory in their disposition and frequent changes . . . militate against efficiency.' Macdonald conveniently disregarded that displacement by non-unionized foreign workers had caused white railroaders' recent unemployment; conscription also accounted for their high turnover rates on the rails . . . .

The CBRE and the Board of Conciliation could not have known the extent of the CPR's duplicity. With a judgment in its favour and presumed support from the Ministry of Labour, CPR agents continued their hunt for more African American railroaders, this time for its sleeping car service. Aaron Mosher of the CBRE contested CPR recruitment of African American would-be porters in Chicago and Minneapolis, notifying the Department of Immigration: 'my information is that Mr Simpson, Superintendent of Sleeping Car Department, C.P.R., Winnipeg . . . went to St Paul and had announcements made in the churches of the colored people there to the effect that the C.P.R., required 500 colored men for work in Canada.' Mosher advised the Ministry of Immigration that over 100 men were 'being fed and housed in C.P.R.

cars at Winnipeg terminals'. He posited that the black immigrant workers were 'not permitted to mingle with the other employees or citizens of Winnipeg'.[21] The CBRE concluded that such strict corporate control over African American railroaders could only mean that they 'have been imported for the sole purpose of action as strike breakers'.[22] Attorneys for the CBRE alleged that the CPR clandestinely imported sleeping car porters from Minneapolis and St Paul in anticipation of postwar labour unrest in the West. CBRE president Aaron Mosher warned the Commissioner of Immigration that the continued importation of foreign labour—particularly African Americans—would 'very possibly . . . lead to further industrial warfare and increased unrest among organized labour' in Canada.[23] . . .

If Canadian railway managers actively solicited a compliant immigrant black workforce, it certainly was not what they got. Black railwaymen in Canada recognized that Canadian industrialists and white trade unionists viewed them as gullible pawns. Canadian railway companies upheld an antiquated racialized mirage in their Pullman Car departments, exploiting black sleeping car porters in the process. When conditions deteriorated with white workers, Canadian railway administrators replaced them with African Americans and West Indians herded into Canada by conniving managers. Since the beginning of the war, conditions on the rails worsened for all workers, even if the work itself became more readily available. Fearing greater unemployment and distracted by the rhetoric of war, white workers begrudgingly worked alongside black railroaders, all the while pressuring for a more rigorous racialized division of the Canadian railway workforce. Their nascent unions targeted black labour, Canadian and foreign-born, making them the scapegoats for unemployment, falling wages, and humiliation at the hands of company men.

Inasmuch as white workers and white managers thought little of black railroaders, West Indian, African American, and Canadian-born black railwaymen envisioned their position on the rails quite differently. Black railroaders understood white workers' growing hostility and sensed the nation's agitation over their presence. In the spring of 1917, Winnipeg-based porters John A. Robinson, J.W. Barber, B.F. Jones, and P. White began holding secret meetings. Robinson, who came to Canada from St Kitts to work on the CPR in 1909, led the charge. If black railwaymen were to survive World War I, he resolved that they needed protection. The men carefully weighed their options. White union men had made clear that they would not accept black workers in their brotherhood. Their white-only membership clause and open animosity affirmed it daily. Though African American sleeping car porters were likely contemplating the value of railway unionization, no such organization existed at the time (Brazeal, 1946).

Robinson and his allies discussed the possibility of forming a union for Canadian sleeping car porters. These clandestine deliberations changed the course of railway unionism in Canada. In April 1917, John A. Robinson and his co-workers chartered the Order of Sleeping Car Porters (OSCP)—the first black railway union in North America.[24] Their organization spread politicized trade union radicalism across Canada. Within two years of its inauguration, the OSCP negotiated successful contracts for all sleeping car porters—black as well as white—on the Canadian Northern and Grand Trunk Railways.[25] By the end of the decade, Robinson emerged as the champion of black railway unionism. His two-fisted approach to Jim Crow on Canadian rails fought segregation at work and in Canadian trade unionism simultaneously.

Black railwaymen in the Order of Sleeping Car Porters targeted white trade unionists, holding union leaders to their rhetoric of working-class solidarity. John A. Robinson began his campaign for national trade union recognition with the Trades and Labour Congress of Canada (TLC), a national coalition of trade and craft unions endowed with official collective bargaining recognition (*Canadian Railroad Employee Monthly*, 1929: 33). The Order of Sleeping Car Porters applied for a charter with the TLC in 1917, soon after its creation.[26] Though fully aware of the CBRE's white-only membership policy, TLC president Tom Moore denied the OSCP's petition, ruling instead that Canadian sleeping car porters seek auxiliary endorsement in the existing national railway union—the Canadian Brotherhood of Railway Employees. In effect, the Trades and Labour Congress of Canada Jim Crowed black unionists into auxiliary status, a station otherwise exclusively reserved for women workers or trade unionists' wives and daughters.

Unwilling to concede such easy defeat, black railway unionists plotted their next move. The OSCP set its sights on the Canadian Brotherhood of Railway Employee's annual convention meeting in Port Arthur in September 1918. Sleeping car porters from across the country protested the CBRE's white-only membership policy, forcing the issue onto the convention floor. The question of black membership rocked the CBRE's 1918 assembly, developing into a tempestuous debate. White railroaders from Western Canada reminded delegates that throughout the spring of 1918, the 'C.P.R. [had] imported a large number of coloured men from the States and promptly put into effect their threat' to replace 'all the white cooks and waiters and putting negroes in their places.'[27] Black workers, stressed field organizer E. Robson, jeopardized white workers and their families, as evidenced by the fact that 'white men are still off and the negroes are on the road.'[28]

Black railwaymen then presented their arguments for membership. George A. Fraser, President of Halifax's Canadian Grand Trunk Railways Sleeping Car Porters Association, seconded John A. Robinson's campaign against white supremacy in the Canadian Brotherhood of Railway Employees. Fraser addressed an open letter to CBRE members meeting in Port Arthur and accused the CBRE of undermining national railway unionism with its racist policies. Fraser emphasized '[w]e wish to point out that we are working in the same capacity as all other railway men and in consequence we are asking for admission into the C.B.R.E.' The continued exclusion of black railroaders from the CBRE, amounted to an egregious breach of African Canadians' citizenship rights, declared Fraser. 'We feel that as British subjects and also Loyal Canadians, that there should be no discrimination shown . . . between different races.' Dismantling racism in the CBRE, Fraser avowed, 'will not only benefit us, but will greatly strengthen your Division No. 36, the [white] members of which are working hand in hand with us'. Fraser requested that members of the Canadian Grand Trunk Railway Porters Association be admitted to the CBRE and hoped that African Canadian railroaders would 'receive a square deal'.[29]

White delegates meeting in Port Arthur were not moved by Fraser's appeal for a 'square deal'. Instead, members buried the matter in the Committee on Constitution and Laws, then boarded a specially commissioned bus for the Orpheum Vaudeville Theatre. There, the men feasted on a banquet, cooled their palates with drink, and washed down the day's events with a minstrel show, 'The Boys from Memphis,' featuring blackface singers Fox and Evans.[30] Whereas CBRE delegates could not fathom a meaningful partnership with black railwaymen, they cheerfully welcomed burlesqued images of black men. They could digest chuckling and jiving black buffoons, if not equal status among workers as proposed by Fraser, Robinson, and other sleeping car porters.

Although the Order of Sleeping Car Porters lost in Port Arthur, black railroaders' initial bid for CBRE membership forced a debate on racial segregation among workers and unmasked the deep-seated resentments of white railwaymen. As such, they laid bare the hypocrisy of working-class rhetoric by a CBRE leadership wedded more to white supremacy than working-class solidarity. . . .

The period between 1880 and 1914 thus held great promise for black railroaders in Canada. After setting tracks and feeding work crews, black railwaymen moved from the fields to the freight yards, finally gaining a footing in the industry poised to dominate the new century. They initially enjoyed a range of employment options and utilized railway work to ensure full employment, countervail ennui, and pursue other commercial enterprises. Wages were good, if the work itself gritty and always dangerous. Black railroaders in Canada soon learned, however, that their welcome on the rails was conditional.

White trade unionists and railway management, defining their new roles in an age of rapid industrialization, held conflicting positions on black labour. Against the threat of industrial strife, both adopted Jim Crow as a rational model for labour relations. Railway management, burdened by what it construed as uppity white railwaymen, manipulated its workforce by fuelling racial tensions on their lines. When they wanted to appease disgruntled white railway workers, Canadian railway companies conceded to unionists' segregationist demands. White Canadian unionists won Jim Crow as one such compromise by 1915.

At other times, Canadian railway executives circumvented white unions by importing foreign black workers, knowing that their race prevented membership in existing unions. Canadian railway companies creatively ignored immigration and labour laws and successfully engaged accomplices in the Canadian government. Consequently, twentieth-century immigration and labour restrictions never meaningfully hampered Canadian railway companies' insatiate appetite for African American and West Indian workers.

The Great War strained labour-management relations on Canadian lines. If the war made Canadian railway companies rich, it also roused trade union activists. Radicalism among white unionized railwaymen intensified and moved west during the 1910s. Railway unionists posited that the introduction of Southern African American and West Indian railroaders demeaned their white manhood, citizenship, and rights as union men. Their resentment, so deep-rooted, thwarted a bid for interracial unionization by sleeping car porters,

favouring hollow white supremacy to equal status for all railway workers.

Likewise, black railroaders took notice of the climate on the rails. As president of the OSCP, John A. Robinson intensified his assault on Jim Crow in white Canadian unionism. The Order of Sleeping Car Porters targeted its first offensive on the Canadian Brotherhood of Railway Employees' white-only membership doctrine. Robinson challenged the CBRE's rank and file, arguing that if the CBRE were really the beacon of Canadian trade unionism, it would set new industrial standards by striking racism out of its constitution. The time had come, Robinson contended, for black workers to get a permanent foothold in the Canadian House of Labour.

Notes

1. Van Horne and Hays, both American-born, transformed Canadian railways during their tenure as general managers for the CPR and GTR respectively. Hays died on the Titanic in April 1914, never having witnessed the GTR's national service. See 'Charles Melville Hays', 1052 and 'William Cornelius Van Horne', *The Canadian Encyclopedia* (Toronto, Historical Foundation of Canada: 2000), 2437.

2. See the *Annual Report of the Canadian Pacific Railway Company*, Montreal, April 1896, 28. In 1885, CPR spent $24,098.99 on the Parlour and Sleeping Car Department. *Annual Report*, May 1886, 27.

3. See Dominion Bureau of Statistics, *Census of Canada 1911*, 372–3.

4. See NAC, RG30-2035, CNR, 'Grand Trunk Railway Payrolls for 1902'.

5. See *Auditor's General Report* 1898–99, R-38.

6. See NAC, RG75-576-816222, Immigration Branch Records (IBR), H.F. Matthews to Thomas Gelley, 20 April 1920.

7. Also see Stanley Grizzle, *My Name's Not George: The Story of the Brotherhood of Sleeping Car Porters in Canada* (Toronto: Umbrella Press, 1998).

8. See Provincial Archives of Nova Scotia (PANS), MG20-2012 and MG20-2218, Union Lodge Records. Pursuant to an agreement with Mr Robert Northup, Grand Secretary of the Grand Lodge, I am unable to release the names of Union Lodge members. Also see Fingard, 49–64.

9. The dismissed porters were eventually rehired by the ICR or accepted positions with the CPR once they were made available. See Fingard, 57–9.

10. See *Globe* (Toronto) 7 April 1898: 4, *Herald*, 25–8 March and 8–15 April 1898. *House of Commons Debates (HCD)*, 31 March–14 April 1898.

11. See NAC, MG28 1215, CBRE, 'CBRE Annual Convention Minutes 1908 and 1919'.

12. All new wage agreements were reproduced in the *Labour Gazette*, pursuant to federal labour law.

13. See *Annual Report of the Canadian Pacific Railway Company*, 1910–19 and M.C. Urquhart, ed., *Historical Statistics of Canada* (Toronto: Macmillan, 1965), 532.

14. NAC, MG28 1215, CBRE, Aaron Mosher to J.E. McGuire, 11 March 1943. Also see NAC, RG76-576-816222, IBR, Aaron Mosher to William D. Scott, 28 May 1919 and Thomas J. Murray to Assistant Commissioner of Immigration, 4 June 1919. Wilfred Israel, 'Montreal Negro Community', MA thesis, McGill University, 1928.

15. Este, only 17 years old when he came to Canada, worked as a bootblack and bellhop before attending the Congregational College of Canada in 1918.

16. See NAC, RG76-566-810666, IBR, William D. Scott to A.W. Macdonald, 12 September 1915.

17. Also see *By-Water Magazine*, October 1916, 1, and Gobin Sawh, ed., *The Canadian Caribbean Connection—Bridging North and South: History, Influences,*

Lifestyles (Hansport, NS: Carindo Cultural Association, 1992), 103–19; and Jean-Pierre Gagnon, 'Canadian Soldiers in Bermuda During World War One', *Histoire Sociale/Social History* 23 (May 1990): 9–36.

18. See Alien Labour Act, 6061 Victoria, c. 11.
19. See Alien Labour Act, *RSC* 1906, c. 97, s. 12.
20. See Immigration Act, 6 Edward vii, c. 19, s. 32.
21. See NAC, RG76-576-816222, IBR, Aaron Mosher to William D. Scott, 28 May 1919.
22. See NAC, RG76-576-816222, IBR, Thomas Murray to Assistant Commissioner of Immigration, 4 June 1919.
23. See NAC, RG76-576-816222, IBR, Thomas Murray to Commissioner of Immigration, 4 June 1919.
24. See NAC, MG28 1215, CBRE, John A. Robinson to J.E. McGuire, 27 March 1941.

25. See NAC, MG28 1215, CBRE, John A. Robinson to J.E. McGuire, 27 March 1941.
26. See NAC, CBRE, 'CBRE Convention Proceedings, 1918', MG28 1215. See also William E. Greening, *Easy*, 59.
27. See NAC, CBRE, MG28 1215, 'CBRE Convention Proceedings, 1918', Port Arthur, 24 September 1918, 60.
28. See NAC, CBRE, MG28 1215, 'CBRE Convention Proceedings, 1918', Port Arthur, 24 September 1918, 61.
29. See NAC, CBRE, MG28 1215, 'CBRE Convention Proceedings', Port Arthur, 24 September 1918, 61.
30. See NAC, CBRE, MG28 1215, 'CBRE Convention Proceedings', Port Arthur, 24 September 1918, 61. Also see *Port Arthur Daily-News Chronicle*, 24 September 1918, 8 and 28 September 1918, 24.

References

Adelaide-Merlande, Jacques. 1994. *Histoire générale des Antilles et des Guyannes: des Précolombiens à nos jours*. Paris: Diffusion.

Arnesen, Eric. 1994. 'Like Banquo's Ghost, It Will Not Down: The Race Question and The American Railroad Brotherhoods, 1880–1920', *American Historical Review* 99 (December): 1601–33.

Auditor General's Report, 1898–99 (AGR). 1900. 'Railways and Canals Department', 63 Victoria A.

Brazeal, B.R. 1946. *The Brotherhood of Sleeping Car Porters: Its Origin and Development*. New York: Harper and Bros.

Calliste, Agnes. 1988. 'Blacks on Canadian Railways', *Canadian Ethnic Studies* 20: 36–52.

Canadian Railroad Employee Monthly. 1929.

Dookhan, Isaac. 1975. *A Post-Emancipation History of the West Indies*. Essex, England: Collins.

Fingard, Judith. 1995. 'From Sea to Rail: Black Transportation Workers and their Families in Halifax, c. 1870–1916', *Acadiensis* 24 (Spring 1995): 49–64.

Foner, Philip. 1974. *Organized Labor and the Black Worker*. New York: International Publishers.

Gilmore, John. 1989. *Swinging in Paradise: The Story of Jazz in Montreal*. Montreal: Vehicule Press.

Globe. 1911. 8 April.

Globe. 1911. 12 April.

'Good Morning with Avril Benoit'. 1998. CBC Radio interview with Stanley Grizzle, Herb Carvery, and Saje Mathieu. Toronto. 11 August.

Greening, W.E. 1961. *It Was Never Easy: A History of the Canadian Brotherhood of Railway, Transport and General Workers*. Ottawa: Mutual Press.

Grossman, James R. 1989. *Land of Hope: Chicago, Black Southerners, and the Great Migration*. Chicago: University of Chicago Press.

Halliday, Hugh A. 1999. *Wreck! Canada's Worst Railway Accidents*. Toronto: Robin Brass Studio.

Herald (Halifax). 1898. 25 March.

Herald (Halifax). 1898. 28 March.

Herald (Halifax). 1898. 6 April.

House of Commons Debates. 1989. 31 March–14 April.

Jacobson, Matthew F. 1998. *Whiteness of a Different Color: European Immigrants and the Alchemy of Race*. Cambridge: Harvard University Press.

Kempton, Murray. 1935. *Part of Our Time: Some Ruins and Monuments of the Thirties*. New York: Modern Library.

Labour Gazette. 1908. December.

Labour Gazette. 1909. December.

Labour Gazette. 1913. October.

Labour Gazette. 1918. June.

Labour Gazette. 1918. August.

Labour Gazette. 1918. 'Testimony of George Hepburn', August.

Lemann, Nicholas. 1991. *The Promised Land: The Great Black Migration and How it Changed America*. New York: Knopf.

Manitoba Free Press. 1911. 5 April.

Mathieu, Sarah-Jane. 2001. 'Jim Crow Rides This Train: The Social and Political Impact of African American Sleeping Car Porters in Canada, 1880–1939'. PhD dissertation, Yale University.

Mika, Nick, and Helma Mika. 1986. *An Illustrated History of Canadian Railways*. Belleville, ON: Mika Publishing Company.

Nelson, Scott. 1999. *Iron Confederacies: Southern Railways, Klan Violence and Reconstruction*. Chapel Hill, NC: University of North Carolina Press.

Palmer, Ransford W. 1995. *Pilgrims From the Sun: West Indian Migration to America*. New York: Twayne.

Santino, Jack. 1983. 'Miles of Smiles, Years of Struggle: The Negotiation of Black Occupational Identity Through Personal Experience Narratives', *Journal of American Folklore* 96: 393–412.

Scott, James C. 1990. *Domination and the Arts of Resistance: Hidden Transcripts*. New Haven: Yale University Press.

Vaughan, Walter. 1920. *The Life and Work of Sir William Van Horne*. New York: Century Company.

Walker, James. 1992. *The Black Loyalists: The Search for a Promised Land in Nova Scotia and Sierra Leone, 1783–1870*, 2nd edn. Toronto: Africana Publishing Company.

Winks, Robin. 1968. 'Canadian–West Indian Union: A Forty-Year Minuet', *Institute of Commonwealth Studies*. London: The Athlone Press.

———. 1977. *The Blacks in Canada: A History*. New Haven: Yale University Press.

CHAPTER 12

'The best men that ever worked the lumber': Aboriginal Longshoremen on Burrard Inlet, BC, 1863–1939

Andrew Parnaby

Aboriginal people in Canada, like Aboriginal people across the continent, have been engaged in wage labour for centuries. Yet despite a long and diverse history of paid employment, this dimension of Aboriginal life is under-studied by Canadian scholars. Generally, anthropologists and ethno-historians have focused on 'traditional' Aboriginal cultures and Native–newcomer relations, while political scientists and legal experts continue to probe questions of treaty rights and government policy. This intellectual orientation is not surprising. To some extent, it reflects scholars' engagement with contemporary Aboriginal politics. Documenting the existence and persistence of a customary way of life—the occupation and use of a certain territory or the practice of a specific ritual—has been, and continues to be, a critical dimension of the ongoing struggle for title to land and rights to resources. As a consequence, however, the significance of wage labour to Aboriginal communities—a phenomenon that suggests change, not continuity; modernity, not custom—has been neglected. It does not fit easily

into scholarship aimed, to varying degrees, at bolstering Aboriginals' historical and moral claim to self-determination.[1]

Yet as the work by Harald Prins (Nova Scotia), Frank Tough (Manitoba), and John Lutz (British Columbia) illustrates, although the significance of wage labour to the history of Aboriginal communities has been under-explored, it has not been neglected entirely.[2] Indeed, on the Pacific Coast, where Aboriginal scholarship comes closest to dominating the provincial historiography, a relatively small yet sophisticated literature on this topic emerged in the early 1970s, when two ground-breaking books—Robin Fisher's *Contact and Conflict* (1992) and Rolf Knight's *Indians at Work* (1996)—were first published. Initially, the debate over Aboriginals and wage labour on the West Coast focused on Fisher's observation that 'with the transition from the fur trade and the consolidation of settlement, the Indian had been reduced from an integral to a peripheral role in British Columbia's economy'—a contention that Knight, James Burrows, and Dianne Newell have since rejected (Burrows, 1986; Fisher, 1992: 210; Newell, 1992). In the wake of this initial exchange, the debate's focus has shifted, due in part to John Lutz's micro-history of the Lekwammen (Songhees) of southern Vancouver Island in the nineteenth and twentieth centuries, and his related, though more general, assessments of Aboriginal workers 'after the fur trade' and the ideological construction of 'Indian' in British Columbia. Of interest, now, is not whether Aboriginal people worked for wages, but why they chose to do so, what that experience meant, and how long it lasted (Lutz, 1992: 199).

This cluster of questions is at the core of this essay, an examination of Aboriginal longshoremen, most of whom belonged to the Squamish First Nation, a linguistic subdivision of the Coast Salish, on Burrard Inlet, British Columbia, from 1863 to 1939. In taking up this topic it joins a growing body of work that rejects Fisher's original formulation about the irrelevance of Aboriginal workers to British Columbia's transition to capitalism. At the same time, however, it offers a different perspective than Lutz, and it does so by tapping historical materialism in a more obvious way. A greater emphasis on the analytic category of class, both as a structured socio-economic presence and a lived daily experience, clarifies the importance of one dimension of Aboriginal workers' lives that Lutz's important contributions on the role of the state, law, and discourse do not: the workplace. . . . Often mentioned in the scholarly literature, but never studied in a systematic way, the 'Indian' waterfront provides a window into the importance of waged work to Aboriginal people on Burrard Inlet and the sophisticated ways that the Squamish responded to Canadian colonialism *and* capitalism.

Cheakamus Tom understood the history of Native–newcomer relations in British Columbia very well. 'For many years, our people could and did gain a living suitable for our wants from the forest and the sea,' he stated in a letter written to the Royal Commission on Indian Affairs, which was holding hearings in the province from 1912 to 1916. 'The different tribes or bands had their own territory in which they fished and hunted, and over which they had control,' he continued. 'But when the White man came he was allowed to go where he pleased to hunt, trap, or fish. Then our troubles began.'[3] Pithy and succinct, Tom's assessment evokes an era prior to European settlement, when his people, the Squamish, utilized a swath of land between Howe Sound and Burrard Inlet in southwestern British Columbia; seasonally harvested aquatic and terrestrial resources in groups of family or extended family members; and, with these resources in hand, periodically held potlatches—a collection of ceremonies that reaffirmed the prestige, status, and influence of particular leaders or families through feasting, dancing, and gift-giving (Barnett, 1955; Suttles, 1987; Harris, 1997). . . .

From the mid-nineteenth century to the early years of the twentieth century, British Columbia underwent a far-reaching economic transformation, a shift illustrated well by the rise of Vancouver as an important Pacific Coast port. Spurred on by the completion of the Canadian Pacific Railway in 1886 and the opening of the Panama Canal in 1914, large piers, grain elevators, and warehouses were constructed up and down Burrard Inlet, while numerous rail lines were laid along both its north and south shores. . . . Like the physical environment of the port, capital was reorganized too. Individually, shipping companies in Vancouver invested in iron hulls, steam technology, and larger vessels; collectively, shipping, railway, and stevedoring companies banded together to form the Shipping Federation in 1912 to better manage the increase in maritime traffic and the waterfront's burgeoning labour force (Yarmie, 1991). . . .

Squamish men and women were important, if unequal, actors in this new industrial context.

They stacked lumber in the mills, acted as guides for recreational hunters and fishers, built fences on farms, felled trees in the coastal forests, gutted fish in the canneries, piloted small boats in the salmon fishery, and loaded and unloaded cargo on the waterfront, usually combining a range of occupations to earn a modest livelihood. That all of the occupational pursuits undertaken by Aboriginal workers were seasonal is important, hinting at the ways in which the temporal and spatial rhythms of a customary, kin-ordered way of life articulated with the logic of a burgeoning capitalist labour market. 'The result was a mixed economy in which Squamish men and women deployed some of their labour power some of the time in a new way—working for wages—while simultaneously maintaining older methods of regulating access to resource sites and affirming links between their families and larger aboriginal groups. There was a culturally specific logic in operation here that was internal to Coast Salish society: it is likely that Squamish men and women engaged in wage labour because their earnings could be used to purchase the goods necessary to hold a potlatch—a rationale shared by the Lekwammen and Kwakwaka'wakw of Vancouver Island. Fragmentary evidence reveals that the Squamish continued to hold potlatches throughout this period of economic adjustment, although it is difficult to assess their size and frequency.[4] In short, cash and culture were connected, the persistence of the latter tied, to some degree, to the successful acquisition of the former.

Decisions about the utility of wage labour were not always made under conditions of the Squamish's own choosing, however. As an 'old man' who could 'remember when there was no Indian agent', Cheakamus Tom knew this: 'The White man thought we ate too much fish, too much game, and passed laws to prevent our people from killing game or fishing except for a short time each year.'[5] From the earliest days of the colonial project in British Columbia, the state played a critical role in setting limits on, and erecting boundaries around, the scope of Aboriginal life—a dynamic particularly obvious in the context of land. By the late 1870s, the Squamish, who, along with other Coast Salish groups bore the brunt of white encroachment, occupied a clutch of reserve sites in and around Howe Sound and on the North Shore of Burrard Inlet, an archipelago of Aboriginal territory in a sea of white pre-emptions (Harris, 2002—see maps 3.6, 5.1 and 5.2). Urban development, population growth, and economic expansion in the Lower Mainland, backed by a state that refused to recognize Aboriginal title to land, eroded this modest land base even further. . . . While the Squamish were drawn into the capitalist labour market by a desire to continue potlatching, they continued to work for wages because, as time went on, they possessed few other options, save for selling their labour power in the canneries or on the waterfront.

For waterfront workers on Burrard Inlet, as for longshoremen the world over, the experience of work was shaped by the demands of both a casual labour market and the 'shape-up' method of hiring—a combination that persisted, in various guises, from the mid-nineteenth century until the 1920s. Typically, when vessels arrived in port, men swarmed the docks, and there, in a ring around a foreman, cargo hooks in hand, they jostled for position in hopes of securing a day's work.[6] In this context, work came in fits and starts, earnings fluctuated, and competition among men was often intense. Not surprisingly, then, waterfront workers tended to stress different skills and abilities in order to carve out a degree of security in an otherwise chaotic labour market. Organized into gangs, some men worked on ship, others laboured on shore, and within both categories men specialized in handling a particular cargo or operating a piece of technology. . . .

Socially constructed, and sometimes bitterly defended, demarcations of skill and ability intersected with cleavages of race and ethnicity on the job to produce a complex and hierarchical occupational milieu. Between 1908 and the late 1930s, the years for which solid evidence is available, white longshoremen dominated general cargo, Italian men tended to work as coal heavers, and Aboriginal workers monopolized logs and lumber (ILWU Pensioners, 1975: 27, 29, 41, 45, 99). . . .

Lumber handling gangs loaded cut wood into a ship's hold. On a sailing ship, lumber was transported by hand over the stern or through a porthole, each piece sliding down a series of ramps to the hold. Alternatively, the cut wood, what longshoremen sometimes called 'boards', 'sticks', or 'timbers', was placed inside a sling, which was then fastened by a series of cables to a portable steam-powered engine called a 'donkey'; the donkey engine, which was situated on a barge or on the wharf, lifted the 'sling load' to the sailing ship to be stowed. Steam-powered vessels, which had all but replaced sailing ships in the lumber trade by the mid-to-late 1920s, utilized deck-mounted winches, as well as derricks or cranes, to accomplish the same task, albeit at a much faster pace. Once inside a ship's hold, the load was disassembled and each 'stick', which ranged widely in length, width, and weight, was carefully packed away (ILWU Pensioners, 1975: 16, 24–9, 36–7, 44–5, 55–6).

. . . In the context of the waterfront, 'Indian' was an elastic category that included individuals born to Squamish parents, as well as those, Aboriginal and non-Aboriginal, who married Squamish women. An assortment of other workers, drawn from a range of national, cultural, and racial backgrounds, including other First Nations, rounded out the ranks of the 'Indian'-dominated gangs. This diversity is captured well by the personnel histories of William Nahanee and Joe Jerome. Nahanee, who started on the waterfront in 1889 and remained a longshoreman for over 50 years, was of Hawaiian and Squamish ancestry, while Jerome, who, it appears, began his career on the docks sometime in the 1930s, was born to Tsimshian parents and married to a Squamish woman.[7]

The 'Indians" status on the waterfront as lumber handlers flowed, in part, from their long history of paid employment in and around Burrard Inlet. They had been handling logs and lumber, either in the sawmills or in the woods, for a long time.[8] With this employment history, it is no surprise that they emerged as adept waterfront workers: both logging and longshoring were physically demanding jobs, and the skills acquired in one occupational context—the ability to run a donkey engine, for example—were easily transferred to another (ILWU Pensioners, 1975: 74; Mortimer, 1981). Specialization in a particular commodity helped Aboriginal longshoremen shore up their prestige as well, for it enabled them to gain greater knowledge of a specific cargo and, over time, a strong reputation for loading and unloading it. 'The Indians were "it" on the sailing ships,' one old-timer recollected. 'They were the greatest men that ever worked the lumber,' observed another (ILWU Pensioners, 1975: 27, 29).

Great, but not quite equal: while Aboriginal dockers chose to work 'the lumber' because they possessed the right skills, and specialization helped to bring some predictability to casual work, they did so in an occupational context in which their options, although not closed off entirely, were constrained. Significantly, white waterfront workers tended to dominate general cargo, which was less dangerous and more lucrative than working the lumber.[9] Their position of relative privilege was girded by a sense of entitlement that all whites possessed by virtue of being white in a society in which race mattered. In British Columbia, this structure of feeling was deeply imbricated in culture, discourse, and space, formalized in law, and bound up in the province's political economy. In the specific context of the waterfront, it was reinforced by employers who benefited from competition from racially distinct gangs and who tended to hire non-Aboriginal men to handle general cargo—day-to-day decisions that, over time, helped to create the conditions in which such divisions were naturalized and legitimated. It is not hard to see how white longshoremen's own sense of powerlessness on the job would make them more receptive to the authority derived from, to borrow from David Roediger, 'the fiction that they are "white"' (1994: 8).

Aboriginal men negotiated the politics of waterfront work in a variety of ways—individual and collective struggles marked by the tensions associated with being both a longshoreman and being an 'Indian'. '[My Indian friend] George Newman, he was always full of fun. He would holler down the hatch in Indian language and then he would start to laugh,' Edward Nahanee observed, the punch line being that white workers ''tween decks' did not understand George's orders: 'Those Indian boys could talk behind their backs.'[10] On the Vancouver waterfront, longshoremen's use of a shared language—nicknames, slang, profanity, and occupational jargon—accentuated the differences between employers and employees, and distinguished dockers from other ostensibly more respectable and skilled workers (De Cries, 2000). As this anecdote suggests, however, the use of the 'Indian language' on the job reinforced *internal* divisions of allegiance and identification as well—a dynamic that likely subverted white workers' sense of racialized camaraderie and entitlement, if only for a moment. . . .

In Vancouver, as in other port cities, a longshoreman's success or failure in the competition for work was dependent on a wide range of factors, not the least of which was the ability of racial groupings to mobilize in defence of their particular occupational niches, no matter how undesirable or difficult the work within that niche was (Nelson, 2000). Use of the 'Indian' language and physical confrontation were part of this process; so, too, was labour recruitment. It was not uncommon for the sons and nephews of Aboriginal longshoremen to follow their fathers and uncles to the waterfront, and, in the process, learn the arts and mysteries of 'working the lumber'. On other occasions, experienced Aboriginal longshoremen could be found enticing 'young fellows' from the Mission and other reserves to work on a specific lumber ship—a manoeuvre facilitated by the extensive familial relationships that characterized Aboriginal life on the North Shore and elsewhere (ILWU Pensioners, 1975: 56; Kennedy, 1995).

The experience of Simon Baker illustrates this final point. Born in 1911, Baker was raised on the North Shore of Burrard Inlet by his grandfather (and longshoreman), Squamish chief Joe Capilano, and his grandmother, Mary Agnes Capilano. As a young man, Baker attended a residential school, where he 'organized' a 'strike' to protest poor food and harsh discipline, and worked in a variety of occupations, including waterfront work. 'After I got back home [from hop-picking], Dan Johnson, who is a relative of ours, asked me to go with him. I knew why he asked me, because we're good longshoremen,' Baker recalled in his autobiography. . . . Baker's first stint as lumber handler did not last long. The next year he worked as a logger followed by a lengthy sojourn to the Skeena River, in northern British Columbia, to take part in the commercial fishery. In 1935, Baker returned to the waterfront, where he remained for nearly 40 years. 'Our legend began in the 1800s during the days of the sailing ships. They had one mill at the time on the North Shore. They hired all the Indians on the North Shore who were able to work,' Baker observed. 'Five generations of our family have worked on the waterfront' (Baker, 1994: 2–4, 8–11, 36–7, 53–60, 76–8).

Baker's recollections are significant for another reason: they illustrate the ways in which longshoremen, in the context of the waterfront labour market, utilized the idea of race to sort out who should have access to the docks, what gang to join, and which cargo to handle. Key to white longshoremen's monopoly on general cargo, race was deployed simultaneously by Aboriginal longshoremen to defend their status as skilled men on the lumber and to facilitate the entry of other 'Indians' into waterfront work, thereby perpetuating their presence on the docks over time. In a more intimate way, working the lumber, and all the associations of race that went with it, helped Baker to further establish a dichotomy between himself as an Aboriginal person and other non-Aboriginal individuals. That understanding of difference, as his autobiography suggests, was critical to the formation of his identity as an Aboriginal man, and to his understanding of the need for political action, on the job and off. . . .

Labour relations on the waterfront were rarely peaceful. Between 1889 and 1935, Vancouver's waterfront workers joined a wide range of unions—from the conservative to the Communist—and went on strike at least 18 times, a pattern of militancy that was matched by few other occupational groups, either provincially or nationally (Parnaby, 2001).[11] Aboriginal longshoremen were deeply involved in these struggles. In 1906, lumber handlers on Burrard Inlet, most of whom were Squamish, founded Local 526 of the Industrial Workers of the World (IWW), a radical organization that offered up a heady mix of revolution and reform to those workers who did not fit well into the established craft union structures: the unskilled, the migratory, and the marginal (Leier, 1990). Its highly decentralized form of

union organization, which was rooted in part in the itinerant lifestyle of its members, likely suited Squamish lumber handlers well, for they continued to hunt, fish, and work seasonally. Limited evidence suggests that Local 526 included approximately 50 or 60 men and held its meetings on the North Shore's Mission reserve (Dunlop, 1989: 80, 166).[12] A nasty waterfront strike in 1907, which, according to one source, was characterized by impressive levels of racial solidarity, apparently marked the local's demise (*Industrial Union Bulletin*, 2 November 1907).

. . . Equally striking is the fact that the IWW emerged at the same time that coast and interior Salish peoples were experimenting with new forms of resistance. In 1906, representatives from both communities met on Vancouver Island. There they nominated a delegation of three chiefs, including Joe Capilano, to take their demands directly to King Edward in London. Although the mission was unsuccessful—the British government maintained that the question of title to land was strictly a Canadian issue—the unity of coastal and interior groups was, as Paul Tennant has argued, 'a step in the evolution of pan-Indianism' that set the stage for future political innovations in the 1910s and 1920s (Tennant, 1990: 85). Without question, the assertion of Aboriginal rights, particularly title to land, was part of a specific history of resistance among the Squamish that stretched back to the earliest days of white settlement and drew upon the cultural resources of their community. At the same time, however, it is important not to underestimate the political contribution of their participation in the industrial economy. Travelling great distances and working in a variety of occupational settings likely enhanced the Squamish's understanding of the breadth and depth of the changes wrought by white society and allowed for the wider dissemination of political ideas among different Aboriginal groups. 'In my young days . . . we lived in shacks with outside toilets. . . . We didn't seem to know that we could have things, the same as the white man,' Simon Baker recalled. 'It wasn't until I was young and travelled to other places in BC [to work] that I realized that we could do better' (Baker, 1994: 98).

The importance of migration, and the realizations it prompted, is particularly evident in the realm of waterfront work. Not only did the existence of Aboriginal-dominated gangs serve as an important framework for the affirmation of Aboriginal culture in a largely white occupational environment, but when those gangs travelled from Burrard Inlet to the sawmills and docks on Vancouver Island, where culturally similar and often related Aboriginal groups also laboured as lumber handlers, that framework, and the beliefs that circulated within it, was stretched wider.[13] In this context, the links between the emergence of the IWW and the first pan-Salish organization comes into sharper focus. Not only were the same people involved in both movements—Joe Capilano paid for his trip to England with money earned on the waterfront—but, on a wider canvas, both were attempting to assert control over an economic and political context in which the balance of power had shifted decisively in favour of white society with the emergence of industrial capitalism and the incursion of the colonial state (Zaharoff, 1978; Knight, 1996: 124). This dialectic of politicization is captured by the nickname adopted by Aboriginal dockers for local 526: It was called the 'Bows and Arrows', an assertion of difference and identity at a time when white society was bent on political marginalization and cultural assimilation.

After the demise of Local 526, Squamish waterfront workers formed local 38-57 of the International Longshoremen's Association (ILA) in 1913, about a year after white workers had established

ILA Local 38-52 in Vancouver. 'The Indians used to handle nothing but lumber and the whites, the general cargo. Sometimes they'd be working in the next hatch to each other and they'd get talking. That's how some Indians learned English and that kind of talk led to the formation of the ILA' one lumber handler recalled. 'Things were dying out and ILA was getting bigger and bigger,' remarked another (Philpot, 1963: 44; ILWU Pensioners, 1975). Communication across divisions of race and specialization was no doubt important in this process of union building, but so too were the broader structural shifts taking place in the shipping industry, which brought larger numbers of workers together to load and unload a wider range of commodities on a single vessel. By the eve of the First World War, only a handful of ships took on large volumes of lumber, while sailing vessels, once the domain of Aboriginal dockers, continued to disappear (ILWU Pensioners, 1975: 46–7).

The decision to disband the Bows and Arrows and join the ILA sparked a debate among Squamish workers. While no transcripts or minutes of this discussion survive, the memories of Ed Long, a lumber handler during these years, suggest that Aboriginal workers were politicized both as workers and as 'Indians'. . . . Long's recollection highlights one dimension of casual work that many longshoremen—Aboriginal or not—valued: the ability to choose when and where to work, even if that choice meant taking one's chances on the daily shape-up.[14] More specifically, it suggests that at the core of the 'Indian boys" critique was an abiding sense of pride in their status as skilled men 'on the lumber' and a desire to protect their usual practice of merging waterfront work with other pursuits, such as waged work in the hop fields or hunting and fishing (Dunlop, 1989: 80, 163–6).[15] In the end, according to one source, about 90 per cent of the Bows and Arrows backed a move into their *own*

ILA local—the men, evidently, opting for political separation in order to maintain control over their union affairs (ILWU Pensioners, 1975: 46–7).

Between 1913 and 1916, when local 38-57 was an independent organization, veteran docker William Nahanee served as its president; his son, Edward, who started on the waterfront in 1911 or 1912 in his mid-teens, occupied the vice-president's post (Philpot, 1963: 44–5; ILWU Pensioners, 1975: 55). They were joined in the union's upper ranks by Andrew Paull. The first child of Teresa and Dan Paull, who once worked as a longshoreman, Andrew was born in 1892 in the Howe Sound area, the Squamish's traditional territory. With the support of his family, which possessed considerable status within the Squamish community, Andrew spent six years in school and went on to study law in Vancouver in 1906, at the time of the Salish chiefs' trip to London (Patterson, 1976). In the years that followed his legal education, Andrew worked as a longshoreman and served as a delegate to the annual convention of the Pacific Coast District of the ILA in Vancouver in 1914; there he was named to the district's grievance committee and introduced a motion pertaining to Aboriginal dockers on Burrard Inlet.[16]

Significantly, Paull's commitment to the labour movement emerged alongside a deepening engagement in the struggle for Aboriginal rights. He was an interpreter for the McKenna-McBride Commission, which examined the question of Aboriginal land claims in British Columbia between 1912 and 1916, and a founder of the Allied Tribes of British Columbia, an organization that formed as the commission's work drew to a close (Dunlop, 1989). Without question, Paull's political aspirations reflected his own history as a Squamish man, and the influence of the Squamish chiefs who, according to E. Palmer Patterson, had been grooming him for leadership from an early age (Patterson, 1976: 63–4). Yet according to Herbert

Francis Dunlop, a Catholic priest who wrote a biography of the Squamish leader, Paull's understanding of the spiritual costs associated with being a 'beast of burden' on the docks was of some consequence as well. Aware of his own feelings of estrangement and powerlessness on the job, and the stark contrast between this condition of alienation and the ways in which life and labour were historically organized in Squamish society, he understood well that in the white man's world, independence, either on the job or on the reserve, was vital to his future and that of the Squamish. For without it, he was headed back 'to the ships with their stinking cargos, and their humid holds, and [the] endless, meaningless loading and unloading' and his community was headed for 'extermination' (Dunlop, 1989: 80–1, 84).

From the emergence of the IWW to the creation of the ILA, Aboriginal men were involved in the political fermentation that characterized working-class life in Vancouver in the early twentieth century. Presumably they took part in the debate surrounding the amalgamation of ILA locals 38-57 and 38-52 in 1916, the new union's subsequent support for the One Big Union, and the strike wave that gripped Vancouver during and after the Great War. Edward Nahanee was among the waterfront workers barricaded inside the ILA hall on 3 August 1918 when it was attacked by returned soldiers who were protesting the dockers' unanimous support for the 'Ginger Goodwin' general strike. 'There were swarms of soldiers storming the doors, and on the roof of one of the warehouses, three machine guns were trained on us by the RCMP, so close I could practically see down their barrels,' he recalled (Mortimer, 1981: 115–16). Woven into this wider pattern of collective action were moments when Aboriginal longshoremen's language and tactics addressed issues that were specific to them as 'Indian' workers in a workplace segmented by differences ascribed to race: the desire to work the lumber, influence the composition of work gangs through labour recruitment, and take on other jobs when the need or desire arose. Significantly, the politics of work influenced, and in turn were shaped by, the emerging struggle for Aboriginal rights. Both played an important role in the political socialization of Joe Capilano, Andrew Paull, and Simon Baker, among others, and addressed issues of powerlessness, identity, and independence.

. . . The 1923 longshoremen's strike was a lengthy all-or-nothing affair that marked a turning point in the organization of the waterfront workplace (Hovis, 1985: 175). In that conflict, the Shipping Federation moved decisively to break the ILA, establish an open shop, and reconfigure the local labour market. For its part, the longshoremen's union, which had played an important role in fomenting 'the spirit of discontent' that accompanied the Great War, was pushing for a five-cent wage increase and greater control of hiring through a union-run despatch hall (*Longshoremen's Strike Bulletin*, 24 October 1923, vol. 37). Fragmentary evidence from the 1923 saw-off suggests that Aboriginal dockers were opposed to going on strike at first, but later took an active role in 'holding the fort'. . . . After two months on the picket line, the ILA, which had mounted 'one hell of a fight', was broken, its efforts undercut by the Shipping Federation's effective use of strikebreakers, limited unity among Pacific Coast waterfront workers, and the conservatism of the labour movement—locally, provincially, and nationally—after the heady days of 1919.

Aboriginal workers paid a heavy price for their activism. After decades of class conflict, the Shipping Federation embraced a new philosophy of workplace relations: welfare capitalism. Inspired by similar innovations in other industries, it sought to secure long-term industrial peace by building institutional and social bridges across the chasm of class difference and decasualizing the local labour market. Dubbed a 'good citizens policy', the latter initiative took aim at the use of the shape-up method of hiring and the overabundance of casual workers who, it was thought, were 'inclined to agitation'. Under the terms of the post-strike settlement, members of the ILA, if they were not blacklisted outright, were entitled to only a small portion of available work; the lion's share of employment opportunities was reserved for strikebreakers who, after the end of the strike, were enrolled in a new company-sponsored association, the Vancouver and District Waterfront Workers Association.[17] In this context of defeat, whatever unity existed between Squamish longshoremen and their white counterparts dissolved. By January 1924, former members of the Bows and Arrows, in particular Andrew Paull, were pressing the Shipping Federation to create a new lumber handlers' organization, the Independent Lumber Handlers' Association (ILHA). Not only did they want to control their own political affairs, but they objected 'to being placed in [full-time] gangs because of the necessity of working whenever the gangs in which they were placed were equipped'—a practice key to the Shipping Federation's vision of decasualization.[18]

Ambivalent about the idea at first, the Shipping Federation later endorsed the new organization, perhaps hoping to ensure that longshoremen remained divided among themselves and thus weaker politically.[19] Shortly after its creation, the membership of the ILHA underwent a significant change: it became smaller and whiter. . . . Without waterfront work, Aboriginal men (and their families) hunted and fished, cut firewood and picked hops, worked in the commercial fishery, and applied for relief from the band's government-administered trust fund.[20] The ILHA persisted until 1933, its remaining, largely non-Aboriginal, membership receiving few opportunities to work (Philpot, 1963: 45; Pine, 1996).[21]

Aboriginal longshoremen were marginalized from waterfront work after the 1923 confrontation. Placed at a considerable disadvantage by the blacklisting of former ILA men and the creation of a company union, their desire for some control over when and where their gangs were 'equipped' was at odds with the Shipping Federation's long-term vision of creating a permanent pool of full-time longshoremen under its direction.[22] The logic behind the ILHA's position reflected a preference among its Aboriginal members for a more migratory working life, one that combined a variety of occupations with other customary forms of support, such as hunting and fishing.[23] Not only did this attachment to mobility resonate with their specific histories as Aboriginal people, but, in the context of waged work, it provided a means to assert their independence on the job. At the same time, however, a migratory working life was born of necessity. The terms of the post-strike settlement, which reduced the earning power of the ILHA's membership, coupled with the limits placed on other Aboriginal economic practices by the colonial state, made it difficult for them to make ends meet without working on the docks, aboard a fishing vessel, or in the hop fields in a single year. 'In ten days it was all over,' Edward Nahanee observed, referring to the 1923 strike. 'We lost our jobs and everything' (Philpot, 1963: 45).

Aboriginal workers' absence from the waterfront lasted until 1935, when they returned to work in the midst of a gruesome six-month confrontation between the Shipping Federation and the Vancouver and District Waterfront Workers Association, which had forged links with the Communist Party of Canada in the early 1930s and become more and more militant as the Depression wore on (McCandless, 1974). Leaflets identifying 'scab' workers circulated by the longshoremen's strike committee contained the names of several Aboriginal men; one Communist-backed newspaper, *Ship and Dock*, asserted that the Department of Indian Affairs was helping waterfront employers in recruiting replacement workers.[24] 'Some would call us strikebreakers,' Tim Moody recollected. 'But that is a matter of opinion. The men whose jobs we took were those who broke the strike in 1923 . . . My father said my grandfather had been a longshoreman and we had to hang on to what he had started. It was all we had' (Philpott, 1963: 47). Hanging on in the aftermath of the 1935 strike meant being members of the North Vancouver Longshoremen's Association (NVLA), a union created by the Shipping Federation, with the assistance of the North Vancouver Board of Trade, to both reward 'Indian' workers for opposing the 'forces of disruption' and act as a bulwark against bona fide unions that were active in other Pacific Coast ports.[25] . . .

Strikebreakers, not strikers, this time around, 'Indian' dockers fared better in the wake of the 1935 confrontation than they did after the 1923 strike. Indeed, in the mid-to-late 1930s, they dominated the union's executive and worked nearly as often as other gangs that handled similar cargo, despite the ongoing effects of the Depression on maritime traffic. After a long hiatus, the Bows and Arrows were back 'on the lumber'— an occupation that they would retain during the Second World War and after.

Aboriginal men on Burrard Inlet figured prominently in the industrialization of British Columbia, taking up longshoring, among other occupations, almost from the moment that sawmills first came to the area in the early 1860s. On the docks, they worked in an occupational setting characterized by turbulent labour relations, strong competition for work, and sharp distinctions of specialization. The intersection of class and race was significant in this complex context, shaping the day-to-day decisions that Aboriginal longshoremen, most of whom were Squamish, made about what job they might do, whom they might work with, and what their political options were, on the waterfront and off. That waterfront unionism and organizations dedicated to Aboriginal rights emerged at the same time illustrates this point well. Men who were politically active on the 'Indian' waterfront were also involved with the Salish delegation to London, the Allied Tribes of British Columbia, and the Squamish Tribal Council—a cross-pollination that persisted into the early 1940s, when Tim Moody of the NVLA joined the Native Brotherhood of British Columbia, a group created by coastal First Nations in 1931 to advance the concerns of Aboriginal commercial fishers (Philpott, 1963: 48–9; Tennant, 1990).

Skilled and knowledgeable longshoremen, Aboriginal workers' longevity on the waterfront was due to many factors, not the least of which was their ability to specialize in a particular cargo and, over the span of several decades, ensure that 'Indian' men were available to work it. Family relations were vital to this process of labour recruitment; so, too, was the passage of workplace knowledge from one generation of Aboriginal waterfront workers to the next. Absent from waterfront work after the 1923 strike, the Bows and Arrows returned to the docks in 1935, and in short order they made up about half of the NVLA's membership and dominated its executive. . . .

Inspired by Rolf Knight's pioneering *Indians at Work*, this analysis illustrates the significance of wage labour to Aboriginal life on Burrard Inlet between 1863 and 1939. Rooted in a specific location, time period, and configuration of power relations, the Bows and Arrows' history of waged work was, simultaneously, part of a more general phenomenon: the expansion of capitalism on a global scale. Indeed, indigenous people from south-east Alaska to Puget Sound faced broadly similar challenges with the advent of paid labour from the mid-nineteenth to the early twentieth century; so, too, did waterfront workers from Seattle to London, Montreal to Mombassa, who struggled with decasualization as it took hold in other labour markets in other ports during the same time (Wyatt, 1987; Crockford, 1991; Barsh, 1996; Cooper, 2000; Weinhauer, 2000). Perhaps the experiences of Tlingit cannery workers or London dockers were known to the Bows and Arrows—information, as well as commodities, circulated in port cities—and, from their vantage point on Burrard Inlet, they recognized a common pattern of conflict, resistance, and adaptation to capitalist development.

For the 'best men that worked the lumber' that pattern was intimately connected to their encounter with colonialism. As a consequence, their struggle for autonomy not only embraced questions of land, resources, and self-government—as the existing literature suggests—but issues related to the day-to-day realities of life 'on the hook' as well. By bringing Aboriginal history and labour history into closer contact, two disciplines that are typically conceptualized and researched separately, the very notion of Aboriginal politics expands and changes shape. Class, as a structured reality and a lived daily experience, mattered to the Squamish. To ignore or downplay this dimension of their lives is to obscure many of the key issues that they thought about often, struggled with daily, and hoped, in the end, to be free from.

Notes

1. For the Canadian context, see Steven High, 'Native Wage Labour and Independent Production during the "Era of Irrelevance"', *Labour/Le Travail* 37 (Spring 1996): 243–64. For the American context see Alice Littlefield and Martha C. Knack, eds, *Native Americans and Wage Labor: Ethnohistorical Perspectives*

(Norman and London: University of Oklahoma Press, 1998).

2. See John Lutz, 'After the Fur Trade: The Aboriginal Labouring Class of British Columbia, 1849–1890', *Journal of the Canadian Historical Association* (1992): 69–94; Lutz, 'Gender and Work in Lekwammen Families, 1843 to 1970', in Kathryn McPherson, Cecilia Morgan, and Nancy M. Forestell, eds, *Gendered Pasts: Historical Essays on Femininity and Masculinity in Canada* (Toronto: Oxford University Press, 1999), 80–105; Harald E.L. Prins, 'Tribal Network and Migrant Labor: Mi'kmaq Indians as Seasonal Workers in Aroostook's Potato Fields, 1870–1980', in Alice Littlefield and Martha C. Knack, eds, *Native Americans and Wage Labor: Ethnohistorical Perspectives* (Norman and London: University of Oklahoma Press, 1998); Frank Tough, *'As their natural resources fail': Native People and the Economic History of Northern Manitoba, 1870–1930* (Vancouver: UBC Press, 1996).

3. Chief Cheakamus (Tom) to 'Honourable Gentlemen', [n.d. likely 1912 to 1916], file 520C, vol. 11021, RG 10, British Columbia Archives (hereafter cited as BCA). I consulted RG 10, the records of the Department of Indian Affairs, in both the British Columbia Archives and Library and Archives Canada (LAC); for this reason, citations for TG 10 may refer to either the BCA or the LAC.

4. References to potlatches held by the Squamish can be found in Byrne to assistant deputy, 3 Feb. 1914, vol. 1479, Letterbook, RG 10, BCA; Devlin to Vowell, 16 July 1896, file 121, 698-53, vol. 3944; Charles Hill-Tout, 'Notes on the Skqomic of British Columbia', in Charles Maud, ed., *The Salish People* (Vancouver: Talonbooks, 1978), 49; testimony of Chief Mathias Joseph and Chief Harry, 1913, Add. Mss 1056, BCA; 'Gilbert Malcolm Sproat's Summarized Report. . .1877', file 3756-11, vol. 3611.

5. Chief Cheakamus (Tom) to 'Honourable Gentlemen'. For the general trend see Newell, *Tangled Webs*. For the Squamish see Paull to Byrne, 3 May 1920, file 167/20-2, vol. 10899, G 10, LAC.

6. The global perspective is detailed in Colin J. Davis, David de Vries, Lex Heerma van Voss, Lidewij Hesselink, and Klaus Weinhauer, *Dock Workers: International Explorations in Comparative Labour History, 1790–1970* (Aldershot: Ashgate, 2000). For Vancouver see John Bellamy Foster, 'On the Waterfront: Longshoring in Canada', in Craig Heron and Robert Storey, eds, *On the Job: Confronting the Labour Process in Canada* (Montreal and Kingston: McGill-Queen's University Press, 1986), 281–308; ILWU Pensioners, *Man Along the Shore! The Story of the Vancouver Waterfront as Told by the Longshoremen Themselves, 1860s–1975* (Vancouver: ILWU Pensioners, 1975).

7. According to 'Squamish Longshoreman Has Watched Vancouver Grow into Great Port', *Vancouver Daily Province*, 10 May 1941, Nahanee's father was Hawaiian and his mother was a 'Capilano Indian'. This suggests that William was born in BC. The 1901 *Census of Canada* presents a different picture. It states that Nahanee was born in Hawaii, came to BC in 1896, and married a Squamish woman shortly after arriving. For Joe Jerome see Stuart Bowman Philpott, 'Trade Unionism and Acculturation: A Comparative Study of Urban Indians and Immigrant Italians' (MA thesis, University of British Columbia, 1963), 48.

8. See 'Agricultural and Industrial Statistics, 1899–1919', vol. 1493, RG 10, BCA.

9. 'Accidents for the 1st Half of 1925', file 1, box 36, Add. Mss 279, City of Vancouver Archives (CVA).

10. Interview with Edward Nahanee, tape 17:9. ILWU records, University of British Columbia Special Collections (UBC-SC).

11. For the national strike trends see Gregory S. Kealey and Douglas Cruikshank, 'Strikes in Canada, 1891–1950', in Gregory S. Kealey, ed., *Workers and Canadian History* (Kingston and Montreal: McGill-Queen's University Press, 1995), 345–418. For an excellent introduction to the debates about longshoremen and strikes see Raymond Miller, 'The Dockworker Subculture and Some Problems in Cross-Cultural and Cross-Time Generalizations', *Comparative Studies in Society and History* 11 (1969): 302–14.

12. See also ILWU Pensioners, *Man Along the Shore!*, 33, 46; interview with Axel Nyman, tape 17:19, ILWU records, UBC-SC.

13. On the movement of Aboriginal longshoremen from one port to another see ILWU Pensioners, *Man Along the Shore!*, 41; Knight, *Indians at Work*, 123, 286 n. 29.

14. On this point see Klaus Weinhauer, 'Power and Control on the Waterfront', in Davis et al., *Dock Labour*, 580–603.

15. See also interview with Axel Nyman, tape 17:19, ILWU records, UBC-SC.

16. See 'Annual Convention of Longshoremen', *BC Federationist*, 22 May 1914; 'The Pacific Coast District, No. 38, I.L.A', 29 May 1914.

17. For an introduction to welfare capitalism see the entire issue of *International Labor and Working-Class History* 53 (Spring 1998). For the Vancouver waterfront see Parnaby, 'On the Hook', 26–74.

18. McVety to Harrison, 23 Feb. 1924, Strike 95 (vol. 2), vol. 332, RG 27, LAC.
19. Crombie to ILHA, 26 and 28 Jan. 1924, file 1, box 36, Add. Mss 279, CVA.
20. See also Ditchburn to Scott, 6 Jan. 1925, file 351,304, vol. 4045, RG 10, BCA; Burke to Perry, 7 Nov. 1925; Halladay to Perry, 21 Oct. 1924; Perry to Billy and Henry Newman, 9 Oct. 1924; Perry to Motherwell, 17 Dec. 1924, file 167/20-2, vol. 10899, RG 10, LAC.
21. Cromiba to Webber, 2 Oct. 1925, file 5, box 32; Greer to Crombie, 7 June 1926, 26 Oct. 1927, 31 Aug. 1931; 'Special Committee re: ILHA', 29 April 1931, file 1, box 36, Add. Mss 279, CVA. Edward Nahanee and Denny Paull (Andrew Paull's son) joined gangs belonging to the company union; see 'VDWWA North Shore Members', 9 July 1928, file 10, box 5, Add. Mss 279, CVA.
22. Crombie to Labour committee, 11 Feb. 1924, file 4, box 23, Add. Mss 279, CVA.
23. On the importance of migration to other Aboriginal workers in BC see Paige Raibmon, 'Theaters of Contact: The Kwakwaka'wakw Meet Colonialism in British Columbia and at the Chicago World's Fair', *Canadian Historical Review* 81, no. 2 (June 2000): 157–90.
24. 'Where are these men working?' file 10, 75-E-5, series 200, Vancouver Police Department fonds, CVA; 'Indian Agency Is Used To Break Strikers' Ranks', *Ship and Dock*, 14 Nov. 1935, Strike 87A, vol. 369, RG 27, LAC.
25. Canadian Transport to Johnson, 18 Feb. 1938, file 2, box 46, Add. Mss 279, CVA.

References

Baker, Simon. 1994. *Khot-la-cha: The Autobiography of Chief Simon Baker*, Verna J. Kirkness, ed. Vancouver: Douglas and MacIntyre.

Barnett, Homer. 1955. *The Coast Salish of British Columbia*. Eugene: University of Oregon Press.

Barsh, Russell Lawrence. 1996. 'Puget Sound Indian Demography, 1900–1920: Migration and Economic Integration', *Ethnohistory* 43, 1 (Winter): 65–97.

Burrows, James. 1986. '"A much needed class of labour": The Economy and Income of the Southern Interior Plateau, 1897–1910', *BC Studies* 71 (Autumn): 27–46.

Cooper, Frederick. 2000. 'Dockworkers and Labour History', pp. 523–41 in Colin Davis, David de Vries, Lex Heerma van Voss, Lidewij Hesselink, and Klaus Weinhauer, eds, *Dock Workers: International Explorations in Comparative Labour History, 1790–1970*. Aldershot: Ashgate.

Crockford, Cairn Elizabeth. 1991. 'Nuu-chah-Nulth Labour Relations in the Pelagic Sealing Industry, 1868–1911'. MA thesis, University of Victoria.

Davis, Colin, David de Vries, Lex Heerma van Voss, Lidewij Hesselink, and Klaus Weinhauer. 2000. *Dock Workers: International Explorations in Comparative Labour History, 1790–1970*. Aldershot: Ashgate.

De Vries, David. 2000. 'The Construction of the Image of the Dock Labourer', pp. 695–700 in Colin Davis, David de Vries, Lex Heerma van Voss, Lidewij Hesselink, and Klaus Weinhauer, eds, *Dock Workers: International Explorations in Comparative Labour History, 1790–1970*. Aldershot: Ashgate.

Dunlop, Herbert Francis. 1989. *Andrew Paull as I Knew Him and Understood His Times*. Vancouver: Order of the OMI of St Paul's Province.

Fisher, Robin. 1992. *Contact and Conflict: Indian–European Relations in British Columbia, 1774–1890*, 2nd ed. Vancouver: UBC Press.

Harris, Cole. 1997. *The Resettlement of British Columbia: Essays on Colonialism and Geographical Change*. Vancouver: UBC Press.

———. 2002. *Making Native Space: Colonialism, Resistance, and Reserves in British Columbia*. Vancouver: UBC Press.

Hovis, Logan. 1985. 'The 1923 Longshoremen's Strike', in Working Lives Collective, ed., *Working Lives*. Vancouver: New Star Books.

ILWU Pensioners. 1975. *Man Along the Shore! The Story of the Vancouver Waterfront as Told by the Longshoremen Themselves, 1860s–1975*. Vancouver: ILWU Pensioners.

Industrial Union Bulletin. 1907. No. 2.

Kennedy, Dorothy Irene. 1995. 'Looking for Tribes in All the Wrong Places: An Examination of the Central Coast Salish Social Network'. MA thesis, University of Victoria.

Knight, Rolf. 1996. *Indians at Work*, 2nd edn. Vancouver: New Star Books.

Leier, Mark. 1990. *Where the Fraser River Flows: The Industrial Workers of the World in British Columbia*. Vancouver: New Star Books.

Longshoremen's Strike Bulletin. 1923. 24 October.

Lutz, John. 1992. 'After the Fur Trade: The Aboriginal Labouring Class of British Columbia, 1849–1890', *Journal of the Canadian Historical Association*: 69–94.

———. 1998. 'Gender and Work in Lekwammen Families, 1843 to 1970', in Kathryn McPherson, Cecilia Morgan, and Nancy M. Forestell, eds, *Gendered*

Pasts: Historical Essays on Femininity and Masculinity in Canada. Toronto: Oxford University Press.

———. 1999. 'Making "Indians" in British Columbia: Power, Race, and the Importance of Place', pp. 61–84 in Richard White and John M. Findlay, eds, *Power and Place in the North American West.* Seattle and London: University of Washington Press.

McCandless, Richard. 1974. 'Vancouver's "Red Menace" of 1935: The Waterfront Situation', *BC Studies* 22 (Spring): 56–70.

Mortimer, Hilda with Chief Dan George. 1981. *You Call Me Chief: Impressions of the Life of Chief Dan George.* Toronto: Doubleday.

Nelson, Bruce. 2000. 'Ethnicity, Race, and the Logic of Solidarity', pp. 655–80 in Colin Davis, David de Vries, Lex Heerma van Voss, Lidewij Hesselink, and Klaus Weinhauer, eds, *Dock Workers: International Explorations in Comparative Labour History, 1790–1970.* Aldershot: Ashgate.

Newell, Dianne. 1993. *Tangled Webs of History: Indians and the Law in Canada's Pacific Coast Fisheries.* Toronto: University of Toronto Press.

Parnaby, Andrew. 2001. 'On the Hook: Welfare Capitalism on the Vancouver Waterfront, 1919–1939'. PhD dissertation, Memorial University of Newfoundland.

Patterson, E. Palmer. 1976. 'Andrew Paull (1892–1959): Finding a Voice for the "New Indian"', *Western Candian Journal of Anthropology* 2 (1976): 63–80.

Philpott, Stuart Bowman. 1963. 'Trade Unionism and Acculturation: A Comparative Study of Urban Indians and Immigrant Italians'. MA thesis, University of British Columbia.

Prins, Harald E.L. 1998. 'Tribal Network and Migrant Labor: Mi'kmaq Indians as Seasonal Workers in Aroostook's Potato Fields, 1870–1980', in Alice Littlefield and Martha C. Knack, eds, *Native Americans and Wage Labor: Ethnohistorical Perspectives.* Norman and London: University of Oklahoma Press.

Roediger, David. 1994. *Towards the Abolition of Whiteness: Essays on Race, Politics, and Working-Class History.* New York: Verso.

Roine, Chris. 1996. 'The Squamish Aboriginal Economy, 1860–1940'. MA thesis, Simon Fraser University.

Suttles, Wayne, 1987. *Coast Salish Essays.* Vancouver: Talonbooks.

Tennant, Paul. 1990. *Aboriginal People and Politics: The Indian Land Question in British Columbia, 1849–1989.* Vancouver: UBC Press.

Tough, Frank. 1996. *'As their natural resources fail': Native People and the Economic History of Northern Manitoba, 1870–1930.* Vancouver: UBC Press.

Weinhauer, Klaus. 2000. 'Power and Control on the Waterfront: Casual Labour and Decasualisation', pp. 580–603 in Colin Davis, David de Vries, Lex Heerma van Voss, Lidewij Hesselink, and Klaus Weinhauer, eds, *Dock Workers: International Explorations in Comparative Labour History, 1790–1970.* Aldershot: Ashgate.

Wyatt, Victoria. 1987. 'Alaskan Indian Wage Earners in the 19th Century: Economic Choices and Ethnic Identity on Southeast Alaska's Frontier', *Pacific Northwest Quarterly* 78, 1 (January–April): 43–9.

Yarmie, Andrew. 1991. 'The Right to Manage: Vancouver Employers' Associations, 1900–1923', *BC Studies* 90 (Summer): 40–74.

Zaharoff, William John. 1978. 'Success in Struggle: The Squamish People and Kitsilano Indian Reserve Number 6'. MA thesis, Carleton University.

PART VI

The Depression Decade

For working-class families in Canada, the 1920s did not exactly 'roar'. The immediate post-World War I years were ones of economic dislocation and unemployment; not until 1922–23 did the situation improve for Canadian workers. Many working-class households found it necessary to have multiple earners, or other means of income such as boarders, in order to survive.

Certainly, the economy was changing. Corporations were becoming more concentrated with mergers producing large conglomerates, and new resource industries like hydroelectric power and pulp and paper were expanding. Financial institutions and large enterprises also required internal bureaucracies, thus providing more white collar jobs for young women who wished to work before marriage, and who wanted to avoid the isolation of domestic work or the drudgery of factory labour. This was also a period when some employers experimented with new forms of 'welfare capitalism', providing benefits meant to solidify labour loyalties to the firm and prevent unionization, a strategy detailed in Joan Sangster's 'The Softball Solution', in Part VII. The flip side of this calculated benevolence was the increased implementation of more regimented technologies and work processes: following Frederick Winslow Taylor's earlier scientific management theory, measures were used to break down jobs into minute parts, speeding up production. This pattern fit new, assembly-line mass production plants, the archetype of which was the increasingly important automobile industry, very well.

To be sure, many young women and men perceived a different social atmosphere in the wake of the devastation and loss of life of World War I; some rebelled by hiking their skirts higher, embracing new pastimes like dancing, and spending more time in movie theatres watching popular films that promoted mass consumption, new standards of beauty care, and passionate romance. Such leisure activities, however cheap, became far less affordable after the Depression hit in 1929.

The economic crisis was unlike anything experienced before by workers and their families. It created mass unemployment, widespread poverty, growing despair, and increasing anger. Within a few years, the Gross National Product declined by almost 30 per cent; one in four workers was unemployed. At least one-tenth of the entire population depended on relief, a form of welfare considered a discretionary privilege rather than a citizen's right. Resource industries, in which male workers were historically responsible for the 'breadwinner wage' that bought the food and paid the rent, were especially hard hit. If women's rates of unemployment were lower than those suffered by men, as some observers claimed, this was partly because they were in 'sex-typed' jobs like domestic service that no man would stoop to take. Their low social value also meant that these occupations often went unrecorded in official statistics. This did not stop some commentators from demanding that married women leave the workforce, assuring jobs for men, an unworkable and unlikely solution that simply reflected gendered anxieties that working-class masculinity was as much in crisis as was the economy.

Working-class people responded to this unprecedented collapse of the capitalist system in a multitude of ways. They tried to 'get by' on less. Some left home to search for work, lessening the strains on households now pressured from many directions. Children who could not leave might be encouraged to look for work, scavenge for useful materials for the domestic economy, such as wood to burn, or contribute in other ways to the faltering household. Many applied for relief, or sought charity of one kind or another. Finally, significant numbers of Canadians also embraced dissident ideas, protesting the state's inadequate, and at times heartless, response to the plight of the jobless by aligning themselves with the voices of the left in the Communist Party of Canada (CP) or the Cooperative Commonwealth Federation (CCF). The former, with the Soviet Union and workers' revolution as its beacons, attracted many of the most alienated and dispossessed to its cause, while the latter, espousing a parliamentary road to a rational, planned socialist society presented a more respectable, but still forceful, challenge to a Canadian capitalism in obvious crisis.

Denyse Baillargeon's article on Montreal homemakers during the 1930s takes us inside the working-class household, where we are able to view the material, spatial, and personal dimensions of women's unpaid domestic labour during the 1930s. Researchers focusing on labouring families have been especially interested in using oral history as a means of recovering aspects of working people's everyday lives. Most Canadian men and women, lacking the authority, power, and material resources to control their own destinies in ways they might like, have seldom had the education, inclination, or time to draft first-hand accounts of their experiences and then deposit them in archives for future historians to consult. Baillargeon thus draws on oral testimonies presenting us with a view of how families coped during a period of acute economic distress. She brings to light a fundamental historical truism, but one too often obscured in the kinds of evidence that have survived and on which so many historical accounts rest uncritically. By probing women's recollections directly, Baillargeon paints a vivid picture of the varied, unheralded labours of the household. Wages, often brought home by males, were of course pivotally important to working-class well-being, but so too was the work of women, which included turning paycheques into clothing, food, and housing, as well as the 'labours of love' associated with child-rearing, caring for the elderly, and other under-appreciated tasks. This motherwork was always critically important, but when the 1930s economic collapse meant that male breadwinner wages were either unavailable entirely, or severely curtailed, it was often all that was left keeping labouring families afloat.

John Manley's account of the efforts of the Communist Party to organize the unemployed during the Depression also points to the importance of women's domestic labour. His article indicates how the crisis of the working-class family in the 1930s served as a stimulus to women's political organization. Poor housewives, as he shows, could be mobilized to protest both the means of paying relief and the meagre amounts allotted, which simply could not provide adequate clothing, housing, and food for those in dire need.

The Communist Party's ways of mobilizing Canadians during the Great Depression changed over the course of the difficult decade, but in general this left-wing party tried to organize the unorganized, be they working in the new mass production industries, or thrown out of paid employment by the destructive downturn in the business cycle. In the early years of the Great Depression, Canadian communists organized spirited rallies in defence of free speech and the right to criticize the state's lack of policies to address unemployment, took the lead in establishing militant unions in work sectors often shunned by mainstream labour organizations, and were forceful in their willingness to support strikes and other class battles.

Communists the world over, including Canadian leftists, relied for instruction on the Moscow-based Communist International and its undisputed leader, Joseph Stalin. As the world capitalist crisis unfolded in 1929–30, communist policy was premised on the view that post–World War I global capitalism had entered a Third Period of intensified crisis in which revolutionaries were urged to do their utmost to fan the flames of class war. There was to be no compromise with class enemies of all stripes, from powerful bourgeois bosses to mild socialists committed to piecemeal reforms. Revolution was supposedly around the corner, communists claimed, the collapse of the capitalist system proving the inevitability of a revolutionary order taking its place. It was necessary to prepare workers to take power as class confronted class. In the early years of the Depression decade, communist practice in Canada thus coincided with Stalin's directives.

By 1935, the global realities confronting the Communist International indicated the folly of this approach. Fascism had come to power in significant parts of Europe, most importantly in Germany, long regarded by communists as perhaps the critical country with the potential making of the European Revolution. Realizing, too late, that Hitler's crushing of the German workers' movement spelled the death of communism, Stalin reversed the policy of the Communist International. Communists, who had refused all alliances with non-revolutionary forces now proclaimed the need for labour and the left to create Popular Fronts of any and all forces, including bourgeois elements and progressives in liberal-democratic governments, through which the working-class and its 'allies' could defeat Hitler. This, communists felt, was the best way to ensure that Nazi armies of aggression did not overrun the Soviet Union. But it also ensured that communists led fewer protests within capitalist countries such as Canada, and were less likely to provide unambiguously radical leadership to workers struggling to build unions or engage in other activities. The independent 'red' unions that had been set up and sustained by Canadian communists from 1930–35, for instance, were disbanded and their leaders, as well as their rank-and-file, were urged to affiliate with the more moderate conventional unions. The Popular Front strategy also advocated forming broad political coalitions, capable of building widespread support for progressive causes and promising to bring radicals in the CP and the CCF together. After years of being denounced as traitors and misleaders, however, many CCFers were understandably reluctant to link arms with the communists.

As Manley shows, some Communist Party efforts to mobilize the unemployed and families on relief were more successful than others. While it is difficult to assess the overall impact of the Party during the Depression, it is clear that campaigns like the national petition to secure work or unemployment insurance, or communist leadership in local anti-eviction struggles, did build on growing working-class resentments, drawing new members into the communist movement, winning the Party political credibility. These successes, as Manley reveals, also resulted in state repression as communist leaders were jailed or deported.

Communists, Prime Minister R.B. Bennett claimed in the early 1930s, were enemies of the state, a dangerous element that needed to be crushed. They were responsible, though small in number, for many of the strikes that erupted in the early years of the decade, and Bennett saw their irksome 'conspiratorial' presence behind the 1935 On-to-Ottawa Trek, perhaps the most well known protest of Canada's jobless during the Depression. As Bill Waiser's book-length study of the Trek reveals, the proposed cross-country march of the unemployed was fuelled far more by the anger and despair of Canada's single, unemployed men than it was by communist agitation. Hoping to get a hearing in government circles by marching from Vancouver to the nation's capital, the out-of-work protesters were fed up with the misery of life in federal relief camps. Herded into isolated barracks far distant from centres of population, subjected to military discipline and required to engage in meaningless physical labour, the trekkers were a lost generation of Canadians, the human casualties of economic crisis. Their plight inspired Irene Baird's *Waste Heritage* (1939), arguably the country's first proletarian novel.

The Trek, which came to an abrupt halt in Regina when the Royal Canadian Mounted Police and the protesters clashed in a violent riot, is often the historical image used to represent the Depression decade. The two articles in this Part reveal another side of this history of labouring people devastated by capitalism's collapse: of families protesting their impoverishment and struggling to retain their dignity; of working-class households marshalling their human resources in order to survive one of twentieth-century Canada's most difficult decades.

Further Reading

Irving M. Abella, *Nationalism, Communism, and Canadian Labour: The CIO, the Communist Party, and the Canadian Congress of Labour, 1935–1956* (Toronto: University of Toronto Press, 1973).

Irene Baird, *Waste Heritage* (Toronto: Macmillan, 1974).

Stephen Endicott, *Bienfait: The Saskatchewan Miners' Struggle of '31* (Toronto: University of Toronto Press, 2002).

Alvin Finkel, *Business and Social Reform in the 1930s* (Toronto: Lorimer, 1979).

Graham Lowe, *Women in the Administrative Revolution: The Feminization of Clerical Work* (Toronto: University of Toronto Press, 1987).

Gabrielle Roy, *The Tin Flute* (Toronto: McClelland and Stewart, 1958) [translation of *Bonheur d'occasion*].

Joan Sangster, *Dreams of Equality: Women on the Canadian Left, 1920–1950* (Toronto: Oxford University Press, 1989).

Veronica Strong-Boag, 'The Girl of the New Day: Canadian Working Women in the 1920s', *Labour/Le Travail* 4 (1979): 131–64.

James Struthers, *No Fault of Their Own: Unemployment and the Canadian Welfare State, 1914–1941* (Toronto: University of Toronto Press, 1983).

Bill Waiser, *All Hell Can't Stop Us: The On-to-Ottawa Trek and the Regina Riot* (Calgary: Fifth House Publishing, 2003).

Labour/Le Travail 56 (Fall 2005). A special issue on communism and the Left.

Visual Resources

NFB, *Born of Hard Times* (1989), 53 minutes (on the origins of the Communist Party of Canada and the Cooperative Commonwealth Federation; from the series *Imperfect Union: Canadian Labour and the Left*).

Cinema Libre, *A Vision in the Darkness* (1991), 90 minutes (a portrait of Lea Roback, a Quebec trade union organizer, social activist, and in the 1930s also a communist).

CHAPTER 13

'Starve, Be Damned!': Communists and Canada's Urban Unemployed, 1929–39

John Manley

Historians have shown relatively little interest in the contribution of the Communist Party of Canada (CPC) to the struggles of the urban unemployed in the 1930s. Although they are prepared to recognize the CPC's leading role in mobilizing the unemployed in this period, they have often questioned the significance of the movement itself. . . . Unquestionably, most of Canada's unemployed masses, who numbered around 800,000 at the trough of the Depression in the winter of 1932–3, and at least 500,000 on the eve of the Second World War, were not politicized. Communist activist George MacEachern has recorded how, even in industrial Cape Breton, an area of highly developed unemployed activity, the jobless often settled for muddling through on '$3.00 a week and stealing your coal' (Frank and MacGillivray, 1987: 49). Nevertheless, all through the decade,

a militant minority refused to starve in silence.[1] The CPC's efforts to build its challenges to Canada's localized relief system into a broader political assault on the state obviously failed, but its revolutionary ambitions—at least until 1935—ensured that a definable movement emerged.[2]

Intellectually, the CPC leadership was ready for the economic crisis. 'Life itself' seemed to be confirming the predictive powers of Communist International (Comintern) theoreticians, who announced in 1928 that capitalism had entered a 'Third Period' of postwar development in which a profound political crisis would be precipitated by the working class's recognition that mass unemployment had become 'normal, inevitable and permanent' (Communist International, 15 March 1930; Morris, 1930; Lozovsky, 1931). Faithful to this 'New Line', party leaders held that only a failure of will on their part could block the emergence of a revolutionary movement of the unemployed. Yet when it launched the National Unemployed Workers' Association (NUWA) early in 1930, the party was ill prepared for combat. Membership had declined steadily since 1925 and, by late 1930, stood at barely 1,400, less than one-third of its peak in the 1920s. Making a virtue of this catastrophe, general secretary Tim Buck claimed that the residual hard core of bolshevik 'fighters' compensated for all the departing faint-hearts and renegades (Penner, 1988).[3]

For most of 1930, the NUWA targeted young, single, transient men, whose 'rowdiness' and lack of 'bourgeois respectability', it was thought, made them willing combatants in the 'struggle for the streets'. NUWA head Tom Ewan remarked of one notably aggressive young fighter that 'the only theory he has is to get a punch at the police . . . [but] that is a very good theory . . . He is a good element, he wants action . . . his type is hard to control, but . . . should not be condemned.'[4] Mobilizing transients in rapid-fire demonstrations demanding 'work or wages' at employment and relief offices proved particularly effective in Vancouver, where two immigrant 'Red Clyde-siders', Allan Campbell and James Litterick, organized over 100 demonstrations in 1930.[5] In central Canada, however, police repression hit the NUWA harder. Montreal and Toronto activists complained that the focus on transients reflected a failure to grasp the permanence of mass unemployment. They called for greater emphasis on work among unemployed families and insisted on fresh tactics and demands, arguing that married men and women were reluctant to confront the forces of law and order on a regular basis and could not take seriously the standard NUWA demand of 'work or full maintenance' at $25 a week—a sum that few had ever *earned*.[6] Comrades debated the issue for three months in the *Worker*, with Vancouver party

chief Malcolm Bruce trenchantly defending the status quo against the easterners' 'tailism'. When a Comintern directive endorsed the moderates' viewpoint, Toronto ended the debate in their favour and warned Bruce against indulging in factionalism.[7]

The resulting tactical shift was limited. Party leaders remained committed to the Third Period thesis that leading social democrats were 'social fascists,' or, as A.E. Smith, the general secretary of the Canadian Labour Defence League (CLDL), put it in a letter to the premier 'social fascist', J.S. Woodsworth, an old Labour Church and Social Gospel comrade, 'the servants of the capitalist class among the working class . . . daily [betray] the workers.'[8] Communists believed that Woodsworth and his fellow Independent Labor Party (ILP) MPs A.A. Heaps and Angus MacInnis (and other labour leaders) should be denied working-class platforms, especially when they sought to muscle in on the unemployed movement. . . .

The NUWA made a turn towards economic demands 'for immediate cash relief, for free electricity, gas and water and against evictions', and organizers followed a standard procedure for developing contacts. Going from door to door, they asked for time to explain the NUWA's purpose and left each household two cards. One contained basic information about the NUWA and an invitation to consult it when faced with difficult landlords and utility companies; the other was a questionnaire eliciting information about local conditions, which would then be used to produce leaflets targeted at rank-and-file concerns. Each card urged: 'ORGANIZE UNEMPLOYED COUNCILS. FIGHT, DON'T STARVE.' Although neighbourhood work did not transform the NUWA's fortunes overnight—the Windsor NUWA was disappointed at the poor response to its call to fight the gas company with a campaign of mass nonpayment—it drew in new members and broadened the base of the movement, not least by facilitating women's participation (Andrews, 1931).[9]

Recognizing past failures to address 'social problems, women's problems outside of [the] economic situation', the party affiliated its Women's Labour Leagues (WLL) to the NUWA and freed them to pursue women's concerns.[10] The party opposed contemporary pressure against women's waged employment and gave the dominant discourse of maternal feminism a militant twist by calling on housewives to *fight* in defence of their homes and families. 'Special' women's issues had considerable mobilizing impact. Demand for health care 'increased enormously' during the Depression, partly as a result of the party's propaganda and demonstrations. With occasional success, the NUWA and the WLLs opposed cuts in services and demanded increased and improved public provision, especially in the areas of antenatal care and contraception. Vancouver activists exposed how the city's private birth control clinics were beyond the means of the jobless and pressed the city council to open a free, public service. Yet, determined not to promote 'separatist' and 'reformist' tendencies, the party insisted that Canadian women would enjoy the sexual equality that applied in the Soviet Union only *after* the revolution.[11]

The difficulty some male comrades still found in perceiving the possibility of struggle outside the mainly masculine domains of the workplace and the street was reflected in the observation that, while the WLLs consisted 'in the main of housewives, they can *nevertheless* play a very important role in the everyday struggles of the workers' ('The Work of WLL', 15 July 1931; emphasis added).[12] Party attitudes towards women's role in class struggle were not static, however. One spokesman ambiguously captured the changing perception of women's role when he suggested that their bolshevism was reinforced by femininity. Women, he argued, were 'the most militant section of the workers', fully capable of achieving 'a high level of class consciousness'. They were the *best* bolsheviks because they were 'more subjugative to the tasks'—they followed orders—and were exemplary on the crucial matter of prompt dues payment (cited in *Unemployed Worker*, 4 February 1933). There was no hint of his equation of bolshevism and good housekeeping in the observations of a female Alberta comrade, who pointed out, simply, that no 'fight is a real fight if only half of those affected are in the front ranks'. Thankfully, she added, the 'old prejudices . . . about the woman staying at home and letting the man do the fighting for his wife and family are disappearing' (Thomas, 1933). The Vancouver *Unemployed Worker* offered a graphic representation of how class consciousness was not essentially masculine: a front cover depicted the interior of a dilapidated working-class household where a defeated male figure sits at the table, head in hands; it is his wife who points through the window at the advancing BC Hunger Marchers and announces: 'STARVE, BE DAMNED! WE'RE GOING TO FIGHT!' Ann Lenihan, a leader of the 1938 Calgary relief projects' workers' strike, was one of several party women who ensured that this was more than an idealized image (*Unemployed Worker*, 20 February 1932; Kealey and Whitaker, 1997).

Side by side with its grass-roots organizing, the party mounted a national campaign in 1931 around the Workers' Unity League (WUL) bill. In line with Comintern directives to unite employed and unemployed, the party in 1930 attached the NUWA to the WUL, its new centre of 'red' labour unions. The WUL bill was really a mass petition, calling for a range of state reforms, notably 'work or full maintenance' and 'state non-contributory unemployment insurance'. The party believed that when the state refused—as it surely would—to grant these reasonable demands, employed and unemployed alike would conclude that they had no option but to take the 'revolutionary way out of the crisis'. A signature drive exceeded all expectations. Between mid-January and mid-April, over 94,000 people signed the bill. Across Canada, 50,000 demonstrated on the Comintern's International Day of Struggle against unemployment in February, and on 15 April, when a WUL delegation delivered the bill to R.B. Bennett, the party claimed that 85,000 attended solidarity rallies. Local NUWA units were overwhelmed by membership applications. As many as 20,000 Canadians joined the NUWA between January and June. While most of them melted away as soon as the excitement died down, the party was thrilled by the experience of genuine mass work. Even the notoriously hard-to-please Comintern was impressed (*Party Organizer*, April 1931).[13]

A measure of the WUL's advance was the state's decision, immediately after the February demonstration, to prepare a pre-emptive strike against the party. The federal Department of Justice, the RCMP, and military intelligence routinely exchanged information on radical activities with provincial and local officials, and there was clear collaboration between the Tory administrations in Ottawa and Toronto in support of the latter's final onslaught against the leadership in August 1931. Constant police raids on party offices, vigorous breaking up of street meetings, and individual intimidation, especially of European immigrants, shattered the optimism engendered by the WUL bill. Few could have imagined that the purge would end with the arrest of Tim Buck and seven other members of the Political Bureau. As the party reconstructed its underground apparatus and tightened up internal discipline, the NUWA sought to open itself up by accelerating its shift towards grass-roots struggles and changing its sectarian stance towards political competitors (Adams, 1978; Bright, 1997).[14]

While repression may have temporarily quelled the Communist advance, it could not end the economic slump. State officials were dismayed that rising unemployment continued to generate fresh NUWA recruits. A military intelligence officer reported from Windsor that even after rumours had been planted that NUWA members were to be removed from the relief rolls, 'many English-speaking people' continued to join. This was a potentially alarming development, since it challenged the widespread view that party organizations attracted only ignorant foreigners who were easily controlled by the threat of deportation, the British being too phlegmatic and sensible to be attracted to revolutionary organizations (*Border Cities Star*, 21 January 1932). New 'united front from below' tactics made it easier for Anglo-Celts to enter the party's ideological orbit. Acknowledging that their own 'sectarian folly' had helped drive a majority of the organized unemployed into reformist groups, the leaders of the now underground party took the NUWA out of the WUL in March 1932, made it formally independent, and renamed it the National Council of Unemployed Councils (NCUC). They set cadres the task of convincing the unemployed that one did not have to be 'a "red" or a Marxist' to join the new organization's permanent 'block' and 'neighbourhood' councils, and freed them to work within reformist organizations in appropriate circumstances (*Workers' Unity*, 30 October 1931; Burns, 1932; *Unemployed Worker*, 14 May 1932). . . .

Activists constructed a culture of solidarity around the many issues arising out of the relief system. The Burnaby Unemployed Council's winter 1932–3 campaign against price increases, for example, incorporated political education, the assumption of representative functions by unemployed council leaders, and direct action. Organizers sought initially to focus unemployed anger on the nearest class enemy—the store-keeping 'gentry'—but then shifted their attention to the responsibility of the local state to sustain the decency of its citizens. After several delegations demanding emergency winter relief returned empty handed from visits to the municipal council, the unemployed council turned to direct action. Around 400 members surrounded three stores to await news of a last appeal. When the appeal was refused, organizers invited the demonstrators to take what they needed in a disciplined manner, announcing as they left that this procedure would be repeated if the need arose (*Unemployed Worker*, 15 October 1932, 21 January 1933).

Behind such actions lay the theory that each success would move the struggle towards the limits of what the state could concede, encourage the unemployed to view concessions as rights, and show them the value of mass pressure. To forestall the possibility that the rank and file might settle for concessions, the party incorporated political education in the life of the neighbourhood councils and tried to recruit the best activists into the party. If few were ready for the personal demands of party membership, many were prepared to join such 'fronts' as the CLDL, Workers' Ex-Servicemen's League (WESL), and Friends of the Soviet Union (FSU).[15]

The significance of the overtly political aspects of the movement should not be exaggerated. One of the most attractive features of the unemployed 'family' was its social life, in which escapism played a prominent role. Every left organization offered diversion from the meanness of life on relief. Between 9 January and 4 February 1932, for example, anyone with the inclination and stamina could have attended seven social functions (dances, concerts, banquets, and get-togethers) organized by five different party organizations. 'Next Friday at 8 p.m.,' the Waterfront Neighbourhood Council announced, 'we will hold a social and dance and there will be some pep to it. This is the real stuff and the admission is free.' House parties, childrens' outings, film shows, drama groups, and team sports were regularly on offer. Most of those originally attracted by a cheap night out probably developed no additional commitments to the left, but the forging of a distinct oppositional culture contributed to the Vancouver left's unusually cosmopolitan vibrancy (*Unemployed Worker*, 13 June 1934; Liversedge, 1973: 33).

The unemployed movement helped the party scrape a foothold even in traditionally hostile centres like Hamilton and Montreal. In Montreal, Communists dominated the mainly anglophone Verdun Workingmen's Association and Rosemount Tenants' League (RTL), two groups well known for successfully resisting forced property sales and evictions![16] An eviction in 1933 precipitated the single event that thrust the CPC into the consciousness of working-class Montreal: the 'murder' of Nick Zynchuk. When the party discovered that Zynchuk's assailant, Constable Joseph Zappa, was a member of a fascist group, it tried to turn the case into a *cause célèbre*. The CLDL rushed out a pamphlet that made the case the centrepiece of an attack on the growing 'fascization' of the Canadian state; Montreal CLDL secretary Bella Gordon pilloried the findings of a coroner's inquest that not only exonerated the police but praised their forthright treatment of the 'foreigners'; the Progressive Arts' League based the agit-prop play *Eviction* on the case, performing it at unemployed conferences, and the WUL issued an appeal calling for the organization of a national unemployed movement strong enough to ensure that no 'cowardly police thugs' ever again 'drew a murderous gun against unarmed workers.' An estimated 10,000 Montrealers followed the cortege at Zynchuk's 'red funeral' (CLDL, 1933; *Nova Scotia Miner*, 1933; *The Worker*, 11 March, 17 June, 1 July 1933; *Toronto Daily Star*, 10 March 1933; Abella, 1977). . . .

Toronto's unemployed councils also found eviction struggles congenial. By 1935 they were involved in so many that CCF Mayor Jimmy Simpson accused them of concocting cases to discredit him (*The Worker*, 29 April 1933).[17] As in Montreal, they increased their participation in non-party groups, especially in the working-class suburbs. Ernest Laurie in Long Branch, Ewart Humphreys in York Township, and Jimmy Wilson in Scarborough all gained leading positions in their respective Workers' Associations despite unconcealed Communist views. Even where no particular leader stood out, the party seemed to be shaping the language of unemployed protest. In March 1933 a deputation of four North York unemployed organizations presented the township council with demands for a 10 per cent increase in the value of relief vouchers and the right for welfare recipients to redeem them in stores outside the municipality. To these they appended a manifesto that espoused the labour theory of value, drew attention to warehouses full 'of the necessities of life . . . while thousands [were] starving', and demanded that 'the needs of the unemployed be looked after before profits are paid'. 'Dividends must be cut,' it stated, 'taxes must be increased on the incomes of the rich, the stored-up food and clothing and the empty houses must be used to satisfy the needs of the million unemployed and their families' (*Toronto Daily Star*, 7 March 1933).

Credit accumulated in neighbourhood work helped the Toronto Central Unemployed Council reclaim the public space the party had lost in 1929–30. Between June and August 1933 a 'Free Speech Fight' revealed a significant shift in opinion. In 1929 Police Chief Dennis Draper's red-baiting inspired little working-class protest; in 1933 large numbers of workers were willing to turn out to defend the party's freedom of speech. Battles raged at most of the seven venues in the unemployed council's open-air circuit, climaxing in a showdown at Allen Gardens on the evening of 15 August. A crowd of over 2,000 turned out for a meeting co-hosted by the unemployed councils and the WESL. When foot police failed to stop the crowd gathering around the speakers, motorcycle officers used a dispersal tactic that had been successful on at least one earlier occasion. Encircling the crowd, they faced their machines outwards and inwardly projected a fog of exhaust. The Allen Gardens crowd, including many veterans (one of whom wrote to the *Star* comparing the assault to German poison-gas attacks in the Great War), knew what to expect. Demonstrators made a stand and battled the police for two hours. Two nights later, 5,000 Torontonians listened in Earlscourt Park as speakers 'shot defiance' at the watching police and cited their non-intervention as a victory for mass action and a sign that Draper's rule was on borrowed time. A few weeks later the Police Commission ordered him to restrain his men from interfering with meetings unless the law had actually been broken (Houston, 1933a, 1933b; *Saturday Night*, 1933; Smith, 1933; *Toronto Daily Star*, 16, 22 August 1933; Betcherman, 1982).

The Toronto Free Speech Fight was part of an explicit attempt to keep politics in the movement's foreground, a purpose also served by national and provincial unemployment conferences and hunger marches. The Workers' Economic Conference (WEC) in Ottawa in August 1932 offered a proletarian counterpoint to the Imperial Economic Conference on Parliament Hill. The chance to play up the symbolic contrast between 'pot-bellied . . . empire economic big shots' and the 'lean and hungry lot' in an abandoned garage they had scrubbed down and whitewashed themselves was too good to miss. Delegates contrasted their class demands with the bourgeois selfishness of the imperial motherland and the white dominions. As the official conference sought to shore up the British imperialist bloc, the anti-imperialist and internationalist WEC called for Canada to fund unemployment insurance—and promote the USSR's 'peace plan'—by cutting the defence budget. . . .

These events invariably provoked coercion. R.B. Bennett ordered continuous armoured car patrols of Parliament Hill during the March 1932 National Unemployment Conference, and, to prevent embarrassment at the Imperial Economic Conference, he had the RCMP conduct a stop-and-search operation to eject possible WEC delegates from Ottawa-bound freight trains. When WEC delegates defied a ban on an open-air rally, they were baton-charged. A delegation from the Provincial Unemployment Conference was so intimidated by the armed police presence in and around the Nova Scotia legislature that it slipped quietly into the building, deposited its demands, and left unnoticed.[18] The Communist Party believed that coercive displays were advertisements for communism. . . .

As displays of armed force struck influential non-party observers as illiberal, immoderate, and un-Canadian, the state gradually reduced the level of anti-Communist coercion (although the On-to-Ottawa Trek showed that it was being held in reserve). The 1933 National Hunger March to Ottawa passed off uneventfully, with only one of many supporting local solidarity marches, at Nelson, British Columbia, producing a significant clash between the police and the jobless (*Globe*, 17, 18 January 1933; *Ottawa Evening Journal*, 17, 18 January 1933; *Toronto Daily Star*, 17, 18 January 1933; *Winnipeg Free Press*, 17, 18 January 1933). . . .

A major weakness of the unemployed effort was that—like the party itself—it mainly attracted the foreign born. Many Anglo-Celtic workers gravitated towards non-Communist groups because the Communist-led movement was identifiably 'foreign' and 'dangerous'. Only weeks after a group of 27 Yugoslavs and Ukrainians formed a NUWA branch in Cranbrook, British Columbia, immigration officials removed several of them for summary deportation. Hungarian activist John Farkas made a militant speech to the Oshawa Unemployed Workers' Association in 1932 and was promptly arrested, convicted of contravening section 98 of the Criminal Code, and deported. A minimum of 'several hundred' immigrants were deported for political radicalism in the 1930s, including, in one sixteen-month period in 1932–3, an estimated 100 party members. Many others were ostensibly deported as public charges, but were in reality victims of political repression.[19] Immigrant workers who risked the double jeopardy of vagrancy and activism displayed a profound degree of political courage. Their commitment may well have stemmed from the CPC's staunch anti-nativism. Although the party was keen for its members to become naturalized citizens, it consistently challenged notions of 'racial' hierarchy. Unemployed demonstrations invariably celebrated proletarian internationalism and sometimes achieved symbolic unity between European immigrants and those of British stock. Ethnic representatives would take turns to insist that 'the status of a hungry, homeless "British" worker in no way differs from that of the foreign born worker . . . [all were] victims of the same system in every country of the world . . . [except] the Soviet Union.' Ethnic rivalries by no means dissolved, but Anglo-Celts *were* joining the party through the unemployed movement; between 1929 and 1934 the 'British' minority rose from around 5 per cent to around 25 per cent.[20]

Middle-class organizations such as the Kiwanis, YMCA, YWCA, Women's Institutes, Imperial Order Daughters of the Empire, Junior Leagues, and the Rotarians joined with business and the churches to ensure that the CPC did not enjoy unopposed access to the 'native' unemployed. Using sporting activities, training schemes, and make-work projects, they sought to 'bring the more and the less fortunate members of the community . . . into active and sympathetic contact' and to detach the jobless from those who were 'intent on "sowing the seeds of discontent"'.[21]. . .

The unemployed movement was too fluid for any single organization to exercise absolute control. Every radical tendency was represented, as were the Liberal and Conservative parties and individuals of no fixed political abode. The executive of the Earlscourt Unemployment Council was a coalition of representatives from the ILP, labour unions, ratepayers' and property owners' groups, the Canadian Legion, the British Imperial Association, and the Orange Order.[22]. . . The classic example of an individual who built a career in the working-class movement through the unemployed struggle was Arthur Williams, who emerged from nowhere to dominate the East York Workers' Association (EYWA), before going on to become township reeve, a leading official in the Canadian Congress of Labour, and a CCF member of parliament (Schulz, 1975: 19–20, 33–41).

. . . Communists could not take the loyalty of the unemployed for granted. The British Columbia party mistakenly assumed that the unemployed councils would readily consent to becoming the basis of the 1933 provincial election campaign of its alter ego, the BC Workers' and Farmers' United Front. When it proceeded to suspend normal unemployed activities, many rank-and-file unemployed council members made it clear that they resented this attempt to exploit the movement for partisan ends. The Burnaby council—which, ironically, had been formed by ILP members before entering the NUWA in 1931—dissolved itself rather than become a 'political' organization. When members reformed it as the Burnaby Workers'

Association, the party no longer enjoyed sole leadership. Paradoxically, some of the unemployed chose to join new unemployed bodies being created by the CCF and the recently reformed Socialist Party of Canada (SPC) (Purvis, 1933; *Unemployed Worker*, 27 December 1933, 13 June 1934).

During 1933–4, changes in the international situation enhanced the party's willingness to look outwards and make conciliatory gestures towards former rivals on the left. Sanctioned by cautious Comintern signals, party leaders felt it was worth running the risk of political dilution to obtain a mass audience (James, 1933; Sims, 1933). United front work developed more rapidly in the unemployed movement than in any other area (much more so than in the labour unions). As early as March 1933 Ewart Humphreys, president of the Mount Dennis branch of the York Township United Workers' Association, drew delegates from 30 organizations, 19 of them non-party, to a United Workers' Conference, to share experiences, pool knowledge, and build a unified township body. Toronto Trotskyists approved of this 'more . . . correct Leninist approach'. There were similar attempts in the Kitchener-Waterloo-Galt-Preston area, Toronto's Lakeshore suburbs, the Niagara Peninsula, and in other provinces. Despite the hostility of CCF national and provincial leaders, a significant degree of unity developed between CPC and CCF rank and filers.[23]

This affinity helped prepare the unemployed for the fresh upsurge in their struggle provoked by the new relief measures Bennett introduced following the August 1934 Dominion-Provincial Conference. Against the background of an eighteen-month-old economic upturn, Bennett found it hard to believe that unemployment stemmed from anything other than fecklessness. He announced that a Public Works Construction Act would be combined with a 22 per cent reduction in federal contributions to the provinces' direct relief funds. Provinces and municipalities, he insisted, should toughen up their relief regimes: too many recipients were squandering an overgenerous dole on 'movies, candy and beer' (*New York Times*, 1 August 1934; *Toronto Daily Star*, 23 August 1934; Struthers, 1983: 116–18). As cuts trickled down to the municipalities, however, they precipitated a new wave of militancy. This was particularly intense in Ontario, where cuts amounted to 37 per cent of direct relief funds, and where Mitchell Hepburn set aside his sympathy for the unemployed, announced plans to 'clean out the fakirs' from the relief rolls, and handed welfare minister David Croll the dubious privilege of launching an austerity drive, to begin in February 1935.

Unemployed groups, fearing a new wave of evictions and humiliated by the welfare department's demand that new relief applicants undergo investigations of their probity, morality, and personal hygiene, made clear, almost in trade union fashion, that they resented being tagged 'fakirs' and 'shirkers' and would oppose any cuts in relief standards. The next two years produced mass resistance, expressed in protest meetings, rallies, occupations, anti-eviction confrontations (an eviction had only to be rumoured for flyers to appear on telegraph polls giving the time and place at which volunteers should gather to keep out the bailiffs), and relief work strikes. When the introduction of direct cash relief in September 1935 was accompanied by a new cut in the value of relief and an increase in the amount of task work needed to obtain it, unemployed leaders countered the implication that they were choosing to stay on the dole and pointed out that, by increasing task-work requirements, the state was actually hampering their chances of finding real employment. An expanded conception of legitimate protest was soon manifested in highly visible ways. Relief recipients locked the mayor of Pembroke in his office until, seven hours later, he withdrew a cut [in relief]. . . .

Female militancy was a much-noted feature in this phase of the struggle. The party pulled non-Communist women radicals to the left, into support of the desperate plight of single unemployed women (Laing, 1935; *Toronto Daily Star*, 15 March 1935; Sangster, 1989). When the Ontario Educational Association stated that working-class mothers needed to be taught the proper nutritional needs of their children, the party cited 12 Long Branch mothers who had besieged the township welfare board, demanding the issue of emergency food rations for their children. These women were 'showing that they need no "educating". They know what their kiddies need and are determined to get it for them.' In a brief report on an unemployed demonstration in Niagara Falls, the *Toronto Star* twice mentioned that the 'angry mob' that 'stormed the relief office' was made up of men and women. Mothers were developing a sense of entitlement for themselves and their children. Those in the EYWA threatened to picket the homes of township council members if they were not provided with children's clothes for the new school year. They then rejected the clothing they were offered a few days later, declaring that *their* children would not be wearing 'easily distinguishable' sweaters—they were printed with Disney characters—visible 'a block away'.[24]

This action suggests the complex character of the class-consciousness generated by unemployed activism: the mothers' resistance to the labelling of their children suggested both assertiveness and a residual sense of shame at their reliance on the state. As the hanging in effigy of David Croll indicated, militancy did not necessarily lead to socialist conclusions. The unemployed often personalized their anger, directing it at 'unfair' housing administrators, relief officers, policemen, and local councillors rather than at the abstraction of an unfair system; demonizing an individual seemed more natural than sustaining a class analysis of the system he or she serviced. Their challenge to authority was invariably accompanied by a willingness to settle for a mixture of paternalism, accountability, and respect. . . .

Between 1935 and 1939 Popular Front imperatives forced the indefinite postponement of socialist revolution and made the party's main objective the construction of cross-class alliances to defend bourgeois democracy. To this end it either dissolved or transformed its front groups into broad mass bodies 'congenial to . . . the petty bourgeoisie, the office employees, and the progressive intelligentsia' and eased itself away from struggles in which its leading role was too exposed or which threatened to frighten away potential allies. It quickly abandoned any attempt to build a national unemployed movement, initially opposing the 1935 On-to-Ottawa Trek on the grounds that 'the fight against the Bennett government must be fought out in each locality.'[25] Although Buck complained to the party's Central Committee in late 1936 that in many key centres the party's unemployed work had 'diminished rather than otherwise,' despite sweeping cuts in relief appropriations, this decline did not presage a revival of the movement (Buck, 1936: 62). Unemployment all but disappeared from the agendas of major national and provincial conventions.

During 1936 and 1937, Communist energies were largely consumed by the Aid to Spain movement (and other anti-fascist campaigns) and by the struggles in mass-production industry precipitated by the dramatic rise of the Committee for Industrial Organization. With unemployment continuing to fall, the party tried—without success—to offload responsibility for the unemployed to the Trades and Labour Congress (TLC) of Canada. Unemployment rose sharply again during the 'Roosevelt recession' that started in the fall of 1937, but the

party no longer saw the unemployed movement as a priority. Though Communists remained in the forefront of important local struggles, such as the dramatic month-long occupations of Vancouver's Art Gallery and post office by the British Columbia Relief Project Workers' Union (RPWU) in the summer of 1938 and the relief strikes that swept metropolitan Toronto in 1939, their leaders were increasingly eager to keep the level of militancy under control. RPWU organizers warned the Vancouver sit-downers against provoking confrontation and to 'refrain from any action which might alienate public sympathy'. In Toronto the party lost support among the single unemployed by 'agitating [them] . . . to the point where they were ready to take militant action and then restraining them from doing so.'[26] Now unashamedly reformist, the party channelled mass protest into representative lobbies (invariably including at least one clergyman) of provincial governments, electoralism, and faith in the state: the way to defeat unemployment was to elect a progressive federal government with the will to finance a massive recovery program of slum clearance and the construction of the St Lawrence Seaway.[27] . . .

The CPC clearly failed to induce insurrection or unify employed and unemployed workers partly because unemployed work always ranked lower than workplace activity. Even during the exceptional period of the WUL bill, Tom Ewan complained that 'we have been so active among the unemployed that we have entirely lost sight of everything else.'[28] If the jobless often sustained the party's contention that they would not 'scab', the employed avoided thinking about unemployment until it became a reality—which, for most, it is worth remembering, it never did. Not only did workers remain hesitant about taking action even in defence of their interests *as* workers but the party tended to provide them with moral exhortation rather than practical advice on *how* to support the unemployed. The extent to which unemployed activism built new solidarities that would later find expression in industrial unionism has still to be seriously examined, but considerable cross-fertilization between the two wings of the workers' movement certainly occurred, and some rank and file workers first perceived the virtues of collective organization as unemployed activists (Cochrane, 1933).

Although local contexts need to be examined to determine whether a specifically Communist presence brought *additional* material benefits to the unemployed, the party's constant agitation on the systemic nature of the crisis and the right of the working class to make demands on the state stimulated popular expectations and greater boldness in expressing them, and almost certainly sustained levels of relief expenditure that would otherwise have been cut. . . .

Ultimately, it is probably impossible to quantify the movement's value. Some of the men and women who chose to fight rather than starve knew they were also fighting the humiliation of being perceived, labelled, and treated as social failures. Collective action broke down personal isolation and gave combatants the dignity and self-worth needed to survive the Depression with their individual personalities intact. Winnipeg unemployed activist Mitch Sago eloquently expressed the psychological and spiritual value of participation in the unemployed struggle. When 'all you could see was a sort of dead end towards any changes year after year,' he observed, 'the organization of the unemployed created a feeling of optimism, it provided certain goals that projected beyond the immediate question of what do we eat today, what do we eat tomorrow' (cited in Abella and Millar, 1978: 284). Brutalized conditions, in other words, did not need to produce brutes—or victims. How many of the tens of thousands of Canadians who passed through the movement discovered and acted on similar feelings is worthy of further investigation.

Notes

1. See National Archives of Canada (NA), Michael Fenwick Papers, interview with Michael Fenwick; University of British Columbia, Special Collections, interview with Alex Fergusson; Harry A. Cassidy, *Unemployment and Relief in Ontario, 1919–1932* (Toronto and Vancouver: J.M. Dent, 1932); James Struthers, *No Fault of Their Own: Unemployment and the Canadian Welfare State, 1914–1941* (Toronto: University of Toronto Press, 1983).

2. For two excellent local studies of urban unemployed protest, see Patricia V. Schulz, *The East York Workers' Association: A Response to the Great Depression* (Toronto: New Hogtown Press, 1975); and Carmela Patrias, *Relief Strike: Immigrant Workers and the Great Depression in Crowland, Ontario, 1930–1935* (Toronto: New Hogtown Press, 1990).

3. Norman Penner, *Canadian Communism: The Stalin Years and Beyond* (Toronto: Methuen, 1988), 89–94; See also Ontario Archives (OA), Communist Party of Canada (CPC) Papers, 8C 0588-66, Tim Buck's reply to discussion, CPC Central Executive Committee (CEC) Plenum, Feb. 1931.

4. See CPC Papers, 8C 0497, Tom Ewan, comments at CEC Plenum.

5. See Vancouver City Archives, Police Commission Files, vol. 15, Chief Constable V.A. Bingham, Report re 'Unemployed Situation and Agitation 1930–1931', 21 Jan. 1931; Harry McShane and Joan Smith, *Harry McShane: No Mean Fighter* (London: Pluto, 1978), 142, 146; Stuart Macintyre, *Little Moscows: Communism and Working Class Militancy in Inter-War Britain* (London: Croom Helm, 1980), 95–9.

6. D. Chalmers, Dave Weiss, and J. Carey, articles in *The Worker*, 6 Dec. 1930, 17, 24, Jan. 1931.

7. Malcolm Bruce, '"Tailism" in the Work among Unemployed', *The Worker*, 18 Oct. 1930; CPC Papers, 1A 0709, Malcolm Bruce to Tim Buck, 3 Dec. 1930; 10C 1850 ff, 'The Resolution of the Anglo-American Section of the Profintern on the Situation and Tasks of the Workers' Unity League of Canada', 28 Nov. 1930; NA, Comintern Fonds (CF), reel 11, file 98, unsigned [probably Stewart Smith] to Tom [Ewan], 24 Dec. 1930. By 'Tailism,' Lenin referred to his Menshevik rivals' habitual tendency to 'tail' behind

the working class's 'trade union' consciousness. See, for example, *What Is to Be Done?* [1902], and *One Step Forward, Two Steps Back* [1904]. In effect, Bruce was charging the central Canadians with a failure of leadership, even political cowardice.

8. NA, J.S. Woodsworth Papers, vol. 6, file 8, A.E. Smith to J.S. Woodworth, 22, 25 April 1930.

9. George Andrews, 'How to Organize Local Councils of the NUWA,' *Party Organizer*, June 1931; See also CPC Papers, 2A 1200, Arthur Seal to Tom Ewan, 6 June 1931; 2A 1201, March 1931; 2A 1119, George Andrews to Sam Carr, 16 March 1931; Stevens, 'Radical Political Movements,' 87–8.

10. 'The Work of WLL,' *Workers' Unity*, 15 July 1931; CPC Papers, 4A 2446, Catherine Lesire to Julia Collins, 20 May 1931; Sangster, *Dreams of Equality*, 71–4.

11. See Leonard Marsh, *Health and Unemployment* (Toronto: Oxford University Press for McGill University, 1938), 92, 132–3, 177; Vancouver *Unemployed Worker*, 6 June, 28 Nov., 5 Dec. 1931, 20 Feb., 3 Sept., 27 Nov., 3 Dec. 1932; Gillian Cresse, 'The Politics of Dependence: Women, Work, and Unemployment in the Vancouver Labour Movement before World War II', in Gregory S. Kealey, ed., *Class, Gender, and Region: Essays in Canadian Historical Sociology* (St John's: Canadian Committee on Labour History, 1988), 134–8; 'Winnipeg Police Use Gas to Quell Riot', *Winnipeg Free Press*, 21 July 1933; 'Four Doctors Are Now Ministering to City's Jobless', *Winnipeg Free Press*, 7 Sept. 1933; *Canadian Medical Association Journal 29* (Nov. 1933), 553–3; Anna Bell, articles on birth control and abortion in *Daily Clarion* (DC), 18, 20 Nov. 1936; 'Russian Mothers, Canadian Mothers,' *Workers' Unity*, 6 Aug. 1931.

12. 'The Work of WLL' (emphasis added); University of Toronto, Fisher Library, Robert S. Kenny Collection, box 2, folder 6, 'Resolution on Women,' and A.M. Cooke, 'Resolution of Work among Women', CPC Eighth National Convention, Oct. 1937; Kenny Pamphlet Collection, Communist Party of Canada, *Resolution of Enlarged Plenum*, Feb. 1931, 54–9; National Committee of Unemployed Councils, *Building a Mass Unemployed Movement* (Toronto, undated [1933]), 21–7.

13. See also CPC Papers, 3A 1842, Charlie Marriott to Sam Carr, 20 April 1931; RILU Letter, 8 May 1931, in *Agents of Revolution: A History of the Workers' Unity League, Setting Forth Its Origin and Aims* (Toronto: Attorney General's Office, no date [Feb. 1934]), 6; Carl Cuneo, 'State Mediation of Class Contradictions in Canadian Unemployment Insurance, 1930–1935', *Studies in Political Economy 3* (Spring 1980): 37–65.

14. See also Robert Kenny Papers, box 26, folder 1, Hugh Guthrie to W.H. Price, 18 March 1931; CPC Papers, 4A 2505, Malcolm Bruce to Tom Ewan, 13 July 1931; 3A 2303-4, Ewan to Bruce, 29 July 1941; Jack Kruger, . . . *Canadian Labour Defender*, March 1931.

15. Report of W. Alexander's talk to a meeting of Kingsway Block Council no. 3, in *Labor Defender*, May 1934. On the CLDL in British Columbia, see *Canadian Labor Defender*, May 1934, March 1935; UBC, Special Collections, interview with Alex Fergusson; Kenny Collection, box 39, folder 4. CLDL, *Report of the Annual District Convention*, Vancouver, 25–6 Aug. 1935. Copious information on the WESL and FSU is available in Gregory S. Kealey and Reg Whitaker, eds, *R.C.M.P Security Bulletins: The Depression Years, Part I: 1933–4, Part 2: 1935, Part 3: 1936* (St John's: Canadian Committee on Labour History, 1993, 1995, 1996).

16. See Comrade Morgan, Report to Anglo-American Secretariat, 2 July 1932; Andrée Lévesque, *Virage à Gauche Interdit: Les Communistes, les Socialistes et Leurs Ennemis au Québec, 1929–1939* (Montreal: Boréal Express, 1984), chaps. 1–2; 'Rosemount Tenants League Scores Another Victory', *The Worker*, 13 May 1933: 'Militant Montreal Jobless Put a Bailiff to Flight', *The Worker*, 1 July 1933; 'Tenants League Stands By', *The Worker*, 29 April 1933; *Unemployed Worker*, 21 Feb. 1934.

17. 'Eight Days of Picketing Makes Welfare Department Act', *The Worker*, 29 April 1933; NA, CF, reel 18, file 152, 'Estimation of Work in District #3 [S. Ontario] on the basis of the Plan of Work adapted at the end of January', 20 June 1933; 'Radicals Warned by Mayor: Eviction Riots Must Cease', *Toronto Daily Star*, 7 March 1935.

18. See *Ottawa Evening Journal*, 2, 4 March 1932; *New York Times*, 24, 30 July 1932; *Workers' Unity*, Aug.–Sept. 1932; Borsook, 'The Workers Hold a Conference'; *Toronto Daily Star*, 18 Jan. 1933.

19. CPC, 4A 2470, 4A 2529, Alex Meronyk to Tom Ewan, undated [c. June 1931] and 16 July 1931; NA, CF, reel 2, file 206, John Navis, Report on Canada to Anglo-American Secretariat of the Comintern, 4 May 1933; Barbara Roberts, *From Whence They Came: Deportation from Canada, 1900–1935* (Ottawa: University of Ottawa Press, 1988), chaps. 7, 8.

20. DND, Directorate of History, file 161.009, Windsor City Police, Reports re: 'Communist Meetings in Lanspear Park', 1 May, 13 Aug. 1932; Robert Kenny Papers, box 1, Comintern Executive Committee, closed letter to the Central Committee, CPC, 8 April 1929; NA, CF, reel 19, file 152, 'Estimation of York in District #3', 20 June 1933; reel 9, file 163,

Report from District #6 [Lakehead], CPC, 21 March 1934; 'Materials on Alliance Recruiting Campaign,' *Communist Review*, Sept. 1934.

21. 'Report of the Department of Labour for 1931', *Ontario Sessional Papers 10* (1932): 34-5; 'A Canadian Plan for Employment', *The Times* (London), 3 Nov. 1932; 'Edmonton Employment Service Plan Successful', *Industrial Canada* 34 (Aug. 1933): 42; 'Mayor Stewart Says Relief Not Perpetual', *Toronto Daily Star*, 10 Feb. 1933; 'Winnipeg Service Bureau . . . Closes . . . This Week', *Winnipeg Evening Tribune*, 30 June 1934; David Croll, speech reported in *Toronto Daily Star*, 5 April 1935.

22. OA, H.G. Ferguson Papers, box 131, A.M. Barnetson to E.G. Ferguson, 14 Aug. 1930.

23. OA, George Henry Papers, box 168, 'Report of Motions Passed at York Township Workers' Conference', undated [11 March 1933]; 'Notes from the Townships', *October Youth*, April 1933; 'Holds Workers' Body Is a Rudderless Ship', *Toronto Daily Star*, 3 March 1933; 'Ask Food Allowances Keep Up with Prices', *Toronto Daily Star*, 9 Feb. 1934; 'Plan for United Activities', *The Worker*, 15 April 1933; John Weir, 'After Calgary Strike', *The Worker*, 19 Aug. 1933; NAC, Sound Archive, interview with Pat Lenihan; University of Toronto, J.S. Woodsworth

Papers, box 1, J. Houston to All Trade Unions, Mass Organizations, CCF Clubs, and All Meetings of Workers, 11 Aug. 1933; CCF Ontario Provincial Council, Minutes, 26 Jan., 19 April, 4 May 1935; 'Evictions,' *New Commonwealth*, 4 Aug. 1934.

24. Anne Smith, 'With Our Women', *Daily Clarion*, 1 May 1936; 'Niagara Falls Mob Threatens Relief Head', *Toronto Daily Star*, 27 April 1935; 'Women Plan to Protest "Brutal Axe of Economy"', *Toronto Daily Star*, 27 Aug. 1935; '"Mickey Mouse" Sweaters Evoke Workers' Protests', *Toronto Daily Star*, 12 Sept. 1935; '"Keep Vigil Till Tots Fed" Say Women after 40 Hours', *Toronto Daily Star*, 18 April 1936.

25. NA, J.L. Cohen Papers, vol. 3, file 2342, CLM, National Convention, 19–20 Oct. 1935, *Main Resolution*, 4–5; 1, 4, 6 June 1935.

26. NA, Communist Party of Canada Papers, Box 2, folder 2–8, 'Labor College: A Short Course on Trade Unionism', undated [c. Jan. 1936], 28–34; Brodie, *Bloody Sunday*, 12; Kealey and Whitaker, eds, RCMP *Security Bulletins, 1938–1939*, 177, 278, 369; Struthers, *No Fault of Their Own*, 192–4.

27. Kenny Collection, box 2, folder 5, CPC, *We Propose. . .Resolutions of the Eighth Dominion Convention*, Toronto, 8–21 Oct. 1937.

28. CPC Papers, Ewan to Drayton, 18 April 1931.

References

Abella, Irving, ed. 1977. 'Portrait of a Jewish Professional Revolutionary: The Recollections of Joshua Gershman', *Labour/Le Travailleur* 2.

Abella, Irving, and David Millar, eds. 1978. *The Canadian Worker in the Twentieth Century*. Toronto: University of Oxford Press.

Adams, Ronald A. 1978. 'The Anti-Communist Role of the RCMP in the Depression'. Paper presented to the Canadian Historical Association, London, ON, June.

Andrews, George. 1931. 'How to Organize Local Councils of the NUWA', *Party Organizer*, June.

Betcherman, Lita-Rose. 1982. *The Little Band: The Clashes between the Communists and the Political and Legal Establishments in Canada, 1928–1932*. Ottawa: Deneau.

Border Cities Star. 1932. 21 January.

Bright, David. 1997. '"The Lid Is Tight Now": Relations between the State, the Unemployed and the Communist Party in Calgary, 1930–1935', *Canadian Historical Review* 78 (December): 537–65.

Buck, Tim. 1936. *What We Propose*. Communist Party of Canada.

CLDL. 1933. *Workers' Solidarity against Fascism: Stop Hitler's Horrors*. Toronto: n.p.

Cochrane, James. 1933. 'Winning Our Way to the Factories', *Worker's Unity*, May.

Communist International. 1930. 6 (1 and 15 March).

Frank, David, and Donald MacGillivray, eds. 1987. *George MacEachern: An Autobiography*. Sydney, NS: University College of Cape Breton Press.

Globe. 1933. 17 January.

Globe. 1933. 18 January.

Houston, James. 1933. 'Letter to the Editor', *Toronto Daily Star*, 1 August.

————. 1933. 'Tasks of the Unemployed Councils', *The Worker*, 10 June.

James, M. 1933. 'The East End Section and the Unemployed', *The Builder*, March.

Kealey, Gregory, and Reg Whitaker, eds, 1997. RCMP *Security Bulletins: The Depression Years*, Part 5: 1938–9. St John's: Canadian Committee on Labour History.

Laing, Jean. 1935. 'Authorities Turn Deaf Ear to Single Women's Needs', *The Worker*, 19 December.

Liversedge, Ronald. 1973. *Recollections of the On-to-Ottawa Trek*, Victor Hoar, ed. Toronto: McClelland and Stewart.

Lozovsky, A. 1931. 'The United Front of Employed and Unemployed', *Communist International* 8 (1 March): 122–5.

Morris, Leslie. 1930. 'The Unemployment Crisis and Our Party', *The Worker* (19 April).

New York Times. 1934. 'Canadian Provinces to Shoulder Relief', 1 August.

Nova Scotia Miner. 1933. 'A Resolution on Murder of Zynchuk', 8 April.

Ottawa Evening Journal. 1933. 17 January.

Ottawa Evening Journal. 1933. 18 January.

Party Organizer. 1931. 'For a Bolshevik Organization', April.

Penner, Norman. 1988. *Canadian Communism: The Stalin Years and Beyond*. Toronto: Methuen.

Purvis, Bill. 1933. 'Recent Experiences of the Coast Unemployed Movement', *The Worker*, 2 September.

Sangster, Joan. 1989. *Dreams of Equality: Women on the Canadian Left, 1920–1950*. Toronto: McClelland and Stewart.

Saturday Night. 1933. 'We Are Sorry for the Police', 12 August.

Schulz, Patricia. 1975. *The East York Workers' Association*. Toronto: East York Historical Association.

Sims, Charles. 1933. 'A Few Lessons to be Drawn from the Relief Strikes', 1 July.

Smith, William. 1933. 'Letter to the Editor', 22 August.

Struthers, James. 1983. *No Fault of Their Own: Unemployment and the Canadian Welfare State, 1914–1941*. Toronto: University of Toronto Press.

The Worker. 1933. 'Eight Days of Picketing Makes Welfare Department Act', 29 April.

The Worker. 1933. 11 March.

The Worker. 1933. 17 June.

The Worker. 1933. 1 July.

Thomas, Ellen. 1933. 'Women at War in the Forefront of the Fight for Existence', *Canadian Miner*, 24 February.

Toronto Daily Star. 1933. 17 January.

Toronto Daily Star. 1933. 18 January.

Toronto Daily Star. 1933. 'Demand Increased Relief in Extremist Manifesto', 7 March.

Toronto Daily Star. 1933. 10 March.

Toronto Daily Star. 1935. 'Unemployed Women Relate Pitiable Tales to Croll', 15 March.

Toronto Daily Star. 1933. 'Some Newspaper Opinions', 16 August.

Toronto Daily Star. 1933. 'Police Tactics Abet the Agitators', 22 August.

Toronto Daily Star. 1934. 23 August.

Unemployed Worker. 1932. 20 February.

Unemployed Worker. 1932. 15 October.

Unemployed Worker. 1933. 21 January.

Unemployed Worker. 1933. 'Unidentified speech to BC Provincial Unemployment Conference', 4 February.

Unemployed Worker. 1933. 'For a New Year of Decisive Struggles against Hunger', 27 December.

Unemployed Worker. 1934. 'Unemployed Organization Gains 200%', 13 June.

Unemployed Worker. 1934. 13 June.

Winnipeg Free Press. 1933. 17 January.

Winnipeg Free Press. 1933. 18 January.

CHAPTER 14

Working for Pay and Managing the Household Finances
Denyse Baillargeon

Housework, by which we mean the various tasks required to feed, clothe, and care for a family, undoubtedly represents the most substantial element of women's domestic labour. Unlike the kinds of care and worry associated with motherhood, for example, household tasks are indeed easier to conform to what we generally see as 'work', because the time they take to accomplish can be measured and because they lead to the production of specifics (meals, clothing) that are also quantifiable. . . .

Since the middle of the nineteenth century, this form of work has undergone numerous transformations, as much in the sort of tasks that had to be done as in the kinds of tools available to do them. Industrialization in fact permitted a growing number of urban housewives to buy certain manufactured articles instead of making them at home: bread and a few other basic commodities; soap, yard goods and, to a certain extent, clothing were among the products that would henceforth be purchased by the majority of these women, at least from time to time. Electricity and running water, which were generally available in working-class districts in the second decade of this century, were certainly the two innovations that had the greatest effect on how they did their work. Finally, from the beginning of the twentieth century, housework became the object of a series of pronouncements aimed at rationalizing its execution in conformance with the new scientific and hygienic standards that were beginning to appear. From the 1920s onward, it would also begin to be invested with an emotional charge that would make it into a 'labour of love'.

Despite all these transformations, it was still the fact that, for the women interviewed, the family represented more an area of production than of consumption, and that would be true until at least the 1940s. In fact, their insufficient incomes meant that the majority of them had no other choice than to produce the most goods and services possible while devoting what little money they had to those expenses that were essential and unavoidable. In this sense, what they produced represented a crucial contribution to the economy of the household, as this production met the needs that their cash income would never have stretched to satisfy. Moreover, it encompassed such a range of products that when the Depression arrived, it was difficult for them to add new tasks to those that they were already doing. Unlike middle-class women, who could substitute their own labour for the purchase of consumer goods during the Depression, the majority of the women in this sample had not as

yet attained mass consumption and thus could not return to practices that they had never abandoned. The Depression, however, did have the effect of expanding their workload while making it more difficult to carry out those tasks they were already doing or increasing the frequency with which they had to be done.

Women's Space and Workplace

The new gender division of roles brought about by industrialization went hand in hand with a spatial segregation for activities appropriate to each sex. Bit by bit, after the middle of the nineteenth century, the urban dwelling becomes the space specifically for domestic labour and the place where in the future only women work. The domestic workspace, however, reaches beyond the narrow confines of the home to extend to all those places where some part of housework is carried out (Chabaud-Rychter, et al., 1985: 23): shops, school, medical clinics, and the like. The conditions in which these housewives had to live and work therefore depended, in part at the very least, on the degree to which their housing provided healthy conveniences, on the general layout of these lodgings, and on the range of services available in the districts in which this housing was situated.

The Neighbourhood

During the l920s and 1930s, the women we interviewed lived in various working-class districts in southwest Montreal and the east end of the city, in Verdun, and in certain newer areas like Rosemont, Villeray, and the Plateau Mont-Royal. . . . The residential areas of Montreal's working-class districts, whether old or new, typically lacked green spaces and contained the highest concentration of population and the least adequate housing. These districts, built to accommodate a rapidly growing working-class population, featured streets lined with two- and three-storey attached houses that held from two to six flats. The oldest of these dated to about 1860—built close to the sidewalk and having neither front yard or balcony, they had interior staircases and sometimes portes-cochères that led to other housing situated at the back of the rear yard.[1] The exterior staircases, which along with rear laneways would become characteristic of the Montreal urban landscape, made their appearance around 1900. These lanes were particularly lively. They were at once playgrounds for the children and passageways for pedlars and for the coal and wood delivery men who could thus reach the rear sheds where the fuel was stored—and represented the quintessential area of urban socializing for the women and children of the working-class neighbourhoods.

While the urban working-class district at the beginning of the century was often polluted and over-populated, it was not transformed during the day into an exclusively female zone, in contrast to the modern suburb. Morning, noon, and night, it was criss-crossed by children on their way to school, by men and young people going to work, and by numerous delivery-men, itinerant salesmen, and pedlars offering their wares door-to-door or shouting them in the street. These neighbourhood bonds, which merged, as often as not, with those of kinship, also contributed to the intense life of the district and helped to keep its housewives from the isolation that was frequently deplored in the period after the war (Pelletier, 1987; Séguin, 1989).

Housing

The working-class districts in Montreal where the informants lived during the Depression had been built in the late nineteenth and early twentieth century, when building standards were not overly demanding. Each of these neighbourhoods,

of course, contained its better-off areas where the local elite lived, such as the streets surrounding Georges Étienne Cartier Park in Saint Henri or the eastern part of de Maisonneuve, also called Viauville, but by and large the amount of money these households had to spend on rent, between 12 and 18 dollars a month, kept them out of the better and larger flats.[2] In the majority of cases, these women had to be satisfied with a four- or five-room flat on the second or third floor, as the occupant-owners commonly kept the first floor, roomier and giving onto the yard, for themselves.

Whether this housing was old or new, the buildings generally filled the whole width of the lot and were attached on both sides. To allow each of the rooms a bit of light, most of these flats had a double room at the front although in some of the older ones the centre room had no window at all. In addition to the absence of natural light and ventilation, these long, narrow flats often had but one room that could offer a modicum of privacy. This was, however, kept for the children, who went to bed early, while their parents had to be satisfied with the room off the parlour, which was simply curtained off.

More often than not, the lack of adequate insulation meant that, especially in the third-floor flat directly under the roof, the tenants sweltered in summer and froze in winter and had to pay considerably more for their heat, which generally came from a stove in the kitchen at the far end of the flat.[3] In these conditions it was very difficult, if not impossible, to distribute heat evenly through the entire flat. For the women, these circumstances meant that they did their work in badly lit and poorly ventilated rooms, in uncomfortable temperatures—conditions strongly reminiscent of the factory floor.

All of the housing inhabited by the informants in the survey was connected to the municipal water mains and had electricity. The hot water heater was not, however, included in the rent and had to be bought or rented by the tenants. Still, the kitchen had to be large enough for one of these boilers and the flat had to be connected to the gas lines that fuelled them. In any event, because of their minimal incomes, most of the informants were not able to afford this luxury—in fact, only three of them had always owned a water heater and just seven more had rented one shortly before the Second World War. These boilers did not work automatically. They had to be lit each time before hot water was desired. Certain kinds were attached to the stove and only worked if the stove was lit, something that was hardly practical in summer. In order to save money or time, the hot water reservoir was often used only for the weekly baths and laundry, which meant that the housewives who had one still continued to heat water on top of the stove to do the dishes or other household tasks that required smaller amounts of water. 'The gas was expensive. You had to save on everything' (E19), said one informant. Another explained, 'It didn't work automatically like today—it was easier to put a kettle on to do the dishes. We heated the boiler more for the laundry or for a bath' (E15).

Though all of the flats had a flush toilet, in several cases this had been added after the house was built and installed in one of the rooms where it was walled off by a flimsy wooden partition.[4] Only 14 of the informants had always lived in accommodations that boasted a bathtub, while seven more had to wait until after the war to achieve a flat with this convenience. Unless she had a hot water boiler already, the housewife had somehow to heat the water the family needed to wash themselves. The absence of a bathtub, as well as the fact that there was almost never a sink in the lavatory, meant that housewives had to rely solely on the kitchen sink, at which the family got washed, meals were prepared, and dishes and laundry done. This sole source of running water was in

heavy demand on washdays and complicated women's work. In certain flats, the kitchen sink was so tiny that they had to wash the dishes on the kitchen table in a basin while others possessed large washtubs that were more useful but that took up a lot of space in the small rooms. The absence of counters and storage space did not make the women's work easier, either. In short, these facilities were far from the functional kitchens recommended by the 'experts' and from which better-off housewives were beginning to benefit (Strong-Boag, 1986). . . .

Lack of money also meant that families often had to sacrifice the parlour to make an extra bedroom. Having neither room nor money, 12 of the women in the sample thus waited several years before acquiring the furniture for this room. Whether they bought it when they were first married or some years later, most of them preferred to get a more versatile sofa bed than a chesterfield. The parlour, even if it was furnished, was thus often transformed into a bedroom by night and was not reserved for a single function, which was a sign of a greater degree of financial comfort. Nevertheless, the youngest child often slept in the parents' room until quite an advanced age, while the children's rooms, and even their beds, were always shared. Some members of the family might have to sleep in the kitchen or the hallway on a folding bed. This crowding and the use of extra beds (folding beds, sofa beds) that had to be put up and taken down daily and the several kinds of activities that took place in each room increased and complicated the work of the housewife who was anxious to have a tidy house.[5] Keeping order was not made easier when the number of persons per room exceeded a critical number, since space to store things was especially lacking. Hooks put up behind the bedroom doors and in the hallway near the entrance did their best to make up for an absence of wardrobes. Large appliances like wringer washers and sewing machines were squeezed in with some difficulty, generally winding up in the kitchen. The space available in some flats was so tight that the idea of buying such equipment could hardly be entertained. The shed, situated behind the building, where coal and wood was stored and an outside cupboard installed along the partition that separated the rear balconies of the attached houses added to the storage space. Among other uses, perishable food could be stored in this cupboard during cold weather.

The costs of moving to new accommodations could severely strain an already tight budget. A popular saying of the time, indeed, asserted that 'three moves equals one fire.'[6] Nevertheless, at least half of the women in the sample moved at least every year or two from the time they were married until the end of their thirties. There are a number of explanations for these frequent moves. Commonly, when a young couple first set up housekeeping on their own, they often picked a two- or three-room flat, which was initially cheaper but which would prove too small after the birth of the second or third child—after a few years, they would have to find something larger. The poor quality of the flats—inadequate insulation, presence of vermin, absence of certain amenities, too-small rooms—would encourage regular moves thereafter. If the head of the family took a new job, this might also be a reason to move, as the men generally preferred to be able to walk to work to save on transportation and to come home to eat their noon meal.

In view of the very low wages, the slightest rise in rent also might force a family to move. 'I sure have moved in my life! When I think about it. . . . If the landlord raised the rent a dollar a month, we moved. It was too much, we couldn't pay it' (P29). The Depression of course contributed to increasing the frequency of these moves, since half of the women we interviewed had to shift to cheaper accommodations, in other words, to a smaller, less comfortable, and often less well-equipped flat, thus giving up what little comfort and convenience they had previously had.[7] If the entire family suffered from the deterioration in their housing conditions, it was the women, for whom the home was the place where they at once both lived and worked, who were the most affected.

For women, moving to new accommodations represented an increase in their work as well. Not only did they have to find the new flat and pack and unpack the family's belongings, but they also had to clean it from top to bottom and, if they had the money, repaint or repaper, run up new curtains, and so on. In order to reduce costs, they often called upon their relatives to help out and, if possible, got a contribution from the landlord:

> So I took another place, but it was so dirty! I cleaned the flat. The landlord gave us wallpaper and he gave us paint, we had to do it all ourselves. . . . We worked like crazy but it didn't cost us anything. When you moved, you rented a truck—if you had a relative with a truck then he'd come help you move and it didn't cost anything. That's why we moved so often. (E29)

Implements of Work

A majority of household appliances, like the washing machine, the vacuum cleaner, and the dishwasher, were patented in the United States in the course of the nineteenth century, very often by women (Strasser, 1980; Bernard, 1981). But it was not until the beginning of the twentieth century that they became available on the market, often to meet the needs of hotels and restaurants and several more decades would have to pass before they would be adapted for use in the home and homemakers could buy them. Certain small appliances, like the electric iron or the electric toaster, became more rapidly available. In general, however, the high cost of the new large appliances as well as lack of space or the absence of the utilities needed to run them (inadequate electrical wiring, no gas connection) meant that working-class housewives had to do their work without modern equipment until at least the Second World War. An examination of the tools available to the women in our sample will allow us to determine which of them could be found in the majority of houses and to consider their advantages and disadvantages for the housewife.

Among the appliances which offered more disadvantages than advantages were the wood, coal, or combination stoves (wood and coal, gas and coal) used by more than two-thirds of the women interviewed during the 1930s. Their surfaces were not entirely enamelled and thus required considerable upkeep if they were not to rust. Another of their considerable disadvantages was that they gave off an intense but local heat, which did not manage to spread the full length of the flat but which did overheat the kitchen, especially in the summer during mealtimes or on laundry day. In addition, these stoves had to be continually fed and they produced ashes which had to be thrown away after they were sifted to retrieve lumps of coal ('clinkers') that had not burnt down. . . .

Considering the astronomical cost of electric refrigerators,[8] it is hardly surprising that only one of the informants possessed one at the time of her marriage. Two others had bought an enamelled icebox, but all the others had to make do with a wooden icebox that most of them kept until the end of the 1940s. Six others did not even have this convenience when they were first married. At any rate, the icebox could keep food for only three or four days and only in small amounts, which was not especially useful to mothers of large families. In addition, one had to keep an eye on the icebox

because it was necessary to empty the container that caught the water from the melting ice. Because of lack of space or in order to avoid water damage, some housewives preferred to put the icebox in the shed or on the back balcony. . . .

Electric washing machines, with a metal tub and an electric or manual wringer, began to appear in the 1920s and were, without a doubt, a marked improvement over the washboard or the washing machine that was agitated by hand[9] or by water. But their high price and the amount of space they took up meant that most of the women interviewed waited until they had one or more children before buying one. More than two-thirds scrubbed their washing on a board for a number of years;[10] a few of them did their wash at their mother's or mother-in-law's, or, unusually, borrowed a neighbour's machine. But even when they had a machine, most of them continued to do their daily wash by hand in a tub, at the kitchen sink, or in the bathtub. 'You didn't bring out the machine every day to wash the diapers' (E2), as several of the informants explained. That was because these machines were not without their disadvantages, especially when they did not work entirely by electricity. As well, the machine had to be moved to the sink where it obstructed access or took up a large part of the kitchen and it was also necessary to heat up large quantities of water to fill it. . . .

The sewing machine was a tool much more important than the washing machine because it allowed the making of clothes and household linen in order to effect appreciable savings.[11] In fact, only five of the women did not have one and most of those who did bought it before they bought a washing machine. Several of the women, especially the youngest in the family, inherited them from their mothers, who had no further use for it after their daughters were married. These were not electric but treadle machines, which meant that a sewing session involved a fairly considerable expense of physical energy. Over the years, however, most of the women had a motor installed, which considerably lightened this particular chore. . . .

Altogether, then, there were few conveniences and a narrow range of rather rudimentary tools available to these housewives. The fact that most of these household appliances did not work automatically, along with the restricted space and lack of amenities of their housing, did not make it easy for women to accomplish several tasks at the same time, a possibility that would increase as the housewife became equipped with increasingly sophisticated appliances. It was indeed difficult to wash dishes and clothes at the same time with but a single sink at one's disposal. This meant that the women often had to drop one chore for another more pressing one, creating considerable discontinuity.

The introduction of electricity and plumbing into workers' housing certainly represented two important improvements that separated these women from those of previous generations and from rural women. But in order fully to enjoy all of the advantages that these utilities could provide, the housewife needed the plumbing fixtures (bathtub, water heater, second sink) and the appliances (electric washing machine, gas or electric stove, refrigerator) that few had available to them. One informant, however, who came to Montreal when she married, summed up the advantages of electricity like this: 'Back home, even if we didn't have electricity, we had Aladdin lamps . . . so I didn't find that there was that much of a difference. There would have been the laundry, a washing machine, that would have been the only change' (E22).

None of the women interviewed had to dispose of their appliances because of the Depression, though it did cause them to put off buying certain articles of furniture and equipment. During the 1940s, as their economic situation improved, the majority of them were quick to change their old wood or coal stove for a new, more practical, gas range.[12] It must be observed that these purchases necessarily coincided with the rental of a flat containing the requisite connections, which often rented for a larger amount. All the same, those who did not already have a washing machine bought one during or immediately after the war, while the others traded their old model in on one that functioned completely electrically (both tub and wringer).

Nevertheless, the Depression did temporarily deprive several of the women of their appliances for various reasons. For example, one informant did the laundry for several months in the bathtub because she did not have the money to get her machine fixed. 'I had a wooden agitator with a handle in the side and the wringer was broken, which meant I had to do the wash in the bathtub. And it was only something that cost thirty-nine cents. I did the laundry for I think five or six months in the bathtub like that' (E27). In order to save on electricity, another woman used a sad iron her mother lent her that she could heat on the stove. Finally, two informants had their electricity cut off because they could not pay their bills. These cuts seriously complicated their work because they had to put off doing some of it until after dark, when they could reconnect illegally, without worrying about inspectors from the company coming by.[13]

Two of the women interviewed went back to live on the land because their husbands were not able to find a job. Without electricity or running water, they had to give up their washing machines and other electric appliances (toaster, iron) and return to making a good number of items at home (bread, soap, preserves, and so on) that they had formerly bought. One of these couples bought a little farm that was already in cultivation, but the other had to set up in a 'colonization zone', and to undertake the hard work demanded by the clearing and ploughing of a tract of land. These two women had already experienced this kind of life, which made it easier for them to adapt to their new situation. It should be recalled that between 42,000 and 52,000 persons took up land in the colonization zones during the 1930s (Linteau, et al., 1989), so that such would have been the fate of a considerable number of women, many of whom would not have been prepared to deal with changes of this sort.

Organizing Household Tasks

The sexual division of labour within the home meant that housework in general remained the almost exclusive responsibility of women. Moreover, the majority of women in this sample viewed this work as theirs and sought no help with it whatever from their husbands. 'When you are married, each one has their own work' (E7). This way of conceptualizing the assignment of tasks and roles within marriage came up on several occasions in the oral histories and shows clearly that these women put their work on the same plane as that of their husbands. In reference to the sharing of housework by young couples, one informant commented:

> When all that began to change, I was really taken aback. For me, a woman who doesn't wash her walls, things like that. . . . well, I said, that's not what a man should be doing, that's women's work. She's the one living in the house. He has his own work, outside. . . . Everything but the ceilings. My husband never wanted me to wash them, or do the painting either—he always did that. He always painted—he painted my house every year. My paint was really good. (E23)

As this recollection suggests, male participation in housework was most often limited to heavy or dirty work—washing walls and ceilings, painting, hanging wallpaper, emptying ashes, taking out the garbage. A few husbands dried the dishes, at least until their daughters were old enough to do it, and washed floors, but in general, the women insisted on doing the housework by themselves. To ask for help was the same as admitting that they were not able to shoulder their responsibilities:

> I was strong enough to do all my work. He didn't help around the house, I have to say. I can't say I ever asked him to. Three rooms, four rooms—it would have been ridiculous to make him do anything. I was quite capable of doing my own work. I had the time. (E22)

Another woman even maintained that men who helped their wives might become the neighbourhood laughingstock:

> The man next door, he helped his wife. So my [husband and brothers] laughed at that guy! They called him the 'diaper-washer.' That was awful, eh? A man who helped his wife—they made fun of him in those days! . . . And we didn't ask them to help us—as far as we were concerned, it was our work. We said, 'We don't want to have them in our pots and pans.' We were the ones who looked after that. (E29)

The idleness brought about by unemployment did not lead to a greater participation by men in housework.[14] Just as wives did not try to take their husbands' place as principal breadwinner, no more did the men meddle in the housework. If they did lend an occasional hand, it was only to do the jobs they had done previously—going to the store, taking care of the children, washing the floors. According to the respondents, most of the men spent the greater part of their time out of the house, looking for work. . . .

In order to get their work done, most of the women had developed a strict schedule. Thus, Mondays and Tuesdays were devoted to washing and ironing as well as the mending. Wednesday was the day for sewing or cooking depending on circumstances, while Thursday and Friday were for the weekly cleaning and shopping. On Saturday, some would take advantage of their husbands' presence to do the baking while he looked after the children. This pattern was generally observed, no matter what happened: 'On Mondays, regardless of what kind of day it was, I did the wash. I always did' (E23). A few of the others maintained that they used to have more flexible timetables, even going so far as to make fun of this rather obsessive regularity:

When I couldn't [maintain the schedule], I didn't give a damn. . . . It all depended on how I got out of bed in the morning. . . . If I didn't feel so well, I'd put it off till the next day . . . I told myself when to do things. I didn't have anyone breathing down my back. I was the boss. I did what I wanted—as long as the work got done, it was all right. I was never that fussy about things like that. (E12)

This attitude, less common, was found more among those women who had learned their domestic tasks on the farm, where housework followed a different rhythm, or among those who had not experienced the discipline of the factory floor. Factory work, which instilled habits of punctuality (by docking wages if necessary) and taught that the least particle of time should be made profitable, certainly helped to accustom these women to respect precise schedules and to carry out their

work according to a virtually unchangeable plan. Several of the women who placed a great importance on their work routine and on a rational allocation of their time, moreover, maintained that their mothers (who had often grown up on the farm and who had never worked in a factory) were less strict in this regard: 'My mother would put things off till tomorrow more easily than me. "If I don't do it today, I'll do it tomorrow." For me, it was today, never tomorrow' (E2). . . .

A heightened concern for cleanliness went along with this discipline. 'We had to have everything just so—we kept our houses more spick and span than our parents had' (E2). For some of the women, cleanliness was almost an obsession: 'I washed by hand like crazy because the washers we had then didn't get clothes clean enough—so I had to scrub my washing. . . . I did a spring cleaning in the fall as well as the spring—two spring cleanings a year. I never went a year without painting' (E23). . . .

Along with the scientific organization of labour, a concern for order and cleanliness were two preoccupations that appeared at the same time as industrialized society.[15] These were associated not merely with hygiene but also with the moral values they served to reinforce—a clean and orderly home at once reflected the presence of an accomplished housewife, preserved the family core from being dispersed, and inculcated in the family members fundamental Christian virtues basic to society (Coderre, 1924). A clean and well-kept home suggested that its occupants, especially the woman responsible for its maintenance, were of high moral character. 'Is not to present a clean and orderly dwelling but a way of showing the will to maintain order everywhere and in everything, as the interior of the home reflects the person?' (Lemieux and Mercier, 1982). In this atmosphere, it is to be expected that the women interviewed were absolutely insistent on their concern for order and cleanliness.

The Cycle of Household Chores

With the passing of days and weeks, the women interviewed performed the same tasks sometimes more, sometimes less, frequently. The laundry, for example, far from being merely a weekly chore, could become a daily one when there were young children.[16] An insufficient supply of diapers, mattress pads, nightgowns, and flannel blankets would make a daily laundry necessary; for women who had several babies, this would mean a number of years of daily washes. 'Every morning, you knew there was a boiler full of diapers waiting for you' (E2), one woman recalled. As one informant, who did nevertheless have a machine, pointed out, these 'little' washes were done by hand, on a washboard placed in a tub or in the bathtub, and the women often 'took advantage' of these sessions to wash out certain articles of clothing. 'When I was washing the diapers, I also did some things that were easy to wash' (E6).

As mentioned earlier, most of the women interviewed did not have a washing machine until after the birth of their first, and sometimes second or third, child. Despite this fact, only seven of them used the services of commercial laundry, most of them on an irregular basis and more frequently toward the end of the decade, and three of these had their own machines. In most cases, only the very large and difficult to launder items, like sheets and towels, were sent to the laundry every two weeks. The rates, by the pound, were not very high—it cost about twenty-five cents to wash the bed linen, towels, and dishcloths. At this price, however, the laundry was not returned dry, but as 'wet wash', to the housewife, who had to hang it out before ironing it. Even this minimal cost represented a major obstacle since the family budget was very tight. That is why even those who used this service only did so occasionally, in order to lighten a particularly heavy week. When the husband was out of work, it was obviously impossible to make use of the service.

There were other reasons offered to explain why the women in the sample made so little use of the laundry services. One of them, for example, could never resign herself to sending her washing out of fear of being considered lazy: 'Oh, no, I would have done the laundry in the bathtub rather than send it out. I would have been ashamed to send my sheets to the laundry. They would have said, "[She] is really lazy, that one—she doesn't wash her own sheets!" Oh no!' (E17). . . .

Doing the washing was a lengthy and arduous chore that everyone remembered as a horror. 'You started at eight o'clock in the morning and were lucky if you were finished before three. Along the way, you had to feed the kids, mop up, make the beds' (E10). For each load of wash, it was necessary to heat huge quantities of water, empty it into the washtubs or the washing machine, add the soap, bleach, and blueing depending on the load, empty the dirty water into the sink, wring out the clothes, and start all over again.[17] Each load had to be washed and rinsed twice, not to mention that certain items had to be soaked before being laundered. If signs of elevated standards of cleanliness might be detected in all this, it must also be noted that some clothing, especially work overalls, could be very dirty indeed. Other items demanded special treatment—diapers, for example, had to be boiled, as much to get them clean as to conform to a notion of hygiene, while cotton had to be rinsed in blueing to keep it white. . . .

Just like the laundry, cleaning the house was something that took place on a weekly and a daily schedule. 'After breakfast,' one informant explained, 'I did the bedrooms. I made the beds and mopped the floor. In those days, we had linoleum everywhere. After that, I did my dusting. That was a regular thing, every day' (E20). This routine, reported by almost every one of the women, was extended at the week's end to include a more thorough cleaning of every room—windows, baseboards, bathroom, and floors all washed. If the floors were softwood, they would have to be scrubbed with a brush and 'lessis' in order get them back to golden; linoleum floors, easier to keep up, nevertheless had to be waxed and, as one woman recalled, 'In those days, floors had to be done with paste wax. We didn't have liquid wax' (E20).

It was also on Fridays that these housewives did their major shopping. From time to time, they would make an excursion to one of the city markets to buy fresh fruit and vegetables, but most often these purchases would be made at one of the numerous grocer-butcher shops that could be found in the area and that did not require a long journey. Unlike a supermarket, these little concerns offered personalized service in that each of the customers was waited on individually. The informants were quite insistent on this point so as to emphasize the attention they received: 'In those days, we didn't wait on ourselves' (E10). Supermarkets, which began to appear in the 1930s, were at first viewed as an aberration because shoppers could take products directly from the shelves. 'When they first started, we said, good heavens, they are going to be robbed! Everybody is going to get at everything' (E15). Rather quickly, however, the women observed that self-service had certain advantages, as they sometimes felt uncomfortable rejecting a piece of meat that had been expressly cut for them or an article they had asked the price of.[18] On the other hand, the small grocery stores offered free delivery, which the supermarkets did not necessarily do. . . .

The women in the sample most often turned to local shops, generally concentrated on a nearby commercial street, for almost all their purchases, including yard goods, clothing, household articles, and furniture. They very rarely visited the downtown department stores except for sales or at Christmas. A few of the poorest women got their clothes and furniture from the outlets of the charitable organizations in their parish, like the Saint Vincent de Paul Society. Pedlars sold clothing door-to-door but their prices were usually higher because they sold on credit and only a few of the women interviewed bought from them: 'It was the Jews who came to the door selling bed linen, sheets, pillowcases, coats, dresses, everything like that. . . . It was a lot more expensive, but we were stuck. . . . They would come to collect from us' (E27).

Thanks both to the variety of products that were delivered to the home and to the nearness of most retail stores, these women spent relatively little of their time shopping or bringing things home. In fact, this last activity was most often undertaken by pedlars or by a young deliveryman employed by the merchant; it would be accurate to say that it was not as yet part of everyday housework.[19]

When it was a question of making purchases involving large sums of money, like furniture and household appliances, husbands more frequently accompanied their wives to the store and some even went on their own. On the other hand, they were rarely involved in buying material or clothing, except for their own, though a majority of them did at least some of the shopping for food. In most cases, this occurred when they were sent to the store now and then by their wives for odds and ends, though almost a third did all of the shopping on a regular basis. . . .

Most of these women spent several hours a week sewing or mending clothes for their families. More than two-thirds of them made most of their children's clothes, only a third made their own clothes, and none sewed for their husbands. Husbands thus accounted for the greatest part of clothing expenditures, but women, more than children, also wore store-bought clothes.

According to these oral histories, if the women did not make their husband's clothes, it was in part because the men were 'too proud' to wear home-made garments, but also because men's clothing required too much work and, if they were to fit properly, greater skill than the women had. As we may recall, most of them had received only a sketchy training in sewing and some of them felt particularly lacking when faced with this task:

I was not a real, one hundred percent seam-stress. I only sewed for my children, for the littlest ones. . . . I made things for my little guys to start out with because I had two in a row . . . I learned, but I had to put my head down on my machine lots of times because I was crying lots of times. I was so discouraged. I didn't know how to go about it and then I was not someone who would ask. (E23)

According to how much money there was, the children's clothes were made out of new material or remade out of their father's old clothes[20] or those of other relatives, which required a lot of work: 'those old things . . . that I took apart, turned inside out, washed, ironed, remade. . . . I even made my daughters' coats. I did a lot of work then' (E19). Just like their fathers, the boys graduated to ready-to-wear more quickly than their sisters. 'I made all my children's clothes, even the little boys' until they started to wear long pants . . . when they were twelve, but I made my girls' clothes all the time, all the time. . . . I even made the clothes they wore to get married in' (E24).

As for themselves, the women did not go out very much and thus had less need of many clothes. Around the house they wore cotton housedresses that cost so little that they were hardly worth sewing at home. 'In the house, I always wore a "duster" and an apron. But I didn't go out, you know' (E28). The low price of these garments made specifically for housewives (the women interviewed used the English term 'duster' for them) allowed them to save precious time to work on clothes for their children who were getting bigger and going to school. . . .

Like knitting, which several of the women did, sewing is a precise undertaking that demands a certain degree of peace and does not improve by being interrupted. This is why the women did their sewing most often at night, when the children were in bed, or in the afternoon, when they were in school or taking a nap. More than any other household task, sewing involved the establish-ment of broad exchange networks among families and reinforced the bonds among the female rela-tives; the richer ones gave their used clothes to the poorer ones and mothers and mothers-in-law lent their sewing machines and sometimes took over sewing for their grandchildren.

Within this weekly cycle of housework, there were of course the daily tasks, like preparing meals. Cooking took up a considerable amount of the housewife's day, since virtually all of the women made all the food, from soups to desserts. Two-thirds of them also did some canning, and made their own pickles, jams, spruce beer, dandelion wine, ice cream, and so on. They also had to cut up and mince the meat: 'They didn't have all the cuts of meat like nowadays—you got a big piece of meat in those days because the families were so big. If you bought a big piece, ten or twelve pounds, it was cheaper' (E16).

Even if some of them reserved one day a week for cooking, still every day they had to prepare the meat, clean and slice the vegetables, and cook or heat up the lot. Preparing meals also involved setting and clearing the table, doing the dishes and the pots, cleaning the stove and sink, and sweeping the kitchen. In fact, many of the women maintained that cooking took up the greater part of their time. 'We spent two-thirds of our time preparing meals' (E5). 'It's the everyday stuff [that takes up the most time]. When you have a lot of kids, of course you have to do more. Fixing the vegetables. . . . That's what takes the most time' (E17). . . .

Cutting Back on Necessities

All in all, the Depression did not seem to have added new jobs to the housewife's roster of tasks. As we have seen, the majority of them were already using all of their resources and skills to get the most out of what they had. Because they were not consuming anything except essentials, however, the Depression forced them to cut to the bone, which meant that they had constantly to search for alternatives and make important changes in the way they shopped, sewed, and cooked, all of which seriously complicated their household tasks.

Buying as little as possible at the best price was already a way of life for these housewives. As far as actual food purchases went, however, it was often difficult to cut back on quantity. Therefore, the housewives sought new ways to economize by buying lower quality and by stocking up in different ways. Therefore, some of the women began to buy their meat directly from the abattoir rather than from the local grocery, which permitted them to obtain greater quantities at the same price. . . . It was also possible to get cut-rate meat by buying it late on Saturday evening, just before the stores closed;[21] a number of grocers who did not have refrigeration preferred to get rid of their stock rather than risk losing their merchandise by storing it until Monday morning. Finally, one of the informants also bought horsemeat, cheaper than the other kinds.

Some of the women would buy fruits and vegetables that had been reduced because they were wilted, even if it meant taking a little more time to prepare them: 'It was a lot of work to make them all right to eat. Sometimes they were starting to go. But if you picked out what was edible' (E5) . . . . Other women would go to the market to pick up fruits and vegetables that were thrown out at the end of the day by the farmers who had given up all hope of selling them. 'My husband would go to Bonsecours market for vegetables. The farmers threw out quite a lot—what was still good, my husband brought home and we ate it. . . . You can't be fussy!' (E25).

As mentioned previously, two-thirds of the women interviewed were in the habit of making pickles and preserves. This activity, however, was not linked to the Depression. On the contrary, a lack of income and the way in which direct relief was dispersed made it difficult to buy the large quantities necessary for their production: 'I never canned anything—in the first place, I never had the money to put things up, to buy the jars and everything else you need. I didn't have the money for that' (E12). . . .

Preparing the same amount of food with fewer means and from inferior quality products required a good pinch of ingenuity to create appetizing meals. Sausage, minced meat, spaghetti, and noodles appeared very often on the table, prepared in every imaginable way. Dishes in sauce, made with a base of flour and water, were also an economical solution, since they generally did not contain meat: 'I made potatoes and white sauce, eggs and white sauce, beans and white sauce, and tinned salmon and white sauce. We ate a lot of paste!' (E25). Desserts were skipped altogether or consisted of 'broken biscuits' sold cheaply in bulk or made from recipes that did not ask for expensive ingredients, like the famous 'pouding chomeur' (literally, unemployed pudding, poor man's pudding): 'If it wasn't going to cost too much, you had to make a cake that didn't take more than one egg' (E25). 'I made all my own cakes and I didn't put in any eggs—just a little milk and some baking powder and my cakes were always light' (E29).

Despite all of these strategies, some of the informants simply had to deprive themselves of food so their children could have it:

> I would make a stew, as we called it. . . . I would make it out of spaghetti and whatever stuff was the cheapest and the most nourishing. But that doesn't mean we were well fed. . . . All it meant is that we had something to eat and even then sometimes we had to leave it all for the children. (E27)

On those days when there was hardly anything in the house to eat, the father might disappear around mealtime, saying he was going to look for work, so that his wife and the children could share whatever food there was. One couple often made do with macaroni and butter and sugar spread on bread, while another informant admitted that she had often eaten sugared bread dampened under the faucet. . . . In regard to nourishment, the Depression made the housewives' task more difficult both in terms of getting provisions and devising meals. Even more serious, however, was that it also forced a significant number of them to deprive themselves of food.

During spells of unemployment, buying clothing was the first thing to go. 'We didn't have much to wear' (E6), a number of the informants said in essence. Very often, the women, but also their husbands, wore their old clothes year after year in order to preserve their limited resources to clothe their children. Two of the women interviewed who had not previously done any sewing took it up to make clothes for their children specifically on account of the Depression. . . . In most cases, however, the women who did not know how to sew were more likely to go to the stores run by the Salvation Army or the Saint Vincent de Paul Society.

Finally the costs of heating, electricity, and gas were reduced as far as possible by cutting back on the time they were in use (at night, for example) or by avoiding the use of electric appliances, as we have already seen. Some families turned to fuel picked up along the railway lines or on building sites, or made from cardboard boxes or old newspapers. It was the men who salvaged these materials:

> He'd go out in the morning to look for wood in Saint Lambert. . . . After that, he'd go to the store so he'd have some cardboard. He'd take the cardboard cartons apart, roll them up, and tie them with wire and stack them in the shed to make wood for next winter. Then . . . he'd soak newspapers in water in a basin . . . and make them into balls . . . and then let them dry. There, that was our coal for the winter. (E25)

According to this informant, this kind of fuel increased the risk of fire and required her to 'mind the fire' all night long, taking turns with her husband.

Despite the fact that they had to move more frequently, do laundry more often, had greater difficulty in stocking the larder, and even suffered deprivation, and constantly had to look for some way to find possible substitutes to satisfy their families' needs, the women interviewed were not unanimous in their view of the effects of the Depression on their household work. Some among them believed that the lack of money did not mean that they had to do much more work. Others agreed that they were forced to do somewhat more, but hastened, however, to add: 'Work around the house never bothered me' (E6), and 'Yes, but it's just like I told you. It was routine. It didn't make much difference to me. I knew how to manage so we had food on the table' (E29). These statements at once communicate the self-denial of these women faced with their families' needs as well as their pride in being able to confront every situation with no exceptional difficulty. Furthermore, they reveal that the women have a most elastic conception of their time and their capacity for work; even in normal times, the list of household tasks represented a significant number of hours of work in a day that began at dawn with breakfast and the care of the smaller children and continued until late in the evening in front of the sewing machine, whereas their husbands could take a little rest: 'You got up in the morning and you never stopped. . . . After supper he [her husband] read his paper—us women, we had the dishes, the kids' homework' (E2).

Several of the women also had to find the time to do work for which they got paid, without, however, neglecting their household responsibilities. Their workday was therefore longer and more broken up, but they asserted that they managed to sort everything out without help and drew a certain satisfaction from having been successful in accommodating everything. One of them, who managed her husband's shop during the day, stated, 'I managed. . . . You can always find some way to work things out. . . . I don't remember having had much trouble. . . . I had a lot of energy' (E7). . . .

When considered in connection with the overall family economy, housework would appear as the essential counterpart to the wage. Indeed, analyzing various household tasks reveals that those occupying the greatest amount of time were allocated to the production of goods and services directed toward satisfying the basic needs of family members. Production in the home could make up for inadequate family incomes by allowing what money there was to be devoted exclusively to the purchase of goods and services that would otherwise be impossible to obtain. The women themselves, moreover, were aware of the economic importance of their labour, which they thought of in the same way as that of their husbands: 'He had his work and I had mine,' they were happy to recall, thus putting both kinds of work on equal footing.

In general, the level of consumption on the part of these families was already at a minimum when the Depression occurred. In these conditions, the extra restraints that they had to impose on themselves in the matter of food and housing, among other things, seriously affected the welfare, if not the actual health, of family members and especially impinged on women in regard to their working conditions and their own subsistence. Obviously, the search for makeshifts to allow families to be fed, clothed, and housed despite a loss of income fell to the housewife.

Notes

1. This kind of housing existed well into the 1930s. Out of the 4,216 workers' homes that were visited during the municipal inquiry of 1936–37, they accounted for 379, or 8.9 per cent of the total. Furthermore, some of the women interviewed had lived in them (Réal Bélanger, George S. Mooney and Pierre Boucher, *Les vieux logements de Montréal* [Montreal: Commission Métropolitaine de Montréal, Département d'urbanisme et de recherché, 1938], 9).

2. At the beginning of the thirties, more than half of the informants were paying less than fifteen dollars a month in rent for a four-room flat. According to *La Gazette du Travail*, a six-room flat without modern facilities or with some of them absent would cost,

in Montreal, from sixteen to twenty-five dollars a month in 1929 and from fifteen to eighteen dollars a month in 1933 (Canada, Minister of Labour, *La Gazette du Travail*, February 1929: 256, February 1933: 257).

3. In 1941, 51.5 per cent of Montreal flats were heated exclusively by a stove, which was the case for almost every flat visited in 1937 during the course of the municipal inquiry carried out in seven working-class districts of Montreal (Canada, *Recensement du Canada, 1941* 5, 54; Bélanger, et al., 1938: 11).

4. The municipal inquiry of 1936–37 noted that in the 4, 216 lodgings visited, only 1,716 had a completely separate toilet; in 1,431 cases, it had been added to

a corner of the kitchen, in 112 cases in the parlour, in 536 in a bedroom, and in 239 in the hallway (Bélanger, et al., 1938: 12).

5. In another connection, this crowding reminds us that the poorest classes do not have the benefit of any sort of privacy: 'room is lacking to provide a private space for each member of the group—private space is thus only the public space of the domestic group' (Antoine Prost, 'La famille et l'individu', in Antoine Prost and Gérard Vincent, eds, *Histoire de la vie privée*. vol. 5: *De la Première Guerre mondiale à nos jours*. [Paris: Seuil, 1987], 72).

6. This saying reminds us that working-class families in this period did not carry fire insurance. Mentioned in 'Housing', a column by Louise in *La Patrie*, 13 February 1932: 14 and in a talk by Mme Louis-F. Coderre on 'The Home' for the *Semaine sociale du Canada* Fifth Session, *La Propriété* (Montreal: Bibliothèque de l'Action française, 1924), 146. According to Mme Coderre, 'A principal way of saving money is to have a steady place of residence, or in other words, to avoid moving house.'

7. The number of relocations in Montreal was in fact constantly on the rise during the first years of the Depression: 54,000 in 1930, 55,000 in 1931, 65,000 in 1932, and almost 82,000 in 1933 according to data furnished by Montreal Light, Heat and Power (*La Patrie*, 17 April 1931: 7 and 17 April 1933: 3). Moreover, the economic situation meant that most of these families were looking for less expensive accommodations. Thus during the Depression, the best flats remained vacant while an overpopulation was noted in the old housing. In this connection, see Marc Choke, *Les Crises du logement à Montréal* (Montreal: Éditions Saint-Martin, 1980), 109.

8. The item that the Woodhouse store advertised as 'the famous Fisher electric icebox' retailed for between $225 and $736, depending on the model, in 1930 (*La Patrie*, 1 March 1930: 37).

9. The tubs of these machines had to be agitated by a wooden handle.

10. Only four owned a washing machine when they married. Seven had to wait between one and two years, four between two and three years, eight between three and five years, and seven for more than five years. These figures do not take into account the period of shared accommodations, when the bride might have been able to take advantage of her mother's or mother-in-law's machine.

11. Elizabeth Roberts recalls that the sewing machine was for a long period the only technological innovation possessed by working-class families ('Women's Strategies, 1890–1940', in Jane Lewis, ed., *Labour and Love: Women's Experience of Home and Family 1840–1940* [Oxford: Blackwell, 1986], 232).

12. In 1941, 17.7 per cent of Montreal households used wood or coal for cooking and only 8.2 per cent in 1951. There are no figures for this subject in the 1931 census. On the other hand, the municipal inquiry of 1937 concluded that almost all the housing visited was heated only by a stove and that in 68.6 per cent of these cases, either wood or coal was used as fuel (Bélanger, et al., 1938: 11).

13. Montreal Light, Heat and Power exercised a virtual monopoly in the Montreal region which allowed it to maintain high rates and to disconnect customers who did not pay their bills. According to Robert Rumilly, more that 20,000 families were deprived of electricity in the depths of the Depression (Robert Rumilly, *Histoire de Montréal* [Fides, 1974] cited in Claude Larivière, *Crise économique et contrôle social: le cas de Montréal 1929–1937* [Montreal: Éditions Saint-Martin, 1977], 175).

14. A number of others have already observed this phenomenon in English Canada and in the United States. See Veronica Strong-Boag, *The New Day Recalled: Lives of Girls and Women in English Canada, 1919–1939* (Toronto: Copp Clark, 1988), 50; Mirra Komorovsky, *The Unemployed Man and His Family* (New York: Arno Press, 1971), 28–130.

15. According to Maïté Clavel, 'Contrary to those societies which allowed them space, industrialized societies excluded dirt, the buried, the hidden. Only what was clean was valued, promoted, and celebrated . . . the current value attributed to cleanliness for its own sake would date from the seventeenth century' ('Propreté: mots, rites, images,' *Cahiers internationaux de sociologie. Le détour anthropologique féminin-masculin* 80 [1986]: 43).

16. Several authors who have studied the evolution of domestic labour have often associated the increase in frequency of certain household tasks, like laundry, with the appearance of more sophisticated machinery. In this regard, see Bernard, 395 and n.4, 410; Ruth Schwartz Cowan, 'The "Industrial Revolution" in the Home: Household Technology and Social Change in the 20th Century', *Technology and Culture* 17 (1976): n.10, 5.

17. As Ruth Schwartz Cowan has observed: 'Studies of energy expenditure during housework have indicated that by far the greatest effort is expended in hauling and lifting the wet wash, tasks which were not eliminated by the introduction of washing machines' ('Industrial Revolution', n.10, 5). These

operations were not without their risks. Newspapers of the period frequently carried stories about children who were scalded when they tipped a washtub over on themselves. In the months of November and December 1929 alone, *La Patrie* reported five accidents of this kind (*La Patrie* 20, 23 November 1929: 3, 11, 24; December 1929: 1 and 26 December 1929: 23). Moreover, one of the families in the sample experienced a similar accident.

18. According to Keith Walden, the 'Toronto-based *Canadian Grocer*, a weekly trade journal, recommended clearly visible price tags on products: "Nowadays, every well-informed grocer makes it a point to have everything marked." This would avoid the embarrassment to customers who would have to ask the shopkeeper for the price, which might turn out to be too expensive' (Keith Walden, 'Speaking Modern: Language, Culture and Hegemony in Grocery Window Displays, 1887–1920', paper presented to the Congress of the Historical Society of Canada, Quebec, June 1989: 10).

19. According to Ruth Schwartz Cowan, delivery services began to disappear in the United States during the 1930s, due to the rise of the automobile and to the ferocious competition among retailers trying to capture the market. This led to their cutting back their costs of operation in order to lower their prices. (*More Work for Mother: The Ironies of Household Technology from the Open Hearth to the Microwave* [New York: Basic Books, 1983], 79–85). The compulsory school attendance of the children who did this sort of work was probably also responsible. According to the oral histories, it was not until the 1940s, in any event, that delivery services began to disappear in Montreal, which coincided with the application of the school attendance law of 1943. In this regard, see Dominique Jean, 'Familles québécoises et politiques sociales touchant les enfants de 1940 à 1960: obligation scolaire, allocations familiales et travail juvénile', PhD dissertation, University of Montreal, 1989.

20. The informants rarely mentioned remaking their own clothes, probably because they had very few of them and they wore them to shreds.

21. In this period, most shops stayed open until eleven o'clock on Saturday night.

References

Bernard, Jessie. 1981. *The Female World*. New York: The Free Press.

Chaubaud, Danielle, Dominique Fougeyrollas-Schwebel and Françoise Sonthonax. 1985. *Espace et temps du travail domestique*. Paris: Librairie des Méridians.

Coderre, Mme Louis-F. 1924. 'The Home', *Semaine sociale du Canada* Fifth Session, *La Propriété*. Montreal: Bibliothèque de l'Action française.

Lemieux, Denise, and Lucie Mercier. 1987. 'Familles et destines féminins. Le prisme de la mémoire, 1880–1940', *Recherches Sociographiques. La famille de la Nouvelle-France à aujourd'hui* 28, 2–3: 259–62.

Linteau, Paul-André, et al., 1989. *Histoire du Québec contemporain*. vol. 2: *Le Québec depuis 1930*. Montreal: Boréal Compact.

Pelletier, Lyse. 1987. 'Au sujet des espaces féminisés', *Cahiers de géographie du Québec* 31, 83: 177–88.

Séguin, Anne-Marie. 1989. 'Madame Ford et l'espace: lecture féministe de la suburbanisation', *Lieux et milieux de vie. Recherches Féministes* 2, 1: 51–68.

Strasser, Susan. 1980. 'An Englarged Human Existence? Technology and Housework in Nineteenth-Century America', in Sara Fenstermaker-Berk, ed., *Women and Household Labor*. London: Sage.

Strong-Boag, Veronica. 1986. 'Keeping House in God's Country: Canadian Women at Work in the Home', in Craig Heron and Robert Storey, eds, *On the Job: Confronting the Labor Process in Canada*. Montreal and Kingston: McGill-Queen's University Press.

PART VII

Workplace, Welfare, and World War II, 1920–1960

Class tensions and struggles are a recurring and inevitable element of working-class history. Yet how those tensions and conflicts manifest themselves, and how they are negotiated and managed, varies dramatically over time and in different workplaces. Moreover, labour history is also at times characterized by workers' acquiescence to the existing social order, and by complex accommodations among class forces. These can be encouraged and sustained by employers, the state, unions, and a wide array of other institutions (churches, schools, voluntary societies), as well as individuals and families.

The following articles deal with mid-twentieth-century examples of the management of class and workplace conflict, drawing particular attention to distinct developments in this formative period. On the one hand, in the immediate aftermath of World War I many corporations experimented with welfare capitalist measures designed to ameliorate class tensions. If the Great Depression tended to undercut the necessity of such concessions, the outbreak of World War II in 1939, and the subsequent need for expanding production with its pressing need for labour to be on the job, created a climate in which the state increasingly tried to address working-class grievances and contain tensions.

Joan Sangster uses a method of historical reconstruction favoured by many social historians: a local 'case study' of one workplace or one group of workers, which is then used to illuminate broader themes and issues. Sangster's focus is on a Peterborough clock manufacturing company, Westclox, which employed a large number of women and was designated an enlightened innovator in the provision of workplace benefits for its employees. She traces relations between workers and managers over four decades, using the Westclox example as a means of exploring how and why workers consent to the rules of particular industrial relations regimes. She thus enters into interpretive debates about ideology, paternalism, and welfare capitalism in North American labour history.

The paternalism of Westclox managers varied dramatically from the nineteenth century paternalism characterizing the fur trade described by Carolyn Podruchny, but it shared with earlier versions of this broad employer strategy an investment in the kind of patriarchal ideology that portrayed the workplace as a 'family'. In this understanding of class relations, paternal employers had a responsibility to care for their workers and provide for them, just as workers owed respect and loyalty to their employers. Paternalism was discretionary and subjective: it did not carry with it 'rights' for employees, but rather involved notions of reciprocity and collaboration in a common economic enterprise.

Welfare capitalism was a specific managerial strategy that emerged especially in the post World War I period, offering certain benefits to workers. These ranged from concrete economic improvements, such as paid vacations and pension plans, to more nebulous workplace beautification schemes and the subsidization of sports and leisure activities for workers. Factory lunch rooms, corporate tennis courts made available to workers, and company-sponsored singing societies or baseball teams might all be parts of elaborate welfare capitalist innovations. In the period after the labour revolt of 1919, many industrial employers experimented with these schemes as a means of facilitating workplace harmony. For example, in the steel industry, historian Craig Heron found that new developments included safety programs, pensions, and an in-house employee newsletter, while in the textile town studied by Joy Parr, the employer sponsored a Pleasure Club with dances and card parties, as well as sporting events and picnics.

Paternalism and welfare capitalism, as Sangster shows, could overlap, reinforcing each other, particularly in hard times such as the Great Depression. They were also fundamentally gendered practices: there were different benefits provided to, even owed, men and women, and the sexual division of labour in the workplace became intertwined with paternalist practices. Interviewing workers, Sangster asked how they experienced work and leisure at Westclox, looking especially at activities, such as the softball team, designed to secure women's loyalty to the firm. By drawing on employers' and workers' experiences as articulated in their recollections, the article attempts to understand paternalism not simply as a manipulative employer strategy but as a negotiated exchange that working women and men engaged in and constructed for their purposes. She thus shows that even employer-initiated approaches to managing tensions arising in workplaces might be both accommodated and adapted to new purpose in the give-and-take of class relations.

A fundamental reason that employers embraced both paternalism and welfare capitalism was to keep unions out of the workplace. In the 1950s, when far more industrial workers were unionized, and the monetary advantages of work at Westclox were disappearing, workers turned their backs on paternalism, and formed a union. Peter McInnis's article explores this critical post-war period in Canadian labour history, examining the origins and impact of the Fordist 'accord', or post-World War II settlement. Taking a different approach from Sangster's microstudy, McInnis provides a national overview of relations among the state, employers, and trade union leaderships, asking how and why this unwritten agreement—often referred to as an 'industrial pluralist accommodation' or the arrival of 'industrial legality'—emerged.

The seeds of the post-war accord, McInnis shows, were planted in the labour relations of World War II, symbolized by the creation of Labour Management Production Committees that were designed to keep output for the war effort at a maximum pace and efficiency. The legal status of trade unions changed substantially during the war. Production, heralded as critical to the national interest, increased dramatically: between 1939 and 1944, economic output rose by two-thirds. After the misery of unemployment during the Depression, jobs were readily available and workers used the opportunity of full employment to try and better wages and secure new rights in the workplace. The number of unionized workers doubled between 1939 and 1945, and a strike wave of considerable strength occurred in the early years of the war, from 1941 to 1943. In response, the federal government passed Privy Council Order 1003, a wartime measure that codified a new industrial relations regime designed to reduce strikes and stabilize class relations. This 'strategic compromise' gave workers the right to their own elected representatives and required employers to engage in collective bargaining in good faith. Unfair labour practices for both labour and employers were defined and fairly stringent regulations on union certification were laid out. In the post-war period, provinces looked to the example of PC 1003, setting up similar legislation as well as provincial Labour Relations Boards to act as legal intermediaries between workers and employers.

Another plank in the Fordist accord was laid in the aftermath of a strike of Ford autoworkers in Windsor, Ontario in 1945. Called in to mediate the rowdy revolt, Supreme Court Justice Ivan Rand sought a means of stabilizing class relations and evening out the power imbalance between labour and capital. His solution, now known as the Rand formula, gave unions new legitimacy by requiring employers to 'check off' union dues from workers' paychecks. An individual worker did not have to join the union, but these dues went to the union, a recognition that unions bargained for and benefited all workers in a given factory or plant.

McInnis's discussion of the Fordist accord takes place against this backdrop of highly significant changes in industrial relations, which, in effect, secured Canadian trade unions collective bargaining rights and material securities unprecedented in the history of the country's development. During the war, Labour Production Committees were intended to facilitate dialogue and collaboration between worker and employer in order to reduce workplace conflict and maintain war production at a high level.

After the war, new forms of accommodation flowed in the wake of the 'industrial pluralist' regime. Premised on notions of mass consumption and high productivity, the Fordist post-war settlement was rooted in the need to tame the turmoil of class relations and ensure uninterrupted production: far-seeing employers and a state struggling to keep the lid on explosive class antagonisms were willing to concede union rights to workers to secure this much-desired end. The Fordist accord ushered into being a modern labour relations system heavily dependent on legalism: both trade unions and employers, once used to battle for control of the production process, now found themselves ensnared in provincial labour codes, complicated collective agreements that grew from a dozen pages to multi-volume tomes, and reliant on lawyers and other expert advisers. For their part, unions grew more bureaucratic, and trade union officialdoms were distanced from their memberships. McInnis also shows how such developments were gendered in their implicit assumptions about working-class life. The high-wage, secure unionism of the mass production industry was the core of the Fordist accord, and it assumed a male breadwinner and a married female homemaker managing 'consumption'. The labour movements' pursuit of purchasing power as its strategy in the post-war period, and its abnegation of workplace militancy, some historians now argue, thus had some negative consequences for the working class as a whole, and especially for women workers. If the post-war settlement provided labour with new legal rights and entitlements that had been fought for over the hard course of many decades, it also tied workers to more 'accommodationist' tactics and perspectives. Moreover, as subsequent articles in this collection indicate, not all workers benefited from the Fordist accord: many women, immigrant, and non-Anglo workers occupied a 'second tier' in the hierarchical labour market. They lacked the high wages, union securities, and other material benefits that the post-war settlement provided to selective groups within the broad Canadian working class.

Carmela Patrias's discussion of employment discrimination and state complicity in the 'racialization' of specific sectors of the Canadian working class in the World War II period underscores the insight that the Fordist accord of this period was weighted down with the wages of whiteness. As Patrias shows, 'race' remained a point of division among the nation's workers, one that employers and the state exacerbated. Her article makes distinctions between the treatment of various ethnic, racialized, and Aboriginal labouring groups during this period. She also shows that many workers and ethnic/ human rights organizations were not only aware of the state's complicity with employer discrimination, but they also tried to counter these practices with evidence gathering and political lobbying. When Canada was promoting a war to supposedly defend 'democracy', they argued, how could it sanction prejudice and racism on the home front? Her article highlights that even in the midst of monumental change, continuities in the history of subordination characterized Canadian class relations. The more some things changed, the more, sadly, others seemed to remain the same.

Further Reading

Irving Martin Abella, *Nationalism, Communism, and Canadian Labour: The CIO, the Communist Party of Canada, and the Canadian Congress of Labour, 1935–1956* (Toronto: University of Toronto Press, 1973).

Michael Earle, ed., *Workers and the State in Twentieth-Century Nova Scotia* (Fredericton, New Brunswick: Acadiensis Press, 1989).

Judy Fudge and Eric Tucker, *Labour Before the Law: The Regulation of Workers' Collective Action in Canada, 1900–1948* (Toronto: Oxford University Press, 2001).

H.M Grant, 'Solving the Labour Problem at Imperial Oil: Welfare Capitalism in the Canadian Petroleum Industry, 1919–1929', *Labour/Le Travail* 41 (Spring 1998): 69–95.

Craig Heron, *Working in Steel: The Early Years in Canada, 1883–1935* (Toronto: McClelland and Stewart, 1988).

Laurel Sefton Macdowell, 'The Formation of the Canadian Industrial Relations System during World War II', *Labour/Le Travail* 3 (1978): 175–96.

Joy Parr, *The Gender of Breadwinners: Women, Men, and Change in Two Industrial Towns, 1880–1950* (Toronto: University of Toronto Press, 1990).

Bob Russell, *Back to Work? Labour, State, and Industrial Relations in Canada* (Scarborough: Nelson, 1990).

Visual Resources

NFB, *A Man and His Job* (1943), dir. Alister Taylor, 17 minutes (traces a 'typical' Canadian worker from the Great Depression through World War II, stressing the creation of unemployment insurance).

NFB, *Defying the Law* (1997), dir. Richard Nielsen, 47 minutes (documents one of the key strikes of the post-World War II period, the 1946 strike of steel workers in Hamilton, Ontario).

NFB, *Canada's Sweetheart: The Saga of Hal Banks* (1985), dir. Donald Brittain, 114 minutes (the story of the Cold War and the destruction of the Canadian Seaman's Union).

NFB, *The Un-Canadians* (1996), dir. Len Scher, 72 minutes (explores the Cold War, the blacklist, and RCMP security investigations in Canada).

NFB, *Needles and Pins* [How They Saw Us] (1955), dir. Ann Pearson and Roger Blais, 10 minutes (shows the life of a factory seamstress and member of the ILGWV, who participates in the annual 'Baldes Midinettes').

CHAPTER 15

The Softball Solution: Female Workers, Male Managers, and the Operation of Paternalism at Westclox, 1923–1960

Joan Sangster

I always said that we didn't need a union there because we were treated so well. It was a nice place . . . I had nice friends . . . Plus we were fairly well paid. A lot of today's troubles come from unions.

Management had the whole picture; they knew the situation best.[1]

These retrospective observations of former workers at a Peterborough clock factory reflect common characterizations of this workplace by women who once assembled the minute, inner workings of the famous Westclox alarm clocks and watches. . . . Within this small Ontario manufacturing city, no other factory with hundreds of employees could claim so effective a management strategy, or so loyal and respectful a workforce. While this cannot be measured 'objectively' through statistics such as workplace longevity, it can be measured subjectively through the way in which former Westclox workers construct their memories, endorsing the familial metaphor promoted by the Company.

It is my intention to examine the rise and decline of paternalism in this factory, exploring both managerial intentions and worker responses, with special emphasis on women's understanding of the workplace hierarchy. . . . Westclox's initial success in this small, ethnically homogeneous Ontario city emerged from its overlapping strategies of nineteenth-century paternalism and twentieth-century welfare capitalism, made possible by the distinct material and cultural conditions in this workplace, industry, and locale. Secondly,

paternalism was a managerial strategy which embodied a gender ideology of male dominance; its operation was intertwined with and aided by a gender hierarchy found in the family, wider community, and the workplace, which ultimately supported women's secondary status as daughters in the Westclox family.

Finally, women's own memories of work at Westclox illuminate the way in which workers understood, utilized, negotiated, and eventually repudiated paternalism; their recollections suggest a more complex relationship between manager and worker than mere rebellion against, or sycophantic acceptance of the Company's aims. In trying to map workers' responses to paternalism, oral history is especially useful as a means of probing the subjective areas of experience and feeling.[2] . . . The structure of memory and the emphasis, tone, and language of interviews provide insight into how experience and ideology shaped the outlook and choices of women workers, and thus how accommodation operated in the factory. If we are to comprehend working-class support for the economic status quo, and attempt to theorize about consent in the workplace,[3] then we must listen to the voices of the workers who embraced or at least tolerated paternalism as part of their daily efforts to survive the difficulties of wage labour.

Paternalism and Welfare Capitalism

Often applied to nineteenth-century industrial experiments, the term paternalism conjures up images of a single entrepreneur who 'ruled his works and his workers directly from some large baronial home overlooking the industrial village' (Heron, 1988: 100). Drawing on previous forms of deference within the church, the community, or especially the household, the owner attempted to incorporate these social relations into the factory regime. . . . Paternalism was intended to avoid labour unrest, to preserve managerial authority, and to satisfy a patrician sense of philanthropy.[4] While often cloaked in a rationale of obligation, duty, or honour, paternalism essentially justified, extended, or at most modified existing power relationships. . . .

The twentieth century supposedly inaugurated a 'professionalism' of paternalism with the introduction of welfare plans and a trained workforce of welfare and personnel specialists (Brandes, 1976; Nelson, 1975; Brody, 1980).[5] Replacing the fatherly factory head was the corporate practice of organized, efficient welfare capitalism, which still contained some of the basic principles of paternalism: the familial metaphor; the endeavour to create a Company culture of consensus, deference, and accommodation; and attempts to maintain a loyal, long-lasting, and of course, un-unionized workforce. . . . In the Westclox case, the introduction of welfare capitalism and modern personnel management did not preclude the persistence of some nineteenth-century forms of paternalism: the two existed together.

In examining the operation of paternalism (a term I use to include both traditional paternalism and organized welfare capitalism), two interlocking power relationships must be highlighted. First, paternalism was premised on fundamentally unequal economic relations, though there were also possibilities of negotiation and bargaining embedded in these power relations. To see paternalism as only a form of clever managerial social control is to simplify its operation and render

the workers in such a system passive, malleable, and without agency. While the labour movement was understandably suspicious of welfare capitalism, some workers were sympathetic to it, and their outlook cannot be dismissed simply as 'false consciousness'. Not only does this obscure the multi-layered and contradictory nature of consciousness (for consent and class consciousness may well coexist), but it also overlooks the fact that struggle between groups with unequal power may proceed on many levels, and that 'class conflict may involve those with power avoiding confrontation with those without it,'[6] and those without power bargaining in sporadic, informal, even unconscious ways.

Nonetheless, the subtle, but powerful process of ideological hegemony sustaining paternalism must still be highlighted.[7] In order to interpret their workplace experiences, workers inevitably drew on the ideological resources at their disposal, and the dominant ideology—experienced as lived, habitual practice, interwoven throughout the culture, discerned as 'common sense'—justified existing corporate leadership and the 'natural' existence of gender and class stratification.[8] One manifestation of the ideological hegemony of those with social and economic power, paternalism encouraged consent to economic hierarchy as an inevitable part of daily life: in a Gramscian sense, it successfully 'universalized ruling class interest with community interest' (Boggs, 1984: 160).

Paternalism was also a power relationship based on notions of gender difference and structures of gender inequality. Feminist historians have argued persuasively that we need to understand the ways in which the family and the workplace were interlocking hierarchies of dominance and negotiation, with class and gender constructed simultaneously.[9] . . . Nineteenth-century paternalism, argues Judy Lown, did not simply draw superficially on familial metaphors; rather, male dominance was an 'organizing principle' (Lown, 1985: 34) of paternalist workplace relations. Similarly, the Westclox example demonstrates the centrality of gender ideology to paternalism, and consequently, the need for a feminist analysis of the material and ideological processes behind its operation.

Establishing the 'Westclox Way' in Canada

. . .The Canadian Westclox plant grew along with the American parent: in 1926, it employed 180, by the late 1930s, approximately 400, and during the Second World War, its payroll hit an all-time high of 800. Although male employees outnumbered women in the Company's infancy, women soon became a majority of about 60 per cent (during the war their numbers, as well as their percentage of the workforce, rose even higher). . . . Until the 1960s, Westclox was seen as a stable Peterborough employer that had a 'complete manufacturing operation', (Company pamphlet, *c.* 1978) including design, industrial engineering, and accounting as well as assembly. One person dominates the history of the Canadian Westclox: its general manager and later president, J.H. Vernor. Originally associated with the export division of the American Westclox, Vernor had given up medical education to work as export manager for Westclox. In 1922, he and his wife returned to North America from their European posting so that Vernor could oversee the construction of the Canadian branch plant. Until his retirement in 1953, Vernor was the guiding force of Company personnel policy,[10] though Company administration was also strongly influenced by the American parent, which trained many Canadian administrators in managerial exchange programs.

Vernor saw himself in the terms familiar to paternalist enterprise: as the concerned, but disciplinarian father. He was referred to in the community as 'Mr Westclox' (*Peterborough Examiner*, 20 July 1966), a term he actually promoted. In their recollections, employees repeat this nickname, and some clearly adopted, at some level, the familial analogy of Vernor watching over his employees like a father. One even mused that because Vernor was childless himself, he invested inordinate interest and energy in his surrogate children, his employees.

Indeed, it is revealing that many employees have constructed their memories of the Company around a narrative theme that stresses the rise and decline of the family—like an epic saga—at Westclox, which roughly (though not completely accurately) coincides with the Company's financial success and decline.[11] In this narrative theme, the 'family' and the business enterprise have merged, their fate tied to the story of a man whose health and spirit went downhill along with the factory: the economic vigour of the factory and workers' job security clearly help to shape the collective script of their stories. . . . In the Westclox script, Vernor, the young, dashing executive, popular with most of his employees, ages rapidly in the postwar years as the closely knit family becomes more troubled and stressed, less cohesive and congenial. In some oral accounts, unionization in 1952 symbolized the inauguration of a new era and the rejection of the older family, along with its father. 'The union broke Vernor's heart—Westclox was his family,' commented one employee.[12]

It was not simply Vernor's use of the familial metaphor, however, which kept Westclox from unionizing until relatively late, prevented any strikes, and produced a paternalistic workplace. First of all, paternalism was necessarily constructed on the edifice of unequal economic power: material constraints should not be minimized in the paternalist equation for they provided the essential backdrop for the factory's authority structure. As Patrick Joyce notes, 'power relations are a precondition for [paternalism] . . . vulnerability sows the seeds of deference' (Joyce, 1980: 94).

The Westclox factory was quite tightly controlled by managerial prerogative: until after World War Two, a number of managers and foreman were influential in hiring and firing, and in assigning work duties. Hiring, remembers some former workers, seemed personal and arbitrary; one worker remembers Vernor talking to him briefly, 'making a few scratchy notes', then saying 'you're hired.'[13] In 1945, a separate personnel department was set up at the urging of the parent company which feared its unorganized workforce would be stirred by the wave of unionization sweeping North America. Even after this, Vernor and other managers took a personal interest in hiring, with recommendations of family and friends carrying weight in their decisions. As a former manager put it, 'there were names that immediately boded well for you, but others that meant instant disaster . . . forget this talk about nepotism . . . it was just a form of reference.'[14]

Securing jobs for kin, keeping a job during the Depression, choosing where one wanted to work within the factory: these were the economic pressures that employees had to consider when interacting with their superiors. Because jobs were often secured through family, women also develop-ed a sense of 'debt' to their employer, particularly during the Depression; as Joy Parr argues in her case study, workers felt 'they owed their jobs to their patrons' (Parr, 1990: 35). During the worst of the Depression, the factory reduced the work week and instituted job sharing in order to keep people at least partially employed, a measure which accentuated a sense of obligation to the Company. Indeed, in comparison to the often-cited American example, the Depression could actually give pater-nalism a new lease on life. . . .

The regulation of the work process also provided clues to the operation of paternalism.

At first glance, the work process, especially for women, appeared tightly controlled. Although some skilled men, like the tool and die makers, exercised considerable authority over their work conditions, women were primarily assigned to repetitive jobs in assembly line work that were often compensated through piece rates or produc-tion targets. In the office, women's work was closely supervised and their polite demeanour noted when it came to promotions and raises, which were individually assigned, as no clear job posting system existed until the 1950s.

Many blue-collar women worked on an assembly line characteristic of the new 'mass industries' of the twentieth century: the principle was based on a carefully engineered, continuous flow work process which could mass produce goods relatively cheaply for a growing consumer market.[15] Women's work was characterized by machine pacing of the job, by 'indirect assembly' (Glucksman, 1980: 154) (as opposed to direct servicing of machines), and by the extensive use of some kind of piece or incentive pay. Jobs could be broken down into minute and exact parts which were repeated again and again. Moreover, some of the assembly line work at the plant was extremely fine work, for which women were given finger dexterity and eyesight tests (though it was also claimed that dexterity and careful attention to detail were inherently-female attributes).

Within this fairly rigid structure, however, there existed a small degree of flexibility which assisted the Company's efforts to 'manufacture consent'[16] by mitigating the intrinsic alienation of wage labour. For one thing, the actual number of different jobs (however monotonous each one was) was greater here than in local factories like the textile mill, and because management was sympa-thetic to mobility within the plant, women could change positions if they really wanted to. Even more important was the degree of autonomy and respect built into the system of supervision. When former women workers describe why they stayed at Westclox, they often emphasize the atmosphere, nature of supervision, and flexibility on the shop floor. Supervision and the practice of paternalism interacted on one another, with the paternalist philosophy of the Company creating the precise shape of authority relations in the workplace. Women, for example, might be allowed to 'sneak out' a few minutes early to catch their train home for the weekend, workplace joking and socializing were given fairly elastic boundaries, and the continuous-flow assembly work, though seen as taxing and difficult, was not continually and arbitrarily pushed to its limit with speed-ups—at least not in the early years before Westclox's financial problems became visible.

Foremen were also trained to listen and mediate, rather than reject complaints, and especially not to embarrass or humiliate women workers. Almost every female informant commented positively on the manner in which their male foremen dealt with conflict and grievances. 'We were taken aside, never embarrassed in front of others on the line,' remembers one woman. 'I learned *never* to dismiss a complaint,' recalls a former manager. J.H. [Vernor] once took a strip off me for brushing off a complaint . . . I listened, even if the complaint didn't seem [justified].'[17] Some women claimed to prefer this conciliatory method to later union practices, as the latter tended to be more confrontational, drawing attention to the griever as 'the union was always looking for an issue to hold over the Company's head.'[18] . . .

Managers were encouraged to deal with men under them in a somewhat different manner, with an eye to creating a feeling of male partnership, even though the workers knew this to be something of an illusion. In one meeting, a foreman was severely and humiliatingly 'chewed out' by a

manager in front of his peers. His response was to pull a different kind of rank on the manager—that of moral superiority and reference to the comradeship preached by the Company. 'I might be a farmer's son and you a university grad' he replied, 'but you can't treat me that way, and if you do, I'm quitting.'[19] The manager backed down, and the foreman's tactics were applauded by his colleagues who had absorbed the Westclox message that position and class differences could not, at least, be flaunted, and that all workers deserved respect. . . .

While styles of supervision were important to workers, material rewards were also part of the paternalist bargain: Westclox's early attempts to establish good pay and benefits compared to other industries in Peterborough helped create an informal peace treaty with labour. By paying one or two cents more an hour than other factories and providing paid vacations, the Company hoped to procure better-educated workers, increase productivity, and secure a stable workforce. From the outset, the Company also carefully 'planned production almost a year in advance in order to regularize employment',[20] thus creating workers' loyalty. Because this was not a one-company town, Westclox management felt it had to compete for skilled male labour, but they also extended this strategy to include female workers. . . .

Given the relative prosperity of the 1920s, and a measure of tariff protection in the interwar years, it made good business sense to inaugurate a personnel policy which utilized the lure of benefits to secure long-term investment in employee stability—something that was to change with different economic conditions 30 years later. These welfare capitalist policies were also clearly motivated by a desire to avoid unionization, but to young women seeking jobs in the interwar period and even the early 1940s, this goal did not worry them.[21] Time and again, women remember the sense of competition for the few openings at Westclox. One woman climbed the hill day after day to ask if there was a position; another, lacking a family member there, babysat for a foreman and persuaded him to speak for her.

While many companies assumed women were not interested in benefit plans, women did consider these part of the allure of employment at Westclox.[22] On top of paid vacations, available after five years of service (one of the most attractive benefits), there was also a group insurance plan, instituted from the beginning, which the employer paid. From the 1930s on, employees could also contribute to a jointly-paid sick leave plan, but a pension plan didn't appear until 1940. There was also a number of less costly benefits, though ones which the company loudly advertised, such as a cafeteria with cheap hot meals, tennis courts on the grounds, and an infirmary. . . .

While many of these benefits were standard ingredients of welfare capitalism, an important element of the company's paternalism was the personal and discretionary way that benefits were imparted: nineteenth-century paternalism thus overlapped with twentieth-century welfarism. In a confidential survey returned to the Ontario Department of Labour in 1927, the company revealed that in 'deserving cases, money was sometimes lent on the quiet for house buying' but at the same time the survey recorded that 'Vernor hates anything paternal.'[23] While understanding the pejorative connotation of the word, he was still willing to apply its principles.

Until a union contract of 1952, there was no official bereavement leave and pay; before that, management created, on an ad-hoc basis, similar benefits for some employees. One long-time blue-collar employee, whom Vernor knew well, remembered the situation when her father died. Not only

was she was given time off, but Vernor lent the family his car for the funeral and when he came to pay his respects, he shook hands and discreetly left a 20-dollar bill behind—a personal contribution to the funeral expenses which families sometimes found hard to meet. While most women report similar instances of sympathetic paternalism, a former secretary noted that when her mother died, the company sent for her at the funeral home to come and finish some special typing only she had done in the past; paternalism, in other words, was arbitrarily applied.

These discretionary benefits were important for they reinforced ties of loyalty and obligation between boss and worker, sometimes so successfully that workers began to *interpret* legal rights as personal gifts. Even after a sick benefits plan was introduced, Vernor told a woman office worker to 'let him know if she needed time off because there was a sickness in the family'[24] so he could arrange it, an incident then translated as evidence of his flexibility and concern. Another blue-collar employee praised Vernor for his concern with the personal safety of his female employees who had to be taxied home after midnight shifts during the war years. Although she was very vaguely aware that this was required by law, she primarily saw Vernor's hand in it: 'the taxi driver had to wait until we were in the door . . . and if he didn't, we were supposed to notify Mr Vernor about [it].'[25]

Women and Men in the Westclox 'Family'

When former workers offered positive interpretations of company paternalism, most did not employ a language of worker deference, as much as they used familial metaphors which were intimately connected to the sexual division of labour in the plant, and to notions of female respectability and male breadwinning. Westclox promoted a sexual division of labour that was characterized by women's exclusion from supervisory positions and apprenticeships, and from heavy work in shipping and automatics, along with their concentration in assembly line work, tasks like washing clock faces that approximated domestic labour, some smaller punch-press jobs, and clerical work. Women's relegation to these job ghettoes was rationalized on two bases: the male breadwinner ideology and women's 'natural' physical differences, especially their nimble fingers and ability to tolerate fine eye work. While a former manager claimed that the Company simply 'hired for the job', he also saw some impermeable gender boundaries: 'you wouldn't hire a man to knit would you? His fingers were too big and clumsy . . . girls are much more adaptable to assembly work.'[26]

Explanations for this sexual division of labour were often interwoven with descriptions of paternalism in the factory; accounts of why and how the sexual division of labour existed are characterized by a familial discourse within which women workers assume the role of daughters and maiden aunts, while men assume the role of sons. The latter role, of course, was constructed in a particularly patriarchal manner, with younger men under the control of older ones, but always with the prospect of advancing themselves into positions of power. . . .

Not only were men promoted internally, but the bonds of male solidarity were also cemented by perks like a club house for foremen and managers on the Westclox property, and by men's social events such as golf stags, poker nights, and Vernor's annual foremen's picnic held at his cottage on Buckhorn Lake. Here, male camaraderie was reinforced with activities like fishing derbies, horseshoes, cards, and, one assumes, drinking as well, as Vernor was not known as an

abstainer. Indeed, some of the men whom Vernor came to know well helped to 'protect' his public image by buying his scotch for him; after a court appearance for an impaired drinking charge in 1954, however, Vernor's reputation became more public (*Peterborough Examiner*, 1 December 1954). Male bonding thus temporarily superseded class hierarchy, even though Vernor always made it clear that respect for his title should take precedence within the factory. Fraternal loyalties may also have played a role in cementing these male ties: both Vernor and the (later) General Manager Cranford were active Masons, as were some of the workers on the shop floor.

What role did women's labour play in this family? As with domestic labour, women's wage labour sustained the enterprise but was also undervalued, and did not lead to possibilities of significant advancement and power. The distinction between the paternalism directed towards men and women was the way in which sons might prosper in the family, but women could only maintain their secondary roles. As daughters primarily interested in temporary wage work and ultimately marriage, women were presumed to be satisfied with smaller wage packets, a view many women, even some single career women, remember endorsing. The one way that women could use the Company's emphasis on internal promotion and discretionary paternalism was to advance from blue- to white-collar work, which offered better working conditions, more interesting work, and higher status, if not better wages. Though this promotion ladder was truncated compared to men's, it was appealing to some working-class women, especially those whose education had been cut short during the Depression.[27]

The one group of women who did not fit into this familial model were single, 'career' women who chose to pursue wage work rather than marry. Interestingly, these women are sometimes described with metaphors which suggest their role as 'spinsters' or maiden aunts—as determined, unusual, even eccentric women—or alternatively as dutiful daughters, who in their own way, were also playing the appropriate familial roles by caring for aging parents. 'You must talk to "Susan", I was told by one manager, you know she was really a "good girl". . . she worked all her life, lived at home, and looked after her mother until she died.'[28] . . .

Even after women were allowed to work after marriage, the paternalism accorded men and women remained a feature of factory life. By rationalizing its hiring decisions and the gendered division of labour with appeals to innate sexual abilities and the male breadwinner ideal,[29] the Company incorporated gender ideology directly into its managerial strategy. These assumptions reinforced the notions that women were less concerned with autonomy and control over their work, were less suited to supervise, and that women's wage work was secondary to domestic duties.

The incorporation of paternal assumptions into the dominant characterization of white-collar work was especially noteworthy; the attributes of a good white-collar worker underlined a paternal relationship between female worker and male supervisor. Good work habits—punctuality, preciseness, politeness, pleasant personality—were essentially seen as 'female' attributes, and as Margery Davies points out, the very language used to describe the ideal secretary—as adaptable, deferential, a good listener, and nice looking—in fact, 'cast her in a female role as office daughter/wife' (Davies, 1982: 155).

Such assumptions both reflected and were bolstered by prevailing gender ideology. Women workers recall accepting the 'natural' placement of men over women on the job, and the characterization of men's work as important, women's

as less important. Blue- and white-collar women alike spoke of the need to respect male supervisors because of their greater experience, skill, and knowledge. 'My manager,' recalled one woman 'said we really didn't know half of what went on' and how the workplace operated, and 'I guess he [was right].'[30] Women's accommodation to the gendered hierarchy at work was reproduced not only through the daily practice of a sexual division of labour, but also through the notions of masculinity and femininity, and the gendered meanings of experience, skill, and the right to work which women absorbed from the wider cultural context. Gender ideology thus assisted the acceptance of male authority as natural and inevitable, and helped create the paternal—and patriarchal—workplace.

Earlier research has argued that both male and female workers were 'rendered childlike' by paternalism, which also 'undermined [men's] sense of identity as breadwinners' (Brandes, 1976: 140), but this obscures paternalism's inherent rationalization of gender divisions within the factory. As in a patriarchal family, some men could assume control, at least in theory, over women. The same was true for Westclox sons, but obviously not for its daughters.

There were other differences between the treatment of sons and daughters; for example, the moral protection of women, not men, was a concern of the Company. It is often assumed that such moral paternalism did not persist past the Progressive-era schemes of employers to emphasize feminine skills and moral protection in their welfare plans for women; yet, at Westclox, quite the opposite was true.[31] Although the image of what a respectable working girl's social life was like did change after 1920, with activities like dancing increasingly taken for granted, anxiety about sexual morality and marriageability remained a subtext of concern. Many veiled references to sexual respectability, to the 'better class' of girl who was hired in the 1930s and 1940s, especially before the company went downhill by the 1960s, indicates how the theme of sexual propriety of the daughters was also tied into the narrative theme of family decline. Other local factories were contrasted to Westclox: the textile mill which employed many women was referred to as 'tough, you know, you had a tough name if you worked there. My wife lived near there, but her father wouldn't let her get a job there.'[32] The way that the word nice was used made it clear that moral respectability was at issue. As one manager commented: 'We hired very nice girls [at Westclox]. We were careful about that, to hire good girls, respectable girls. You could be a preacher's daughter and work at Westclox, you know.'[33] Former workers made the same connection, implying that it drew in a more educated, and thus respectable class of women: 'We took the cream of the crop . . . we even had schoolteachers there. . . . But after the war, it was harder to find people and we had to take some we didn't really want.'[34] . . .

It was assumed that a 'good' female worker also meant one who was above moral reproach. Extremely revealing is the incident involving a woman who had already been interviewed and offered a job in the postwar period only to be phoned back and told there were no openings available; a male worker who had witnessed part of the interview had informed a manager that she was living immorally with a married man. Notwithstanding the many implications of this episode—including the gender solidarity evidenced and how easily small-town gossip can ruin a woman's reputation—the message was quite clear: she was promiscuous and therefore should be denied the job. 'If you hire a few like that,' one male interviewee commented, then 'all the girls are tainted with the same brush.'[35] . . .

The company's attempt to champion the morality and respectability of its women workers was not entirely unwelcome among female employees in the 1930s and 1940s. This dimension of paternalism offered women, especially those in the plant, some reciprocal psychological benefits, by countering a prevailing image of the 'tough' factory girl, which many women workers resented. Women who worked in other heavier industries in the city like General Electric and Outboard Marine lamented that factory women were viewed as less feminine or refined: tough and rough were the two words commonly used. Apprehension about blue-collar work was symbolized in the references to cleanliness and dress; the sight of coveralls, even during World War Two, carried with it fears of endangered femininity. Women who worked at Westclox, on the other hand, constantly cited their clean workplace and the fact that they could wear what they wanted as evidence of their better class of employment, especially in comparison to the 'dirty, dark'[36] General Electric. It is noteworthy that one of the few women who worked in a dirtier area of Westclox, automatics, sometimes felt slighted by the girls on the upper floors who she thought believed themselves superior to her. Other historians have pointed to the symbolic importance of dress for working women as signs of their 'orderly',[37] successful, or respectable character; for Westclox women, dress, cleanliness, and an impeccable reputation offered them a modicum of respectability which they felt was denied them by prevailing images of factory workers.

The appeal to a sense of respectability may have also been shaped by ethnic homogeneity and exclusivity as well. Like the city itself, the plant was predominantly Anglo-Celtic in character.[38] Although there was occasional Catholic/Protestant rivalry in the plant, women were ultimately drawn together more from a sense of being upright and respectable than they were separated by religious differences. Those religious differences which did occasionally surface were tempered by the company's conscious personnel strategy of hiring Catholics in proportion to their numbers in the city and opening up skilled positions 'elsewhere under control of the Masons' to Catholic men. 'I remember our priest saying out how good [Vernor] was to East City' remembers a male worker. 'He praised J.H. up and down for hiring Catholics.'[39] By carefully attending to religious tensions, Vernor was able, again, to bolster his image as fair-minded and generous to the local community.

Company Sports and Newspapers

It was not only through the provision of material benefits and support for notions of respectability that Westclox sustained its paternalism. The company's on-site clubhouse and tennis courts as well as its careful maintenance of extensive gardens and lawns (and its advertisement of its civic awards for the best kept industrial workplace) all were designed to create a 'homelike' atmosphere. Company rituals, especially those geared to Westclox children, such as picnics and Christmas parties, and those geared to long service, such as retirement dinners and the Quarter Century Club events, were also very important. Many who attended the Quarter Century Club and retirement dinners characterize these events as lavish affairs, which they see as evidence of the company's magnanimity. One employee proudly repeated, in her interview, word for word, the acceptance poem she delivered when she received her 25-year award.

Other initiatives were probably more important: one of these was the encouragement of recreation and athletics for employees. J.H. Vernor supported the creation of industrial league teams for both men and women and donated money to rent the YWCA for team sports, sometimes personally passing on the cheque through an employee. Westclox's community name, however, was best known for its women's softball team. When I began to interview employees, I was repeatedly urged to seek out the women ballplayers; Westclox's name was still intimately associated with sports in many former employees' minds.

Women workers were sometimes ballplayers scouted out by coaches concerned more with team than with manpower needs in the plant. One woman remembers that even before she finished high school 'they were hot and heavy after me to play softball for them . . . but my mother put her foot down as she wanted me to finish my business training.'[40] When another teenager was approached by the coaches before her sixteenth birthday, her parents were also consulted, a sign not only of her youth, but also of company scruples against interfering with traditional family authority. One woman was recruited by her sister, already a Westclox athlete: 'I went there to play in the sports. I think you'll find a lot of the girls did the same thing. They got jobs to play softball, basketball. My sister got the job first, then Mr Vernor, who was the president needed another player [so I was hired].'[41]

Women on the Westclox team practised regularly, competed fiercely, and did well: in 1945 they were runner-up for the provincial championship. The company outfitted the women with uniforms, paid for buses to transport them across the province, and, although the women were not supposed to get extra perks at work, some lateness might occasionally be accepted when they were playing for championships out of town. When one ballplayer sprained her ankle, Vernor sent a truck to pick her up every day so that she could make it to work.

Sports were meant to create a sense of company loyalty, suggesting competition with the outside, but team effort inside; they were supposed to create a loyal, disciplined, and committed workforce that strove to give its best performance on and off the job. Anxious to cash in on the popularity of amateur sports in the interwar years (Betke, 1975),[42] the company also saw sports teams as a good source of advertising: they made the Westclox name known outside of Peterborough, and reinforced a positive view of the company in the town. Nor did this end with the war; if anything, an emphasis on sports increased in the 1940s.[43] . . .

Listening to women's subjective memories of industrial sports suggests a different perspective: the actual meaning sports had for players might differ from the intentions of team promoters (Adilman, 1989). Women who played on Westclox teams enjoyed the physical competition and public visibility involved. When a woman from the Westclox basketball team remembered her exhibition game with the famous Edmonton Grads, she noted how exhilarating it was to play, by boys' rules, and to a large crowd, if only to lose to such competitive, top-notch players. Ballplayers recall with pride the spectators, especially other Westclox employees, who filled the stands; there was no mistaking the sense of public presence articulated by one woman who told me 'that [baseball diamond] at [Riverside park] *belonged* to us girls . . . then later, the men took it over.'[44] 'Years later,' a star player remembered nostalgically, 'someone would come up to me on the street downtown and say, "I remember you pitching for Westclox"!'[45]

Women's teams drew together a 'specially bonded' (*Peterborough Examiner*, 1990)[46] female community, and at Westclox united office and plant workers, who rarely socialized in other companies. Teams also became a way for married women to continue work and friendly contacts that homemaking denied them after they left the company. One woman, self described as 'ball crazy',[47] continued to play and tour after she left work to have children; she used to take her children to practices and another Westclox friend looked after them. The strong identification of these women with sports may well point to a class dimension missing in the feminist analysis of Canadian sport: Veronica Strong-Boag has suggested that working-class women were perhaps 'less intimidated by stereotypical assumptions' about femininity and thus uniquely placed to take advantage of new team opportunities (Strong-Boag, 1988). The early experience of many of these women playing ball in the streets and fields with brothers and friends, and their later, hearty embrace of sports, indicates this to be true.

To the company, of course, promotion of these teams was a form of boosterism, a means of encouraging company loyalty and keeping good workers. Some women ballplayers remained for years with the company; once established there, the existence of benefit and pension plans encouraged one's decision to remain. And while workers who participated in sports may not have directly shared in the company's goals, sports still had a positive influence on their attitude towards their employer: these women's recollections of work and their attitude towards their employer are clearly coloured by their positive experience of sports. Moreover, for some women, excellence in sports seemed to provide a source of personal identification that helped to overcome the limitations of the glass ceiling encountered at work. . . .

If team sports supplied one glue to cement the Westclox family together, another was the company publication, *Tic Talk*. As Stuart Brandes has argued, company publications were a well-planned strategy to persuade the worker that she had a stake in the company's success, that the company had the economic sense to run the show, and also cared about their personal goals and family life (Brandes, 1976). . . . Like other in-house publications, the Westclox one attempted to create support for company objectives. Basic lessons in economics were standard fare. The hazards of running a profitable business were stressed and concepts like capital formation were made familiar with comparisons to homes and gardens: 'capital formation . . . is just [the same] as when you set up a garden, you buy the necessary tools, fertilizer. . . . It is what every company or country needs to provide jobs for *all of us* [my emphasis] in the coming years' (*Tic Talk*, June 1954). The Horatio Alger myth was also a staple theme, as was the company's good will and connections to the community, its commitment to full employment, and especially its concern for health and safety (though accidents, it was stressed, were invariably the result of individual failings). Changes in company structure were rationalized, particularly down-sizing exercises, increasingly accompanied by veiled warnings that the company was 'vulnerable' because its 'costs of assembly'—especially wages—were too high.[48] Finally, the company's fate, it was stressed, lay in the response of 'Joe Customer' to the quality of its product (*Tic Talk*, December 1956, December 1962). Workers were simultaneously encouraged to see themselves as consumers, thus making the point that workers were the architects of their own employment fate.[49] Indeed, the theme of consumerism ran throughout the publication; the company included ads for its own products and gossip columns abounded with notices of workers' consumer purchases: 'Ethel . . . came in all smiles this morning' noted one writer for *Tic Talk*, 'Her hubby has given her a new radio and hi fi. Add to this the new automatic dryer she got recently and she isn't doing badly!' (*Tic Talk*, December 1959). That Ethel's own wages had been used to make these purchases is not noted.

Tic Talk also promoted a vision of Westclox as a family, and in doing so, reinforced certain images of women's and men's gendered work and family roles: for instance, women's domestic and mothering duties were lauded approvingly, while biographies of long-time employees often confirmed their status as 'good family men'. Family ties were often mentioned as a theme underlying plant relationships; as Fathers' Day approached one year, the editor urged everyone to have a very special 'Westclox Fathers Day' celebration because so many kids had 'followed their dads into the plant' (*Tic Talk*, June 1954). . . .

Nowhere are distinct gender roles more clearly accented than in the extensive gossip columns sent in by worker-writers. The births, deaths, and marriages columns were obviously meant to reinforce a sense of community and overcome the impersonal alienation of factory life. But it was the mating and dating game that clearly drew most reader interest. Here, the dominant social prejudices of the period are replicated with little or no critical comment. Women are supposedly consumed with mating impulses and bliss is achieved when a diamond ring appears. Especially after the war years, women came close to being man hunters: 'she may not be in the RCMP, but she got her man!' (*Tic Talk*, December 1956). Once mated, a woman was then 'out of circulation' (*Tic Talk*, June 1954), no longer fair game for other interested bachelors. Male reporters were almost as concerned with romance, ridiculing fellow workers who were smitten with the 'love bug' and thus would soon lose their manly independence to the trap of marriage (*Tic Talk*, June 1966).[50] Particular relish is shown for in-house romances, which then become a focus for further teasing. Once official, engagements are followed by a number of rituals: departmental showers, parties, and a public gift-giving. With marriage, it is assumed that 'women will now retire to take up another job, home-making' (*Tic Talk*, December 1966), while men will continue to work at the plant. Few references to married working women are made, save for one reporter who notes that the married women are easily noticed by their 'weary faces' (*Tic Talk*, July 1966), a rare comment on the double day. Until the 1960s, one image of the family is made to seem natural and inevitable in these columns: the nuclear, home-owning, mother-at-home, father-at-work family.

The sexes are bound together by dating and mating, and ultimately, 'marriage comes highly recommended' (*Tic Talk*, September 1959) but at the same time, men and women are oceans apart in character and ability—an implicit justification for a division of labour. Women are concerned with beauty and appearance, men with technical knowledge and physical strength. Women's 'known' love of shopping is mentioned frequently, while fishing and hunting are clearly pursuits which preoccupy male departments. Cars are a man's joy, but women are 'the plague of our highways' (*Tic Talk*, September 1959). While car ownership is clearly offering some women new independence by the 1940s, depictions of women's car trips and vacations often carried a punchline describing mishaps or teasing about the potential perils of female independence.

Tic Talk's use of graphics and pictures also exhibited the familial theme; not only were company events showing workers and managers happily leisuring together profiled but many employees sent in their own pictures of family and fellow Westclox friends. . . . Pictures were off-centre, sometimes ill-focused, and completely homegrown; it is this lack of professionalism, ironically, that characterized *Tic Talk*'s success for a feeling of active involvement rather than Company manipulation was created, consciously or not, by this 'family album' approach. Moreover, while both Companies used the publication to promote things like pension plans, GE once used its paper to denounce the union, a mistake Westclox never made.

Although *Tic Talk* columns were occasionally edited, they were also the product of shopfloor banter, which many workers clearly enjoyed. One of the ways in which workers cope with the workplace, Louise Lamphere argues, is to create their own social networks which celebrate life rituals, offer mutual support, and break down the anonymity of the factory (Lamphere, 1985). These social networks may be particularly important to women because they reproduced care-giving roles learned in the family and because women's wage work, which was characterized by little control and autonomy, needed a strong antidote of sociability on the shop floor. By integrating these social networks into its own publication, Westclox was able to promote the image of a humane workplace concerned with workers lives outside the factory. While the company calculated this as a means of securing worker satisfaction and loyalty, workers participated for different reasons: to alleviate boredom, engage in daily gossip (surely one of the most important social staples of our lives), and connect with other people. . . . At the same time, by participating in the company magazine, by endorsing images of male breadwinner and female dependent, male competence and female technical scatterbrain, workers were also legitimizing the division of labour and the existing hierarchy in the factory and in the household. While trying to make the workplace livable, they were unconsciously reproducing its gendered hierarchy.

Conclusion: Paternalism in Decline

Westclox's paternalism was, from the very beginning, part of a conscious strategy to avoid unionization, but the company was ultimately unable to defeat a powerful postwar trend, and in 1952, after more than one union attempt, the plant chose the International Union of Electrical Workers (IUE) as their bargaining agent. Still, the office workers consistently resisted unionization, the plant never went on strike, and the union was considered 'moderate' by others in the vicinity.

Plant workers became sympathetic to unionization when they saw the material benefits of paternalism seriously eroding. As other major Peterborough plants secured good benefit packages, Westclox's former generosity began to look deficient. Once the gap between the promise of paternalism and the reality became quite wide, disappointment set in, perhaps even more strongly because of previously raised hopes of fair dealing on the company's part. With more economic pressure on the company, the shop floor also became more pressured by the 1960s, and the previous bargain of flexibility in work relations deteriorated. . . .

Unionization was an indication that the negotiated partnership and paternalist bargain fostered from the 1920s to the 1940s had begun to erode. As Gerald Zahavi points out, workers tried to use paternalism for their own ends, extracting certain economic and moral obligations from the employer in return for their loyalty (Zahavi, 1988). Women and men at the Westclox plant used the rhetoric of paternalism, and obtained their own rewards, as much as possible, from the company. Men could benefit from a degree of autonomy on the shop floor, hope of upward mobility, a sense of male privilege and camaraderie, and reinforced identification with the image of the masculine breadwinner. Women could also try to use paternalism to make their working conditions humane and flexible; to provide mobility within female job ghettos; and also to reinforce a sense of dignity secured through their status as moral working women. For some individuals, like the favoured softball players, there were other sources of pride and compensation. But decent benefits and wages were always part of the 'deal' that the company fashioned with its workers. If the company let down its part of the bargain, workers felt justified in shifting their allegiance as well. . . .

For many years, Westclox successfully synthesized favourable local and international economic conditions with a policy of moderate benefits and discretionary paternalism. . . . The company's paternalist strategy was perhaps more easily realized in the small-town atmosphere of Peterborough. The geographical proximity of worker and manager in some neighbourhoods and churches, close knowledge of family networks, and a stable social hierarchy bolstered the ideological hegemony operating within the factory, creating the illusion of an 'organic community' in which class and community interest were one and the same. Earlier work has suggested that class consciousness could be 'reinforced by the community solidarity of small towns with stable, homogeneous and familiar populations' (Heron and DeZwaan, 1985).[51] The Westclox example, however, indicates that the social relations of small cities might also inhibit class conflict. Furthermore, Peterborough's distinct labour history, in particular the failure of an industrial strike in textiles in 1937, and the inability of industrial unions to make significant inroads until the later 1940s, also meant that workers did not have at hand institutional or ideological alternatives to the paternalist bargain.

Finally, the resilience of paternalism must also be explained by the ideological creation of consent. Already-existing dominant notions of 'natural' economic hierarchy and inevitable gender differences were diffused through daily workplace practices, company symbols, and rituals. Gender was not peripheral, but rather central to this ideological hegemony. Paternalism was sustained by its assimilation and reproduction of a gender ideology that reinforced an image of female transience and marriageability, male independence and camara-derie, and female obedience and male authority. The workplace hierarchy was fused with gender roles supposedly found in the household and given strong sanction by society. A familial language justified *both* the gendered division of labour in the plant *and* the paternal placement of male managers over female workers; notions of sexual difference explained why males might go from being sons to fathers, while women remained forever daughters.

Significantly, when the company called for a wage roll-back in 1969, it targeted *only* the women workers. When the union appeared to waver on the issue, one female union execu-tive had to write an indignant letter to the union negotiator warning him that women workers were upset about reported 'secret negotiations' between the (male) union and management, and that women would not tolerate union leaders making a backroom deal to sell out the women.[52] When the General Time Empire began to fold in Canada, Westclox women were first asked to pay the price and become even more dependent on the 'father' with lower wages. The fact that the women refused indicates that the paternalist bargain, while appealing, always had its limits.

Notes

1. Westclox Interview #18, February 1990, and #1, July 1989. I have deliberately chosen one quote from a blue-collar worker and one from a white-collar worker.

2. On oral history, see Ronald Grele, *Envelopes of Sound: The Art of Oral History* (Chicago: Praeger, 1975); M. Frisch, 'The Memory of History', *Radical History Review* 24 (1981); or more recently, Sherna Gluck and Daphne Patai, eds, *Women's Words: The Feminist Practice of Oral History* (New York: Routledge, 1991).

3. As Ava Baron points out, in working-class history 'while women's resistance has been documented, their "consent" to oppression, like that of men, remains undertheorized.' Ava Baron, 'Gender and Labor History: Learning from the Past, Looking to the Future', in Baron, ed., *Work Engendered: Toward a New History of American Labor* (Ithaca: Cornell University Press, 1991), 16.

4. On Britain see Patrick Joyce, *Work, Society, and Politics* (London: Methuen, 1980), and more recently Judy Lown, *Women and Industrialization: Gender and Work in Nineteenth Century England* (London: Blackwell, 1990), which addresses the question of gender as a central part of her thesis. See also Donald Reid, 'Industrial Paternalism: Discourse and Practice in Nineteenth Century French Mining and Metallurgy', *Comparative Studies in Society and History* 27 (1985); Charles Dellheim, 'The Creation of a Company Culture: Cadburys, 1861–1961', *AHR* 92, 1 (February 1987). American studies range from those starting with the mid-nineteenth century textile mills to those extending their focus into the twentieth century. See Phillip Scranton, 'Varieties of Paternalism: Industrial Structures and the Social Relations of Production in American Textiles', *American Quarterly* 36 (Summer 1984); Jacqueline Dowd Hall, *Like a Family: The Making of a Southern Cotton Mill World* (Chapel Hill: University of North Carolina Press, 1987); Frances Couvares, *The Remaking of Pittsburgh: Class and Culture in an Industrializing City, 1877–1919* (Albany: SUNY Press, 1984), chap. 7; Tamara Hareven, *Family Time and Industrial Time* (New York: Cambridge University Press, 1982); Stephen Meyer, *The Five Dollar Day: Labor Management and Social Control in the Ford Motor Company, 1908–21* (New York: SUNY Press, 1981); Stanley Budner, *Pullman: An Experiment in Industrial Order and Community Planning* (New York: Oxford University Press, 1979). The best recent book is Gerald Zahavi, *Workers, Managers and Welfare Capitalism: The Shoeworkers and Tanners of Endicott Johnson, 1890–1950* (Urbana and Chicago: University of Illinois Press, 1988).

5. Nelson, for example, sees paternalism and welfare capitalism as distinct and claims in some situations, traditional paternalism 'deterred' the adoption of welfare work. Daniel Nelson, *Managers and Workers: Origins of the New Factory System in the United States, 1880–1920* (Madison, WI: University of Wisconsin Press, 1975), 115.

6. Genovese paraphrased from Jackson Lears, 'The Concept of Cultural Hegemony: Problems and Possibilities', *AHR* 90 (June 1985).

7. Recent writing has shied away from the very word ideology, influenced by post-structuralist critiques

of the concept and understandably wary of a very traditional Marxist categorization of 'false' or illusory ideology mystifying the 'true' picture of society. Instead of jettisoning the concept, it may be useful to use it, in a Gramscian and feminist manner, as one means of understanding how class and gender inequalities become 'naturalized' and universalized, in the workplace and in larger society.

8. My thinking here is indebted to interpretations of Gramsci by both labour historians and social theorists: three examples are Robert Gray, *The Labour Aristocracy in Victorian Edinburgh* (Oxford: Oxford University Press, 1976); Anna Pollert, *Girls, Wives, Factory Lives* (London: Palgrave Macmillan, 1981); and Terry Eagleton, *Ideology: An Introduction* (London: Verso, 1991).

9. For workplace studies incorporating this perspective, see, for example, Mary Blewett, *Men, Women and Work: Class, Gender and Protest in the New England Shoe Industry* (Urbana and Chicago: University of Illinois Press, 1988); Patricia Cooper, *Once a Cigar Maker: Men, Women and Work Culture in American Cigar Factories* (Urbana and Chicago: University of Illinois Press, 1987); Cynthia Cockburn, *Brothers: Male Dominance and Technological Change* (London: Pluto Press, 1983); and Joy Parr, *The Gender of Breadwinners: Women, Men, and Change in Two Industrial Towns, 1880–1950* (Toronto: University of Toronto Press, 1990).

10. Although financial and production management was guided by others, including long-time manager, Newfoundland-born Herbert Cranford.

11. Of the interviews with blue- and white-collar workers, about half made reference to the congenial, family atmosphere. Others, while they did not describe the workplace in familial terms made observations such as: 'Westclox was a wonderful place to work when I started . . . management and employees got on so well; I could hardly wait to get back to work the next day.' Westclox Interview #22, July 1989. A minority certainly saw this simply as a job like any other; these were more often shorter-term employees.

12. Quote from Interview #2, June 1989. Although this was a manager speaking, similar observations were made by other white- and blue-collar employees, though they did not describe the situation quite so tragically.

13. Westclox Interview #9, April 1991.

14. Westclox Interview #23, July 1989.

15. Miriam Glucksman argues that women were the primary—and crucial—workforce in many mass production industries making food and small appliances; this resulted not from a de-skilling process, but rather from the initial, conscious decision of management to hire cheaper female labour. See Miriam Glucksman, *Women Assemble, Workers and the New Industries in Inter-War Britain* (London: Routledge, 1990).

16. This term is taken from Michael Burawoy, *Manufacturing Consent: Changes in the Labor Process under Monopoly Capitalism* (Chicago: University of Chicago Press, 1979).

17. Westclox Interview #6, June 1989; Interview #23, July 1989.

18. Westclox Interview #6, June 1989. It is possible that women's own methods of conflict resolution learned in the family, or even their different sense of privacy, made them appreciate this mediated approach. This is not an ahistorical claim that women are, by nature, conciliatory, but rather a suggestion that, in this time period, women often learned mediating roles in the family and community. While labour historians have documented women's different work cultures and different approaches to resistance, there is less research on women's accommodation in the workplace. More recent feminist literature on women's methods of organizing have suggested that our gendered experience, as well as feminist ideology, produces different methods of organizing. See Jeri Wine and Janice Ristock, eds, *Women and Social Change: Feminist Activism in Canada* (Toronto: Lorimer, 1991). It is worth noting that a contemporary study of activist women suggests different conclusions about the relationship between family and work than I do: See Karen Sachs, *Caring by the Hour: Women, Work and Organizing at Duke Medical Centre* (Urbana and Chicago: University of Illinois Press, 1988).

19. Westclox Interview #9, April 1991.

20. See Archives of Ontario (OA), Department of Labour, RG 7-57, file: Industrial Relations, pre-1936.

21. It is also important to note that the city as a whole was largely ununionized until the later 1940s.

22. Women's attitudes towards benefits were also shaped by their age and longevity of employment. Still, many industries made generalizations about all women workers. For example, General Electric in the US assumed women were interested in 'sociability not security'. Ronald Schatz, *The Electrical Workers: A History of Labor at General Electric and Westinghouse, 1932–60* (Urbana and Chicago: University of Illinois Press, 1983), 22.

23. OA, RG 7, Department of Labour, 7-57, 3, file: Industrial Relations pre-1936. It is revealing that other Peterborough industries listed in the same file indicated similar patterns. Quaker Oats, for

instance, said there 'was no pension plan but the company takes care of needy and deserving cases. No one is allowed to suffer.'

24. Westclox Interview #18, February 1990.
25. Westclox Interview #20, August 1990.
26. Westclox Interview #2, June 1989.
27. On department stores' successful use of paternalism, including the encouragement of upward mobility of women into white-collar jobs, see Gail Reekie, 'Humanizing Industry: Paternalism, Welfarism and Labour Control in Sydney's Big Stores, 1890–1930', *Labour History* 53 (November 1987).
28. Westclox Interview #2, June 1989.
29. As other authors have noted, company promotion of the ideal of a family wage also provided ideological and economic reinforcement for women's role in unpaid domestic labour. See Martha May, 'The Historical Problem of the Family Wage: The Ford Motor Company and the Five Dollar Day', *Feminist Studies* 8 (Summer 1982). See also Linda Frankel, 'Southern Textile Women's Generations of Survival and Struggle', in Karen Sachs, ed., *My Troubles are Going to Have Trouble with Me: The Everyday Trials and Triumphs of Women Workers* (New Brunswick, NJ: Transaction Publishers, 1980), for the argument that 'paternalism . . . depended on women's continued responsibility for domestic life', 46.
30. Westclox Interview #13, August 1989.
31. From the chaperoned boarding houses of Lowell to lessons in culture at Heinz, employers utilized various tactics to create the impression that under their tutelage, working-class women would be better able to maintain their pure character, and thus become respectable and sought-after wives. On distinct programs for women see Daniel Nelson, *Managers and Workers*. On nineteenth century paternalism and the protection of women's respectability see Joy Parr, *The Gender of Breadwinners*, chap. 2. In *Workers, Managers and Welfare Capitalism*, Zahavi argues that Endicott Johnson defended the morality and respectability of wage earning *mothers*, primarily because these women's labour was needed in his factory—indicating the malleability of paternalism according to the needs of capital. In the context of the Peterborough labour market, married women were not a crucial necessity to the company (at least until the war years) and so the company could endorse the family wage and ignore the issue of wage-earning mothers.
32. Westclox Interview #2, June 1989.
33. Westclox Interview #2, June 1989.
34. Westclox Interview #1, July 1989.
35. Westclox Interview #23, July 1989.
36. Westclox Interview #4, December 1990.
37. For discussion of how dress, image, and gesture were used to express gender identity for working-class women, see J. Dowd Hall, 'Disorderly Women: Gender and Labor Militancy in the Appalachian South', *Journal of American History* 73 (Summer 1986), and Kathy Peiss, *Cheap Amusements: Working Women and Leisure in Turn-Of-The-Century New York* (Philadelphia: Temple University Press, 1986).
38. Census material from 1921 to 1941 confirms this characterization. For example: Canada, *Census* of 1921, vol. 1, Table 28 shows those listing British origins to be 92 per cent of the city's population. Canada, *Census* of 1931, vol. 2, Table 34 shows 91 per cent of the population listing British origins. Table 47 showed that 80 per cent of the population born in Canada and 16 per cent born in the British Isles. Canada, *Census* of 1941, vol. 1, Table 34 indicates 90 per cent listed British origins; Table 45 indicates that 83 per cent were Canadian born and 12 per cent were born in Britain. This was a predominantly Anglo city.
39. Westclox Interview #9, April 1991.
40. Westclox Interview #12, July 1989.
41. Westclox Interview #7, September 1989.
42. American sports historians point to the commercialization of sports in this period, but this was not so visible in a smaller community. See Mark Dyreson, 'The Emergence of Consumer Culture and the Transformation of Physical Culture: American Sport in the 1920s', *Journal of Sport History* 16, 3 (Winter 1989).
43. On the increasing use of recreation programs by companies during World War II, see 'Industrial Recreations, Canadian Style', *Recreations*, December 1944. For a revisionist view which suggests that US companies renewed their interest in welfare capitalism during World War II, see Elizabeth Fones-Wolf, 'Industrial Recreation, the Second World War and the Revival of Welfare Capitalism, 1934–60', *Business History Review* 69 (Summer 1986).
44. Westclox Interview #20, August 1990.
45. Westclox Interview #12, July 1989.
46. See *Peterborough Examiner*, undated clipping, 1990. This term was used by a woman interviewed about her memories of war-time industrial softball leagues.
47. Westclox Interview #7, September 1990.
48. By the 1960s these warnings were hardly veiled. In *Tic Talk*, December 1966 the paper asked 'Do these names mean anything to you?' It offered the names

of plants that had gone out of business in Peterborough, then concluded: 'The key to job security is in your hands.'

49. At GE, interestingly, it was *Mrs* Consumer who was featured in their paper. For a discussion of companies like GE which deliberately pursued promotion of consumerism among its workers, see John Cumbler, *Working Class Community in Industrial America: Work, Leisure and Struggle in Two Industrial Cities, 1880–1930* (Westport, CT: Greenwood Press, 1979).

50. The humour relating to marriage in these columns bears a striking resemblance to themes presented in James Snell, 'Marriage Humour and its Social Functions, 1900–39', *Atlantis* 11, 2 (1986).

51. It is important to note that many of the businesses (except for GE) in this city were, like Westclox, small enough to facilitate the cultivation of paternalism.

52. See National Archives of Canada, IUE Collection, 28-I-264, vol. 83. P. Drysdale to George Hutchens, President, Canadian IUE, 15 September 1969. This issue is taken up by other women outside the factory who write to the Ontario Women's Bureau complaining that such a roll back would be 'discriminatory'. OA, RG 7, Department of Labour, Women's Bureau Correspondence, Series 8, Box 1.

References

Adilman, Melvin. 1989. 'Baseball, Business and the Workplace: Gelber's Thesis Re-examined', *Journal of Social History* 23 (Winter).

Barrons. 1962. 'General Time Ticks Off Swift Earnings Rebound'. 19 February.

Barrons. 1967. 'On the Uptick'. 16 October.

Betke, Carle. 1975. 'The Social Significance of Sport in the City', in A.R. McCormack and I. Macpherson, eds, *Cities in the West*. Ottawa: National Museums of Canada.

Boggs, Carl. 1984. *The Two Revolutions: Gramsci and the Dilemmas of Western Marxism*. Boston: South End Press.

Brandes, Stuart. 1976. *American Welfare Capitalism, 1880–1940*. Chicago: University of Chicago Press.

Brody, David. 1980. *Workers in Industrial America: Essays on the Twentieth Century Struggle*. New York: Oxford University Press.

Company pamphlet. *c.* 1978. 'The Westclox Story'. Personal copy.

Davies, Margery. 1982. *Woman's Place is at the Typewriter: Office Work and Office Workers, 1870–1930*. Philadelphia: Temple University Press.

Forbes. 1959. 'What the Clock Watchers Didn't See'. 15 February.

Forbes. 1961. 'No More Puffs Please'. 15 April.

Glucksman, Miriam. 1990. *Women Assemble, Workers and the New Industries in Inter-War Britain*. London: Routledge.

Heron, Craig, and George DeZwaan. 1985. 'Industrial Unionism in Eastern Ontario: Ganonoque, 1918–21', *Ontario History* (September).

Heron, Craig. 1988. *Working in Steel: The Early Years in Canada, 1883–1935*. Toronto: McClelland and Stewart.

Joyce, P. 1980. *Work, Society and Politics*. London: Methuen.

Lamphere, Louis. 1985. 'Bringing the Family to Work: Women's Culture on the Shop Floor', *Feminist Studies* 11 (Fall).

Lown, Judy. 1985. 'Not so much a Factory, More a Form of Patriarchy: Gender and Class during Industrialization', in E. Gamranikow, ed., *Gender, Class and Work*. London: Gower.

Nelson, Daniel. 1975. *Managers and Workers: Origins of the New Factory System in the United States, 1880–1920*. Madison, WI: University of Wisconsin Press.

Parr, Joy. 1990. *The Gender of Breadwinners: Women, Men, and Change in Two Industrial Towns, 1880–1950*. Toronto: University of Toronto Press.

Peterborough Examiner. 1954. 1 December.

Peterborough Examiner. 1966. 'Mr Westclox Dies'. 20 July.

Peterborough Examiner. 1990. Undated clipping.

Strong-Boag, Veronica. 1988. *The New Day Recalled: Lives of Girls and Women in English Canada, 1919–39*. Toronto: Addison Wesley.

Tic Talk. 1954. June.

Tic Talk. 1956. December.

Tic Talk. 1959. December.

Tic Talk. 1962. December.

Tic Talk. 1966. June.

Tic Talk. 1966. July.

Tic Talk. 1966. December.

Zahavi, Gerald. 1988. *Workers, Managers and Welfare Capitalism: The Shoeworkers and Tanners of Endicott Johnson, 1890–1950*. New York: University of Illinois Press.

CHAPTER 16

Race, Employment Discrimination, and State Complicity in Wartime Canada, 1939–1945

Carmela Patrias

Sometime in 1941 a group of 'Slavic' workers travelled from Alberta to Ontario in search of skilled jobs in war industries. All the workers were Canadian-born and all had been trained under the government's War Emergency Training Programme. Yet despite shortages in skilled labour in Ontario, they were unable to obtain work. Upon learning their names, Ontario employers refused to hire them, and the workers were eventually forced to return to Alberta.[1] The rejection of these workers, despite their Canadian birth and training, baffles the contemporary reader. Were these workers of Polish, Ukrainian, Czech, Slovak, Serbian, or Croatian descent? Did they trace their origins to countries at war with Canada or ones allied with it? Ontario employers apparently considered such information irrelevant. Not the national heritage of these 'Slavic' workers, but their 'race' convinced prospective employers that they were unfit to work in war industries.

In 1941 'foreign' names were widely understood as markers of racial difference. The introduction to the volume on Canada's population in the 1941 census, for example, stated that 'knowledge of one's racial origin' could be 'perpetuated in a family name'. Census analysts found it necessary to explain the criteria by which 'racial origin' could be known, because the basis for racial classification in the census varied for different groups. 'Colour' was the basis for classifying the 'Indian, Eskimo, Negro, Hindu, Chinese and Japanese races', religion for classifying Jews, and language for Ukrainians. For some groups 'racial origin'

implied 'geographical area—the country from which the individual himself came or that which was the home of his forebears.' While in most cases racial origin could be traced through the father, children of 'mixed Blood'—those born of mixed marriages between whites and 'Negro, Japanese, Chinese, Hindu, Malaysian etc.'—were classified as belonging to those racial groups if either parent belonged to the 'black, yellow or brown races'. The racial designation for people of mixed 'white and Indian blood' was 'Half-breed' (Canada, Dominion Bureau of Statistics, 1950: 218–19).

That the names of the 'Slavic' workers from Alberta signified 'racial' difference of sufficient magnitude to disqualify them from obtaining work in war industries suggests that however imprecise its definition, the racial origin designation was economically and socially very significant. One goal of this article is to examine the nature and extent of racist employment discrimination during World War II. It will show that, in wartime Canada, racializing minority groups—attributing to them substantial, inborn distinguishing characteristics—greatly disadvantaged group members in the labour market and prevented their full incorporation within the body of the nation.[2] A second and related goal is to demonstrate that despite officially prohibiting employment discrimination based on race, nationality, and religion during the war, state officials colluded with racist employers and workers in such discrimination.

The focus on the war years offers a unique opportunity for studying racist employment discrimination because evidence of such discrimination on the home front abounds. Unprecedented intervention by the federal government in the labour market generated some of this evidence. State officials intent on maximizing labour productivity during the war were forced to pay close attention to employment discrimination because members of racialized minority groups constituted an indispensable source of labour. On the one hand, discrimination threatened productivity both by creating tensions among workers and by excluding some of them from certain occupations. On the other, after 1942, when employment was plentiful and menial jobs went unfilled, racialization could be useful in channelling workers into undesirable yet essential jobs. This study draws extensively on the records of federal government agencies. Minority group members—not necessarily from the same groups that attracted official attention—had their own reasons for documenting employment discrimination. They believed that the blatant contradiction between Canada's declared war aim of fighting the racism of the Nazis and racist discrimination at home, combined with the high demand for labour and state control over the labour force, created propitious circumstances for challenging employment discrimination. The records of voluntary organizations established by racialized minority groups, especially by Jews and African Canadians, comprise the second important body of evidence on which this study relies.[3]

Studying employment discrimination during the war can do more, however, than illustrate the nature and significance of racism between 1939 and 1945. That the national heritage of the 'Slavic' workers from Alberta made so little difference to Ontario employers suggests that employment discrimination on the home front owed far less to wartime alliances on the international stage than to longstanding association between 'race' and suitability for certain types of employment and for

citizenship in Canada. To be sure, state officials anticipated—and some of them shared—security concerns about the participation of 'enemy aliens' in home defense and war production. As we shall see, however, many employers, workers, and state officials also racialized Canadian-born and naturalized people of Japanese, central, eastern, and southern European, and Jewish origin: many Canadians saw these racialized groups as 'foreigners', suspected them of disloyalty, and therefore believed that they were undeserving of certain types of economic and political rights. The war also brought sharply into focus and even intensified racist assumptions that African Canadians, eastern and southern Europeans, and Native people were suitable only for menial jobs and that the aggressive and greedy Jews, and Chinese and Japanese Canadians constituted unfair competition for 'true' Canadians because they placed economic gains above patriotic duty. Such racist assumptions served to legitimize the marginalization of minority groups in Canadian society.

The inclusion of minority groups of southern and eastern European parentage—such as the 'Slavic' workers introduced above—as well as of African, Asian, and Native Canadians, is central to the analysis of the meaning and impact of race offered here. Some of the most influential recent studies of racism in Canada make clear that characterizing groups that we would describe today as 'white', as racially distinct and inferior, reveals the social construction and hence fluidity of racial classification.[4] Even in these studies, however, the attention given 'visible' minorities generally outweighs examinations of the racialization of groups of European origin. Such a focus is understandable because people of colour have been the targets of the most extreme and most overtly state-sanctioned racism in Canada, in the form of immigration restrictions, denial of the franchise, and legal exclusion from certain types of jobs. It is also easier to study such racism than the less formalized racialization of groups of European descent. This study's focus on employment discrimination allows us to explore the meaning and impact of racist ideas and practices for minority groups of peripheral European as well as African, Asian, and Native parentage, because the mobility of all these groups in the labour force was impeded during the war.[5] . . .

Here, as in the United States, the status of people from the peripheries of Europe was ambiguous. Encouraged to come by the hundreds of thousands prior to World War I, such immigrants were classified 'non-preferred' during the interwar years. They were allowed into Canada before the Depression only in the numbers needed to perform work that Canadian residents avoided. One clear expression of their perceived inferiority in Canada was their exclusion, along with immigrants of Asian and African descent, from 'better neighbourhoods' by legally accepted covenants. But, with the exception of the 1917 elections, when even naturalized members of these groups were deprived of their vote, European immigrants could secure citizenship rights. Such rights were denied to people of Asian descent, but not to African Canadians. Nevertheless, as Constance Backhouse has argued, although the racial identity of the dominant white group was splintered in many directions, a 'racial chasm' separated such groups from Native people, and from people of African and Asian descent (Backhouse, 1999: 9). . . .

Yet, although skin colour was so significant to racial assignment in Canada, purported racial inferiority and superiority were most often not expressed in terms of colour. Even more tellingly, colour was not central to the self-definition of 'inbetween' people. Indeed, given the uneven distribution of people of colour in Canada, eastern and southern Europeans were the only racialized 'others' in many communities. The differences

between the make-up of the populations of Canada and the United States go a long way toward explaining the difference in racial discourse in the two countries. Most importantly, the weakness of the institution of slavery in Canada's past and racist immigration policies meant that, in contrast to the United States, the number of people of African descent in Canada remained small until the last decades of the twentieth century. Consequently, the type of black–white polarization that some scholars place at the core of American racial thought did not develop in Canada. To claim that immigrants from the peripheries of Europe were initially perceived as 'non-white', and that they 'became white' in the course of their integration into Canadian society would . . . oversimplify a complex and multifaceted process of racialization. This article examines only part of this process: the construction of racial classification in wartime by Anglo-Canadian (and to a lesser extent French Canadian) state officials, employers, and workers, and the impact of such classification on minority workers. . . .

By illuminating state complicity in the racialization of workers, the study's focus on racist employment discrimination also sheds new light on the role of the state in wartime Canada. Studies of the relationship between the state and minority groups in wartime Canada have hitherto concentrated largely on the Nationalities Branch of the Department of National War Services and the Cooperative Committee in Canadian Citizenship. Because these two agencies were created by the federal government specifically to mobilize minority groups behind Canada's war effort, and to increase group harmony by familiarizing English and French Canadians with minority groups and their contributions to Canadian society, their records offer rich and readily accessible sources for studying state-minority relations in wartime. Some scholars believe that such endeavours marked the first step in citizenship training, or in Canada's progress toward a tolerant and inclusive national policy of multiculturalism (Drisziger, 1988; Pal, 1993). Others characterize these undertakings as Eurocentric and ineffectual (Young, 1988; Thompson, 1991).[6] Whatever their conclusions, the focus of scholars on the Nationalities Branch and the Cooperative Committee offers only a partial view of state-minority relations in wartime. The officials of many other government departments and agencies also dealt with racialized minority workers, and as this study will show, their collusion with racist employers and workers helped to block the mobility of minority workers in the labour force throughout the war. The state's complicity both reflected and legitimized racist views widely held in Canadian society both prior to and during World War II.

The Denial of Employment and Relief

Calls for the dismissal of 'foreigners' from their jobs arose almost immediately after the outbreak of World War II and intensified in 1940, following the sudden and rapid successes of German troops in western Europe and Italy's entry into the war. Thousands of people across Canada lost their jobs. They came from a wide variety of occupations: miners in Cape Breton, steel workers in Hamilton, department store and hotel employees in Toronto and Winnipeg, municipal employees in Windsor and Calgary, and shipyard workers in Vancouver. They included not only workers who were born in, or could trace their origins to, countries now at war with Canada, such as Germany, Italy, and Japan, but also men and women born in, or whose ancestors were born in, countries allied with Canada. They also included both naturalized British and foreign subjects.

The difficulties of many of these 'foreign' workers were compounded by their inability to obtain relief. Many dismissed able-bodied workers were denied relief on the grounds that they were capable of working. This placed them in a 'state of suspended animation with no means of support', in the words of T.C. Davis, Associate Deputy Minister of the Department of National War Services [DNWS].[7] Because immigrant workers had been disproportionately represented among the unemployed during the Great Depression, the hardship caused by the combined loss of jobs and the denial of relief was great, especially in Ontario and Alberta, where the provincial governments decided to cut off relief to all non-naturalized immigrants (Hurd, 1937).[8]

The ostensible reason for dismissals and the denial of relief was that these workers were potentially disloyal—enemies capable of all manner of subversive activity, including sabotage. Reports from Europe concerning fifth-column activity in the Netherlands and Norway fired the imagination of many Canadians—private citizens, public servants, and elected officials—and convinced them of the need to be vigilant.[9] Some of them harboured quite specific fears: that Japanese Canadian women employed in British Columbia fish canneries would poison herring intended for British soldiers, that Finnish loggers would destroy lumber required for making airplanes, or that German miners with Nazi sympathies would sabotage Nova Scotia mines.[10] . . .

The reasons for the participation of municipal and provincial governments in anti-alien campaigns at the war's outset are not difficult to find. Both levels of government stood to gain materially and politically from denying relief to 'foreigners'. In 1939, when large numbers of Canadians were still unemployed, responsibility for relief was split among the three levels of government: municipal, provincial, and federal. When Ontario Premier Hepburn and Toronto Mayor Daly spoke out against foreign-born recipients, they may have been hoping to force the federal government to assume the costs of caring for resident aliens. The premier also may have been influenced by anti-foreign letters, such as the one from the town council of Kenora, declaring that precious resources should not be spent in wartime on the foreign-born who did not see fit to assume the responsibilities of citizenship.[11] Whatever their motivations, the public statements of such influential figures as the Ontario premier and the Toronto mayor were clearly inflammatory. They could not have been unaware that their official communications and public statements could fuel anti-foreign sentiments. They may even have been counting on the appeal of such sentiments to Anglo-Canadian voters.

A clear indication that more than war-created anxiety concerning enemy aliens was at work in the years between 1939 and 1941 was the vulnerability of people with accents or foreign-sounding names, even if they were born in Canada or in countries allied with Canada. These women and men lost their jobs because employment was still scarce in Canada in the early war years, and many Canadians of British descent believed that they had greater claim to them than so-called foreigners.[12] Their anti-foreign sentiments were based on their understanding of race, not nationality. The author of a letter to the *Windsor Daily Star*, for example, drew no distinctions among them when he asked why 'the foreign element such as Italians, Jews, Russians, Pol[es were] all working and holding down good jobs, while our English-speaking boys are on welfare, walking the streets' (*Windsor Daily Star*, 22 September 1939: 9). . . .

The case of mine workers of Italian origin in Nova Scotia, dismissed from their jobs following Italy's entry into the war in June 1940, sheds light on the nature and causes of such discriminatory attitudes as well as on the hardship they created. While District 26 of the United Mine Workers

of America [UMWA] voted to allow foreign-born men to return to work, Anglo-Canadian miners in two collieries refused to work with them. That summer the unemployed 'foreigners' provided for themselves and their families by supplementing their small relief allowances with the produce of their gardens. By the fall of 1940, however, the workers were finding it impossible to subsist. As winter approached, their children's clothing was so threadbare that some were unable to go to school.[13] Clarence Gillis, Co-operative Commonwealth Federation [CCF] MP for Glace Bay South, Nova Scotia, believed that for local young Anglo-Canadian men, who had never had any work because of the Depression, Italy's participation in the war was just an excuse to throw 'foreigners' out of work. They resented the fact that 'such a large number of foreigners are gainfully employed while they, the natives of the country, are walking the street'.[14]

The seriousness of this type of discrimination—even after the economic boom generated by war eliminated unemployment—came to light as part of a study conducted by the Manpower Labour Supply Investigation Committee, established in July 1941. The Committee put at 15,096 in rural Manitoba alone, the number of men of Polish, Russian, Ukrainian, Czech, and Slovak descent, who should be considered 'as one' with Canadians in the war effort because they were 'of the same stock as the races actively engaged in fighting the Axis Powers in Europe'. Yet, even when shortages in skilled labour began to develop, 'eastern' employers resisted hiring such workers. Employers interviewed for the manpower study declared that they would not hire these men 'unless they are forced to do so by circumstances'.[15] . . .

Canada's leading newspapers took notice of this type of discrimination and clearly identified it as racist. In December 1941, for example, both the *Globe and Mail* and the *Montreal Star* reported the case of Myrm Chknoski, convicted in the Toronto Police Court of a breach of the National Resource Mobilization Act. The act required registration by all Canadian residents over the age of 16, men and women alike. The purpose of national registration was to create an inventory of the mechanical and industrial skills of Canada's workforce, as well as of men available for home defense. Racial origin formed part of the information sought by the government, and was duly noted on the card each worker received upon registration. In principle, only those possessing registration cards were eligible for employment. Although Chknoski complied with the Act and obtained a registration card, his 'foreign-sounding name' prevented him from getting work. He was arrested and tried because in desperation he gave himself an 'Anglo-Saxon' name on a second card, on which he forged the signature of a deputy registrar. A *Globe and Mail* editorial sympathized with Chknoski's plight and ascribed the inability of men like him to obtain work to 'racial prejudice' (*Globe and Mail*, 26 December 1941). . . .

The widely held—though inaccurate—belief that foreigners were not volunteering to serve overseas and were not required to train for home defense exacerbated hostility towards them. The *Vancouver Sun,* for example, reported that:

> While Canadian young men are volunteering and having to enter training for home defense . . . many hundreds, perhaps some thousands of alien youths are having a good time in British Columbia. They are taking the jobs of the Canadian boys. They are earning better pay than they have ever known before. They are acquiring new skills that will serve them well when the war is over. They are digging in.

The article went on to suggest that foreign-born males who could be trusted be conscripted, and those who were not trustworthy be compelled to perform some other public duty, lest this state of affairs breed racial hatred (*Vancouver Sun*, 16 October 1941). The complaints of some Vancouver residents that Chinese Canadians were becoming rich because of the war, and now refused to remain within the confines of Chinatown, confirmed the *Vancouver Sun's* predictions about the intensification of racial hatred (Laviolette, 1978: 32n.5). Without knowledge of enlistment figures, many English Canadians concluded that while their sons were away fighting, the sons of 'foreigners . . . stay home and make money' (Giffen, 1947: 155). Members of the Vancouver Island Farmers' Council, for example, maintained that 'Oriental' farmers benefitted from unfair advantages over 'European' farmers because they did not have to train for home defense and were not enlisting in the armed forces. 'The result has been that large numbers of white farmers have had to plant their land to grass while the Oriental . . . is taking up land formerly used by European farmers.'[16] Farmers around Cooksville, Ontario, were 'stewing because their sons and husbands are in the thick of war while those damn foreigners [Jews and Italians] are running Toronto markets and fruit stands and growing rich'.[17] Suspicions that Jews were profiteering through black market activities instead of enlisting were especially widespread.[18]

Dangerous 'Foreigners'

Some employers found it advantageous to stoke the flames of anti-alien sentiments. Blaming 'foreigners' for labour activism and unrest was a convenient way to discredit the labour movement, especially the CIO which was making inroads among Canadian workers. In 1941, when the Packinghouse Workers Organizing Committee [PWOC] successfully enlisted workers at the Canada Packers plant in Toronto, for example, J.S. Willis, the company's personnel director, accused the union of attempting to sabotage the war effort by slowing down production so that 'Canadian' men who could have been at the front were held back in Canada. His 'proof' of the union's disloyalty to the allied cause was the assertion that about 70 per cent of the men who chose to support the PWOC, rather than the company union already in place, were 'foreigners', and that one of their leaders, Adam Borsk, was of German origin and sympathetic to the German cause. Based on surveillance of the plant, the RCMP supported Willis's allegations.[19] Police reports described Borsk as a 'White Russian' Nazi sympathizer, and warned that he was in a position to set the pace of production in the plant.[20] Any fears about the influence of 'foreigners' at Canada Packers were put to rest when the CIO organizing efforts were defeated by the company's insistence that the vote on the union be conducted in all its plants, and by the dismissal of Adam Borsk (Murray, 1942: 334–5). By then, however, the publicity surrounding the case no doubt intensified suspicions against foreign-born workers. . . .

Jews and African Canadians

Racism was clearly at work when Canadian-born Jews and African Canadians, who could hardly be accused of harbouring loyalties to Canada's wartime enemies, were barred from certain types of employment. Such racism, of course, predated the war, but it came to light during the war because activists in these two minority groups believed that the incongruity of calling upon them to make sacrifices on behalf of the nation through enlistment, while simultaneously denying them the right to equal treatment in the labour market, created a unique opportunity to fight against racism and discrimination in Canada. For ammunition in this fight, they actively collected evidence of employment discrimination.

The Joint Public Relations Committee of the Canadian Jewish Congress and B'nai B'rith [JPRC], established in 1938 to oppose anti-Semitism specifically and racial and religious discrimination generally, decided to take action because state-owned or crown companies, as well as private industry involved in war production 'consistently refused employment to Jews solely on racial or religious grounds'.[21] The JPRC assembled copies of job application forms that included questions about the 'race' and 'religion' of prospective applicants, and solicited information from Jews who had experienced or witnessed employment discrimination. Despite fears that such testimony could render them unemployable, Jews in various lines of work responded. Some of them, probably those less proficient in English, provided oral accounts and then signed affidavits, while others wrote letters describing their experiences.

The cases of Hy Lampert and Gertrude Green illustrate the nature of discrimination against Jewish blue-collar workers. In 1942, Lampert responded to a newspaper advertisement for general machine shop help, in which he was trained and had some experience, at a Toronto plant. When he identified himself as Jewish in response to a question concerning his religion, he was informed that the job was filled. Yet advertisements for the same position continued to appear in Toronto newspapers. Wary of anti-Semitism, Gertrude Green inquired whether a 'Jewish girl would be employed', before going to an interview for a job at the Canadian Acme Screw and Gear in Toronto. The answer she received was unequivocal: 'they had never done so and had no intentions of hiring them in the future, and therefore, I should not bother coming down to see them.'[22]

According to the Ontario Division of the Canadian Jewish Congress [CJC], the extent of employment discrimination against Jews was best illustrated by their 'infinitesimally' small numbers in war industries.[23] H.M. Caiserman, of the CJC's head office in Montreal, identified Canadian Marconi, RCA Victor, Royal Typewriters, and Canadian Car & Foundry as some of the Montreal companies not hiring Jews.[24] As late as the spring of 1943, the CJC claimed that, because the National Selective Service [NSS] was not sending them to jobs consonant with their skills and goals, thousands of Jewish men, boys, and girls were standing in line for hours at the Montreal Selective Service to obtain open permits which would allow them to approach places of employment on their own.[25]

African Canadians also publicized, and protested against, employment discrimination. War production actually somewhat reduced segregation of this group within the labour force. For example, African Canadian women, the majority of whom were forced to work as domestic servants until the 1940s, could now find employment in factories. As one of them explained, 'we weren't allowed to go into factory work until Hitler started the war, and then they would beg you, "Would you like a job in my factory"' (Brand, 1994: 179). Yet by no means did all factories welcome African Canadian workers. A *Globe and Mail* reporter discovered in October 1942 that only a small number of the 4,000 African Canadians in Toronto were able to find work in industry. Although their own acceptance of racist stereotypes played an important part in job allocation, employers sometimes blamed objections raised by other employees for this type of discrimination (*Globe and Mail*, 31 October 1942).[26] . . .

White-Collar Work

Even as a booming economy enhanced chances for upward mobility for many other Canadians starting in 1941, racism continued to block Jews, African Canadians, and people of eastern and southern European descent from white-collar occupations.

Reverend Harvey Forester, superintendent of the All People's Mission for the Niagara Peninsula, reported such discrimination in Welland, an industrial community with an exceptionally high proportion of people of eastern and southern European descent. Officials of a war plant, seeking clerical workers at the end of the school year in 1942, requested the names of the best high school graduates from the local school board, on which Forster served. The list sent by the board included the names of pupils of central European origin. 'Don't send us foreigners; send us white men!' responded war plant officials.[27] . . .

The entry of Jewish women and men into white-collar occupations was similarly restricted. During the war years, Jews were employed by state agencies. They found it difficult to obtain clerical and professional jobs in private businesses, however, even ones engaged in war production. For example, after trying unsuccessfully to enlist in the armed forces, Norman Cowan, a trained accountant, sought work in Toronto. Despite having excellent references from previous employers and auditors, Cowan was turned down by six different firms. Three of the six, including Price Waterhouse, told him outright that they did not employ Jews. Small wonder that the disappointed Cowan wrote the JPRC about a 'boycott against the Jews'.[28]

Adeline Natanson had similar experiences. An interviewer at the war plant of the John Inglis Company in Toronto, having declared that her educational background and experience qualified her for the job, was ready to hire her as a typist. As an afterthought he inquired as to her 'nationality and racial origin'. When she told him that she was Jewish, he replied that 'unfortunately, for simply *that* reason *only*', he would be unable to hire her, explaining that he had to abide by office policy. The interviewer apparently regretted turning Adeline away and tried to place her by calling a friend who managed a department of another war plant, only to discover that concerning the employment of 'those of Hebrew nationality for clerical work' the Small Arms Branch adhered to the same policy as the John Inglis Company.[29]

African Canadians also continued to be barred from white-collar occupations. In Montreal, Janet Long, field secretary of the Girls' Cottage School, protested publicly on behalf of 'coloured girls'. 'Most employers did not wish coloured employees for office work,' she stated (*Montreal Daily Star*, 8 December 1942; Potter, 1949: 74–5). Frances E. Upton, registrar and school visitor of the Association of Registered Nurses in Quebec, explained restrictive practices in nursing in Montreal by observing that if 'Negroes were admitted to the profession, white mothers would decline permission to their daughters to train as nurses'. She added that coloured girls did not work as hard as white girls, did not like to be disciplined, and would not bring the same 'refinement' to their jobs (Potter, 1949: 119–20).[30] . . .

State Intervention

We will never know the precise number of those affected by dismissals, the denial of relief, and restriction to menial jobs. The problem was sufficiently great, however, to concern Canada's Ministers of Labour, Justice, and National War Services, and such leading civil servants in Ottawa as Norman Robertson, Deputy Minister of External Affairs, and T.C. Davis, Associate Deputy Minister of the DNWS. These officials recognized that those affected included many naturalized British subjects and so-called friendly aliens.[31] Officials in charge of the federal–provincial training programme also complained about employment discrimination. In November 1941, J.H. Ross, regional director for Alberta, wrote to alert R.F. Thompson, supervisor of training in Ottawa, that a difficult situation was

developing in Alberta and northern Saskatchewan because employers 'will not accept Canadian born trainees who are of foreign but naturalized parentage'. 'This action is most unfair,' he added, because such men 'are accepted without question for the Armed Forces.' Thompson in turn thought the matter grave enough to inform the Department of Munitions and Supply.[32] . . .

Since a large proportion of Canada's labour force was comprised of groups facing employment discrimination, Ottawa could simply not afford to ignore their plight. Officials in the Department of External Affairs [DEA] were among the first to consider acting against employment discrimination. Although only the fate of nationals of other countries fell within their mandate, they knew that such discriminatory treatment was not limited to enemy aliens but extended to naturalized Canadians of German and Italian origin and even to Canadian residents of other European origins, 'irrespective of their status under the Naturalization Act'.[33] By 1940, a small, interdepartmental committee under the leadership of the DEA—consisting of representatives of the DNWS, the RCMP, the Censorship Branch, the Custodian of Enemy Property, and others—started meeting to explore the possibilities of enabling fuller, smoother participation of these groups in the war effort.[34] They focused almost exclusively on groups of European descent.

One of the first proposals of the Committee on Aliens was to create labour battalions in which men unemployable because of their nationality or 'race' 'could be enlisted and put to useful work of national importance for the duration of the war'. The plan both acknowledged the existence of employment discrimination and sidestepped it. The proposed battalions would be open to individuals other than enemy aliens, who 'for one reason or another could not be usefully employed either in the defense forces, on essential war work or public work'. . . . In the end this plan was not adopted, probably owing to fears that the battalions would displace other workers and thus intensify resentment against 'foreigners'.[35]

Another early plan called for the Minister of Labour to approach employers through the Canadian Manufacturers' Association, the Canadian Chamber of Commerce, and the Canadian Association of Boards of Trade, as well as labour unions, to put a stop to employment discrimination against workers of foreign extraction.[36] On 14 March 1941, the Department of Labour issued a circular urging employers and secretaries of trade unions not to discriminate against persons of foreign name or birth, whether citizens or residents, so long as they had demonstrated unquestioned loyalty to Canada.[37]

These state plans, however, were designed to deal only with the problems of workers of European descent. Although the circular stated that the help of 'various nationalities . . . regardless of creed or racial origin' would be required to win the war, the fate of people of Asian origin—Japanese Canadians especially—was considered separately throughout the war. This was ostensibly because their situation was different—most were concentrated in British Columbia. In fact, however, their distinct treatment had to do with the intensity of racism against Asian Canadians. The Committee on the Treatment of Aliens and Alien Property, for example, stated that the loyalties of Japanese Canadians were 'racial not national'.[38] . . .

Racism against people of Asian descent was . . . a key reason for Ottawa's failure to consider legislative remedies for employment discrimination. In 1942, when the Department of Labour proposed an order in council that would prohibit racial discrimination in war industries, Henry Angus, now an official of the Department of External Affairs, advised that such an order would conflict with pre-war provincial legislation limiting the employment of 'persons of the Chinese race' and limiting the employment of 'persons of other races by Chinese'. Angus added that such an order would place employers in a difficult situation if their employees, customers, or communities harboured racist attitudes toward Japanese Canadians.[39]

State Complicity

Not only did government officials not stop racist employment discrimination, they in fact actively colluded in racist practices, including ones that targeted people of eastern and southern European descent. As we have seen, the directors of the Emergency War Training Programme complained in 1941 that racist employment practices undermined the efficacy of the programme. But instead of challenging such exclusion, officials in charge of vocational training in some cases reinforced it by barring members of some racialized minority groups. During the first two years of the war, for example, some of those who trained young men for skilled work in the armed services believed there was no point in training 'Asiatics' and members of the 'coloured races' since they would not be admitted into the RCAF in any event.[40] In 1942, employment discrimination led those in charge of training in Toronto to classify 'Jews, Negroes, Chinese' as 'problem cases', along with 'Canadian children not of British origin (e.g., Canadian children of Italian or German origin)', 'people with relatives in the warring countries', and 'people with foreign-sounding names'. In order not to 'waste time and money', applicants from these groups were admitted to the training programmes only if they were sponsored by future employers.[41] Thus, minority workers could not always avail themselves of government training programmes to move out of the marginalized sectors of the economy to which they had been relegated.

Officials of the [National Selective Service] NSS, an agency established in 1942 to mobilize and ensure the most efficient use of the civilian labour force in war production, also collaborated with discriminatory employers, as did employees of the Unemployment Insurance Commission [UIC] whose offices were formally incorporated into the NSS structure. In principle every potential worker required the permission of an NSS officer to enter any employment, including changing jobs. Recent research suggests that many Canadians ignored NSS officers altogether, moving from one job to another on their own (Stevenson, 2001: 20, 122–3). But some minority workers whose occupational mobility was constrained by racism attempted to use government offices to find better jobs. All too frequently they were sorely disappointed.

Guided by prevailing racial stereotypes, some NSS officials used information on 'racial origin' to discriminate against minority group members. In Windsor, for example, although the United Auto Workers district council pointed out that 'Chinese' were 'doing an excellent job of work in Ford', NSS officials were sending Chinese workers to work in restaurants and laundries.[42] . . . Racist stereotypes were even more damaging in the case of African Canadians. When the executive director of the Negro Community Centre in Montreal consulted the head of the city's NSS about employment of African Canadians, he was told, 'I can't do anything for your people, their IQ is too low' (Potter, 1949: 70). Such attitudes no doubt explained why 'coloured boys and girls' were being offered 'menial jobs, without regard for qualifications' (Potter: 1949: 71). Anti-Semitism led some NSS officials in Montreal to direct Jewish applicants only to jobs in 'lower or lowest brackets'.[43] It could not have been irrelevant in all these cases, that the lower-paid, lower status occupations were becoming more and more difficult to fill.

To be sure, not all NSS officials were racist. Some of them even belonged to racialized minority groups. A few Anglo-Canadian officials, moreover, spoke up against racist discrimination. For example, Verna McClure, an employment and claims officer for NSS, chaired the London Japanese Advisory Committee, which protested against racism that prevented Japanese Canadians from contributing to national life by earning a living in the occupations for which their training and experience qualified them.[44] Some Montreal NSS officials, not all of them Jewish, supplied the Canadian Jewish Congress with evidence of the anti-Semitic attitudes of their colleagues and with lists of employers who specified that they were unwilling to employ Jews.[45]

Many more state officials, however, who may or may not have subscribed to racist ideas, accepted such requests as 'no aliens and no Jews' from prospective employers.[46] The clearest evidence of such official collusion came from Jewish employers who sought to fill positions through the NSS or the UIC. UIC employees asked prospective employer J.H. Gringorten of Canada Motor Products Limited in Toronto, a plant for the assembly of aircraft and automobile fuses, on several occasions, 'whether nationality made any difference', and upon receiving a negative response, added 'not even if they are Jewish?' These questions troubled Gringorten, who believed that they planted the idea of discriminating against prospective Jewish employees in the minds of otherwise neutral employers. When he confronted one of the officials, she explained that the questions were asked in the interest of the Jewish applicants, 'who all too often have been sent to places whose practice was to discriminate against them, and it simply meant a waste of time and car fare and general disillusionment for the applicant.'[47]

Targeted minorities, especially Jews and African Canadians, protested against such discrimination. In November 1942, representatives of labour unions with large Jewish memberships such as the International Ladies Garment Workers Union and the Fur Workers Union, along with community activists, presented evidence of discrimination against Jews to Elliott M. Little, who as chief of the Selective Service Board stood at the helm of civilian and military mobilization in Canada. Percy Bengough, acting president of the Dominion Trades Congress, accompanied the delegation. African Canadian community organizations, church groups, and youth clubs similarly publicized discrimination through interviews with the press, petitions, and delegations to the federal and provincial governments. Given what we know about the complicity of their employees in racist employment practices, the skepticism with which NSS authorities initially greeted these allegations appears disingenuous, to say the least (*Ottawa Evening Journal*, 13 October 1942). The ensuing publicity nevertheless convinced the NSS to warn employers that it would not tolerate discrimination 'for reasons of race, color or creed'.[48] It prohibited the inclusion of questions concerning race and religion on official registration and employment forms and warned employers that 'the practice of discrimination' might mean a 'shutting off of all labor supplies for their plants' (*Globe and Mail*, 16 November 1942).

Even after such classification on official forms was prohibited, however, employers continued to express their racial preferences, and NSS officials attempted to comply. They inquired about the background of applicants not in writing, however, but over the telephone or during interviews. About a year after discrimination based on race was officially prohibited, the Director of NSS issued an internal directive encouraging such collusion with racist requirements of employers. The new directive suggested that applying the anti-discrimination provisions too rigidly had 'caused

embarrassment both to applicants and employers'. 'Where good judgement would indicate that there is some possibility of real difficulty in the assimilation of the applicant into the organization of the prospective employer,' the instructions suggested, 'a preliminary enquiry should be made preferably by telephone to determine whether there are insurmountable obstacles in the way of acceptance of the applicant.'[49]

Whatever the motivation of NSS officials, state intervention in the labour market in wartime Canada had the effect of reinforcing the racialization of minority workers. . . .

Equally blatant was state complicity with efforts to channel Chinese, Japanese, and Native Canadians into farm labour, lumber work, light industries, and service jobs, precisely those sectors of the economy that other groups were abandoning for more lucrative employment elsewhere. Although skilled and white-collar jobs in many parts of Canada remained closed to Jews and other minorities from eastern and southern Europe, and to African Canadians, by 1942 the expanding wartime economy did offer them some new employment opportunities. Such workers could and did abandon seasonal or temporary, ill-paid, dangerous jobs or those in isolated areas, to which they were relegated before the war, in favour of more regular, better-paid work in war industries. . . .

Consequently, serious labour shortages developed in agriculture, food processing, lumbering, mining, railroad maintenance, and the service sector—the very sectors staffed by 'non-preferred' immigrants before the war.[50] Since the war had put a stop to immigration, worried government officials were desperately searching for new sources of labour to fill such jobs. Alarmed by crops left rotting in the fields, uncultivated farm lands, the closure of food processing plants, and declining production in the resource sector, state officials increasingly turned to those groups most marginalized by racism in the Canadian economy. . . .

Japanese Canadians

In the case of Japanese Canadians state collusion with racist attitudes, policies, and practices was even more flagrant. Here racist attitudes eventually converged with labour needs. After the removal of Japanese Canadians from coastal British Columbia deprived them of their means of livelihood, the British Columbia Security Commission [BCSC], charged with the removal, faced a Herculean task: to make Japanese Canadians self-supporting so they would not constitute a financial burden for the federal government, when most Canadian communities adamantly opposed the settlement of Japanese Canadians within their boundaries. Its initial plan entailed the separation of families. Women, children, and unemployable men were moved into ghost towns in the interior of British Columbia. Only a few men of prime working age were allowed to accompany them, to make the towns liveable. Most Japanese Canadian men between the ages of 18 and 45, whether Japanese nationals, naturalized, or Canadian-born, were moved to road camps. Canadians who refused to let the men move into their communities were quite happy to allow them to build new highways under strict government supervision. The men were expected to stay in the road camps, unless given permission to leave by the RCMP. They were not free to take commercial employment, and were required to assign $20 from their monthly earnings (unskilled labourers earned 25 cents per hour) for the maintenance of their dependants, a sum supplemented by the government by no more than $5 per dependent child per month.[51]

At the time of the evacuation, the only way that Japanese Canadian families could stay together was to agree to go to the sugar beet fields of Alberta and Manitoba.[52] Nearly 4,000 Japanese Canadians were sent to such fields in Alberta, Manitoba, and eventually Ontario (Laviolette, 1978: 74). Because the work was seasonal, the Japanese Canadians required either additional work or government assistance for part of each year. Initially, only males could find such work in northern lumber camps. Although work deemed appropriate for women, in canning and domestic service, was available in communities near the beet fields, Japanese Canadian women could not take up this work because they were formally excluded from such communities as Lethbridge.[53] Eventually, some communities did allow Japanese Canadians to undertake some of this work, in canning factories, for example, on condition that they return to sugar beet farms at the end of the work season (Adachi, 1976: 282). . . .

By the end of 1942, at least in part because of the development of great shortages of labour throughout Canada, the federal government decided that 'dispersal' east of the Rocky mountains, especially in areas of lumbering and agriculture, was the solution to the Japanese Canadian problem. State officials chose to place Japanese Canadians in localities and occupations where they would not 'compete seriously with white workers' and where they would not be required to meet the public regularly. Occupations for young women initially included domestic work, basketmaking, dress factories, laundries, and canneries, and for young men gardening, domestic work, truck driving, painting, or work in garages, tanneries, foundries, lumbering, or railway work as section men and repairmen.[54] Plans for Japanese Canadian families included settlement on abandoned farms, where they would grow specialized crops. These were largely the jobs abandoned by all who could find more lucrative employment in war production. . . .

Federal government officials—even those who protested that these workers could not be treated like indentured labour—at times used travel permit requirements to direct Japanese Canadians to or keep them in undesirable jobs. They advised, for example, that travel documents could be withheld from families seeking to leave sugar beet fields in Manitoba.[55] In principle, of course, all Canadians of working age required permission to change employment starting in 1943. But while many other Canadians ignored this requirement, Japanese Canadians could not do so (Stevenson, 2001: 35). The case of Hikowo Masuda offers a dramatic illustration of the consequences of defying restrictions on their movements. Masuda, a shipyard designer by profession, was scheduled to work on building the trans-Canada highway near Scheiber, Ontario. Angered by the restriction of Japanese Canadians to such menial jobs, he travelled to Montreal instead, where he was arrested and tried for lacking the required permit. The presiding judge described his behaviour as indicative of the untrustworthiness of the 'Japanese', and sentenced him to an internment camp for having failed to report to Scheiber (*Montreal Gazette*, 14 September 1943). . . .

Despite the degree of state control over them, Japanese Canadians attempted to resist such policies. Resistance in British Columbia, for example, threatened to undermine the government's plans for dispersal. Japanese Canadians who ventured east wrote letters warning those still in the British Columbia interior about the hard labour required in the beet fields in Alberta, Manitoba, and Ontario, and the lumber camps in Ontario, and about the hostile reception they could expect. They also knew that even if they agreed to go east and attempted to rebuild their lives there, they could be forced to leave at war's end. Facing passive resistance and fearing sit-down strikes, state officials campaigned to make relocation more attractive. They tried to

rescind guarantees to remove Japanese Canadians from any community that requested it. They also tried to find work more appropriate to the experience and training of Japanese Canadians. Although they suspected that this would be difficult, they believed that men might be more willing to accept beet work, lumbering, and railway section work, if they were promised that they could move on when more suitable jobs came up.[56]

Native People

The other racialized group of workers over whom the state exercised an exceptional degree of control was Aboriginal peoples. Although all First Nations were still officially wards of the federal government during the war years, and some state officials viewed them as so marginal to the economy that they exempted 'Indians' from national registration, their employment patterns, and hence the ability of the Indian Affairs Branch [IAB] to control their participation in the labour force, varied greatly. By the 1940s, Native peoples who lived in proximity to white settlements in Canada and the northern United States had well-established traditions of working for wages away from their reserves. These patterns continued and even strengthened during the war. They worked in steel plants in Sorel, Sault St Marie, and Michigan; an aluminum plant in Massena, New York; a foundry in Fort William; Munition Plants in Owen Sound and New Toronto; a synthetic rubber plant and other industries in Sarnia; harvesting wheat on the Prairies and hops in Oregon; and fishing, ranching, and shipyards in British Columbia. In some areas where Native people had been denied employment during the Great Depression on the grounds that they were the responsibility of the federal government, labour shortages now reopened doors to them.[57]

On remote reserves, however, poverty was so great that Native people seeking employment away from home were unable to relocate without IAB assistance. On one reserve in Saskatchewan, for example, large numbers of girls and women wanted to work in war industries in Ontario, but only two of them actually managed to go to Kingston because their parents could afford to pay their fares. Some Native people in Saskatchewan lacked the necessary funds to buy appropriate work clothing after they paid train fares to eastern Canada.[58] In such cases, the goals and prejudices of local agents and IAB bureaucrats could shape employment patterns of Native people. . . . The bureaucrats were far more concerned with ensuring that their wards would not be dependent on relief, and with satisfying labour priorities, than with opening new opportunities for Native people. Many of them also believed that Native people were inherently suited only for menial tasks.

Although they believed that wage work in lumbering would 'look like heaven to Indians', IAB officials had so little confidence in the abilities and industry of Native workers that they agreed only with great reluctance to pay the way of a small group from the Red Pheasant Reserve in Saskatchewan to Kapuskasing, where the Spruce Falls Pulp and Paper Company was desperately short of workers. The white men who had worked there seasonally before the war had been lured to the south by better prospects.[59] The reluctance of IAB officials was based on an unsuccessful arrangement with an Ontario lumber company a few years earlier, when Native workers failed to remain on the job for an entire season. Instead of recognizing that labour turn-over—whatever the workers' background—was a widespread problem in lumbering, the officials ascribed the failure of the earlier experiment to the character of 'Indians'.[60]

When the Spruce Falls company expressed great satisfaction with the workers from the Red Pheasant Reserve and sought many more Native

workers, the IAB made the necessary arrangements. IAB officials still worried, however, that the men would not on their own initiative use their wages to support their families, who would continue to depend on relief from the IAB. Unless they 'are willing to assign 20 to 30 dollars a month to their families', wrote one official, 'little benefit will accrue to the Department from this experiment'. Accordingly, the employer sent some of the men's wages directly to their families and, to ensure that the men stayed on the job, retained the remainder until the season's end. Only then was their trip home paid for and their remaining wages handed over to the Indian agent on their reserve.[61]

By contrast, the IAB was quite willing to pay the costs of sending Native labourers to the sugar beet fields of Manitoba, where harvesting was especially difficult because heavy soil on low-lying lands clung to beet roots. The Japanese Canadians who had been sent there earlier were unable to support themselves despite hard labour.[62] Yet Superintendent Hoey believed that this was work to which 'the Indians . . . could readily adapt themselves, and the experience gained would no doubt prove very valuable.' . . .

Although newspapers wrote in glowing terms about the contributions of Natives as agricultural labourers, even in this sector they encountered deep prejudices. Edna Jaques, reporting to the Writers' War Committee from Alberta, expressed views prevailing around Edmonton: 'You know as well as I do, how much work an *Indian* will do. In a pinch, he works about three hours and then you can't *find* him. Yet they are talking of sending Indians to help the farmers in the spring.'[63]

In some cases, the view of Native workers as shiftless and undependable may have been related to white perception of their preference for casual employment which could be combined with their own seasonal round of work (High, 1996). In the

Kenora district, for example, Native workers were willing enough to work as track men provided that they would be allowed to return to trapping, which provided better income, in season. There was no great difference between their pattern of employment and that of farmers who took up other types of work in winter on condition that they would be able to return to farming in the spring. In the case of the track men, employers were so short of workers that they were willing to be flexible vis-à-vis their Native employees. In other sectors, the non-acquisitive attitude of Native people toward work continued to create problems. In some cases, they simply left their jobs once they earned a certain amount of money. Insensitive to cultural differences, employers and some officials of IAB ascribed this behaviour to inherent or racial attributes of Indians.

Toward the end of the war, the participation of Native workers in war production seemed to transform the perceptions of employers and IAB officials.[64] Some employers and nutrition experts recognized that malnutrition had at times been the cause of what appeared to be laziness and indolence among Native people.[65] Officials on the west coast of British Columbia discouraged Native men from enlisting 'because they were of far more value to the country to take the place of the Japanese in the fishing industry'.[66] The Indian Agent in Williams Lake, in the interior of British Columbia, reported after the war that 90 per cent of the labour required for cattle shipped out of the Cariboo during the war was provided by Native people.[67] Such approbation was echoed in Ontario as well. Gifford Swartman, Indian Agent from Sioux Lookout, reported that, according to local mine managers, only the labour of Native people kept the mines from closing during the war. The war years also witnessed the development of better understanding of the tremendous variation in Native people's employment patterns, which depended in part on their access to wage labour.

So deeply rooted was the view of Native workers' inferiority, however, that despite this recognition of their important contribution to the war effort and the serious constraints under which Native workers operated, IAB officials simply accepted that in the more competitive post-war labour market, the 'Indian' would be the 'first man to lose his job' and the 'last to get it',[68] and that Native people would have to rely on trapping and handicrafts for their livelihood. Some officials presented these prospects in positive terms by suggesting that trapping was the chosen occupation of Native men, the only life they knew, and one they found appealing because their friends and relatives were in the 'wilds'. Others acknowledged that Native workers would return to trapping not by choice but because 'competition in more preferred employment' would force them to.[69] . . .

Conclusion

This examination of the fate of racialized minority groups in the labour market between 1939 and 1945 reveals that the crisis of war reinforced pre-existing social and economic inequality based on racist views and practices. War-induced anxieties intensified suspicion of 'foreigners'—a term that encompassed large numbers of Canadian-born and naturalized people of Japanese, central, eastern and southern European descent as well as Jews—as unpatriotic, disloyal, radical, and incapable of becoming truly Canadian. The war also reinforced racist assumptions that African Canadians, eastern and southern Europeans, and Native people were fit only for menial jobs; that Jewish, Chinese, and Japanese Canadians were economically aggressive; and that Jews in particular were given to shady practices. Such racist stereotypes in turn legitimized ongoing employment discrimination.

The state colluded in racist practices. Although by no means were all state officials or all Canadians racist, the pragmatism that informed official complicity with employment discrimination underscores the pervasiveness of racism in wartime Canada. State officials—some of whom held racist ideas—were willing to accept employers' and workers' racist preferences because they believed that to do otherwise would create social unrest and disrupt war industries. Moreover, officials found that the relegation of minority groups such as Chinese Canadians, Japanese Canadians, and Native people to menial work offered the important benefit of filling jobs that Canadians with wider options avoided.

Racist assumptions in wartime Canada clearly affected some groups more adversely than others. People of colour, or 'visible minorities', targets of the most extreme, state-sanctioned racism before World War II, continued to suffer most from employment discrimination during the war. Southern and eastern Europeans, however, were also racialized, and hence disadvantaged as workers and citizens. At the same time, state officials were most keenly aware of and most willing to tackle discrimination against these groups.

Indeed, the varying extent to which racism shaped the experiences of racialized minority workers during the war serves as an important reminder of the complexity and historical specificity of the meaning of race. On the one hand, limits to the mobility of all these workers amidst wartime labour shortages reflect both the depth of racist views in mid-twentieth-century Canada and the practical advantages of racist assumptions in filling undesirable but essential jobs in the economy. On the other hand, the selective allocation of different groups within the labour market expressed their placement in a racial hierarchy that privileged those from northern and western Europe—especially 'Anglo-Saxons'—while disadvantaging eastern and southern Europeans, people of African and Asian origin and Indigenous Canadians to differing degrees. Anti-discrimination campaigns by racialized minorities themselves—with the help of their English and French Canadian allies—were required to begin to dismantle this hierarchy after the war and thus to pave the way toward greater, if imperfect, equality for minority groups in Canadian society. As the status of workers of eastern and southern European descent improved, the chasm that separated them from people of African and Asian origin and Indigenous Canadians unfortunately deepened.

Notes

1. Library and Archives Canada [hereafter LAC], Ralston Papers, MG 27 III B11, vol. 113, Manpower Labour Supply Investigation. Committee's Report to the Labour Coordination Committee, October 1941, p. F31. My attention was drawn to this important report by Thomas M. Prymak, *Maple Leaf and Trident: The Ukrainian Canadians During the Second World War* (Toronto: Multicultural History Society of Ontario, 1988).

2. For discussions of racialization in Canada see the following works by Vic Satzewich: *Racism and the Incorporation of Foreign Labour* (London: Routledge, 1991); 'The Political Economy of Race and Ethnicity,' in Peter S. Li, ed., *Race and Ethnic Relations in Canada*, 2nd edn. (Toronto: Oxford University Press, 1999); 'Whiteness Limited: Racialization and the Social Construction of 'Peripheral Europeans', *Histoire Sociale/Social History* 33 (November 2000): 271–89.

3. The study also relies on wartime newspapers and magazines. The papers of government departments and voluntary associations consulted for the study contained a large number of newspaper clippings. The *Hamilton Spectator* archive of World War II,

available online through the Museum of Civilization, provided access not only to the *Spectator*, but also to *The Globe and Mail*, the *Toronto Telegram* and *The Toronto Daily Star*. With the help of Larry Savage, I consulted *Le Devoir*, the *Montreal Gazette*, *Niagara Falls Review*, the *St Catharines Standard*, *Welland Tribune*, the *Winnipeg Free Press*, the *Canadian Forum*, and *Saturday Night* systematically for the war years.

4. See Satzewich, 'Whiteness Limited'; Constance Backhouse, *Colour-Coded: A Legal History of Racism in Canada, 1900–1950* (Toronto: University of Toronto Press, 1999), 6. In his path-breaking *Patterns of Prejudice: A History of Nativism in Alberta* (Toronto: McClelland and Stewart, 1982), Howard Palmer used the term nativism to describe prejudice against groups of European origin, arguing that racism was inapplicable to white groups. More recently, *The Colour of Democracy: Racism in Canadian Society*, 2nd edn. (Toronto: Nelson, 2000), by Frances Henry et al., questioned the application of 'racism' to groups of European origin on grounds that it diminishes the 'colonization' of coloured people (22), while Eric W. Sager and Christopher Morier, 'Immigrants, Ethnicity and Earnings in 1901: Revisiting Canada's Vertical Mosaic', *Canadian Historical Review* 83 (2002): 196–229, a quantitative analysis of the 1901 census, suggested that ethnicity had no significant impact on the class position of Canadians.

5. 'Peripheral' Europeans is Vic Satzewich's term for eastern and southern Europeans. See Satzewich, 'Whiteness Limited'.

6. Mark Kristmanson, *Plateaus of Freedom: Nationality, Culture and State Security in Canada* (Toronto: Oxford University Press, 2002), sees a link between state cultural policy and security concerns in multicultural states.

7. LAC, Department of National War Services fonds [hereafter DNWS], RG 44, vol. 36, file: 'German and Italian Unemployables', T.C. Davis, Associate Deputy Minister of DNWS, to Norman McLarty, Minister of Labour, 21 December 1940.

8. LAC, DNWS, RG 44, vol. 36, file: 'German and Italian Unemployable', Harry Hereford, Dominion Commissioner, Dominion Unemployment Relief, Department of Labour, to Justice T.C. Davis, Associate Deputy Minister of National War Services, 18 October 1940.

9. LAC, DEA, RG 25, vol. 1964, file 855-E, Pt. II, Ernest Lapointe, Minister of Justice, to Prime Minister King, 30 May 1940.

10. LAC, Ian MacKenzie fonds [hereafter IM], MG 27111 B5, vol. 81(1), file J-25-1, Japanese in Canada

problem, Jan 1942, R.W. Mayhew, Member for Victoria to Prime Minister King, 17 February 1942; LAC, Norman Robertson fonds, MG 30 E 163, vol. 12, file 145, E.W. Bavin, Supt. Intelligence Officer, RCMP, memo to interdepartmental committee, 22 June 1940; LAC, W.L. Mackenzie King papers, MG 26, J1, vol. 325, reel C6806, p.276562, Olof Hanson MP to King, 1 June 1942.

11. LAC, DNWS, RG 44, vol. 36, file: 'German and Italian Unemployable', Harry Herreford, Commissioner, Dominion Unemployment Relief, to T.C. Davis, Associate Deputy Minister of National War Services, 18 October 1940. OA, Hepburn Papers [hereafter HP], RG 3-9, Gen Cor (Public), box 213, file: Public Welfare Department, Clerk, Town of Kenora to Hepburn, 11 June 1940.

12. LAC, DNWS, RG 44, vol. 36, file: 'German and Italian Unemployable', T.C. Davis, Associate Deputy Minister of National War Services, to Norman McLarty, Minister of Labour, 21 December 1940.

13. LAC, CSB, RG 26, vol. 36, file: 'German and Italian Unemployable', Clarence Gillis, CCF MP, Glace Bay South, to Ernest Lapointe, Minister of Justice, 26 September 1940.

14. LAC, CSB, RG 26, vol. 36, file: 'German and Italian Unemployable', Clarence Gillis, CCF MP, Glace Bay South, to Ernest Lapointe, Minister of Justice, 26 September 1940.

15. LAC, RP, MG 27111 B11, vol. 113. Manpower Labour Supply Investigation. Committee's report to the Labour Coordination Committee—with appendix and index. October 1941, p. F14.

16. LAC, DL, RG 27, vol. 632, file 77, Farm Labour Problems, Raymond W. Pincott, Secty, Vancouver Island Farmers' Council to the Honourable Minister of Agriculture, 20 May 1941.

17. LAC, Canadian Authors' Association, MG 28 I2, Special Projects or Awards, Writers' War Committee, report of Mary Weekes, Cooksville, Ontario, 30 July 1943. The Writers' War Committee, with Watson Kirkconnell as chairman, was appointed in 1942 by the Canadian Authors' Association 'to put the abilities of all Canadian authors at the disposal of the Wartime Information Board'. As part of the Committee's efforts, writers from almost every part of Canada submitted fortnightly reports to the WIB, giving their impressions of the trend of public opinion in their districts. Watson Kirkconnell, *A Slice of Canada: Memoirs* (Toronto: University of Toronto Press, 1967), esp. ch. 23.

18. See, for example, *Winnipeg Free Press*, 14 October 1939; Jeffrey Keshen, *Saints, Sinners, and Soldiers:*

Canada's Second World War (Vancouver: University of British Columbia Press, 2004), 39.

19. LAC, DL, RG 27, vol. 638, file 202: Canada Packers Limited, J.S. Willis, Personnel Director, Canada Packers Ltd., Toronto, to Professor Gilbert Jackson, Montreal, 12 July 1941.

20. LAC, Tracy Philipps fonds [hereafter TP], MG 30 E350, vol. 1, file 22, Correspondence July 1941, M. Black, RCMP to Tracy Philipps, 25 July 1941.

21. OA, Drew Papers, RG 3-17, box 436, file 87-G: Fair Employment Practices Act, 'Brief Presented to the National Selective Service by the Canadian Jewish Congress in 1942' [hereafter CJC Brief].

22. CJC Brief, Hy Lampert to Mr Hoffman, 31 July 1942; Gertrude Green to Mrs Sherwin, 21 July 1942.

23. CJC Brief, 2.

24. Canadian Jewish Congress Charities Committee National Archives [hereafter CJCCNA], CJC Organizational Records, Chronological File Series [hereafter CJCCF], ZA 1943, box 3, file 26, undated confidential memorandum by H.M. Caiserman.

25. CJCCNA, CJC, CJCCF, ZA 1943, box 3, file 26, H.M. Caiserman to Mrs S. Levitt, 22 March 1943.

26. CJCCNA, CJC, CJCCF, ZA 1943, box 3, file 22, note from Bernice Marshall, Verdun, dated 3 February 1943.

27. LAC, TP, MG 30 E350, vol. 2, file 15: Eisner Report.

28. CJC Brief, Norman Cowan to Mrs Sherwin, 17 June 1942.

29. CJC Brief, Adaline Natanson to Mrs Sherwin, Jewish Employment Service, Toronto, 1 October 1942.

30. On discrimination against Jewish and 'coloured' girls in Toronto, see LAC, DL, RG 27, vol. 1522, file XI-2-12, Pt. 3, B.G. Sullivan to Mrs Rex Eaton, 5 July 1943.

31. LAC, DNWS, RG 44, vol. 35, file: 'Bureau of Public Information—Foreign Section', Davis to H.R. McMillan, 28 February 1942; AUA, WKP, vol. 48, file 20, T.C. Davis, Associate Deputy Minister, Department of National War Services, to Professor Watson Kirkconnell, 3 January 1941.

32. LAC, Department of Munitions and Supply, RG 28, vol. 144, file: Inter-Departmental Committee on Labour Co-ordination, General Correspondence, Pt 3, H.H. Kerr, Regional Director, Ontario, Dominion Provincial War Emergency Training Programme to J.H. Ross, Regional Director, Alta, 17 November 1941; Joe H. Ross, Regional Director, Alta, Dept of Ed, to Mr Thompson, Supervisor of Training, Department of Labour, Ottawa, 24 November 1941; R.F. Thompson to A.W. Crawford, Director General of Labour Relations, DMS, 27 November 1941; LAC, Privy Council Office fonds, RG 2, vol. 6, file M5, re: Armed Services Industry. A.D.P. Heeney analysis of manpower supply for Cabinet War Committee.

33. LAC, DNWS, RG 44, vol. 36, file: 'German and Italian Unemployable', Memorandum of the Interdepartmental Committee on the Treatment of Aliens [by Norman Robertson], 13 August 1940.

34. LAC, Robert England fonds, MG 30 C181, vol. 3, file: Report on the Reorganization of Nationalities Branch, Department of National War Services. By Robert England, 12 June 1944.

35. LAC, DNWS, RG 44, vol. 36, file: 'German and Italian Unemployable', memorandum to Labour Co-ordination Committee from A.W. Crawford and W.J. Couper, re: discrimination in employment against certain nationality groups by war industries, 13 January 1942.

36. LAC, DNWS, RG 44, vol. 36, file: 'German and Italian Unemployable', T.C. Davis, Associate Deputy Minister, DNWS to Norman McLarty, Minister of Labour, 21 December 1940.

37. LAC, DNWS, RG 44, vol. 36, file: 'German and Italian Unemployable', to Employers of Labour and Secretaries of Trade Unions from N.A. McLarty, Minister of Labour, 14 March 1941, To Employers of Labour and Secretaries of Trade Unions, 14 March 1941, 'Re—Employment of Citizens and Aliens.'

38. LAC, Ian MacKenzie fonds, MG 27111 B5, vol. 32, file X-52, Committee on the Treatment of Aliens and Alien Property, first interim report and file 81 (1), Japanese in Canada problem, January 1942, 'Meeting to consider questions concerned with Canadian Japanese and Japanese Nationals in BC, 8 January 1942'.

39. LAC, DEA, RG 25, box 3008, file 3542-40, H.F. Angus to W.J. Couper, Department of Labour, 28 August 1942.

40. OA, RG 7-16-0-93, R.F. Thompson, Supervisor of Youth Training to J.F. Marsh, Dept. of Labour, 2 May 1940.

41. CJC brief, M.W. Wright to Martin Cohn, CJC, 22 January 1942; Confidential, the Board of Education, Toronto, 19 March 1942. Sponsored classes in four Vocational Toronto Schools.

42. Walter Reuther Library, United Auto Workers Toronto Sub-Regional Office, box 11, file: Meeting November 1943. Minutes of District Council 26, 7–8 November 1942.

43. CJCCNA, CJCCF, ZA 1943, box 3, file 26, Conversation with Mr Shecter of the National Selective [sic] of Montreal H.M. Caiserman, 11 March 1943.

44. LAC, DEA, RG 25, vol. 3005, file 3464-V-40. London Japanese Advisory Committee to Prime Minister King, 29 June 1944.

45. CJCCNA, CJC, CJCCF, ZA 1943, box 3, file 26, confidential memo; CJCCCNA, CJCCF, ZA 1943, box 3, file

26; Conversation with Mr Shecter of the National Selective [sic] of Montreal H.M. Caiserman, 11 March 1943.

46. CJCCCNA, CJCCF, ZA 1942, box 5, file 57, Affidavit by Simon Yasin, 9 September 1942.

47. CJC Brief, J.H. Gringorten to Rabbi Maurice N. Eisendrath, 2 October 1942.

48. CJCCCNA, CJCCF, ZA 1943, box 3, file 26, Selective Service Circular No. 81, 'Discrimination in Employment', *Winnipeg Free Press*, 14 October 1942. 'Race Prejudice Stories Result in Ottawa Step', Clipping, Spectator Collection.

49. Ontario Jewish Archives [OJA], JCRC, MG 8 S, file 78, NSS Circular No. 81A, Discrimination in Employment. For a discussion of the new instructions see CJCCCNA, CJCCF, ZA 1943, box 3, file 26, Louis Rosenberg to Saul Hayes, 24 February 1944; LAC, Jewish Historical Society of Western Canada Collection, Records of the Canadian Jewish Convess, Western Division, MG 28, V 114, vol. 3, file: Executive, Louis Rosenberg, 1944.

50. LAC, RP, MG 27 III B11, vol. 113, Manpower Labour Supply Investigation. Committee's report to the Labour Coordination Committee, October 1941, pp. 91–6. LAC, RG 27, DL, Labour, vol. 632, file 77, 'Farm Labour Patterns', vol. 975, file 1: NSS Canning.

51. LAC, DEA, RG 25, box 1964, file 855-E-39, Pt. 2, Order in Council, P.C. 1348, 29 February 1942.

52. On the nature of beet work and the difficulty of labour recruitment in this field before World War II, see John Herd Thompson and Allen Seager, 'Workers, Growers and Monopolists: The "Labour Problem" in the Alberta Beet Sugar Industry', *Labour/Le Travail* 3 (1978): 153–74.

53. LAC, DL, RG 27, vol. 170, file 614.02:11, re: Placement of Certain Japanese Families in the Province of Alberta, vol. 2, Japanese conditions in Canada generally, 21 October 1943, Report by Const J.S. Connor, RCMP, Lethbridge. Ken Adachi, *The Enemy That Never Was: A History of Japanese Canadians* (Toronto: McClelland and Stewart, 1976), 281.

54. LAC, DL, RG 27, vol. 644, file 23-2-3-7-1, Pt. 1, 'Placement and Relocation, Southern Ontario', Mactavish, Acting Eastern Supervisor, BCSC to George Collins, Commissioner, BCSC, 15 January 1944.

55. LAC, DL, RG 27, vol. 170, file 614.02:11, Transference of Japanese from BC to Province of Manitoba, vol. 2, from 1 Dec. 1942, R.H. Brown (Commissioner's representative for Manitoba) to MacNamara, 22 March 1943.

56. LAC, DL, RG 27, vol. 169, file 614.02:11, MacNamara to J.M. Wardle, Directory, Surveys and Engineering Branch, Dept of Mines and Resources, 2 June 1943;

LAC, DL, RG 27, vol. 169, file 614.02:11, Collins to MacNamara, 13 March 43; LAC, RG 27, vol. 169, file 614.02:11, MacNamara to George Collins, 26 April 1943; RG 27, DL, vol. 169, file 614.02:11, MacNamara to Collins, BCSC, 28 April 1943.

57. LAC, DL, RG 27, vol. 1485, file 2-153, Pt. 2, DNWS, Native Indians, Memorandum, W.S. Arneil, Inspector of Indian Agencies, to Dr McGill on Indian Reserves and Indian administration in Nova Scotia, 23 August 1941.

58. LAC, Department of Indian Affairs fonds [hereafter DIA], RG 10, vol. 3236, file 600,337, M. Christianson to T.R.L. MacInnes, Secretary of Indian Affairs Branch, 7 November 1941.

59. LAC, DIA, RG 10, vol. 7236, file 600,337, J.P.B. Ostrander, Indian Agent, Battleford, Sask, to M. Christianson, General Superintendent of Indian Agencies, Regina, 6 November 1941.

60. LAC, DIA, RG 10, vol. 7236, file 600,337.

61. LAC, DIA, RG 10, vol. 7236, file 600,337.

62. LAC, DL, RG 27, vol. 170, 614.01.11, Transference of Japanese from BC to Man, vol. 1. RCMP Report concerning Sugar Beet workers strike against Manitoba Sugar Co. In Fort Gary, Man, 2–3 October 1942.

63. LAC, Canadian Authors' Association, MG 28 I 2, Special Projects or Awards, Writers' War Committee, file: Edmonton district reports from Edna Jaques, n.d.; *Winnipeg Tribune*, 12 March 1943.

64. My attention was drawn to these discussions by Vic Satzewich, 'Indian Agents and the "Indian Problem" in Canada in 1946: Reconsidering the Theory of Coercive Tutelage', *The Canadian Journal of Native Studies* 17 (1997): 227–57. For a detailed study of changing attitudes toward Native people during the war see R. Scott Sheffield, *The Red Man's on the Warpath: The Image of the 'Indian' and the Second World War* (Vancouver: University of British Columbia Press, 2004).

65. *Special Standing Committee on Reconstruction and Reestablishment, Minutes of Proceedings and Evidence No. 8* (Standing Committee), (Ottawa 1944), testimony of D.J. Allan, Indian Affairs Branch, 242–3.

66. *Special Standing Committee on Reconstruction*, 242–3.

67. Satzewich, 'Indian Agents'. LAC, DIA, RG 10, vol. 6811, file 470-2-8, Pt. 1, reel C-8534 Wm. Christie, Indian Agent, Williams Lake, BC, to Glen, 5 February 1946.

68. *Special Standing Committee on Reconstruction*, testimony of D.J. Allan, superintendent of Reserves and Trust Service, IAB, 243.

69. *Special Standing Committee on Reconstruction*, testimony of D.J. Allan, 238.

References

Adachi, Ken. 1976. *The Enemy That Never Was: A History of Japanese Canadians*. Toronto: McClelland and Stewart.

Backhouse, Constance. 1999. *Colour-Coded: A Legal History of Racism in Canada, 1900–1950*. Toronto: University of Toronto Press.

Brand, Dionne. 1994. '"We weren't allowed to go into factory work until Hitler started the war': The 1920s to the 1940s", in Peggy Bristow et al., eds, *'We're Rooted Here and They Can't Pull Us Up': Essays in African Canadian Women's History*. Toronto: University of Toronto Press.

Canada, Dominion Bureau of Statistics. 1950. *Eighth Census of Canada, 1941*, vol. 1, *General Review and Summary Tables*. Ottawa: Bureau of Statistics.

Dreisziger, N.F. 1988. 'The Rise of a Bureaucracy for Multiculturalism: The Origins of the Nationalities Branch, 1939–1941', in Norman Hillmer, Bohdan Kordan, and Lubomyr Luciuk, eds, *On Guard for Thee: War, Ethnicity and the Canadian State, 1939–1945*. Ottawa: Canadian Committee for the History of the Second World War.

Giffen, P.J. 1974. 'Rural Adult Education in Manitoba', MA thesis, University of Toronto.

Globe and Mail. 1941. 26 December.

Globe and Mail. 1942. 31 October.

Globe and Mail. 1942. 16 November.

High, Steven. 1996. 'Native Wage Labour and Independent Production during the "Era of Irrelevance"', *Labour/Le Travail* 37 (Spring): 243–64.

Hurd, W. Burton. 1937. 'Racial Origin and Nativity of the Canadian People', in *Seventh Census of Canada*. Ottawa: Bureau of Statistics.

Laviolette, Forrest Emmanuel. 1978. *The Canadian Japanese and World War II: A Sociological and Psychological Account*. Toronto: University of Toronto Press.

Montreal Daily Star. 1942. 8 December.

Montreal Gazette. 1943. 14 September.

Murray, Ross. 1942. 'The End of the Canada Packers Myth', *The Canadian Forum* 21 (February): 334–5.

Ottawa Evening Journal. 1942. 'Want Congress to Substantiate Charge Made', 13 October.

Pal, Leslie. 1993. *Interest of State: The Politics of Language, Multiculturalism and Feminism in Canada*. Montreal and Kingston: McGill-Queen's University Press.

Potter, Harold Herbert, 1949. 'The Occupational Adjustments of Montreal Negroes, 1941–48', MA thesis, McGill University.

Stevenson, Michael D. 2001. *Canada's Greatest Wartime Muddle: National Selective Service and the Mobilization of Human Resources during World War II*. Montreal and Kingston: McGill-Queen's University Press.

Thompson, John Herd. 1991. *Ethnic Minorities During Two World Wars*. Ottawa: Canadian Historical Association.

Vancouver Sun. 1941. 'Foreigners Dig In', 16 October.

Windsor Daily Star. 1939. 22 September.

Young, William R.1991. 'Chauvinism and Canadianism' in Norman Hillmer, Bohdan Kordan, and Lubomyr Luciuk, eds, *On Guard for Thee: War, Ethnicity and the Canadian State, 1939–1945*. Ottawa: Canadian Committee for the History of the Second World War.

CHAPTER 17

Teamwork for Harmony: Labour–Management Production Committees and the Post-War Settlement in Canada

Peter S. McInnis

In October 1942 Prime Minister William Lyon Mackenzie King addressed a convention of the American Federation of Labor in Toronto, and called for the formal establishment of labour–management committees 'in every industry in our country' (King, 1944: 200–6). His remarks signalled the start of one of the most successful and long-lived cooperative experiments in Canadian industrial relations: the Labour–Management Production Committees (LMPCs). Designed to encourage teamwork and harmony among competing interests in the workplace, these committees were to counter the critical wartime problems of worker absenteeism and low industrial productivity. They were also to function as conduits for the exchange of productivity information between workers and management in a way that did not usurp collective bargaining procedures.[1] To this end, a plethora of guidebooks, films, posters, and other propaganda extolled the virtues of labour–management cooperation schemes. Supported by both the Trades and Labour Congress (TLC) and its rival, the Canadian Congress of Labour (CCL), as well as the Canadian Manufacturers' Association and the Canadian Chamber of Commerce, LMPCs rapidly expanded, so that by the war's end, hundreds of committees existed in many large- and medium-sized industrial settings.[2] As well, many individual unions, including the United Automobile Workers, the United Steelworkers, and the United Electrical Workers, lobbied government officials for the inclusion of such forms of cooperation.[3] . . .

In the broader context of the frenetic war years, the modest plans to establish labour–management production committees drew scant attention or comment. The overall cause justified such innovation, since the war was to be won at any cost. On one level, asking Canadian workers and managers to pull together was both common sense and the patriotic duty of citizens facing a national emergency. Where patriotism itself would not suffice, LMPCs offered a concrete response to workers' demands for stability in industrial settings that were undergoing rapid transformation. . . .

For many engaged in industrial work, LMPCs provided routine access to the boardrooms of management, a bonus that not even compulsory collective bargaining had ensured.[4] This program came at a time when collective agreements were beginning to assume their modern form as a complex list of rights and responsibilities minutely enumerating the actions of labour and management.[5] Formal and informal mechanisms for

labour–management cooperation allowed for the negotiation of issues not specifically encompassed in contract language. As such, LMPCs were an important adjunct to the achievement of compulsory collective bargaining. In the two decades following the war, the number of committees rose as their mandates were broadened to include issues such as health and safety and the quality of working life. Eventually, LMPCs served as springboards to full collective bargaining activities in settings where traditional recruitment methods had failed.

Analysis of Labour–Management Production Committees may offer an opportunity to learn how the routine of industrial relations functioned, in the words of historian David Brody, to mediate the polarity between 'sources of stability' (traditionally pragmatic trade union leadership) and 'sources for change' (a militant rank and file) (Brody, 1960). This study addresses the issue of industrial legality, with reference to the familiar dichotomy of consent and coercion. But whereas we know how organized labour found itself increasingly entangled by a web of legal and procedural encumbrances, we learn little of the role consent played in the shaping of the postwar milieu. How, then, did cooperation, in the mundane routine of workplace interactions, serve to cement the bonds of labour–management interactions in the next four decades?[6] By tracing the history of this cooperative venture, we may discover how collective-bargaining procedures were successfully inculcated into the workplace; we may understand the gender assumptions by which trade union jobs were allocated; and, more broadly, we may learn how LMPCs helped to consolidate a new era of routine state intervention under the rubric of cooperation. As a result, union members were locked into a model of behaviour premised upon productivity bargaining and material consumption that formed the basis for the postwar compromise in Canada.[7] . . .

Labour–Management Production Committees, as they functioned in the Canadian context, were not examples of the overarching tripartism found in European corporatist structures in countries such as Sweden or Austria. Canadian unions did not possess the economic and political leverage to assure such a redistribution of workplace control, just as they lacked the strongly unified central organizations requisite for such tripartism.[8] Instead, LMPCs emerged from the desire for corporatist consensus-building seen in the American Wagner Act of the New Deal era and the post-Second World War epoch (Lichtenstein, 1982). These committees were concerned with the 'achievement of peaceful and integrative bargaining with a high recognition of a mutuality of interest' (Kelly, 1987: 48–9). In 1945 Paul Martin, then parliamentary assistant to the minister of labour, described this corporatist cooperation as part of a new 'democratic citizenship' for the postwar era, one where unionized labour would gain entitlement to substantive economic benefits if it conducted itself as a mature and responsible junior partner (Martin, 1945: 24–5). . . .

In January 1944 Ottawa decided to boost the development of LMPCs and, by Order-in-Council PC 162, established the Industrial Production Cooperation Board (IPCB). This body was to act as an intermediary to facilitate the resolution of conflicts at the point of production. Because of the opposition of both business and unions towards government interference with established contractual procedures, the IPCB's mandate noted gingerly that it would concern itself exclusively with 'problems of production and should leave problems relating to wages, working conditions and similar matters to the appropriate collective bargaining procedure' (*Labour Gazette*, February 1944: 144). The federal government moved to institute labour–management committees so as to ensure a harmonious balance in the workplace.

It based its cooperative program on the British National Joint Advisory Council and, after 1941, the American War Production Board.[9] The original impetus for a formal cooperative structure stemmed not from the Department of Labour, but from its rival 'super-ministry', the Department of Munitions and Supply, and it was this department that most directly shouldered the mandate for war production.[10] By the war's end, almost 400 functioning LMPCs covered nearly 300,000 workers, and, between 1943 and 1945, more than 1,000 committees were created. As a percentage of the industrial labour force these figures show a higher rate of compliance than in Britain or the United States (*Labour Gazette*, October 1945: 1415).[11]

The establishment of the IPCB was but one initiative among many with organized labour in the years since 1939. Most efforts proved unsuccessful, as unionists questioned whether the true motivation of the federal government was to foster corporatism or something less functional. Although Canadian trade union officials were consulted in many state-sponsored initiatives, ranging from the National Selective Service and the National War Labour Board to the Unemployment Insurance Commission, the experience usually proved frustrating for labour because real influence was retained by the country's traditional power brokers in the corporate sector (Bothwell and Kilbourne, 1979). All civilian industrial workers were subject to strict governmental controls issued through a complex series of orders-in-council regulating wages and closely monitoring transfers between jobs. Workers saw their opportunities to take advantage of high pay and better jobs mired in bureaucratic red tape. . . .

After the war, the federal government continued to promote LMPCs as a tool for redressing economic uncertainty in the immediate reconstruction period. The numbers of committees and overall worker percentages continued to climb, though as war contracts began to dwindle, government enthusiasm for LMPCs was questioned.[12] The advisory committee of the IPCB did not meet for several months, and the CCL executive wrote to federal officials to complain that the IPCB budget was insufficient for its mandate.[13] Change came quickly, however, with the upsurge in union militancy and strike activity in the immediate postwar era. For trade unions, numerically strong but still weak politically, much was at stake, including their very survival in a hostile and often reactionary climate. As a statement of sheer economic power, the strike wave was an important and necessary gesture.[14] Commenting before a federal committee in the midst of the tumult, Pat Conroy, secretary-treasurer of the Canadian Congress of Labour, glibly noted that 'the lid had, figuratively, been put on wages for a period of nearly six years, and it was inevitable that, unless the pressure was eased, the lid would blow off.'[15]

The ensuing explosion surpassed all predictions, as strikes disrupted numerous industrial sectors between 1946 and 1947. Woodworkers on Vancouver Island struck for better wages and conditions, automotive workers protested long-festering issues of job security in southern Ontario, coal-miners in Alberta and Nova Scotia stopped production, as did steelworkers at the country's primary producers. Miserable conditions in Quebec's textile industries resulted in bitterness and violence on the picket line. These events were compounded by significant disputes in the electrical and rubber industries. Members of the United Packinghouse Workers of America held their first-ever national strike against Canada's meatpacking industry, one of the most notorious anti-union sectors.[16] This postwar strike wave was an indication that rank-and-file unionists in their tens of thousands were determined not only to consolidate their wartime gains but also to situate themselves better in the era of reconstruction. These events built on

precedents of an earlier strike wave in 1943.[17] It was also a stark reminder that, despite planning and cooperative efforts, the essential rights of free association and collective bargaining would have to be secured through economic struggle—as neither the state nor private businesses were willing to concede anything for which labour was not prepared to strike. Again government action made clear its intention to use coercion to quell industrial disputes. Plans for the postwar period may have continued apace, but state-sanctioned violence and repression always waited offstage.

The strike wave, however, compelled the state to encourage consensual, rather than coercive, measures in the workplace. Suddenly, official support for the LMPC idea was gaining, not losing, momentum and, consequently, the program was extended (Department of Labour, 2 February 1946; Black, 1947–8: 226–7). Under the National Emergency Transitional Powers Act the federal government retained the power to extend such measures until May 1947. Specifically, LMPCs were to be promoted through a new agency, functioning under the Department of Labour's Industrial Relations Branch, known as the Labour–Management Cooperation Service. Government intervention had to be applied, with due circumspection for the political liabilities. Canadians were tired of wartime controls, tired of sacrificing for the common good of the nation and the Commonwealth. Unless LMPCs could be adjusted to coincide with the shifting public mood towards consumerism, the project was unlikely to survive in the postwar era.

The mood for experimentation, induced by wartime pressures for industrial productivity, continued to hold sway among the ranks of the federal civil service. Whatever future faced the country as it emerged from a costly and protracted war would depend on an aptitude for rapid conversion to peacetime production. In Ottawa, not only had the absolute number of bureaucrats expanded considerably but the war itself had greatly enhanced the prestige of a group long considered drab minions toiling in obscurity. In an address before the Canadian Political Science Association, John Deutsch, an economist with the Bank of Canada who had served during the war as special assistant to the Department of External Affairs, commented that the government had, of necessity, become 'a highly centralized machine' capable of much innovation and experimentation (Deutsch, 1957). This view was shared by Leonard Marsh, a man renowned for progressive reform. In retrospect, Marsh recalled, 'the war, whatever it was in death and destruction, was a vortex in terms of social ideas and political ferment' (Marsh, 1975: xiii).

In this spirit of ferment, the government turned to the continuing problems of industrial strife and planned to fashion a permanent mechanism to further labour–management cooperation. Part of the task was to reaffirm the concept of cooperation with business leaders. In a series of articles appearing in *Industrial Canada* and *Canadian Business*, the respective publications of the Canadian Manufacturers' Association and the Canadian Chamber of Commerce, LMPCs were touted as part of the solution to postwar uncertainty. Observers noted that such committees coincided with the move in many larger unions, such as the United Steelworkers, towards centralizing of negotiation procedures and industry-wide pattern bargaining (Goldenberg, 1945: 27–9, 72). The propaganda zeroed in on key postwar issues stating that labour–management committees '[must] seek to shift the emphasis from production for victory to production geared to the needs of the postwar competitive era, in terms of wage levels, and job security'. . . .

Along with the pleas for postwar productivity, an important message was included that any Canadian worker who had survived the Depression could not fail to grasp. Accompanying these articles were numerous photographs of labour and management representatives sitting across boardroom tables discussing the future in an atmosphere of mutual respect. For unionists accustomed to the unrelenting management hostility of the 1930s and much of the war years, this potential for recognition must have seemed enticing. The new arrangement was to leave intact the adversarial process of collective bargaining, where labour and management could often agree only to disagree, and combine it with LMPCs, where the two sides would discover points of harmony. . . .

The IPCB actively solicited correspondence from businesses, particularly factory personnel managers, on the efficacy of LMPCs. Many of these comments would be incorporated in future brochures and booklets published by the government. Most accounts explained how labour–management committees had 'intangible benefits' as they encouraged improved relations between employers and unionized workers in breaking down the 'invisible wall' that separated the two. The rhetoric is instructive, since LMPCs were touted as encouraging 'operational efficiency', instilling 'common sense' on the shop floor, and providing an avenue for the 'flow of ideas' or the 'frank and open discussions' necessary to assure corporate profitability in the uncertain postwar era.[18] Joint labour–management cooperation was pitched not only as a matter of common interest (some committees were given the moniker 'mutual interest boards') but also as an appeal to the assumed *rationality* incumbent in mature industrial relations policies. . . .

The concept of industrial democracy was in need of all the support it could garner. Throughout the war, organized labour had continually pursued the issue of fair procedures to ensure that its members were represented before employers and government boards. In many instances these efforts had met with frustration. Unions continued to participate in government-directed procedures not only because they were the law, but also because there was little else to replace this process. To some extent, LMPCs provided just the sort of quietly effective mechanism for workplace cooperation that many business executives and union officials desired. The Industrial Production Cooperation Board frequently reminded LMPC participants to carry out shop-level policies that *immediately* responded to any instances of workers' participation, however slight. The central focus of this approach was transmitted through company 'suggestion plans'.

Suggestion plans, by which workers contributed advice on matters from workplace safety to production efficiency, had long been a feature of many corporate polices. Collective bargaining offered an imperfect apparatus of grievance resolution, and many unionists came to resent the 'obey now—grieve later' policies that relegated their complaints to a process that seemed as mystifying as it did interminable. LMPCs offered a contrast to the standard grievance route in both style and substance, since they were intended to function in a more congenial atmosphere and their benefits could be instantly gratifying and financially lucrative. Workers who suggested cost-saving tips or new production methods were to be rewarded with cash bonuses that ranged from $2 to $25 for minor improvements to $750 for major ideas (May, 1944: 10).[19] Many companies developed elaborate formulae for calculating these bonus rewards. Government brochures instructed employers to make sure that their suggestion plans provided for the 'continuous publicity' of each program. All participants were to receive personal letters of commendation (regardless of the utility of the proffered advice), while beneficiaries garnered

prominent notice in company newsletters or on posters for factory bulletin boards. . . .

Union business agents also considered that the habit of filing suggestion plans was useful, since each successful program reinforced the procedures of participatory cooperation with rank-and-file members. A new spirit of cooperation would prevail and would carry over to all aspects of the job. Suggesting how an employer could, for example, save time by more efficiently transferring supplies arriving at the loading dock melded smoothly with the orderly filing of grievance claims dealing with broader contractual matters. In both instances, workers were told to stand aside and trust in the functioning of due process—to fill out the proper forms and leave the matter to others. Such boundaries on worker activity served to define expected roles for all concerned. . . .

On the shop floor, the war years had done much to erode the standing and prestige of foremen. Government-imposed controls on job mobility, combined with relentless pressures for industrial production meant that few companies wished to lose skilled personnel. Workers knew that the power of foremen in this situation was diminished and foremen themselves were increasingly alienated from corporate decision making.[20] Cooperative programs were adapted to reverse this state of affairs. An IPCB publication, *The Foreman and the LMPC*, discussed strategies for enhancing the status of foremen 'caught in the crossfire of labour–management differences'. Foremen would be active in various LMPC subcommittees, while they attempted to appear neutral in votes or decision-making. Other booklets suggested training projects to be known as management forums; they were intended to train prospective foremen or subforemen in the art of workplace cooperation by emphasizing that 'we're all human beings rather than labour and management.'. . .

Figure 17.1 LAC, C-142803

Figure 17.2 LAC, C-142804

Throughout the latter stages of the war, the Industrial Production Cooperation Board published its monthly newsletter, *Teamwork for Victory*. In appearance, the newsletter was a crudely mimeographed report, typewritten on legal-sized paper, which adhered to the common format of most war-era 'news bulletins' and conveyed the impression that it held timely, unsifted accounts taken from the factories and workshops of the nation. Compared with slick governmental publications, *Teamwork for Victory* resembled a club newsletter. Whether understated by design or default, this publication represented one tool for broadcasting the idea of industrial cooperation. The National Film Board was enlisted to produce films with titles such as *Workers at War* (1943), *Coal Face—Canada* (1943), *Smoke and Steel* (1944), and *Work and Wages* (1945), and to distribute similar films from Britain, all in an effort to exhort workers to new levels of patriotism through industrial production. Film footage culled from the British shorts

Partners in Production (1944), *Democracy at Work* (1944), or *The New Pattern* (1945) was combined with Canadian-produced 'discussion prefaces and trailers' under the overall title, *The Joint Labour–Management Production Committee* (1945).[21]

In another approach, a series of posters and pay-packet inserts commissioned under the general theme 'Produce for Prosperity' were devised to publicize the importance of continuing the spirit of cooperation that had won the war, since 'the security of Canada's industries no less than the workers' jobs depends on cooperation' (*Teamwork in Industry*, September 1945: 4).[22] The first poster issued in the series portrayed a horse-drawn cart in which was piled a cornucopia of goods intended both for export and for domestic consumption. Holding the reins to the vehicle of Canada's future were two male figures, dressed respectively in a business suit and overalls, depicting labour and management working together in harmony (see Figure 17.1). The postwar industrial world would be one of unbridled aspirations and, in terms of employee composition, an implied return to the status quo.

Women may have found their way into the workplace in record numbers during the wartime crisis, but from now on their roles would return to those of wife, mother, and creator of the idealized postwar household. Elaine Tyler May suggests that the tendency towards highly organized and bureaucratized blue-collar jobs led to an image of the home as a 'warm hearth' of freedom and individuality (May 1988).[23] Poster 9 (Figure 17.2) in the series made the connection even more explicit. Arranged around the central figure of a dollar sign that was coloured bright red in the original were images of household necessities (a dress, kitchen pots, shoes, and a new house in which to place them), while presented diagonally were the objects of desire (a radio, a refrigerator, an automobile). The caption 'Everything we need—everything we want—depends on greater production' frames these pictures. In both sets of images the appeal was to be transmitted to the male breadwinner as well as his spouse. The grouping 'everything we need' includes kitchen utensils and a dress, while 'everything we want' makes reference to durable goods—even to a full-length fur coat, the epitome for many women of conspicuous consumption. Moreover, the image of a house was that of a suburban single-family dwelling, the type most likely to appeal to the aspirations of the upwardly mobile and those with a steady, secure income.[24] Thus, the intended postwar social formation was revealed: the home would remain the locus for consumption and leisure of material wealth, which was secured by male breadwinners whose unions had signed wage contracts premised on a strategy attuned to the national drive for industrial productivity. With the timely application of state assistance, labour and management could now move to accommodate each other.

A further poster in the series demonstrated the 'before' and 'after' situations. It depicted columns of stylized tanks rolling off wartime military assembly lines with the caption 'Then it was quantity,' contrasted with an image of a single domestic automobile and the phrase 'Now it's quality' (Figure 17.3). Text accompanying the poster clarified what was at issue: 'You have a personal stake in the quality of the goods you help produce. A growing demand for the goods or services of your firm means steady employment, greater opportunity for advancement, and the possibility of increased pay for you.'[25] The connection between labour–management cooperation and job security, future promotion, and higher wages would prove a powerful incentive for many Canadian workers terrified of returning to the despair of the Depression or afraid of losing the precious gains secured during the war years. For organized labour, the stability of the postwar family was to be anchored to a base of workplace standards that would provide the required financial and social security for the happiness and prosperity of the nation.

Just as the prosecution of the Second World War had dominated most activities of the state and civil society, the debate about the future of the nation in the postwar era engaged a diverse group of participants. By 1943–4 Canadians may have expressed cautious optimism as to the eventual outcome of the war, but many citizens viewed the task of postwar reconversion with consternation. Loath to repeat the events that had followed the Armistice in 1918, many now looked to the state for direction and planning.[26] It was, after all, an obvious solution. Had not the dominion government amassed unprecedented powers during the war years, and were not its citizens led to believe that these powers were generally successful in coordinating the nation's activities? If the 'command economy' had served this role since 1939, could it not suffice for the aftermath? . . .

PRODUCE FOR PROSPERITY

then it was **QUANTITY**

now it's **QUALITY**

GIVE YOUR IDEAS ON QUALITY CONTROL TO YOUR L.M.P.C. REPRESENTATIVE
OR PLACE IN THE SUGGESTION BOX

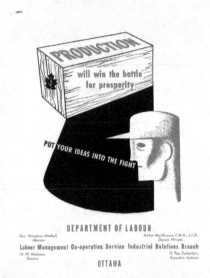

Figure 17.3 LAC, C-142802

Figure 17.4 LAC, 142805

The emphasis would change after the Allied victories in the European and Pacific theatres. The constant cajoling of workers to use industrial production to win the war was transformed in the postwar years to focus on global competitiveness, a trend in keeping with the emphasis on international exports articulated in the 1945 White Paper on Employment and Income (Figure 17.4).[27] LMPC pamphlets with such wartime titles as *Victory in the Making* and *Back the Attack* were rephrased to become *Partners in Production*, *Industrial Democracy at Work*, or *Working Together in a Democratic Society*. . . .

Full employment, made necessary to satisfy a modern war machine, was fast becoming something from which many employers sought to withdraw their commitment. The extension of formal mechanisms for labour–management cooperation offered the hope of maintaining high productivity despite the 'inevitable' layoffs that were to accompany the cessation of hostilities.

The initial economic indicators for the immediate postwar period were not at all positive, as experts were divided over what the future would bring. In their annual state-of-the-economy forecasts, the country's major chartered banks warned that although organized labour posed a threat to the nation's stability, the problem lay not with unions themselves but with their 'maladministration'. This threat could be overcome if labour and management worked together to 'unselfishly distribute their earnings' (*Saturday Night*, 16 December 1944: 48).[28]

Not all economic predictions for the postwar period suggested a recession; indeed, several polls identified a pent-up desire among Canadians to purchase the consumer goods they had so long been denied by wartime restrictions. Generally high wages and a long work week meant that the money for these goods was in ready supply. Trade publications in the manufacturing sector confidently spoke of a high potential demand for durable goods. MacLean-Hunter, the nation's largest publisher of specialized trade magazines, established a Post-War Research Department to survey Canadian citizens and industrialists about their plans, going so far as to determine that exactly 762,568 new cars would be needed for 'V+2', the two years immediately following victory. Another survey of 1,526 housewives found strong markets not only for 'big ticket' domestic appliances such as washing machines, refrigerators, and electric stoves but also for radios, vacuum cleaners, and other consumer items. . . .

Gary Cross, one of the few historians who has assessed the culture of mass consumption in the immediate postwar era, writes that 'a consumerist consensus emerged after 1945. It had been built upon mass production, balanced with high wages, and buttressed by Keynesian macro-economic management and manipulated needs creation' (Cross, 1993: 184). Male workers in heavy industries were offered the option of maintaining their longer week and the opportunity for abundant overtime hours or accepting a sharp reduction of hours if the work week was more evenly distributed among others, including women restricted to part-time jobs. LMPCs may have played a role in establishing that further benefits take the form of increased wages rather than a shorter work week. If LMPCs were intended to assuage workplace conflict, they were not felt to be the vehicle for redressing the standard hours of work. Economist Juliet Schor notes how the desire for consumer goods led in turn to personal debt, and how that debt forged ever stronger chains of dependence to the job and the dictates of employers (Schor, 1991: 60–6). She argues that 'workers want what they get,' and that the ideological pressures associated with a society that creates material desire leads people to look for ways to accommodate those urges (Schor, 1991: 128–9). For many workers this meant acquiescence and cooperation, rather than struggle and resistance through vehicles such as an LMPC. . . .

Other aspects of the postwar world were also subject to renegotiation. Historians Ruth Roach Pierson and Gail Cuthbert Brandt have suggested that the Second World War and the reconstruction period posed an ideological challenge to accepted definitions of marital and familial relationships, just as they modified social constructions of gender and sexuality.[29] As seen in previous wars, gender boundaries were first extended and then retracted during the war and its immediate aftermath. Serious concern was expressed about the state of the postwar family and its adjustment in the reconstruction period.[30] Many Canadians, men and women trade unionists among them, wished to move away from the overt patriotism or civic-mindedness of the war years and retreat to the private realm of the family. Although some working women said they would fight to retain these higher-paid jobs after the war, the sentimental image of the 'home and family' as a bastion from society's troubles continued to have widespread appeal both during the war and after.[31] The Produce for Prosperity poster series emphasizing working men's responsibilities to provide economic sustenance for their wives and families found constant emphasis, and it did so in a manner that was often uniquely Canadian in perspective.[32] Part of the country's opportunity for national renewal would come from a more holistic redefinition of economic security.

Although the trade union movement would continue to lobby for broad legislative reforms, the focus shifted to comparatively narrow and specific measures likely to be secured through contractual negotiations and greater cooperation. To a large extent organized labour withdrew from the challenge to reformulate the gender dynamics of the workplace in a way that would address the inequalities that chronically afflicted female wage-earners. The priority for postwar jobs continued to privilege unionized male wage-earners. Women were informed they could best benefit from these specific contractual reforms, and the modestly expanding welfare state, indirectly as spouses of these men rather than as paid workers outside the home (Lewis, 1992: 36–9, 92–4). The grudging acceptance by male unionists of family allowances (in lieu of demands for a minimum industrial wage) was made more palatable with the promise of financial benefits to be secured through close cooperation with government and employers. Organized labour in Canada consented to this arrangement and continued its support for LMPCs.

The gender assumptions of labour–management cooperation are revealed in case studies published by the IPCB. In industrial settings employing large numbers of women workers, such as the textile/clothing sectors, government literature encouraged the use of LMPCs, not in the 'masculine' sense of problem-solving devices to resolve non-contractual issues, but as 'feminine' committees promoting recreational or social clubs outside the workplace. An issue of *Teamwork in Industry*, that proclaimed that 'LMPCs Help Women Adjust to Industry' detailed how labour–management cooperation had proved useful in 'acclimatizing' women to their postwar job opportunities (*Teamwork in Industry*, September 1948). Examples drawn from the St Thomas, Ontario, plant of the Monarch Knitting Company, organized as Local 777, Textile Workers Union of America (CCL-CIO), described how LMPCs mainly took the form of recreational subcommittees that helped in boosting morale and maintaining high productivity. LMPC subcommittees sponsored contests for regular job attendance and 'good housekeeping' that offered cash rewards for compliance. Compared with LMPC literature intended for male-dominated workplaces, the contrast in subject and in editorial tone is notable. Women were assumed to be most interested in

social interactions, while men focused on health and safety or production efficiency.[33] . . .

The ongoing discussions and experiments with industrial relations blended into the larger debates surrounding the future of the Canadian welfare state. The war had provided the opportunity to establish long overdue policies such as unemployment insurance, and the prospect of peace offered hope that more comprehensive welfare measures would be introduced. In Britain, plans for a cradle-to-grave state, outlined in the influential Beveridge Report of 1942, led some Canadians to hope that this model might set the tone for reforms in Canada.[34] The Advisory Committee on Reconstruction and its Subcommittee on the Post-War Problems of Women were kept busy throughout 1942–3 with representations from various groups concerned with the postwar state.[35] Another significant part of this reformist milieu was the 1943 Marsh Report, with its pessimistic economic forecast for the immediate postwar era. That the efforts of both the James Committee and Leonard Marsh were largely shunted aside in favour of political expediency and a more conventional view of the Canadian state does not detract from what historian Doug Owram refers to as a 'bureaucratic enthusiasm for reconstruction' (Guest 1985; Owram 1986: 287). Trade unions appearing before the House of Commons Committee on Reconstruction and Rehabilitation in support of many of the recommendations for an expanded welfare state emphasized the relationship between the achievement of collective bargaining and a broader postwar vision of social security for Canada. . . .

The willingness of unions to consent to a structure of workplace cooperation in the immediate postwar era may have spurred the development of a 'split-level' economy that privileged only the strongest trade unions with high wages and favourable working conditions at the expense of their less well-positioned confederates.[36] Beyond the goal of mere legal recognition, participating unions sought inclusion in the emerging regulatory regime. But not all unions were welcome. Cold war politics served to narrow greatly the range of dialogue on progressive social reform. In the postwar atmosphere of hostile name-calling, violence, and dirty tricks, official support for expanded welfare provisions, and equality for wage-earning women, were easily conflated with intrusive state planning regimes of nations situated on the wrong side of the 'iron curtain'. In what was a startling example for the domestic use of a foreign threat, any evocation of Stalinist intrigue forced closure on vital domestic issues of social policy. Canada's communist labour movement, now exposed to withering attacks from its many opponents, retreated from the public sphere, leaving the debate on the future of industrial relations to those groups who were prepared to adopt more conciliatory positions in their transactions with government and management representatives. In return for purging Canada's labour movement of its 'disreputable' communist-led organizations, those unions who remained were rewarded for their cooperation with an entrée as legitimate interests into the new regulatory state. This tacit precondition was achieved by the end of the 1940s, as both the CCL and the TLC engaged in rancorous internal battles.[37] Those labour leaders remaining in the fold were now deemed eligible to participate on various tripartite boards, commissions, and advisory panels. Union cooperation with management brought a concurrent linkage with the state.

Following the war and the initial transition phase to a peacetime economy, government officials redirected LMPCs to health and safety issues. While improved productivity remained a key element of the program, the focus during the 1950s was to link industrial production with job security. Throughout the 1950s, interest in labour–management cooperation continued to

gain momentum. Between the fiscal years of 1950 and 1955, the number of LMPCs grew from 684 to 1,029, covering 260,000 and 310,000 workers, respectively (Department of Labour, 1950: 29–31, 1955: 29–30; *Teamwork in Industry*, October 1953: 1–2). Small industrial plants started to account for a large number of new committees. At the level of union locals, this increase resulted in bridges that eventually led to co-management schemes between labour and business. Not all of these developments were positive. The federal Labour–Management Cooperation Service sponsored its bulletin *Teamwork in Industry*, as well as commissioning films and radio projects intended to broaden the appeal of this concept. At times these tactics degenerated to the level where a mawkish cartoon character, known as Tommy Teamwork, was enlisted to remind production workers of the importance of cooperation and the commonality of interests they shared with their employers and the state.[38] . . .

By the early 1960s, the idea of labour–management consultation had spread into many areas of state and parastate institutions—notably hospitals. In 1964 almost 300 LMPCs acted as 'dual capacity' committees, serving the traditional role of stimulating greater productivity, as well as taking on the capacity to negotiate terms hitherto restricted to collective agreements (Wood, 1964: 16).[39] Through institutions such as the National Productivity Council (1961–3) and the Economic Council of Canada (1963–92), organized labour sought out new liaisons with business and the state. . . . Echoes of LMPCs resonate in recent experiments with Quality Circles, Quality of Working Life (QWL), and Total Quality Management (TQM), initiatives launched by many provincial governments and corporations eager to increase employee productivity, reduce payrolls, and still retain a semblance of workplace 'harmony'.[40] . . .

The arrival of a 'professional' stratum of labour officials shifted the focus of decision-making away from the shop stewards and their rank-and-file constituency. Industrial legality stifled spontaneous self-activity, replacing it with complex, routinized collective bargaining procedures, activities that posed no serious threat to capital's essential property rights. LMPCs and their materialist focus on productivity and consumption blended smoothly with the postwar prospects for a select and privileged cohort of predominately male trade unionists in Canada's resource, transportation, and manufacturing sectors. In the immediate postwar era, Canadian trade unions were presented with a choice that many found congenial. In return for the promise of unprecedented wealth and stability, workers were counselled by management and the state, as well as by their union and political leaders, to consider only their pay cheques—and what these could purchase. Teamwork and harmony served to reinforce an active but rigidly circumscribed sphere for labour's actions. Contentious issues of workplace control or class solidarity were shunted aside in the rush to consumerism.[41] Recent efforts by the nation's largest unions to resurrect a class-conscious 'social unionism', sensitive to the changing nature of both the workplace and Canada's workers, have failed to deliver on the promise

that this new approach differs substantively with traditional 'business unionism'.[42] The choice made from the mid-1940s onward, to step onto the escalator of regular and predictable material gain, still guides the intent of current union strategy.

In the years following the Second World War, Labour–Management Production Committees presented a model of a shared community of interests premised on the mutuality of productivity and consumption. For Canadians emerging triumphant from another global conflict, with collective memories of wartime sacrifices and privations, this postwar 'social contract' proved highly seductive. Aspects of the hegemonic notions of the postwar settlement continue in the limited institutional forms and practices of the state and labour. It was not the first instance, nor the last, where organized labour championed reforms they would live to regret in later years. The decisions made during the Second World War and the immediate postwar era simultaneously opened up opportunities for progressive change *and* led to complacency. For labour, such complacency has resulted in political atrophy that has left it ill equipped to confront a resurgence of employers' reactionary incursions within today's 'global' economy.

Notes

1. While government-sponsored materials made it clear that wages or basic working conditions were not in the purview of LMPCs, the line delineating these activities was often unclear.
2. See *Saturday Night*, 27 June 1942, 6–7; Canadian Manufacturers' Association, *The War and After* (Toronto: CMA, 1944), 12; H.A. Logan, *Trade Unions in Canada: Their Development and Functioning* (Toronto: Macmillan, 1948), 521–8.
3. LMPCs were not new, for a similar concept of 'production councils' had originated with unions associated with the Labour Progressive Party (Communist Party of Canada) to promote the Allied war effort. See, for example, pamphlets of the United Electrical Workers (UE), including *We Produce for the Second Front* and *Victory* (Toronto: Eveready Printers 1942).

The politically left Canadian leadership of the United Automobile Workers (District Council 26) advocated this form of cooperation in early 1942; see Charlotte A.B. Yates, *From Plant to Politics: The Autoworkers Union in Postwar Canada* (Philadelphia: Temple University Press, 1993), 37–40.
4. The wartime rules and procedures for compulsory collective bargaining culminated with Order-in-Council PC 1003, 'The Wartime Labour Relations Regulations' (17 February 1944). For details, see John A. Willes, *Contemporary Canadian Labour Relations* (Toronto: McGraw-Hill Ryerson, 1984), 75–9.
5. For examples of the way that contractual language rapidly assumed a formidable complexity, see Peter Warrian, '"Labour Is Not a Commodity": A Study of the Rights of Labour in the

Canadian Postwar Economy, 1944–48', PhD dissertation, University of Waterloo, 1986.

6. An assessment of the Canadian situation is offered in H.C. Pentland, 'The Canadian Industrial Relations System: Some Formative Factors', *Labour/Le Travailleur* 4 (1979): 9–23. Revisionist accounts of an American perspective, taken from the 'critical legal studies' school, include: Karl E. Klare, 'Judicial Deradicalization of the Wagner Act and the Origins of Modern Legal Consciousness, 1937–1947', *Minnesota Law Review* 62 (1978): 265–339; James B. Atleson, *Values and Assumptions in American Labor Law* (Amherst: University of Massachusetts Press, 1983); Christopher L. Tomlins, *The State and the Unions: Labor Relations Law and the Organized Labor Movement in America, 1880–1960* (Cambridge: Cambridge University Press, 1985). The best synthesis of this literature is Nelson Lichtenstein and Howell John Harris, eds, *Industrial Democracy in America: The Ambiguous Promise* (Cambridge: Cambridge University Press, 1993). For Canada, see David W.T. Matheson, 'The Canadian Working Class and Industrial Legality, 1939–1949', MA thesis, Queen's University 1989.

7. The phrase 'postwar compromise' describes the peace treaty brokered by the state between labour and capital which established the rudimentary framework for industrial peace following the end of the Second World War. See Claus Offe, *Contradictions of the Welfare State* (Cambridge, MA: MIT Press, 1982), 147–61.

8. The European model of tripartism involves the allocation of a permanent place for organized labour on administrative bodies alongside state and corporate representatives; it also provides substantive procedures for long-range planning, instead of defaulting into a highly adversarial approach within a traditional market economy. For a discussion of these themes, see Leo Panitch, 'The Tripartite Experience', in Keith Banting, ed., *The State and Economic Interests* (Toronto: University of Toronto Press, 1985), 37–119.

9. See James E. Cronin, *The Politics of State Expansion: War, State and Society in Twentieth-Century Britain* (London: Routledge, 1991), 138–45; Dorothea de Schweinitz, *Labor and Management in Common Enterprise* (Cambridge: Harvard University Press, 1949); *Labour Gazette*, May 1945, 595.

10. The term 'superministry' is drawn from John Smart, 'Administrative Outline', *Records of the Department of Labour*, General Inventory Series (Ottawa: National Archives of Canada, 1988), 25–6.

11. In the United States a total of 5,300 committees was established, with 3,800 active at one time, involving more than eight million workers. The British participation figures approximate those of the Americans; see Carol Reigelman, *British Joint Production Machinery* (Montreal: International Labour Office, 1944). See also de Schweinitz, *Labor and Management in a Common Enterprise*, 1–27; Carol Reigelman, *Labor–Management Cooperation in United States War Production* (Montreal: International Labour Office, 1948); G.D.H. Cole, *The Case for Industrial Partnership* (London: Macmillan, 1957).

12. At a three-day conference of the Industrial Production Co-operative Board, LMPCs were declared 'essential to the successful solution of the problems of peace', *Labour Gazette*, January 1945, 2; February 1945, 126–7.

13. NA, CLC Records, RG 28, I 103, vol. 145. IPCB, *Quarterly Report*, March 1946.

14. For details, see Donald Kerr and Derek W. Holdsworth, eds, *Historical Atlas of Canada,* vol. 3 (Toronto: University of Toronto Press, 1990), plate 62; Wayne Roberts and John Bullen, 'A Heritage of Hope and Struggle: Workers, Unions, and Politics in Canada, 1930–1982', in Michael S. Cross and Gregory S. Kealey, eds, *Modern Canada: 1930–1980s* (Toronto: McClelland and Stewart, 1984), 105–40.

15. NA, Records of the Department of Labour, RG 27, B 6, vol. 896, CCL National Wage Coordinating Committee submission, 1 August 1946.

16. For commentary and statistical analysis of these strikes, see Gregory S. Kealey and Douglas Cruikshank, 'Strikes in Canada, 1891–1950', *Labour/Le Travail* 20 (Fall 1987): 85–145; Jamieson, *Times of Trouble: Labour Unrest and Industrial Conflict in Canada, 1900–66* (Ottawa: Task Force on Labour Relations, 1968), 295–305; Morton, *Working People* (Montreal and Kingston: McGill-Queen's University Press, 1998), 175–200. For details of the packinghouse strikes, see Alton W.J. Craig, 'The Consequences of Provincial Jurisdiction for the Process of Company-wide Collective Bargaining in Canada', PhD dissertation, Cornell University, 1964; Bryan Mahn and Ralph Schaffner, 'The Packinghouse Workers in Kitchener', in J.T. Copp, ed., *Industrial Unionism in Kitchener* (Elora, ON: Cumnock Press, 1976).

17. A strike of 13,000 steelworkers in January 1943 caused severe production shortages. See Laurel Sefton MacDowell, 'The 1943 Steel Strike against Wartime Wage Controls', *Labour/Le Travailleur* 10 (Autumn 1982): 65–85.

18. See, for example, Department of Labour, *Common Sense in Labour Relations* (Ottawa: King's Printer, 1945); *Partners in Production* 2 (1949): 8–9, 12–19. See also de Schweinitz, *Labor and Management in a Common Enterprise*, 78–9, 142.

19. During the latter stages of the war, the aircraft manufacturers alone paid out an estimated $38,000 in suggestion awards.

20. In the United States, employers were alarmed about a nascent union, the Foreman's Association of America, fearing it would spread across the continent. See Lichtenstein, *Labor's War at Home,* 118–20.

21. For a listing of these wartime films, see Donald W. Bidd, ed., *The NFB Film Guide: The Productions of the National Film Board of Canada, 1939–1989* (Montreal: NFB, 1991).

22. Workers were also encouraged to make their own home-made posters to add credibility to the campaign. See also Marc H. Choko, *Canadian War Posters: 1914–1918, 1939–1945* (Ottawa: Éditions du Méridien, 1994).

23. See also Stephanie Coontz, *The Way We Never Were: American Families and the Nostalgia Trap* (New York: Basic Books, 1992), 92–121; Joanne Meyerowitz, ed., *Not June Cleaver: Women and Gender in Postwar America, 1945–1960* (Philadelphia: Temple University Press, 1994).

24. The postwar push for women to return to the household is addressed in Veronica Strong-Boag, 'Home Dreams: Women and the Suburban Experiment in Canada, 1945–60', *Canadian Historical Review* 72 (December 1991): 471–504; Doug Owram, 'Home and Family at Mid-Century', Paper presented to the Canadian Historical Association, 1992. On the subject of government-sponsored domesticity, see Margaret Hobbs and Ruth Roach Pierson, '"A Kitchen That Wastes No Steps": Gender, Class and the Home Improvement Plan, 1936–1940', *Histoire Sociale/Social History* 31 (May 1988): 9–37.

25. See Department of Labour, Industrial Relations Branch, Poster 7 (5946). Other posters dealt with workplace health and safety in the (apparently) all-male world of the postwar factory. In this context, the image of a workman tripping over shop debris with the caption 'Good Housekeeping Is Important to Safety' held a particular irony.

26. Representative of this literature is Wartime Information Board, *Canadian Affairs* 1, 18 (October 1944), Leonard Marsh and O.J. Firestone, 'Will There Be Jobs?'; Department of Labour, *Dismiss—But What of a Job?* (Ottawa: King's Printer, 1945). See also Canadian Broadcasting Corporation, *The Soldier's Return* (Toronto: CBC, 1945), 1–48.

27. For details on Canada's export market orientation, see Paul Phillips and Stephen Watson, 'From Mobilization to Continentalism: The Canadian Economy in the Post-Depression Period', in Cross and Kealey,

eds, *Modern Canada,* 20–45; Glen Williams, *Not For Export: Towards a Political Economy of Canada's Arrested Development* (Toronto: McClelland and Stewart, 1983).

28. Annual report by C.H. Carlisle, President, Dominion Bank. Similar positions were expressed by the Bank of Montreal, Commerce Bank, and the Bank of Nova Scotia. This coincided with Ottawa's interpretation. See *Annual Report of the Bank of Canada* (1994): 11–15; (1946), 8–12.

29. See Ruth Roach Pierson, *They're Still Women After All: The Second World War and Canadian Womanhood* (Toronto: McClelland and Stewart, 1986); Gail Cuthbert Brandt, '"Pigeon-Holed and Forgotten": The Work of the Subcommittee on the Post-War Problems of Women', *Histoire Sociale/Social History* 15 (March–May 1982): 239–59.

30. For example, see Charlotte Whitton, *The Dawn of Ampler Life* (Ottawa: Macmillan, 1943). See also Annalee Gölz, 'Family Matters: The "Canadian Family" and the State in the Postwar Period', *Left History* 2 (Fall 1993): 9–49; Owram, 'Home and Family at Mid-Century'; Strong-Boag, 'Home Dreams'; Margaret Higonnet, et al., *Behind the Lines: Gender and the Two World Wars* (New Haven: Yale University Press, 1987); Barry Broadfoot, *The Veteran's Years: Coming Home from the War* (Vancouver: Douglas and McIntyre, 1985).

31. For a contemporary example of this debate see Agnes MacPhail and Helen MacGill, 'Do Women Expect to Go Back to Kitchens after the War?', *Monetary Times* (October 1943): 29–31, 103.

32. It must be noted that women wage-earners continued to increase numerically in the immediate postwar era, but structural barriers often maintained gender inequalities. For one case study of this issue, see Pamela Sugiman, *Labour's Dilemma: The Gender Politics of Autoworkers in Canada, 1937–1979* (Toronto: University of Toronto Press, 1994).

33. For example, compare the subject matter of the IPCB booklet, *Pattern for Production* (1948), which dealt with the case study of LMPCs at the Market Street plant at Massey-Harris in Brantford, Ontario. In this factory with an overwhelmingly male labour force of more than 1,100, LMPCs were assumed to deal with issues closely related to the workplace, not the home. An LMPC was later established at the Massey-Harris 'M' Foundry (Brantford), one of the nation's largest.

34. For background on the Beveridge Report, see Paul Addison, *The Road to 1945: British Politics and the Second World War*, rev. ed. (London: Pimlico, 1994), 210–28.

35. The Advisory Committee on Reconstruction (also known as the James Committee, after its chairman, McGill president Cyril James) was established in 1941. Associated with the project was a study of postwar social programs, the *Report on Social Security for Canada,* prepared by social scientist Leonard Marsh.

36. On the stratification of trade unions, see Mike Davis, *Prisoners of the American Dream* (London: Verso, 1986); Kim Moody, *An Injury to All: The Decline of American Unionism* (London: Verso, 1988), 41–69; Robert Brenner and Mark Glick, 'The Regulation Approach: Theory and History', *New Left Review* 188 (July–August 1991): 45–119.

37. For details of the anti-communist battles, see Irving M. Abella, *Nationalism, Communism, and Canadian Labour* (Toronto: University of Toronto Press, 1973), 44–53, 66–85, 168–87.

38. In what became the focus of considerable worker derision, General Motors Corporation used a similar strategy in the 1980s for its automotive assembly plants with the characters of 'Quality Cat' and 'Howie Makem'. See Ben Hamper, *Rivethead: Tales from the Assembly Line* (New York: Warner Books, 1991), 111–16.

39. The author observes that 'by 1964, almost 50 per cent of the total were committees covering fewer than 100 employees.'

40. For example, the Ontario QWL Centre (1978–88). See also Charlotte Gold, *Labour–Management Committees: Confrontation, Cooperation, or Cooperation?* (Ithaca: ILR Press, 1986); Jerome M. Rosow,

Teamwork: Joint Labor–Management Programs in America (New York: Pergamon Press, 1986); Donald V. Nightingale, *Workplace Democracy* (Toronto: University of Toronto Press, 1982); Noiman Eiger, 'Organizing for Quality of Working Life', *Labor Studies Journal* 3 (Fall 1989): 3–13; Don Wells, *Empty Promises: Quality of Working Life Programs and the Labor Movement* (New York: Basic Books, 1987). For two views of Total Quality Management schemes, see Cathryn Klassen, 'TQM-Improving Quality Means Improving Communication', *Canadian Business Review* (Summer 1993): 15–18; Mike Parker and Jane Slaughter, 'TQM: Lean Production Is Mean Production', *Canadian Dimension* (January–February 1994): 21–2.

41. For further discussion of this point, see David Brody, *Workers in Industrial America: Essays on the 20th Century Struggle* (New York: Oxford University Press, 1980), 173–257; Lichtenstein, *Labor's War at Home,* 203–45; Michael Goldfield, *The Decline of Organized Labor in the United States* (Chicago: University of Chicago Press, 1987), esp. 180–230. Juliet Schor, *The Overworked American* (New York: Basic Books, 1991), 60–6; Joshua Freeman, et al., *Who Built America,* American Social History Project, vol. 2 (New York: Pantheon, 1992), 469–77.

42. For discussions on this point, see Bryan D. Palmer, *Working-Class Experience: Rethinking the History of Canadian Labour, 1800–1991* (Toronto: McClelland and Stewart, 1992), 370–7; Carla Lipsig-Mumme, 'Unions Struggle with New Work Order', *Policy Options* 16, 9 (October 1995): 3–6.

References

Blake, G.R. 1947–8. 'Employee Participation with Management in Business Administration', *Quarterly Review of Commerce* 13, 4: 226–7.

Bothwell, Robert, and William Kilbourne. 1979. *C.D. Howe: A Biography.* Toronto: McClelland and Stewart.

Brody, David. 1960. *Steelworkers in America: The Nonunion Era.* Cambridge, MA: Harvard University Press.

Cross, Gary. 1993. *Time and Money: The Making of Consumer Culture.* London: Verso.

Department of Labour. 1946. Information Division, 2 February.

Department of Labour. 1950. *Reports of the Deputy Minister.*

Department of Labour. 1955. *Reports of the Deputy Minister.*

Deutsch, J.J. 1957. 'Some Thoughts on the Public Service', *Canadian Journal of Economics and Political Science* 23 (February): 83–9.

Goldenberg, H. Carl. 1945. 'Labour–Management Cooperation', *Canadian Business* (February).

Guest, Dennis. 1985. *The Emergence of Social Security in Canada,* 2nd ed. Vancouver: University of British Columbia Press.

Kelly, Matthew A. 1987. *Labor and Industrial Relations.* Baltimore: Johns Hopkins University Press.

King, W.L. Mackenzie, 1944. *Canada and the Fight for Freedom.* Toronto: Macmillan.

Labour Gazette. 1944. February.

Labour Gazette. 1945. October.

Lewis, Jane. 1992. *Women in Britain since 1945: Women, Family, Work, and the State in the Post-War Years.* Oxford: Blackwell.

Lichtenstein, Nelson. 1982. *Labor's War at Home: The CIO in World War II.* Cambridge: Cambridge University Press.

Marsh, Leonard. [1943] 1975. 'Introduction', in Michael Bliss, ed., *The Report on Social Security for Canada, 1943*. Toronto: University of Toronto Press.

Martin, Paul. 1945. 'Labour's Post-War World', *Behind the Headlines* 5, 1: 24–5.

May, Allen. 1944. 'Letting Labour into the Front Office', *Liberty* 28 February.

May, Elaine Tyler. 1988. *Homeward Bound: American Families in the Cold War Era*. New York: Basic Books.

Owram, Doug. 1985. *The Government Generation: Canadian Intellectuals and the State, 1900–1945*. Toronto: University of Toronto Press.

Saturday Night. 1944. 16 December.

Schor, Juliet B. 1991. *The Overworked American: The Unexpected Decline of Leisure*. New York: Basic Books.

Teamwork in Industry. 1945. September.

Teamwork in Industry. 1948. September.

Teamwork in Industry. 1953. October.

Wood, W. Donald. 1964. *The Current Status of Labour-Management Cooperation in Canada*. Kingston, ON: Industrial Relations Centre, Queen's University.

PART VIII

Managing the Marginal

Working-class historians have been concerned not only with men, women, and children's paid labour, but also with the social lives of people marginalized by their poverty, by behaviour considered less than 'respectable' by middle-class norms, or by their sexual practices. As indicated by Bonnie Huskins in Part II, nineteenth-century Canada was characterized by distinct class differences in the kinds of leisure, festivities, and social interaction in which people engaged. Studies have explored the tavern as a site of collective masculine class sociability; the severe seasonal impact of poverty on the underemployed; and the distinctions between the rough and respectable elements of the labouring classes. A major demarcation within working-class life thus separated those who were sober, held down jobs, believed in the work ethic, and spent their wages on the necessities of life and the pursuit of propriety, as opposed to those given to dissipation and debauch. If workers were encouraged to embrace lives that were pious, productive, and proper through choices and activities of their own, those who refused such routes often had to be guided by more formal regulations. Or so those in positions of authority often thought.

The essays in Part VIII address these themes for the twentieth century, looking at groups for whom the dominant norms of society seemed less than decisively influential. Working-class people like this often faced either legal regulation by the state, or more informal, but nonetheless powerful, forms of moral censure. Both studies draw on the concept of moral regulation, indicating the intellectual cross-fertilization of working-class history with legal studies and criminology, in which discussions concerning the why and how of control and regulation are centrally important.

In the 1970s and 1980s, the concept of 'social control' sometimes framed similar studies. Social control referred to the 'planned and programmed response of society to people regarded as problematic, "deviant", threatening, worrying, [or] troublesome', as John McLaren, Robert Menzies, and Dorothy Chunn have written. Many writers addressing this kind of effort to manage the marginal focused especially on the formal, legal, and state means of creating proper kinds of working-class people. Drawing partly on Michel Foucault's influential writing, the concept of moral regulation emerged as a way of addressing forms of non-state social disciplining. This interpretive accent drew attention to the more subjective, as opposed to institutional, ways in which the marginal could be made more mainstream. Powerful professional or reformist discourses, for instance, might emanate from influential institutions or sites of knowledge ranging from schools and churches to the medical and helping professions. Their importance in managing the marginal complemented the more overtly coercive regulations of legal prohibitions.

Forms of regulation, as well as examples of resistance, have often concerned historians combining the history of sexuality and the study of workers. Gay and lesbian history, and studies of the subjective dimensions of female delinquency, for instance, have shown that the experience, regulation, and representation of sexuality were profoundly shaped by class, as well as by gender, ethnicity, and race.

Such a multi-faceted analysis animates Robert Campbell's discussion of Vancouver beer parlours. Campbell extends the interest of nineteenth-century historians in the local tavern into a twentieth-century study of the far more regulated taprooms, asking who frequented them, whether attitudes towards drinking changed over time, and how bars were licensed and monitored by the state. The historical records available to working-class historians on issues of 'marginalization' and moral regulation are sometimes heavily biased towards the state and those with the power to judge. Yet, by reading these records 'against the grain', with a critical eye to deciphering and uncovering the voices and experiences of those who were being surveyed and regulated, it is possible to gain considerable insight into the lives of working people who have left little in the way of conscious records of their views and everyday pastimes. In this case, the Liquor Control Board records tell us much about the inspectors' class, race, and gender understandings of conventional behaviour. Concerns about 'loose' women, interracial liaisons, and gay encounters in the bars surface, as does a history of working-class patrons' attempts to set their own standards for social interaction, which sometimes developed in defiance of the codified understandings of proper 'morality' set out by state regulators.

Becki Ross's article on stripping as work also employs the analytic categories of race, class, and gender to guide her interpretation, drawing as well on key concepts and debates from the published work in the history of sexuality. Her study is a welcome challenge to scholarly literatures that moralize exotic dancing by placing it within the paradigm of 'deviance', an approach that also undermines understanding of sex-trade work by simply exploring the state's attempts to ban or constrain this area of women's employment, which became increasingly significant in the last decades of the twentieth century. Instead, Ross examines stripping, also referred to by some authors as the 'skin trade', in the context of the working conditions women encountered, the cultural and artistic influences on their work, and the way in which race and ethnicity affected dancers' presentation of sexual spectacle. Like Campbell, she explores issues of legal and moral regulation, but she also wants to understand the flip side of the coin: how did exotic dancers experience this regulation? How did they attempt to create their own meanings about the work they were doing, and its worth and dignity? Ross's essay is thus a pioneering statement about the making of a particular occupation, a 'trade' the moral regulators constructed as marginal and too often understood only as vice.

Further Reading

Nancy B. Bouchier and Ken Cruikshank, 'The War on the Squatters, 1920–1940: Hamilton's Boathouse Community and the Re-Creation of Recreation on Burlington Bay', *Labour/Le Travail* 51 (Spring 2003): 9–46.

Chris Bruckert, *Taking It Off, Putting It On: Women in the Strip* (Toronto: Women's Press, 2002).

Craig Heron, *Booze: A Distilled History* (Toronto: Between the Lines, 2003).

John McLaren, Robert Menzies, and Dorothy Chunn, eds, *Regulating Lives: Historical Essays on the State, Society, the Individual, and the Law* (Vancouver: UBC Press, 2002).

Steven Maynard, '"Through a hole in the lavatory wall": Homosexual Subcultures, Police Surveillance, and the Dialectics of Discovery, Toronto, 1890–1930', *Journal of the History of Sexuality* 5 (October 1994): 207–42.

Steven Maynard, '"Without working?" Capitalism, Urban Culture, and Gay History', *Journal of Urban History* 30 (March 2004): 378–98.

Joan Sangster, *Regulating Girls and Women: Sexuality, Family, and Law in Ontario, 1920–1960* (Toronto: Oxford University Press, 2001).

CHAPTER 18

Managing the Marginal: Regulating and Negotiating Decency in Vancouver's Beer Parlours, 1925–1954

Robert A. Campbell

For the few Canadian historians involved in alcohol history, temperance and related issues remain alluring themes. Little historical work has been done in Canada on public drinking in general and public drinking after prohibition in particular. This neglect is a real oversight in British Columbia because hotel saloons were transformed into hotel beer parlours after the province's brief experience with prohibition between 1917 and 1921. The first parlours opened in Vancouver in 1925, and, like saloons, they catered to a working-class clientele. Parlours held sway until 1954 when a new Government Liquor Act provided for additional venues of public drinking. One did not have to sit long in a Vancouver parlour to realize that more than alcohol consumption was being regulated. Parlours also regulated class, gender and sexuality, and race.[1]

As Jack Blocker has noted, alcohol historians have adopted two broad explanatory approaches to analyze drinking. The first emphasizes social control in which the state and allied elites 'define the conditions under which ordinary drinking takes place'. The second is a 'cultural model' that 'emphasizes the power of group norms in determining individual drinking behaviour, whether the group is defined by gender, nationality, social class, ethnicity or race'. He argues that historians must use both models to understand drinking and its regulation. Without a doubt, though, social control has been the dominant perspective (Blocker, 1994: 229–30).[2] . . .

Social historians seeking some more flexible analytical tools have delved into moral regulation literature. Much, but not all, of this work is grounded in Foucault's idea of governmentality, 'the contact between the technologies of domination of others and those of the self'. Joan Sangster has described moral regulation as 'the process whereby some behaviours, ideals, and values were marginalized and proscribed while others were legitimized and naturalized.' Moral regulation refers to a process of normalization, the attempt to render natural and obvious what is actually constructed and contested. Ultimately, as Mary Louise Adams has noted, 'moral regulation limits the forms of expression available to us by masking difference with an illusion of social unity. What are taken for "normal" are, for the most part, representations of dominant interests' (Adams, 1994: 119; Dean, 1994: 158; Sangster, 1996: 241).[3] . . .

Carolyn Strange and Tina Loo have described the history of moral regulation in Canada as 'a way of managing the marginal, whether that marginality was conferred by race, class, or gender'. While the behaviour of people was important, it was so because behaviour categorized individuals. Much of the power of regulation was derived from defining people and space, and regulation was closely linked to status and place. Most of the regulatory initiative came from state officials, but Strange and Loo emphasize that state success was often less than spectacular. The 'lofty goals and high hopes' were well-nigh impossible to achieve, and regulation often 'failed by its own standards'. Moreover, regulation was expensive, complex, and time consuming. In the end negotiating morality often proved to be cheaper and easier than eliminating vice (Strange and Loo, 1997: 149–51).[4]

Moral regulation is a useful analytical perspective because it blends cultural and control approaches to regulation. Yet moral regulation and state power are not necessarily in conflict. An examination of the regulation of Vancouver's beer parlours, particularly in regard to parlour patrons, leads to the conclusion that the state remained a powerful regulator. Despite the complexity of regulation and the multitude of regulators, the state's influence should not be minimized to a point that obscures the significance of internalization, acquiescence, and coercion.

* * *

Vancouver beer parlours opened in former hotel saloons in the downtown core. The bulk of the male patrons were drawn from the city's casual labourers, dock, mill, and railway workers, and itinerant loggers. They often stayed in the hotels attached to parlours before they headed back to the woods. A few Vancouver parlours were located in first-class hotels and they generally attracted little official attention. Liquor Control Board (LCB) expectations and policies were oriented to the lower-end hotels with their overwhelmingly working-class clientele.[5]

State officials sought to create licensed facilities that would not offer opportunities for what they considered deviance. As so-called workingmen's clubs, parlours were designated as suspect space occupied by suspect people. The basic assumption was that parlours and the people in them needed to be closely regulated. While temperance groups had lost the battle over the return of public drinking, they had been successful in defining the traditional saloon environment as immoral. Hence the parlours had no stand-up bar, no food, and

no entertainment—just beer served by waiters to people seated at small tables. Parlour policy was clearly linked to conceptions of decency. No one issued a document that defined decency, and it remained flexible and unwritten, as much of parlour policy was unwritten. In practice decency generally meant moderate consumption, appropriate comportment, and heterosexual propriety.[6]

The comportment expectations of decency were clearly linked to class. In most parlours inspectors were always prepared for a rough crowd, and they seemed surprised when they did not find trouble. After touring the Melbourne Hotel in February 1928 an inspector commented that 'considering that this premises, caters largely to the Longshoremen trade and Fishermen, the patronage is kept pretty well in hand.'. . . .

The authorities attempted to curb the excesses of working-class sociability. The inspectors tried hard to enforce the ban against games, dancing, and music, including singing, all of which officials believed encouraged a saloon-like atmosphere and excessive camaraderie. Singing caused the most problems for the Board because patrons' voices were difficult to regulate, and some operators condoned it. A convivial atmosphere with thirst-inspiring songs could enhance beer sales. . . . The British Columbia Hotels Association (BCHA) posted signs in parlours that warned patrons about singing and playing musical instruments. Yet with ingenuity and defiance customers still sang, sometimes with the assistance of operators.[7]

Parlour decency was also quite gendered. Hotel saloons had been closed to women, and provincial regulations barred women from working in the parlours, unless they were part of the parlour business. Yet parlours, technically at least, were open to female patrons. Some observers claimed the presence of women would curb the excesses of male camaraderie. Initially many parlours banned women both to placate male customers who did not want them there and to prevent temperance groups from being able to damn parlours as havens for prostitutes. Soon, however, in concert with the LCB, operators created a separate area for men only and another for women and couples, or 'ladies and escorts'. The goal was to separate unattached men from unattached women, ostensibly to limit prostitution and the spread of venereal disease. These areas became more rigidly separated by partitions erected during World War II.[8]

In April 1942, when the LCB ordered all Vancouver parlours to install barriers, the partitions had to be a least six feet high and constructed to 'permit no visibility' between the two parlours. In 1947 the LCB received statutory authority to force hotels to improve their facilities. Parlour restrictions became more elaborate. Higher, more permanent, partitions moved closer to the service bar, as one bar usually served both parlours. Of some parlours the LCB demanded a partition right to the bar or a gate between the partition and the bar. When simple swing gates failed to control patrons, the Board asked for locked gates or those with electric devices to open and close them. The Board also required that some parlours hire floormen to guard the gated area or the increasingly common separate street entrance for women and escorts.[9]

Still, LCB inspectors grew frustrated with their inability to check what they called 'crossovers' or 'wandering'. Crossing over most commonly referred to unattached men entering the ladies and escorts' parlour or walking from the men-only side to the mixed side. 'Wandering' was often used in the same way, but it also referred to movement within a beer parlour, particularly male movement from table to table on the mixed side. Inspectors claimed that some parlour operators did little to stop unauthorized movement. In June 1951 an inspector described an unusually blatant example of wandering in the New Fountain on Cordova Street: 'two men—unattached—were observed carrying their table, full of beer, over to two unattached females.'[10]

While the Inspectors' files are full of references to male crossovers and wanderers, occasionally women took the initiative. In May 1949, for example, an undercover investigator in the Royal Hotel on Granville Street noticed 'Ladies in the mens [sic] section. One woman standing at the bar drinking beer.' From the agent's point of view their behaviour may have been brazen, but it was also brave. Men, properly accompanied, were expected to be on the ladies' side, but the Men's side was completely closed to women. Unescorted women who wanted male company usually encouraged or coaxed men to come to their side where the women could exert more power over space. A woman who received unwanted male attention on her side could have her harasser ejected as an unattached man.[11]

Despite the frustration of the inspectors, we should be mindful of their files. A parlour that caused little trouble warranted little attention or record keeping. Even temperance groups, which damned *all* parlours from the beginning, had to acknowledge during the initial intense debate over them that some parlours were quiet, orderly places. . . .

Moreover, the LCB used its coercive powers to encourage parlour compliance. The Board worked closely, if not always harmoniously, with police and health officials. It also had statutory authority to 'suspend or cancel any beer licence for such reason as to the Board may seem sufficient'. In addition, liquor authorities sent lists of interdicted persons to parlour operators. People under interdiction orders had lost their right to purchase liquor in stores or parlours.[12]

With full support of the LCB, parlour operators took the initiative to ban specific individuals who were considered troublemakers. The LCB and parlour operators often named women drinkers as suspected prostitutes, which had real regulatory effect. After a December 1947 inspection of the West Hotel, the LCB sent an undercover investigator to watch the parlour. On 23 December he commented that 'no open soliciting was seen, but the women companions of the men patrons were rather of the easy virtue type.' On 29 December he still saw no soliciting, but 'some of the women present did not come under heading of "Ladies".' On 11 January 1948 he again saw nothing untoward, but 'some of the women present looked as if their professions were more ancient than honorable.' Later that year the hotel banned all single women from registering as guests.[13]

Effective restrictions placed on male behaviour were less obvious. On the men-only side, small tables and the ban on standing while drinking usually prevented large gatherings, but in small groups men could still chat, boast, and treat. Treating remained the mainstay of beer purchase by men in groups. It reinforced male reciprocity, and opponents had long argued treating promoted excessive consumption since a man would lose face if he left before he had bought his round. Even if treating *per se* did not encourage consumption, men were fairly free, and more free than women, to consume a lot of cheap beer. Serving intoxicated people violated the rules, but intoxication was a subjective and gendered assessment. An unattached woman could find herself ejected from a parlour for intoxication, even if she had little or nothing to drink. The real limits for men were excessive rowdiness, its opposite, sleeping, or the loss of control over bodily functions. In short, parlour regulation circumscribed male sociability, but it certainly did not eliminate it.[14]

Many men continued to long for the old days of a completely-male drinking environment. It was a common opinion that women restricted sociability as much if not more than the state. In 1926 the *Vancouver Province* had supported a proposed ban on all women, even though the paper accepted that women had caused no trouble in the parlours. The paper claimed there was 'an instinctive aversion in the public mind—it exists, so the hotelmen say, among many of the men who frequent beer halls—against the idea of women in these places.' Mr Charles Hurt, who supported women in parlours, allowed that 'there are many men who can not be happy unless they are telling or listening to lewd stories or punctuating their conversation with a series of oaths, and such men do, no doubt, find their liberty of action circumscribed by the presence of ladies in the parlor.' As late as 1954, Jack Johnson, at 75 still a waiter in the Princeton Hotel parlour, remembered his time in the old saloons. He claimed, 'there wasn't half the trouble there is today.' Saloons were better than parlours 'because there were no women allowed in the bars in those days.' In 1963, when the partitions began to come down, one male customer lamented, 'where can we go if we want to have a quiet beer and tell a few good jokes?' (*Vancouver Province*, 29 July 1926, 8 August 1926, 23 November 1954, 4 December 1963; Hey, 1986).

As for the public expression of masculine sexuality, the LCB obviously tried hard to prevent unaccompanied men from encountering unescorted women. At best, the results were mixed. These official efforts regulated women more than men and were directed to the Ladies and Escorts side.

On the men-only side the Board tried to make sure male interaction remained non-sexual. By the early 1950s the Castle Hotel on Granville Street was known as a rendezvous for gay men. What provoked the inspectors was not so much gay men drinking together but their attempts to have sex in beer parlours. For example, in July 1952 an inspector responded to a complaint about a hole in the wall between two toilets in the men's washroom of the Stratford Hotel on Keefer Street.

He interviewed the manager and bartender who admitted that this was actually the second hole they had found. The inspector did not leave until a janitor had 'put a metal sheet covering over hole.' He also warned the operators that 'they must keep a sharp look out for anyone going in Gents washroom for immoral purposes,' and that he intended to notify the police (Trower, 1996: 166, 210).[15] . . .

By the early 1950s the New Fountain on Cordova Street was also known for its homosexual clientele. Located in the heart of skid road, it appealed to lesbians as well as gays. . . . The LCB considered the New Fountain one of the more notorious beer parlours, but its recorded notoriety was not linked to lesbians or gays. In the summer of 1951 an inspector submitted a long, detailed report on the wild conditions of the New Fountain. His antipathy toward the New Fountain was obvious, but his concerns were prosaic by parlour standards: drunkenness, crossovers, and prostitutes.[16]

The regulatory priority in parlours was the suppression of illicit heterosexuality. The formal regulations prohibited the presence of 'persons of a notoriously bad character, or disorderly persons', and since the terms were undefined, they could have been used against just about anyone. Yet they were confined primarily to women named as prostitutes. Inspectors may have conflated 'lesbian' with prostitute, especially after World War II. As Donna Penn has argued, in Cold War United States, officials attempted to make lesbians more visible and dangerous by linking them to prostitutes as examples of sexual degeneracy.[17]

In any event, parlour inspectors were attuned to a variety of gestures and behaviours that brought men and women together. Some inspectors probably did not see or were fooled by the fluidity of gendered behaviour. While a single woman entering a parlour often aroused suspicion, two women or a group of women might not, especially if they were femme rather than butch lesbians. Gay men could pass as straight, but be visible to other gay men with the use of well understood codes. The performance could be much more complex with women acting as men and men as women. They could make a mockery of the separate sections for men only and ladies and escorts, as could more transgendered people whose appearance, performance, or physical attributes defied any simple or fixed categories of 'male' or 'female'.[18]

Ironically, the requirement of a men-only parlour facilitated the gathering of gay men and transformed some parlours into gay sites, but not sites exclusively for gay men. Just as important, the LCB did not appear to make the suppression of gay sociability a high priority, as long as the sociability remained non-sexual.' . . .

Beer parlour decency was also quite racialized, and white, Anglo-Celtic, males were the standard by which others were judged. Yet, like gender, 'race' was not only a fluid category, it also was sometimes difficult to see because of its behavioural qualities. As Elaine Ginsberg has argued, while appearance is important, racial categories are also performative. The term 'passing' refers to how a variety of identities, be they of gender, sexuality, or even class, are constructed and shed. Yet the rationale and agency in passing can be more complex than an individual simply choosing a different identity (Ginsberg, 1996: 2–4).[19]

Racial appearance and performance came together in the regulation of the gender relations of parlour customers. In many circumstances men of colour could drink in parlours without incident, but in the company of white women their behaviour marked them as coloured and liable to censure from state authorities, parlour operators, and other customers. The potential for miscegenation threatened the dominance of white men and ultimately destabilized the category of 'white'.

For example, in October 1952 a man and a woman entered the ladies and escorts side of the Martin Hotel beer parlour. At first the waiter ignored them, and then, according to the couple, they were told that mixed-raced couples were not served. Quite embarrassed, the woman wrote the LCB and said that, on his own, her 'Hindu' friend had been served without incident in three other parlours. . . . The Chief Inspector only informed the woman that the operator had 'the right to refuse service to anybody he does not wish to serve'. While the LCB did not have an official policy on mixed-race couples, it carefully watched those parlours that did not ban them.[20]

The most explicitly negative racial comments are about black men, and race, gender, and class all interacted. When H.Y. complained about the Martin Hotel's refusal to serve her and her 'Hindu' companion, she stressed that he was a businessman engaged in both the lumber and petroleum industries. She added that 'after all a Hindu is a British subject and not a negro.' Many black patrons were railway workers, probably porters on the two major railways. Both the Canadian National and Canadian Pacific stations were in the beer parlour district. In a 1946 complaint against the St Helen's hotel for refusal of service to a black man, his white colleague, who lived in Ontario, stressed that they regularly travelled 'every province from Halifax to Vancouver'. A black man who was refused service with his white wife at the Regent sent his complaint on letterhead of the 'Brotherhood of Sleeping Car Porters'. In beer parlours black men had more than their race against them. Some of them were transient railway workers who were perceived to be here for a good time, not a long time.[21]

In the records and in the parlours the racializing of a 'mixed-race couple' was narrowly defined. A mixed couple referred to a white woman with a man of colour. As categories of official and popular concern, women of colour with white men, or mixed-race couples that included no white member simply did not exist. As real people, though, these couples drank in beer parlours. In particular, aboriginal women were often linked with white men and sometimes with non-native men of colour. Little emphasis was placed on the racialized coupling aspect of these relationships. Instead aboriginal women with non-native men were usually dismissed as prostitutes or concubines (Lemert, 1954: 309, 319–20; Hawthorn, Belshaw and Jamieson, 1958: 330, 380).[22]

In British Columbia legislation pertaining to liquor and aboriginal people had been on the books since the 1860s. Yet the primary emphasis of provincial law was to uphold federal restrictions, which banned access to alcohol to status Indians until 1951.[23]

Some aboriginal people did drink in Vancouver beer parlours, and the LCB cautioned parlour operators to use 'the utmost precaution in serving liquor to Minors and Indians'. Yet official documents say little about how aboriginals were defined and assessed in beer parlours. As James Frideres has argued, 'Indian' was a legal category under the Indian Act that changed many times. It did 'not reflect social, cultural, or racial attributes', and it did not express how First Nations defined themselves. In beer parlours waiters and operators did not generally rely on identity cards. The only natives who had any incentive to offer documents were those enfranchised and thus eligible to drink. 'Indianness' was a constructed assessment based on appearance and behaviour. For example, in 1948 a Mrs K., who was not a legal Indian, was denied service in the Regent Hotel because she looked like one. The LCB Secretary suggested that Mrs K. obtain an official letter 'to the effect that she is not deemed to be an Indian within the meaning of the Indian Act'.[24]

Behaviour, however, was just as important as appearance in defining Indians. Aboriginal men, even status Indians, who drank quietly and moderately might never be bothered in a beer parlour. They could pass as whites. Assessing the extent of individual passing is impossible. Natives who fooled parlour workers and inspectors were not captured in the records generated by the state. Yet passing was not just trickery; it could also be a more negotiated process of racial definition. Aboriginal women had both race and gender working against them, but they too could be accepted in parlours. In 1950, for example, an LCB undercover agent claimed he saw, among many infractions, 'an Indian girl' drinking in the Dodson Hotel. He did not link her to any of the other problems with the parlour. In the warning letter sent to the Hotel, the Chief Inspector never mentioned the woman. She had not caused any trouble and thus, for the moment, was accepted as white.[25]

Once Vancouver beer parlours legally opened their doors to aboriginal people, status Indians no longer had to pass as whites. Yet the 'beer parlour Indian' did not disappear from the official record. For example, in April 1953 an inspector noted that too much beer (the limit at the time was two per person) had been served to a table 'at which five Indians were seated' in the Melbourne Hotel. The Chief Inspector wrote a blistering letter to the operator citing the 'excessive amount of beer on a table where five Indians were seated'. In his letter of apology the operator admitted 'an excessive amount of beer was being served on the table where five Indians were seated.' Yet the legal infraction was over-service, not over-service to Indians. Too much beer and native people remained a tenacious conceptual link.[26]

Asians, especially the relatively large population of Chinese, stood out prominently in Vancouver. Popular and official assumptions about the impossibility and undesirability of Asian assimilation translated into policies of exclusion from the

dominant society and concentration, geographically in segregated areas and occupationally in menial jobs. Yet it was their alleged behaviour, especially the historic association with gambling and drugs, which racialized them in Vancouver beer parlours. The LCB took a noticeably firm approach to regulating illegal gambling or book-making, and race likely provided at least a subtext for that firmness. Just as significant, racialized conceptions of decency resulted in Asian exclusion from parlour operations.[27]

The original 1925 regulations required that a parlour operator be eligible to vote. Since Asians were denied the provincial franchise until after World War II they could not obtain licences. This official exclusion extended to working in parlours because the regulations also required that parlour workers be eligible to vote.[28]

The Chinese received the provincial franchise in 1947, but that did not alter their inability to obtain beer licences. In January 1952 the lawyer for a Mr P.C. asked the Chief Inspector 'of the policy of the Board as to Canadian born Chinese holding the licence of a beer parlour?' The next day the Chief Inspector replied that 'an application from a Chinese is not favourably looked upon by the Board as it has been found that Chinese are not able to handle this type of business.' Moreover, even after Asians received the vote, obvious Asian surnames did not appear on the list of parlour employees (Barman, 1991: 363).[29]

Yet the racial regulation of Asians in parlours was more dynamic than simple exclusion. No specific efforts appeared to have been made to bar Asians as customers, and some drank in beer parlours. Asians, again particularly Chinese, worked around and in beer parlours. Some managed the hotel operations that were often separate from parlours until well after World War II. At the New Empire in 1952 an inspector thought it important enough to note that the Chinese room manager 'supervises the clerks, who are white persons'. Finally, between 1947 and 1954 at least 15 Vancouver parlours employed Chinese as janitors. As long as Asians did not occupy positions of responsibility within the parlours, in many ways they remained invisible.[30]

* * *

Vancouver beer parlour regulation was a complex process that involved a number of actors. Despite its almost exclusive jurisdictional authority, the provincial state certainly was not the only regulator. From the beginning temperance groups defined the moral limits of regulation as they had successfully discredited a saloon environment, and they kept a watchful eye on the parlours. Parlour operators, both as individual licensees and members of the BCHA, had an impact on the direction of regulation. Some operators took the formal regulations seriously. Some paid lip service to them, and a few, perhaps with a megaphone in hand, defied them.

Parlour patrons played a particularly active role in parlour regulation. Separate facilities are a good example of the state's attempt to morally engineer working-class public drinking after prohibition. Yet liquor and health authorities could not simply decide what was appropriate behaviour in beer parlours, issue the decrees, and exercise the proper sanctions. Patrons challenged the dominant discourse, notably decency's ideal of unattached men separated from unattached women. Their success can be measured by both the imaginative ways they bypassed the partitions and the state's ever increasing physical and policy efforts to control them. Parlour partitions were both a material manifestation of decency's expectations and a monument to the undermining of them. Some patrons also exerted regulatory power and undermined the partitions by defying simple definitions of 'male' or 'female'. Patrons and the state, however, were not always at odds. In some

parlours customers reinforced official views that mixed-race couples were unacceptable.

In general women in parlours were able to expand the boundaries of heterosocial leisure, but they did not eliminate them. Parlour partitions revealed the gendered, spatial dimensions of decency. For women the partitions were walls. 'Female' and 'decent' were linked only on the ladies and escorts side. Even there decency was defined in narrow ways. Unattached women were often treated as or akin to prostitutes. . . .

For men the partitions were more porous as male leisure space embraced female space. Porous, however, did not mean invisible. On the ladies and escorts side appropriate male behaviour was tied to the company of women. On the men-only side patrons were freer to practice variations of traditional public drinking rituals. Some men saw the partitions as protection as they tried to re-create saloon sociability as best as they could in an institution that was designed to prevent it. Men's sexuality was also far less regulated than women's. Men were chastised but not condemned for illicit sex, as long as their actions remained heterosexual. . . .

Still, the state remained a powerful manager of the marginal. Although the records could tempt one to conclude that the parlour was bedlam born of beer, the impact of the state regulation should not be dismissed. Orderly parlours simply did not warrant much comment. The silence can be read as a measure of decency's achievement. Well-behaved patrons could be construed as regulation by internalization, or government of the self. The state could not control this process, but internalization upheld the values of the state and enhanced legitimacy.

Moreover, state regulation did not require complete success to be successful. While internalization was the ideal, in the end the state required only acquiescence to achieve many of its objectives. Certainly the state counted on compliance, especially on the part of operators. In the 1920s three inspectors covered the province. By the late 1940s about that many watched only Vancouver, but with 63 parlours in the city, the human resources devoted to regulation were minimal. Yet the state's ability to suspend or cancel licences encouraged operators to act as regulators.[31] . . .

At the same time, however, acquiescence should not be confused with consent. As Philip Corrigan and Derek Sayer have argued, compliance does not always mean incorporation or internalization. A collective response is not necessarily a unitary one. People may act the same way for a variety of motives. Mark Leier went a step further. He argued that whenever the reality or threat of 'unpleasant consequences' exists, 'whether these be overt or implied, material or psychological, it is impossible to distinguish between consent and coercion.' Coercion operates both formally and informally, and what passes for consent 'may be manipulated in a number of ways'. Reward and punishment are two sides of the same coin. Leier's intent was to declare that 'all authority is illegitimate,' but his argument reveals some of the subtleties of coercion (Corrigan and Sayer, 1994: 197; Leier, 1995: 36–8).

Coercion remained a powerful state tool in parlour regulation. While liberal states have developed a variety of means to negotiate what appears to be consent, the state still has a monopoly on the legitimate use of force. In Vancouver's beer parlours the state's authority was fragmented, but regulation was not a process that engaged equals on a level playing field. Officials arrested people, had them barred, and ruined reputations. Parlour operators had their licences suspended or cancelled. In general Foucault was wise to shift our gaze away from power as state-centred repression. Certainly the state risks legitimacy if it resorts to coercion too often or too intensely. Yet state coercion used judiciously and creatively is an effective means of regulation.[32]

Moral regulation and state power are not in contradiction. Understanding the state requires going beyond structures and institutions and placing more emphasis on processes. Colin Hay has argued that the state is a 'constantly changing network of relationships and institutional practices and procedures'. The state is not an object, but rather a process of rule embedded in material relations. From this vantage one neither attributes a single mentality to the state or its institutions. Philip Corrigan and Derek Sayer emphasized that the power of the state is not just external and objective, but also internal and subjective. The state 'works through us'. The state produces knowledge. It helps to organize individual and collective representations. The results are not necessarily consistent, but the effects help keep the state a powerful regulator, as seen, in this case, in Vancouver's beer parlours.

Notes

1. Despite the title of Cheryl Krasnick Warsh's collection, *Drink in Canada: Historical Essays* (Montreal and Kingston: McGill-Queen's University Press, 1993), the majority of the essays are oriented to temperance subjects. The same is true, of course, of Jan Noel's award-winning *Canada Dry: Temperance Crusades Before Confederation* (Toronto: University of Toronto Press, 1995). As for Sharon Cook's study of the Ontario WCTU, it is as much a work on evangelicalism as temperance. See Sharon Anne Cook, *'Through Sunshine and Shadow': The Woman's Christian Temperance Union, Evangelicalism, and Reform in Ontario, 1874–1930* (Montreal and Kingston: McGill-Queen's University Press, 1995). *The Changing Face of Drink: Substance, Imagery, and Behaviour* (Ottawa: Social History, Inc., 1997), a collection edited by Jack S. Blocker Jr and Cheryl Krasnick Warsh, is more diverse. Yet of the three articles devoted to Canada, temperance is an important theme in two of them. On prohibition and its aftermath, see Robert A.

Campbell, *Demon Rum or Easy Money: Government Control of Liquor in British Columbia from Prohibition to Privatization* (Ottawa: Carleton University Press, 1991), especially Chapters One and Two.

2. See also, Patricia E. Prestwich, 'The Regulation of Drinking: New Work in the Social History of Alcohol', *Contemporary Drug Problems* 21 (Fall 1994): 369–71; Gareth Stedman Jones, 'Class Expressionism versus Social Control? A Critique of Recent trends in the Social History of "Leisure"', *History Workshop Journal* 4 (Autumn 1997): 162–77.

3. See also, Michel Foucault, 'Governmentality', in Graham Burchell, Colin Gordon, and Peter Miller, eds, *The Foucault Effect: Studies in Governmentality* (London: Harvester, 1991): 102–3; Philip Corrigan and Derek Sayer, *The Great Arch: English State Formation as Cultural Revolution* (Oxford: Blackwell, 1985), 4.

Another stream of moral regulation literature winds its way back to Marx, usually via Gramsci's concept of hegemony. Mariana Valverde has argued that Marxian and Foucaultian approaches to moral regulation share much 'political common ground' because they both focus on 'power and domination'. See Mariana Valverde, 'Editor's Introduction', *Canadian Journal of Sociology* 19 (1994): vi–vii (quotations).

4. See also, Tina Loo and Carolyn Strange, 'The Traveling Show Menace: Contested Regulation in Turn-of-Century Ontario', *Law and Society Review* 29 (1995): 639–67. On space and regulation see Daphne Spain, *Gendered Spaces* (Chapel Hill: University of North Carolina Press, 1992), 15–21; Mary Louise Adams, 'Almost Anything Can Happen: A Search for Sexual Discourse in the Urban Spaces of 1940s Toronto', *Canadian Journal of Sociology* 19 (1994): 217–32; Nicholas K. Blomley, 'Text and Context: Rethinking the Law–Space Nexus', *Progress in Human Geography* 13 (1989): 512–34.

5. On the working world of Vancouver see Robert A.J. McDonald, 'Working', in Working Lives Collective, ed., *Working Lives: Vancouver 1886–1986* (Vancouver: New Star Books, 1985), 25–33. In his semi-autobiographical novel, *Deadman's Ticket*, Peter Trower captured the spirit of the urban environment of beer parlours in the early 1950s:

The usual crew of tenderloin regulars thronged the sidewalk around me—knots of carousing loggers lurching noisily from bar to bar; shabbily dressed East End housewives looking for bargains at the Army and Navy or the Save-on-Meat store; scrofulous winos with grimy paws cadging dimes

in raspy voices; cut-rate hookers wearily heading for toast and black coffee at some greasy spoon café; a furtive heroin pusher bound for the Broadway Hotel—Vancouver's notorious 'Corner' [Hastings and Main]—to set up shop at a dim beer parlour table. . . . (See *Deadman's Ticket* [Madeira Park, BC: Harbour Publishing, 1996], 27).

6. See Campbell, *Demon Rum or Easy Money*, 50–5. The original parlour regulations can be found in British Columbia, Liquor Control Board (hereafter LCB), *4th Annual Report* (hereafter *4th AR*) (Victoria, 1925); *Vancouver Province*, 31 May 1925.

7. See BCA, LCB, GR52, Box 8, File 121-327, Chief Inspector to Chairman, 27 March 1951 (quotations); File 121-327, Secretary to Dominion Holdings, 28 March 1951; BCHA notice is from BCA, LCB, GR770, Box 5, File 1999. For other examples of singing see the list of notations for the Yale Hotel (BCA, LCB, GR52, Box 9, File 121-367), the West Hotel (Box 9, File 121-366), the Anchor Hotel (Box 7, File 121-310) and Marr Hotel (Box 8, File 121-355). Music initially caught the authorities off guard. The original regulations only banned games, sports, and dancing. Music and musical instruments were explicitly prohibited the next year. See LCB, *4th AR*, and *5th Annual Report* (Victoria, 1926). On pub singing as a form of popular radicalism, see Iorwerth Prothero, *Radical Artisans in England and France* (Cambridge: Cambridge University Press, 1997), 290–8. On public drinking and sociability in general see Thomas Brennan, *Public Drinking and Popular Culture in Eighteenth-Century Paris* (Princeton: Princeton University Press, 1988), 14; Roy Rosenzweig, *Eight Hours For What We Will: Workers and Leisure in an Industrial City, 1870–1920* (New York: Cambridge University Press, 1983), 40–59; Madelon Powers, 'The "Poor Man's Friend": Saloonkeepers, Workers, and the Code of Reciprocity in U.S. Barrooms, 1870–1920', *International Labor and Working-Class History* 45(Spring 1994): 3–5; W. Scott Haine, *The World of the Parisian Café: Sociability Among the French Working Class* (Baltimore: Johns Hopkins University Press, 1996).

8. All of these issues are discussed in much greater detail in Robert A. Campbell, 'Ladies and Escorts: Gender Segregation and Public Policy in British Columbia Beer Parlours, 1925–1945', *BC Studies* 105–106 (Spring/Summer 1995): 119–38.

9. BCA, LCB, GR770, Box 5, File 199A, Wyllie to Sir, 23 April 1942; British Columbia, *Statutes*, 1947, c.53 ('An Act to Amend the "Government Liquor Act"'),

s.11; British Columbia, LCB, *28th Annual Report* (Victoria, 1949); see for example, BCA, LCB, GR52, Box 8, File 121-337, Kimberly to Chief Inspector, 12 November 1949 (partitions, Ivanhoe to Director of Licensing), 5 August 1952 (gate and floorman, Niagara Hotel); File 121-362, list of notations (electric gate lock, Stanley Hotel).

10. For examples on the flexible use of 'wandering' see BCA, LCB, GR52, Box 8, File 121-329, list of notations; Box 9, File 121-349, Inspector to Chief Inspector, 24 June 1951 (quotation).

11. BCA, LCB, GR52, Box 9, File 121-358, '?' to Chief Inspector, 2 May 1949 (Royal). On women coaxing men see, for example, Box 8, File 121-332, Haywood to Chernecki, 10 March 1952 (Grand Union).

12. British Columbia, *Revised Statutes of British Columbia*, 1924, c.146 ('Government Liquor Amendment Act'), s.27(5) (quotation); BCA, LCB, GR52, Box 9, File 121-368, Murray to Secretary, 22 April 1954 (interdicted list). On interdiction in general see British Columbia, *Statutes*, 1921, c.30 ('Government Liquor Act'), s.57–60.

13. The three investigator's reports are in BCA, LCB, GR52, Box 9, File 121-366, as is the 1948 inspector's report noting that single women could not register.

14. The Temperance League continued to link treating with a saloon environment; see, for example, *Vancouver Province*, 14 May 1940. The new Government Liquor Act of 1953 did ban treating, but only on the part of parlour operators. See British Columbia, *Regulations Made Under the Government Liquor Act*, (BC Reg. 528/59), Division 5 [5.16(a)].

15. See also BCA, LCB, GR52, Box 9, File 121-364, Pettit to Haywood, 10 July 1952.

16. On the New Fountain see previously cited inspector's report dated 24 June 1951 and BCA, LCB, GR52, Box 9, File 121-349, Chairman to Ely, 17 July 1951.

17. LCB, *4th AR* (quotation). On conflating 'lesbian' with 'prostitute', see Donna Penn, 'The Sexualized Women: The Lesbian, the Prostitute, and the Containment of Female Sexuality in Postwar America', in Joanne Meyerowitz, ed., *Not June Cleaver: Women and Gender in Postwar America, 1945–1960* (Philadelphia: Temple University Press, 1994), 359; see also, Mary Louise Adams, 'Youth, Corruptibility, and English-Canadian Postwar Campaigns against Indecency', *Journal of the History of Sexuality* 6 (1995): 108–15.

18. On the performative qualities of gender see Judith Butler, *Bodies That Matter: On The Discursive Limits of 'Sex'* (New York: Routledge, 1993); see also Holly Devor, 'Gender Blending: When Two is Not Enough', MA thesis, Simon Fraser University, 1985, iii–iv; George Chauncey, *Gay New York: Gender, Urban*

Culture, and the Making of the Gay Male World (New York: Basic Books, 1994), 348–9; Vern L. Bullough and Bonnie Bullough, *Cross Dressing, Sex, and Gender* (Philadelphia: University of Pennsylvania Press, 1993), 238; Leslie Feinberg, *Transgender Warriors: Making History from Joan of Arc to Rupaul* (Boston: Beacon Press, 1995), 88–9. On sexuality in general see Gail Hawkes, *A Sociology of Sex and Sexuality* (Buckingham: Open University Press, 1996).

19. On the discrediting of the biological assumptions of race see Kay J. Anderson, *Vancouver's Chinatown: Racial Discourse in Canada, 1875–1980* (Montreal and Kingston: McGill-Queens University Press, 1991), Chapter One. For a good empirical study of the complexities of race passing see Graham Watson, *Passing For White: A Study of Racial Assimilation in a South African School* (London: Tavistock Publishing, 1970).

20. BCA, LCB, GR52, Box 9, File 121-344, Pettit to Director, 24 October 1952 (first quote); H.Y. to Sir, October 1952; Haywood to H.Y., 27 October 1952 (second quotation). In a similar incident at the American Hotel in 1953 a waiter refused to serve a party that included three white men, one Chinese man, and a white woman. An inspector interviewed the operator and was told that American Hotel had a house rule 'that no mixed couples were to be served'. See Box 7, File 121-309, Bruce to Director, 27 March 1953. For official attitudes on parlours that did not bar mixed-race couples, see the correspondence on the Stratford Hotel: Box 9, 121-364, "#1" to Chief Inspector, 1 October 1950; Haywood to Stratford, 3 October 1950. In 1948 an agent had described the ladies section of the Stratford as 'full of drunks, mixed couples of white women and male negroes'. See '?' to Chief Inspector, 3 June 1948.

21. BCA, LCB, GR52, Box 9, File 121-344, H.Y. to Sir, 20 October 1952; Box 9, File 121-359, Buckley to LCB, 9 February 1946 (St Helen's); Box 9, File 121-357, Lawrence to Wyllie, 9 March 1950 (Porter letterhead).

22. See also Jean Barman, *The West Beyond the West: A History of British Columbia* (Toronto: University of Toronto Press, 1991), 170–2; Jean Barman, 'Taming Aboriginal Sexuality: Gender, Power, and Race in British Columbia, 1850–1900', *BC Studies* 115/116 (Autumn/Winter 1997/98): 264.

23. BCRMB, AG Files, Reel 372, 'B.C. Laws pertaining to liquor control'; British Columbia, *Statutes*, 1921, c.30 ('Government Liquor Act'), s.11, 36, 57–60. On natives and liquor in general see, Peter C. Mancall, *Deadly Medicine: Indians and Alcohol in Early America* (Ithaca: Cornell University Press, 1995); Joy Leland, *Firewater Myths: North American Indian Drinking*

and Alcohol Addiction (New Brunswick: Transaction Publishers, 1976); Brian Maracle, *Crazywater: Native Voices on Addiction and Recovery* (Toronto: Viking, 1993); Jan Noel, *Canada Dry*, 183–8.

24. BCA, LCB, GR52, Box 8, File 121-327, Wyllie to Dominion Hotel, 4 July 1939 (1st quotation); James B. Frideres, *Native People in Canada: Contemporary Conflicts* (Scarborough: Prentice Hall, 1983), 6–9 (2nd quotation); BCA, LCB, GR52, Box 9, File 121-357, Wyllie to Peterson, 21 September 1948 (3rd quotation).

25. BCA, GR25, Box 8, File 121-326, '#1' to Chief Inspector, 1 November 1950; Haywood to Dodson, 3 November 1950. A similar lack of official interest was shown at the Stanley in July 1951. See Box 9, File 121-362, '#1' to Chief Inspector, 27 July 1951 and Haywood to Secretary, 30 July 1951.

26. BCA, LCB, GR52, Box 9, File 121-345, Bruce to Director of Licensing, 18 April 1953 (1st quotation); Haywood to Melbourne Hotel, 22 April 1953 (2nd quotation); Brandolini to Haywood, 14 May 1953 (3rd quotation). For a similar example from the Stanley see Box 9, File 121-362, Bruce to Director, 18 April 1953.

27. On the long history of anti-Asian hostility in British Columbia, see Peter Ward, *White Canada Forever: Popular Attitudes and Public Policy Toward Orientals in British Columbia* (Montreal and Kingston: McGill-Queen's University Press, 1978) and Patricia Roy, *A White Man's Province: British Columbia Politicians and Chinese and Japanese Immigrants, 1858–1914* (Vancouver: University of British Columbia Press, 1989). On the Chinese and gambling see, Strange and Loo, *Making Good*, 75–8, 121–2; Kay Anderson, *Vancouver's Chinatown*, 101–4; Ward, *White Canada Forever*, 9–10; Roy, *A White Man's Province*, 16–17; David Chuenyan Lai, *Chinatowns: Towns Within Cities in Canada* (Vancouver: University of British Columbia Press, 1988), 195, 229–30; Greg Marquis, 'Vancouver Vice: The Police and the Negotiation of

Morality, 1904–1935', in John McLaren and Hamar Foster, eds, *Essays in the History of Canadian Law, Vol. 6, The Legal History of British Columbia and the Yukon* (Toronto: University of Toronto Press, 1995), 248–51.

28. LCB, *4th AR*. On Asian licensing exclusion before prohibition see Mimi Ajzenstadt, 'The Medical-Moral Economy of Regulations: Alcohol Legislation in B.C., 1871–1925', PhD dissertation, Simon Fraser University, 1992, 111–12.

29. BCA, LCB, GR52, Box 8, File 121-340, Bradshaw to Haywood, 9 January 1952; Haywood to Bradshaw, 10 January 1952. The LCB required that parlours submit lists of employee names and where they were eligible to vote.

30. BCA, LCB, GR770, Box 5, File 2 (126), Kennedy to McIntyre, 2 September 1944. Hotels that employed Chinese janitors: Ambassador, American, Balmoral, Carlton, Castle, Commercial, Grandview, Drake (Haddon), Main, Marble Arch, New Fountain, Regent, Royal, St Helen's, and Stanley. The references are all taken from BCA, LCB, GR52. For the comment of the inspector at the New Empire, see Box 8, File 121-329, Bruce to Supervisor, 5 May 1952.

31. In 1929 chartered accountant Albert Griffiths completed a report on liquor for the newly-elected Conservative government. He concluded that of three inspectors, only one had 'the faintest idea of his duties and responsibilities'. See BCA, Attorney General Files, GR1323, Reel B2307, 'Report of Investigations and Inquiries in Connection with the Administration of the Liquor Control Board', 31 December 1929, 4; Chauncey, *Gay New York*, 347. The LCB's regulatory resources also included a few undercover agents. The LCB was also assisted by the police, health officials, temperance and other observers, and even the press, which had an appetite for alleged parlour debauchery.

32. On coercion and consent, see Colin Hay, *Re-Stating Social and Political Change* (Buckingham: Open University Press, 1996), 25–7.

References

Adams, Mary Louise. 1994. 'In Sickness and in Health: State Formation, Moral Regulation, and Early VD Initiatives in Ontario', *Journal of Canadian Studies* 28, 4 (Winter): 117–30.

Barman, Jean. 1991. *The West Beyond the West: A History of British Columbia*. Toronto: University of Toronto Press.

Blocker, Jack S. 1994. 'Introduction', *Histoire Sociale/Social History* 27 (November).

Corrigan, Philip, and Derek Sayer. 1985. *The Great Arch: English State Formation as Cultural Revolution*. Oxford: Blackwell.

Dean, Mitchell. 1994. '"A Social Structure Of Many Souls": Moral Regulation, Government and Self-Formation', *Canadian Journal of Sociology* 19 (1994): 145–68.

Ginsberg, Elaine K. 1996. 'Introduction: The Politics of Passing', in Elaine K. Ginsberg, ed., *Passing and the Fictions of Identity*. Durham: Duke University Press.

Hawthorn, H.B., C.S. Belshaw, and S.M. Jamieson. 1958. *The Indians of British Columbia: A Study of Contemporary Social Adjustment*. Toronto: University of Toronto Press.

Hey, Valerie. 1986. *Patriarchy and Pub Culture*. London: Tavistock.

Leier, Mark. 1995. *Red Flags and Red Tape: The Making of a Labour Bureaucracy*. Toronto: University of Toronto Press.

Lemert, Edwin M. 1954. *Alcohol and the Northwest Coast Indians*. Berkeley: University of California Press.

Sangster, Joan. 1996. 'Incarcerating "Bad Girls": The

Regulation of Sexuality through the Female Refuges Act in Ontario, 1920–1945', *Journal of the History of Sexuality* 7, 2 (1996): 239–75.

Strange, Carolyn, and Tina Loo. 1997. *Making Good: Law and Moral Regulation in Canada, 1867–1939*. Toronto: University of Toronto Press.

Trower, Peter. 1996. *Deadman's Ticket*. Madeira Park, BC: Harbour Publishing.

Vancouver Province. 1926. 'Editorial', 29 July.

Vancouver Province. 1926. 8 August.

Vancouver Province. 1954. 23 November.

Vancouver Province. 1963. 4 December.

CHAPTER 19

Bumping and Grinding on the Line: Making Nudity Pay

Becki L. Ross

. . .In this paper, I ruminate on complicated entanglements of sexuality, labour, and social class in the history of twentieth century erotic entertainment in North America. I utilize preliminary archival and ethnographic findings from my case study on burlesque and striptease culture in Vancouver, 1945–1980,[1] to explore the working conditions and artistic influences of former dancers, the racialized expectations of erotic spectacle, and the queer dimensions of strip culture. Accepting 'business insiders' as the expert practitioners of their own lives means discovering not only the identities of the women who performed striptease in postwar Vancouver, but the meanings that these entertainers attached to their craft.[2] And because men have been indispensable to the production and consumption of striptease as club owners/staff, musicians, choreographers, booking agents, costume designers, photographers, and patrons, their recollections must be solicited, and will be integrated in upcoming research reports.

Popular lore within striptease culture laments the decline of the glamorous, golden era of the tasteful, lavish art of 'the tease' in burlesque, and the gradual rise of the vulgar, anti-erotic, generic 'cunt show' by the late 1970s (Jarrett, 1997: 192). Reflecting on her exit from the business in 1979, Montreal-based dancer Lindalee Tracey observes: 'Striptease fell from grace because the world stopped dreaming' (Tracey, 1997). . . . In what follows, my entrée into striptease history wedges open a window onto deep-seated cultural anxieties about gender and sexual norms, working-class amusements, and racial otherness. I conclude with some comments about the imbrication of sex and nation in the history of erotic entertainment.[3]

Nice Girls, Smart Girls, Good Girls Don't Disrobe in Public

Female burlesque, go-go, and striptease have been perceived by religious, civic, and moral reformers as commercialized sexual vice that inflame men's passions (already fuelled by alcohol), propel them to seek adulterous liaisons, abandon their families, and jeopardize their workplace productivity (Corio,

1968; McCaghy and Skipper, 1972; Jarrett, 1997). For almost a century, popular conflations of strip-tease with nymphomania, illiteracy, drug addiction, prostitution, and disease, have labelled female erotic performers dangerous to the social order, the family, and the nation (cited in Skipper and McCaghy, 1971).[4] In the 1920s and 1930s of the US and Canada, striptease within the broad rubric of burlesque was a unique combination of sexual humour and female sexual display, with a focus on sexual suggestiveness aided by the 'tease' factor (Allen, 1991: 244). Historian Andrea Friedman notes: 'The key to the striptease was not how much a woman stripped, but how much the people in the audience thought she stripped, as well as how successfully she encouraged their desire that she strip' (Friedman, 1996: 204). It was maintenance of the illusion of nudity that afforded the business some legal protection from obscenity laws. . . .

Cameos of stripteasers in Hollywood film have worked to stabilize the age-old dichotomy between good, middle-class girls and wayward, working-class sex deviants. In the decorated blockbuster, *The Graduate* (1967), newly minted, aimless university graduate Benjamin Bradock (Dustin Hoffman) is pressured to escort Elaine Robinson (Katherine Ross), the daughter of his lover, Mrs Robinson (Anne Bancroft), on a date. By insisting on accompanying Elaine to a downtown stripclub, Benjamin succeeds in sexually, publicly humiliating and punishing the white, upper-class, virgin by forcing her to witness the sullying, sickening debauchery of stripteasers who twirl ornamental tassels from jeweled pasties (double-dutch style) for a living. However, at the horrifying sight of Elaine's tears, Benjamin is jolted into class-conscious chivalry and proceeds to lunge angrily, violently at the dancer on stage. Pursuing a fleeing Elaine out of the club, he later comforts her with kisses and food in the safety and style of his red convertible sportscar.

In the post World War II era, burlesque and striptease flourished in Vancouver's blind pigs or afterhours booze cans, and a handful of nightclubs and mainstream theatres. Marketed as adult entertainment for both locals and tourists in the port city, erotic performance was 'most legal' and 'most respectable' in large, soft-seat nightclubs such as the Palomar and the Cave Supper Club that routinely staged swing bands, large-scale musicals, and big-name lounge acts.[5] In smaller nightclubs such as the Penthouse Cabaret, the Kobenhavn, and the Shangri-La, in poorer, working-class neighbourhoods, including Chinatown, striptease acts that overlapped with 'high art', though packaged to emphasize partial, and later, full, nudity, faced multi-voiced opposition. Clergy, public officials, women's groups, and police argued for the careful scrutiny of 'low class' venues associated (ideologically and spatially) with the 'criminal classes', and at different times, mobilized a range of municipal by-laws, provincial liquor laws, and federal Criminal Code provisions, to turn up the heat on unscrupulous hoteliers, cabaret owners, and dancers.[6] Indeed, the flourishing of striptease, first on the stages of quasi-legal, unlicensed bottle clubs (which themselves traded in the forbidden), and later, post-1969, when 'bottomless' strip acts were legalized, contributed to the city's reputation as home to the hottest nightclubs north of San Francisco (Davis, 1997).

In Vancouver in 1941, a special Police Delegation of religious and temperance leaders toured and inspected the city's night spots: they were known as the 'special constables', and were part of a long tradition of anthropological treatment of the city as, quoting Carolyn Strange, 'a laboratory full of troubling specimens of urban life' (Strange, 1995: 106). When they roamed city streets in search of flourishing vice both inside and adjacent to well-known red-light districts, they became social geographers, mapping the locations of moral evils. Upon visiting a local cabaret, Mrs McKay of the Vancouver Local Council of Women, representing 78 women's groups, told reporters for the *Vancouver News Herald*: 'The floor show was objectionable, . . . with girls naked except brassieres and loin clothes.' . . .Years later, in 1976, the Attorney General's office instructed the BC Liquor Control Board to enforce a ban on 'bare-breasted waitresses' in Vancouver nightclubs (*Vancouver Sun*, 31 August 1976). A key paradox in the history of the nightclub scene in British Columbia and elsewhere, is the subjection of striptease to a concerted proliferation of speech and acts intended to prohibit it.[6]

The Penthouse Cabaret, which opened on Seymour Street in downtown Vancouver in 1947, was owned and run by the Filippone brothers Joe, Ross, Mickey, and Jimmy—and their sister Florence.[7] It started out as Joe's penthouse apartment where he 'privately' entertained guests above the family's Diamond Cabs and Eagle Time Delivery service, and it was raided for liquor infractions the first night it opened. Still operating in 2000, and continuing to be run by members of the Filippone family, it is the longest-standing striptease venue in Canada. In 1968, reporter Alex MacGillivray wrote that The Penthouse was 'a watering spot for bookies and brokers, doctors and dentists, guys and dolls, ladies and gentlemen, and just about anybody who could smell a good time' (MacGillivray, 1968). . . . By the early 1960s, the Penthouse had a reputation as the best place in the city to meet elite prostitutes who frequented the club, bought food and drinks, and charmed a loyal clientele of tourists and locals.

For decades, the Penthouse was habitually raided and closed down. Between 1951 and 1968, nightspots like the Penthouse were strictly bottle clubs—patrons brought bottled liquor to the club or purchased drinks from the illegal stash behind the bar, as well as ice and mix. In so doing, they made themselves vulnerable to police busts. According to Ross Filippone, his brother Joe arranged for a lookout on the roof who buzzed a waiter downstairs when he spotted the 'Dry Squad'. The waiter then warned patrons to hide their booze on built-in ledges under the tables, and to deny any wrong-doing to the gun-and-holstered boys in blue. In 1968, after decades of lobbying by the West Coast Cabaret Owners Association, Penthouse was finally awarded a liquor licence which legalized liquor sales years after hotel and parlours in the city had been granted the right to sell beer (only, and by the glass). In December 1975, after a five-month-long undercover operation,[9] the Filippone brothers, a cashier, and a doorman, were charged with living off the avails of prostitution and conspiring to corrupt public morals (*Dick MacLean's Guide. . .*, 1978: 112–15). In his testimony, Joe Filippone vowed that he never allowed total nudity on the stage at the Penthouse's Gold Room. All the dancers were cautioned to keep their g-strips firmly in place (*Dick MacLean's Guide. . .*, 1978: 27). Finally, in 1978, after a forced, padlocked closure lasting two-and-a-half years, convictions, fines, appeals, and $1.5 million in litigation fees, all of the accused were fully acquitted (*Dick MacLean's Guide. . .*, 1978: 113; Didon, 1978). So, though Vancouver nightclubs were never closed down *en masse* à la New York City in 1942, hotspots like the Penthouse, as well as the Kobenhavn, Zanzibar, and Oil Can Harry's, were consistently under the gaze of moral and legal authorities, scapegoated as dens of immorality, obscenity, and indecency. Stripteasers, who were commonly assumed to moonlight as prostitutes, were never exempted from the scrutiny of those who damned nightclubs as the playgrounds of gangsters, bootleggers, bookies, pimps, hookers, and sex fiends.

Working the Stage: The Good, The Bad, The Ugly

Headliners Sally Rand, Gypsy Rose Lee, Lili St Cyr, 'Queen of the Strippers', and Tempest Storm, all of whom performed in Vancouver during the 1950s and 1960s, netted top salaries. Their price of upwards of $4,000 per weekend (even when they were over 40) meant they earned more than women in any other job category (Jarrett, 1997: 170). However, a handsome pay cheque did not necessarily translate into respect. In 1969, American sociologists Jesser and Donovan interviewed 155 university students and 122 parents of students, all of whom assigned stripteasers a lower occupational ranking than what were seen to be traditionally low status jobs: janitor, artist's model, and professional gambler (Jesser and Donovan, 1969). Interviews with five former dancers suggest that female erotic dancers who performed in Vancouver clubs such as the Penthouse and the Cave, and later, the No. 5 Orange Hotel, the Drake Hotel, and the Cecil Hotel, negotiated salary and working conditions in a stigmatized, male-controlled profession.[10]

Commonly perceived as sex deviants (alongside unwed mothers, homosexuals, prostitutes, and unattached wage-earning women), female erotic dancers were subjected to surveillance, police arrest, detention, forced venereal disease testing, extortion, violence, and rejection by family and friends. One 50-year old former dancer we interviewed has never told her twenty-something children about her years in burlesque. At the same time, a dancer like Val who was working-class and British-born, made more money, had more freedom, worked fewer hours, and had more control over her work than the waitresses, nurses, teachers, chambermaids, and secretaries she knew. Others like Michelle and Noelle, neither of whom had a high school education, told stories of long,

12-hour days, split shifts 'on an invisible leash', and six-day weeks cooped up in 'ratty hotels with broken-down beds and cockroaches . . . in small towns with people who had more keys to your room than you did.'

Dancers were customarily paid in cash; they ear-marked a standard ten per cent of their earnings for their booking agent and, on occasion, paid fines to club owners for minor infractions such as showing up late or skipping a gig without adequate notice. Some like Val managed money wisely— saved it, got investment advice, and left the business after three years—and later secured a real estate licence. Others like Michelle had a tougher time: 'I was raised Catholic, so it was like, you gotta have savings, but I had no money management skills whatsoever. When I retired, I pissed it all away on living for a year and a half, and on love. A dollar was like a penny to me. I could piss away money faster than anything . . . that career did not set me up for being good with money.'

The amount of pay, the quality of dressing room and performance space, lighting and music, food services, accommodation, promotion, and treatment by management and staff, depended on the nightclub. Headliners could clear $2,000 a week, placing them in an economic position of superiority compared to women in any other occupation, but these were the privileged few. Stratified on a scale from high end to low end, Vancouver nightclubs varied greatly in the downtown core: booking agents in the late 1960s graded 'their girls' as A, B, or C, and slotted them into the corresponding clubs. Upon retiring from the scene in Vancouver in 1975, Val, who often felt like a counselor and 'the one bright thing' in her customers' lives, received a 'solid silver tea service from the gentlemen, the skid row types' who were her regulars.

Some occupational hazards were unique to the business; others were common to female-dominated service work. Val and Michelle recall fears of carrying around wads of cash at the end of the night. Jack Card tells the story of Las Vegas show girls in the 1950s running out at rehearsal breaks to get silicone injected directly into their breasts prior to the invention of implants. Diane Middlebrook, author of *Suits Me: The Double Life of Billy Tipton*, quotes a male nightclub goer who recalls that in the 1960s across the US, 'guys would try to scrub out cigarettes or cigars on a stripper. Entice her over, use a cigarette to burn her leg, sometimes try to light their silken gowns on fire. I know one girl was burned to death when that happened, and many strippers carried burns on their bodies (Middlebrook, 1998: 221). . . .

One male narrator who booked strippers for fraternity house parties on the campus of the University of British Columbia in the 1950s recalled that 'college boys could be monsters.' One evening, he escorted a dancer to a campus stag only to rescue her from 'an ugly scene', and then 'drove her home along back alleys, with the headlights out, in order to lose crazy kids who were following us.'[11] Two dancers told stories about club owners offering cocaine to underage prospects as a recruitment ploy, and all of the dancers recalled the low-grade, lewd heckling from male customers. At the most extreme end of the spectrum, former booking agent Jeannie Reynolds was called to the Vancouver city morgue to identify the bodies of two strippers who had been murdered in downtown Vancouver nightclubs in the late 1960s.

Regardless of the venue, none of the former dancers had access to vacation pay, sick leave, disability leave, or pension plans. On the unionization front, in Vancouver in 1967, three 'topless dancers' staged a two-night picket at a local nightclub (*Vancouver Sun*, 18 and 19 October 1967). They demanded higher wages, staff privileges, and a dressing room heater. They expressed the desire to organize dancers at six other nightclubs,

though as far as we know, dancers never certified in Vancouver. In Toronto, the Canadian Association of Burlesque Entertainers (CABE) was a local of the Canadian Labour Congress in the 1970s, though it did not survive long, nor did the American Guild of Variety Artists, which represented sex performers in central Canada until the early 1970s.[12] Former dancer Barbara noted that waves of union agitation in Vancouver throughout the 1970s and 1980s often corresponded with times of economic affluence in the city, though club owners and booking agents consistently and fervently opposed the labour agitation. Additionally, Barbara recalled the competitive conditions under which dancers secured paying gigs, the lack of pro-union consciousness among the women, and the need for dancers to tour, all of which impeded worker solidarity and thwarted unionization. Stripteasers were migrant labourers whose travel and performance schedules were similar to those of employees of the Ice Capades, Barnam & Bailey's circus, and the National Hockey League. . . . However, unlike professional skaters, jugglers, and hockey players, stripteasers *explicitly* sold sexual allure and teetered on the edge of legality, which likely confounded efforts to attract union backing.

On occasion in postwar Vancouver, erotic dancers supplemented their nightclub earnings by modelling, movie work, all-male stag events (which date back to the late 1800s), magazine work, and legitimate dance in chorus lines and with jazz troupes. In the 1960s, a number of Vancouver-based strippers were hired to perform a 15-minute act between porn reels on the stage of the Chinese-owned Venus movie house on Main Street, at the edge of Chinatown. I suspect that a small percentage of former strippers combined striptease with prostitution, though no one has disclosed their involvement in the exchange of sex for money. Instead, several dancers emphasized their careers as artists, and either implicitly or explicitly set themselves apart from 'no-talent' prostitutes, which is an important division to flesh out further.

(Un)dressing For Success

Under the rubric of striptease as production and consumption of spectacle, we turn our attention to the nature of the performances themselves—the artistic, cultural, aesthetic, and musical traditions that influenced dancers and choreographers. . . . Jack Card, a well-known choreographer who was born in Vancouver, and worked the West Coast wheel, remembers that every dancer had a gimmick: at 'Isy's Supper Club, strippers worked with live doves or did fire shows, Yvette Dare trained a parrot to pluck her clothes off, another stripper was a magician, Jane Jones had a tiger in her act, another dancer sat on an electric trapeze and stripped while swinging.' . . .

Regardless of how much nudity was allowed, or required (by the early 1970s), female bodies were expected to conform to male-defined standards of female sexiness: pretty face, medium to large breasts, long, shapely legs, small waist, long hair. 'Bombshells' like Annie Ample, Morganna, and Chesty Morgan had legendary breast sizes; Mitzi Dupré was a super-feature who sprayed ping pong balls and played a flute with her vagina.[13] According to Michelle, when Mitzi was on stage, she had people laughing in stitches while they played mock baseball games with the flying-ping pong balls. For almost nine years, Bonnie Scott perfected her show-stopping extravaganza in Vancouver and across the country: on stage, under pink lights, she stripped off her super-deluxe, twelve-hundred dollar beaded gown, . . . climbed a wrought-iron ladder, and once inside her five-foot tall, plexiglass champagne flute, she struck sexy poses amidst the bubbles.

Jack Card worked and travelled with headliner Gypsy Rose Lee who performed in Vancouver and,

more regularly, in the extravagant Las Vegas revues where each of her costumes carried a $5,000 price tag. Underneath the sequined gowns and furs, in addition to jeweled pasties and g-strings (which were often worn layered over one another), rhinestone clips were popular in the 1950s and 1960s: v-shaped and glittery, they fitted over the pubic area, were made of sprung steel, and inserted into the vagina. In Montreal in 1951, Lili St Cyr was arrested and subjected to a trial for 'giving an obscene performance', and arrested again in 1967 before tourists arrived for Expo (Campbell, 1999). Perhaps because of St Cyr's brush with the law, dancers in Montreal in the 1960s were known to wear 'muckettes'—patches of artificial pubic hair glued to the pubic region in order to avoid arrest for indecency, all the while perpetuating the illusion of nudity.

The Colonial Carnivalesque Under Big Tents

Lured by the promise of a 20-week season and a steady pay cheque, many burlesque dancers packed their trunks and joined the travelling exhibition or carnival, often in the twilight of their career. Girl shows had become staples of the touring carnival and circus across North America, beginning after the Chicago Columbia Exhibition in 1893.[14] Alongside the merry-go-rounds, arcades, shooting galleries, and sideshows spotlighting bearded ladies, alligator-skinned boys, and 'midgits', stripteasers were main features.[15] Borrowing from big revues like the Ziegfeld Follies, carnival showmen added 'spice and less wardrobe' to give their tent-shows more edge than downtown cabaret acts (Stencell, 2000: 13). While other show girls paraded their (hetero) femininity by baking cakes in competition, or strutting their stuff as beauty pageant contestants vying for the crown of Miss Pacific National Exhibition (PNE), strippers on 'carnival stages sang, danced, told jokes, and shed their elaborate costumes.[16]

In the 1950s in Vancouver, impresario Isy Walters, who owned the Cave Supper Club, and later, Isy's Supper Club, also booked strip acts at the PNE. Isy's Black Tent Show,[17] which was next door to his White Tent Show, invited patrons to pass between the legs of a 50-foot plywood cut-out of a black burlesque dancer at the tent's entrance on the fairgrounds. As Jack Card recalls, inside the neon-lit tent, the talker introduced: 'The African Queen, DIRECT from the jungles of Africa', and behind her there'd be Nubian slave girls in chains, a bumping and a thumping.' Here, the colonial trope of African primitivism, bound up with the imperialist custom (and fantasy) of captivity, was remade as titillating foreignness at the same time, and in the same city, that African-American singer Lena Horne was refused hotel accommodation for 'being a Negro'. A decade later in Vancouver, Hogan's Alley—the city's working-class African-Canadian enclave—was bulldozed into the ground.[18] Significantly, the discourse of burlesque under the Big Tent was never about sex alone. It was tangled up with the economic, cultural, and political privileges of a white body politic.[19]

. . . In circuses and carnivals across North America throughout the 1900s, black performers who were paid consistently less than their white counterparts, were routinely consigned to the role of cannibals, 'Zulu warriors', bushmen, and bear-women from the darkest Africa (Strange and Loo, 1996: 179–80). In addition, for more than a century, some white burlesque dancers disguised themselves as Algerian, Egyptian, Hawaiian, or Arabian in an effort to feed white appetites for the exotic, what Mary Douglas calls 'radical strangeness' (Douglas, 1985: 201–4).

Gawking at dancers of colour and white women who impersonated the Other, white consumers were reassured of their own normality and cultural dominance; social boundaries between spectators and performers, the civilized and the uncivilized, were conserved, and the near homogeneity of Anglo, postwar Vancouver, affirmed. Pre-existing racial and gender stereotypes were animated in the interests of carnies or showmen smartly fluent in the common-sense, naturalized precepts of mass entertainment. The speech of the talker, the colourful images on the bally front, and the hand-bills advertising the event, were rooted in a racial, gender, and class grammar that distinguished native instinct from white self-discipline, and native lust from white civility.[20] . . .

Racism in burlesque and striptease played out in myriad ways. In the US in 1956, Princess Do May—'the Cherokee Half Breed' (Figure 19.1)—was photographed in full feather headdress, beaded headband, and a (sacred) drum, freeze-framed in time and space anachronistically as an Indian artefact displaced from community and territory, and repositioned against an untouched, untamed wilderness ripe for conquest (Rothe, 1997: 29). A picture of condensed and standardized symbols of Indianness, and of imperialism as commodity spectacle, she served to make invisible the multiple identities and multiple interests of diverse first nations (McClintock, 1995: 56). All colonial histories of slaughter and subjugation are absented in this rendition of the myth of the noble savage. The Princess, and not her degenerate sister—'the drunken, broken-down, and diseased squaw'—was employed in burlesque to excite the sexual imagination of white men who engineered Euro-Canadian and Euro-American expansion, settlement, and industry on the frontier.[21]

Counterpose this image of Princess Do May against the seductive Lili St Cyr (Figure 19.2) (Rothe, 1997: 97). The American-born St Cyr of Swedish/Dutch heritage, spent many famous years

Figure 19.1 Princess Do May

Figure 19.2 Lili St Cyr

in Montreal, beginning in 1944, and was well-known for her on-stage bubble-baths, elaborate props, and her penchant for eccentric story-telling on stage (Weintraub, 1996). The Nordic, voluptuous cowgirl, replete with ten-gallon hat, holster and guns, leather boots and lariat, is equally burdened by a condensation of symbols and metaphors—in this case, those of the conquerors of aboriginal peoples, and the keepers of Euro-Canadian myths of colonial rule. St Cyr stands in for the brave, heroic, pioneering men and women who have been memorialized as the founding ancestors of the contemporary nation, emblems of national identity, pride, and prosperity. St Cyr embodies the colonial myth of the rough and tumble Wild West, the promise of abundant resources free for the taking, and the danger of encountering Indians who had never seen a white man or a white woman (Furniss, 1997–8: 29). Decked out in traditional cowboy garb, St Cyr fetishized the triumph of

European colonizers, and reminded white men in the audience that force was always at their disposal if they needed or wanted it. At the same time, she sent up the machismo of the Marlboro man.

Hoochie Coochie Queers?

In their 1965 study of women's prisons in the US, Ward and Kassebaum found that a 'disproportionate number' of strippers (and models) were likely to be homosexuals. . . . In my 'Striptease Project', I have learned that gay dancers and choreographers, make-up artists, prop-makers, costume designers, wig-makers, and customers, found a home in the business.[22] According to Jack Card, some of the most beautiful showgirls he knew were gay, as were the dancing boys with their bare chests and false eyelashes. Former erotic dancers Maud Allan, Josephine Baker, Gypsy Rose Lee, and Tempest Storm are rumoured to have had women lovers. . . .

If stripteasers identified as gay women, what relationship (if any) did they develop to Vancouver's butch and femme bar culture?[23] Kennedy and Davis reveal that in the 1940s and 1950s, femmes in Buffalo, New York typically had steady paid employment while their butch lovers struggled with long stretches of unsteady, sporadic labour and financial uncertainty as car jockeys, elevator operators, and couriers (Kennedy and Davis, 1993). What we don't yet know is: did the wages of femmes in g-strings subsidize the earnings of their butch lovers? Given the tendency of butches to bind their breasts, wear men's clothing, and spurn feminine artifice, was stripteaser a primarily femme occupational category?

Almost twenty years before the invention of *Xena: Warrior Princess* on prime-time TV, Klute—a butch lesbian in disguise successfully reworked themes from 'Conan the Barbarian' as an s/m dominatrix, and played with the fantasies of men who longed to be topped. As she recalled, she never fit the 'high femme, mega-feature look'. Instead, she played with gender ambiguity by adopting the personae of Michael Jackson and Grace Jones on stage until she was ostracized for being 'too dykey'. Notwithstanding Klute's impressive transgression, we suspect that butches were principally spectators who sought out striptease as exciting, titillating entertainment wherever it was staged; femme spectators likely balanced the opportunity to be mentored with pangs of envy. It is also probable that queer female customers in gay pubs that staged striptease—the Vanport and the New Fountain— were working-class gay girls who were less invested in the rigours of respectability than their middle-class, professional sisters (Gilmartin, 1996). . . .

The presence of queers on and off striptease stages troubles the naturalized presumption that nightclubs and carnivals were indisputably straight milieux. Acting out moments of what Judith Butler calls 'insurrectionary queerness' (Butler, 1997: 159) inside cabarets, stripclubs, and under big tents, queer stripteasers, staff, and fans interrupted the heterosexual imperative. What is not yet apparent to us is the complexity of queer relationships to the closet, as well as to communities beyond the borders of the nightclub world. Given the criminalization of homosexuality prior to 1969, combined with the stigmatization of striptease, we suspect that most queers in the business prior to gay liberation in the 1970s sought the same subterfuge that sheltered Hollywood he-man Rock Hudson for so long.

The Imbrication of Sex and Nation

In the end, a fundamental paradox governed the business of erotic entertainment before 1980, and arguably still does today. On the one hand, stripteasers were, in the main, well-paid, glamorous entertainers who, as working-class women with limited employment options, stripped first for the money. The women we've interviewed took pride in putting on a good show, they loved the applause, and the challenge of developing new routines, costumes, and props. On the other hand, they were subjected to criminal and social sanctions that pressured them to be ashamed of their work, to pretend that they did something else for a living, or to abandon their careers as dancers altogether. Their skills and expertise, their dedication, flare, and originality as workers, were overshadowed, if not entirely discounted, by moral reformers, police, and civic officials who, at various times and for a variety of purposes, were in the business of scapegoating non-conformists. While professional female dancers in ballet, modern, and jazz increasingly inspired awe and veneration in the second half of the twentieth century, stripteasers were consigned to the interstices between adoration and attention, and fear, resentment, and hostility.

It seems clear that female erotic dancers did not qualify as full-fledged citizens dedicated to the ideal family, the social order, and the health of the Canadian nation (Scott, 1996: 12). Perceived by many as no better than disgraced whores who haunted the quasi-legal underworld in postwar Vancouver, dancers were positioned outside of discourses that elaborated what it meant to be a normal, moral, and patriotic citizen. As a result, they could never take for granted the fundamental constituents of substantive citizenship such as inclusion, belonging, equity, and justice.[24] Like prostitutes and other sex trade workers, in an era of suburbanized, privatized domesticity, and marital nuclearity, erotic dancers were presumed to be devoid of real jobs, families, and meaningful, intimate relationships.[25] No dancer raising children, especially if she was non-white, was ever honoured for her role as mother and moral guardian of 'the race'.

Because strippers were commonly perceived as anti-family, they were presumed to possess no maternal honour worth protecting. Rather than being extended dignity, security, and safety, their family forms were stigmatized as a menace to the stability of the nation state (Räthzel, 1995: 168). Two retired dancers we interviewed who balanced child-rearing and their careers as strippers recall the painful judgment of other parents, day care workers, coaches, and teachers who disapproved of their chosen field of work. . . .

[Even now], all across North America, the paradox persists. More money is spent at stripclubs than at large-scale commercial theatres, regional and non-profit theatres, the opera, the ballet, jazz, and classical music performances—combined (Schlosser, 1997: 44). In the US, the number of strip clubs has doubled in the past decade, with the fastest growth in upscale 'Gentlemen's Clubs' which have reframed striptease as adult entertainment that upholds the highest standards of the hospitality industry. Over the past decade, Canada's Immigration Department has granted thousands of temporary six-month work permits to women from Romania, the Czech Republic, Hungary, and Poland, to serve Canada's burgeoning stripclub business as 'burlesque entertainers' (Oziewicz, 2000). At the same time, striptease continues to be a lightning rod for cultural/legal and political conflicts all over North America (Hanna, 1998: 62). Unresolved debates swirl around the legal and moral character of lap dancing, peep shows, live sex acts on stage, the physical location of 'exotic dance', and nightclubs as venues for prostitution. . . .

The combination of old-fashioned police pressure, residents' associations dedicated to protecting property and family values, media sensationalism, and the manipulation of zoning ordinances, has meant heated attacks on stripclub culture with sobering results. Since 1993, striptease has been the number one topic of Free Speech litigation in the US (DeWitt, 1995). According to anthropologist Judith Lynne Hanna, over 62 communities across North America have enacted laws to restrict striptease, including Seattle, Tacoma, Fort Lauderdale, Syracuse, and Phoenix. New laws continually resurface. Only time will tell whether or not similar, discriminatory prohibitions will be invoked to control (or obliterate) erotic dancing in Vancouver, or any other Canadian city. So long as stripper bodies conjure up popular associations of worthless, diseased, lazy, drug-addicted, oversexed, dangerous, and un-Canadian bodies, the erotic labour performed by dancers, past and present, will never be appreciated *as labour*: it will be forever figured as something else. And age-old struggles by dancers for improved working conditions, union certification, and destigmatization of their artform will continue in the absence of a titanic transformation in the cultural meanings attached to bump and grind.

Notes

1. There is an important sociological literature that focuses on the business of striptease or 'exotic dancing' in the 1980s and 1990s, though much of the work is uncritically rooted in the tradition of the sociology of deviance. See Craig Forsyth and Tina Deshotels, 'A Deviant Process: The Sojourn of the Stripper', *Sociological Spectrum* 18 (1998): 77–92; William Thompson and Jackie Harred, 'Topless Dancers: Managing Stigma in a Deviant Occupation', *Deviant Behaviour* 13 (1992): 291–311; Scott Reid, Jonathon Epstein, and D.E. Benson, 'Does Exotic Dancing Pay Well But Cost Dearly?', in A. Thio and T. Calhoun, eds, *Readings in Deviant Behaviour* (New York: Pearson, 1995), 284–8; and G.E. Enck and J.D. Preston, 'Counterfeit Intimacy: A Dramaturgical Analysis of an Erotic Performance', *Deviant Behaviour* 9 (1988): 360–81.

2. See Dorothy E. Smith, *The Everyday World As Problematic: Toward a Feminist Sociology* (Boston: Northeastern University Press, 1987), 154.

3. For stunning insights into the place of sexuality in the process of Canadian state formation, see Steven Maynard, 'The Maple Leaf (Gardens) Forever: Sex, Canadian Historians and National History', unpublished paper, Department of History, Queen's University, 1999.

4. Also see James Skipper and Charles McCaghy, 'Stripteasers: The Anatomy and Career Contingencies of a Deviant Occupation', *Social Problems* 17 (1970): 391–404.

5. Robert Campbell makes a similar argument when he distinguishes the sale of alcohol in first-class hotels from lower-end hotels with their overwhelmingly working-class clientele. See his article, 'Managing the Marginal: Regulating and Managing Decency in Vancouver's Beer Parlours, 1925–1954', *Labour/Le Travail* 44 (Fall 1999): 112.

6. Robert Campbell, in *Demon Rum or Easy Money: Government Control of Liquor in British Columbia from Prohibition to Privatization* (Ottawa: Carleton University Press, 1991), 50–5, argues that the BC Liquor Control Board enforced a 'no food, no entertainment, no dancing' policy in Vancouver's beer parlours (in hotels) until 1954.

7. Here, I am adapting insights of Judith Butler, *Excitable Speech: A Politics of Performative* (New York: Routledge, 1997), 130–5.

8. Filippone is the anglicized version of the original Philliponi, invented by a racist immigration officer when Joe (the eldest) and his parents arrived in British Columbia from San Nicola, Italy, in 1929.

9. According to a cover story in *Dick MacLean's Guide: the Fortnightly Restaurant Magazine*, 4–18 October 1978, 'The full operation, which involved 12 officers, included surveillance by means of electronic eavesdropping devices, hidden cameras, motor vehicle surveillance, and male officers entering the club to pose as prostitutes' clients' (13).

10. For autobiographical writings on striptease from 1970 to 2000, see Misty, *Strip!* (Toronto: New Place Press, 1973); Janet Feindel, *A Particular Class of Woman* (Vancouver: Lazara Publications, 1988); Margaret Drague and A.S.A. Harrison, *Revelations: Essays on Striptease and Sexuality* (Gibson's Landing: Nightwood Editions, 1988); Annie Ample, *The Bare Facts: My Life as a Stripper* (Toronto: Key Porter Books, 1988); Lindalee Tracey, *Growing Up Naked* (Vancouver: Douglas & McIntyre, 1997); Dianna

Atkinson, *Highways and Dancehalls* (Toronto: Vintage, 1988); Shannon Bell, ed., *Whore Carnival* (New York: Autonomedia, 1995); Gwendolyn, 'Nothing Butt: The Truth about the Sex Trade', *Toward the Slaughterhouse of History* (Toronto 1992), 16–23; Chris Bearchell, 'No Apologies: Strippers as the Upfront Line in a Battle to Communicate', *The Body Politic* 123 (February 1986): 26–9; Kim Derko, 'A High-Heeled Point of View', *Independent Eye*, 12 (Spring/Summer 1991): 1–8; Sasha, 'Taking It Off is One Thing. . .', *Globe and Mail*, 22 January 2000, A15; Merri Lisa Johnson, 'Pole Work: Autoethnography of a Strip Club', in Barry Dank and Roberto Refinetti, eds, *Sex Work and Sex Workers* (New Brunswick, NJ: Transaction Publishers, 1999), 149–58.

11. Interview with George P., 17 June 2000.
12. For more on efforts to unionize, see Amber Cooke, 'Stripping: Who Calls the Tune?' and Mary Johnson, 'CABE and Strippers: A Delicate Union', both in Laurie Bell, ed., *Good Girls/Bad Girls: Sex Trade Workers and Feminists Face to Face* (Toronto: Canadian Scholars Press, 1987), 92–9, 109–13.
13. In a fascinating article, Kristina Zarlengo characterizes the 'bombshell' as a 'deeply desirable, unattainable woman with an inflated body and intense sexuality—a steadfast atomic age feminine ideal. . .who represented raw power of a kind frequently associated with the atom bomb.' See Zarlengo, 'Civilian Threat, the Suburban Citadel, and Atomic Age American Women', *Signs: Journal of Women in Culture and Society* 25 (Fall 1999), 946.
14. According to A.W. Stencell, *Girl Show: Into the Canvas World of Bump and Grind* (Toronto: ECW Press, 1999), in the 1860s it was said that in the various saloons and parlours, girls pretending to be can-can dancers, as practised in Parisian cabarets in Montmartre and Montparnasse, would do private dances without clothes for a dollar (4).
15. See Robert Bogdan, *Freak Show: Presenting Human Oddities for Amusement and Profit* (Chicago: University of Chicago Press, 1988). For her inspiration, I am grateful to Helen Humphreys whose historical research for her prize-winning novel, *Leaving Earth: A Novel* (London: Picador, 2000), 96, turned up evidence of women stripping underwater on the fairgrounds of the Canadian National Exhibition in Toronto in the 1930s.
16. Candace Savage tackles the world of beauty pageants in *Beauty Queens: A Playful History* (Vancouver: Greystone Books, 1998).
17. In the US, the 'black show' was typically referred to as the 'Nig Show'. See Carolyn Strange and Tina Loo, 'Spectacular Justice: The Circus on Trial and the Trial as Circus, Picton, 1903', *Canadian Historical Review* 77 (June 1996): 159–84.
18. See 'Hogan's Alley', directed by Andrea Fatona and Cornelia Wyngarten, 1994. Distributed by Video Out, Vancouver.
19. See Ann Laura Stoler, *Race and the Education of Desire: Foucault's History of Sexuality and the Colonial Order of Things* (Durham: Duke University Press, 1997), 190.
20. See Stoler, *Race and the Education of Desire*, 178–9.
21. See Elizabeth Furniss, 'Pioneers, Progress and the Myth of the Frontier: The Landscape of Public History in Rural BC', *BC Studies* 115/116 (Fall/Winter 1997–8): 7–44; Jean Barman, 'Taming Aboriginal Sexuality: Gender, Power, and Race in British Columbia, 1850–1900', *BC Studies* 115/116 (Fall/Winter 1997–8): 237–66.
22. African American jazz singer Teri Thornton, who died in May 2000 of cancer, found work as the intermission pianist for strippers at the Red Garter nightclub in Chicago in the 1950s. She performed in Vancouver at Isy's Supper Club in January 1967, though it's not clear whether or not she accompanied strippers at that gig. In Ben Ratliff's obituary in the *Globe and Mail*, 'Singer was a favourite of Ella Fitzgerald', there is no mention of Thornton's sexuality, which suggests that she may have been gay (8 May 2000, R6).
23. On butch and femme culture in Vancouver in the 1950s and 1960s, see Vanessa Cosco, 'Obviously Then I'm Not Heterosexual: Lesbian Identities, Discretion, and Communities', MA thesis, Department of History, University of British Columbia, 1997; and 'Forbidden Love: The Unashamed Stories of Lesbian Lives', dir. Aerlyn Weissman and Lynne Fernie, National Film Board of Canada, 1992.
24. See Jeffrey Weeks, 'The Sexual Citizen', *Theory Culture and Society* 15 (August/November 1998): 35–9.
25. On the post-World War II era, see Mary Louise Adams, *The Trouble with Normal: Postwar Youth and the Making of Heterosexuality* (Toronto: University of Toronto Press, 1997); Doug Owram, *Born at the Right Time: A History of the Baby Boom Generation* (Toronto: University of Toronto Press, 1996); Joan Sangster, 'Doing Two Jobs: The Wage-Earner Mother, 1945–1970', in Joy Parr, ed., *Diversity of Women, Ontario 1945–1980* (Toronto: University of Toronto Press, 1995), 98–134; and Joanne Meyerowitz, ed., *Not June Cleaver: Women and Gender in Postwar America, 1945–1960* (Philadelphia, PA: Temple University Press, 1994).

References

Allen, Robert. 1991. *Horrible Prettiness: Burlesque and American Culture*. Chapel Hill, NC: The University of North Carolina Press.

Butler, Judith. 1997. *Excitable Speech: A Politics of the Performative*. New York: Routledge.

Campbell, Murray. 1999. 'Memories of Montreal's Skin Queen', *Globe and Mail*, 3 February, A3.

Corio, Ann, with Joseph DiMona. 1968. *This Was Burlesque*. New York: Madison Square Press.

'Dancers End Picket at Club: Deal Reached'. 1967. *Vancouver Sun*, 19 October.

Davis, Chuck. 1997. *The Greater Vancouver Book: An Urban Encyclopedia*. Surrey, BC: Linkman Press.

DeWitt, Clyde. 1995. 'Legal Commentary', *Adult Video News*, 112–27.

Dick MacLean's Guide: The Fortnightly Restaurant Magazine. 1978. 4–18 October, 112–15.

Didon, Pino. 1978. 'A Candid Interview: Philliponi Disapproves of Nudity', *L'Eco D'Italia* 20 January, 1–3, 8.

Douglas, Mary. 1985. 'My Circus Fieldwork', *Semiotica* 85: 201–4.

Friedman, Andrea. 1996. 'The Habitats of Sex-Crazed Perverts: Campaigns Against Burlesque in Depression-Era New York City', *Journal of the History of Sexuality* 7: 203–38.

Furniss, Elizabeth. 1997–8. 'Pioneers, Progress and the Myth of the Frontier: The Landscape of Public History in Rural BC', *BC Studies* 115/116 (Fall/Winter): 7–44.

Gilmartin, Katie. 1996. '"We Weren't Bar People": Middle-Class Lesbian Identities and Cultural Spaces', *GLQ: A Journal of Lesbian & Gay Studies* 3: 1–51.

Hanna, Judith Lynne. 1998. 'Undressing the First Amendment and Corsetting the Striptease Dancer', *The Drama Review* 42, 2 (Summer): 38–69.

Jarrett, Lucinda. 1997. *Stripping in Time: A History of Erotic Dancing*. London: Rivers Oram Press.

Jesser, C., and L. Donovan. 1969. 'Nudity in the Art Training Process', *Sociological Quarterly* 10: 355–71.

Kennedy, Elizabeth Lapovsky, and Madeline Davis. 1993. *Boots of Leather, Slippers of Gold: The History of a Lesbian Community*. New York: Penguin.

McCaghy, Charles, and James Skipper. 1972. 'Stripping: Anatomy of a Deviant Life Style', in Saul Feldman and Gerald Thielbar, eds, *Life Styles: Diversity in American Society*. Boston: Little, Brown and Company.

McClintock, Anne. 1995. *Imperial Leather: Race, Gender, and Sexuality in the Colonial Contest*. New York: Routledge.

MacGillivray, Alex. 1968. 'Column', *Vancouver Sun*, 20 December, A2.

Middlebrook, Dianne Wood. 2000. *Suits Me: The Double Life of Billy Tipton*. Boston: Mariner Books.

Oziewicz, Estanislao. 2000. 'Canada's Bare Essentials', *Globe and Mail*, 19 February.

'Picket Still On—Three Dancers'. 1967. *Vancouver Sun*, 18 October.

Räthzel, Nora. 1995. 'Nationalism and Gender in West Europe: The German Case', in Helma Lutz, et al., eds, *Crossfires: Nationalism, Racism and Gender in Europe*. London: Pluto Press.

Rothe, Len. 1997. *The Queens of Burlesque: Vintage Photographs from the 1940s and 1950s*. Atglen, PA: Schiffer Publishing.

Schlosser, Eric. 1997. 'The Business of Pornography', *US News and World Report*, 10 February.

Scott, David. 1996. *Behind the G-String: An Exploration of the Stripper's Image, Her Person and Her Meaning*. Jefferson, NC: McFarland and Company.

Skipper, James, and Charles McCaghy. 1971. 'Stripteasing: A Sex-Oriented Occupation', in James Henslin, ed., *Studies in the Sociology of Sex*. New York: Appleton-Century Crofts.

Stencell, A.W. 2000. *Girl Show: Into the Canvas World of Bump and Grind*. Toronto: ECW Press.

Strange, Carolyn. 1995. *Toronto's Girl Problem: The Perils and Pleasures of the City*. Toronto: University of Toronto Press.

Strange, Carolyn, and Tina Loo. 1996. 'Spectacular Justice: The Circus on Trial and the Trial as Circus, Picton, 1903', *Canadian Historical Review* 77 (June 1996): 159–84.

'The Penthouse Papers'. 1978. *Dick MacLean's Guide: The Fortnightly Restaurant Magazine*, 4–18 October, 27.

Tracey, Lindalee. 1997. *Growing Up Naked*. Vancouver: Douglas and McIntyre.

Vancouver Sun. 1976. 'Cover Up, Says A-G'. 31 August.

Weintraub, William. 1996. 'Show Business: Lili St Cyr's Town—and Al's and Oscar's', in *City Unique: Montreal Days and Nights in the 1940s and 50s*. Toronto: McClelland and Stewart.

PART IX

The Changing Face of Class Struggle in the Post-War Period

The post-World War II 'Fordist' accord, described by Peter McInnis in Part VII, was an informal compromise involving labour, capital, and the state. It rested, first, on the tacit agreement of organized labour and capital to adhere to certain 'rules of the game' in a state-monitored industrial relations system. Trade unions secured the right to organize and bargain collectively for their members; capital received certain guarantees that production would not be disturbed during the life of collective agreements binding workers and their employers to specific legal obligations. The entire system rested on the economic prediction that in a post-war age of affluence increasing output of commodities would be absorbed by rising mass consumption, fueled by the high wages and job securities of a well-remunerated and reasonably protected workforce. This workforce, moreover, was understood to be accepting of the need to behave in respectable ways, a process of accommodation reinforced by the Cold War's anti-communism. In the late 1940s and 1950s—a period that saw the establishment of a kind of industrial pluralism—Canada's unions underwent a period of 'political cleansing' in which many radicals, including union leaders and members affiliated with the Communist Party of Canada, were driven underground or out of positions of authority.

As many historians are now pointing out, this 'Fordist' agreement was actually developed in ways that benefited and applied to one predominant sector of the labour force: white, male workers, especially those in large, unionized, mass production and resource extractive industries. Obviously, many workers did not fit into this model. Displaced Persons (DP) from refugee camps in Europe brought to work in farmers' fields, women in low-paid domestic service, sweatshops, or small, marginal factories, and immigrants confined to unskilled or semi-skilled jobs in a host of service occupations or employed on the periphery of economic sectors like construction, were all part of a growing 'second tier' of workers. They could not count on the benefits of the Fordist post-war settlement, nor did they share equally in the expansion of consumption that we associate with the 1950s and 1960s. To address such people, who seemed to be falling through the cracks of the post-war period's advances, the welfare state's growth promised certain protections, albeit ones always limited, partial, and, as Ann

Porter shows in a recent study of unemployment insurance, gendered in ways that reproduced traditional understandings of women and work.

These were thus years of contradictions. Despite images of affluence, there remained many workers locked into the insecurities and uncertainties of material marginality; pockets of dire poverty scarred the social and economic landscape of Canada. To try to purchase a piece of the image of the successful, consuming family that began to be promoted in popular magazines, newspapers, radio, and the new medium of television, more and more women were joining the workforce, supplementing the male breadwinner wage that was supposedly able to secure 'the good life' in post-World War II Canada. Slowly in the 1950s, and more rapidly in the 1960s, women's paid employment expanded with the fastest growing group: married women with families. Despite unions continuing to be seen as institutions of blue-collar workers in private industry, the most significant growth area within organized labour from the mid-1960s forward was the public sector, which of course grew dramatically in size with the expansion of the welfare state. Civil servants, health care workers, teachers, and many others employed by the state were thus new recruits to both the labour movement and class struggle.

The following articles deal with aspects of the post-war period of key significance to working-class history, but they do not necessarily tell a traditional story. Pamela Sugiman's chapter from her study, *Labour's Dilemma: The Gender Politics of Autoworkers in Canada, 1937–1979* (1994), looks at women autoworkers at a time and in an industry that captures the quintessential experiences of Fordism. Following a major battle with employers and the state in 1937, Oshawa autoworkers took the first steps toward the establishment of the United Automobile Workers of America (UAW), an international industrial union associated with the United States-based Congress of Industrial Organization, or CIO, the Canadian equivalent of which was the Congress of Canadian Labour (CLC).

Women remained a distinct minority in the auto industry, confined to gender-defined jobs that were considered appropriate to their femininity. Less vocal and prominent than men in union affairs, women in Canada's automobile industry faced an uphill battle in fighting their way into the labour movement. Drawing on interviews with women workers as well as union archives, Sugiman offers an explanation for why both women and men accepted the prevailing gendered division of labour in the plants, and how women used the more sophisticated union agreements of the period to improve their working conditions. The female workforce was changing, with a more diverse and older group of women in the plants, and unionized women were learning how to use the grievance procedure as well as union concepts of 'justice and fairness' to create spaces of dignity for themselves in the workplace. It is not surprising that the next chapter in Sugiman's book documents the efforts by women in the 1960s to go further, challenging the sexual division of labour and masculine power structures within their own unions.

Mobilization of teachers, both in terms of union affiliation and of militant job action, are often associated with the post-1970 period, when they and other public sector workers secured the right to strike. Magdalena Fahrni documents an illegal strike of Montreal teachers in 1949. By the early 1970s, teachers were recognized as one of the most militant groups in the Quebec labour movement. They participated in the 'Common Front' described in Ralph Guntzel's article (Part X), but this late 1940s walkout was unprecedented for the time. Despite the illegality of their action, these lay Catholic teachers, the majority of whom were women, were able to secure a substantial measure of public support for their protest. Using the teachers' strike as her focus, Fahrni explores the urban family in this period, asking how notions of parenthood were used by both the striking teachers and those mothers and fathers who mobilized to support or oppose the withdrawal of services in the education sector.

The teachers' strike was one of a number of struggles in post-World War II Quebec that signalled a new militancy on the part of working people. Other significant class confrontations, such as the momentous Asbestos strike of 1949, the 1952 strike at Montreal's Dupuis Frères department store, or the violent United Steel Workers-led battle at Murdochville, also signalled an upsurge in militancy both within international unions and in Quebec's Catholic unions. Indeed, as Quebec workers struggled to secure better conditions they were part of an advance guard of reform-minded combatants, including journalists and professors, who broke decisively from past traditions to chart a new future for French Canadians. The Quiet Revolution of the early- to mid-1960s would be one consequence of this as, ironically, so too would be the rise of Pierre Elliott Trudeau, an influential figure who came to public prominence through his associations with this world of late 1940s and 1950s working-class upheaval, only to clamp down on it repressively as he occupied the Prime Minister's Office in the late 1960s and 1970s.

Alvin Finkel illuminates a further irony. He charts the ways in which trade unions contributed to the emergence of the welfare state, with its premise that all Canadians were entitled to a minimal standard of living with respect to health care, security in old age, housing, and other basic necessities. Finkel's broad overview suggests that there were currents within the trade union movement that worked diligently to achieve the betterment of all Canadian workers, regardless of their affiliation with unions. This commitment to universal social programs and the redistribution of income as ways of creating a more egalitarian society were at the very core of an understanding of what trade unions were meant to be doing in the post-war period. But the actual history of the labour movement, while indicating some successes in the struggle for social justice, also reveals failures. Finkel shows that in post-war Canada, as trade unions gained legitimacy and power and strengthened their capacity to pressure the state and achieve broad reform, they could also retreat from this project of social transformation. If gains were registered in many quarters, it was also sadly the case that at some points and in some sectors, Canadian labour organizations cultivated the narrow concerns of a traditional business unionism interested only in the wage advances and job conditions of a 'sheltered proletariat', whose key privilege was trade union affiliation and its benefits.

Further Reading

Gillian Creese, *Contracting Masculinity: Gender, Class, and Race in a White Collar Union, 1944–1994* (Toronto: Oxford University Press, 1999).

Sam Gindin, *The Canadian Auto Workers: The Rise and Transformation of a Union* (Toronto: Lorimer, 1995).

Cy Gonick, Paul Phillips, and Jesse Vorst, eds, *Labour Gains, Labour Pains: 50 Years of PC 1003* (Halifax: Fernwood, 1995).

Bryan D. Palmer, 'System Failure: The Breakdown of the Post-War Settlement and the Politics of Labour in our Time', *Labour/Le Travail* 55 (Spring 2005): 334–46.

Ann Porter, *Gendered States: Women, Unemployment Insurance, and the Political Economy of the Welfare State in Canada, 1945–1997* (Toronto: University of Toronto Press, 2003).

Pierre Elliott Trudeau, ed., *The Asbestos Strike* (Toronto: James, Lewis & Samuel, 1974).

Charlotte B. Yates, *From Plant to Politics: The Autoworkers Union in Postwar Canada* (Philadelphia: Temple University Press, 1993).

Visual Resources

NFB, *Canada's Sweetheart: The Saga of Hal Banks* (1985), dir. Donald Brittain, 114 minutes (the story of the Cold War and the destruction of the Canadian Seaman's Union).

NFB, *The Un-Canadians* (1996), dir. Len Scher, 72 minutes (explores the Cold War, the blacklist, and RCMP security investigations in Canada).

CHAPTER 20
Becoming 'Union-Wise', 1950–1963
Pamela Sugiman

When auto manufacturers reconverted their operations to domestic production in the mid-to-late 1940s, many women lost their jobs. However, with bursts of economic growth in the early 1950s and renewed prosperity in the early 1960s, employers recalled some war workers and hired additional women. What were the experiences of this new cohort of female workers in times of relative social and economic stability?

Predictably, women's responses to auto work were similar before, during, and immediately after the Second World War. In each of these periods, women's gender identity and subordinate position in society strongly shaped their relation to auto work. Newly hired workers in the industry upheld conventional beliefs about the sexes and did not challenge sex-segregated work arrangements. Like the cohort that preceded them, these women made strong investments in friendships and family.

After the war, however, as the UAW gained strength and legitimacy, and as women secured a more permanent position in the industry, they developed a stronger self-identification as wage earners and as unionists. By the 1950s many women recognized that they were in the plants to stay. Consequently, they paid greater attention to the terms of their employment, and they formally protested a number of shop-floor conditions. . . .

In this chapter we will see that the resistance strategies of women auto workers were largely shaped by the gendered politics of earlier times—a politics that led to the dominance of a masculine agenda and male discourse in the union. The UAW,

the women's most viable resource for change at this time, embraced working men's vision of social justice—a vision that upheld conventional gender ideologies, accepted sex-based inequalities, and was premised on the unquestioned assumption that because women were different from men, it was reasonable to treat them differently (less well). At the same time, however, unionists continued to promote the ethos of worker solidarity and unity, and the universal pursuit of social justice. Guided by this contradictory outlook, male union leaders entrenched and legitimated blatant gender inequalities in collective agreements, while they simultaneously championed female workers' rights as dues-paying unionists.

These contradictions resulted in a fractured workers' struggle. Yet this fracture only constrained the *nature* of struggle. It did not obstruct *struggle per se*. Throughout these years, women auto workers became increasingly 'union-wise' and with their knowledge of unionism, they lodged battles that would ultimately have great consequence for the organization, and experience, of wage labour.

A New Cohort of Workers in a Changing Context

By the late 1940s and early 1950s, auto manufacturers were again expanding their operations and recalling some of the women they had laid off at the war's end. In addition, they were hiring women who had never before worked in the industry. In 1948, 350 women were employed out of a total of 4,850 plant workers in GM's Oshawa complex (representing 7 per cent of the total workforce). Local union officials reported that all of these employees were white.[1] . . .

Women's relation to wage work after the war was consistent with the past in many ways. Notably, close friendships and social ties continued to be an important feature of their shopfloor life. . . . Yet the women's talk also reflected subtle changes in their lives and in their outlook on life. They revealed, for instance, greater candour about female sexuality than in the past. [Pat] Creighton [who worked in GMs cutting and sewing room] remarked, 'Some of the girls were having babies out of wedlock and at that time you didn't keep it. Very rarely they kept their babies . . . And then there was no unemployment [insurance] . . . You had six weeks sick leave . . . I've seen them work till Friday night and have the baby on Saturday because they only had six weeks . . . If they were having a rough time at home or if they were single, it was just like a bunch of mother hens around you . . . There was like family. We took care of them . . . Kind of a nice time then.'. . .

More striking, however, is that women began to vent their discontents about wage work. While they consciously avoided the topic of auto work during the war, it became an important part of their conversations in the post-war years. Auto employee Doris Lepitsky said, 'When we got mad, we'd be talking about work . . . at our lunch hour. [In the lunch room, the women would] bitch at that girl that gets away and doesn't do nothing and that one has to work harder and all that stuff . . . They'd bitch about the foreman too, but not so that he could hear.'

Women's growing shop-floor protest can be linked to some intersecting developments. First, the structural framework in which they were living had changed significantly. In spite of recessionary periods and growing foreign competition, the employment of women became more stable than in the past. Simultaneously, the UAW was growing in strength and legitimacy. With the lifting of wartime controls, unionists could make greater demands on employers, the grievance procedure became increasingly effective, and in 1945 organized labour won the union 'check-off', known as the Rand formula. With the check-off in place, the company's payroll department automatically deducted union dues from the paycheque of every worker in the bargaining unit. All of these developments fuelled the labour movement and contributed to a more economically secure working class.

In addition, a parallel change was occurring in the workforce itself. After the war, women auto workers could be divided into three main groups. Unmarried, high-seniority employees who had worked in the industry prior to the Second World War comprised one cohort. By the post-war years, many of these women were 35 to 40 years old. They recognized that they would most likely remain single, and they strongly valued their work for both its material and its social rewards. Another group included women who entered auto employment as war workers. These women married either during the war or immediately after. Because of company restrictions on the employment of married women, most of these workers lost their jobs when war production ceased. Manufacturers eventually recalled some of these women when companies faced labour shortages in the 1950s. Third, and most important, a new cohort of women entered the auto plants during the late 1940s and throughout the 1950s. According to one observer, GM periodically hired large groups of women during these years. When they entered the industry, most of these women were between 20 and 30 years old. Some were married, while others were single, divorced, or widowed.

The female workforce was thus far more diverse than it had been in the past. Women auto workers had always varied widely in age, and both married and unmarried women had worked in the plants during the war. However, in the post-war years, the women had more diverse employment experiences and perspectives on wage work. In addition, since GM hired greater numbers of Eastern European and some Dutch immigrants after the war, the labour force became more ethnically heterogeneous.[2]

Importantly, much of the post-war female workforce was familiar with industrial employment. Women in the first two categories had experience in the auto industry itself, and many of the new employees had previously worked in some sort of factory setting. These women were not bewildered by a huge industrial complex. Although many of them still feared their supervisors and were hesitant to openly assert their rights, others were bold and defiant. The bold and defiant frequently stood up for their more timid sisters. . . .

While they continued to work out of economic need, few women expressed an overwhelming sense of gratitude for their employment. Furthermore, while many women planned to leave employment upon marriage, others viewed wage work as a lifetime endeavour. Over time most of the women adjusted their aspirations to the material realities of their lives. These realities forced them to recognize that they were permanently tied to the labour force. And as they accumulated seniority and pension rights, they were less inclined to quit their jobs. . . .

Developing a Union Consciousness

After the war, women remained peripheral to the union administration. Few women held an elected office and consequently they still had little input in the union's agenda. Similarly, their attendance at membership meetings, representation on union standing committees, and participation in conferences remained disproportionately lower than men's. By 1961, there were 3,612 female members in the UAW Canadian Region; however, only 22 women held office in a UAW local. They included two presidents, six recording secretaries, three financial secretaries, 10 trustees, and one sergeant-at-arms.[3]

Nevertheless, women workers continued to firmly support the philosophy and goals of industrial unionism. While the figures on women office holders hint at the extent of their access to the UAW power structure, they do not, in turn, tell us about women's allegiance to the union. Bev McCloskey, committeewoman in the cutting and sewing departments, pondered the complex, contradictory relationship between women and the UAW. About the female sewing room workers she said, 'They'd call you up—the boss would give them hell and they'd be cryin'. It took me years to get them to stop cryin', you know, because their feelings would be hurt . . . But I don't know . . . Women—when we had strikes, they were right there. They were the best people going. Right out on that picket line. And they had to fight just as hard as anybody.' . . .

As these statements illustrate, women's weak formal participation in the UAW was rooted in the social organization of the union, industry, and society, not in women's ideological stance. As noted, female members had trouble getting elected to office and attending meetings and conferences because of inadequate child care and transportation, as well as their confinement to women's departments in the plants. The masculine culture of the labour movement also hampered their involvement. These obstacles explain women's seeming indifference to the union in normal times, but active commitment during periods of crisis. . . .

Women's Grievances and Perceptions of Gender on the Shop Floor

The women most clearly revealed their growing union citizenship by taking full advantage of the strengthened UAW grievance procedure. Throughout the 1950s and early 1960s workers filed grievances on a wide range of issues. 'Everything you could ever think of that's a grievance, we had them,' said Bev McCloskey. On the basis of fragmentary archival data we cannot make a conclusive statement about the number of grievances filed by women. However, the records and interview data available indicate that some women used the grievance procedure extensively and that during these years there was a notable increase in their formal complaints compared with earlier times.[4]

Although it was not overwhelming, women's use of this form of protest is striking given the historical context. After the war organized labour was stronger than ever, but it was still attempting to establish itself in a highly conservative era. This was an era in which legislators, private individuals, and even some labour leaders themselves were attempting to purge unions of a 'Communist threat'. In addition, conservative voices strongly enforced the view that woman's proper place was in the home. Through both the experience of wage work and participation in the union, however, women auto workers adopted values and expectations that in a contradictory way overshadowed, as well as highlighted, gender prescriptions. Throughout these years, union officials encouraged all workers to use the grievance procedure to uphold their contractual rights. Notably, they directed this recommendation at women as a distinct group.

During the 1950s, employers in mass production industries increasingly relied on the intensification of work or 'speed-up', as part of a classic Fordist/Taylorist strategy to increase productivity and assert control of the shop floor.[5] Indeed, the production standard was one of the most contentious issues facing workers. Given the sex-segregated nature of auto work, women could not compare their production quotas with those of men. Nevertheless, they did evaluate their work requirements by their physical capacity to keep up, and on this basis they believed the quotas were unjust. According to Phyllis Yurkowski, supervisors in all the women's departments made excessive demands on the workforce. In the cutting and sewing room in Oshawa, for instance, 'some foremen . . . just wanted women to keep their nose to their sewing machine. They just wanted so much work done . . . But some jobs were heavy and harder and that made them slower . . . You got so many pieces off of that job when you were doing it and that was that. But then if they come along and speeded something up . . . then that's when you'd call the union in.' About the wire and harness department, she stated, 'I had everything to complain about there. Speedups and putting terminals in fuse boxes . . . oh, your fingers would be bleeding. And the . . . foreman and the group leader would get their heads together and go and speed up lines and . . . you were just going like this and here you're trying to get those terminals in the fuse boxes to work. And oh, your fingers were so sore! Oh! . . . It would get on your nerves.' Similarly Elsa Goddard recalled, 'You had to produce or they let you know that you weren't producing . . . They used to come around every so often and time the job . . . We'd always hope that the person that was the fast one never got timed because if that's the time they chose everybody had to work at that speed. And there could be a lot of problems because there was a lot of women that just couldn't do it at that speed.'

Women's gendered learning heightened their susceptibility to supervisors' demands. Like many women, these workers took pride in their diligence, efficiency, and high productivity. In addition, some of the older workers placed an emotional stake in securing the bosses' approval. In order to prove that they were reliable workers and good women, they pushed themselves hard. This hard work took its toll on many individuals. Indeed, in 1950 a Local 199 representative in McKinnon Industries reported that in trying so desperately to keep up with the demands of the line, 'the girls were breaking down'.[6]

Wire and harness worker Ann Brisbois described her experience.

> I worried terrible, just awful, about it. I got very nervous when I was being timed. They'd tell us the day before. And I would be almost sick to my stomach to think that I was going to be timed . . . They all knew that we didn't like it.

. . . Such working conditions forced some women to leave their jobs for work in lower-paying but less demanding industries. Others resisted the labour process through small acts of sabotage. For instance, when GM management increased their quota from 10 pieces to 15 pieces per hour, a group of angry women in the Oshawa plant 'beat' the time study men by putting a block of wood under the machine so that it could work only at a limited pace.[7] . . . Encouraged by their union leaders some women also protested unfair work standards through formal channels. 'The dictionary defines the word intimidation to mean, inspire with fear; to overawe, cow, making afraid. This seems to be the practice lately in the Sewing Department,' declared union representative Bev McCloskey. 'The foreman's idea of a "Fair Day's Work" is to stand behind the employees with the

Standard Men for a period of 8 hours, 2 or 3 days a week. The employees in this department are well aware of the tactics the Company used to get increased production out of the workers, without increasing manpower. This situation will not be allowed to prevail. The dignity of the workers means something to the Union, even if it doesn't to the Company. I'm requesting all the affected employees, to call their committeeman' (Gibson, 1963: 4).

Women responded to such requests by filing a series of individual and group grievances against GM.[8] 'I . . . protest the action of my foreman in asking me to do more than a fair day's work,' read one of many such complaints.[9] 'We feel we are definitely performing to the best of our ability and every time we manage to produce more he [the foreman] reprimands us for . . . not performing a fair day's work and we request that this practice cease immediately,' declared four women from the McKinnon plant.[10] In May 1951, 27 women in the Delco division protested a rate change without a time study of their work operations.[11] In April 1957, 15 women protested speed-ups in department 63.[12] And in March 1959, 10 women in department 64 grieved management's use of a light to monitor the work output of the first operator on their line.[13] . . .

Underlying women's attempts to assert control over the labour process was an effort to maintain some personal dignity in the workplace. Some women understood that the exercise of power and dominance on the shop floor was inextricably tied to gender relations within society as a whole. Many women, for instance, claimed that foremen harshly disciplined them specifically because of their sex. As well, some women were reluctant to assert themselves because their bosses were men. . . .

Another GM employee, Fay Bender, claimed that supervision was unjustly 'hard' on women for absenteeism. 'We didn't have any more absenteeism than men,' she stated, 'but it was just the point that they could hassle the women. And a great number of them wouldn't say anything back to them . . . it was just their continual hassle of us. It even got to the point that if you took a day off, so that you wouldn't get too much of a hassle even for a headache—you went to the doctor and said I have to have a doctor's note.'

Women also resented the sometimes flagrant favouritism of supervisors. According to McKinnon worker Rose Taylor, 'There was an awful lot of favouritism, so I wouldn't want to work in a place like that without a union.' Helen Beaugrand, formerly of GM and later a Chrysler employee, served as a union steward in Local 1090 for six years. In deciding to run for this position, she said to herself, 'Why should some get this and others turned down all the time? And you seen different little things that you didn't like and I thought well, I'll run.'

Some women believed that favouritism had a basis in men's attitudes towards female sexuality. 'If you had hair colour that might be right, could be blonde, could be brunette, you know, or a red head . . . they could do no wrong and other girls weren't favoured,' said Laura Saunders. 'And they would get the dirty jobs.' McKinnon employee Doris Lepitsky believed that the middle-aged and older females paid for the foremen's preference for young women. She explained, 'Say you're 17, 18, and I'm 40. And I got 20 years seniority and you only got 5, but because the foreman likes you because you're young and everything else, he gives you soft jobs and he gives the older women harder jobs. Then you gotta call the union and fight it out 'cause you got more seniority.'[14] . . .

With chivalry, male unionists also defended their sisters against the sometimes boorish behaviour of management. For example, in May 1952,

when the Local 199 Shop Committee met with McKinnon representatives to discuss the transfer grievance of a woman, union officials protested the company's conduct towards the griever. According to the unionists, the employee went to the restroom 'white as a ghost' as soon as she left the management office. When her foreman asked her what was wrong, she burst into tears. According to the union, she did not want to give management the satisfaction of seeing her in this state. UAW chairman Gordon Lambert stated to H.W. McArthur, McKinnon personnel director, 'The manner you treated Letta in the office, I wouldn't talk to a lady in that manner. The union feel you have no right bringing a lady in the office and treating her in the manner you did.' Lambert claimed that the griever was home sick because of this episode. 'I can't use the language you used because there's a lady present,' he remarked.[15] . . .

Working Within the Parameters of the Collective Agreement

During the 1950s and early 1960s women auto workers left unchallenged the two most outstanding and fundamental instances of sex-based discrimination—sex-based job classifications and wage rates, and separate seniority systems based on sex and (women's) marital status. This strategy needs to be understood in the light of the women's protests regarding other aspects of their employment.

Gender Segregation and Sex-Based Wage Rates

In the 1950s, despite increased hiring, women were still confined to a few departments. For example, in GM's Oshawa facility, women remained in the radiator room, the wire and harness, and the cutting and sewing departments (McCloskey,

1956: 4). At one time, a small group of women also worked in the parts and service department.[16] Within these departments, they continued to occupy a narrow range of jobs. For example, in 1955, there were approximately 19 female and 25 boy's job classifications in the Oshawa plant, compared with roughly 393 adult male classifications.[17] . . .

Sex-based job classifications furthermore provided the foundation for unequal wage rates for women and men. Without a thorough analysis of work content, it is difficult to equate women's and men's jobs; however, a few classifications permit comparison. In 1953 in GM's Oshawa plant, an adult male assembler received between $1.49 and $1.60 per hour, while a female general assembler earned between $1.24 and $1.31. In comparison, general assemblers in the boys' group received $1.24 to $1.39 per hour.[18] In 1956 the job rate for male bench hands was $1.69, while the rate for female bench hands was $1.45. . . .

Insofar as the gendered division of labour and sex-based wage rates were sanctified in the collective agreement, women rarely challenged them. Such a challenge would be considerable. Without sufficient resources women instead sought fair rates for jobs they performed within female classifications and work groups.[19] Admittedly, some women attempted to reduce sex-based differentials in pay. For instance, in January 1951 four female core makers in McKinnon's foundry complained that the differential between male and female core makers was 24 cents, whereas the differential between male and female production workers was only 12.5 cents. They did not, however, challenge gender segregation, the basis of these differences in pay.[20]

Foreshadowing emerging feminist debates, many women did forcefully protect their restricted contractual rights, though. When management gave them work that officially fell within a man's classification, some women demanded that they be paid the appropriate *male* rate (Sutton, 1957: 4–5). Employers paid men the 'male rate' when they temporarily performed a woman's job,[21] and they continued to pay women a 'female rate' when they performed a man's job. In 1956, on behalf of women employees, the union demanded that McKinnon Industries pay the adult male rate to women who assembled glove-box doors, a job which the local wage agreement defined as 'properly belonging to an adult male'. Upholding the contract, a UAW official declared 'that where a job is allocated seniority wise to adult males then the rate for that job should certainly be that of adult males' (*Oshaworker*, 4 October 1956: 6).

Some women also protested management's violations of the local seniority agreement. Again, however, insofar as they occupied non-interchangeable sex-based seniority groups, they directed most of these grievances against other women.[22] For example, in March 1950 a UAW committeeman reported that GM junior supervisors were acting like 'nasty little brats' in violating the seniority rights of sewing room workers. The union official claimed that because the general foreman selected the twenty-fourth woman on the seniority list for a highly rated job, he had 23 'wild women on his hands, every one of them with a grievance' (*Oshaworker*, 1 March 1950).

Management infrequently replaced women with male workers. However, when this happened women upheld gendered divisions with equal resolve.[23] For instance, in March 1957 a female inspector in McKinnon Industries wrote, 'I . . . protest being transferred from my group when an employee from a Male Seniority Group is employed on work normally performed by female employees.'[24] In December 1961 24 women from one department formally protested the lead-man working overtime on their job, and they demanded that this practice cease.[25] . . .

In 1954 several women from GM's radiator department also upheld the contract when the company replaced them with boys (males under the age of 18). At the time approximately 20 women were working in this department, and for over 30 years (prior to 1950) women had exclusively performed the operation in question—'fold and form and centre machine operator—female'. The exception was during the Second World War (1939–40 to 1944–45) when boys alone did the work. On 20 June 1950, however, GM again placed a boy on the job. The following month the company instituted a second (night) shift in the department, and because provincial legislation prohibited night work for women, they hired additional boys for this shift. The boys worked steady nights and the women worked steady days. In an attempt to increase productivity, management informed the boys that if they heightened their efficiency, they could move onto the day shift. Responding to this incentive, the boys began to outperform the women and consequently by 1953 they had entered the day shift, labouring alongside the very same women who had trained them in their jobs.

When management eliminated the night shift the following year, they laid off seven women but retained the boys. Maurie Shorten, one of the displaced women, recalled that management gave the women their layoff notice roughly five minutes before the plant shut down for the day. 'They didn't even let us back into other departments,' she said. This prompted her to go to the women's homes and convince them to file grievances.[26]

The women formally complained that in laying them off while retaining the boys, GM had violated their seniority rights. In November 1954 their cases went to arbitration. . . . The arbitrator . . . noted that by 1945 at the latest, women had taken over the job and that it had remained

an exclusively female operation until June 1950. He further acknowledged that boys worked on the night shift only because the law forbid women to work these hours. In addition, he declared that the company's interpretation of the agreement meant that it 'has it in its power to destroy completely the seniority rights of all female employees who presently enjoy such rights. The Company would not only be entitled to retain at work male employees with greater 'seniority' than the female doing identical work . . . but, since there could be no limitation upon the Company's authority in this regard, it would also be entitled to establish such new groups to parallel every female classification and staff them with low 'seniority' male employees whom it could retain at work while long-service female employees could be laid off . . . It could scarcely be said that in such a state of affairs female employees would be given 'an equitable measure of security based on their length of service Company.' The arbitrator upheld the women's complaint and directed GM to rectify the situation. The grievers each received $200 from the company in back pay, but women ultimately left this department.[27]

As this example indicates, women auto workers relentlessly protected their restricted position in the industry, yet they were bound by a collective agreement that institutionalized sex-based job classifications, wage rates, and seniority systems. Their efforts were therefore limited. A struggle to change the collective agreement would be formidable because of the nature of the undertaking and thus the effort that would be involved. A change in contract language required direct input in the bodies that set the UAW agenda, the resources to launch an organized campaign, and considerable bargaining leverage over management. Moreover, because of the give-and-take nature of collective bargaining in North America, eliminating sex-based contract clauses necessitated that UAW place priority on this demand and relinquish another item on their agenda. However, we have seen that women had restricted powers in the union, their resistance was largely confined to isolated and sporadic acts, and management strongly opposed changes in the division of labour. Furthermore, dominant gender ideologies powerfully legitimated segregation in the workplace. Bev McCloskey aptly described the consequent limitations on women's workplace resistance. 'We used to fight like hell about different things . . . but not really . . . because we were in a mould. We'd been socialized, you know, to think, well this is the status quo, so therefore that's where you stay. That's your job . . . And there wasn't any arguments or fights about well, we want that job and we want that job. We did try to transfer [into men's jobs]—which we couldn't do. Nobody could transfer at that time. It wasn't in our contract.'

Married Women and the 'Victory Shift'

During this period a few pioneering women did, however, successfully contest the unfair treatment of pregnant women and married women. Yet these struggles were also inspired by a growing union citizenship, not a critique of women's specific subordination as a sex in industry. The grievers left intact beliefs that married women were financial dependents, and they did not openly challenge the premise of gender discrimination. Again, women were limited by a masculine discourse.

Both union men and employers treated the job-related rights of married and pregnant women with far more ambivalence than the other concerns of female employees. Nevertheless, women were able to successfully challenge the unfair treatment of married women because the collective agreement categorized workers by sex only, not by marital status or pregnancy status.

For example, in March 1953 an unmarried woman applied for employment at GM. On the

job application, she answered 'no' to the question 'Any known physical defects?' At the time, she was over three months pregnant, but the company was unaware of this. They hired her and she worked for slightly under six months, until the day before she gave birth. Roughly two weeks later, the company dismissed this woman on the grounds that she had provided false information on her employment application. Desperately in need of the job, this woman protested the company's actions through the UAW grievance procedure.[28] During the arbitration hearing of this case, company representatives clearly indicated that if they had known about the worker's pregnancy, they would not have employed her. They further argued that this decision was their prerogative given that, under the collective agreement, management had the right to hire and fire as it saw fit. Consequently, the union's representatives fought this case around the issue of the worker's honesty and integrity rather than the more general and fundamental matter of the firm's policy against pregnant women. In reviewing the case, the arbitrator stated, 'Admittedly, the aggrieved employee failed to disclose that she was pregnant. On the other hand, she was not asked specifically whether she was pregnant; she was asked whether she suffered any physical defects.' Taking a strategic and unprecedented stance, the union argued that the term 'physical defect' refers to 'an incapacity accompanying or resulting from illness or injury, and that pregnancy is not looked upon as a physical defect but rather as a natural and normal physiological condition.' On this premise, they claimed, the employee properly answered the question on the application form. The arbitrator accepted this view and concluded that management had improperly discharged the griever and must reinstate her (CAW, 1953).

Throughout this period the question of marital status as grounds for discharge also came to the fore as a few married women, too, tried to protect their right to employment. . . . Because the GM plants in Oshawa did not immediately expand production after the war, they reinstated their restrictions on the employment of married women, and many women consequently lost their jobs. However, when GM increased production in the 1950s, they again relaxed their policy and recalled and hired married women. . . . 'It was an understanding when they came back they just worked in this busy season and then they were automatically off again,' explained GM employee Jane McDonald. 'During the busy season, they didn't acquire seniority . . . They come back just for that. It might have been maybe three months, two months . . . and that was it.' Without seniority rights, married women could be easily 'let go' when production declined. . . .

Married women had long resented this arrangement, yet it went unchallenged for many years. It was not until September 1953 that a worker named Rosina Saxby decided to openly contest it.[29] Saxby, a married sewing machine operator in GM, had been laid off because of a shortage of work. While on lay-off, however, she discovered that the company had recalled an unmarried woman who was junior to her.[30] . . . Perplexed, Saxby asked questions. Rosina's husband, Bill Saxby, a UAW shop steward at Houdaille Industries, informed her that insofar as married women were paying union dues, they should have some seniority protection. 'This is why I come out and fight,' said Rosina. 'When I went into General Motors, they started to take money [union dues] out of my paycheque.' She said to Bill, 'I can't see the point in this. If we're not in the union, why are they taking money out of us?'. . .

Most local unionists were indifferent to her concerns. Nevertheless, Saxby persisted, stating, 'I want to go on a seniority list where, along the line, I've got protection.' In a private meeting, local union officials discussed her concerns with management, and in January 1954 they cleverly side-stepped her complaint by establishing a separate seniority group for married women. This measure gave married women the right to accumulate seniority among themselves, but it did not give them the seniority rights enjoyed by other workers, either male or unmarried female. . . .

This measure, however, was also in violation of UAW International policy. In June 1954 the UAW International Office had issued an administrative letter in which they advocated the fair treatment of married women and upheld the union's seniority principle. In addition, a recent UAW Convention had resolved to protect married women's employment rights (CAW, 1954). When Caroline Davis, director of the UAW Women's Bureau, heard about the local's actions she immediately requested an explanation. Echoing arguments that were typical among solid unionists at the war's end, she asked, 'How long will it be before they will suggest separate seniority lists for single men, who have less home responsibility than married men, and then older men, whose children have married and left home. And what about the person who has a small farm, filling station or store? Do we in turn put them on separate seniority lists—and what, then, happens to our unity? . . . Our safest position,' she concluded, 'is to not vary from established seniority.'[31]

While the local wavered, Bill Saxby appealed directly to Walter Reuther, the UAW President, for a just resolution. Saxby also sought the help of his friend Doug Sutton, a UAW committeeman at GM. On 10 December 1953 Rosina filed a grievance with Sutton, but in the meantime the company discharged her. GM also issued 'removal notices' to 27 other married women, declaring that none of them had seniority rights (*Oshaworker*, 4 February 1954: 2). . . .

After much stalling by the union, Saxby's grievance made its way through the various stages of the procedure, and in December 1954 it went to arbitration. . . . At the hearing UAW International Representative John Eldon argued that GM both failed to recall Saxby in accordance with her seniority rights and had improperly discharged her. In turn, the company claimed that as a married woman Saxby had no seniority rights under the contract. GM spokespersons also stated that they had recalled another woman before Saxby because the former was better trained to perform the work required. . . . The company argued that long before unionization, GM acted on 'the premise that married women did not acquire seniority rights and that, immediately upon marriage, females forfeited whatever seniority rights they had acquired during their unmarried state'. Company representatives added that because the union had never in the history of their bargaining relationship opposed this practice, one must view them as consenting to it.

The arbitrator contended that where a provision in an agreement is 'vague or ambiguous', the interpretation should concur with past practice. However, he did not see any vagueness or ambiguity in this case. . . . 'Nowhere in the Section is there so much as a word or a phrase from which it could be inferred that the parties intended to deprive married women, solely by reason of their marital status, of the rights to which employees are entitled under the Section.' On this basis, he reasoned that Saxby acquired seniority rights in the same way as unmarried women and that GM should have recalled her in line with her seniority. He therefore directed the company to compensate the griever for lost time.[32] Saxby received $1,200 in back pay, yet the company refused to reinstate her. Regardless of the validity of her protest, because the union had failed to take her grievance to the third stage of the procedure within the established time limit, they lost their chance to dispute this matter.[33] . . .

These cases all had significant implications for women's perceptions of their rights as wage earners, as well as for their structural position in the industry. Although they were rare and isolated, these grievances set precedents and generated important debates among the union membership. Rosina Saxby recalled that her case 'was brought up on the floor at a big union meeting with General Motors. And of course there was men that were for, there was men that was against married women. And I got up and I did my thing and I can remember being extremely nervous about it . . . I can recall one man gettin' up and telling me I had no business being in General Motors. He felt that . . . married women should not work . . . There was a lot of that way back in the '50s . . . They figured you're married you should be at home with the kids and all that kind of stuff.' Witnessing these struggles, some women began to think about the larger questions they raised. . . .

Yet despite these outcomes, the women who initiated the complaints did not directly contest the gendered division of wage labour. Indeed, both workers and employers tended to uphold the belief that married women were essentially financial dependents and therefore less deserving in the sphere of employment. What then prompted these women to file their complaints? Fundamentally, they felt that management had violated their rights as unionists. As dues-paying UAW members they believed that they were entitled to seniority protection. Although they did not demand equality with men, they felt that they should have the same contractual privileges as other women.

Rosina Saxby did not refer to her rights as a woman nor did she criticize the company's assumptions about the female sex. Likewise, Bill

Saxby, a solid trade unionist, stated, 'I agree in principle with the argument that if two people want a job, two women, I think the . . . single woman should get preference because they need the money more. But the fact is if the company hired the married woman and . . . and they took . . . union dues out of her paycheque, she has the right. She should have the same rights as everybody, as a single woman.' . . .

Nevertheless, some male unionists could not reconcile these principles with their patriarchal beliefs. They consequently used their authority and knowledge of the union and industry to circumvent the contract and deny their sisters' rights. Ultimately, however, these men were challenged by the very system (industrial unionism and its tool, the collective agreement) that they themselves instituted. In many ways, the union contract 'froze' the gender inequalities that existed in the workplace and society. Yet it also granted women workers limited rights to protect themselves against management and encouraged them to regularly exercise these rights. The union therefore pushed women forward and drew them back. The agreement shaped worker resistance. It both embodied and contained workers' struggles.

Summary

Although the women did not openly challenge sex-based inequalities, they attempted to better their conditions of work with the recognition that, as women, they held a different, albeit unequal, place in society. By no means acquiescent, they protested particular aspects of their sexual subordination by management. Insofar as classes are gendered, any attempt to improve their working life indirectly affected their treatment as a sex. These protests, however, were not couched in a feminist critique, nor did they openly challenge contemporary gender ideologies and prescriptions of masculinity and femininity.

Women's shop-floor protest was primarily guided by a narrow union perspective, a masculine discourse. Female employees waged their struggles within the parameters of a collective agreement that working men negotiated according to their gender-biased vision of social justice. Within this framework, there was only a weak link between gender-based difference and equal rights. Thus, it was predominately by drawing on longstanding union principles and their rights as dues-paying unionists that women were able to win many grievances.

This strategy was based on ideological concerns and practical considerations. The degree as well as the nature of the struggle determined women auto workers' partial resistance. Insofar as sex-based job classifications and seniority systems were entrenched in the collective agreement, they were far more difficult to challenge than workplace issues such as speed-ups and washroom facilities, matters that could be negotiated directly and immediately by workers on the shop floor and in meetings between local union committeemen and first-line managers. Given women's lack of power in the union, and their hesitancy to directly participate in this masculine domain, movement on these issues was more within their reach. In the absence of an alternative ideology and social movement, women's strong gender identity was not channelled into a fully developed feminist consciousness. Rather, like men's gender identity, it was channelled into a union consciousness that presented the workforce as uniform in need.

Through both the experience of wage work and their participation in the union, however, women adopted certain values and expectations that overshadowed, as well as highlighted, their gender prescriptions. According to GM worker Betty Murray, 'I think that if you didn't have a union,

I'm not too sure how a shop would operate. Let's say a couple of hundred women would they get together to discuss their problems? I don't know. It starts with your union and with your union hall.'

Notes

1. See ALUA, George Addes, Secretary-Treasurer Collection, Box 80, Plant Survey Cards.
2. Baldwin interview, 9 July 1990, by author.
3. See ALUA, UAW Canadian Region, General Files Collection, Box 25, File 11, 'International UAW Women's Department and Canadian Region Women's Department, 1960–64', Caroline Davis to George Burt, 1 March 1961.
4. This discussion is based on a systematic review of all grievances and arbitration decisions in the archival collections and private papers for the period of study. Until the 1970s grievances filed by women were easy to isolate because of the given name of the grievant, and because reports often identified the grievant's sex, if the employee was female.
5. See, for example, Richard Herding, *Job Control and Union Structure* (Rotterdam: Rotterdam University Press, 1972).
6. ALUA, UAW Local 199 Collection, Box 20, File 'Bargaining, 1950', Bargaining Committee Meeting, 27 October 1950.
7. Bender interview, 22 July 1990, by author.
8. For example, ALUA, UAW Local 199 Collection, Box 6, File 'Grievances, Step 1 & 2, 1957', Employee Grievance No. 1087; Ibid., Employee Grievance No. 1080; Ibid., Box 7, File 'Grievances, Step 1 & 2, 1959–60', Employee Grievance 1776; Ibid., File 'Step 3, January–August, 1958', H.W. McArthur to James Connell, 18 February 1958; Ibid., Employee Grievance No. 2312; Ibid., Box 8, File 'Grievances, Step 1 & 2, 1963', Employee Grievance No. 3103, 18 December 1963; Ibid., Employee Grievance No. 1718; Ibid., File 'Grievances, Step 3, January–June, 1962', H.W. McArthur to Gordon Lambert, 1 February 1962; Ibid., File 'Grievances, Step 1 & 2, 1963', Employee Grievance No. 3117; Ibid., Box 11, File 'Meetings with Management, July–December 1962', Employee Grievance 2444; Ibid., File 'Meetings with Management, 1958', Minutes of Meeting with Shop Committee, 13 February 1958.
9. For example, ALUA, UAW Local 199 Collection, Box 8, File 'Grievances, 1962, Step 1 & 2' (second file), Employee Grievance No. 1718; Ibid., Employee Grievance No. 1717; Ibid., Employee Grievance 2592; Ibid., File 'Grievances, Step 1 & 2, 1963', Employee Grievance No. 2932; Ibid., Box 11, File 'Meetings with Management, January–May, 1963', Employee Grievance 2608.
10. ALUA, UAW Local 199 Collection, Box 6, File 'Grievances Step 1 & 2', 1957, Employee Grievance No. 10832.
11. Ibid., Box 5, File 'Miscellaneous, 1951', Employee Grievance No. 2610.
12. ALUA, UAW Local 199 Collection, Box 6, File 'Grievances, Step 1 & 2', 1957, Employee Grievance No. 107799.
13. ALUA, UAW Local 199 Collection, Box 11, File 'Grievances, Step 3, 1959–60'; Ibid., Box 7, File 'Meetings with Management, January–June, 1959', Employee Grievance No. 1777.
14. For example, ALUA, UAW Local 199 Collection, Box 8, File 'Grievances, Step 3, January–March 1963', H.W. McArthur to Gordon Lambert, 21 February 1963; Ibid., Box 11, File 'Meetings with Management—January–May 1963', Employee Grievance 2614. At times, working men lodged similar complaints, but the tone of their grievances was different. Unlike the women's complaints, they expressed an indignation that supervisors yell or swear at them, but they did not entail a notion of female sensitivity.
15. ALUA, UAW Local 199 Collection, Box 10, File 'Meeting with Management, March–May 1952'.
16. In comparison, boys (under the age of 18) were employed in the Radiator Room, Rods and Tubing, Sheet Metal Stamping, Truck Body and Hardware, Window Regulator Assembly and Packard Cable, Inspection, Material Handling, Heavy Reject, Final Finish, Passenger Primary Hardware, and Final Body Fit-Up departments. Pat McCloskey, 'Zone 31 Sewing Room', *Oshaworker*, 4, 5 (17 May 1956): 4.
17. PAC, MG 28, I 119, Acc. 83/215, Box 8, File 'General Motors Negotiations, 1955', Proposed Occupational Classifications, 25 June 1955. Women's jobs included sewing machine operator, door and arm rest trim assembler, bench hand, clicker machine operator, headlining piler and marker, tag writer, vertical and horizontal taping machine operator, wiring harness utility operator, service wiring operator, wiring harness repair operator, Fisher body wiring harness, miscellaneous press operator, solder dipper, rest room supervisor, and matron.

18. Ibid., Box 1, File 'Agreements, 1953', McKinnon Industries Supplement No. 7 to the Local Wages Agreement, 6 July 1953.
19. For example, Ibid., Box 1, File 'Appeal Cases 1960, CI 29-30, Record of Case CI-30; Ibid., Box 2, File 'Appeal Cases CJ 54-66,' Record of Case CJ-56; Ibid., Series I, Acc. No. 297, Box 6, File 'Working Conditions, 1952', Employee Grievance No. 1318; Ibid., File 'Wage Classification Rates, 1952–53', H.W. McArthur to John Kramer, 8 May 1952; Ibid., Box 7, File 'Grievances, Step 3, 1960', H.W. McArthur to Gordon Lambert, 6 October 1960; Ibid., File 'Step 3, January–August, 1958', Employee Grievance No. 2312; Ibid., 'Grievances, Step 1 & 2, 1959–60', Employee Grievance No. 1781; Ibid., Box 8, File 'Grievances, Step 3, January–March 1963', Employee Grievance No. 3119; Ibid., J.H. Morrow to Gordon Lambert, 7 March 1963; Ibid., Employee Grievance No. 3083; Ibid., Box 11, File 'Meetings with Management, January–May 1963', Minutes of Meeting with Shop Committee, 9 May 1963; Ibid., File 'Meetings with Management, August–December 1960', Minutes of Meetings with Shop Committee, 14 October 1960; Ibid., File 'Meetings with Management, 1958', Minutes of Meeting with Shop Committee, 13 February 1958; Ibid., File 'Meetings with Management, August–December, 1960', Minutes of Meetings with Shop Committee, 14 October 1960.
20. Ibid., Box 4, File 'Wage Classification and Rates, 1949–51', K.J. Barbeau to Gordon Lambert, 31 January 1951; Ibid., Box 4, File 'Wage Classification and Rates, 1949–51', Employee Grievance No. 3079, 30 January 1951.
21. For example, ALUA, UAW Local 199 Collection, Box 7, File 'Grievances, Step 3, January–June, 1961', Ibid., Box 11, File 'Meetings with Management, 1957', Minutes of Meeting with Shop Committee, 11 April 1957.
22. For example, ALUA, UAW Local 199 Collection, Box 1, File 'Appeal Cases, 1960', C.I. 29-31, Record of Case CI-37; Ibid., Box 2, File 'Appeal Cases, 1961', C.I. 52-60, Record of Case CI-54; Ibid., Box 5, File 'Miscellaneous, 1951'.
23. For example, ALUA, UAW Local 199 Collection, Box 7, File 'Grievances, Step 1 & 2, 1958', Employee Grievance No. 660, No. 621; Ibid., File 'Grievances, Steps 1 & 2, 1959–60', Employee Grievance No. 2434.
24. Ibid., Box 6, File 'Grievances, Step 1 & 2, 1957', Employee Grievance No. 1327.
25. Ibid., Box 7, File 'Grievances, 1961, Step 1 & 2', Employee Grievance No. 1168, No. 2066.
26. Shorten interview.
27. PAC, MG 28, I 119, Acc. 88/324, Box 87, 'General Motors Arbitrations', Arbitration Case 23-54, 18 November 1954; Shorten interview.
28. Shorten interview.
29. For example, in December 1951, Canadian UAW member, Zita Bowers, reported that at a recent meeting of the UAW Women's Advisory Council both Canadian and American women discussed, at length, how employers force women to quit working when they marry. They also noted that in some cases, married women would continue to work, without seniority rights. ALUA, UAW Canadian Region—Locals Collection, Box 85, File 12, 'Local 195, Windsor, 1950–51', Zita Bowers to George Burt, 4 December 1951; Saxby interview; PAC, MG 28, I 119, Acc. 88/324, Box 87, Binder 'General Motors' Arbitrations', Arbitration Case 22-54, Case No. GMO-23, 30 December 1954.
30. PAC, MG 28, I 119, Acc. 88/324, Box 87, Binder 'General Motors' Arbitrations', Arbitration Case 22-54, Case No. GMO-23, 30 December 1954.
31. ALUA, UAW Canadian Region—Series V Collection, Box 146, File 'GM of Canada Limited, Oshawa, 1953–54', Caroline Davis to Douglas Sutton, 11 February 1954.
32. PAC, MG 28, I 119, Acc. 88/324, Box 87, Binder 'General Motors' Arbitration', Arbitration Case 22-54, Case No. GMO-23, 30 December 1954.
33. Ibid.; Saxby interview, 9 August 1990, by author.

References

CAW. 1953. Arbitration Case 29-53. 17 October.
———. 1954. *UAW Administrative Letters,* Volume 1 (1948)–Volume 10A (1958), 1958. Book 1: 'UAW-CIO Administrative Letter', 16 June.
Gibson, Beverley. 1963. 'Department 32', *Oshaworker* 21, 8 (9 May): 4.
McCloskey, Pat. 1956. 'Zone 31 Sewing Room', *Oshaworker* 4, 5 (17 May): 4.
Oshaworker. 1950. Volume 8, Number 5 (1 March): 1.
Oshaworker. 1954. 'GM Shop Report', 12, 3 (4 February): 2.
Oshaworker. 1956. 'GM Shop Committee Report', 4, 13 (4 October): 6.
Sutton, Doug. 1957. 'GM Shop Committee Report', *Oshaworker* 5, 9 (16 May): 4–5.

CHAPTER 21

Parents, Pupils, and the Montreal Teachers' Strike of 1949
Magdalena Fahrni

In January 1949, for one cold week in the middle of a Montreal winter, the city's Catholic lay teachers went on strike. Across the metropolis, the classrooms normally run by these teachers remained empty, although nuns and teaching brothers continued to go to work. Children hung about school playgrounds or stayed home; parents listened to radio reports on the strike in order to decide whether to send their children to school. Nearly 1,500 francophone teachers congregated daily in a downtown hall to listen to speeches and strategize; more than 300 English-speaking Catholic lay teachers joined them in solidarity.[1]

This strike by Montreal teachers was unprecedented.[2] Since the teachers were considered public service workers, it was also illegal (*Le Devoir*, 18 January 1949). Although the teachers ultimately achieved some of their salary demands from the school board, their union's certification was suspended by Premier Maurice Duplessis and the Quebec Labour Relations Board, and was not restored until 1957.[3] The strike has thus attracted some attention from scholars interested in labour relations and Duplessiste politics (Thwaites and Perron-Thwaites, 1995).[4] A dimension of the strike that has not been dealt with by labour historians or industrial relations scholars, however, is the role played by parents—and, to a lesser extent, children—in the dispute.

This was principally a strike about wages. The union representing Montreal public-school teachers, the Alliance des professeurs catholiques de Montréal (APCM), had been trying to negotiate better wages with the school board, the

Commission des écoles catholiques de Montréal (CECM), for almost two years. Wages for lay teachers in Quebec had historically been low, particularly in rural areas. In part, this was because lay teachers competed with nuns and teaching brothers, who were paid very little on the assumption that they had taken vows of poverty and had few expenses. The APCM, led by Léo Guindon, pointed out that Montreal's Catholic teachers earned less than teachers in other provinces and, particularly grating, far less than Protestant teachers in the city itself.[5] When arbitration failed to resolve the problem, members of the APCM voted to strike and, on the morning of 17 January, refused to show up to work.

By all accounts, the teachers enjoyed a great deal of public support. The school board complained that newspapers and radio stations were biased in favour of the teachers. Union files overflowed with telegrams of support from the city's Protestant teachers, from teachers elsewhere in Quebec and Canada, from other unions, from the Co-operative Commonwealth Federation (CCF), and from concerned individuals. Likewise, the school board archives are filled with telegrams urging commissioners to take the teachers' needs seriously and to act responsibly in order to end the strike. The Canadian Congress of Labour, the Confédération des travailleurs catholiques du Canada, and the Fédération provinciale du travail du Québec all backed the APCM's stand, offering financial assistance if need be. Prominent Montreal activists such as Thérèse Casgrain and Frank Scott also offered the union financial support.[6] Streetcar drivers, students at the Université de Montréal, and, as we will see, public school pupils, rallied to the teachers' support (*Le Devoir*, 17, 19, 24 January 1949; *Montreal Gazette*, 17, 24 January 1949). Teachers were seen to be fighting for the city's children, a perception that teachers capitalized on by publicly expressing their concern for their 'dear students'.[7] Commentators spoke of children's 'right' to education (*Le Front Ouvrier*, 22 January 1949)—a right that was, of course, only recently acquired.

The majority of these striking Catholic lay teachers were women, and the central role played by female teachers in the strike was acknowledged and commended by the press. A reporter for *Le Devoir* noted that women had assumed leadership roles in this strike, and had played a large part in sustaining morale and solidarity. The commitment of the striking female teachers to their cause had earned them, this journalist claimed, the support of 'les mères de famille' (*Le Devoir*, 22 January 1949).[8] *Le Front Ouvrier* also highlighted women's importance to this strike by publishing a photograph of picketing female teachers, alongside a photograph of an empty classroom with the caption 'La maîtresse n'y était pas.'[9]

Because of the particular mix of lay teachers and teaching brothers and nuns in Montreal's Catholic school system, most schools were not shut down completely. Those with lay principals and a preponderance of lay teachers were much more affected by the strike than those run and taught primarily by members of religious orders. Religious personnel continued to teach during the strike. As Sœur Marie-Anne-Françoise of the Sisters of Sainte-Anne told the school board president six months after the strike, 'Nos religieuses, il me semble, ont donné, comme les autres communautés, une preuve tangible de leur zèle héroïque, de leur absolue fidélité à votre cause, lors de la suspension du travail des instituteurs

laïques.'[10] Yet there is little evidence of hostility on their part toward the lay teachers. Religious and lay personnel had a long tradition of working together in the city's schools, and knew that they would once again be sharing the school corridors after the strike was resolved.[11] Religious directors of schools appeared reluctant to report striking teachers to the board. Sœur Sainte-Anne-des-Miracles, the principal of École Ville-Marie, neglected to inform the school board about the actions of two militant female lay teachers during the strike because, as she explained to the CECM's president, Eugène Simard: 'Vraiment, je n'ai pas pensé que les incidents qui se sont produits pouvaient être considérés comme des faits saillants. Souvent dans notre vie d'éducatrice, nous avons affaire à des jeunes filles nerveuses ou surrexcitées et nous pensons que la meilleure attitude à prendre dans la circonstance est le calme et l'oubli. C'est pourquoi, en recevant la feuille du rapport le 19 janvier, j'ai omis de mentionner les faits du 17 janvier.'[12]

Another female member of a religious community, the director of l'École Ste-Jeanne-d'Arc, met with 80 pupils and five homeroom teachers on the first morning of the strike. Called to the telephone, she returned to find that all 80 students had vanished. Yet in her report to the school board she refused to blame the female lay teachers and instead attributed the students' disappearance to 'une manœuvre extérieure.'[13]

Once the strike began, the union and the school board reached an agreement on wage demands relatively quickly, but the teachers refused to return to work until the board agreed not to inflict reprisals on the teachers who had participated in the strike (*Montreal Gazette*, 24 January 1949). Seven days into the strike, it ended when, at a meeting of the teachers that lasted through the evening and into the early hours of the next morning, Archbishop Joseph Charbonneau and two Catholic parents' groups, the École des Parents and the Catholic Parents' League, promised the teachers that they would lobby for wage increases for them and would attempt to ensure that no reprisals were taken, if only they would return to their classrooms later that day.[14]

But what of the pupils? On the Monday that had marked the first day of the strike, children had appeared at a loss as to what to do: they hung around schoolyards and crowded around teachers' cars for information. As it became clear that classes run by lay teachers would not he held, most children stayed home. The APCM reported on the first day of the strike that 'les classes laïques sont vides, les élèves sort repartis.'[15] Activist pupils, or simply restless ones (those the assistant director of the city police called 'quelques écoliers turbulents')[16] participated in the strike. *Le Devoir* described children parading in front of their school with banners reading, 'Nous appuyons nos professeurs' (*Le Devoir*, 17 January 1949). Boys from Le Plateau and Saint-Stanislas schools travelled in packs to other schools, encouraging fellow students to leave class and to rally behind striking teachers. In the wake of the strike, the school board claimed that 200 to 300 pupils had marched in the streets and had demonstrated in front of the school board offices and various schools. Madeleine Vézina, a ninth-year student at the École Baril, organized a sympathy strike and led 100 fellow students from school to school gathering support for the teachers.[17] . . .

The role played by the École des Parents and the Catholic Parents' League in ending the strike, which I will address later in this chapter, was but the tip of the iceberg—they were the most visible, articulate, and organized of parents. Unorganized parents, or parents organized in ways *other* than as parents, also expressed their support for the teachers. Fathers, in particular, sent letters and telegrams to the union in support of the strike. Henri Verroneau, for instance, wrote to the

teachers of the first day of the strike. 'Mesdames, Mesdemoiselles, Messieurs', he began. 'J'accomplis ce matin mon devoir dans ma faible capacité en gardant mes deux filles d'âge scolaire à la maison.' Roland Barrette wrote to the APCM president, Léo Guindon, 'Je suis père de trois enfants qui vont à l'école St-Barthélemy, et je sais tout le dévouement de nos instituteurs et institutrices laïques, et je souhaite que votre cause triomphe. Nul doute que l'immense majorité des parents sont avec vous de tout cœur.'[18]. . .

Members of other unions wrote to advise the teachers that they were keeping their children home from school. André Plante and L. Perreault, of La Fraternité canadienne des employés civiques, told the APCM that they were recommending that their Montreal members not send their children to school until the school authorities showed a willingness to come to an agreement.[19] This support from members of local unions, acting as parents, made a difference in the 1940s, when unionization was widespread and memberships were relatively militant.

Parents also wrote to the school board to defend the strikers. One mother told the board, 'Mon mari & moi, nous opposons fermement à la manière dont vous traitez actuellement le corps proffessoral [*sic*] de Montréal et nous vous obligeons à garder dans nos classes nos professeurs respectifs [*sic*] si non [*sic*] nous garderons nos enfants un temps indéfini.'[20] The principal of l'École Dollier-de-Casson stated that most of the neighbourhood fathers were union members who refused to send their children to school during the strike. Certainly the majority of children attending CECM schools came from working-class or lower-middle-class families; wealthier parents tended to send their children to private, Church-run schools (Gagnon, 1996; Ewen, 2000). Yet even those parents who may not have approved of unions appear to have heeded the requests of striking teachers, broadcast across the local radio waves, to keep children at home rather than sending them to unsupervised classrooms.[21]

Not all parents supported the teachers' actions, however. The files of the school board (unlike those of the union) contain a few letters from parents who opposed the strike.[22] One father wrote to Eugène Simard, the president of the school board, to say:

> C'est plus fort que moi, ça me commande, il faut que je vous écrive pour vous dire que la plus part [sic] des parents sont avec vous et vous appuient dans votre tenacité [sic]. Je suis un père d'une famille de 5 enfants et je gagne $40.00 pour 55 heures de travail dur, je dis dur parce que c'est de *nuit*, et pourtant je suis satisfais [sic] et je suis seul pour gagner. Pour mon opinion je serais plus que satisfais [sic] avec un salaire d'instituteur. Ils ont tort. Continuez de tenir votre bout et je suis sur [sic] qu'avec le temps et l'organisation et l'aide du public vous pourrez avoir le succès sur votre côté.
>
> Je suis âgé de 38 ans et j'ai déjà passé par un [sic] grève, *fini*, pour moi les unions, telles qu'elles soient.[23]

Another father wrote to advise Simard of his opposition to the strike. In abandoning their classrooms, teachers were, he argued, neglecting their responsibilities.[24] Quebec Premier Duplessis likewise expressed his regret that people in charge of young minds should exhibit such lack of respect for law, order, and properly constituted authority. Children, he argued, were the strike's main victims (*Le Devoir*, 17 January 1949; *Montreal Gazette*, 17 January 1949).

The resonance of parenthood in the immediate postwar years is suggested by the fact that the striking teachers themselves articulated their interests as parents. They claimed, understandably, that they were unable to meet the needs of their own families on their current salaries and in the context of the high cost of living. A union representative told Montrealers gathered around their radios during the strike, 'C'est justement de 1944 que date le début des difficultés actuelles. Devant l'inflation qui se faisait déjà sentir à ce moment, les instituteurs ont voulu, au même titre que tous les pères de familles, que tous les citoyens conscients de leurs responsabilites, assurer a leurs families un rampart contre l'insécurité.' This speaker hoped that Montreal parents would understand that 'en menant leur propre lutte, les instituteurs mènent en même temps la lutte de toutes les familles qui sont actuellement aux prises avec le coût de la vie.[25] Striking teachers, not surprisingly, kept their own children home from school.[26] Invoking family could be a prudent way to defuse hostility to strikes.[27] Implicitly, however, this was an argument that applied only to married *male* teachers. The needs of female teachers—who were, of necessity, unmarried and therefore unable to make the claims of parents—were overshadowed.[28] The union's wage demands, for instance, maintained a gendered wage discrepancy, requesting salaries of up to $2,500 per year for women and up to $3,500 per year for men (*Le Devoir*, 17 January 1949). Female teachers were, it seemed, among the few actors in this dispute unable to claim the rights of parents.

Teachers were seen to have returned to work on 24 January both 'for the good of the children' and because they recognized the desires of Montreal parents (*La Presse*, 24 January 1949; *Le Devoir*, 24 January 1949). The decisive intervention of the École des Parents and the Catholic Parents' League, in a successful bid to resolve the strike, speaks to parents claiming a voice in public matters in the wake of the Second World War and in the context of Quebec children's new universal rights. In a resolution distributed to the teachers, the school board, and the press, the École des Parents insisted that parents were 'les premiers responsables de leurs enfants,' who had merely delegated their power to other authorities. As parents, members of the École des Parents felt compelled to demand that the parties involved resolve the strike as quickly as possible.[29]

Begun by a group of young, francophone, Catholic parents in 1940, the Montreal-based École des Parents du Québec was a cornerstone of Quebec's *mouvement familial*, and by the end of the decade claimed more than one thousand members. The École described itself as 'une association fondée par un groupe de parents, convaincus comme beaucoup de leurs compatriotes, que pour donner à leurs enfants la préparation à la vie à laquelle ils ont droit, il leur fallait faire l'effort de mieux comprendre leurs enfants, d'adopter les méthodes les plus susceptibles d'en faire des personnalités fortes, efficientes et bien équilibrées. Ils ont compris aussi l'importance de conserver à la famille canadienne-française ce qui lui a donné à date la force de lutter : sa foi, ses traditions, ses mœurs, tout en lui permettant de suivre le progrès.'[30]

Its early members included Montrealers active in intellectual, political, and union circles in the postwar years, many of whom had been involved with the Action catholique youth movements.[31] The École invited speakers—including Thérèse Casgrain, Florence Martel, Germaine Parizeau, and Édouard Montpetit—to share their thoughts on parenthood and parenting techniques.[32] It offered courses, held study groups, screened documentary films and, beginning in 1943, spoke to an even broader audience through its Radio-Canada series called RADIO-PARENTS.[33] The École des Parents had a particular interest in building bridges between parents and schools.[34]

The intervention of the École des Parents, alongside Montreal Archbishop Joseph Charbonneau and the English-language Catholic Parents' League (led by Dr Magnus Seng and Dr J.G. Howlett), played upon the loyalties of Catholic teachers to the postwar Church. But their entreaties to the strikers were made principally in the name of parents and children (*Montreal Gazette*, 24 January 1949). The irony is that although the École des Parents and the Catholic Parents' League supported the teachers, by pressuring them to return to work for the children's sake, they were, in effect, putting the needs of parents and children ahead of the needs of wage-earners—including, in this case, many unmarried female wage-earners. In promising the teachers that they would lobby for their interests if they would only go back to work, they exercised a moral pressure that encouraged workers to subordinate their own rights to those of parents and children.[35] . . . And the interests of parents—even parents supportive of the teachers' demands—could trump the interests of workers in an era that celebrated family.

André Laurendeau's columns in *Le Devoir*, written during and after the strike, provide insight into these debates (*Le Devoir*, 18, 24 January 1949).[36] Laurendeau, a well-known journalist and politician, certainly empathized with the striking teachers. Yet his principal concern was that children would be the first to suffer and that parents had no way of making their voices heard in the dispute. Laurendeau approved of the interventions of the École des Parents du Québec and the Catholic Parents' League, but noted that these organized groups of parents had only moral suasion, not direct authority, on their side. His columns reveal discomfort with the idea that parents were to relinquish control of their children's education to the state. Parents, he argued, bore the primary responsibility for the education of their children—before the state and the church. . . . Laurendeau especially lamented the loss of authority of the 'chefs de famille' and, more precisely, the 'père de famille'. Civil authorities, he insisted, did not listen to fathers anymore. Was there no way to reintegrate them into 'la cité'?

This concern about the 'chefs de famille' and the 'pères de famille' was expressed at a time when the state was perceived to be stepping in to replace fathers and breadwinners through measures such as family allowances and compulsory schooling. It was shared by other commentators. . . .

The Jesuit publication *Relations* likewise printed an article in the wake of the strike supporting the teachers and arguing that the labour dispute had demonstrated parents' desire for a greater role in their children's education. The provincial government appointed four of the seven commissioners on the Montreal school board, and the church appointed the other three. Yet 'les chefs de famille', taxpayers all, had no representation on the board ('Éducation et grève', 1949).[37]

Nadia Fahmy-Eid (1986) judiciously warns against assuming a consensus favourable to the implementation of compulsory schooling in 1943. She is surely correct: only five years before the strike, Opposition leader Maurice Duplessis, in the context of wartime controls, had described provincial compulsory schooling legislation as the conscription 'des enfants pour l'école'.[38] We might, in fact, see the controversy over the teachers' strike as one way in which conflicting opinions over compulsory schooling were still being worked out, six years after the fact. Yet the strike also suggests that the view that schooling was a 'right' for Quebec's children had become quite quickly entrenched— indeed, it had probably existed in some form, and in certain circles, prior to the 1942 legislation.[39]

The children of a victorious postwar democracy were seen to belong in school. The strike suggests, moreover, that compulsory schooling allowed parents to claim a public voice as parents, as they negotiated the terms of their children's education with the state. In the wake of the strike, for instance, the École des Parents demanded that parents be represented on the Montreal school board.[40] Such demands contrasted with a very recent past, when schooling was seen by many working-class parents to conflict with family needs and with their needs in particular. Indeed, Dominique Marshall's work demonstrates that for the poorest of Quebec families, such conflict continued to exist through the 1940s (Marshall, 1998).

While the École des Parents and the Catholic Parents' League were the most organized and vocal of parents, other parents also voiced their opinions (both for and against) the strike by writing letters to the teachers' union or to the school board. All parents spoke through their actions, choosing whether or not to send their children to school during the strike. Even parents who opposed the strike could be seen as claiming citizenship rights—in this case, children's (new) right to education. Thus the idea of family could be used to legitimate parents' claims to a public voice—but the use of family in this way could also have conservative results. In this case, the rights of children took priority over the rights of unmarried female wage-earners. Children were a particularly powerful argument in the immediate postwar years; it was difficult to respond to the critics of the strike who invoked children deprived of their right to education.[41] . . .

Notes

1. For the union's statistics on the percentage of teachers who struck, see Archives de l'Université Laval (AUL),   Fonds de l'Alliance des Professeurs de Montréal (APM), 250, File 250/5/3, Livre VI, Assemblées

générales tenues par l'APCM du 12 janvier 1949 au 7 novembre 1951, Assemblée générale de l'APCM tenue le 18 février 1949.

2. On Catholic lay teachers' earlier attempts at organizing, see Geoffrey Ewen, 'Montreal Catholic School Teachers, international Unions, and Archbishop Bruchési: The Association de bien-être des institutrices et institutrices de Montréal, 1919–20', *Historical Studies in Education / Revue d'histoire de l'éducation* 12, 1–2 (2000): 54–72.

3. See 'Le statut des instituteurs', *La Presse*, 24 January 1949, 1: 'Striking Teachers' Return Urged by Local Parents' Associations', *Montreal Gazette*, 24 January 1949, 3; Robert Gagnon, *Histoire de la Commission des écoles catholiques de Montréal* (Montreal: Boréal, 1996), 223.

4. See also the brief summaries of the strike in Jacques Rouillard, *Histoire du syndicalisme québécois* (Montreal: Boréal, 1989), 275–8; Gagnon, *Histoire de la Commission*, 219–24.

5. This was by no means a new situation: on the post-First World War period, see Ewen, 'Montreal Catholic School Teachers', 57.

6. See AUL, APM (250), File 250/15/2, Handwritten list on letterhead of La Fédération des Instituteurs et des Institutrices catholiques des Cités et Villes de la Province de Québec: 'Ceux qui ont offert aide et secours financier à L'Alliance'.

7. Caption to photographs, *Le Front Ouvrier*, 22 January 1949, 10; *Le Devoir*: '1,500 instituteurs en grève ce matin', 17 January, 1, 3; 'Ce que femme veut. . .', 22 January 1949, 9.

8. On the high proportion of lay teachers in the public system who were women, see Nadia Fahmy-Eid, 'Un univers articulé à l'ensemble du système scolaire québécois', 36: 43–4, in *Les couventines: L'éducation des filles au Quebec dans les congrégations religieuses enseignantes 1840–1960*, eds, Micheline Dumont and Nadia Fahmy-Eid (Montreal: Boréal Express, 1986); Micheline Dumont, 'Les congrégations religieuses enseignantes', in *les couventines*, 263–4; Gagnon, *Histoire de la Commission*, 225.

9. Caption to photographs, *Le Front Ouvrier*, 22 January 1949, 10.

10. See Archives de la Commission des écoles catholiques de Montréal (ACECM), Dossier: Alliance—Convention collective—Généralités—Grève—1949—III. Soeur Marie-Anne-Françoise to Eugène Doucet, 9 July 1949.

11. On the importance of clerics to the teaching staff of both the private and public systems in Quebec, see Micheline Dumont, *Girls' Schooling in Quebec,* *1639–1960* (Ottawa: Canadian Historical Association, 1990); Dumont and Fahmy-Eid, *Les couventines*.

12. See ACECM, Dossier: Alliance—Convention collective—Généralités—Grève—1949—I, Soeur Sainte-Anne-des-Miracles to Eugène Simard, 1 February 1949.

13. See ACECM, Dossier: Alliance—Convention collective—Généralités—Grève—1949—I, La Commission des écoles catholiques de Montréal, Service des études, District numéro 4, Énumération des actes posés. The teaching brothers of l'École Christophe-Colomb likewise claimed not to have noticed whether a particular lay teacher was picketing. Dossier: Alliance—Convention collective—Généralités—Grève—1949—I, La Commission des école catholiques de Montréal, Service des études, District numéro 5, Énumération des actes posés. See also AUM, ACC, P16/N6, 1, 2, News clipping, 'Blocs-Notes', *Le Devoir*, 22 January 1949.

14. AUL, APM (250), File 250/5/3, Livre VI, Assemblées générales tenues par l'A.P.C.M. du 12 janvier 1949 au 7 novembre 1951. Dimanche le 23 janvier 1949; 'L'aide des parents est bien reçue', *La Presse*, 24 January 1949, 1; 'Les parents et la grève des professeurs', *Le Front Ouvrier*, 22 January 1949, 10; 'Striking Teachers' Return Urged by Local Parents' Associations', *Montreal Gazette*, 24 January 1949, 3; 'Les instituteurs retournent en classe', *Le Devoir*, 24 January 1949, 1, 3; 'Les instituteurs one entendu l'appel des parents', *Le Devoir*, 24 January 1949, 1.

15. AUL, APM (250), File 250/5/3, Livre VI, Assemblées générales tenues par l'A.P.C.M. du 12 janvier 1949 au 7 novembre 1951. Cessation de travail, lundi le 17 janvier 1944. See also *Le Front Ouvrier*, 29 January 1949, 20; '1,500 instituteurs en grève ce matin', *Le Devoir*, 17 January 1949, 1, 3. Note the photograph of an empty classroom published in *Le Front Ouvrier*, 22 January 1949, 10.

16. AUL, APM (250), File 250/5/3, Livre VI, Assemblées générales tenues par l'A.P.C.M. du 12 janvier 1949 au 7 novembre 1951. Cessation de travail, lundi le 17 janvier 1944.

17. ACECM, Dossier: Alliance—Convention collective—Généralités—Grève—1949—I, La Commision des écoles catholiques de Montréal, Service des études, District numéro 4, Énumération des actes posés; La Commission des écoles catholiques de Montréal, Service des études, District numéro 1, Énumération des actes posés; Eugène Simard to Joseph Dansereau, 19 January 1949; Joseph Dansereau to Messierus les Commissaires, 17 February 1949.

18. AUL, APM (250), File 250/15/2, Henri Véronneau to APCM, 17 January 1949; Roland Barrette to Léo Guindon, 17 January 1949. See also Mr and Mde Rodolphe Nadeau to Mlle Marie Lessard and Mlle Marguerite Dubois, 18 January 1949.

19. AUL, APM (250), Dossier 250/15/2, André Plante and L. Perreault to APCM, 14 January 1949. For similar letters see, in the same file: Telegram from Local 102, Ouvriers unis des textiles d'Amérique, to APCM, 17 January 1949; Telegram fro United Brewery Workers, CIO-CCL, to APCM, 17 January 1949; Telegram from J. Eucher Corbeil, president-général, Fraternité canadienne des employés de chemin de fer et autres transports, to APCM, 18 January 1949.

20. See ACEM, Dossier: Alliance—Convention collective—Généralités—Grève—1949—I, M and Mme M. Deniger to CECM, 15 January 1949.

21. See ACEM, Dossier: Alliance—Convention collective—Généralités—Grève—1949—I, La Comission des écoles catholiques de Montréal, Service des études, District numéro 6, Cas des écoles où le principal et plusieurs professeurs étaient presents mais les élèves absents.

22. I have found six letters in school board files opposing the strike. At least two of these came from parents; the authors of the other four letters did not indicate whether they had children in the school system.

23. ACECM, Dossier: Alliance—Convention collective—Généralités—Grève—1949—I, Albert Cesari Jessery to Eugène Simard, 18 January 1949. Emphases in the original.

24. ACECM, Dossier: Alliance—Convention collective—Généralités—Grève—1949—I, R. Messier to Eugène Simard, 18 January 1949.

25. AUL, APM (250), Dossier 250/13/4/3, 'Radio, conférences. Mardi, 18 janvier 1949, Programme: CCF. Poste: CHLP'.

26. ACECM, Boîte 216, École St-Stanislas, Département de l'Instruction Publique, Journal de l'École pour l'année scolaire 1948–1949. Many younger brothers and sisters of teachers also stayed home from school. ACECM, Dossier: Alliance—Convention collective—Généralités—Grève—1949—I, Joseph Dansereau to Messieurs les Commissaires, 17 February 1949.

27. On the federal government sidestepping the thorny question of workers' rights to promote instead the innocuous rights of children, see Marshall, 'Reconstruction Politics, the Canadian Welfare State and the Ambiguity of Children's Rights, 1940–1950', in Greg Donaghy, ed., *Uncertain Horizons. Canadians and their World in 1945* (Ottawa: Canadian Committee for the History of the Second World War, 1996), 265–6.

28. On the policy of the Commission des écoles catholiques de Montréal (CECM) not to hire married women, see Gagnon, *Histoire de la Commission*, 225–6. The CECM appears to have suspended this policy for the duration of the 1949 strike. ACECM, Dossier: Alliance—Convention collective—Généralities—Grève—1949—I, Copie de resolution adoptee par la Commission des écoles catholiques de Montréal, Séance du 14 janvier 1949 suite de la session régulière du 13 janvier, 15ième.

29. ACECM, Dossier: Alliance—Convention collective—Généralities—Grève—1949—I, Odile P. Ranet-Raymond, Présidente, L'École des Parents du Quebec, to Eugène Simard, Président, CECM, 21 January 1949; 'L'École des Parents', *Le Devoir*, 24 January 1949, 1.

30. AUL, APM (250), File 250/17/2. *École des Parents, section Longueuil*. See also Denyse Baillargeon, '"We admire modern parents": The École des Parents du Québec and the Post-war Quebec Family, 1940–1959', in Nancy Christie and Michael Gauvreau, eds, *Cultures of Citizenship in Post-war Canada, 1940–1955* (Montreal and Kingston: McGill-Queen's University Press, 2003).

31. For instance, André Laurendeau, Gérard and Alexandrine Pelletier, Claude Ryan, and Simonne Monet-Chartrand all participated in the École's activities. Simonne Monet Chartrand, *Ma vie comme rivière: Récit autobiographique, vol. 2, 1939–1949* (Montreal: Éditions de remue-ménage, 1982), 251.

32. See Simonne Monet Chartrand, *Ma vie comme rivière: Récit autobiographique, vol. 2, 1939–1949* (Montreal: Éditions de remue-ménage, 1982), 174, 327–8; AUM, ACC, P16, File: P16/O5/45, Programme des cours de l'École des Parents de Québec, 1949–50.

33. AUL, APM (250), File 250/17/2, *École des Parents du Québec*; AUM, ACC, P16, File: P16/O5/45, Programme des cours de l'École des Parents de Québec, 1949–50; Marie-Paule Malouin, *Le Mouvement familial au Québec. Les debuts: 1937–1965* (Montreal: Boréal, 1998), 46. English-language CBC Radio also broadcast a show entitled *School for Parents* between 1954 and 1962; see Mona Gleason, *Normalizing the Ideal: Psychology, Schooling, and the Family in Postwar Canada* (Toronto: University of Toronto Press, 1999), 50.

34. AUM, Collection Gisèle Morin-Lortie, P 272, École des Parents du Québec, Coupures de presse, Vol. 2. 'Parents et instituteurs s'entendent. La geste de l'École des Parents fait retourner les petits à l'école', *La Presse*, 24 January 1949. See also AUM, ACC, P16/

O5, 45, École des Parents du Québec, news clipping, 'Clinique de l'École des Parents du Québec', *Le Devoir*. Mona Gleason notes that psychologists in English Canada also argued 'that parents and teachers should forge a powerful alliance in the battle to ensure well-adjusted, democracy-loving children.' *Normalizing the Ideal*, 123.

35. In a slightly different context, Dominique Marshall argues that the rights of families often superseded those of workers in the postwar period. Family allowances, for instance, were Ottawa's answer to unionized workers' demands for higher wages. Marshall, *Aux origins sociales*, 144.

36. See also AUM, ACC, P16: File: P16/N6, 1, 2, News clipping, 'Bloc-Notes', *Le Devoir*, 22 January 1949; File: P16/R57, News clipping, 'Pour un mouvement des familles', *Le Devoir*, 22 November 1950.

37. This division of the school board commissioners had been established by Duplessis's provincial government in 1947. Previously there had been nine commissioners: Three appointed by the municipality; three by the provincial government; and three by the Archbishop's palace. Thwaites and Perron-Thwaites, 'Une petite grève', 784.

38. See York University Archives (YUA), Maurice Duplessis Fonds, 1980-008/001, Reel 7. 'Schéma–Discours' [1944], p. 3. He did not, however, revoke the legislation once he returned to power in 1944.

39. Dominique Marshall also argues, 'By the 1940s, there was a widespread belief in education, and cases where parents opposed the fourteen-year-old leaving age were exceptional.' See 'The Language of Children's Rights, the Formation of the Welfare State, and the Democratic Experience of Poor Families in Quebec, 1940–55', *Canadian Historical Review* 78, 3 (September 1997): 414.

40. AUM, Collection Gisèle Morin-Lortie, P 272, École des Parents du Québec, Coupures de presse, Volume 2. 'Droits des parents en éducation revendiqués', *La Presse*, 25 February 1949.

41. On the new rights of children, see 'Égalité de préférence à autorité', *La Presse*, 26 March 1949, 28; Dominique Marshall, 'Reconstruction Politics, the Canadian Welfare State and the Ambiguity of Children's Rights, 1940–1950', pp. 261–83 in Greg Donaghy, ed., *Uncertain Horizons: Canadians and their World in 1945* (Ottawa: Canadian Committee for the History of the Second World War, 1996); Dominique Marshall, 'The Language of Children's Rights, the Formation of the Welfare State, and the Democratic Experience of Poor Families in Quebec, 1940–55', *Canadian Historical Review* 78, 3 (September 1997).

References

Éducation et grève'. 1949. *Relations* 98 (February): 30–1.

Ewen, G. 2000. 'Montreal Catholic School Teachers, International Unions, and Archbishop Bruchesi', *Historical Studies in Education* 12, 1: 54–72.

Fahmy-Eid, Nadia. 1986. 'Un univers articulé à l'ensemble du système scolaire québécois', in Micheline Dumont and Nadia Fahmy-Eid, eds, *Les couventines: L'éducation des filles au Quebec dans les congrégations religieuses enseignantes 1840–1960*. Montreal: Boréal Express.

Gagnon, R. 1996. *Histoire de la Commission des écoles catholiques de Montréal: Le développement d'un réseau d'écoles publiques en milieu urbain*. Montreal: Boréal.

La Presse. 1949. 'Fin de la grève; retour en classe', 24 January: 1, 3.

Le Devoir. 1949. 'Ce que femme veut. . .', 22 January 1949: 9.

Le Devoir. 1949. 'Déclaration du ministère du travail', 18 January: 3.

Le Devoir. 1949. 'Et les parents?', 18 January.

Le Devoir. 1949. 'Les instituteurs ont entendu l'appel des parents', 24 January: 1.

Le Devoir. 1949. 'Les instituteurs retournent en classe', 24 January: 1, 3.

Le Devoir. 1949. 'Me Simard empêche le reglement de la grève', 19 January: 1.

Le Devoir. 1949. '1,500 instituteurs en grève ce matin', 17 January: 1, 3.

Le Front Ouvrier. 1949. 'Les parents et la grève des professeurs', 22 January: 10.

Marshall, Dominique. 1998. *Aux origins sociales de l'État-providence*. Montréal: Presses de l'Université de Montréal.

Montreal Gazette. 1949. 'Catholic Schools Strike Is On; English Teachers Join French', 17 January: 3.

Montreal Gazette. 1949. 'Duplessis Scores Teachers' Strike', 17 January: 3.

Montreal Gazette. 1949. 'Striking Teachers' Return Urged by Local Parents' Associations', 24 January: 3.

Montreal Gazette. 1949. 'Teachers' Strike Ended, Classes Resume Today; Walk-Out Now Week Old', 24 January: 1.

Thwaites, James D., and Nadine L.C. Perron-Thwaites. 1995. 'Une petite grève d'envergure: L'Alliance contre la C.É.C.M. en 1949 et ses suites', *McGill Law Journal* 40: 780–801.

CHAPTER 22

Trade Unions and the Welfare State in Canada, 1945–1990

Alvin Finkel

In December 1952, while the Canadian economy was experiencing rapid economic growth thanks partly to Korean War expenditures, Andy Andras, the assistant research director for the Canadian Congress of Labour [CCL], wrote a pointed note to CCL secretary-treasurer Donald MacDonald. After observing labour's collective bargaining achievements for its members in the years since 1944, Andras, on behalf of himself and CCL research director Eugene Forsey, listed questions that the CCL should debate. Among them:

> Is organized labour going to slow down its drive for social security for *all* Canadians by getting it for its own members? Is there a danger that we are creating a sort of 'sheltered proletariat' who are relatively comfortable while the rest of the working class does without? . . .
>
> Are the hundreds of thousands of new trade unionists of the past ten years seeing in the labour movement something more than a slot machine? Is there really an ideological (and idealistic) content to our movement or is that merely window dressing? . . .
>
> Are we getting Convention decisions through to the rank and file? Are we passing, often with enormous enthusiasm, a lot of resolutions which, for all practical purposes, fall like a stone into a barrel of tar? If this is happening to any appreciable degree, why is it, and what can we do about it?[1]

In considering labour's role in the struggle for comprehensive social security programs for Canadians the questions that Andras and Forsey raise are central. Did the postwar labour movement want to create a 'sheltered proletariat' in the larger firms that were most susceptible to union organizing drives or was it attempting to achieve social justice for all working people? Was labour willing to fight for social entitlements for the entire working class rather than simply its unionized members? And, given that most of those members were male, what were labour's perspectives on how the welfare state was to be 'engendered'? . . .

Politics and Vision of Postwar Labour

When we analyze labour's response to proposed social programs, we must distinguish between several wings of the labour movement in Canada at different periods. In the late 1940s and early 1950s there were four identifiable, though unequal, segments of organized labour in Canada. The largest trade union central was the Trades and Labour Congress of Canada (TLC), formed in 1883 and home to most of the skilled-trades unions in the construction and railway sectors. These were mainly affiliates of US unions active in the American Federation of Labor. By the 1950s the TLC, had also made significant inroads in signing up semi-skilled industrial workers. The second largest trade union body, the Canadian Congress of Labour, was composed mainly of industrial unions affiliated with the Congress of Industrial Organizations (CIO) in the United States. The CCL was the result of a merger in 1940 between the CIO unions and some of the national unions that had established the All-Canadian Congress of Labour in 1927. In 1956 the two giants of Canadian labour united to form the Canadian Labour Congress [CLC]. That still left two groups outside the big tent of Canadian labour. Communist-led unions, such as the United Electrical Workers, were refused entry into the CLC thanks to the hold of Cold War ideology over the leaders of the new federation. Catholic unions in Quebec, organized in the Canadian and Catholic Congress of Labour (CCCL), chose not to give up their separate identity, and when that federation shed its confessional past in 1960 to become the Confederation of National Trade Unions (CNTU), it confirmed its desire not to submerge its Québécois national identity in a pan-Canadian organization.[2]

Among these unions the most politically progressive were the CCL and the Communist-led unions. The CCL had endorsed the socialist Co-operative Commonwealth Federation as early as the 1943 provincial elections in Ontario, but in the postwar period it was at pains to distinguish itself from the Communists and to purge Communists from its ranks (Abella, 1973). Its social vision would be compromised both by its desire to appear anti-Communist at all times—it would try not to appear to say things Communists might say—and by its conservative appraisal of what political demands made sense in the midst of postwar prosperity. The TLC, by contrast, had always been somewhat conservative. It was non-partisan, except in the 1945 federal election when it supported Mackenzie King's Liberals, but it did support comprehensive social security for Canadians, although always within a framework that stressed a male-breadwinner ideal. So did the CCCL and later the CNTU, although their policies had both nationalist and (in the case of the CCCL) Catholic overtones that made them favour provincial control over social programs and, in the CCCL's case, sometimes led to strident opposition to programs of benefit to women workers.[3]

The limits of the social vision of the trade unions before the 1970s (and on many issues still today) are best demonstrated perhaps by looking first at issues unions did not support. Worker control of industry was considered a non-issue, as was public provision of daycare for children of working mothers. In large part union positions on these issues reflected a conservative, patriarchal vision of the social order: male breadwinners, defended by trade unions and state planning, were supposed to bring home sufficient wages to care for the needs of nuclear families, in which wives restricted their labours to the domestic sphere and received no pay. But the unions' stance also reflected Cold War ideology, which thundered against both worker control and feminism as potential communist perversions of 'democracy' and 'free' enterprise.

Before it had expelled communists and presumed communists, the CCL, imbued with the wartime bug for major social change that infected many working Canadians, had been willing to challenge the notions that workers should always be dependent on owners and/or managers and that women should always be dependent on men. In its presentation before the House of Commons Reconstruction and Re-establishment Committee in 1943, the CCL proclaimed that 'free enterprise' no longer performed its historic function and 'a considerable sector' of the economy ought therefore to be placed under public control (*Gazette* [Montreal], 16 July 1943). A CCL pamphlet of 1945, *Political Action by Canadian Labour*, emphasized full-employment policies and public ownership, advocating that 'useful jobs at union wages and under union conditions must be provided for every man and woman able and willing to work.' Recognizing the special problems faced by women in finding and holding jobs, the CCL, called for maternity benefits and 'day nurseries for working mothers, either within individual establishments or on a community basis, whichever seems more effective'.[4]

Daycare disappeared totally from the agenda of the CCL after 1945. The patriarchal notion of the 'family wage' re-emerged, and the CCL's search for respectability also led to a withdrawal of support for a cause that Cold Warriors labelled as a Red attempt to destroy 'the family'.[5] There were no resolutions on daycare at CCL conventions from 1946 to the organization's amalgamation with the TLC in 1956. Affiliates that were usually regarded as socially progressive, such as the United Auto Workers, ignored childcare, refusing to give it even a token mention in such documents as the 'Official Program for Social Security of the UAW-CIO in Canada' (1946). This program, also called the 'UAW-CIO Win the Peace Plan', clearly assumed that women would win the peace by marrying the men for whom the 'Official Program' proposed wall-to-wall job security and wage protection.[6] Provincial federations of the TLC and CCL and later the CLC were equally uninterested in daycare, maternity pay, and other primarily women's issues before the 1970s.[7] The CTCC, along with other Catholic organizations, was actively hostile to married women workers and strongly denounced public daycare, while the more secular CNTU simply joined the rest of Canadian labour in ignoring the issue altogether (Gagnon, 1974).

The CCL did prove to be somewhat more progressive on the issue of women's right to unemployment insurance on the same basis as men. Women's access to UI had, from its inception, been limited compared to men's as a result of exclusions of occupations mainly held by women. After the war, women laid off from high-paying war-related jobs were cut off from UI if they failed to take poor-paying 'women's ghetto' jobs, and from 1950 to 1957 a regulation discriminating against married women further enforced the gendered character of the UI program. While the CCL initially made

no protest against this regulation, it changed its position fairly quickly mainly because of 'thin edge of the wedge' arguments as opposed to any concerns about the rights of working women to equality per se. Even such arguments, however, did not persuade the leaders of the TLC, and that organization appears to have remained divided on the issue. With the formation of the CLC in 1956, a firm stance against discrimination on the basis of gender in the unemployment insurance field became official policy (Porter, 1993).

Labour's position on the need for public ownership and worker involvement in the management of industry also softened in the climate of the Cold War. The CCL's denunciations of capitalism gave way to anodyne calls for labour-management cooperation. CCL president Aaron Mosher's Labour Day message in 1949 proclaimed: 'Labour unions are now more and more providing an agency by which the energies and aspirations of the workers may be directed, in cooperation with employers, toward greater production in industry and higher living standards for the people of Canada.'[8]

The Trades and Labour Congress was particularly at pains to assure owners and managers that labour intended no attack on their prerogatives. 'We in organized labor do not want to interfere with management. We do not want any part of the management of the enterprise,' Gordon Cushing, general secretary of the Trades and Labour Congress, told the Canadian Chamber of Commerce at its annual convention in 1955. The worker, Cushing said, was interested only in a good rate of pay, a short workday, and safe conditions in the workplace. 'He doesn't want to be or to share management.' Nor, for the most part, did he (and the worker, in Cushing's address, as in most TLC discourse, was a 'he') want to work for the state, although the TLC continued to advocate that resource industries, like utilities, be operated by the state.[9]

But Cushing stressed that labour wanted governments 'to provide more of social security for the people', including a nationwide scheme of prepaid medical and hospital insurance. He argued to his largely unbending business audience that 'broad social security schemes' would encourage greater mobility on the part of the workforce.[10] In general, as the Cold War and prosperity provoked a retreat on labour's part from a more general attack on the capitalist system as such, the labour movement's new focus was on social programs that would make life for workers under capitalism less insecure.

But labour was by no means unanimous about the relative importance of social security programs on the political agenda. After the June 1945 federal election, Mackenzie King, having beaten back the CCF challenge by promising a program of comprehensive social security measures, called a federal–provincial conference to implement the programs in a Green Book drafted by federal bureaucrats. The conference was essentially bogus because King and his ministers, relieved by the fact that there was no postwar depression, were anxious to cave in to conservative calls to cut government spending and taxes. The government was intransigent in the face of provincial demands about cost-sharing and revenue-raising and decided cynically to blame the premiers for the conference's failure. Relative postwar apathy on the part of popular organizations played into the government's hands (Bothwell, Drummond, and English, 1981; Gotlieb, 1985; Finkel, 1993). The CCL proved to be one of the few national organizations that paid much attention to the deliberations of this conference, which buried issues of social justice under a mound of constitutional wrangles and personal recriminations. The CCL and its affiliates made clear their view that the country required national programs of social insurance and that if necessary Canada should change its constitution to make

unlimited intervention by the federal government in the area of social security possible.[11] The CCL also indicated that while its members believed that the taxation system should be revamped to make the wealthy pay their fair share, they recognized that cradle-to-grave social security would be expensive. Thus they were prepared to pay increased taxes to secure it.[12]

Not all unions were so prepared. While the conference was meeting—with Mackenzie King and his ministers besieged by business advocates of smaller budgets and a huge tax cut—the railway brotherhoods, while claiming support for social insurance measures, indicated that the government's chief priority should be a tax cut to stimulate postwar spending.[13]

On the whole, then, the trade union movement moved quickly away from a brief wartime flirtation with radical ideas of transforming social relations of production and gender relations. It made its peace with capitalism and focused both on winning benefits for its members through collective bargaining and benefits for all working people through an expansion of state social insurance and social service programs. For the TLC unions the first of these two goals largely eclipsed the second; but for the CCL, whose leaders maintained socialist commitments, however mellowed, the battle for social melioration was an important part of the job. The industrial union movement never became totally the 'slot machine' that the CCL researchers feared it was becoming.

Successes, Failures, and Contradictions

Perhaps the key area where the union movement's advocacy played a key role—and a role that historians generally underrate—was in the area of universal medical insurance.[14] On the surface, a campaign by the unions for medicare may seem to have been superfluous. From the mid-1940s onwards about 80 per cent of Canadians supported a national, universal program of prepaid medical insurance (Taylor, 1978: 166). But by the late 1940s the opposition of both the Canadian Medical Association and the Canadian Chamber of Commerce, among other conservative groups, made it appear that, as in the United States, popular support for medicare would not be enough to convince politicians to implement a program (Finkel, 1993: 136–9). When John Diefenbaker announced a royal commission of Conservative appointees headed by Justice Emmett Hall to examine the need for national medicare, onlookers widely assumed that this conservative committee would conclude that there was no need for a compulsory state program. Instead the commission concluded the very opposite.

It did so despite a well-organized, well-documented campaign by the Canadian Medical Association, private insurers, and business groups that emphasized the growth in private medical insurance coverage since World War II.[15] The opponents of a universal state program rallied around the notion that only about 15 per cent of Canadians could not afford private coverage and that this group alone should be covered by a state insurance program for their basic medical needs.[16] In any case the doctors assured the commission that they did not turn away patients who could not afford to pay their bills and that they provided first-rate care to all patients regardless of the size of their pocketbooks. The popular support for medicare might cause one to believe that thousands of ordinary people came forward to tell their stories and cast doubt upon the vested interests' version of private medicine. In fact, a search through the thousands of pages of testimony before the Royal Commission on Health Services reveals that only one individual came forward to claim that she received second-rate medical treatment because

she was poor. Her physician's swift denunciation of her testimony explains the general reticence: most people are intimidated by their physicians and afraid to publicly question their wisdom or authority.[17] So, whatever they were willing to tell anonymous pollsters, individual Canadians were simply unwilling to go before a public royal commission and suggest that a doctor had provided them with no service or inferior service.

It was left then to organizations to provide the horror stories that individuals would not tell. Organized health-care groups, including pharmacists, dentists, and medical supply firms joined physicians and business organizations in opposing medicare outright and were not about to provide ammunition to the commission; nurses' organizations, primarily concerned with having their professional status enhanced, ignored issues that linked access to medical care with wealth and took no position on whether universal medicare should be legislated.[18] This left only three significant groups to explain to the commission members why they should give in to popular opinion and endorse a universal medicare program: farmers' organizations, social workers, and the trade union movement. The Canadian Federation of Agriculture and several other farm groups appeared before the commission and indicated that the majority of farmers could not afford private health insurance.[19] Social workers' representatives told countless stories of poverty-stricken individuals and families with health problems that were unattended because of lack of money.[20]

The trade unions probably landed the best punches against private insurance and private medicine. Many, after all, had won private health insurance coverage for their members at the bargaining table. But national, provincial, and local labour federations provided abundant evidence of the limitations of these profit-driven insurance schemes. The plans generally ignored preventive health services, rehabilitation, mental health, dental needs, and follow-up social services. Of course, as implemented by the federal and provincial governments, Canadian medicare programs are also deficient in these areas. But the Hall report certainly envisioned a comprehensive medical coverage scheme, and it was only the unions that made the point to them that private insurance ignored many important areas of medical well-being.

Effectively, the unions managed to limit the medical establishment's success in phrasing the terms of the debate purely in terms of how much of the population was already covered by private medical plans and what percentage could realistically be expected to eventually be covered by such plans. Opponents of medicare could respond to the farmers and spokespersons for the poor by conceding that there should be a state plan for the poorest Canadians. Such a plan could ensure that medical practitioners received some payment for treating people who otherwise would simply not seek help or would seek help but then not pay. At the same time it would leave them the continued right to charge what the market would bear for everyone else. It was more difficult to respond to complaints from representatives of large groups covered by insurance that the coverage was limited and did not stress health promotion.

The Canadian Labour Congress, which had already presented a significant brief early in the deliberations of the royal commission, was the only organization with the audacity to respond point by point to the extensive submission of the Canadian Medical Association. The CMA had suggested making publicly funded medical insurance available on a means-tested basis. The CLC observed that, using the CMA's own figures on who was too poor to pay for medical services, the government would end up paying for coverage for 4.5 million Canadians. This would involve

considerable costs both for medical coverage and for administration of means-testing. It would place a stigma on millions of people because of the 'loss of self-respect with which a means test is associated in the minds of many of our people'. Means-tests, the CLC indicated, were necessary for some programs of government assistance, but the organization questioned whether such tests 'should be more than marginal in its application'. Summing up the views that many other labour bodies had presented to the commission, the CLC noted:

> There is in addition the very obvious fact that private prepayment plans, whether of the non-profit or commercial variety, have so far signally failed to provide dental services, and have restricted the provision of drugs, nursing, and appliances (while excluding eye glasses or hearing aids) to coverage under the so-called major medical benefit plans with their costly deductible and co-insurance charges. It is too much to expect that a complete range of services can be made available on a universal basis to the Canadian people within the near future through the mere extension of the private pre-payment schemes. It is not physically, financially nor administratively possible. (Welfare Council of Ottawa, 1962)

Trade union groups also dissected regional disparities in health provision resulting from a market driven medical system. The Newfoundland Federation of Labour, for one, documented the dismal state of medical care in the island province. The proportion of doctors to population was less than half the Canadian average, and many areas of the province had no doctor. The ratio of registered nurses to population was also only about half the Canadian average. Dentists were scarce outside the two main centres, and St John's institution for the aged and infirm was 'a blot on the decency of the

Canadian nation'. The NFL noted that to overcome a history of poverty the province would need far more than a national health insurance program: it would need a national health plan that would ensure the building and staffing of regional hospitals and clinics. The NFL concluded: 'The regional differences show only the need for flexibility and adaptability in such a national health plan—the need for its comprehensiveness to comprehend the diversities of the Canadian nation as well as the diversities of need between one individual and the next.'[21]

Labour did not win an absolute victory in the medicare debate by any means. The medicare scheme that the Pearson Liberals agreed to fund left control over medical planning in Canada in the hands of the medical profession, rejecting the community-control vision of medical care that both labour and farm organizations had struggled to put forward over several decades (Swartz, 1977; Rands, 1981). Doctors were paid on a fee-for-service basis rather than salaried; no special provisions were made for community clinics; and services such as dental health and mental health that labour wished to integrate into community clinics were left out of what the Liberals called the 'first stage' of Canadian medical insurance (the second stage has yet to arrive). Nonetheless, labour's victory in the medical services area was far greater than in other domains of social welfare, particularly housing.

Push for Social Housing

In many capitalist countries, one of the victories of 'welfarism' has been the establishment of a large social-housing sector that co-exists with the private shelter market, generally providing shelter to those of modest income on a means-tested basis.[22] It is testimony to the greater hegemony of capital in North America that social housing provides an insignificant proportion of homes. The growth of private ownership and the prevalence of the model of the single-family detached home did not occur by accident or because of 'sovereign consumer' choice. Rather, they have been the product of government policies consciously designed to discourage social housing in favour of a model that extols nuclear families, privacy for the family unit, and the notion of shelter as capital (Moscovitch, 1981; Bacher, 1993). The trade union movement has never developed a critique of this model, but in the 1940s and 1950s, at least, a significant section of the labour movement questioned its universal desirability.

The rallying point for postwar housing reformers was the report prepared in 1944 by the Housing and Community Planning subcommittee of the federal government's Advisory Committee on Reconstruction. Chaired by Queen's University economics professor C.A. Curtis, the subcommittee revealed the shabby housing conditions in which much of the Canadian population lived. While the Curtis committee supported public policies to encourage more private-sector development of new homes and maintenance of existing homes, its members concluded that to provide decent shelter for all Canadians regardless of income, a relatively large social-housing sector would be necessary to house poorer Canadians (Canada, Advisory Committee on Reconstruction, 1944).[8] Although the Curtis committee's evidence and conclusions proved anathema to the governing Liberals, they were a catalyst to the labour movement's involvement in public housing campaigns concentrated in the country's big cities.[23]

In April 1945, with victory for the Allies around the corner, the Canadian Congress of Labour submitted a memorandum to the federal government indicating its displeasure that the recommendations of the Curtis report were being ignored by the government and insisting that low-rent housing for wage-earners 'could be provided only by public enterprise, through Municipal Housing Authorities subsidized by the Federal Government. Private enterprise simply cannot do the job at all.'[24] Over the next decade the CCL would join with the Canadian Legion, the Canadian Welfare Council, and other organizations to fight for a greater government role in providing housing for working people. As late as 1953 the CCL's official position, while somewhat softened regarding the respective roles of the private and public sectors in housing, was that extensive social housing was required.[25]

The Trades and Labour Congress did not join the call for social housing, focusing instead on having the federal government expand its mortgage subsidy programs, which favoured the better-off, to include most working-class households. By 1954 the CCL, whose opposition to a purely private housing market was based solely on economic considerations with no wider thought given to the impact on working-class or community life of developer-driven models of community development, had moved partially to that position as well. The federal government, in an effort to boost loans for new housing, had changed the operations of the Canada Mortgage and Housing Corporation to provide federal guarantees for loans to qualified mortgage-holders. The CCL correctly noted that this was 'in effect a subsidy to home ownership' and a windfall for the financial institutions making loans because they would have government guarantees against risks normally associated with loans. Rather than reject the scheme in its entirety, and mindful that its members were being successfully bombarded with various forms of propaganda in favour of single-family suburban housing, the CCL called for the government to make loans directly to homebuyers, simply bypassing financial intermediaries. It could then substantially decrease the loan rate, bringing housing within the purview of a large section of the working class.[26] Such a policy would

have been consistent with practice in Norway and Denmark, where social-democratic governments favoured home ownership for workers rather than social housing (Epsing-Anderson, 1985). The CCL did reiterate its support for 'more subsidized public low-rental housing' as the best means, along with co-operative housing, 'to provide decent housing for the people who need it most.' But, as the prosperity of the 1950s allowed more and more working-class households, particularly those with two incomes, to buy modest single-family homes, the involvement of the CCL and later the CLC in campaigns for social housing became token.

Conclusion

The labour movement did continue to express an egalitarian vision. In Canada's centennial year, Andy Andras, who had asked such pertinent questions 15 years earlier about labour's role as a catalyst for social change, was director of legislation for the CLC. Writing in *Canadian Welfare*, Andras made clear that the labour movement was only partly mollified by the spate of Pearson legislation—the Canada Assistance Plan, the Canada Pension Plan, and medicare being the jewels in the crown—extending the welfare state in Canada. Wrote Andras: 'The market economy produces poverty. It has always produced poverty. Short of very extensive economic planning by government, together with a massive redistribution of wealth and advantage, it is likely to continue producing poverty. All the social security measures which have been enacted and which have brought Canada pretty well into the welfare state, have served merely to mitigate the effects of poverty rather than to do away with it' (Andras, 1967: 29).

But the CLC, reflecting the Cold War retreat of the CCL from earlier positions and perhaps responding as well to TLC conservatism, was loath to consider extensive public ownership as a solution to the greatly unequal distribution of wealth under capitalism. Its view was that government direction of the economy and 'massive distribution of wealth and advantage' could be imposed on the existing economic system. Such a stance assumed that capitalism—as historian R.H. Tawney had once said, critiquing British Labour Party thinking—was an onion to be torn away leaf by leaf rather than a tiger responding to an attempt to remove a single paw. The models generally mentioned favourably by labour leaders included the Scandinavian states and Britain, where somewhat greater equality in the distribution of wealth had been established. The exception to this embrace of moderate social-democratic solutions was the three major Quebec labour federations which, for a brief period in the early 1970s, committed themselves to a socialist vision of society rather than a reconciliation with capitalism (Drache, 1972). They were fuzzy, however, about what steps labour should take to achieve this vision and gradually returned to more traditional social-democratic stances and eventually to a nationalist corporatism (Lipsig-Mummé, 1984, 1991; Rouillard, 1988).

In the 1970s and especially the 1980s the labour movement dropped, at least in part, its commitment to one-earner families and began to recognize the right of women not only to work,[27] but also to have equal access with men to all jobs. Labour also began to work much more regularly with a variety of social movements, including women's, visible minority, gay, environmental, and disabled groups, to press for a wide variety of legislative changes. As the economy stagnated and neoconservatism gained ground, labour fought to protect existing social rights and extend Canada's social programs to include a national daycare program (Schutz, 1982).

Arguably, the labour movement is still further than it ever was from having a coherent vision that links social and economic policy. There has rightly been labour disappointment over the failure of New Democratic provincial governments to protect and extend social programs as well as the salaries and rights of provincial government employees. But the labour movement, like the NDP, has, in effect, no economic policy and no clear line of defence when the tiger comes striking with all its paws. Although, as we have seen, the CCL did have such a policy and a social vision to accompany it in the immediate aftermath of World War II, it lost some of that vision during the Cold War. While the emphasis of that earlier period on social ownership alone may now seem too limited, it is incumbent on the labour movement to fashion a vision that links its egalitarianism to concrete economic policies.

In the prosperous years of the 1950s and 1960s, it may have seemed less naive to argue that a rapidly growing economy could pay for new programs with little redistribution of wealth being necessary. Now that we know that the biosphere cannot tolerate this solution to poverty, the options seem fewer. It remains to be seen whether the labour movement, subject to many different ideological pulls, can recover a sense of social purpose.

Notes

1. National Archives of Canada, Canadian Congress of Labour Papers, MG 28 1 103, Vol. 127, Andy Andras to Donald MacDonald, 30 December 1952.
2. The best history of union development in Canada is Bryan D. Palmer, *Working Class Experience: Rethinking the History of Canadian Labour, 1800–1991*, 2nd edn. (Toronto: McClelland and Stewart, 1992).
3. The CCCL, for example, joined with other Catholic groups in 1942 to oppose the Wartime Day Nurseries Act, which created a limited number of publicly subsidized daycare spaces for mothers employed in war-related industries; *Le Devoir*, 22 October 1942. On the evolution of Quebec unions' attitudes to women in the labour force after World

War II, see Mona-Josee Gagnon, 'Les Centrales Syndicales et la Condition Feminine', *Maintenant* 140 (novembre): 25–7. The Catholic context of the unions' anti-feminism is emphasized in Francine Berry, *Le Travail de la femme au Québec* (Montréal: Les Presses de l'Université du Québec, 1977).

4. CCL Papers, Vol. 345, Congress of Canadian Labour, *Political Action by Canadian Labour* (Ottawa: Mutual Press, 1945).

5. On the battles for public financial support for daycare, see Susan Prentice, 'Workers, Mothers, Reds: Toronto's Postwar Daycare Fight', *Studies in Political Economy* 30 (Autumn 1989): 115–41, and Alvin Finkel, 'Even the Little Children Cooperated: Family Strategies, Childcare Discourse, and Social Welfare Debates, 1945–1975', *Labour/Le Travail* 36 (Fall 1995): 91–118.

6. National Archives of Canada, Mackenzie King Papers, MG 26, J1, Vol. 398, George F. Addes, international secretary-treasurer, UAW-CIO, to Mackenzie King, 26 April 1946, 33910-20.

7. Judging by the records of the Manitoba Federation of Labour and the Alberta Federation of Labour. When the MFL cautiously endorsed public support for childcare in 1974, it broke a silence that had prevailed since at least 1955. The Alberta Federation of Labour failed to address women's issues at any convention from 1945 to 1970. Provincial Archives of Manitoba, Manitoba Federation of Labour papers, 'Report of Proceedings' for annual conventions 1955–1979; Provincial Archives of Alberta, 'Proceedings' for conventions 1945 to 1970.

8. CCL Papers, Vol. 174, 'A Message for Labour Day', 2 September 1949.

9. National Archives of Canada, MG 28, 3, 62, Canadian Chamber of Commerce Papers, Vol. 2, 'Canadian Chamber of Commerce 26th Annual Meeting Addresses', Gordon G. Cushing, General Secretary-Treasurer, TLC, Address, 6 October 1955.

10. National Archives of Canada, MG 28, 3, 62, Canadian Chamber of Commerce Papers, Vol. 2, 'Canadian Chamber of Commerce 26th Annual Meeting Addresses', Gordon G. Cushing, General Secretary-Treasurer, TLC, Address, 6 October 1955.

11. So, for example, the Oshawa and District Labour Council advertised in the *Oshawa-Times Gazette* its support for the federal proposals at the Dominion-Provincial Conference, indicating: 'It goes without saying that organized labor is interested in social legislation which would give the ordinary man the right to work, the right to shelter, the right to a decent education and protection from unemployment, sickness and other social evils' (*Oshawa-Times*

Gazette, 15 October 1945). The Labour Council took out another ad two days later, calling on the federal government to adopt policies that had full employment as their central focus. The ads were sent by M.J. Fenwick to Mackenzie King and are found in Mackenzie King papers, Vol. 381, Fenwick to King, 15 and 17 December 1945.

12. Canadian Congress of Labour papers, Vol. 314, File 4-26, 'Memorandum Submitted to the Dominion Government by the Canadian Congress of Labour', 5 April 1946.

13. King papers, Vol. 406, 'Memorandum of Proposed Legislation Submitted by the Dominion Joint Legislative Committee of the Railway Transportation Brotherhoods', submission to cabinet, 366859-61.

14. The standard account of the introduction of medicare mentions the role of unions in promoting medicare only in passing. See Malcolm G. Taylor, *Health Insurance and Canadian Public Policy: The Seven Decisions That Created the Canadian Health Insurance System* (Montreal and Kingston: McGill-Queen's University Press, 1978).

15. National Archives of Canada, RG 33, Series 78, Royal Commission on Health Services. Among key anti-medicare briefs were those of the Canadian Health Insurance Association, Vol. 7, File 13, October 1961; Honourable Duff Roblin, Premier of Manitoba, Vol. 8, January 1962, File 48; Canadian Medical Association, Vol. 6, File 67, 16 October 1962; and Canadian Chamber of Commerce, Vol. 14, File 188.

16. This percentage was mentioned in both the Canadian Medical Association and Canadian Chamber of Commerce briefs.

17. Royal Commission on Health Services, Vol. 22, File 355, Brief of Mrs Marguerite Miles, Toronto, n.d.; Brief 375, Dr C. Collins-Williams, Toronto, n.d.

18. Submission of Canadian Nurses Association, Royal Commission on Health Services, Vol. 15, File 205, March 1962.

19. The CFA's brief is found in Royal Commission on Health Services, Vol. 14, File 190, 27 March 1962.

20. One particularly excruciating brief because of the number of detailed examples provided came from the Welfare Council of Ottawa, *Royal Commission On Health Services*, Vol. 15, File 208, 23 March 1962.

21. Submission of Newfoundland Federation of Labour, Vol. 7, File 25, October 1961.

22. On the British experience, see Michael Ball, *Housing Policy and Economic Power: The Political Economy of Owner Occupation* (Montreal and Kingston: McGill-Queen's University Press, 1983). On the Scandinavian countries, see Gosta Esping-Anderson, *Politics*

against Markets: The Social Democratic Road to Power
(Princeton: Princeton University Press, 1985), 186–8.

23. There had been campaigns for public housing in which the unions participated before the war as well, particularly in Vancouver. See Jill Wade, *Houses for All: The Struggle for Social Housing in Vancouver, 1919–1950* (Vancouver: UBC Press, 1994).

24. Canadian Congress of Labour papers, Vol. 314, 'Memorandum Submitted to the Dominion Government by the Canadian Congress of Labour', 25 April 1945.

25. National Archives of Canada, MG 28, I 10, Canadian Welfare Council/ Canadian Council on Social Development papers, Vol. 54, File 471, 'CCL, Statement on Housing Submitted to Canadian Legion National Housing Conference, 1953'.

26. CCL Papers, Vol. 220, File 220/16, 'Memorandum Submitted by CCL, to the House of Commons Standing Committee on Banking and Commerce, on Bill 102, an Act to promote the construction of new houses, the repair and modernization of existing houses and the improvement of housing and living conditions', 23 February 1954.

27. The support of all major trade union federations for publicly subsidized daycare during the hearings of the Royal Commission on the Status of Women marked the beginnings of a reassessment by the labour movement of its traditional support for the universal desirability of the nuclear, one-income household model. National Archives of Canada, Royal Commission on the Status of Women, *Briefs*, Canadian Labour Congress, Vol. 17, Brief 440, October 1968; Confédération des syndicate nationaux, Vol. 17, Brief 347, June 1968; Quebec Federation of Labour, Vol. 17, Brief 393, June 1968.

References

Abella, Irving Martin. 1973. *Nationalism, Communism and Canadian Labour: The CIO, the Communist Party, and the Canadian Congress of Labour, 1935–1956*. Toronto: University of Toronto Press.

Andras, Andy. 1967. 'Relief and the People on It', *Canadian Welfare* (May–June).

Bacher, John C. 1993. *Keeping to the Marketplace: The Evolution of Canadian Housing Policy*. Montreal and Kingston: McGill-Queen's University Press.

Bothwell, Robert, Ian Drummond, and John English. 1981. *Canada Since 1945: Power, Politics and Provincialism*. Toronto: University of Toronto Press.

Canada, Advisory Committee on Reconstruction. 1944. *Final Report, IV: Housing and Community Planning: Final Report of the Subcommittee*. Ottawa: King's Printer, March 24.

Drache, Daniel, ed. 1972. *Quebec—Only the Beginning: The Manifestoes of the Common Front*. Toronto: University of Toronto Press.

Esping-Anderson, Gosta. 1985. *Politics against Markets: The Social Democratic Road to Power*. Princeton: Princeton University Press.

Finkel, Alvin. 1993. 'Paradise Postponed: A Re-examination of the Green Book Proposals of 1945', *Journal of the Canadian Historical Association 1993*, New Series 4: 120–42.

Gagnon, Mona-Josee. 1974. 'Les Centrales Syndicales et la Condition Feminine', *Maintenant* 140 (novembre): 25–7.

Gazette (Montreal). 1943. July 16.

Gotlieb, Marc J. 1985. 'George Drew and the Dominion-Provincial Conference on Reconstruction of 1945–46', *Canadian Historical Review* 66, 1 (March): 27–47.

Lipsig-Mummé, Carla. 1984. 'The Web of Dependence: Quebec Unions in Politics Before 1976', in Alain G. Gagnon, ed., *Quebec State and Society*. Toronto: University of Toronto Press.

———. 1991. 'Future Conditional: Wars of Position in the Quebec Labour Movement', *Studies in Political Economy* 36 (Autumn): 73–107.

Moscovitch, Allan. 1981. 'Housing: Who Pays? Who Profits?', in Allan Moscovitch and Glenn Drover, eds, *Inequality: Essays on the Political Economy of Social Welfare*. Toronto: University of Toronto Press.

Porter, Ann. 1993. 'Women and Income Security in the Post-War Period: The Case of Unemployment Insurance, 1945–1962', *Labour/Le Travail* 31 (Spring): 111–44.

Rands, Stan. 1981. 'Recollections', in Donald C. Kerr, ed., *Western Canadian Politics: The Radical Tradition*. Montreal: Boréal.

Rouillard, Jacques. 1989. *Historie du syndicalism au Québec: Des origins à nos jours*. Montreal: Boréal.

Schulz, Pat. 1982. 'Minding the Children', in Maureen Fitzgerald, Connie Guberman, and Margie Wolfe, eds, *Still Ain't Satisfied: Canadian Feminism Today*. Toronto: The Women's Press.

Swartz, Donald. 1977. 'The Politics of Reform: Conflict and Accommodation in Canadian Health Policy', in Leo Panitch, ed., *The Canadian State: Political Economy and Political Power*. Toronto: University of Toronto Press.

Taylor, Malcolm G. 1978. *Health Insurance and Canadian Public Policy: The Seven Decisions That Created* *the Canadian Health Insurance System*. Montreal and Kingston: McGill-Queen's University Press.

PART X

The 1960s and Legacies of Conflict

In 1969, the women autoworkers described in the article by Pamela Sugiman in Part IX joined other women lobbying for new anti-discrimination laws. They wanted to put an end to the firmly entrenched sexual division of labour in workplaces, job advertisements, and seniority lists. Their protest joined a chorus of other voices calling for, if not demanding, radical social change in the 1960s. Popular culture often paints a picture of the 1960s—sometimes said to extend from 1965 to 1975—as an era characterized by the rebellion of university students and middle-class youth. In reality, sixties protests were much wider in scope: Meg Luxton, for example, argues that the early 'second wave' women's movement drew on working-class feminist activists and spoke to the need for change in the workplace and the labour movement. The wildcat strikes described by Bryan Palmer also show that youth protest did not simply take place on university campuses but was an integral part of new challenges by young workers to the constraints of their situation in the mid-1960s.

A new generation of workers, he argues, led a wave of defiant wildcat strikes that challenged the basic premise of Justice Ivan Rand's post-war settlement: that the collective agreement was sacred, and work stoppages within the life of the contract were illegal acts that would subject unions and their leaders to jailings, fines, and other sanctions. Yet, hundreds of such wildcats erupted from 1964 to 1966, taking not only employers and the state by surprise, but also trade union officials. Young workers' pent up frustrations over protracted contract negotiations, technological change, or the disciplining of their fellow unionists boiled over in rebellious, spontaneous strike action. The percentage of wildcat strikes in this two-year period was 'earth shattering' in comparison to preceding years, and surpassed as well similar activities in the next decades.

Wildcatting workers created difficult dilemmas for labour leaders. Many such trade union officials had fought for collective bargaining rights to be enshrined in law and they regarded the post-World War II Fordist accord as a great victory, one that needed to be honoured and preserved. They were caught off guard by the youth revolt that seemed to treat the terms of a now codified and state-monitored industrial legality with such disrespect. They often ordered, or begged, their union members to return to work. Yet seldom were they obeyed: wildcats became scenes not only of violent class revolt against employers, but also raucous denunciations of the union bureaucracies, which were often seen as complacent and incorporated into large, impersonal structures of oppression.

Wildcat strikers understandably focused their ire on laws, such as those used to impose injunctions that purported to be fair and neutral but that were invariably seen as being used in ways detrimental to the interests of workers. Industrial legality, these critics argued, disguised the ongoing power of the state and capital to 'set the rules of the game' in the employers' favour. Such perspectives indicated how working-class experience was becoming more politicized.

This increased politicization of workers was then articulated in Quebec through, and with, a growing nationalist movement. Quebec's labour movement had always been distinct from that of English Canada, shaped historically by its ties to the Catholic Church and also by particularly repressive provincial labour and anti-communist statutes in effect from the 1930s until the 1960s. Catholic trade unions, gathered under the umbrella of the CTCC (Confédération des Travailleurs Catholiques du Canada), founded in 1921 and originally led by priests, lent Quebec's labour movement a distinct character. In the immediate post-World War II years, these religiously-ordered labour organizations remained a strong presence, enrolling in their ranks about one-third of the unionized workers in the province. As these Catholic labour organizations grew in significance, they came to advocate a more 'secular humanist' world view and, according to Jacques Rouillard, developed into more and more militant vehicles of working-class protest in which committed organizers displaced Catholic clergy as key leaders. In 1961, these Catholic *syndicats* dropped the religious component of their name, becoming the Confederation of National Trade Unions or Confederation des syndicats nationaux (CNTU/CSN). This was perhaps the most dynamic and radical of the three union centrals discussed by Ralph Güntzel in his article on Quebec labour and the politics of sovereigntism. As the CNTU exploded in significance over the course of the 1960s, it grew from 80,000 to 250,000, rivaling the traditional craft unions organized in the Federation des Travailleurs du Québec, or FTQ. Public sector workers have come to be affiliated with the former teachers' union body, the Centrale des syndicats du Québec (CSQ).

Güntzel explores the changing political platforms of these three main union centrals in Quebec—the FTQ, the CSN and the CSQ—from the 1960s through to the 1990s. He examines how different labour organizations address the issue of Quebec's separation from Canada and details the debates within unions about which political parties, ideas, and strategies to support. While all the union centrals supported federalism in the mid-1960s, all three increasingly moved towards an embrace of sovereignty as the best political option for Quebec workers and, for a brief period in the late 1960s and early 1970s, some trade unionists advocated an extremely radical and Marxist view of Canadian and international politics. For French Canadian workers whose experience of class exploitation was one and the same with the cultural/linguistic oppression of francophones, Güntzel shows, sovereignty simply 'made political sense' as a means of confronting the historic dominance of English-speaking Canadians. The same was true of CSQ members whose jobs involved teaching and protecting the French language. For many Quebec trade union leaders, the possibility of securing radical, or even social democratic reforms, was increasingly linked to a political nationalism that would allow the Québécois to be 'masters in their own house'. Güntzel's article thus underscores some of the key differences between Quebec and English Canadian labour, not the least of which is the centrality of the national question to Quebec unions, and the ways in which this contrasts to the implicit federalist inclinations of the pre-1985 Canadian Labour Congress.

The 1960s were also characterized by important changes in the field of immigration: in 1967, the federal government finally swept away the provisions in official immigration policy which had allowed the state to discriminate on the basis of race in the selection of immigrants. Until this point, the unstated intent of Canadian policy, with some minor exceptions, was the maintenance of a 'white' Canada. In the post-World War II period, of course, there had been a significant surge of immigration from Europe, with preference initially given to British immigrants, though large groups of eastern and southern Europeans also arrived, usually gravitating towards major metropolitan centres. Canada's immigration policy has always been shaped by the perceived needs of the labour market, with special recruitment efforts often focused on finding foreign-born workers for jobs that native-born Canadians could or would not fill—such as domestic service.

If there is one constant theme in the intertwined histories of immigration and women's work it is that of the recruitment of domestic servants. At the turn of the century, the largest group of women in the labour force worked in domestic service, and countless efforts were made by the state and women's reform groups to entice more women to emigrate to fill these jobs. Although the numbers of women in domestic service declined after World War I, many women were forced back into this isolating and often lowly paid work during the hard times of the Depression.

Over the course of the twentieth century, homemakers have increasingly performed domestic labour themselves rather than using paid help. There was nevertheless an unfilled demand for domestics in the post-World War II decades and, in recent times, programs have been developed to import child minders and nannies for affluent families. Their contemporary presence remains a sharp reminder that the experiences and interests of working-class women are often quite distinct from those of middle-class, professional women.

Sedef Arat-Koç's article explores the search for domestic workers from the late nineteenth century to the post-World War II period, looking at both the changes and continuities in Canada's recruitment policies and priorities. Her overview of the state's efforts to bring in domestics indicates how tenacious the equation of women with domestic labour has been, and secondly, how important this labour of social reproduction is to the ongoing maintenance of families and society. An analysis of ethnicity and race is central to her argument; she shows how and why Canada targeted different national and racial groups as potential domestics. A woman's ethnic and racial background in turn dictated if she was welcomed as a permanent resident or brought in only as a temporary worker. While white, British women were sought as immigrants at the turn of the century in the hopes that they would settle here and become 'mothers of the nation', later efforts shifted to the recruitment of white European women and, finally, to women of colour who were not imagined as 'mothers of the nation'. Ironically, as Arat-Koç shows, the liberalization of immigration laws in the late 1960s that led to a more 'colour blind' policy did not aid immigrant domestics from the Caribbean and Philippines who wished to become citizens. Their labour as domestics, still undervalued and perceived to be unskilled, placed them in a new category of state-defined temporary workers that left them without the rights of citizenship. As will be evident in reading Part X, what the state gives workers as 'rights', it can also withhold or take away under the guise of national necessity.

Further Reading

Agnes Calliste, 'Canada's Immigration Policy and Domestics from the Caribbean: The Second Domestic Scheme', in Jessie Vorst, ed., *Race, Class and Gender: Bonds and Barriers* (Toronto: Between the Lines, 1989).

Daniel Drache, ed., *Quebec—Only the Beginning: The Manifestoes of the Common Front* (Toronto: New Press, 1972).

Franca Iacovetta, *Such Hard Working People: Italian Immigrants in Postwar Toronto* (Montreal and Kingston: McGill-Queen's University Press, 1992).

Meg Luxton, 'Feminism as a Class Act: Working-Class Feminism and the Women's Movement in Canada', *Labour/Le Travail* 48 (Fall 2001): 63–88.

Stuart Marshall Jamieson, *Times of Trouble: Labour Unrest and Industrial Conflict in Canada, 1900–1966* (Ottawa: Task Force on Labour Relations/Queen's Printer, 1971).

Jacques Rouillard, *Histoire du syndicalisme au québécois: Des origines à nos jours* (Montréal: Boréal, 1989).

Pamela Sugiman, '"That wall's coming down": Gendered Strategies of Resistance in the UAW Canadian Region, 1963–1970', *Canadian Journal of Sociology* 17 (Winter 1992): 1–28.

Visual Resources

NFB, *On Est Au Coton* (1970), dir. Denys Arcand, 159 minutes (deals with early unionization and workers trying to save their jobs as large firms leave the country).

NFB, *Who Will I Sentence Now?* (1977), dir. Boyce Richardson and David Newman, 28 minutes (the toll of workplace diseases and occupational health hazards are explored).

Full Frame and Video, *A Wives' Tale* (1980), dir. Martin Duckworth and Sophie Bissonette, 73 minutes (follows the establishment and actions of the Wives Supporting the Strike during the 1978–79 strike of Local 6500 steelworkers versus Inco in Sudbury).

CHAPTER 23
Wildcat Workers in the 1960s: The Unruly Face of Class Struggle
Bryan D. Palmer

The wildcat strike might be regarded as the trade union equivalent of the students' sit-in. (Finn, 1965: 17)

Workers and their unions appeared relatively secure as they entered the 1960s. With the apparent attainment of collective bargaining rights secured at the end of the 1940s an historic breakthrough seemed to have been realized in what was championed as a new era of 'industrial pluralism'. The Cold War vanquishing of the communists in the labour movement seemed to secure trade unions a measure of respectability, although, to be sure, there were always rough patches in the accord reached among employers, workers' organizations,

and the state in the immediate post-World War II period. With fractious components of the Canadian workers' movement coming together in the Canadian Labour Congress in 1956, old divides separating craft and industrial unions now seemed overcome, and there were signs that an awakening trade unionism in Quebec could well link arms with its counterparts across the country. Combined with the general climate of post-World War II affluence, in which employment possibilities were strong and employers' capacities to offer concessions seemingly expansive, the times seemed propitious for Canadian workers and the prospects for trade unions to continue their upward trajectory good.

Few recognized the contradictions at the heart of labour's new found security. Older trade unionists and most labour leaders, for instance, knew well that it had taken a century to establish a state-monitored system of industrial relations that recognized workers' legal rights to join unions and bargain collectively with businesses and their management. They were hardly in a position to guard against the ways in which the post-war settlement would move trade unions in increasingly legalistic directions, nor were they, understandably, all that concerned with problems that would be posed for workers and their organizations as the labour movement necessarily grew more and more bureaucratized. Basking in the warm glow of working-class accomplishment, barely a labour eyebrow was raised in recognition that what the state gave it could also, when pressures were brought to bear, take away. It would take decades before such concerns surfaced. They would not really be discernible until the fiscal crisis of the Canadian state manifested itself blatantly in the mid-1970s, and Pierre Elliott Trudeau's Liberals imposed Wage and Price Controls, initiating a legislative assault on trade union freedoms that would be picked up with a vengeance by Conservative, even New Democratic Party, governments in the 1980s and 1990s. Masking the cracks in the edifice of the post-war settlement were a host of 1960s developments, including the expanding infrastructure of 'social safety net provisioning', which encompassed tremendous growth and stabilization of health and education programs and facilities, state commitment to principles of universality in family allowances and unemployment insurance, and a range of initiatives that took aim at the reduction of poverty or targeted youth as specific beneficiaries of state largesse, training, and aid.[1]

But the emergence of resentment and grievance in the arena of class struggle did nevertheless emerge in the 1960s.[2] In particular, it surfaced with a vengeance in 1964–66, at precisely the same point that radical nationalist agitation was developing in Quebec, students were gravitating toward both countercultural alternative and the politics of challenge and dissent, and women were beginning to voice their discontents with a status quo that kept them confined to the constrained possibilities of a feminine sphere. Not surprisingly, as was the case elsewhere, the young led the way. Their vehicle of protest, driven by a rage and violence that was itself an expression of the frustrations of alienation and marginalization common to a wider generational revolt, was the single working-class expression of rebellion that a major architect of the post-war settlement, Justice Ivan Rand, had been at pains to suppress. Rand's historic post-war packaging of trade unionism's rights and obligations in the era of 'industrial pluralism' had emerged out of his arbitration decision settling the tumultuous 1945 strike at Windsor's massive Ford plant. As the so-called Rand formula became the guiding light of Canada's modern industrial relations system, unions were recognized as legitimate agents in the new order, but they were expected to enforce certain standards on their ranks, the most exalted of which was the sanctity of the collective agreement. The traditional weapon of workers, the withdrawal of their services in strike action, was thus never to be used until the collective agreement had run its course, bargaining efforts to reach new agreement had failed, and both labour and capital had exhausted all measures to keep the production that Rand thought pivotal to Canada's 'good life' going. Wildcat strikes, protests in which workers walked off the job in defiance of their contractual obligation not to disrupt the economics of peaceful class co-existence during the life of collective agreements, were the mid-1960s voice of an aggrieved, and youthful, layer of workers waging a most difficult war. For not only did this military-like campaign array itself against the traditional enemy, capital, it also found itself confronting two other powerful structures: the seemingly benevolent state and the embodiment of workers' mechanisms of defence, the trade union and its increasingly hierarchical officialdom.

The Demography of Dissent[3]

The Canadian labour force, like Canadian society in general, grew younger over the course of the 1960s. Whereas people between the ages of 15 and 24 accounted for 15.3 per cent of the country's population in 1951, by the 1970s this figure was approaching 19 per cent.

In the pivotally important 1964–66 years male youth were overwhelmingly concentrated in waged employment. If these young workers were the best schooled generation of working-class youth in Canadian history, they were nevertheless not yet the beneficiaries of a mid-to-late 1960s education boom that saw a tremendous expansion of college and university facilities and the first serious possibility of lower income youth taking advantage of what higher education had to offer. Only 11 per cent of Canadians aged 18–24 were enrolled in university in 1965, with slightly less than 15 per cent of those 20–24 having any university experience at all.[4] Unlike young, working-class women, moreover, males in this age bracket were less likely to be confined to family responsibilities, whether that involved care of the young or the old. The result was that in the mid-1960s, roughly 88 per cent of all 20–24 year old males were in the civilian labour force, compared to approximately 54 per cent of women of the same age cohort. This gendered demographic explains much of the wildness of the wildcats, which were most emphatically male undertakings, marked by bravado and the macho posturing of youth in a pre-feminist working-class cultural moment. Understandably, as well, younger workers entered the workforce

with less security than their older counterparts, and unemployment rates for the young in the mid-1960s indicated that their employment was far more precarious than those in the 25–44 and 45–65 age groups. Young workers from 14–24 years of age faced unemployment rates of from 16.4 to 9.7 and 11.8 to 5.3 per cent over the first half of the 1960s; comparable rates for older workers never reached much more than seven per cent and sometimes bottomed out at just under three per cent.[5]

Working-class youth, of course, were drawn into the same countercultural cauldron as their non-proletarian peers.[6] Many young workers lived at home, and resentments of adult, often patriarchal, authority, fused domestic and workplace resentments in a populistic assault on 'the Establishment', an imprecise target that often seemed to lump together anyone over the age of 30 with the bastions of social and economic power, both groups seemingly rigidly separated from the experience of being young. One 1968 study, addressing Canadian industrial relations, noted 'an undeniable tendency in this generation to question and challenge authority itself and those in a position to exercise it' (Woods, 1968: 99).[7] As music, drugs, sex, fashion, and a generational tendency to refuse all authority congealed in an increasingly public and often consumer-paced popular culture of age differentiation,[8] a 'them vs us' discontent coalesced among Canadian youth, who echoed the lyrics of the 1965 British rock anthem, 'My Generation'. Recorded by Peter Townshend and The Who, the song, presented with a patented stutter, was among the hardest-hitting statements of a newly-combative rock 'n' roll:

People try to put us d-down, talking 'bout my
  generation
Just because we get around, talking 'bout my
  generation

Things they do look awful c-c-cold, talking
'bout my generation
Hope I die before I get old, talking 'bout my
generation
Why don't you all f-fade away, talkin' 'bout
my generation
And don't try to dig what we all s-s-say, talkin'
'bout my generation
I'm not trying to cause a big s-s-sensation,
talkin' 'bout my generation
I'm just talking 'bout my g-g-g-generation,
talking 'bout my generation.

(Townshend, 1965)

Often perceived as a product of campus rebellion, this widening youth culture of discontent
was, in actuality, far more widespread, and it
affected the trade unions as well as the university
classroom. 'Less cerebral, less able to articulate his
discontent than the young student demonstrator,'
the youthful rebel within the mid-1960s trade
union cause was nonetheless animated by the same
spirit of discontent and alienation as his campus
counterpart according to senior labour commentator Ed Finn. As Finn's use of the masculine to
identify discontent suggests, the wildcats were
largely perceived as a male phenomenon (Finn,
1965: 17).[9]

Eight years later one union old-timer in Winnipeg's Transcona and Symington railway yards
looked back on decades of labour-capital conflict,
commenting on the rebelliousness of his younger
co-workers, who were seething with anger after
their union leaders forced the end of a strike and
the provincial New Democratic Party government
'sold [them] out for 4 cents an hour'. 'We've got
three enemies,' asserted the veteran militant, 'the
company, the government and the union. We can't
beat them all now, but we are starting something.
It's the young guys that are responsible for this.
They started it. If it weren't for them we wouldn't

be here now. They're different. They're fearless.
They don't give a damn for the company or the
government or the union.' Memories of 1966
reverberated in this account. Young workers drew
on this reservoir of a recent past to frame stories of
how supervisors had to be kept in line; strike duty
they thought 'more fun' if it was voluntary and
spontaneous. The rebel workers insisted that they
were no more likely to snap to attention if the boss
shouting orders at them was from the union or the
company. 'We're our own boss now.' The old-timer
nodded in agreement. 'It's a new generation,' he
proclaimed ('Trouble on the Line', 1973: 10–11).

The revolt of the young within unions thus had
a profound impact on class relations in the mid-
1960s. It not only upped the level and nature of
the conflict with employers, it also threatened the
capacity of the state to contain struggles within
respected boundaries of legalism and industrial
pluralism as well as rocking the boat of trade
unionism itself. Youthful rebels had none of the
political baggage of their older labour movement leaders: they had not experienced the anti-
communist purges of the 1950s, cultivated no
intense loyalties to a layer of social democratic
trade union officials, and had not, for the most
part, known the difficult, insecure, and often
violently vindictive times of the Great Depression
and before, to which their fathers and mothers had
a more organic connection through family, even
direct experience ('Wildcat Strike Poses. . .', 1965).
Younger workers took for granted much that their
older predecessors and union leaders had struggled, often at great cost and considerable sacrifice,
to achieve. And as the post-war settlement delivered tangible benefits to unions, older leaders had
grown cautious in their protections of the valued
stabilities that had resulted. As Finn noted:

Approximately 80 per cent of Canada's top
labour leaders are between the ages of 50 and

70. Many of them have grown more conservative with the passing years, more wedded to the old ways and the old traditions. They fail to see the need for drastic changes in the structure and policies of the labour movement if it is to cope with automation, industrial and technological change, and other pressing challenges of the 1960s and 1970s. And while the leaders of most unions have aged, the turnover in their membership has brought in many thousands of young workers who are not tied to old union methods and traditions. Better educated, more aggressive, these younger workers have strong ideas about what they want and how to get it. They are taking over the leadership at the local level, and their radicalism often brings them into sharp conflict with the comparatively conservative leaders at the top. (1965: 17)

Writing in *Saturday Night*, Mungo James discussed the mid-1960s 'new ferment' in the trade unions, attributing it 'to the arrival, for the first time in any numbers, of the young, swinging, questing generation'. In Quebec, one local labour activist noted that, 'It used to be that we waited for orders from the union representative, but that is not the way with the young people.' Murray Cottrell, a veteran unionist associated with the powerful United Steel Workers of America (USWA), summed up the problem of class relations as it appeared in the mid-1960s: 'These kids won't take it. They expect to be treated like human beings' (James, 1966: 27–8; Dumas, 1974: 117).[10]

The Meaning of Wildcatting

One aspect of Cottrell's conclusion that youthful workers were refusing to 'take it' not drawn out by the older unionist was that this stand placed them not only in revolt against the employers and the state, but against the union as well. An illegal railway striker in Montreal said, simply, that dissidents were 'fed up with excuses from their union leaders' (Carrothers, 1966: 396–7). The 1968 Task Force on Canadian Industrial Relations, headed by McGill University's H.D. Woods, pointed out that worker dissatisfaction in the mid-1960s was sometimes running 'as deeply against the union and collective bargaining as against management', producing a worrisome 'rebellion of union members against their leaders' (Woods, 1968: 98).[11] Wildcat strikes were *the* most decisive articulation of this process, violating the legality of a contract, posing a threat to union security. Labour organizations found such rank-and-file rebellion threatening, for if they failed to uphold their legal responsibilities within the Canadian post-war settlement, trade unions could be subject to crippling financial penalties in the form of fines, often calculated as a daily sum per union member in defiance of the contract. Depending on the duration of the wildcat, such financial penalties might total hundreds of thousands, even millions, of dollars. As local and international treasuries were the material and symbolic measure of trade unionism's new-found security, this hit labour's developing bureaucracy where it truly hurt. Adding personal insult to the cash injury, these very same trade union tops who failed to stave off or muzzle wildcat strikes might well be jailed if they did not demonstrate sufficient zeal in getting their members back to work.

Wildcat strikes tend to be a combination of informal, but ongoing, organization, and exuberant spontaneity, which marks them out from legal strikes. The latter are planned, coordinated, and announced by union officials well in advance. They have a timetable, which wildcats never do. Everyone involved in a legal strike knows that a collective agreement has run its course and management and labour have been unable to reach a consensus that a new contract will be signed. Wildcats are far less likely to be about wages, pensions, or what business unionists often see as the core issues of contract negotiations, than are legal strikes. If the legal strike is about securing a contract, the wildcat strike can either be about skirting the contract or, alternatively, present itself as a forceful statement from the shop floor that workers are tired of waiting for one. No labour *movement* has ever been built without the enthusiasm and mobilizing potential of the illegal work stoppage, just as no *business* unionism, concerned overwhelmingly with narrow wage issues, has ever been comfortable with wildcats. As one observer told the *Canadian Forum's* Louis Greenspan, 'The union leaders have fought the old fights and won the old battles; they no longer negotiate ideas, they only negotiate money' (Greenspan, 1967: 245).

Often the concerns involved in wildcats are unclear to many of the workers who decide that they will make common cause with their fellow unionists in closing down the plant for an unspecified period. But there is an essential trust in the old trade union maxim that 'an injury to one is the concern of all,' and that some grievance of importance, or the buildup of a series of resentments, necessitates direct action, outside of the usual slow, cumbersome, and officially mediated procedures of resolution. Implicitly a blow against the hierarchy of state-monitored labour organization, and the distance of an increasingly bureaucratized layer of officialdom from the discontents of waged working life, some wildcats can even be explicit protests against a contingent of trade union tops judged inadequate in their response to rank-and-file needs and grievances. As John H. Crispo and Harry W. Arthurs reported in 1968, Canadian wildcats were an expression of 'rank-and-file restlessness' that was sometimes 'as much against the "union establishment" as against the "business establishment"'. One investigator found that a diffuse sense of 'participatory democracy' animated the 1965–66 Canadian wildcat wave, with workers

demanding an expansion of their role in decision-making, especially on critically important issues such as technological innovation and automation. The intensity of commitment to a 'new version of Trade Unionism', surprised this commentator, who concluded that, 'just as the bureaucratized universities have created the militant student and faculty so have the bureaucratized plants created the new generation of union militants.' Talk of a 'new unionism' and 'the just society' spread in labour circles, prompting rebelliousness and commitment to widening the effort to eradicate poverty and create more equitable income distribution (Waisglass qtd in James, 1966: 26; Greenspan, 1967: 245; Jamieson, 1976: 401).

The wildcat strike, then, was the perfect vehicle (in both form and content) for the expression of youthful rebellion in the mid-1960s. It was often a spontaneous eruption of anger, alienation, and anxiety, ordered by workers themselves, rather than channelled through conservative union leaders and the procedural morass of the legally-ordered trade union settlement. Like student protest meetings and demonstrations, wildcat strikes were happenings rather than highly structured and routinely scripted events. They took place outside of the boundaries of what had come to be conventional class relations, and they struck blows against the peaceful co-existence the postwar settlement was designed to secure for capital, labour, and the state.[12]

Class Struggle's Temperature Rising: Wildcat Fever and Youthful Labour Revolt

The mid-1960s seemed wild enough, without the drama of illegal work stoppages being thrown into the mix. A *Globe and Mail* review of 'threatening labour disputes' suggested that Canadians needed to be jolted into awareness that they were being flooded with 'disastrous strikes'. Such upheavals, according to a statement by the Minister of Labour, John Nicholson, in the House of Commons, 'threaten[ed] the Canadian economy'. Nicholson was put off by 'a near epidemic of labour disputes and the hair trigger atmosphere that attends so many negotiations', and he feared a 'long summer of uncontrolled labour strife' that would 'exact its toll from every Canadian' ('A Plague. . .', 1966; 'The More Sensible Course. . .', 1966).

A precise count of the strikes and lockouts of these years is difficult to arrive at because the major government publication upon which such a tally would necessarily be based, 'The Strike and Lockout Reports' published annually in the Department of Labour's Economics and Research Branch *Strikes and Lockouts in Canada*, under-reported the level of conflict. Nevertheless, two separate calculations, one conducted by Stuart Marshall Jamieson, a Professor at the University of British Columbia's Institute of Industrial Relations in the 1960s, and another by Joy McBride, a PhD candidate at Queen's University in the late 1980s, confirm the unmistakable dimensions of an upturn in the class struggle. Jamieson, who ascertained the numbers of strikes and lockouts by surveying official statistics, records a total of 1,118 such conflicts in 1965–66, while McBride, studying the same period, but drawing on the aggregate data rather than reproducing the final published government statistics, suggests that 1,147 strikes occurred. Both scholars place the accent on the dramatic rise in class conflict, with the workers involved, worker-days lost to strikes and lock-outs, and percentage of estimated working time sacrificed to such struggles soaring. The number of worker days lost almost quadrupled over the course of 1963–65, climbing to 7.5 million in the two years of intense mid-1960s conflict. Esti-mated working time that evaporated in the heat of class struggle tripled to .33 per cent, with almost

600,000 workers battling employers on picket lines in 1964–66.

Unemployment having been brought under control, contained at roughly four per cent, infla-tion was the primary scourge of the organized working class. Its rising wage demands, which in the case of some sectors appeared outra-geously excessive, peaked with a 1966 Canadian Union of Postal Workers announcement that the union would seek a mammoth 50 per cent wage hike. When railway workers seemingly insisted on a 30 per cent raise in 1966, politicians from Liberal Prime Minister Lester B. Pearson on down to Ontario's Minister responsible for provincial highways cried foul, claiming the government would be bankrupted. Contractors in Montreal were shocked when 10,000 building tradesmen and labourers associated with the Confederation of National Trade Unions (CNTU) brought $100 million worth of projects to a standstill, rejecting an agreement providing 'the largest and most rapid wage and fringe increases ever negotiated in Canada' for workers in the construction sector. Newspaper editorials and tavern talk turned on 'big unions' and their crippling inflationary wage demands.[13]

More telling (and more open to dispute in terms of differences in the numbers) is the tally of wildcat strikes in 1965–66. Certainly their importance is obvious, but Jamieson's reliance on official statistics alone probably understates signifi-cantly the number of wildcats in these years. He puts the figure at 359, while McBride's survey of illegal strikes approaches 575. What is undeni-able is that such wildcat statistics, encompassing by 1965–66 anywhere from 20 to 50 per cent of all strikes, highlight an earth shattering departure from the practices of the past. Even official statis-tics, such as those gathered for Ontario, conceded that 27 per cent of the strikes in the province in 1966 were illegal, having been launched during the life of the collective agreement. And with this wave of wildcats, Canadian workers served notice that they were prepared to defy law and order, often resulting in violence. This was not so much new, since workers often had their backs placed against walls in ways that necessitated physical refusals and resistance, as it was a challenge to the post-war settlement's attempt to structure class relations in ways that effectively contained such turbulence and undermined the ability of militants in the union movement to reenact the confrontational class struggles of the past. 'The peaceable kingdom', with its attachment to orderly understandings of British constitutional practices, was being assailed from within by an increasingly unruly, wildcatting working class (Woods, 1968: 131; Jamieson, 1976: 400–4; McBride, 1987; Gindin, 1995: 145).

Many of these wildcat battles were epic confrontations that won workers considerable concessions from capital. Often strikers—legal and illegal— were forced to defy court injunctions ordering them to cease and desist from specific picket-line activities and return to their work. So blatant was the hostility to injunctions in mid-1960s labour circles that it threatened to shatter the hegemonic hold of the law. It was difficult to mask the extent to which injunctions prohibiting picket lines were not obvious tools relied on by capital to crush working-class resistance, exposing the class prejudices of the state and its infrastructure of 'justice'. Central Ontario became a particularly hot site of contestation as strikes of typographers at the *Oshawa Times* and poorly paid female workers at the Tilco Plastics Company, both of which were slapped with restraining orders, culminated in a well coordinated and province-wide Ontario Federation of Labour campaign against injunctions. Unionists declared that 'the war is on' and that they had 'no respect for the law'. When a sheriff in Oshawa tried to read an injunction to

a huge crowd of union supporters he was pelted with snowballs and the offensive legal document was torn from his hands, shredded by its opponents. The New Democratic Party's Ontario leader, Donald C. MacDonald, told one group of defiant strikers that 'people who defy laws have in the past been at the center of historic events.'[14]

Labour spokesmen could barely stomach the crude way in which the proliferation of injunctions kneecapped striking workers. Paddy Neale, Secretary of the Vancouver and District Labour Council, made no bones of his disdain for a judiciary that would grant employers injunctions without even glancing at sworn affidavits. 'The law is an ass,' he railed. 'We must try to have it changed, but if we can't, then we may have to ignore it. . . . If labour leaders and workers are forced by law and injunctions into going to jail, let's go. But let's make an issue out of it and keep the problem in the public eye.' Injunctions, by 1965, were a particularly dirty word in British Columbia's militant labour circles. 'We used them to decorate the office as wallpaper,' snorted one strike leader when asked what he thought of the proliferating court orders. Young workers heard such statements and no doubt considered them a license to flaunt the law in general, especially as the class war gave every sign of heating up in the 1965–66 years (*Globe and Mail*, 21 June 1966).[15]

Typical of the complex levels of developing antagonism were strikes of Hamilton and Sudbury steelworkers and miners and Montreal longshoremen in 1966. Contract negotiations at the northern Ontario International Nickel Company (Inco) plant were disrupted by a 16,000-member wildcat walkout that union officials subdued only after three weeks. In spite of the leadership's opposition to the job action, it helped win Sudbury's miners and metal processors an impressive pay hike, making them, according to one newspaper report, 'the highest paid group in the Steel Workers' Union'. When the contract was eventually approved, however, only 57 per cent of the union membership thought it good enough and voted for ratification. To the south, in Hamilton, discontent erupted in a violent wildcat at the Steel Company of Canada, where workers fought police and union officials, destroyed property and won themselves a reputation for militancy and the highest steelworking wage in the world. On the Montreal docks, the first illegal strike in years was fought by longshoremen resisting the stevedoring companies' demands that new cargo-handling machinery be used and gangs reduced in size accordingly. Workers refused to recommend a settlement that contained lucrative wage increases until a Royal Commission was established to inquire into the shipping firms' insistence that the size of work crews be pared down, cutting 600 jobs, thus guaranteeing that traditional long-shoring gangs would be preserved for the duration of the contract, until 1968.

Similar developments on the railways forced parliament to sanction 18 per cent wage increases before it ordered strikers back to work after an October 1964 protest in which 2,800 Canadian National Railway employees booked off sick in an *en masse* protest. Meanwhile, 12,000 postal workers were poised to lead one of the largest nationwide wildcats in the 1965–66 upheaval, partly improving the depressed wage environment in which they had been incarcerated for some time and which saw their pay markedly less ($2,000–$3,000 in some high wage locales such as Vancouver) than policemen and firemen of comparable seniority and unskilled municipal labourers. A *Globe and Mail* editorial worried over the spread of wildcat fever, seeing the postal conflict as a reflection 'of the loss of control by union leaders', noting that the mail carriers' walkout 'spread like wildfire across the country despite efforts by the union leadership in Ottawa to douse it'.[16] Many strikes of

the period, commentators were quick to point out, ended up headed by rebel leaderships and factions that 'refused to obey their national officers', as was evident among postal workers in 1965, the Stelco eruption of 1966, and in the rising militancy of Ontario's 8,500 teamsters.[17]

The demographics of youth figured centrally in these class battles. Time and time again, commentators underscored the origins of the wildcat movement in the impatience, intransigence, and volatility of workers 'new' to the game of stable, industrial relations, uninitiated in the procedural practices of post-war settlement unionism, layered as they were in bureaucratic legalism. The Secretary Treasurer of the CBRT noted in 1966 that three years earlier, during the most recent set of contract negotiations, fully half of his members had not been around at the time of the last strike in the industry, in 1950. 'It is doubtful whether many of these new members even know the names of the leaders, and they certainly have no personal identification, as was the case in the past' ('Wildcat Strike Poses. . .', 1965).

Henri W. Joli, President of the Canadian Manufacturers' Association, feared that the escalating union demands of the mid-1960s imperiled the nation and its prosperity, fueling inflation with strikes for 30 per cent wage hikes and extravagant fringe benefits. 'Sparked by the younger members of the labour force,' these job actions needed to be crushed and Joli advocated the use of injunctions prohibiting pickets and other efforts to 'blockade' legitimate business. Recoiling in indignant horror at the 'growing militancy' and the 'picket line turmoil and violence' associated with many worker walkouts, Joli attributed the worsening climate of industrial relations to those young workers swelling the workforce, 'fresh from school who have no idea what the pre-war world was like and who always have got what they wanted. Many of them appear shocked when they find their demands are not going to be met automatically' (Carrothers, 1966: 452).

At Hamilton's Stelco plant, site of one of the more robust and ribald wildcats, it was young men in their twenties, according to various accounts, who precipitated the walkout. Some of these youthful workers had entered the Stelco workforce, and the union, through family connections, their fathers having long histories in the steelworking community. With contract negotiations having dragged on from May into August, stalling in a deadlock that stretched past the expiration date of the contract, resentments mounted in the massive steelworks. With a foreman taunting an evening shift that, 'You guys haven't got the guts to walk out,' 20 young men marched to the plant gate and formed pickets. Two hundred others were quickly enlisted to circulate throughout the plant, calling workers out. Within a day the illegal walkout had spread throughout the sprawling Stelco works, idling 16,000 workers. Of 29 workers initially targeted as militants, arrested and charged with assault and various other picket line criminal acts, suspected as well of sabotage, the average age was 28.6 years, the oldest being 42, the youngest 20. Fully one-third of those arrested were 23 years old or less. When the reinstatement of these wildcatters became an issue of contention, management refusing to hire some of them back, one union leader responded to criticism with the comment, 'Look, Jesus Christ couldn't have got the jobs back of some of those guys. I know one. He was a good kid, too. His father was a personal friend of mine. He'd only been working at Stelco for six months, but he got caught inside the plant cutting electrical cables and that sort of thing. . . . Now what are you gonna do about a case like that?'[18]

Even the upper echelons of labour leadership were not immune from what seemed the spreading mood of defiance in working-class ranks. At the head of the CLC, for instance, a youthful Associate Research Director, Russell Irvine, moved with the times to embrace positions that labour organizations should not trap negotiations with employers in the cul-de-sac of a traditional *quid pro quo*, in which capital's expectation was that any increase in labour's remuneration had to be met with rising productivity. Irvine refused such a profit-wage bargain, arguing that if workers accepted 'this line about being a responsible citizen and tying . . . income to productivity, not only will [labour's] share not increase—it will get even smaller.' Tired of the assumption that unions had to act within the rules of a game that seemed to have been conceived and constructed by capital and the state, Irvine snorted, 'We're sick of being told to act responsibly. Let *them act* responsibly for a change' (James, 1966: 26). But if this was the rhetoric of militancy emanating from the upper echelons of the trade union bureaucracy, as the wildcat wave peaked many a trade union top imploded in frustrated antagonism to young 'hotheads', who seemed to take labour spokesmen like Irvine at their word.

'Listen to the voice of reason,' one Steelworker official pleaded, begging wildcatting workers to end their protest and allow the union to 'get back to the bargaining table'. As railway workers employed by the express delivery wings of the Canadian National and Canada Pacific railways waged an illegal wildcat in the summer of 1966, a union official, prodded to get the workers back on the job, threw up his hands in despair: 'They said they weren't ready to go back, so what's the point of talking to them?' The strikers' words offered an elaboration on their antagonisms: 'This is a non-confidence vote (in the union executive), we are taking things into our own hands.' When Local 1005 President John Morgan and Steelworkers' area supervisor Stewart Cooke implored wildcat pickets at Stelco's gates to open the lines and return to work they were shocked by the vehemence with which they were denounced. 'We're fed up with you, we don't want you,' one picketer jeered in derision at his local union president. Morgan left in tears. One of his supporters reported, 'It was an ugly scene. . . . They were shouting at us like some of them had gone mad. We were lucky to get out of there alive' (Carrothers, 1966: 373–5, 402; Flood, 1968: 12–19; Freeman, 1982: 103).

The Wildness of the Wildcat

This report of fear and loathing on the illegal picket line trail conveys something of the unique wildness of the 1965–66 labour rebellion. If it did not manage to achieve the conscious radicalism or secure the decisive breakthroughs of previous strike waves in 1917–20, 1941–43, and 1946–47, it nevertheless marked a point of departure, suggestive of the limits that segments of labour were placing on their containment by the bureau-cratic legalism of modern class relations. Writing a year after the wildcat wave, Ed Finn summarized the general importance of the new mood of labour militancy, drawing on his particular familiarity with railway workers:

> Impatient with the interminable delays, and with the seeming lack of assertiveness by their elected negotiators, they took measures into their own hands by staging several wildcat strikes. When they were ordered back to work by the strike-ending legislation, many thousands of them defied the government edict for several days before reluctantly submitting. Had they received the slightest encouragement from the leaders, Canada would have witnessed the spectacle of a mass defiance of Parliament by 120,000 citizens. These workers are now completely disillusioned with the whole railway labour-management system. Many are fed up with their own unions, or at least their present union leaders. The debacle that ended

their strike last summer put the finishing touch to their disenchantment. The only thing that prevented them from engaging in further mass demonstrations of their displeasure was the size of the final wage settlement . . . more than double the 1964–65 wage increase.

Finn concluded that the bitterness engulfing Canadian labour ranks was liable to unleash a new round of 'illegal work stoppages', and if it did not it 'certainly bodes ill for any peaceful settle-ment of the next round of negotiations'. More repression, he prophesied, would make working-class upheavals of 1966 seem 'like a tea party by comparison' (Finn, 1965: 5). It is critical to appreciate the wildness of the wildcat wave, for it proved a forceful, if transitory, reminder that the much-heralded post-war settlement was less than universally welcomed by the first generation of workers tasting the actual fresh fruit, both bitter and sweet, of its offerings.

Not all of the wildness made front-page news and generated editorial attack in the nation's mainstream press. Some of it was so mundane that it often went unnoticed. But it was no less wild for being unheralded. It was not particularly surprising that young auto workers at Chrysler, Ford, and de Havilland plants routinely rebelled against the company imposing compulsory over-time, but when they wildcatted, and won, the right to be let off work early to attend a St Thomas, Ontario hockey tournament in which their buddies were playing, it was a sign that the times were definitely changing (Gindin, 1995: 147). A general malaise at being subject to 'barnyard disci-pline', arbitrarily dispensed by junior executives, prompted a wildcat walkout of Chrysler auto-mobile assembly plant workers. Peterborough's Firestone employees wildcatted in March 1966, fed up with managers treating them 'like imbeciles, like cattle' (Carrothers, 1966: 387, 437; 'Firestone

Wildcat Ends. . .', 1969). A walkout at a Canadian Westinghouse Limited plant involving 185 unionists developed when the Local's President refused to be time-studied. With both the company and the International union contending that the work stoppage was illegal, the wildcatters met with a representative of the union leadership, but 'voted overwhelmingly to remain out and tell the executive to go to hell' (Carrothers, 1966: 425, 433; McBride, 1987: 23).

Stevedores seemed particularly susceptible to wildcat fever, usually of the kind that many would dismiss as rather frivolous. They walked off the Montreal docks, 3,500 strong, on a spring April 1966 day to voice their displeasure at police ticketing their cars parked adjacent to the waterfront. If any of their longshoring brethren were disciplined for transgressions involving drinking, job action was often immediate. The Toronto docks were shut down in June 1966 when harbour police manhandled a longshoreman accused of having an open bottle of beer in a public place, slapping the unionist with a summons against his protestations that he had not been drinking and had merely found the half empty brew as he was unloading cargo. Hamilton's lakeside facilities were subjected to three wildcat walkouts over the course of ten days in November 1965. 'All three apparently were in protest against suspensions that followed liquor violations,' the Globe and Mail reported soberly, noting that the job actions, unsupported by the union, were 'frustrating work at the docks at the peak of the busy end of the season' (Carrothers, 1966: 539–40).

Given what the post-war settlement was supposed to accomplish, and the order unions were expected to achieve in Canada's workplaces, this was all fairly wild. But the wildcats often got even wilder as pent-up frustrations exploded in violence. The largest wildcat in the 1965–66 upsurge, the illegal walkout of thousands of Inco workers, was a key case in point. As contract negotiations faltered in the summer of 1966, the wildcat spread from one operation to another and eventually, outside of all official union control, it took on the trappings of a 'wartime military machine', with illegal strikers using 'walkie-talkies' to communicate and threatening to disable a transport helicopter Inco was using to get supervisory personnel into company facilities. With provincial police appearing on the scene, the wildcatters armed themselves with lengths of pipe, baseball bats, steel bars, and ominous clubs. Roads were blockaded, hydro and telephone lines sabotaged, and a supply truck en route to the plant was stopped, overturned, and rolled down a hill. Shipments of nickel to the United States were stopped dead in their tracks. The Toronto Telegram reported that some pickets carried shotguns and were prepared 'to take on all comers'. Reports of firearms being discharged at Inco's Port Colborne refinery, where 1,800 employees soon joined their Sudbury counterparts, left a management team quaking in their air-lifted boots, incarcerated behind picket lines and awaiting supplies from the company helicopter. When a settlement was finally reached, and the dissident picket lines came down, worker discontent was barely assuaged by the company's wage concessions, which saw increases of almost 30 per cent for skilled tradesmen, a bonus of five-week vacations on top of regular holiday time for all workers with half-a-decade of service under their belts, and greatly enhanced indemnity benefits for those unable to work because of sickness or accident. Some strikers refused to report for the midnight shift as the Inco rebellion ground to a halt in mid-September 1966. One steelworker official confessed his wonderment at the wildness, obviously relieved that it was winding down: 'I saw the Molotov cocktails, the guns, and the dynamite.

The union lost control of the situation. Eventually we took truckloads of arms of one kind or another away from the picket lines.'[19]

The situation was equally explosive in August 1966, as Hamilton's imposing Stelco operations were brought to a standstill by an illegal work stoppage. When USWA leaders invited picket captains at the four struck Stelco gates to send a dozen representatives each to the Union Hall to meet with the Negotiating Committee between 200–300 angry workers rushed the building. Panicked by what they interpreted as a growing 'mob psychology', union officials called the police, which merely made matters worse. 'Get the fuzz out of here. This is our hall. They have no right here!' screamed a militant striker. Union leaflets declaring that there was no authorized strike at Stelco, deploring 'leaderless, direction-less, and futile' actions of 'irresponsible' elements, reminding the militants that there would be no strike relief or welfare for those engaging in the walkout, and insisting that all must return to work at their normal shifts, were torn from stewards' hands, crumpled, piled in the street, and burned. Then, according to one obviously less than progressive union official, the militants danced and howled around the pyre, 'just like a load of . . . indians'. The USWA placed newspaper adver-tisements urging the wildcatters to terminate their illegal actions, took to radio airwaves to suppress the strike, and asked police to close down taverns in the vicinity of Stelco, thereby depriving the discontented workers of both venues to meet and places to bolster their bodies with food and drink. Eventually idling 12,500 production workers and 3,500 non-union office staff, the Stelco strike, soon supported by wives of the wildcatters, erupted in a 'fist-swinging, gouging' battle between police and company guards, on the one hand, and a 'surging mob of 2,000 steelworkers' on the other. Arrests, assaults, and arson characterized the day, which also witnessed a mass sit-down of strikers that clogged a major Hamilton thoroughfare. Hanging over the USWA until 1 September 1966, the uprising at Stelco eventually cooled, but not until the company bumped its contract offer consider-ably, workers had an opportunity to turn down one union-endorsed potential agreement, and management promised it would at least review the cases of 51 workers fired or suspended for their role in the violent early August illegal job action.[20]

These were not blips on the class struggle radar screen. Labour violence in 1965–66 seemed endemic.[21] This wildness of the 1965–66 strike wave prompted the Ontario state to haul an 82-year-old Justice Ivan Rand out of his judicial mothballs, setting him up to inquire into the increasingly tempestuous climate of industrial 'disputes'. Ostensibly instigated by the Peterborough Tilco strikers' violation of an injunction limiting them to 12 pickets, the Rand inquiry ranged broadly over a number of issues relating to strikes, lock-outs, and the legal responsibilities of contending parties in the camps of labour and capital. Rand and his provincial royal commission entourage traversed the province (and undertook some inter-national junkets as well), accumulating testimony that totalled 5,000 pages. So masculinist were the assumptions of the inquiry, which undoubtedly pegged the problematic nature of class struggle on the picket line behaviour of combative males and the ascending *machismo* of union bargaining teams, as well as the stereotypical passivity and hen-pecking anti-unionism of women, that, as Joan Sangster notes tellingly, *not one woman* testified before the whole commission. Ironically enough, as the Rand Commission convened in Toronto, 100 workers at Hiram Walker Limited wildcatted when their bosses refused three of their number an opportunity to attend the hearings.[22]

Rand was no longer the far-seeing progressive that he had been heralded as in 1946. Instead, his approach to the wildness of class battle as it had been enacted in 1965–66 was increasingly troubled. An advocate of progressive, responsible, freedom-loving unionism, Rand prided himself on his expertise in law *and* labour relations, and had no time for the new breed of unionist who refused to see the courts and the police as esteemed protectors of basic rights. Haranguing one labour figure who failed to bow in deference to the majesty of the law, instead arguing that it dripped with class unfairness and collusion, Rand railed: 'I am astonished you have the opinion of the police and the courts that you do when they protect you from thugs you talk as if they are utterly irresponsible. I know more about the courts than you do and I say there is nothing of the sort.' Rand recoiled from civil disobedience, mass picketing, and strike discipline that prevented scabs from entering workplaces—in short, the entire 1945 edifice of militant tactics that Windsor's Ford workers had used to good effect in prompting his arbitration decision that would stand for two decades as the cornerstone of the post-war settlement. In a stumbling statement, Rand reiterated the fundamental importance of law (and the necessary legality of any strike action), retreating into a defence of beleaguered employers who now faced, in his view, a trade unionism that was more often than not an all-too-powerful adversary (Rand, 1968: 6, 18, 29–30).[23]

The learned Justice was no fan of the wildness of wildcat workers. He claimed that history had not exactly absolved them. Small wonder, for Rand's survey of wildcat strikes showed that the law had been anything but a friend to the wild: in the approximately 110 Ontario strikes that Rand's data identified as having taken place during the life of collective agreements in the 1965–66 wildcat

wave, almost 75 of these walkouts were slapped with some kind of disciplinary retribution. Fines were levied, arrests made, injunctions granted, employees dismissed, suspended, or reprimanded, and strikes declared illegal. Rand agreed with the notion that this kind of restraining rod should not be spared. Even granting that many union officials also took umbrage at the wildness of the wildcatters, few in the ranks of the workers' movement had much good to say about the final published Rand report. For the most part, it was regarded as 'a textbook for the promotion of conflict and turmoil in Ontario's industrial relations'.[24]

Politics and the Wildness of Working-Class Upheaval

Justice Ivan Rand saw little politics in the 1965–66 labour revolt, save for the bad manners of those who did not accept the boundaries of restraint in civil society. There was nevertheless no disguising the extent to which some of the wildness of the mid-1960s was related to a working class experiencing an often intense politicization.

This was evident in Quebec, for instance, where some of the violence associated with working-class upheaval blurred into the class-ordered struggles of the rising independence movement. A shoe factory, for instance, was the site of ongoing picket line violence pitting non-union workers against striking unionists. *Independantistes* associated with the Front de Libération du Quebec (FLQ) stepped into the fray. Dragging on for the better part of a year, the 1965–66 battle culminated in a bomb explosion that killed a 64-year old secretary and left eight others injured, closing the plant (Carrothers, 1966: 544; Black Rose Editorial Collective, 1972: 21; Kostash, 1980: 216–17). May 1965 saw a flurry of FLQ-associated bombings at various work sites and struck companies. In Drummondville, the Dominon Textile works were bombed as 5,000 CNTU-affiliated workers walked picket lines, their job action having commenced in March. Twenty-four hours before 4,000 Montreal postal workers commenced wildcat strike action a bomb was defused at the Peel Street Post Office. Job actions in a variety of economic sectors were marred by violence, dynamite, and Molotov cocktails being the incendiary devices of choice. In an underground memo written in 1966, the FLQ's Pierre Vallières indicated that the organization's 'military action is limited to sabotage, bombings, and organizing strikers' self defence,' largely through detonating 'token explosions' during workers' walkouts (Fournier, 1984: 81, 97–9). Some Quebec strikes of these years were also joint efforts of unionists and members of the Rassemblement pour l'indépendence nationale. One such confrontation, involving the Dominion Ayers Company, a plywood concern in Lachute, began in the summer of 1966 and reached into early autumn. It culminated in a huge solidarity rally that was broken up by company guards on 'Tear Gas Sunday', as security forces battled workers and their supporters with batons, tossing tear gas canisters into the crowd. Molotov cocktails sailed back in reply. The next day a bomb was left near the Ayers plant. Even the company President's domestic residence did not go unscathed, rampaging strikers and their allies stoning the house and setting its grounds on fire (Fournier, 1984: 109; McBride, 1987: 27).

Paced by Montreal's Central Labour Council and its fiery President, Michel Chartrand, the CNTU unions moved aggressively to the left in the 1965–68 years, challenging imperialist war in Vietnam and issuing radical manifesto-like statements that widened the political parameters of trade unionism. Pressing for labour to struggle not only for the rights of organized workers, the CNTU embraced the causes of the unorganized, the unemployed, tenants, and consumers. This, in turn, paved the way for the tremendous explosion of class militancy in Quebec's Common Front mobilizations of 1970–72. Industrial unionists and teachers, craft unions and radical supporters marched arm-in-arm as French Canadian workers launched massive work stoppages and general strikes in March–April 1972, the rebelliousness tamed only with back-to-work legislation, crippling fines levied by the courts against the unions, and selective imprisonment of labour leaders (Black Rose Editorial Collective, 1972; Drache, 1972; Palmer, 1992: 312–13; Palmer, 2003: 37–8; McKay, 2005: 185–8).

None of this class conflict was unrelated to the emergence of a radical nationalist movement that identified with the oppressed and exploited proletariat and found itself increasingly at odds with the centralized power of Canadian federalism. Montreal May Days in the 1960s became huge festivals of alternative thought and practice, the vessel of parade overflowing with working-class and radical nationalist content. The CNTU embraced the cause of incarcerated Front de Libération du Quebec members, demanding their release, and separatists such as Pierre Vallières steeled themselves in class conflict defeats like the *La Presse* journalists' strike of 1964–65. Taxi drivers and students waged war at Montreal's airport, battling police in a 1968 show of force protesting the monopoly held by the Anglo-Canadian firm, Murray Hill, over prime limousine and cab service pick-up properties. At an October 1969 demonstration of the Mouvement de Libération du Taxi, a violent encounter at the entryway to the Murray Hill Limousine Company, in which a Molotov cocktail was thrown, ended with a security guard firing a twelve-gauge shotgun into the crowd. An undercover Quebec Provincial Police officer, rumoured to have been functioning as an *agent provocateur* among the militant protesters, was mysteriously killed. Montreal mail-truck drivers formed their own cooperative company and eventually secured certification as a CNTU affiliate, managing, as well, to win the lucrative federal contract from Canada Post. This victory was soon undermined by the federal Liberal Party's decision, in February 1970, to divide the delivery of mail among four different companies. For two-and-a-half years *les gars de Lapalme*, as the drivers dubbed themselves, battled Ottawa and eventually their own union. They employed sabotage, intimidated drivers who took their jobs, and were not shy about the use of violence. In the short span of six months, the striking mail drivers damaged 1,200 postal boxes, attacked 662 postal trucks, vandalized 104 postal stations, and inflicted and suffered 75 reported injuries. Seven dynamite explosions were attributed to them, their ranks thinned by 102 arrests. Still, *les gars de Lapalme* turned out in force to give Pierre Elliott Trudeau the proverbial jeering raspberry on Parliament Hill. They were not pleased at experiencing Trudeau's shift in gears from his days as a 1950s advocate of Quebec's working class to the federal government's Minister of Justice and, eventually, Prime Minister of the country. Faced with their taunts, Trudeau snapped back in kind: 'Mangez de la merde!' (Allnutt and Chodos, 1969: 20–8; auf der Maur, 1970: 19–25, 1971: 32–40; Vallieres, 1971: 208–9; Chodos and auf der Maur, 1972: 43; Kostash, 1980, 217–19; Morton, 1980: 267; Fournier, 1984). The post-war settlement was impolitely imploding.

In English Canada, youthful, militant working-class nationalism often took the mid-to-late 1960s form of antagonism to the old guard, international unions, headquartered in the United States.[25] Fully 1,125,000 workers, or almost 72 per cent of the ranks of organized employees in Canada, belonged to 110 such American-affiliated unions,

the largest of which were the USWA, the UAW, and the Brotherhoods of Carpenters & Joiners, Woodworkers, Electrical Workers, and Pulp & Paper Mill Workers. Only the rising public sector unionists, concentrated in the 84,000-strong Canadian Union of Public Employees, as well as the 32,100 CBRT railway workers, cracked the top ten unions in Canada in terms of their memberships. By the mid-1970s, public sector unionism in Canada, necessarily organized in national unions and thus different than the internationals of old, had expanded considerably and created a dramatic shift in the relations within the upper echelons of the labour movement. The percentage of organized workers belonging to international unions in 1975 had dropped to just over 51 per cent, and CUPE and the Public Service Alliance of Canada, with their combined memberships of 250,000 in 1970, now rivaled steelworkers and autoworkers in terms of numerical significance. In the mid-1960s these developments were in the making, rather than already accomplished. Canadian workers often represented small minorities within their international unions: in the early 1960s, USWAers from Canada constituted just under 11 per cent of the International's dues payers, while the comparable percentages for machinists, labourers in the auto sector, and packinghouse workers ranged from 4.5 to 6.7 to 21.9. Among Quebec workers, of course, nationally-organized unions were stronger, headed by the powerful CNTU, and the francophone state was even known to launch assaults on the American-based internationals ('U.S. Union. . .', 1965).[26] But in English Canada there was no mistaking the weight of so-called international (really bi-national) unionism.[27]

As the rebellious atmosphere of the 1960s permeated the unions, the American-based internationals were often, rightly or wrongly, subject to critique by dissident Canadians, who regarded them as ossified junior partners in a project of imperialist colonization and class collaboration.[28] In the USWA the critique of American domination grew out of a highly politicized left–right factional split in the union that related to the longstanding feud between the ultimately victorious Steelworkers and their communist rivals, the Mine Mill and Smelter Workers Union. That battle was settled by the time of the wildcat wave of 1965–66, but advocates of Canadian unionism revived discontent with their calls for an autonomous labour movement. In Hamilton, the Stelco wildcat of 1966 was led by an Autonomy Group, described by Bill Freeman as 'a loosely organized collection of young inexperienced activists' who, in spite of their rather lacklustre coherence, effectively parlayed a fusion of popular nationalism, militancy, and anti-establishment bravado into loud attacks on 'sell-out' contracts and the complicity of the local and International leadership with management. During the illegal walkout there was much talk that the American leadership had cajoled Hamilton's USWA officials to force their dissident ranks back to work so that precious strike funds could be preserved in the event they were needed to support job actions in the United States (Flood, 1968: 68–9; Freeman, 1982: 97). If the Steelworkers were not necessarily guilty of bleeding Canadian unionists for dues (in the 1968–70 years Canadian USWA members contributed just over $4 million to the International's coffers, but drew out well over $12 million, in what amounted to a $55 subsidy for each Canadian member), other American-based unions could not make the same claim. In 1962–67 the Internationals collected a massive $166,322,000 in Canada, but returned less than $99,000,000 to union locals north of the border. American-based leaderships were not shy in using heavy-handed methods to coerce Canadians into compliance with their wishes. As the wildcat wave

wound down, fully 26 Canadian union locals had been placed under trusteeship by their American headquarters (Finn, 1970: 770, 774).

A series of breakaways and successions by Canadian union locals in the late 1960s and early 1970s wracked the International Brotherhood of Pulp, Sulphite, and Paper Mill Workers, International Union of Operating Engineers, the International Molders and Allied Workers Union, and the Retail, Wholesale and Department Store Union, as well as other unions headquartered in the US. This represented, in Finn's words, 'the first stirrings of the nationalist ferment now bubbling up within Canadian labour'. If stifled, Finn warned, the result would be that these 'incipient rumblings' would lead to a 'titanic—and ultimately successful—struggle for Canadian union emancipation'. The body of workers organized in truly independent English-speaking Canadian unions was small by the end of the 1960s, roughly 124 organizations with a membership of 60,000, but they were nevertheless a voice of discontent with the Internationals and their often staid leaderships. They had served vocal notice that they would not allow themselves to be easily subordinated to American leaders. Particularly among metal trades and smelter workers in British Columbia, there existed an ongoing challenge to the bureaucratized leaderships of the established Internationals, which included a successful raid of the nationalist Canadian Association of Smelter and Allied Workers (CASAW) against the USWA local at the Alcan works in Kitimat. As a former President of the Trail Steelworkers local proclaimed in 1969, 'The younger workers, because of the environment they've been brought up under and seeing the fallacies of their society, these have a stronger feeling of anti-Americanism. It's there, let's not kid ourselves, not only in Canada but all over the world.' One Inco wildcatter had declared in 1966 that Canada was 'on the verge of a revolution . . . when we see what is being taken out of this country by the Americans we are fed up. We want action' (Finn, 1968: 40, 1970: 766–74; Morris, 1972: 90–100; Knox and Resnick, 1974; Resnick, 1977: 178–89; Palmer, 1988; Palmer, 1992: 318–20; King, 1998).

Labour Walking a New Line

As young workers rampaged outside of plants closed by wildcats, as injunctions prohibiting picketing brought forth a deluge of denunciation in which the law was questioned if not repudiated, and as established unions and their conventional structures of collective bargaining, as well as their respectable leaderships, were chastised and jeered, labour seemed to be walking a newly unruly line in the mid-1960s. It threatened the post-war settlement. We are used to seeing this labour-capital accord undermined by capital and the state, a process that Leo Panitch and Donald Swartz have outlined rigorously in a detailed examination of post-1973 socio-economic trends and government 'back-to-work' and other kinds of restrictive, anti-labour, legislation (Panitch and Swartz, 1993). But the irony of the 1965–66 wildcat wave was that an initial blow at the system of so-called industrial pluralism was struck from within the House of Labour, albeit by workers who did not see

themselves as owners of the respectable domicile. As this happened, long established understandings of workers' place, in company and union, were challenged and, in particular instances, came under violent assault.

Journalists referred to a 'new labour revolution, with all its threat of turmoil', suggesting that it had 'only just begun' (James, 1966: 29). They spoke with more insight than they knew. For the true possibility of revolution lay in politicizing young and rebellious workers in the ideas and programmatic commitment to social transformation that grew out of workplace relations but that necessarily reached past the confining experiences of life on the assembly line or in the mine or mill. The task was to expand the political horizons of those trapped in the limitations of industrial legality and unions, which were brokered at every point by their own containments. Around the corner of the wildcat wave of 1965–66 was a growing left challenge, one that, had it co-joined youth of the university and the unions, could well have reconfigured the nature of twentieth-century Canada. Class difference is a difficult hurdle to leap, however, and as campus youth and women joined the unruly workers of the 1960s in an explosive embrace of militance and opposition, they did so, ultimately, divided from one another, in separate and unequal mobilizations.

Notes

1. As an introduction to the unravelling of the post-war settlement and the contours of contemporary class struggle unfolding in its wake see Panitch and Swartz, *The Assault on Trade Union Freedoms*; Yonatan Reshef and Sandra Rastin, *Unions in the Time of Revolution: Government Restructuring in Alberta and Ontario* (Toronto: University of Toronto Press, 2003); Bryan D. Palmer, 'System Failure: The Breakdown of the Post-War Settlement and the Politics of Labour in our Time', *Labour/Le Travail* 55 (Spring 2005): 334–46; Steven High, *Industrial Sunset: The Making*

of North America's Rust Belt, 1969–1984 (Toronto: University of Toronto Press, 2003).

2. For a preface to the class confrontation of the decade see G.F. MacDowell, *The Brandon Packers Strike: A Tragedy of Errors* (Toronto: McClelland and Stewart, 1971); Sam Gindin, *The Canadian Auto Workers: The Rise and Transformation of a Union* (Toronto: Lorimer, 1995), 139–66; Wayne Roberts, *Cracking the Canadian Formula: The Making of the Energy and Chemical Workers Union* (Toronto: Between the Lines, 1990), 91–104.

3. The following section draws directly on evidence and argument in Bryan D. Palmer, *Working-Class Experience: Rethinking the History of Canadian Labour, 1880–1992* (Toronto: McClelland and Stewart, 1992), 278–80. Much of the raw data is drawn from the 'Labour Force' tables in F.H. Leacy, ed., *Historical Statistics of Canada*, 2nd edn. (Ottawa: Statistics Canada, 1983). See, as well, Panitch and Swartz, *Assault on Trade Union Freedoms*, 14–16; Stuart Marshall Jamieson, *Times of Trouble: Labour Unrest and Industrial Conflict in Canada, 1900–1966* (Ottawa: Queen's Printer, 1968), 480–483; and for a more general discussion of youth and its influence in the 1960s, Doug Owram, *Born at the Right Time: A History of the Baby Boom Generation* (Toronto: University of Toronto Press, 1996).

4. As evidence from Paul Axelrod, *Scholars and Dollars: Politics, Economics, and the Universities of Ontario, 1945–1980* (Toronto: University of Toronto Press, 1982), esp. 141 suggests, while enrolment in and expenditure on higher education rose substantially from 1962–68, it would not be until the later years of this period that such trends would register in relevance for working-class youth. See as well John Porter, *The Vertical Mosaic: An Analysis of Social Class and Power in Canada* (Toronto: University of Toronto Press, 1965), and for numerical data for the mid-1960s, Dimitrios I. Roussopoulos, 'Towards a Revolutionary Youth Movement and an Extraparliamentary Opposition in Canada', in Roussopoulos, ed., *The New Left in Canada* (Montreal: Our Generation Press, 1970), 136; Julyan Reid, 'Some Canadian Issues', in Tim Reid, ed., *Student Power and the Canadian Campus* (Toronto: Peter Martin, 1969), 7.

5. Aside from the quantitative data drawn from *Historical Statistics of Canada* note, as well James W. Rinehart, *The Tyranny of Work* (Don Mills, Ontario: Academic Press, 1975), 4, 57, 70; Michael Humphries, 'The Insensitivity of the Union Movement to the Real Need of Union Members', *Relations Industrielles/Industrial Relations* 23 (October 1968): 610 [hereafter *IR*]; Gil Levine, 'The Coming Youth Revolt in Labour', *Labour Gazette* 71 (November 1971): 722–32.

6. As introductions only see Myrna Kostash, *Long Way from Home: The Story of the Sixties Generation in Canada* (Toronto: Lorimer, 1980), esp. 107–44; Kenneth Westhues, 'Inter-Generational Conflict in the Sixties', in Samuel D. Clark, J. Paul Grayson, Linda M. Grayson, eds, *Prophecy and Protest: Social Movements in Twentieth-Century Canada* (Toronto: Gage, 1975), esp. 394–8.

7. H.D. Woods, Chairman, *Canadian Industrial Relations: The Report of the Task Force on Labour Relations* (Ottawa: Privy Council Office, 1968), 99. Although from a slightly later period, note as well Levine, 'The Coming Youth Revolt in Labour', 722–30.

8. For a particularly virulent attack on the superficial aspects of youth revolt see Peter Desbarats, 'The Most Forgettable Generation: A Sad Glance at the Exhausted New Wave of Revolutionary Youth', *Saturday Night* 84 (September 1969): 35–6.

9. In the United States a number of journalistic commentators focused on the growing alienation of young workers in the late 1960s, and the consequent eruption of 'blue collar blues' and trade union rebelliousness. See Judson Gooding, 'Blue Collar Blues on the Assembly Line', *Fortune Magazine* July 1970; 'Strike Fever . . . And the Public Interest', *Life Magazine* 26 August 1966; Ken Weller, *The Lordstown Struggle and the Real Crisis in Production* (London: Solidarity, n.d. circa 1970); Bill Watson, *Counter-planning on the Shop Floor* (Somerville, MA: New England Free Press, 1971); Emma Rothschild, *Paradise Lost: The Decline of the Auto-Industrial Age* (New York: Random House, 1973). William Serrin, *The Company and the Union* (New York: Knopf, 1973), 39 notes that the number of official grievances at General Motors in the United States rose from 6,000 in 1960 to 256,000 in 1969.

10. Note as well, J.H.G. Crispo and H.W. Arthurs, 'Industrial Unrest in Canada: A Diagnosis of Recent Experience', *IR* 23 (April 1968): 237–64; Levine, 'Coming Youth Revolt of Labour'.

11. See also Sam Gindin, *The Canadian Auto Workers: The Birth and Transformation of a Union* (Toronto: Lorimer, 1995), 143.

12. Standard statements on wildcat strikes can be found in Alvin W. Gouldner, *Wildcat Strike* (Yellow Springs, OH: Antioch Press, 1954); Martin Glaberman, *Wartime Strikes: The Struggle Against the Nonstrike Pledge in the UAW during World War II* (Detroit: bewick/ed, 1980), 35–61; James W. Rinehart, *The Tyranny of Work* (Don Mills, ON: Academic Press, 1975), 71–3; Maxwell Flood, 'The Growth of the Non-Institutional Response in the Canadian Industrial Sector,' *IR* 27 (1972), 603–15; Maxwell Flood, 'Some Reflections on Wildcat Strikes', *Summation* 1 (June 1968): 1–14; Maxwell Flood, *Wildcat Strike in Lake City* (Ottawa: Queen's Printer, 1968).

13. The above paragraphs draw on Palmer, *Working Class Experience*, 280, summarizing Jamieson's data; Jamieson, *Times of Trouble*, 371, 397; Joy McBride, 'The Wildcat Wave: Rank-and-File Rebellion in the

Canadian Labour Movement, 1965–1966', unpublished paper, Queen's University, 17 August 1987, in possession of the author. On inflation and wage demands see James, 'Labour Lays it on the Line', 25; Greenspan, 'Wages and Wildcats', 244; Carrothers, *Study of the Labour Injunction*, volume 2, 399–408, 586; 'Construction Workers End Montreal Strike', *Labour Gazette* 66 (July 1966): 349.

14. On the opposition to injunctions see A.W.R. Carrothers, *Report of a Study on the Labour Injunction in Ontario*, volume 1 (Toronto: October, 1966); and the illuminating article by Joan Sangster, '"We No Longer Respect the Law": The Tilco Strike, Labour Injunctions, and the State', *Labour/Le Travail* 53 (Spring 2004): 47–88. Carrothers, *Report of a Study on the Labour Injunction in Ontario*, volume 2 (Toronto: October 1966), contains reprints of *Globe and Mail* articles from September 1965 to September 1966 relating to the 1965–66 labour upsurge. This collation of material was prepared for Carrothers by M.T. Mollison and is an extremely valuable source. Specific items relating to the *Oshawa Times*, Tilco, and other injunction-related strikes and actions are found on 313–56, 520–31. See also Donald C. MacDonald, Letter to the Editor, *Globe and Mail*, 2 August 1966; *Globe and Mail*, 12 February 1966; Ed Finn, 'The Lessons of Oshawa', *Canadian Dimension* 3 (January–February 1965): 7–8; P. Kent, 'Ontario Unionists Defy Injunctions', *Workers Vanguard*, March 1966. On the British Columbia context see Benjamin Isitt, 'Working Class Agency, the Cold War, and the Rise of a New Left: Political Change in British Columbia, 1948–1972', Preliminary draft of PhD dissertation, presented to University of New Brunswick, 2007, Chapter 10.

15. See also Carrothers, *Study of the Labour Injunction*, volume 2, 409; Roberts, *Cracking the Canadian Formula*, 100; Paul Phillips, *No Power Greater: A Century of Labour in B.C.* (Vancouver: BC Federation of Labour, 1967), 164; Ross Dowson, 'Urge General Strike as Judge Jails BC Leaders', and 'BC Labor Debates Injunctions Policy', *Workers Vanguard*, mid-September 1966 and mid-October 1966; and for background to the BC labour opposition to the injunction, A.W.R. Carrothers, *The Labour Injunction in British Columbia, 1946–1955: With Particular Reference to the Law of Picketing* (Toronto and Montreal: CCH Canadian, Limited, 1956).

16. The above paragraphs draw on standard accounts of such battles in Jamieson, *Times of Trouble*, 422–46, which contains the report on Inco's wage offer (432); Flood, *Wildcat Strike in Lake City*; Bill Freeman, *1005: Political Life in a Union Local* (Toronto:

James Lorimer, 1982), 99–116; Mr Justice Samuel Freedman, *Report of Industrial Inquiry Commission on Canadian National Railways 'Run-Throughs'* (Ottawa: Queen's Printer, 1966), 69–80; Stephen G. Peitchinis, *Labour–Management Relations in the Railway Industry* (Ottawa: Queen's Printer, 1971); Ed Finn, 'Why Canadian Workers Are Kicking', *Canadian Dimension* 4 (January–February 1967), 4–6; Stephen T. Wace, *The Longshoring Industry: Strikes and their Impact* (Ottawa: Queen's Printer, 1968); 'Longshoremen's Strike Ends—With Reservations', *Labour Gazette* 66 (September 1966), 497; Jean-Claude Parrot, *My Union, My Life: Jean-Claude Parrot and the Canadian Union of Postal Workers* (Halifax: Fernwood, 2005), 5–20. For the comment on postal workers' and union leadership see 'Wildcat Strike Poses Question: Are Leaders Out of Touch with Members?', *Globe and Mail*, 19 November 1965. Note as well Marvin Gandall, 'The Labour Movement: Two Decades Ago', *Canadian Dimension*, 18 (October–November 1984): 35–37.

17. A sense of the Teamster strike's volatility can be gleaned from press reports culled from the *Globe and Mail* and gathered in Carrothers, *Study of the Labour Injunction*, volume 2, 357–367, 383, 431. See, as well, Jamieson, *Times of Trouble*, 427–9; Arthur Kruger, 'Strike Wave—1966', *Canadian Forum* (July 1966): 73–4; 'Brief Trucker Strike Sparked by Rebels', *London Free Press*, 4 October 1965; Graeme McKechnie, *The Trucking Industry* (Ottawa: Queen's Printer, 1968); P. Kent, 'Ontario Teamster Lockout Projects Battle Cry—No Contract, No Work!' and 'Teamsters Solid, 40-hr. Week Now', *Workers Vanguard*, mid-January 1966 and April 1966.

18. On the role of youth in the Stelco wildcat see Freeman, *1005*, 100–8; Flood, *Wildcat Strike in Lake City*, 9, 70–2; 'Vote to End Stelco Strike', *Globe and Mail*, 8 August 1966, also in Carrothers, *Study of the Labour Injunction*, volume 2, 381.

19. On the Inco wildcat see especially Carrothers, *Study of the Labour Injunction*, volume 2, 367–78; Jamieson, *Times of Trouble*, 429–32; Flood, 'The Wildcat Strike', 253, quoted in McBride, 'Wildcat Wave', 43; and Bryan D. Palmer, *Working-Class Experience: Rethinking the History of Canadian Labour, 1800–1991* (Toronto: McClelland and Stewart, 1992), 317.

20. The most detailed account is in Flood, *Wildcat Strike in Lake City*, which forms the evidence base for the discussion in Freeman, *1005*, 99–114. See also Carrothers, *Study of the Labour Injunction*, volume 2, 378-383; Jamieson, *Times of Trouble*, 433–5.

21. For official recognition of the problem of violence see Woods, *Canadian Industrial Relations*, 133.

22. In this paragraph and below I draw on Joan Sangster's account of Ivan Rand, *Report of the Royal Commission Inquiry into Labour Disputes* (Toronto: Queen's Printer, 1968) in 'Tilco Strike', 71–82. Sangster notes the Hiram Walker wildcat (73), citing *Toronto Telegram*, 23 March 1967.
23. See also, Sangster, 'Tilco Strike', 77–8.
24. My rough calculations from the tables in Rand, *Report Into Labour Disputes*, 232–49; Douglas Fisher and Harry Crowe, *What Do You Know about the Rand Report?* (Don Mills, ON: Ontario Federation of Labour, 1968); Ed Finn, 'Labour: The Rand Report,' *Canadian Dimension* 5 (September–October 1968), 7–8.
25. For a brief, popular introductory statement see Walter Stewart, *Strike!* (Toronto: McClelland and Stewart, 1977), 117–31.
26. 'U.S. Unions Attacked by Lesage', *Montreal Star*, 16 June 1965. This kind of state attack on international unionism was rare in English Canada, although

politicians seeking office could voice it in specific circumstances. See John Crispo, *International Unionism: A Study in Canadian–American Relations* (Toronto and New York: McGraw-Hill, 1967), 294, citing 'Home Rule Asked for Labour Unions', *Globe and Mail*, 16 July 1964.
27. The standard account of international unionism in Canada in the mid-1960s is Crispo, *International Unionism*. For the figure on international union members as a percentage of all Canadian unionists in 1975 see Stewart, *Strike!*, 131.
28. See, for period-type critiques, Roger Howard and Jack Scott, 'International Unions and the Ideology of Class Collaboration', and Charles Lipton, 'Canadian Unionism', in Gary Teeple, ed., *Capitalism and the National Question in Canada* (Toronto: University of Toronto Press, 1972), 68–87, 102–19; Jack Scott, *Canadian Workers, American Unions: How the American Federation of Labour took over Canada's Unions* (Vancouver: New Star, 1978).

References

Allnutt, Peter, and Robert Chodos. 1969. 'Quebec into the Streets', *Last Post* 1 (December): 20–8.

auf der Maur, Nic. 1970. 'Montreal's Cabbies Fight City Hall', *Last Post* 1 (April): 19–25.

———, 1971. 'Les Gars de Lapalme', *Last Post* 2 (October): 32–40.

Black Rose Editorial Collective. 1972. *Quebec Labour: The Confederation of National Trade Unions Yesterday and Today*. Montreal: Black Rose.

Canadian Dimension. 1973. 'Trouble on the Line', 9 (August–September): 10–11.

Carrothers, A. 1966. *Report of a Study on the Labour Injunction in Ontario*, volume 2. Toronto: n.p.

Chodos, Robert, and Nic auf der Maur, eds. 1972. *Quebec: A Chronicle, 1968–1972*. Toronto: James, Lewis, and Samuel.

Drache, Daniel, ed. 1972. *Quebec: Only the Beginning: The Manifestoes of the Common Front*. Toronto: New Press.

Dumas, Evelyn. 1974. 'The New Labour Left in Quebec', in Dimitrios I. Roussopoulos, *Quebec and Radical Social Change*. Montreal: Black Rose.

Finn, Ed. 1965. 'The New Militancy of Canadian Labour', *Canadian Dimension* 3 (November–December).

———. 1967. 'Why Canadian Workers Are Kicking', *Canadian Dimension* 4 (January–February).

———. 1968. 'Prospects for an Autonomous Labour Movement', *Canadian Dimension* 6 (September–October).

———. 1970. 'The Struggle for Canadian Labour Autonomy', *Labour Gazette* 70 (November): 766–74.

Flood, Maxwell. 1968. *Wildcat Strike in Lake City*. Ottawa: Privy Council Office.

Fournier, Louis. 1984. *FLQ: The Anatomy of an Underground Movement*. Toronto: NC Press.

Freeman, Bill. 1982. *1005: Political Life in a Union Local*. Toronto: James Lorimer.

Gindin, Sam. 1995. *The Canadian Auto Workers: The Rise and Transformation of a Union*. Toronto: Lorimer.

Globe and Mail. 1965. 'Wildcat Strike Poses Question: Are Leaders Out of Touch with Members?', 19 November.

Globe and Mail. 1966. 'A Plague of Strikes', 31 May.

Globe and Mail. 1966. 'The More Sensible Course', 2 June.

Globe and Mail. 1966. 21 June.

Greenspan, Louis. 1967. 'Wages and Wildcats', *Canadian Forum* (February): 245.

James, Mungo. 1966. 'Labour Lays it On the Line', *Saturday Night* (December): 27–8.

Jamieson, Stuart Marshall. 1976. *Times of Trouble: Labour Unrest and Industrial Conflict in Canada, 1900–66*. Ottawa: Task Force on Labour Relations.

King, Al, with Kae Braid. 1998. *Red Bait! Struggles of a Mine-Mill Local*. Vancouver: Kingbird.

Knox, Paul, and Philip Resnick, eds. 1974. *Essays in BC Political Economy*. Vancouver: New Star Books.

Kostash, Myrna. 1980. *Long Way from Home: The Story of the Sixties Generation in Canada*. Toronto: Lorimer.

McBride, Joy. 1987. 'The Wildcat Wave: Rank-and-File Rebellion in the Canadian Labour Movement, 1965–1966'. Unpublished paper, Queen's University.

McKay, Ian. 2005. *Rebels, Reds, Radicals: Rethinking Canada's Left History*. Toronto: Between the Lines.

Morris, R.B. 1972. 'The Reverter Clause and Break-Aways in Canada', in Gary Teeple, ed., *Capitalism and the National Question in Canada*. Toronto: University of Toronto Press.

Morton, Desmond. 1980. *Working People: An Illustrated History of Canadian Labour*. Ottawa: Deneau and Greenberg.

Palmer, Bryan D. 1992. *Working-Class Experience: Rethinking the History of Canadian Labour, 1800–1991*. Toronto: McClelland and Stewart.

———. 2003. '40 Years of Class Struggle', *Canadian Dimension* 37 (November–December): 37–8.

———, ed. 1988. *Jack Scott and the Canadian Workers Movement, 1927–1985*. St John's, NL: Committee on Canadian Labour History.

Panitch, Leo, and Donald Swartz. 1993. *Assault on Trade Union Freedoms: From Wage Controls to Social Contract*. Aurora, ON: Garamond Press.

Peterborough Examiner. 1966. 'Firestone Wildcat Ends as Workers Return', 7 March.

Rand, Ivan. 1968. *Report of the Royal Commission Inquiry into Labour Disputes*. Toronto: Queen's Printer.

Resnick, Philip. 1977. *The Land of Cain: Class and Nationalism in English Canada, 1945–1975*. Vancouver: New Star Books.

Townshend, Peter. 1965. 'My Generation'. Recorded 13 October 1965, Pyle Studios, London, England. Towser Tunes, Inc/Fabulous Music, Ltd/ABKCO Music, Inc.

Vallières, Pierre. 1971. *White Niggers of America: The Precocious Autobiography of a Quebec 'Terrorist'*. New York: Monthly Review Press.

Woods, H.D. 1968. *Canadian Industrial Relations: The Report of the Task Force on Labour Relations*. Ottawa: Privy Council.

CHAPTER 24

'Rapprocher les lieux du pouvoir': The Québec Labour Movement and Québec Sovereigntism, 1960–2000

Ralph P. Güntzel

In recent years the Québec labour movement has undertaken great efforts to advocate the idea of a sovereign Québec nation state. Having made the promotion of sovereignty a keystone in their respective political action programs in 1990, the province's three major labour union centrals, the Fédération des travailleurs et travailleuses du Québec (FTQ), the Confédération des syndicats nationaux (CSN), and the Centrale des syndicats du Québec (CSQ), actively campaigned for a 'yes' in the 1995 referendum on sovereignty. Even after the sovereigntist option had been defeated in the referendum, the three centrals reiterated their commitment to propagating sovereignty. However, Québec labour's recent policy stands in stark contrast to its initial reaction to the rise of sovereigntism. During the first half of the 1960s, when modern sovereigntism first emerged, the three centrals defended Canadian unity. During the second half of the 1960s and the 1970s this position gave way to an increasingly pro-sovereigntist orientation. It will be the purpose of this essay to trace and explain Québec labour's sovereigntist turn.

The Three Federations and the Emergence of Sovereigntism, 1960–1967

Since the mid-1960s unionization rates in Québec have oscillated between 35 and 40 per cent, thus making Québec the most densely unionized society in all of North America, except for Newfoundland (Rouillard, 1982; Dionne, 1991; Allaire, 2000). During the period from 1960 to the present, the vast majority of Québec's unionized labour force belonged to affiliates of either the FTQ, the CSN, or the CSQ. Of the three centrals, the FTQ was—and continues to be—the largest. At present, almost half a million workers, or nearly 45 per cent of unionized workers in the province, hold FTQ membership cards. The CSN has about a quarter of a million members, while about 140,000 workers belong to the CSQ. While the FTQ membership has traditionally been dominated by private- and secondary-sector workers, currently about one third of its members work in the public sector. The CSN underwent a transformation from a central, dominated by private- and secondary-sector workers, to one dominated by public- and tertiary-sector workers during the 1960s and early 1970s. Having originally served as the corporate body of Québec's francophone primary- and secondary-school teachers, the CSQ added other public sector-workers since the late 1960s and, thus, became a veritable public-sector central (Dionne, 1991).[1]

During the last four decades, the three centrals devoted considerable energies to political action. During much of the 1960s, the three centrals subscribed to social-democratic reformism, which aimed at 'civilizing' rather than destroying capitalism. The centrals' social-democratic vision entailed state interventionism, economic planning aimed at providing for full employment, extended welfare-state services, the democratization of the workplace, redistributive taxation policies, and the abolition of poverty. During the late 1960s and early 1970s, the centrals espoused an increasingly radical discourse, largely in response to a series of public-sector conflicts with the provincial government. While the FTQ radicalized its rhetoric, but continued to adhere to social-democratic reformism, the CSN and CSQ espoused anti-capitalist positions inspired by a Marxist analysis of capitalism and the role of the state. . . . The two centrals continued to promote socialism until the early 1980s. Not having made much headway in raising an anti-capitalist consciousness among their members, the CSN and the CSQ discontinued their socialist discourse and began to undergo a deradicalization process. By the mid-1980s they once again adopted social-democratic positions (Rouillard, 1982; Fournier, 1994).

Québec labour was first confronted with the idea of a sovereign Québec nation-state in the early 1960s when the Rassemblement pour l'indépendance nationale (RIN) and several other small sovereigntist organizations sprang up. Most of these organizations were influenced by anti-colonial struggles in Africa and Asia. . . . The RIN stressed that Québec was the political embodiment of the French-Canadian nation and that nations must strive for sovereign nation-state status. The RIN also argued that Québec must separate from Canada in order to provide an effective framework for the cultural survival and economic development of the French-Canadian nation (Chaput, 1961; Bourgealt, 1982).

Most parts of Québec labour rejected the RIN's arguments. Many unionists regarded nationalism as an inherently conservative ideology (*Monde ouvrier*, 1969; Keable, 1998). Some unionists also rejected sovereignty because they approved of Canadian federalism. . . . Other unionists took a more critical attitude toward Canadian federalism, but feared that an independent Québec would jeopardize, rather than improve, the condition of the French-Canadian nation. They were particularly concerned that sovereignty might entail economic turbulence, rising unemployment, and declining standards of living (*Labour Gazette*, February 1962: 136–7). Thus, during the early and mid-1960s, both the FTQ and the CSN flatly opposed the notion of a sovereign Québec (Cyr and Roy, 1981; Güntzel, 1993).

By the mid-1960s, however, more and more members of FTQ and the CSN became attracted to Québec nationalism. Nationalist attitudes were particularly strong among the mine workers who belonged to the FTQ-affiliated Québec section of the United Steelworkers of America (QcUSWA). The mine workers had a long history of acrimonious conflict with their English-Canadian or American employers. Having created the mining towns of northern Québec, English-Canadian companies such as Noranda Mines Ltd. or American companies such as the Iron-Ore Co., dominated life in the small communities and exercised a tremendous hold on the miners' lives even outside the workplace. The economic division in the mining towns was accentuated by a cultural division of labour. As one high-ranking civil servant in the Québec Ministry of Natural Resources noted in 1965:

> Attez à Rouyn-Noranda. Là-bas, vous allez voir deux economies qui vivent une côté à l'autre. La petite économie, celle qui est le lot des Canadiens français: les garages, les postes d'essence, les épiceries, les mineurs bien entendu. Tout ce monde-là c'est en grande majorité des Canadiens francais. A côte d'eux, ou plutôt en marge d'eux, vous avez la Noranda, la grande économie de la place. A partir d'un certain niveau dans l'echelle de cette économie, on vit en anglais, on travaille en anglais, on habite un quartier qui n'est pas celui du pompiste ou de l'épicier, d'ailleurs—ce n'est pas par hasard—on est entre Canadiens anglais surtout. (Bamber, 1965: 69)

French-speaking workers were disgruntled with this ethnic hierarchy. . . .

The anguish of French-speaking miners in the company towns of northern Québec was further aggravated by the companies' opposition to the workers' attempts to unionize. Even if they managed to establish local union sections, the miners were forced to negotiate in English and continuously faced staunchly anti-union policies aimed at crushing local union sections (Gérin-Lajoie, 1982: 76–87; Rouillard, 1982). In this situation the miners enthusiastically welcomed the reform of the Québec labour code in 1964, which increased union security and stipulated that the workers could choose the language of the collective agreement (Gérin-Lajoie, 1982: 125–8, 142). The revision of the labour code was one of the reforms the Québec Liberal government undertook under the instigation of René Levesque, its Minister of Natural Resources. . . . In 1965, Jean Gérin-Lajoie, candidate of the nationalist wing, was elected QcUSWA director. Following Gérin-Lajoie's election victory the QcUSWA began to advocate special status for Québec within Canada (Gérin-Lajoie, 1982: 174).

The CSQ opted for a similar constitutional solution. As teachers using the French language as a medium of instruction, CSQ members reproduced an essential part of French Canada's distinctive culture. Hence, cultural survival played a crucial role in their outlook on the question of Québec's constitutional status. This vantage point led many CSQ members to a critical assessment of Canadian federalism's ability to safeguard the French language and French-Canadian culture (Gervais, 1961). In a memorandum adopted in 1964, the CSQ charged that Canadian federalism promoted English Canada's culture to the detriment of French Canada's culture. . . . The original draft of the document had even advocated, 'la souveraineté politique et économique du Québec' in combination with, 'une structure pan-canadienne composé à part égale des représants des Etats nationaux'.[2] The central's enlarged executive, however, eschewed the associated-states model as not reflective of the opinion held by the majority of the membership and replaced it with a call for an ill-defined, but less controversial, special status for Québec.[3]

For both the QcUSWA and the CSQ espousal of the special status formula constituted but a temporary step on their way to an endorsement of sovereignty. For the time being, however, they were held back by two concerns: first, the economic risks involved in sovereignty; and second, their distrust of pro-sovereignty politicians and parties. Soon the sovereigntist movement began to evolve in a way that greatly diminished both concerns.

The FTQ and the Ascendancy of Social-Democratic Sovereigntism, 1967–1976

Having broken with the Liberal Party over the issue of Québec's constitutional status, in 1967 Lévesque founded the Movement Souveraineté-Association (MSA). In 1968 the MSA merged with another sovereigntist party to form the Parti Québécois (PQ), with Lévesque at its helm. The PQ significantly changed the outlook of sovereigntism in two respects. First, it discontinued the use of the term 'French-Canadian nation' and instead used the term 'Québec nation'. Second, it departed from the pure separatism of the RIN and other earlier sovereigntist organizations and espoused sovereignty-association, a constitutional formula, which advocated political sovereignty for Québec alongside continued economic association with Canada. . . . Drawing on Lévesque's political clout, the PQ developed a social-democratic programme and soon became the province's most important left-of-centre political party (Murray, 1976; McRoberts, 1988: 218–19, 238–62).

The arrival of the PQ had a profound impact on Québec labour, since after 1968 support for sovereignty increased significantly among union activists. While the PQ's sovereignty-association formula

failed to entirely eliminate fears about the potential risks involved in severing Québec's political ties with Canada, it did reduce them. Indeed, growth of prosovereignty sentiment was not limited to public-sector workers, who enjoyed a certain safety valve due to relatively high employment security. It also spread to private-sector unions including, most noticeably, the QcUSWA. When Lévesque left the Liberal Party, his popularity with QcUSWA members was such that many of them spontaneously adopted a more sympathetic attitude toward sovereignty. . . .

Political events during the late 1960s and early 1970s further increased the appeal of the PQ among organized labour. In 1969 the provincial government passed Bill 63, which provided for English-language education wherever it was demanded. Many French-speaking Québecers feared that the bill might accelerate the integration of newly arrived immigrants into the English-speaking community and, thus, adversely affect their own upward social mobility and even threaten the survival of the French language in Québec. In this situation, the three federations joined the PQ in calling for French unilingualism. Meanwhile, the federal government headed by Pierre Elliott Trudeau pursued centralist policies based on the premise that Québec was a province like all others. These policies collided with many Québecers' hopes for the devolution of federal powers to the Québec government. Frustration with Trudeau's policies reached a peak in 1970, when the federal government invoked the War Measures Act in response to activities of the terrorist Front de libération du Québec (FLQ). Under the Act, several hundred sovereigntists, including many labour activists, were arrested. While some saw the military intervention as justified, others, including the PQ and the three centrals, opposed it as an undue infringement on civil liberties and human rights.

The language debates, Trudeau's centralism, and the October Crisis, polarized Québec society, but also increased the size of the sovereigntist camp.[4]

In the 1973 provincial elections the PQ won one third of the popular vote (Fraser, 1984). In the elections several union members ran as PQ candidates. One of them was QcUSWA staff member Clément Godbout. Like other unionists, Godbout saw sovereignty as a means to end the cultural division of labour which he had experienced in his formative years as a mine worker in Abitibi-Témiscamingue. . . . According to Godbout, sovereignty and social democracy were interconnected. . . .

Godbout professed not to fear the possible economic repercussions of sovereignty. When members of a QcUSWA local at International Harvester aired their concern that the company might transfer production outside Québec in case of a PQ election Victory, Godbout replied that companies made decisions about production transfers solely on the basis of business considerations. Companies would stay or move out of Québec if doing so would increase their profit margin, regardless of the constitutional status of Québec (Richard, 1972: 3). . . .

In the absence of any polls or internal estimates, it is difficult to assess the degree of popularity which sovereignty attained within the FTQ as a whole during the early and mid-1970s. Given the QcUSWA estimates, it is unlikely that rank-and-file support for sovereignty across the FTQ exceeded 40 per cent. The majority of the central's executive, including president Laberge still opposed sovereignty for economic reasons (Fournier, 1992). Support for the PQ, however, was more widespread than support for sovereignty, because even federalist unionists were attracted to the PQ's social-democratic program.[5] In 1975, the FTQ convention adopted a resolution endorsing the PQ. The resolution noted that the PQ did not constitute a workers' party, but emphasized that it was the party closest to organized labour (Fournier, 1994). Most convention delegates agreed. About 80 per cent of the delegates polled indicated their preference for the PQ over other parties (*Monde ouvrier*, January 1976: 3). The 1975 FTQ convention sealed a rapprochement with the PQ that had been in the making since 1968.

The CSN, the CSQ, and the Rise of Socialist Sovereigntism, 1970–1976

While the PQ's social-democratic programme elicited favourable responses among some unionists, in particular in the private sector, it met with suspicion among others, in particular in the public sector. By the early 1970s, the CSN and the CSQ underwent a radicalization process whereby both centrals adopted anti-capitalist positions which became increasingly incompatible with social-democratic reformism. As a result of the radicalization process, by 1972–73, the leadership of both centrals became dominated by socialists. Most of these socialists opted for sovereignty. They did so because they saw it as an essential component of national liberation and because they believed that pan-Canadian solidarity did not constitute a viable option to achieve socialism. As the CSN's Montreal regional council argued in a 1972 position paper, progressive movements born in English-speaking Canada were doomed to fail in Québec, while progressive movements born in Québec were consigned to the same fate in the rest of Canada. . . .

The CSN's and CSQ's socialist sovereigntists took their cue not from the PQ, but from ideas that had been diffused during the mid-1960s in left-wing journals such as *Parti pris* and *Révolution québécoise*. The left-wing contributors to these journals had claimed that national liberation was meaningless without social emancipation and called for the creation of an independent and socialist Québec. While one group of writers affirmed that independence constituted a first step toward the creation of a socialist society in Québec (*Parti pris*, September 1964: 14), another group declared that independence and socialism must come about simultaneously (Bourque and Dostaler, 1980). Adherents of the two-step model argued that Québec's working class lacked political consciousness and, thus, was incapable of leading the struggle for national liberation. Partisans of the one-step model retorted that neither the petty bourgeoisie nor the bourgeoisie, but only the working class, could be counted upon to bring about national liberation. Despite lengthy debates, the two groups did not arrive at a consensus. Although their discourse had led a marginal existence in the shadows of mainstream sovereigntism, as propagated by the RIN and the PQ, it attracted a sizeable following among young intellectuals. During the second half of the 1960s many of them joined public-sector unions or began to work for CSN and CSQ suborganizations. . . .

Although socialist sovereigntists dominated the CSN and CSQ executives by the mid-1970s, they remained a minority in their respective organizations. An internal CSQ poll conducted in 1973 suggests that about 42 per cent of the central's members supported sovereignty-association. About 12 per cent opted for independence without economic association. Without doubt, the level of support for sovereignty in the CSQ exceeded that in the CSN. CSQ members possessed higher employment security than many CSN members, and thus tended to be less moved by considerations of sovereignty's potentially adverse economic repercussions. Moreover, as noted previously, CSQ members had a direct stake in the status of French as the dominant language. As the poll revealed, almost all of those in favour

of sovereignty-association or independence were convinced that sovereignty would be beneficial for the maintenance and development of Québec's distinct cultural identity centered around the French language. Only a minority of them were persuaded that sovereignty would ameliorate the situation of the working class. In short, most CSQ unionists were swayed by mainstream sovereignty ideas as propagated by the PQ rather than by socialist sovereigntists (Güntzel, 1999).

CSN and CSQ leaders staunchly believed in the need to create a workers' party to the left of the PQ. Since there was little support for such a project among the rank-and-file, the leaders of the two centrals decided to stick to their organizations' traditional neutrality regarding party politics. Unable to nudge along the process of creating a workers' party, they were caught in a vicious circle. Although they resented the PQ, for the time being they had nowhere else to go. Among the major parties in the province only the PQ advocated a progressive program and stood a chance of toppling the liberal government, which the CSN and CSQ leaders loathed. . . . Paradoxically, on the eve of the 1976 provincial elections, the CSN and CSQ both hoped for and feared a PQ victory (Fournier, 1977: 15–16).

The FTQ and the First Referendum on Sovereignty, 1976–1980

In 1976 the Lévesque-led PQ won the provincial elections with about 40 per cent of the popular vote and, thus, came to power a mere eight years after its creation. Having promised to hold a referendum on sovereignty-association, preparing the referendum constituted one of the priorities of the Lévesque administration. In the meantime, the new government also implemented various reforms in areas of direct concern to organized labour. In 1977, the government adopted Bill 101, which strengthened the status of French in Québec. The bill contained a stipulation, which gave workers the right to work in French in all enterprises with at least 50 employees. In the same year, the PQ government also revamped key aspects of the provincial labour code. The new labour code simplified certification procedures, increased union security, and limited employers' rights to hire strike breakers. In 1979, the government passed an industrial health and safety bill, which introduced improved health and safety standards in the workplace and set up a system by which employers and employees became jointly responsible for putting the new standards into practice. Although the reforms addressed long-held union grievances, they did not meet with uniform approval among the three centrals.[6]

The FTQ warmly applauded the government's reforms and maintained a cordial relationship with the Lévesque administration. . . . Unlike the FTQ, both the CSN and the CSQ eschewed a cooperative type of relationship with the Lévesque administration. Two reasons accounted for this approach. First, the socialists who dominated the federations wished for the emergence of a socialist workers' party. Such a party, however, could get off the ground only if a sufficient number of PQ sympathizers would switch allegiances. Thus, criticizing the PQ government was the first step toward the creation of a political alternative to its left. Second, since most CSN and CSQ members worked in the public sector, both federations perceived the Lévesque administration not only as the provincial government but also—and perhaps most importantly—as the employer and, hence, antagonist. To cooperate with the employer might well have meant to weaken one's bargaining position. An attack on the PQ government's shortcomings, in contrast, constituted a promising build-up for the

1979 public-sector negotiations (Güntzel, 1993, 1999).

The same attitudes that guided the three centrals' policies in relation to the PQ government's reformism, also coloured the positions they adopted in view of the impending referendum on sovereignty-association. At the November 1979 FTQ convention the executive presented a working paper which noted that . . . the parallel jurisdiction of the governments in Ottawa and Québec City in economic matters translated into a waste of resources and the absence of an effective economic development policy in Québec. Thus, a concentration of powers either in Ottawa or in Québec City was necessary. The federal government could not be trusted to make the right decisions for Québec, the paper claimed, since it had traditionally given priority to the industrial development of southern Ontario and the agricultural development of the Prairie provinces. Having thereby ruled Ottawa out, the paper concluded that Québec needed complete jurisdiction over economic policies and manpower training.[7] Since the working paper stopped short of endorsing sovereigntism without, however, rejecting sovereignty, it met with approval among both sovereigntists and federalists.

In December 1979, the PQ government announced that the referendum question would ask for a mandate to negotiate sovereignty-association. Given the content of the referendum question, consensus-building for an official FTQ position in view of the referendum became an easy task. Obviously, partisans of sovereignty were only too willing to recommend a 'yes' vote in the referendum. Federalists, too, rallied around a recommendation to vote 'yes'. To endorse a 'yes' vote meant to avoid alienating FTQ sovereigntists and the Lévesque administration without actually having to endorse sovereignty. Moreover, given their penchant for a special status for and a massive transfer of powers to Québec, FTQ federalists had reason to see negotiations *d'égal à égal* as the most promising means to bring about the change which they aspired to. . . .

The FTQ, though, was not content to merely recommend a 'yes' vote. Rather, the federation undertook great efforts to convince as many of its members as possible to vote 'yes.' At the end of the special convention Laberge called on his troops to give their best. 'D'ici le 20 mai vous n'avez plus le droit d'être fatigués ou malades, tout le monde à l'ouvrage.' Following the convention, the FTQ embarked on a full-fledged internal propaganda campaign. Numerous union meetings were devoted to convincing the undecided; FTQ officers toured the province; *Monde ouvrier* devoted its pages to the referendum; and FTQ affiliates set up a 'Regroupements des travailleurs pour le oui' and urged workers to sign lists in support of a 'yes' (*Monde ouvrier*, May 1980: 3; see also *Devoir*, 21 April 1980: 6, 15 May 1980: 8).

The CSN, the CSQ, and the First Referendum on Sovereignty, 1976–1980

Referendum-related debates in the CSN and the CSQ differed markedly from those in the FTQ. At the CSN's special convention in 1979, the central's enlarged executive presented a working paper on the national question, which was largely devoted to designing a socialist vision of society. The position paper charged that the federal government was responsible for Québec's economic underdevelopment relative to Ontario, because it had favoured southern Ontario to the detriment of Québec. The paper also accused the federalists of wanting to perpetuate Québec's national oppression and dismissed sovereignty-association as insufficient, since it did not envisage complete liberation from

the federal stranglehold. In order to end Québec's national oppression, the paper argued, the people of Québec needed to create a regime that would wrestle the strategic sectors of the economy from the hands of foreign capitalists. All essential industries must be nationalized and savings be centralized in a public capital fund, which would then become the centrepiece of a new industrial development policy. Publicly owned enterprises and the central capital fund would have to be controlled and administered '[par] la classe ouvrière en fonction des intérêts des travailleurs' (CSN, 1979: 74–5).

Subsequent to the reading of the working paper, the convention debated whether or not to go on record in favour of independence. The motion to endorse independence failed to get the support of CSN president Norbert Rodrigue and most other high-ranking CSN officers. Despite being favourable to independence, Rodrigue and his associates feared that such a stand might lead to internal divisions. Many CSN members remained opposed to sovereignty. Sovereigntists were divided between PQ sympathizers and socialist sovereigntists, who were split between moderates advocating the two-stage model and radicals promoting the one-step model. Fear of internal strife was not the only reason that motivated Rodrigue and his lieutenants. Like many public-sector unionists they felt that an endorsement of independence might strengthen the hand of the government in the approaching public-sector negotiations. In the absence of support from the central's most prominent leaders, the motion in favour of independence failed (Güntzel, 1993: 167–9). . . .

After further internal debates, the confederal council, the CSN's highest decision-making body between conventions, met in April 1980 to decide whether or not to recommend a 'yes' in the referendum. This time, all high-ranking CSN officers were in agreement. As Rodrigue told the council members, a victory of the 'yes' side would improve the chances of success in the struggle for a socialist society. Since the CSN had sufficiently established its critical distance to the Lévesque administration, a CSN recommendation to vote 'yes' could not be interpreted as an endorsement of either the PQ or its vision of society (Güntzel, 1993: 169). . . .

Unlike the FTQ, the CSN did not try to mobilize its members for a victory of the 'yes' forces. As the referendum campaign unfolded, the CSN looked on from the sidelines. The CSQ remained similarly aloof, albeit for different reasons.

At the 1978 CSQ convention, the executive presented a position paper, which argued that the Québec government needed to obtain more powers to redress Québec's weak economic structure and to defend and promote the French language. The CSQ executive also recommended that the central 'se prononce en faveur de l'indépendance du Québec et considère que la lutte pour l'indépendance est indissociable de la lutte pour une société que les travailleurs québécois ont à définir et à bâtir sur les plans économique, social, culturel et politique, en fonction de leurs intérêts.'[8] The convention resolved that the CSQ take a stand only after an internal referendum on Québec's constitutional status. There was severe disagreement, however, over the question to be asked in the internal referendum. PQ sympathizers wanted a question which offered a choice between independence as defined by the CSQ executive, sovereignty-association, and federalism. The socialists insisted that the question be limited to either accepting or rejecting the recommendation of the CSQ executive. After acrimonious debate, the socialists' proposal carried the day (Güntzel, 1999: 77–8).

In March 1979, all CSQ members received a questionnaire which asked them whether the central should participate in Québec's referendum debate and promote independence as a means of building a workers' society (Güntzel, 1999:

79). Many CSQ social democrats were irate. They supported sovereignty but opposed socialism. Their wish to be able to choose the former without having to endorse the latter had been repeatedly ignored. In this situation, the leaders of several CSQ affiliates decided to strike back against the CSQ's socialist executive. 'Nous n'acceptons pas,' they stated in a joint declaration to the media, 'que le débat [interne] soit mené de telle façon que le oui à l'indépendance soit assoçie automatiquement à un oui inconscient à une vision marxiste de la société québécoise.' Thus, they decided to oppose any participation of the CSQ in Québec's referendum debate (Rivières, 1979: 9). During the following weeks the front of rejection broadened. In the end, almost two thirds of those who returned the questionnaire rejected participation of the CSQ in Québec's referendum debate. Only 17.4 per cent had followed the CSQ executive and endorsed independence and socialism. In accordance with these results, the CSQ's special convention in June 1979 resolved non-intervention of the central in the referendum debate (Güntzel, 1999: 79–80).

The May 1980 referendum dealt the sovereigntist movement a severe blow as almost 60 per cent of the voters voted 'no'. There are no data indicating the voting behaviour of unionized workers in the referendum. Laberge subsequently estimated that about two thirds of the FTQ membership voted 'yes' (Fournier, 1992: 300). While this may be a somewhat exaggerated estimate, it is probable that more than half of the members of the three centrals voted 'yes'. Most likely, support for the 'yes' option was highest among QcUSWA miners and CSQ members. Irrespective of the voting pattern among unionized workers, the referendum outcome ended debates on sovereignty in all three centrals as well as within Québec society in general. Québec sovereigntism went into a prolonged decline.

The Three Centrals and the Decline of Sovereigntism, 1980–1985

Soon after the defeat of sovereigntism, the Trudeau-led federal government instigated negotiations on constitutional reform. After much acrimony, in November 1981 these talks resulted in agreement between the federal government and all provincial governments except Québec. The Québec government judged the constitutional revisions as unacceptable for Québec and refused to endorse them. Thus, when the British North America Act was officially replaced by the Constitution Act in July 1982, Québec remained outside the Canadian constitutional family (although the revised constitution did apply to Québec). Rather than having made Canadian federalism more attractive to Québec, the reform of 1981–82 enlarged the gulf between Québec and the rest of the country. The imposition of the Constitution Act further disillusioned Québecers who had been frustrated by the referendum defeat (Fraser, 1984: 279–301).

The decline of sovereigntism and the imposition of constitutional reform coincided with other developments, which left Québec labour morose. Against the backdrop of a severe economic crisis, both the CSQ and the CSN began to undergo a political-ideological deradicalization. The economic and political developments of the mid- and late-1980s further forced labour on the defensive. Like unions elsewhere, Québec labour found it difficult to come to terms with new issues such as privatization, deregulation, globalization, and free trade. Moreover, despite all consciousness-raising efforts during the 1970s, the creation of a socialist society remained as utopian and remote as ever. In this context, the CSN discontinued its socialist discourse by the mid-1980s. The CSQ had already ended its anti-capitalist rhetoric a few years earlier, as a direct result of the stalemate between reformists and radicals, which ensued from the referendum debate. By the end of the decade, both centrals had watered down their visions of social change and joined the FTQ in promoting social-democratic reformism. . . .

The crisis of the early 1980s increased unemployment and put increasing pressures on the provincial budget. In this situation the PQ government, which had been reelected in 1981, decided to cut expenses in the public sector. In April 1982, the government asked the public-sector unions to give up wage increases, which had been negotiated in 1979, for the period from August to December 1982. After the unions' refusal, in June 1982 the government legislated severe wage cuts for the first three months of 1983. In the fall of 1983 the government and the public-sector unions began negotiations for a new collective agreement. As the negotiations dragged on and a consensus remained elusive, the government legislated wages and working conditions in the public sector for the period from 1982 to 1985. The unions retaliated by going on strike in January 1983. The government passed back-to-work legislation and succeeded in splitting the common front of public-sector workers. By February 1983, the epic struggle came to an end when the CSQ, which had been the last part of the common front to hold out, agreed to a conciliation process. The conciliation verdict improved the government's terms only marginally (Rouillard, 1982: 388–93).

After the events of 1982–83, relations between the PQ and organized labour reached a low point. The government's treatment of public-sector workers left so much bitterness that even the FTQ, which had long been the PQ's ally in the labour movement and which was dominated by private-sector workers, did not endorse the PQ in the 1985 provincial elections (Fournier, 1992: 328–30). The elections resulted in a return to power of the Liberal Party under Robert Bourassa. In an ironic twist of fate, the Liberal reign during the second half of the 1980s and the first half of the 1990s resulted not only in a rapprochement between the PQ and the three centrals but also a resurgence of sovereigntism.

The Three Centrals and the Resurgence of Sovereigntism, 1985–1995

During the mid-1980s, the PQ undertook little to recuperate the social-democratic credentials it had lost in 1982–83. Under the leadership of Pierre-Marc Johnson, who had taken over from Lévesque as PQ president in 1985, it even shelved sovereignty in favour of autonomist nationalism, which it referred to as 'national affirmation'. In 1988, however, Jacques Parizeau, one of Lévesque's former lieutenants, succeeded Johnson as PQ leader. Under Parizeau the PQ once again stressed its social-democratic aspirations and reintroduced sovereignty as the centrepiece of its program. Prior to the 1989 provincial elections, Parizeau expressed his regret and apologies for the imposition of the wage and salary cuts in 1983. Shortly thereafter the FTQ returned to its tradition of recommending to vote for the PQ. . . . Although it lost the 1989 provincial elections, the PQ managed to recuperate some of the labour vote that had deserted the party in 1985 (Fraser, 1989: A7; Fournier, 1992: 348–9).

The resurgence of sovereigntism was intimately tied to the demise of the Meech Lake Accord. Signed by the first ministers in 1987, the accord was meant to make the constitution acceptable to Québec by adding several amendments including, most notably, a clause which recognized Québec as a 'distinct society'. The recognition of Québec's distinctiveness initially appeared as a significant victory for Bourassa, who had been one of the prime movers in the negotiations which had led to the accord. By 1989–90, however, the ratification

process of the amendment got bogged down. At the same time, public opinion polls revealed that more and more English-speaking Canadians opposed the notion that Québec constituted a distinct society. . . .

In Québec, the demise of the Meech Lake Accord revived old fears about cultural survival and increased skepticism about the capacity of the Canadian federal system to accommodate Québec. More importantly, it imbued many francophone Québecers with a strong urge to reassert their sense of group worth in the face of massive disparagement and rejection. In this situation, support for sovereignty quickly soared to the 60 per cent mark (Clouiter, Guay, and Latouche, 1992: 45). Economic considerations no longer acted as an elective counterweight, since Québec's economy had made great strides in the course of the 1980s. . . . By the summer of 1990, more Québecers than ever jumped on the sovereigntist bandwagon.

The developments convinced labour leaders that the time had come to commit their organizations to the promotion of sovereignty. Many leading unionists, such as CSN president Gérald Larose, had already supported sovereignty in the debates of the 1970s and 1980s. Others, such as FTQ president Laberge, had joined the sovereigntist camp subsequent to the 1980 referendum (Fournier, 1992: 262–3). For some time the leaders of the three centrals had regarded sovereignty as an important strategic goal which remained beyond reach. Yet, by 1990, sovereignty no longer appeared as elusive as it had during the 1980s. Unlike in the late 1970s and 1980s, in 1990 there were no major internal obstacles that made it difficult or undesirable for the centrals to endorse sovereignty. A decade earlier, some leaders and many rank-and-file members had opposed sovereignty. In contrast, by 1990, recalcitrant leaders and rank-and-file members had either espoused sovereignty in the course of the 1980s or became infected with the sovereigntist spirit that spread like wildfire through Québec society in 1990. Moreover, the differences between the sovereigntist factions, which had shaken the CSN and temporarily paralyzed the CSQ a decade earlier, faded as a result of the two centrals' de-radicalization. Thus, the fear of internal factionism no longer prevented the centrals from taking the next step in their sovereigntist evolution.

At its convention in early May 1990, the CSN became the first of the three centrals to endorse independence and commit itself to promoting sovereigntism (Berger, 1990: A4; Boileau, 1990: 3). In mid-May, Laberge informed the media that the FTQ would begin to actively promote sovereignty on 24 June, Québec's national holiday (Lortie, 1990: G3). A few weeks later, the CSQ followed suit. In the wake of an internal poll revealing that 74 per cent of the central's members supported sovereignty, the CSQ convention adopted a resolution which committed the CSQ to struggle for Québec independence (Berger, 1990: A20; Lévesque, 1990a: A12, 1990b). The sovereigntist pamphlets and memoranda, which the centrals produced in the summer and fall of 1990, stressed four points: first, Québec must attain sovereign nation-state status, because it is natural for nations to do so. 'We want Québec to be a country rather than a province,' the FTQ stated, 'because it is normal for a people to have a country and Canada will always be the country of others'; second, a sovereign Québec would be in a better position to safeguard the distinct character of Québec society; third, Canadian federalism constituted a burden without which Québec could conduct more efficient economic development policies; fourth, sovereignty would democratize Québec society. Sovereignty, the CSN declared, 'will strengthen the people's capacity to influence those who make

the decisions. It will help democracy to grow and function.' Hence, the CSN concluded, 'sovereignty will bring about more favorable conditions for fulfilling many demands of the unions and mass organizations' (Fiedler, 1991: 122–50).

In order to back up their sovereigntist discourse, the centrals became involved in several important political battles fought in Québec during the first half of the 1990s. After a renewed round of constitutional negotiations with first ministers from the rest of Canada, the Bourassa administration agreed to the Charlottetown Accord of August 1992. The accord included a watered-down version of the distinct-society clause which had played such a prominent role in the Meech Lake Accord (Fraser, 1992: A5; Picard, 1992: A5). On 26 October 1992, the Charlottetown Accord was put to a referendum vote in all parts of Canada. During the referendum campaign, the three centrals vociferously opposed the accord (*Devoir*, 9 September 1992: A2; Montpetit 1992: A6; Trudel, 1992: A2). Their efforts were rewarded as more than 55 per cent of voters in Québec voted 'no'. Having met with rejection in most other parts of Canada as well, the Charlottetown Accord became defunct (Bumsted, 1998: 387). The FTQ also supported the Bloc Québecois (BQ), which had been created in 1990 by a group of independent members of the House of Commons previously belonging to the Progressive Conservative Party. Led by Lucien Bouchard, a former Tory cabinet minister, the BQ espoused sovereignty and, thus, become the federal wing of the sovereigntist movement. In the 1993 federal elections, the FTQ urged its members to vote BQ. Bound by their traditional neutrality regarding party politics, the CSN and the CSQ refrained from following the example of the BQ. They both, however, supported individual BQ candidates. Again, the centrals' efforts were rewarded as the BQ won the vast majority of Québec ridings (Boileau,

1990: 20, 1993: A1, A12; O'Neill, 1993: A5; Truffaut, 1993).

The centrals also became involved in the 1994 provincial elections. Once again, the FTQ supported the PQ, while the CSN and the CSQ stopped short of officially endorsing the PQ. Their formal neutrality barely veiled their sympathies for the PQ. . . . It was thus with great satisfaction that the three centrals greeted the PQ election victory in 1994 (Cauchon, 1994: A2; Godbout and Massé, 1994: A11; Lévesque, 1994: A4). The coming to power of the PQ headed by Parizeau also set the stage for the second referendum on sovereignty. The referendum took place on 30 October 1995, and asked Québecers to agree that Québec become sovereign after having made a formal offer to Canada for a new economic and political partnership (Bumsted, 1998: 421–2).

During the months preceding the referendum, the three centrals once again engaged in a major propaganda effort. Besides reiterating earlier arguments in favour of sovereignty, they contrasted the social and collective nature of Québec's political culture with the liberal values of English-speaking Canada. . . . To strengthen Québec, the argument implied, meant to strengthen a political culture incompatible with the cold-blooded, neo-liberalism that had become popular in English-speaking Canada. The centrals also attacked the federalists' negative propaganda. Larose, for instance, dismissed statements by federal finance minister Paul Martin, who declared that the federal government would not negotiate a new partnership with Québec following a sovereigntist referendum victory. . . .

Despite the propaganda efforts of the three centrals and their allies, the referendum campaign got off to a poor start. For the first few weeks of the campaign, the sovereigntist camp trailed by a large margin in public opinion polls. The momentum

shifted though, a few weeks before the referendum, when Parizeau stepped to the side to make room for Bouchard. Once he had taken the helm of the sovereigntist campaign effort, Bouchard infused his troops with new energy and optimism. Drawing on his tremendous popularity with Québecers and stressing the need for self-respect and reparation for the humiliations of the past, Bouchard almost succeeded in turning a disastrous campaign into a triumph. When millions of Québecers and Canadians turned on their television sets, on the evening of 30 October 1995, the outcome of the vote remained very much in doubt. In the end, the sovereigntists garnered 49.4 per cent of the vote. Some 50.6 of the voters voted 'no'. The difference between the two camps was less than 55,000 votes out of a total of almost 4.7 million voters (Bumsted, 1998: 422–3). Like their sovereigntist allies, the three centrals shrugged off the narrow defeat and renewed their commitment to promoting sovereignty.[9]

Recent Developments and Prospects for the Future

As was the case after the first referendum on sovereignty, the 1995 referendum ushered in a period of public disinterest in the sovereignty option. Despite their efforts to the contrary, Québec sovereigntists have so far failed to recreate the enthusiasm for sovereignty that preceded the second referendum. While Québec's constitutional status has been relegated to the backburner, organized labour and the PQ government have focused on fiscal policies and their impact on the public sector.

In February 1996, Bouchard took over from Parizeau as Québec Premier. In this function, Bouchard promised to work toward building the conditions under which the sovereigntists could win the next referendum on sovereignty. Bouchard saw elimination of the deficit as one of the winning conditions. Soon after his inauguration, the new Premier declared that eradicating the deficit was unavoidable if Québec did not want to run the risk of losing potential investors to Ontario or New Brunswick, where governments pursued pro-business fiscal policies. According to Bouchard, the drastic treatment he envisaged was inspired by pragmatism, not neo-liberalism. . . .

While labour leaders had initially welcomed Bouchard's arrival at the helm of the PQ government (Cantin, 1995: B1), they lost much of their enthusiasm when confronted with Bouchard's deficit-elimination plan. By 1997–98, relations between organized labour and the government deteriorated, as the centrals tried in vain to shield the public sector from government cuts. Frustrated by the cuts, CSN and CSQ leaders accused the PQ government of pursuing neo-liberal policies. Yet, while labour's anti-government discourse became increasingly accusatory, it did not reach the hostility reserved for the oppositional Liberal Party, which the centrals' denounced for wanting to return to the savage capitalism of the nineteenth century (Cloutier, 1997; Lessard, 1997: B5). Relations between the Bouchard administration and the three centrals improved somewhat after the government balanced Québec's budget in 1998. . . .

Despite the temporary return to a certain degree of cordiality between organized labour and the government, both sides remain apart on social and economic issues. Organized labour continues to adhere to social democracy, while the PQ government combines pro-business policies with social-democratic elements. In all likelihood, there will be more conflicts over resource allocation between labour and the PQ government. Still, as long as the PQ will remain somewhere to the left of the liberals, these conflicts will not cause labour to turn its back on sovereignty. Although not entirely unconnected to the PQ's degree of progressivism, labour's support for sovereignty rests on more fundamental arguments. As Larose pointed out in May 2000, labour sees Québec society as more community oriented and Québec political culture as more social than the society and political culture of English-speaking Canada. Thus, sovereignty would diminish the influence English-speaking Canada's individualist social values and liberal, political-culture exercise on Québec via the federal government. In short, Québec sovereignty would create better conditions for implementing social-democratic policies. Political realignment in a sovereign Québec might even entail the creation of a workers' party, which would be a more faithful ally of organized labour than the PQ has been (O'Neill, 2000).

As long as labour continues to be inspired by its analysis of the fundamental differences between Québec and English-speaking Canada, it will pursue its sovereigntist orientation. Only a fundamental change in Québec's political culture may put this analysis into question. The PQ's recent cutbacks did not constitute such a change, especially if viewed in the context of the austere policies pursued by various governments in English-speaking Canada. Yet, even if Québec's social values and political culture, as well as the PQ's programme, were to take a turn to the right, Québec labour might hesitate to embrace federalism. After all, the political influence of the three centrals is limited to Québec. Since extension of this influence to Ottawa does not constitute a viable option, it is a much more rational strategy to demand increased powers for the government that Québec labour *can* influence. Thus, there are good reasons to expect that Québec labour will continue to support sovereigntism for some time to come.

Notes

1. See also FTQ, 'Membres affiliés', www.ftq.qc.ca/html/membres.html; CSN, 'La CSN au Québec', www.csn.qc.c/Pageshtml/MvntCSNque.html; CEQ, 'Profile of the CEQ', www.ceq.qc.ca/ceq/proa3.htm.
2. See Archives de la CEQ, Sainte-Foy, Québec (henceforth ACEQ), CIC, Procès-verbal, conseil provincial, 24–25 October 1964, 18.
3. ACEQ, CIC, Procès-verbal, conseil provincial, 17–19, 22–3.
4. On the language debate: Richard Jones, 'Politics and the Reinforcement of the French Language in Canada and Quebec, 1960–1986', in Michael Behiels, ed., *Quebec Since 1945: Selected Readings* (Toronto: Copp Clark Pittman, 1987), 228–30. On Trudeau's centralism: Kenneth McRoberts, *Misconceiving Canada: The Struggle for National Unity* (Toronto: Oxford University Press, 1997), 55–148. On the October Crisis: Jean-François Cardin, *Comprendre Octobre 1970: la FLQ, le crise et le syndicalisme* (Montréal: Éditions du Méridien, 1990).
5. ANQ, USWA Collection, P 144, 1A, 2, 200, R. Lemoine to J.M. Carle, 25 September 1972, 3; Louis Fournier, '"Changer le régime. . . avec le PQ!"—Louis Laberge', *Québec-Presse*, 27 May 1973, 11; Rob Bull, 'New steel union chief defends his PQ ties', *Toronto Star*, 26 February 1977: B4; Cyr and Roy, *Eléments d'histoire de la FTQ*, 134, 138.
6. On Bill 101: McRoberts, *Quebec*, 277–80. On the reform of the labour code and the health and safety bill: Rouillard, *Histoire du syndicalisme au Québec*, 424–5.
7. Archives de la FTQ, Montréal (henceforth: AFTQ), FTQ, *La FTQ et la question nationale: Congrès tenu à Québec du 26 au 30 novembre 1979* (Montreal, 1979).
8. ACEQ, CEQ, Procès-verbal, congrès, 1978, annexe, 80.
9. www.cam.org/_poursouv/presentation.html.

References

Allaire, Luc, and Nicole de Sève. N.d. 'La CEQ deviendra-t-elle la Centrale syndicale du Québec?', www.ceq.qc.ca/noubelle/mars00/congres.htm.

Bamber, James. 1965. 'Lévesque contre la Noranda', *Magazine Maclean* (November).

Berger, François. 1990. 'La CSN s'engage à promouvoir l'indépendence', *Presse*, 9 May: A4.

Boileau, Josée. 1990. 'La CSN travaillera à l'élection du souverainiste Gilles Duceppe dans Laurier/Sainte-Marie', *Devoir*, 14 July: 2.

———. 1990. 'Vote massif des délégués de la CSN pour le principe de l'indépendence du Québec', *Devoir*, 9 May: 3.

Boileau, Josée. 1993. 'Les syndicates investissent le Bloc québécois', *Devoir*, 11 April: A1, A12.

Bourgeault, Pierre. 1982. *Ecrits polémiques*. Montréal: Boréal.

Bourque, Gilles, and Gilles Dostaler. 1980. *Socialisme et Indépendance*. Montréal: Boréal.

Bumsted, J.M. 1998. *A History of the Canadian Peoples*. Toronto: Oxford University Press.

Cantin, Philippe. 1995. '"Nous sommes en danger d'opération dévastatrice", selon Gérald Larose', *Presse*, 30 November: B1.

Cauchon, Paul. 1994. 'Une rupture avec le discours néolibéral', *Devoir*, 2 December: A2.

Chaput, Marcel. 1982. *Pourquoi je suis séparatiste*. Montréal: n.p.

Cloutier, Edourad, Jean H. Guay, and Daniel Latouche. 1992. *Le Virage: l'évolution de l'opinion politique au Québec depuis 1960*. Montréal: Hurtubise.

Cloutier, Mario. 1997. 'Larose s'oppose à Bouchard', *Devoir*, 22 February.

CSN. 1979. *Procès-verbal, congrès special, 1979*. Montréal: n.p.

Cyr, François, and Rémi Roy. 1981. *Eléments d'histoire de la FTQ: La FTQ et la question nationale*. Montréal: Éditions Saint-Martin.

Devoir. 1980. 'Selon la direction de la FTQ, 70% des members de cette centrale centrale diront Oui', 15 May.

Devoir. 1992. 'Pour bien des raison la CEQ invite ses members à voter NON', 9 September: A2.

Dionne, Bernard. 1991. *Le syndicalisme au Québec*. Montréal: Boréal.

Fiedler, Richard. 1991. *Canada, Adieu? Quebec Debates its Future*. Lantzville, BC: Oolichan Books.

Fournier, Louis. 1977. 'La CSN: du PQ à un socialisme d'ici', *Jour*, 27 May.

———. 1992. *Louis Laberge: Le syndicalisme c'est ma vie*. Montréal: Éditions Québec Amérique.

———. 1994. *Histoire de la FTQ: 1965–1992: La plus grande centrale syndicale au Québec*. Montréal: Éditions Québec Amérique.

Fraser, Graham. 1984. *PQ: René Lévesque and the PQ in Power*. Toronto: Macmillan.

———. 1989. 'PQ elated over wins in semi-final', *Globe and Mail*, 27 September.

————. 1992. 'Parizeau says deal ensures decline', *Globe and Mail*, 26 September: A5.

Gérin-Lajoie, Jean. 1982. *Les métallos 1936–1980*. Montréal: Boréal.

Gervaise, Albert. 1961. 'Repenser la Confédération à neuf ou l'envisager . . . à 9', *Enseignement* (November).

Godbout, Clément, and Henri Massé. 1994. 'FTQ-PQ en neuf engagements', *Devoir*, 10 October: A11.

Güntzel, Ralph P. 1993. 'The Confédération des syndicates nationaux (CSN), the Idea of Independence, and the Sovereigntist Movement, 1960–1980', *Labour/Le Travail* 31 (Spring).

————. 1999. 'The Centrale de l'Enseignement du Québec and Quebec Separatist nationalism, 1960–80', *Canadian Historical Review* 80, 1 (March).

Keable, Jacques. 1998. *Le monde selon Marcel Pepin*. Outremont, QC: Lanctôt Éditeur.

Labour Gazette. 1962. 'Sixth Annual Convention of the Quebec Federation of Labour (CLC)', February.

Lessard, Denis. 1997. 'Les négociations ont refroidi l'ardeur syndicale pour le Bloc', *Presse*, 23 April: B5.

Lévesque, Lia. 1990a. 'Le congrès de la CEQ appelé à se prononcer en faveur de l'indépendence', *Devoir*, 26 May: A12.

————. 1990b. 'Les trois grandes centrals syndicales s'engagement à promouvoir la souveraineté', *Devoir*, 3 July: 2.

————. 1994. 'Les syndicates sont emballés, le patronat reste sur sa faim', *Devoir*, 30 November: A4.

Lortie, Marie-Claude. 1990. 'Plus souverainiste que jamais, la FTQ promet de mobiliser dès le 24 juin', *Presse*, 19 May: G3.

McRoberts, Kenneth. 1988. *Quebec: Social Change and Political Crisis*, 3rd edn. Toronto: McClelland and Stewart.

Monde ouvrier. 1966. 'Les deux solitudes se rencontrent. . .', January–February: 6

Monde ouvrier. 1976. 'Les délégues au congrès de la FTQ: Qui sont-ils?', January.

Monde ouvrier. 1980. 'Créer un "regroupement pour le oui" dans chaque milieu de travail', May.

Montpetit, Carole. 1992. 'Les centrals louent la lucidité des Québécois', 27 October: A6.

Murray, Vera. 1976. *La Parti québécois: de la fondation à la prise du pouvoir*. Montréal: Hurtubise.

O'Neil, Pierre. 1993. 'Une première: la CEQ se mouille', *Devoir*, 24 September: A5.

————. 2000. 'Gérald Larose au Devoir: l'heure n'est pas venue pour la gauche', *Devoir* [electronic edition – www.ledevoir.com], 27 May.

Parti pris. 1964. 'Manifeste 64-65', September.

Picard, André. 1992. 'Deal will bring era of security, Bourassa says', *Globe and Mail*, 23 September: A5.

Richard, Pierre. 1972. 'Le syndicat des métallos opte pour l'indépendence', *Devoir*, 14 January.

Rivières, Paule des. 1979. 'Trois syndicats d'enseignants contestent l'analyse marxiste de la CEQ', *Devoir*, 12 April.

Rouillard, Jacques. 1989. *Histoire du syndicalisme au Québec: Des origins à nos jours*. Montréal: Boréal.

Trudel, Clément. 1992. 'Congrès extraordinaire de la FTQ pour préciser son NON à l'entente', 17 September: A2.

Truffant, Serge. 1993. 'Le Bloc québécois plutôt que le NPD', *Devoir*, 20 September: A1, A8.

CHAPTER 25

From 'Mothers of the Nation' to Migrant Workers: Immigration Policies and Domestic Workers in Canada

Sedef Arat-Koç

In the last two decades, the legal status of domestic workers in Canada has worsened. In all countries where there are paid domestic workers, gender and class inequalities have largely structured their socio-legal status and working conditions. In Canada, however, historical variations in the status and conditions of domestic workers have more directly been linked to the histories of racism and immigration. Precisely at a time in Canadian history when citizenship rights were generally improving for women, the status and conditions of foreign domestic workers significantly deteriorated.

In line with other analyses (Daenzer, 1993; Villasin and Phillips, 1994; Bakan and Stasiulis, 1997), this chapter argues that changes in the racial/ethnic composition of migrant domestic workers have played an important part in this deterioration. This chapter traces the historically differential treatment domestic workers from different racial/ethnic backgrounds and different source regions have received from Canadian society and the state until 1970. It focuses in particular on the different state and societal interests, policies, and practices regulating British domestics and those foreign domestics deemed to be from 'less desirable' backgrounds.

Race, Citizenship, and Domestic Workers

Hidden in the household and considered 'women's work', domestic service has never enjoyed a favourable status. Even though subordination as women and as workers has been a universal condition of domestic workers in industrial capitalism, there is a specific relationship between the rights enjoyed by domestics and their relationship to, or membership in, the Canadian nation and the state. Most modern states are characterized by hierarchies of citizenship rights. Contrary to a model of universal citizenship whereby citizenship rights are accessible to all members of a society, some groups lack many or most such rights. Such groups can be said to exist within the boundaries of state regulation but outside the boundaries of the national collectivity, and with lesser access to state-provided citizenship rights. Women of colour, who have made up the majority of immigrant domestic workers arriving in Canada in the postwar period, are considered to be neither members of the Canadian nation nor citizen-members of the state. Yet highly regulatory immigration practices ensured that they were very much *inside* the state.[1]

Racism, Immigration, and Domestic Service

In Europe, class and gender inequalities were the main determinants of relationships in domestic service. In Canada, as well as in other settler colonies, racial and ethnic inequalities also played a very important role.[2] Immigration schemes, policies, and practices have been important mechanisms in regulating the racial/ethnic composition of society and determining the status and conditions of those who have been allowed in.

In Canada, domestic service has historically been often associated with forms of unfree labour. Contrary to popular opinion, slavery did exist in Canada until it was gradually eliminated in the late eighteenth and early nineteenth centuries. The first Canadian slaves were Native peoples, frequently Pawnee or Panis. Black slaves were also brought by their employers, who were often United Empire Loyalists. Most female slaves were employed as domestic servants (Bolaira and Li, 1985: 165; Barber, 1991: 3). Pervasive anti-black racism continued even once slavery was abolished in Canada and meant that black women had few labour market options beyond domestic service. Dionne Brand estimates that at least 80 per cent of black women in Canadian cities worked in domestic service as late as the 1940s (Brand, 1991).

At different times, some groups of white immigrant women who were recruited to provide domestic service also entered as unfree labour, but this did not have the same consequences for their future status and conditions in Canada. For many white women, domestic service was only a stage of life and a bridge to a different life. In New France, domestic service was often perforated by *engagés*, indentured servants from France whose passage had been paid in advance by their future employers. Given the small population of the white colony and the even smaller numbers of women, *engagés* were encouraged to marry immediately after the end of their bond. In some cases, they were even allowed to break their contract on condition of marriage (Prentice et al., 1988: 46; Barber, 1991: 3).

In the early nineteenth century, in the rural areas of Canada and the northern United States, local white women who were hired as domestics experienced less rigid status differences in relation to their employers. Called 'help' instead of 'servant', these were women who were hired for short periods of time to contribute to their families' income and/or to help a neighbour (Dudden, 1983; Barber, 1991: 4). The conditions of help contrasted sharply with relations in bourgeois households in the cities, where the social distance between employers and employees was growing. So significant were the rural/urban differences that *The Canadian Settlers' Handbook* advised prospective immigrant domestics that they would enjoy 'social amenities' in rural Canada, but that 'no lady should dream of going as a home-help in the cities, for there class distinctions [were] as rampant as in England' (cited in Lenskyj, 1981: 10).

The character of domestic service changed from the middle of the nineteenth century to the 1920s. As the urban middle-class family became more privatized, its emphasis on domestic comforts and luxury increased, and therefore it became dependent on outsiders to actualize its standard of a private haven. Changes in the nature of work, and among the workers performing this type of work, precluded improvements in working and living conditions for domestic workers. The separation of the public and private sphere and the decline in the general status of the domestic sphere corresponded with a rapid feminization of domestic service. Between early and late nineteenth century, within a period of approximately

60 years, the percentage of women among urban domestic workers grew from 50 per cent to 90 per cent (Lacelle, 1987).

Further contributing to a decline in the status of servants, or alternatively, in certain regions, to the persistence of their low status, was the availability of groups of vulnerable workers. In American regions where there were large concentrations of people of colour, it was usually women of the oppressed racial/ethnic groups who had no choice but to accept domestic service positions (Glenn, 1992). In Canada and the northeastern United States, different groups of white immigrants who were perceived as socially and indeed 'racially' inferior provided a source of vulnerable labour. Irish women who were fleeing economic desperation at home found almost no alternatives to domestic work and therefore became particularly vulnerable. In the 1870s, in all urban centres in Canada except Quebec City, Irish immigrants were so highly represented among domestics that domestic service came to be identified with Irish women. Claudette Lacelle found that over the course of the nineteenth century, popular perceptions of domestics became more unfavourable, the level of discipline to which domestic workers were subjected increased, and their working conditions deteriorated (Lacelle, 1987).

It was in the late nineteenth century that immigration began to be used systematically to recruit and control domestic workers. This was a time when the demand for domestic workers increased while the supply from among native-born women declined. The growth in demand corresponded to the high standards of housekeeping of a rising urban middle-class at a time when household technology remained underdeveloped and housework extremely laborious. The decline in supply was due to industrialization, which opened up new labour market options for working-class women—in factories, hospitals, offices, retail outlets, and schools. The conditions of domestic work, especially live-in service, were so unfavourable that working-class women with any other choice took the latter even if the pay was lower. As Canadian-born women came to shun the isolating and menial conditions of domestic service, ever-greater efforts were made to recruit immigrant women to meet the unabating demand.

The solutions sought to this shortage by both the state and a vibrant middle-class social reform movement 'focused more on maintaining the supply of workers through carefully supervised immigration than on reforming the conditions of household work' (Barber, 1987: 100). In the early twentieth century, more than one-third of domestic workers in Canada were foreign-born. In western Canada, the proportion was much higher. In 1901, in Winnipeg, as much as 84 per cent of domestic workers were born outside of Canada (Barber, 1987: 100, 1991: 7–8).

While the demands of the labour market for domestic workers encouraged recruitment of workers from abroad, the dominant forces in Canadian society and the state were selective about where domestics would be recruited from. After Confederation, the state began to regulate immigration through legislation and to use immigration policy as the major means of actively controlling the racial composition of Canada. Immediately after the completion of the railway in 1885, which relied on the back-breaking labour of some 15,000 Chinese male workers, the government passed a Chinese Immigration Act, which imposed steep head taxes on Chinese immigrants (Law Union of Canada, 1981: 20–2). Unique sets of regulations also severely restricted the entry of South Asians, Japanese, black Americans, and West Indians, and restricted their access to state entitlements and citizenship rights.

In the early twentieth century British women constituted more than three-quarters of immigrant domestics coming to Canada. A number of immigration schemes introduced in the late nineteenth and early twentieth centuries were aimed specifically at attracting British women to Canada. The treatment of British domestics under these schemes reflects a complex and sometimes contradictory intersection of gender, class, race, and nationality. While the amount of planning and energy involved in immigration schemes tells us a great deal about how desirable these women were as immigrants in terms of their racial/ethnic stock and the demand for their intended occupation, their working conditions as well as their paternalistic treatment reflect a subordinate class and gender status.

British Domestic Schemes and Nation-Building in Canada

To make sense of Canada's approach to and treatment of British domestic workers in the late nineteenth and early twentieth centuries, we need to place these issues in the context of changes in Canadian society and its discourses of nation-building. White, and especially white British, women were a powerful symbol in the transition of Canada from a fur-trade to a settler society in the Canadian West. The arrival of white women decreased the prevalence of marriage between white men and Native and mixed-descent women, and underlined attempts to define Canada as a British society (Van Kirk, 1983). In their roles as mothers and culture-bearers, white British women were expected to help entrench British culture in Canada and pass it on to future generations. Through their role as 'God's police', they would also contribute to the creation of a more 'stable' and 'respectable' colonial society (Buckley, 1977).

The importance of women in colonies was stressed on both sides of the Atlantic. In Britain, female emigration was emphasized by some as perhaps the most important part of empire-building: 'as respects morals and manners, it is of little importance what colonial fathers are in comparison to colonial mothers.' The absence of the civilizing influence of white women could result in irresponsibility and immorality for men in a colony of all white males. In a colony with a balanced sex ratio between male and female colonizers, on the other hand, 'every pair of immigrants would have the strongest motives for industry shrewdness, and thrift' (cited in Roberts, 1976: 108).

In the racist discourse of nation-building, class biases also shaped the perceived appropriateness of women as settlers. 'Civilization' was not thought of as a universal attribute of all women. Helen Reid, a well-known social worker in Montreal, expressed why working-class women needed to be kept out of Canada. In her view, working-class women would 'bring with them only too often, serious mental and moral disabilities. These women either glut the labour market here, reducing the wages of working men, or end up alas! too frequently in our jails, hospitals or asylums' (cited in Valverde, 1991: 126). Only women from a certain class background and of a certain moral character could embody and transmit the virtues of civilization as defined by British and British Canadian authorities and moral reform leaders.

There was often a contradiction or even a conflict between the economic dimension of colonization and its political and ideological dimension as a 'civilizing' force. The labour requirements of the colonies demanded the strenuous labour of women on farms and in domestic work. Women of the middle and upper classes, who were thought to be the ideal colonizers and civilizers, could hardly be ideal candidates for the drudgery of domestic

service or the challenges of pioneer farming. The tension between the conflicting demands of colonization was partially solved in the nineteenth century with the availability in Britain of 'surplus' or 'distressed' gentlewomen. These were single women from middle-class and educated backgrounds who were impoverished by economic circumstances or the death of a spouse (Jackel, 1982: xxi).

The late nineteenth century was still a period when immigration was not totally formalized and bureaucratized by the state. As part of the reform movement, many middle-class women took an active part in female immigration work through women's organizations. These women were also usually the employers of domestic workers. Active in social reform work, charitable, or sometimes feminist organizations, middle-class women in late nineteenth-century Canadian society 'were urged to delegate the household tasks which had previously occupied most of their time, in order that their civilizing influence no longer be confined to home and family' (Lenskyj, 1981: 4). Immigration work by female reformers was directed at recruitment, 'protection' during transportation, and their placement upon arrival. While class interests were important motivations leading women reformers to this work, their interest in immigration needs to be distinguished from that of business, of transportation agents, or even sometimes of the state. Aware that British female immigrants would become the 'daughters of the Empire' and 'mothers of the race', they were concerned as much about the 'quality' of recruits as about their numbers and the potential economic benefits they would bring to Canada (Roberts, 1990).

The incessant concern for the 'quality' of female immigrants was not always experienced as a privilege by immigrant domestics even if they were of the 'right stock' and of a respectable-class background. For women, true 'belonging' in the nation was conditional upon demonstration of Victorian morality. Poor, single women, even those from a 'gentle' background, could not be trusted to maintain high moral standards. Therefore, middle-class women who were involved with emigration and immigration societies in Britain and in Canada did not hesitate to recruit selectively and to closely monitor and curtail the freedom of the chosen ones. British emigration societies, in collaboration with Canadian organizations like the National Council of Women of Canada, required very strict recruitment and screening procedures. In addition to references and a personal interview, they introduced a compulsory medical examination, which was extended to all immigrants later (Lenskyj, 1981: 8; Valverde, 1991: 126). Women's organizations also overtook the responsibility to 'protect' and supervise women during overseas voyages. Immigrant women usually travelled under the supervision of matrons, who were women from a middle- or upper-class background. Matrons supervising parties of women carefully watched their charges to make sure they would not waste their time or befriend unsuitable acquaintances. Once they arrived in Canada, women were taken into hostels and shelters approved by and supervised by women's groups and then accompanied to their final destination (Roberts, 1990). While claiming that their philanthropic immigration work was for the protection of women and their respectability, women's groups often did not hesitate to cooperate with the police and the state to help deport 'unsuitable' immigrants. In what Valverde calls 'philanthropic deportation', women reformers participated in the deportation of significant numbers of domestic workers (Valverde, 1991: 124–7).

Compared to domestics from other racial/ethnic backgrounds who came before and after them, British domestics enjoyed a very privileged position. Unlike domestics from other backgrounds, not only were they seen as unquestioned members of Canadian society and the nation, but if they lived up to 'appropriate' Victorian standards of 'true womanhood', they were also regarded as civilizers and nation-builders. Unlike other groups, British domestics at the turn of the century were brought to Canada for more than their capacity to labour as domestic workers. Like the few groups of 'desirable' immigrants, British domestics benefited from assisted passage in their arrival to Canada (Barber, 1987, 1991: 9–10). The sense that white British domestic workers were 'privileged' must be moderated by the knowledge of their subjection to extensive social control. Neither the demand for their work nor the desirability of their background guaranteed better working conditions. The ways in which British domestics were 'protected' and 'helped' by women reformers not only limited the freedom of domestics as women and as persons, but generally reflected the class differences between the two groups and served the needs of women reformers as employers, rather than those of domestics as workers.

Between 1888 and the 1920s, when the government did not directly provide assisted passage, private agents arranged for advanced loans from employers, which would tie domestics to them for a specific length of time. The Department of Immigration sometimes evaded legislation in order to fulfill its policing function. For example, around the turn of the century, most of the provinces passed master and servant legislation, which aimed to protect domestics from an exploitative contract which they might have signed in order to immigrate. According to this legislation, contracts signed outside the province were not legally binding. The Immigration Department, however, aiming to enforce indentured status, avoided this legislation by having domestics re-sign their contract upon arrival in Canada (Leslie, 1974: 122).

Being of the desirable racial/ethnic stock was also not necessarily experienced as a privilege by the 80,000 British children who were brought in as indentured farm and domestic help to Canadian farms. Between 1868 and 1925, concerns with imperial nation-building and the health of the British race led to efforts by emigrationists to remove working-class children from urban slums and rescue homes in Britain and place them in the good environment and the 'healthy family life' of colonial farms. At a period when changing conceptions of childhood and approaches to child labour were already affecting working-class children favourably in Britain, these children were not only exploited as workers but sometimes shunned for potential criminal tendencies and moral and physical degeneracies (Parr, 1980).

Domestic Workers from Europe

As the Canadian state failed to fulfill its objectives to populate western Canada and meet Canada's labour needs through an exclusively British source of immigration, it looked to other sources of immigrants. In the late nineteenth century, continental Europe and the United States were considered the least objectionable alternative sources to Britain. There was a substantial increase in the numbers of non-British domestics in the 1920s. By the early 1930s, as many as one-fourth of immigrant domestic workers coming to Ontario were from continental Europe (Prentice et al., 1988: 222).

Scandinavian Domestic Workers
In the early twentieth century, Scandinavian countries were a favoured source of domestic workers second only to Britain. Even in the midst of the Depression, in 1937 Canada started a special scheme to bring in domestics from this region. To encourage immigration of Finnish and other Scandinavian domestics, the Canadian government

'bent immigration regulations, created special categories and made easier travel arrangements'. The overwhelming majority of Finnish women who came to Canada in the early twentieth century worked as domestic servants. In Winnipeg, for example, all Finnish women, except a few who worked in restaurants, were domestic workers. When native-born women and British immigrants were starting to move to other jobs in the labour-market, Finnish women, despite the diversity of skills they brought to Canada, remained concentrated in domestic work, mainly because of language problems (Lindstrom-Best, 1986: 34–6).

Lindstrom-Best argues that Finnish domestic workers were 'proud maids' who enjoyed a high status in the Finnish community and relatively favourable conditions at work. Class, gender, and ethnocultural solidarity facilitated the emergence of a proud collective image and organizations dedicated to improving working opportunities and conditions. Because most women in the Finnish community in Canada were domestic workers, class divisions were absent among women of the same ethnocultural background. The labour and socialist organizing traditions many Finnish immigrants brought with them to Canada meant that some ethnic organizations served as virtual labour locals. The Finns built 'immigrant homes' in several cities and started employment services for domestic workers. In this climate of class and ethnic solidarity, Finnish domestics were able to share information and refuse low wages and bad working conditions. Even in their first year in Canada, many were able to change jobs frequently in order to ensure improved conditions and resist the abysmal treatment normally accorded to recent immigrant domestics (Lindstrom-Best, 1986, 1988).

Central and Eastern European Domestics
The number of immigrants from the British Isles was insufficient to fulfill the defined objectives

of populating western Canada—securing the territory from the United States and developing an agrarian economy. In response, the Canadian state began accepting immigrants from the non-preferred sources. In 1925, the government signed a Railways Agreement with the Canadian Pacific Railway and the Canadian National Railway, which authorized the two companies to recruit and place farmers and domestics. In the years following the Railways Agreement, the number of domestic workers coming to western Canada from continental Europe grew significantly. In Manitoba, in 1921, the British made up 60 per cent of immigrant domestics and Europeans accounted for 30 per cent. By 1931, the ratios were almost reversed (Barber, 1987: 109). Unlike the preferred British domestics, domestic workers coming from continental Europe were not given assisted passage. Most domestics coming from Central and Eastern Europe were considered to be 'of the peasant type' and insufficiently familiar with standards and equipment of housework in middle-class homes to work anywhere but in rural households (Barber, 1985: 16).

Among Central and Eastern Europeans, however, there was one group of domestics who were preferred for urban employment. These were the daughters of Russian Mennonites who came to Canada as refugees and were themselves from servant-employing backgrounds. The Mennonites were able to establish Maedchenheim, or Girls' Homes, in several cities including Winnipeg, Saskatoon, Vancouver, Regina, and Toronto. Similar to the hostels for British domestics run by women reformers, the Maedchenheim offered temporary shelter for new arrivals and served as social centres. Unlike the hostels but like the Finnish immigrant homes, these centres had no connections to employers and therefore worked to protect domestic workers. They would accompany the domestic to her place of employment,

inspect the house with her, remove domestics from unfavourable working environments, and keep a blacklist of employers to whom they would refuse to send domestic workers (Barber, 1985: 16–18, 1987: 112).

During and following the Great Depression, when many native-born women lost the few alternative sources of employment open to them, domestic work became once again the major employer of women as a whole. Despite the dire state of the economy, there was actually an increase in this period in the number of domestic workers. A generalized fall in wages and prices meant that families with fixed or steady incomes who could not previously afford domestic workers could now do so (Prentice et al., 1988: 235–6). In this period, married women joined single women in returning to domestic work on a live-out, or sometimes live-in, basis while their unemployed husbands stayed home with the children. Central and Eastern European domestics who had come to Canada in the late 1920s faced special difficulties. They could only find work with very low wages and very bad working conditions (Barber, 1985: 18–19).

Following the trend begun in the nineteenth century, the demand for domestic workers in the postwar period again exceeded the supply. And once again, the Canadian state turned to recruiting from foreign sources, with vulnerable groups providing the obvious recruits. And as usual, racism would play an important role in determining who among the vulnerable would be recruited. In the postwar period, the first group of immigrant domestic workers came from among refugee women in the displaced persons (DP) camps in Europe. Between 1947 and 1952, Canada accepted around 165,000 displaced persons on the condition that they would work under a one-year contract in specific occupations whose wages and conditions were unacceptable for Canadians. Men were accepted as agricultural workers, miners, and loggers; women as domestic workers in institutions—as cleaners and kitchen workers in hospitals, sanatoria, orphanages, and mental institutions—or private homes. Humanitarian considerations took a back seat to economic motivations and ethnic considerations in the selection and immigration of DPs. The Canadian state not only specified the occupations in which refugees would work but also indicated ethnic and religious preferences. Racial considerations are apparent in Department of Immigration memos. They articulate a clear preference for domestic workers coming from the Baltic countries of Estonia, Latvia, and Lithuania because of their perceived similarities to Scandinavians. There was also a preference for Protestants, even though they were a minority among DPs. With the exception of an experiment placing a few Jewish women in Jewish homes, Jewish women were considered an unsuitable source, ostensibly because very few Jews had previous experience in domestic service (Barber, 1985: 19–20; Danys, 1986: 76–7, 130).

The recruitment criteria reflected the gender and class assumptions that had been long applied to domestic servants but that seemed harsher given the conditions of refugees in postwar Europe. To qualify under the program, women had to be single or widowed, between 18 and 40 years of age, and of 'good average intelligence and emotional stability', and had to go through strict medical examinations which included tests for pregnancy and venereal diseases, as well as X-rays. Those who qualified signed a contract to remain in domestic service for one year. Even though prospective employers also filled out a form specifying wages and conditions of work, they did not have to show it to the domestic when she was hired (Danys, 1986: 133).

Daenzer argues that the case of DP domestics constitutes a turning point in the nature and meaning of indenture for immigrant domestic workers. In this period, the agreement to stay in domestic service for one year changed from a friendly 'gentlepersons agreement' to a mandatory imposition (Daenzer, 1993: 19). There were, however, no serious sanctions as yet for the non-fulfillment of contract, and domestics could easily change employers. Arthur MacNamara, the deputy minister of labour who designed the DP program, made it a policy that any DP who asked for a transfer was to be given one (Danys, 1986: 157). Despite the relative flexibility of the program, though, most DP domestics fulfilled their contract. Usually they remained with the same employer, motivated in part by gratitude to the Canadian government for the chance of a new life distant from their war-torn (and often Soviet-occupied) countries, as well as by fear of jeopardizing the chances for emigration of DPs still in camps (Barber, 1985: 20).

Southern European Domestic Workers

Refugee domestics were only a temporary solution to the problem of domestic shortage. In the early 1950s, Canada once again introduced assisted passage and made several attempts to recruit from the preferred Great Britain and Western Europe. With the exceptions of Germany and Holland, these attempts were futile. With the entrenchment of the Cold War came the end of any possibility of emigration from Eastern Europe. Only then did Canada decide to experiment with domestic schemes drawing from the least-preferred part of Europe: southern Europe (Barber, 1985: 21–3).

The Canadian state's approach to Italian immigration in the 1950s demonstrates how the conflicting immigration priorities of meeting labour market requirements and populating Canada with people of preferred races were played out. In the dominant racist view, Italians, especially those from the rural areas in southern Italy, were equated with hot climate, hot temperaments, dark skins, cultural backwardness, and undemocratic traditions 'better suited to the . . . "fragile" politics of Latin America'. Despite this perception, however, pressures from business in the booming economy of the postwar period compelled the government to decide that the presence of southern Italians could be tolerated provided they offered hard work and cheap labour in agriculture, mining, railway repair, and construction (Iacovetta, 1986, 1992).

A domestic scheme was also started in 1951 but ended the following year after only 357 women were recruited. The Italian scheme was similar to the one that brought in refugee women from DP camps. Prospective employers in Canada would submit 'orders' for domestic workers, and interested workers in Italy would sign a contract obliging them to stay in the designated occupation with the assigned employer for one year. Even though Canada had reintroduced the Assisted Passage Loan Scheme for domestics from Western Europe and Britain, it refused initially to extend it to Italian domestics and tried to persuade the Italian government, instead, to advance passage fares. The short life of the program had as much to do with the negative evaluation of domestics by the employers and by the state as it did with the lack of enthusiasm on the part of Italian women. Italian domestics were seen as ignorant, 'primitive villagers', whose backward cultural background had failed to prepare them for the high standards and sophisticated technology of Canadian housekeeping. They were also found to be feisty employees who complained about working conditions, demanded to change employers, or simply left domestic work before the end of their contracts to work in the factories and/or to join other family members in Canada (Iacovetta, 1986: 13–16). Such demonstrations of freedom could not be tolerated in a group of women who were not considered 'mothers of the race' or carriers of culture. Like other non-British domestics, Italians were brought into Canada solely for the cheap labour they could perform in jobs that Canadians, when and if they had the choice, would not do.

Canada also organized domestic schemes with Greece and Spain in the postwar years. In a period of otherwise restricted immigration from Greece, domestic workers started to be admitted in 1956 to be placed with Greek employers. The program lasted until 1966 and brought in approximately 300 Greek women per year. A much more limited experiment involving 50 Spanish women took place in 1959–60. Placement difficulties brought an end to this program: Spanish authorities wanted Catholic homes, but most prospective employers were Protestant (Barber, 1985: 22–3).

Women of Colour in Domestic Work

Domestic workers from different regions of Europe experienced different levels of vulnerability in their relations with the Canadian state and society, depending on British-Canadian stereotypes, political circumstances, and their own traditions and prospects for resistance. Thus, while all foreign domestics have experienced varying degrees of coercion by the state and more powerful groups, European domestics have fallen along different points in the continuum of the treatment of immigrant domestic workers in Canada. Non-white domestic workers stand at the opposite end of this continuum. The Canadian government recruited women of colour only as a last resort. Since the 1960s, the 'liberalized' immigration policies have not expressed any explicit bias against domestics from non-European sources. Indeed, women from the Third World have predominated among immigrant domestic workers since the early 1970s. That status and conditions for domestic workers that would have been unacceptable half a century ago are currently considered acceptable suggests that racialized sexism and gendered racism are still alive and well in Canadian society and immigration policy.

Women of colour in Canada have been a source of domestic work during most of Canadian history largely because they have historically been excluded from other possibilities in the labour market. At the turn of the century, Mi'kmaq women in Nova Scotia were excluded from industrial employment and were considered suited only for domestic work (Prentice et al., 1988: 121). Black women did find industrial employment at a time of labour shortage during World War II but were subsequently the first group to be laid off (Brand, 1991). In the postwar period, Canadian employers also utilized the cheap labour of 'Canada's own displaced persons, the Japanese Canadians' (Light and Pierson, 1990: 258).

Even though employers demonstrated that they would accept domestic labour from any background providing the workers were cheap and docile, racial and ethnic considerations often dictated against an open-door policy in immigration. As long as recruits could be found from 'preferred' or 'not-so-objectionable' sources, Canada avoided non-white immigrants. The Immigration Act of 1910, in a clause that was not removed until 1978, gave the government of Canada the legal power to discriminate on the basis of race. The clause said that the government could 'prohibit for a stated period or permanently, the landing in Canada . . . of immigrants, belonging to any race unsuited to the climate or requirements of Canada' (cited in Calliste, 1993–4: 133; see also Satzewich, 1989).

In 1911, there was a very short-lived experiment with domestic workers from the Caribbean. With permission from the government, employers in Quebec arranged the immigration of approximately 100 French-speaking domestics from Guadeloupe. Racist assumptions about black women's sexuality played an important part in the public's perception of these domestics. The press also fabricated stories and fuelled fears of immorality. Even though the employers, in their own sexist, classist, and paternalizing way generally responded positively, finding the women preferable to 'fussy' Canadian domestics, the government rejected most domestics in the second party on the grounds of physical and moral unsuitability (Mackenzie, 1988; Calliste, 1989).

During the recession of 1913–15, when unemployed Canadians were willing to do domestic work, the government deported many Caribbean domestics already in Canada, arguing that they could become 'public charges'. More important than economic considerations was the fact that black domestic workers were, unlike their British counterparts, accepted only for their labour power, not as 'permanent assets' to contribute to the social and cultural life of Canada (cited in Calliste, 1989: 138). Department of Immigration memos suggest that Canada lost interest in Caribbean domestics even as a temporary and expedient measure when authorities calculated that the World War would result in 'better' types of immigrants (cited in Calliste, 1989: 138). Long after the end of the short-lived Guadeloupe arrangement, the alleged 'immorality' of these women was still being used to explain the restrictions on Caribbean immigration (Mackenzie, 1988: 128). Immigration of black domestic workers did not occur again until the 1950s.

In 1955, after exhausting attempts to secure domestic workers from Europe, and with mounting pressure from Caribbean governments and Britain, Canada finally entered into a domestic scheme with Jamaica and Barbados. Because the scheme involved a breach of immigration regulations in place, the government used its Order-in-Council powers to put it into effect. Rather than acknowledging its gratitude for a much needed and qualified workforce, the Canadian government reasoned that the scheme was a favour to the countries of emigration. Caribbean domestics were not eligible to apply for the interest-free loans under the 1950 Assisted Passage Loan Scheme. Significantly different from many of Canada's prior domestic programs, the Caribbean scheme required the sending countries to bear the responsibilities and the costs for recruiting, training, medically testing, and arranging the transportation of domestics to Canada. To qualify under the program, women had to be unmarried, between the ages of 21 and 35, and willing to do domestic work for at least a year with an assigned employer. Upon their arrival in Canada, the domestics, who had already undergone extensive medical tests, were also subjected to gynecological examinations (Mackenzie, 1988: 133–5).

The gynecological tests and emphasis on the women's single status were intended to ensure that these women would be in Canada solely to fill a labour requirement and to eliminate the possibility of sponsoring spouses and children. Temporary migration, instead of permanent landed status, was contemplated for Caribbean domestics during the development of the scheme. However, the Canadian government decided against such a move on the grounds that it could be interpreted as a practice of forced labour and a blatant case of discrimination. The government also decided against temporary status on the assumption that, unlike European domestics, the Caribbean women would face discrimination in the labour market and thus most probably stay in domestic work past their one-year contract obligation. A third reason for the decision against temporary status was the possibility that the government could use 'administrative measures', instead of blatantly discriminatory policies, to prevent domestics from 'abusing' the scheme by moving on to other occupations (Mackenzie, 1988: 133; Calliste, 1989: 143). In an unusual deal made with the governments of sending countries, Canada ruled that Caribbean domestics, if found unsuitable for domestic work,

would be deported to the country of emigration at the expense of the Caribbean government concerned. No definition of 'unsuitable' was given in the agreement, which implied that Canadian immigration authorities could use unlimited discretion (Daenzer, 1993: 53–4).

At least initially, the Caribbean domestic scheme was considered to be the most successful domestic program initiated in the postwar period (Mackenzie, 1988: 136). Canada was receiving an overly qualified workforce at no cost to itself. Many of the women recruited under the program were so highly educated that their emigration contributed to a brain drain from Barbados. Despite their qualifications, Caribbean women tended to stay in domestic service longer than European domestics arriving under similar schemes (Calliste, 1989: 145).

Soon after the start of the Caribbean domestic scheme the immigration officials started raising concerns when some domestic workers made application to sponsor relatives. This perceived 'explosion' of sponsorship, with a consequent increase in numbers of undesirable immigrants, spelled an end to the usefulness of the program (Mackenzie, 1988: 138; Satzewich, 1989: 91). Immigration officials were also disappointed with the fact that despite the discrimination in the labour market, Caribbean domestics had a high mobility rate out of domestic service. Once again, measures were considered to ensure that immigrant domestics remained in domestic service. The deputy minister of immigration ruled against forceful tactics in this direction, arguing that it was 'unfair in a free market economy to try to freeze anyone in a lowly occupation' (Mackenzie, 1988: 139). Despite the ambivalence towards the Caribbean domestic scheme, the state, fearing charges of racism from the black community in Canada and a breakdown in trade relations with Caribbean countries, continued the program until 1967, when the point-system became the basis of immigration policy.

Non-Racist Immigration or 'Justified' Discrimination? Foreign Domestic Workers Under the Point-System

Immigration criteria were 'rationalized' in the 1960s to make labour market needs the explicit basis for the recruitment of immigrants. In defining labour market needs, the point-system emphasizes Canada's need for highly educated and highly skilled immigrants, with education and skill measured in formally recognized terms. The new system has been celebrated as marking a liberalization of immigration policy. It has been declared a form of recruitment which has ended discrimination on the basis of ascribed criteria such as race and sex. Ironically, however, the use of the point-system has enabled the Canadian state to treat foreign domestic workers in the most unfavourable conditions legally possible in Canadian history since the abolition of slavery.

Because the definitions of 'skill' and 'education' in modern capitalist society approach domestic work as an unskilled and 'naturally' feminine job, domestic workers have been unable under the point-system to qualify as independent immigrants. Since the 1970s, the Canadian government initiated a temporary program to bring in domestics as migrant workers—that is, as workers lacking the freedom and rights of citizenship or landed immigrant status (Bakan and Stasiulis, 1997). Indeed, immigration authorities deliberately and arbitrarily lowered the points awarded to domestic servants under the system so as to ensure that domestic workers did not qualify for entry as landed immigrants. Thus, indentured status for domestic workers, which in the 1950s was considered unacceptable in a free market economy, has become acceptable since the 1970s and remains acceptable at the beginning of the twenty-first century. Even though this practice is seemingly 'non-racist' and 'legitimate' within the sexist

discourses of 'skill', 'education', and a potentially 'self-sustaining' immigrant, how this practice can be acceptable in an otherwise liberal democratic society should be subject to severe questioning (Arat-Koç, 1992). It is not a coincidence that this change has taken place at a time when Third World women from previously unwanted sources constitute the major supply of foreign domestic workers in Canada for the foreseeable future.

Conclusion

Social, economic, and legal conditions of paid domestic workers are generally characterized by forms of subordination based on the gender and class status of the workers. In settler colonies like Canada, race and ethnicity have played a very important part, over and above gender and class, in shaping the status and conditions of domestic workers. This chapter has traced the differential treatment domestic workers from different racial/ethnic backgrounds have historically received from the Canadian society and the state.

While middle-class biases and paternalism were definitely a part of the schemes designed to bring British domestic workers in the late nineteenth and early twentieth centuries, these schemes also treated immigrant domestics as 'mothers of the nation' who were welcome to Canada as central participants in nation-building. Compared to British domestics, Scandinavian and Central and Eastern European domestic workers arriving in the twentieth century faced linguistic and cultural disadvantages. Even though they were not recognized as full members of a Canadian nation, they were able to improve their conditions of work to the extent that they enjoyed class and ethno-cultural solidarity in their respective communities. In the postwar period, as the efforts to import domestics from the preferred source regions of Britain and Western Europe failed, Canada first tapped 'displaced labour' camps for Eastern European domestic labour and then entered into 'bulk' recruitment schemes with Italy, Greece, and Spain. Employers generally treated southern European domestics as ignorant, 'primitive villagers', who were culturally unprepared for the standards of Canadian housekeeping. Most of these schemes lasted for only a short time due to class, racial/ethnic, and religious biases against southern European women and the unwillingness of the workers to put up with unfavourable working conditions.

In immigration schemes designed to recruit domestic workers for Canada, women of colour were only considered as a last resort, when recruitment from all European sources failed. Since the late 1950s, the Caribbean and, since the mid-1970s, the Philippines have become the major source countries for foreign domestic workers. A very drastic change in immigration policies

concerning domestic workers coincided with this shift in source countries from Europe to the Third World. It is ironic that the recent emergence of migrant, as opposed to immigrant, status for foreign domestic workers has come precisely at a time in Canadian history when Canada claims to have rid its immigration policies and procedures of racial and ethnic biases. Precisely at a time when Canada has started to define itself as 'multicultural', it has become easy to define some groups of immigrants as 'workers only' (Carty, 1994), as disposable nonmembers who, despite their indispensable contributions, are given no acknowledged part in the 'nation' or 'nation-building' project. The easy acceptability by many Canadians of migrant status for foreign domestic workers may have as much to do with racial/ethnic status of domestics as it does with the ever devalued status of domestic labour in modern society.

Notes

1. The term 'inside the state' has been used by Beckett to characterize the overregulated lives of Aboriginal people. See J. Beckett, 'Aboriginality, Citizenship and the State', *Social Analysis* 24 (1988).
2. See Daiva Stasiulis and Radha Jhappan, 'The

Fractious Politics of a Settler Society: Canada', in Daiva Stasiulis and Nira Yuval-Davis, eds, *Unsettling Settler Societies: Articulations of Gender, Race, Ethnicity, and Class* (Thousand Oaks, CA: Sage, 1995).

References

Arat-Koç, Sedef. 1992. 'Immigration Policies, Migrant Domestic Workers, and the Definition of Citizenship in Canada', in Vic Satzewich, ed., *Deconstructing a Nation: Immigration, Culturalism, and Racism in the 90s Canada*. Halifax: Fernwood.

Bakan, Abigail B., and Daiva Stasiulis. 1997. 'Foreign Domestic Worker Policy in Canada and the Social Boundaries of Modern Citizenship', in Abigail B. Bakan and Daiva Stasiulis, eds, *Not One of the Family: Foreign Domestic Workers in Canada*. Toronto: University of Toronto Press.

Barber, Marilyn. 1987. 'The Servant Problem in Manitoba, 1896–1930', in Mary Kinnear, ed., *First Days, Fighting Days: Women in Manitoba History*. Regina: Canadian Plains Research Centre.

———. 1991. *Immigrant Domestic Servants in Canada*. Ottawa: Canadian Historical Association.

Bolaria, Singh, and Peter Li. 1985. *Racial Oppression in Canada*. Toronto: Garamond Press.

Brand, Dionne. 1991. '*No Burden to Carry': Narratives of Black Women in Ontario, 1920–1950s*. Toronto: Women's Press.

Buckley, Suzanne. 1977. 'British Female Emigration and Imperial Development: Experiments in Canada, 1885–1931', *Hecate* 3, 2 (July): 26–40.

Calliste, Agnes. 1989. 'Canada's Immigration Policy and Domestics from the Caribbean: The Second Domestic Scheme', in Jesse Vorst et al., eds, *Race, Class and Gender: Bonds and Barriers*. Toronto: Garamond Press and Society for Socialist Studies.

————. 1993–4. 'Race, Gender, and Canadian Immigration Policy: Blacks from the Caribbean, 1900–1937', *Journal of Canadian Studies* 28, 4: 131–48.

Carty, Linda. 1994. 'African Canadian Women and the State: "Labor Only" Please', in Peggy Bristow et al., eds, *'We're Rooted Here and They Can't Pull Us Up': Essays in African Canadian Women's History*. Toronto: University of Toronto Press.

Daenzer, Patricia. 1993. *Regulating Class Privilege: Immigrant Servants in Canada, 1940–1990*. Toronto: Canadian Scholars Press.

Danys, Milda. 1986. *DP: Lithuanian Immigration to Canada*. Toronto: Multicultural History Society of Ontario.

Dudden, Faye. 1983. *Serving Women: Household Service in Nineteenth-Century America*. Middleton, CN: Wesleyan University Press.

Glenn, Evelyn Nekano. 1992. 'From Servitude to Service Work: Historical Continuities in the Racial Division of Paid Reproductive Work', *Signs* 18, 1: 1–43.

Iacovetta, Franca. 1986. '"Primitive Villagers and Un-educated Girls": Canada Recruits Domestics from Italy, 1951–2', *Canadian Women's Studies* 7, 4: 14–18.

————. 1992. *Such Hardworking People: Italian Immigrants in Post-War Toronto*. Montreal and Kingston: McGill-Queen's University Press.

Jackel, Susan. 1982. *A Flannel Shirt and Liberty: British Emigrant Gentlewomen in the Canadian West, 1880–1914*. Vancouver: UBC Press.

Lacelle, Claudette. 1987. *Urban Domestic Servants in Nineteenth-Century Canada*. Ottawa: Environment Canada.

Law Union of Canada. 1981. *The Immigrant's Handbook*. Montreal: Black Rose.

Lenskyj, Helen. 1981. 'A "Servant Problem" or a "Servant–Mistress Problem"? Domestic Service in Canada, 1890–1930', *Atlantis* 7, 1: 3–11.

Leslie, Genevieve. 1974. 'Domestic Service in Canada, 1880–1920', in Janice Acton, ed., *Women at Work: 1850–1930*. Toronto: Canadian Women's Educational Press.

Light, Beth, and Ruth Roach Pierson. 1990. *No Easy Road: Women In Canada, 1920s–1960s*. Toronto: New Hogtown Press.

Lindstrom-Best, Varpu. 1986. '"I Won't Be a Slave"— Finnish Domestics in Canada', in Jean Burnett, ed., *Looking into my Sister's Eyes: An Exploration in Women's History*. Toronto: Multicultural History Society of Ontario.

————. 1988. *Defiant Sisters: A Social History of Finnish Immigrant Women in Canada*. Toronto: Multicultural History Society of Ontario.

Mackenzie, Ian. 1988. 'Early Movements of Domestics from the Caribbean and Canadian Immigration Policy: A Research Note', *Alternate Routes* 8: 124–43.

Parr, Joy. 1980. *Labouring Children: British Immigrant Apprentices to Canada, 1859–1924*. Montreal and Kingston: McGill-Queen's University Press.

Prentice, Alison, et al. 1988. *Canadian Women: A History*. Toronto: Harcourt Brace.

Roberts, Barbara. 1976. 'Daughters of the Empire and Mothers of the Race: Caroline Chisholm and Female Emigration in the British Empire', *Atlantis* 1, 2: 106–27.

Roberts, Barbara. 1990. 'Ladies, Women and the State: Managing Female Immigration, 1880–1920', in Roxanne Ng, Gillian Walker, and Jacob Muller, eds, *Community Organization and the Canadian State*. Toronto: Garamond.

Satzewich, Vic. 1989. 'Racism and Canadian Immigration Policy: The Government's View of Caribbean Migration, 1926–1966', *Canadian Ethnic Studies* 21: 2: 77–97.

Valverde, Mariana. 1991. *The Age of Light, Soap and Water: Moral Reform in Canada, 1885–1925*. Toronto: McClelland and Stewart.

Van Kirk, Sylvia. 1983. *'Many Tender Ties': Women in Fur-Trade Society, 1670–1870*. Winnipeg: Watson and Dwyer.

Villasin, Felicita, and M. Ann Phillips. 1994. 'Falling Through the Cracks: Domestic Workers and Progressive Movements', *Canadian Women's Studies* 14, 2 (Spring): 87–90.

PART XI

The State of the Unions

Canada's workers and their main organizations of defence—trade unions—have faced a difficult time in the three decades since the mid-1970s. The numbers of workers organized climbed from just under 1.5 million to roughly 2.9 million over the 1960s and early 1970s, with the percentage of the non-agricultural workforce unionized reaching almost 37 per cent in 1975. This rising union density peaked in the mid-1980s, with 40 per cent of Canadian workers organized in trade unions, but thereafter the toll on labour organization has been registered in figures of decline: by 2005 barely 30 per cent of working Canadians carried a union card. If a growing stronghold of labour organization, the public sector employees in the health, education, and government spheres, were excluded then less than 20 per cent of private sector workers in the former bastions of union militancy in mass production and related industries were enrolled in unions. Trade unions and the lot of working-class people in general had fallen on hard times.

The woes of the contemporary labour movement can be dated to a generalized global crisis of capitalism that first showed signs of manifesting serious disorder as early as 1973. That year was marked by an energy crisis that signalled the high cost that western economies were going to pay for their dependence on foreign oil. Soon it was evident that the advanced capitalist nations of Europe and North America were caught in the throes of 'stagflation': economic stagnation, persistent unemployment, seemingly unstoppable inflation, overproduction of goods, and falling rates of profit spelled the end of what had been promised, in the exuberant period of the late 1940s, as a century of affluence. The emergence of the New Right in the United States and the United Kingdom thus brought to the forefront demands that capital had to be freed from the fetters of the post-World War II reconstruction, in which powerful labour unions had seemingly been allowed to dictate levels of production and crippling annual wage increases, while the state taxed the rich and the corporations to provide social safety nets for the ostensible non-deserving poor.

Given Canada's dependency on international trade and exports, the global slump precipitated in the 1973–75 years quickly translated into a fiscal crisis of the state.

Tax revenues, on which governments depended to pay for social services, dried up. With Canada's capacity to compete in the manufacturing sector slipping as the costs of labour rose, and international demand for Canadian natural resources declining, a 1970 Canadian trade balance surplus of $3 billion turned into a $450 million deficit five years later. Under such economic pressures, the political climate changed markedly, with 1960s talk of 'just societies' and 'wars on poverty' giving way to a later 1970s rhetoric of 'restraint' that often took on the appearance of repression. Canada's largely liberal and social democratic federal and provincial states, while not speaking the language of the New Right, actually followed its lead, waging war on the working class, especially targeting government employees in the public sector. Pierre Elliott Trudeau, a liberal advocate of workers in the 1949 Asbestos Strike, played an entirely different role as Liberal Prime Minister in the mid-to-late 1970s, cracking down on trade unions with his Anti-Inflation Program, governed as it was by wage controls that angered Canadian organized labour to the point of a threatened General Strike in 1976.

The 1980s and 1990s saw the continuation, even intensification, of these trends. Free trade agreements such as those brokered among Mexico, the United States, and Canada in 1989 and 1994 were the codes of a new age of neo-liberal globalization. Under pressures of the World Trade Organization, the Canada–United States Auto Pact, which protected jobs in the pivotal auto-producing sector of central Canada, was jettisoned over the course of 1999–2001: the result was a massive restructuring of the industry, the closing of many small parts plants, and the 'downsizing' of major 'Big Three' (Chrysler, Ford, General Motors) auto complexes in Windsor, Brampton, and Oshawa. Capital was now increasingly mobile, and with this mobility came the capacity to undermine the old union powers of the post-World War II Fordist accord. As Bryan Palmer shows in his book on the establishment of a massive Goodyear tire-producing plant in the eastern Ontario town of Napanee, technologically obsolete factories that were once strongholds of organized labour are being allowed to die, so that new, union-free, 'team'-oriented facilities can be built. Given the extent to which capitalist production is increasingly premised on global, rather than national or regional, considerations, the modern industrial production units of our time relocate where costs are lower and encumbrances fewer, whether this is 150 miles down the road or on another continent. The prospects for workers in advanced capitalist economies like Canada are increased insecurity, declining real wages, weakened unions, and deteriorating conditions on the job.

Leo Panitch's and Donald Swartz's essay represents perhaps the first serious academic attempt to come to grips with the post-1973 assault on Canadian trade unionism. Originally published in 1984, it has grown into a much-republished book-length study. Arguably one of the most influential perspectives on 'the state of the unions' in the current crisis of the labour movement, Panitch and Swartz explore how the post-war settlement unravelled under the pressures of capitalist restructuring. It details the extent to which the liberal state initiated an attack on trade union freedoms, with the initial assault directed at public sector workers, whose pivotal place in Canadian organized labour and whose vulnerability to state legislation made them targets of a new crusade to define exceptions to the old rules of the Justice Ivan Rand-constructed industrial relations system. This exceptionalism, however, soon became the norm, as Canadian unions, in both public and private sectors, faced wave after wave of state attack throughout the 1980s and 1990s and into the first decade of the twenty-first century. As David Camfield shows well in his treatment of hospital employees in British Columbia in the 2002–4 period, the dismantling of the post-war settlement has forced trade unionists to struggle, but too often their leaderships are incapable of seeing that these new battles are being fought on terrain entirely different than that of the 1950s and 1960s.

Nandita Rani Sharma provides us with insights into the difficult conditions of contemporary labour by addressing how globalization's reliance on mobility constructs workers in specific ways. Considering a particular 1973 piece of legislation, the Non-Immigrant Employment Authorization Program (NIEAP), Sharma examines how migrant workers to Canada are forced to enter the labour market in ways that construct them as non-citizens, classified, not unlike Panitch's and Swartz's unions under attack, as 'exceptional', or 'temporary'. Like labour organizations designated outside of past industrial relations entitlements, these migrant workers are excluded from citizenship's rights. This exclusion is justified on many grounds of supposed difference separating out the migrant worker from the Canadian citizen, including of course the longstanding markers of gender and race, but as Sharma suggests, this merely perpetuates certain understandings of what constitutes a Canadian nationality. Her article thus links, importantly, the struggle for workers' rights to the struggle for a different kind of nation. Like Panitch and Swartz, and Camfield, who are writing about the assault on workers, Sharma is not content to let state definitions and a legalistic exclusion 'reform the game of domination'.

Further Reading

Dimitry Anastakis, *Auto Pact: Creating a Borderless North American Auto Industry* (Toronto: University of Toronto Press, 2005).

A. Bakan and D. Stasiulus, 'Foreign Domestic Policy in Canada and the Social Boundaries of Modern Citizenship', *Science & Society* 58 (1994): 7–33.

Barry Brennan, 'Canadian Labor Today: Partial Successes, Real Challenges', *Monthly Review* 57 (June 2005): 46–61.

Mike Burke, Colin Mooers, and John Shields, eds, *Restructuring and Resistance: Canadian Public Policy in an Age of Global Capitalism* (Halifax: Fernwood, 2000).

Andrew Jackson, 'Solidarity Forever? Trends in Canadian Union Density', *Studies in Political Economy* 74 (Autumn 2004): 125–46.

Bryan D. Palmer, *Solidarity: The Rise and Fall of an Opposition in British Columbia* (Vancouver: New Star, 1987).

Bryan D. Palmer, *Capitalism Comes to the Backcountry: The Goodyear Invasion of Napanee* (Toronto: Between the Lines, 1994).

Leo Panitch and Donald Swartz, *From Consent to Coercion: The Assault on Trade Union Freedoms* (Toronto: Garamond, 2005).

David Rapaport, *No Justice, No Peace: The 1996 OPSEU Strike Against the Harris Government in Ontario* (Montreal and Kingston: McGill-Queen's University Press, 1999).

Yonatan Reshef and Sandra Rastin, *Unions in the Time of Revolution: Government Restructuring in Alberta & Ontario* (Toronto: University of Toronto Press, 2003).

Alan Sears, *Retooling the Mind Factory: Education in a Lean State* (Peterborough: Broadview, 2003).

Visual Resources

NFB, *Shutdown* (1980), dir. Laura Sky, 26 minutes (follows the closing down of an American-owned branch plant and the effect on the workers).

NFB, *A Time to Rise* (1982), dirs. Anand Patwardhan and Jim Monro, 39 minutes (details the difficult conditions faced by Chinese and East Indian farmworkers in BC, and the discontent that led to the formation of the Canadian Farmworkers Union).

NFB, *Too Dirty for a Woman* (1984), dir. Diane Beaudry, 16 minutes (female workers at Newfoundland's Iron Ore Company discuss their experience of 'non-traditional' labour).

NFB, *Final Offer: Bob White and the Canadian Auto Workers' Fight for Independence* (1985), dir. Robert Collison, 78 minutes (inside look at the 1984 negotiations between the UAW and GM. Tensions within the union lead to the film's conclusion—Bob White's walkout and the formation of the Canadian Auto Workers).

Les Productions Virage, *Un Syndicat Avec Ça?* (2001), dir. Magnus Isaacson, 63 minutes (examines the struggle to organize a McDonalds in St Hubert, Quebec).

NFB, *Westray* (2001), dir. Paul Cowan, 80 minutes (focuses on three miners and three widows following the 1992 Westray disaster, which killed 26 Nova Scotia miners).

NFB, *El Contrato* (2003), dir. Min Sook Lee, 51 minutes (follows Mexican workers from their homes to Canada on their annual migration to southern Ontario to work as migrant farm labourers).

CHAPTER 26

Towards Permanent Exceptionalism: Coercion and Consent in Canadian Industrial Relations

Leo Panitch and Donald Swartz

We are witnessing today the end of the era of free collective bargaining in Canada. The era being closed is one in which the state and capital relied, more than before World War II, on obtaining the consent of workers generally, and unions in particular, to participate as subordinate actors in Canada's capitalist democracy. The era ahead marks a return, albeit in quite different conditions, to the state and capital relying more openly on coercion—on force and on fear—to secure that subordination. This is not to suggest that coercion was in any sense absent from the post-war era or that coercion is about to become the only or even always the dominant factor in labour relations. But there is a changing conjuncture in the Canadian political economy, and it marks a change in the form in which coercion and consent are related to one another, a change significant enough to demarcate a new era.

The era of free collective bargaining began 40 years ago with the federal government's 1944 Order-in-Council PC 1003. This Order-in-Council established legal recognition of the rights of private sector workers across Canada to organize, to bargain collectively, and to strike, and backed these rights with state sanctions against employers who refused to recognize and bargain with trade unions. In 1948, PC 1003 was superseded by the Industrial Relations Disputes Investigation Act (IRDIA) giving these rights a 'permanent' legislative basis for private sector workers under federal jurisdiction. Similar legislation was adopted by the provinces for private sector and municipal

workers in their jurisdiction, with notable delay only by Quebec. These legally-established rights have been universally seen, and not least by the Canadian trade union movement itself, as the point at which Canada extended democracy to include 'free collective bargaining' and finally met the International Labour Organization's (ILOs) 1919 declaration that 'a free society cannot coerce any of its citizens into working conditions that are not truly and generally acceptable.' Despite continuing exclusions and limitations on free trade unionism in Canada, it was widely assumed, in a way that was typical of the reformist ideology that predominated in Canada in the post-war era, that there would be steady if slow progress towards the ever fuller realization of trade union rights. The reforms achieved in the 1940s were thought to be irreversible and cumulative. Such a world view inevitably tends to outlive the social realities which gave rise to it. The social realities of the 1980s may have finally put it to rest.

It is one of the greater ironies of the present conjuncture that just as the Canadian state finally moved in the 1980s to guarantee formally liberal democratic freedoms in an indigenous constitution, so has it simultaneously moved towards foreclosing those aspects of liberal democracy that specifically pertain to workers' freedoms. Canada's new constitution with its Charter of Rights and Freedoms notably excluded the right to strike from its list of fundamental freedoms, but in guaranteeing the right to freedom of association, it might have been thought that the federal and provincial governments were implicitly recognizing that the right to strike alone makes viable workers' rights to freedom of association. Significantly, however, within months of the proclamation of the constitution the right to strike was abrogated for well over 1,000,000 of the 3,500,000 organized workers in Canada through a series of federal and provincial legislator measures.

The most important of these measures, because it most clearly symbolized the significance of the Charter's silences on the right to strike, was the federal Public Sector Compensation Restraint Act introduced in June 1982. This act has tended to be treated as imposing a two-year period of statutory wage restraint on federal employees in conformity with the slogan '6 and 5' (increases of 6 per cent and 5 per cent in the ensuing two years). But the act did much more. It completely suppressed the right to bargain and strike for all those public employees covered by the legislation, and it abrogated existing collective agreements. What it lacked in comprehensiveness as compared with the Anti-Inflation Act of 1975–78 (which covered both public and private sector workers), it more than made up for in the severity of treatment of the workers it covered. The abrogation of the right to strike and to bargain was accomplished by the extension of existing agreements for two years. Since strikes during agreements were proscribed under the earlier legislation, the new act used the legislation which established free collective bargaining today to deny it, a denial which included the 'rolling back' of already signed agreements which provided for increases above '6 and 5' during the life of the act.

The provinces, with the exception of Manitoba and New Brunswick, quickly followed suit. In autumn 1982, Ontario introduced legislation which followed the federal act in form, but was even broader in scope. As well as provincial government and crown corporation employees, Ontario's Inflation Restraint Act covered the employees of municipalities, schools, hospitals, and privately-owned, para-public sector companies contracted to, or funded by, the province (including nursing homes, ambulance services, etc.). The Maritime provinces, Alberta, and Saskatchewan legislated ceilings on wage increases, without explicitly abrogating the right to strike, except for particular groups of workers, for example, hospital workers in Alberta. In Quebec and British Columbia events took a somewhat different but perhaps even more menacing course. The Parti Québécois government of Quebec actually decreed unilaterally one- to three-year collective agreements for public sector workers in 1983, thereby pre-empting their right to strike. These agreements not only required pay reductions of up to 20 per cent (meaning that many of the workers affected would be earning less at the end of 1985 than in 1982), but also rewrote the terms of their collective agreements regarding job security and working conditions.

It is perhaps not surprising that most of the attention has recently focused on British Columbia. The Social Credit government began the whole current trend with their wage restraint legislation at the beginning of 1982. After winning re-election in spring 1983, however, it went a great deal further by proposing to restrict permanently union rights. The form of free collective bargaining was to be preserved, while its substance was dramatically curtailed. Bill 2 sought to deprive provincial government employees of the right to bargain over working conditions and the organization of work, while Bill 3 stripped them of bargaining rights with regard to job security. Bill 16 would empower the government to prohibit strikes and/or picketing at any work site classified as an 'economic development project.' All this was, of course, part of a broader package of legislative assaults on the welfare state.

Taken together, the above-mentioned acts have affected approximately 1,500,000 unionized workers. They have been presented, in most cases, as 'temporary' legislation which merely 'suspends' the right to strike and free collective bargaining. Yet there are good reasons for thinking that this is indeed a case where the old French saying— *c'est seulement le proviso ire qui dure*—has particular merit. These temporary measures are part of a long-term trend that includes the growing use of back-to-work legislation, the adoption of the statutory incomes policy in 1975, the jailing of prominent union leaders for the first time in the post-war era, and the increased designation of public sector workers as 'essential', thereby removing their right to strike.

It is true that the Ontario Supreme Court, in a rather weak ruling coming towards the very end of the life of Ontario's Inflation Restraint Act, declared the act unconstitutional because the act's blanket removal of the right to strike was inconsistent with the freedom of association guaranteed in the Charter. The significance of this ruling is unclear, however, not least because of the ambiguity of the status of the Charter itself. In any case, the federal legislation has remained unaffected by the ruling; no government has explicitly accepted its implications; and Alberta has explicitly promised to use the 'notwithstanding clause' in the constitution to ensure that its legal prohibitions of public sector workers' right to strike remain unaffected by the ruling. Simultaneously, the federal and some provincial governments have moved to facilitate the employment of non-union labour in the construction industry, thus signalling that private as well as public sector workers are coming under the scope of the new, more permanent restrictions of the rights of labour. This paper examines the rise and fall of the era of 'free collective bargaining' and speculates on the shape the new era will take in the future. . . .

The Post-War Decades

The passage of the 1948 Industrial Relations and Disputes Investigation Act by the federal government, accompanied by similar provincial legislation, signified that legal protection of workers' freedom to organize and to bargain would be a central element of the post-war 'settlement'. The labour movement undoubtedly expected that the reforms were 'permanent' gains which would be gradually extended to other workers and perhaps liberalized (Swartz, 1977).[1] Moreover, given that the settlement also expanded the role of the state, substantial growth in the number of public sector workers was ensured. It might have been expected that the extension of bargaining rights would have begun among public employees.[2] There was, however, little growth of bargaining rights in the post-war decades. In general, the unionized proportion of the nonagricultural work force remained close to the 1948 figure of 30 per cent until the mid-1960s. Until that time, there was no extension of legislative protection in the fast growing public sector; indeed, the only changes involved the imposition of additional restrictions on existing collective rights (Jamieson, 1973: 130 ff).[3]

The end to this impasse came not gradually but suddenly, sparked by the Quiet Revolution in Quebec in the mid-1960s. This decade is frequently portrayed as one of university student radicalism and militancy contrasted with working-class consumerism and acquiescence.[4] This contrast is overdrawn, as the 'revolt' of the 1960s was, in broad measure, a generational one. More importantly, consumerism is not without its contradictions. As Ralph Miliband observed, in taking issue with the omnipotence ascribed to corporate demand management through advertising by John Galbraith and others: 'The point is rather that business is able freely to propagate an ethos in which private acquisitiveness is made to appear as the main if not the only avenue to fulfillment, in which "happiness" or "success" are therefore defined in terms of private acquisition. . .' (Miliband, 1969: 217). 'Happiness' and 'success' are of course, relative terms. By the 1960s, the character of the working class was being transformed by the post-war generation no less than the universities. Their frame of reference did not include the Depression or the Cold War, and they grew up when the myth of a classless, affluent society was being incessantly propagated. The contrast between this image and their reality did not so much tarnish the image as inspire them to make it part of their own reality.[5] Increasingly, the only way to achieve incomes consistent with the image was through collective bargaining. This development was manifest in the mid-1960s wave of strikes, an uncommonly large number of which were wildcats (marked by occasional violence) conducted in defiance of union leaders and at times partially against them.

An even more profound set of changes was at work in Quebec.[6] The previous 25 years had seen a transformation of the economic base of Quebec and of its working class, including the growth of unionization. Despite this transformation, the provincial state remained in the grip of conservative, rural interests headed by Duplessis and the Catholic church. The Quebec government's response to a succession of strikes from the 1949 Asbestos Strike through to Murdochville in 1957 was hostile and repressive, fostering a relatively radical working class and intelligentsia. The 1961 election victory of the Lesage Liberals formally broke the hold of the *ancien régime* on the Quebec state, and initiated a belated and rapid political

modernization. For this, no less than in Canada at the close of World War II, a political settlement with labour was essential. The basis of this settlement was the extension of bargaining rights to Quebec's public sector workers in 1965.

The breakthrough in Quebec sent shockwaves reverberating throughout Canada because the reforms went well beyond what had been achieved in English Canada. Moreover, federal public sector workers in Quebec were part of the politicization process of the Quebec working class and were galvanized to intensify their efforts to win the same demands from their own employer. Pressure from Quebec was a powerful boost to the growing insistence of federal workers generally for bargaining rights after the Diefenbaker government, faced with the 1958–61 recession, broke precedent by rejecting the pay increase proposed by the bi-partite National Joint Council, which since 1941 had advised the government on these matters (Arthurs, 1971).

It was inevitable that significant political restructuring would take place, not only in Quebec but at the federal level as well. The Quebec Liberal Party, reflecting the initiatives of a radicalized petit bourgeois intelligentsia, provided a beacon to the federal Liberals who needed to find a new image after the conservative St Laurent–C.D. Howe government of the 1950s was routed by the populist Diefenbaker Conservatives in 1958. This need was intensified by the apparent appeal of the recently formed NDP, an appeal which was sufficient to block a quick return of the Liberals to power.

The new reality at the federal level was reflected in the fanfare surrounding the co-optation of the 'three wise men', Trudeau, Pelletier, and Marchand, into the leadership of the Liberal Party. The second wave of the welfare state in Canada undertaken by the minority Liberal governments of the mid-1960s was in good part an outcome of these developments. A significant element of this, apart from medicare and pension reforms, was the appointment of the Heeney Commission in 1963 to examine the question of collective bargaining rights for federal workers. That Heeney would recommend in favour of collective bargaining for federal workers was a foregone conclusion; what was at issue was how free it really would be.

The government's commitment to the rights of its workers was no deeper than that of capital. As employers, governments have a unique rationale for restricting their employees' freedom of association—the supremacy of parliament. As a result, while finally conceding federal employees' collective bargaining rights in 1967, the federal government insisted on restrictions beyond those imposed on private sector workers. Vital issues, including pensions, job classifications, technological change, staffing, and use of part-time or casual labour, were wholly or partly excluded from the scope of bargaining. Serious consideration was given to denying federal workers the right to strike as well. That the right to strike was granted was due in large measure to the willingness of postal employees, particularly in Quebec and BC, to wage a number of what, in effect, were recognition strikes in the mid-1960s. These strikes did much to persuade the government that making strikes illegal was no guarantee of preventing them.'[7]

The reverberations of the Quiet Revolution in Quebec were also felt in the provinces, where collective bargaining became the order of the day for most public sector workers. While the meaningfulness of these reforms is beyond doubt, it is nonetheless striking how cramped a version of trade union freedoms was conceded. In most provinces a number of crucial issues were decreed to be outside the scope of bargaining. Secondly, in Alberta, Ontario, PEI, and Nova Scotia, provincial employees, and often others, such as hospital workers, were denied the right to strike (Goldenberg, 1973).[8]

The Limits of Reform

The 'breakthrough' of the 1960s in the extension of free collective bargaining must be seen in terms of the continuing narrow limits of trade union rights in Canada. It would be wrong to ascribe these limits just to the resistance of particular sections of capital or to the ideology of liberal politicians. An equally important, and largely ignored, factor has been the remarkable conservatism of the English Canadian labour movement, which has repeatedly proved itself incapable of taking the initiative in generating demands and mobilizing support for reforms to challenge the terms of the post-war settlement. Few Canadian trade unionists, for example, have questioned the principle of the ban on strikes during the life of a collective agreement, although they have sought specific exemptions from its application (for example, unsafe working conditions and technological changes). They have even accepted the requirement that unions act as agents of the law by formally notifying their members of the legal obligation to abide by this ban.

This conservatism can be attributed in part to the effects of the Cold War on the labour movement. The anti-communist crusade after World War II was directed against the tradition of socialist ideas and militant rank-and-file struggle, as much as at members of the Communist Party who symbolized, albeit imperfectly and not exclusively, that tradition. As a result, control of the labour movement was assumed by people who were characterized, as David Lewis delicately put it, 'by the absence of a sense of idealism' (Lewis, 1981: 393). There is no little irony in Lewis providing this description given his own central role in building a base for the CCF in the union movement by trying 'to wrest control from the communists where ever possible' (Lewis, 1981: 151). In this struggle, the CCF allied with the most conservative and opportunistic elements of the union leadership, who, upon winning this internecine struggle, placed their own indelible stamp on the labour movement.

But other factors are involved as well, not least because objective circumstances typically exert more influence over action than subjective intention. In this respect, the adverse effort of the 1940s legislation on the character of the Canadian labour movment must enter into our consideration. Bourgeois reforms, however much they are the product of class struggle, are not without their contradictions. Left unchallenged they can undermine the very conditions which called them into existence, opening the way for future defeats. In reflecting on the approach to union recognition of the IDIA, H.A. Logan observed that: 'The powerful weapon of the strike as an aid to negotiation through militant organization, was weakened in its usefulness where the approach to recognition had to be certification' (Logan, 1956: 76). Logan's reference to the way the legislation devalued militant organization is of crucial importance. Unlike the capitalist firm with its singularity of purpose, unions aggregate discrete individuals with their own purposes. The power of unions lies in the willingness of their members to act collectively, for which a common purpose must be developed (Offe and Wiesenthal, 1979). This is a social process—an outcome of education and organization involving sustained interaction between leaders and members—and one requiring particular skills. Moreover, the incessant centrifugal pressures of a liberal consumerist society make this a never ending process.

The certification approach to recognition did not just weaken the apparent importance of militant organization, but directed the efforts of union leaders away from mobilizing and organizing towards the juridical arena of the labour boards. In this context, different skills were necessary; it was crucial above all to know the law—legal rights, procedures, precedents, etc. These activities tended to foster a legalistic practice and

consciousness in which union rights appeared as privileges bestowed by the state rather than democratic freedoms won and to be defended by collective struggle.[9] The ban on strikes during collective agreements and the institution of compulsory arbitration to resolve disputes while agreements were in force had a similar effect. Under these circumstances, it was unnecessary to maintain and develop collective organization between negotiations. Indeed, union leaders had a powerful incentive to do the reverse, to suppress any sign of spontaneous militancy. Industrial relations legislation inevitably tends to treat unions as legal entities distinct from the people who comprise them. This was reflected in the typically much greater penalties for union officials who violate the law as compared to those for members, which intensifies the pressure on the former to act as agents of social control over their members rather than their spokespersons and organizers.

The corrosive effects on union democracy of this kind of juridical and ideological structuring have been severe.[10] The trade unionism which developed in Canada during the post-war years bore all the signs of the web of legal restrictions which enveloped it. Its practice and consciousness were highly legalistic and bureaucratic, and its collective strength accordingly limited. These characteristics were reflected in the acceptance of the greater restrictions on public employees' freedom of association by the broader labour movement. Moreover, the existing labour movement provided no other inspiration or example than legalism for public sector unions granted partial collective bargaining in the 1960s. This model has been particularly debilitating for those public sector unions which have had to engage in little of the mobilization and struggle for recognition that shaped the early labour movement prior to the post-war settlement. Thus, a union like the Public Service Alliance of Canada (PSAC), in contrast to the Canadian Union of Postal Workers (CUPW), was one born almost entirely of legalism rather than mobilization and struggle.

This, of course, is not to suggest that all the newly-recognized public sector unions have been content to accept what has been offered to them. For many the limited rights acquired were seen only as a way station on the path to their final destination of trade union rights equivalent to those enjoyed in the private sector. As events unfolded, however, this proved to be a naively optimistic view. By the time the unions reached this way station in the late 1960s the roadbed was already crumbling because the state had to contend with the wage pressure from its workers, while adjusting to the constraints placed upon it by the emerging crisis of capitalism.

Towards Exceptionalism

The wave of industrial militancy which arose in the mid-1960s continued on into the early 1970s when it crested as public sector workers, inspired by material aspirations similar to those of private sector workers, exhibited a willingness to fight to achieve them (Swimmer, 1984). This heightened degree of industrial conflict, however, reflected not just greater worker militancy but also opposition to union demands by capital and the state because of the deepening economic crisis. The long post-war boom had led many observers to believe that sustained economic growth was unproblematic. If capitalism had not quietly passed away, they argued, at least its anarchic character had been subdued by governments armed with Keynesian theory.[11] But the post-war boom could not, and did not, last. In the 1970s the economy was characterized by 'stagflation'; growth rates below the level necessary for full employment, combined with severe inflationary tendencies. In these conditions, the margin for concessions to secure labour's

consent no longer existed. It was capital that increasingly required concessions. Faced with stagnant or shrinking markets, rising resource prices, increased foreign competition, and a labour movement ready to defend its living standards, capital experienced reduced profit margins on existing investments and few new profitable opportunities.

One response by governments in Canada, and elsewhere, involved additional subsidies to capital through loans, grants, and tax concessions. Thus governments underwrote investment and further shifted the cost of the welfare state onto employed workers.[12] But these initiatives had little impact on economic growth; indeed, they tended to exacerbate inflation because organized workers responded militantly to preserve their real incomes. Government deficits ballooned as expenditures on corporate subsidies, the unemployed, and public sector wages rose. The other major response by the state to the economic crisis was its attempt to restrict the bargaining power of organized labour. Governments attempted to obtain the 'voluntary' agreement of union leaders to limit members' wage demands to some agreed level, in exchange for a union role in state economic decision making and/or reforms enhancing union security, marginal extensions of the welfare state, etc.[13] At the same time, government increasingly deployed the state's coercive powers against the labour movement. These two strategies were not mutually exclusive. Coercive measures served, intentionally or otherwise, to prompt unions to rethink their opposition to 'voluntary' restraint. On the other hand, the inability of the state to deliver a *quid pro quo* in a form of the 'social wage' because of the growing economic crisis, undermined the viability of the voluntary restraint option and forced the state to adopt more coercive measures.

Government policy at the federal and provincial levels initially reflected both strategies. In 1969–70 and again in 1974–75 the federal

Table 26.1 Back to Work Legislation in Canada

	Federal	Provincial	Total
1950–1970	4	9	13
1971–1975	4	11	15
1976–1978	6	13	19
Total	14	33	47

Source: A. Price, 'Back to Work Legislation' (Price, 1980).

government held discussions with the Canadian Labour Congress (CLC) aimed at securing voluntary wage restraint.[14] In a number of jurisdictions there were reforms enhancing union security and workers' collective rights; for example, the relaxation of the restrictions on secondary picketing (BC), expansion of the right to refuse unsafe work (Ontario, Saskatchewan, federal government), provisions for imposing first agreements on recalcitrant employers (BC, Ontario, Quebec), and limitations on the use of strikebreakers (Quebec). Nonetheless, what became particularly striking as the decade of the 1970s wore on was the state's shift towards new coercive measures. This change was graphically reflected in the rising incidence of *ad hoc* back-to-work legislation at both federal and provincial levels.

The first post-war use of such legislation was by the federal government in 1950 against railway workers striking for a 40-hour week and a pay increase. The justification then, as subsequently, for the legislation was, to quote Prime Minister St Laurent, that 'the welfare and security of the nation are imperilled' (qtd in Price, 1980, 98).[15] Not surprisingly, St Laurent insisted that it was 'not designed to establish precedents or procedures for subsequent bargaining negotiations' (Price, 1980: 99). Events were to prove otherwise, as railway workers were threatened with similar legislation

in 1954 and actually subjected to it in 1960 and 1966. The increased frequency and wider application of back-to-work legislation was not the only notable trend in the state's use of this weapon. Governments have introduced such legislation with greater dispatch after the onset of a dispute and with less parliamentary debate. They have also legislated increasingly onerous penalties for union members defying the law.

This new reliance on back-to-work legislation was part of a broader pattern of developments, which characterized the onset of a new era in state policy towards labour. What marked this transformation was a shift away from the generalized form of coercion (whereby an overall legal framework both establishes and constrains the fights and powers of all unions), towards a form of selective, *ad hoc*, discretionary state coercion (whereby the state removes for a specific purpose and period the rights contained in labour legislation). We have witnessed a return to the pre-PC 1003 era of '*ad hoc* suspension of hostilities', not to avoid or delay the establishment of freedom of association, but to contain or repress manifestations of class conflict as practised within the institutionalized freedom of association. In the last decade, actions legal under general legislation have increasingly been declared unlawful for particular groups of workers or for all workers for a particular period of time. The state's resorting with increasing frequency to emergency rhetoric and powers to override the general framework of freedoms clearly indicated that there was a crisis in the old form of rule. This is precisely what has happened in Canada over the last decade, and today characterizes the state's response to labour.

The treatment accorded to CUPW by the federal government in 1978 illustrates this crisis as it is manifested through back-to-work legislation. The government publicly stated in advance of a strike that it would not tolerate the union's exercise of its legal right to strike. Once the strike began, the government immediately invoked back-to-work legislation (Postal Services Continuation Act, Bill C-8), which revived the previous collective agreement and overrode the relatively small penalties in the Public Service Staff Relations Act to allow for potentially unlimited penalties. Finally, the government charged the union's leader, J.C. Parrot, not for encouraging his members to defy the back-to-work law, but for remaining silent (not publicly urging them to obey the law) (Glasbeek and Mandel, 1979: 10–14). Similar requirements on union leaders specified in previous back-to-work legislation had escaped public notice because they were either obeyed, or if not, were disregarded by the government. In charging Parrot, and in the courts making bail for Parrot conditional upon his telling CUPW members what the law required, the state not only set aside the general legal provisions for the union's right to strike, but also the Bill of Rights protection of free speech.

The increased use of back-to-work legislation is only one sign of the end of the era of free collective bargaining. Equally significant is the use of designations in the public sector to remove the right to strike from a much broader group of workers, and the use of statutory incomes policy to suspend free collective bargaining. Under the 1967 legislation extending collective bargaining to federal public employees, the government reserved the right to 'designate' certain jobs as 'essential for the safety and security of the public' and hence to deny the workers performing these jobs the right to strike. As interpreted by the Public Service Staff Relations Board (PSSRB), the definition of 'safety and security' was a relatively narrow one, so that the right to strike was not vitiated by indiscriminate use of designations,[16] and the government traditionally accepted the PSSRB's definition. This practice was shattered in 1982 when the government, intent on withdrawing the right to strike of virtually the whole Air Traffic Controllers group, successfully challenged the Board's definition of 'safety and security' in the Supreme Court.[17] This ruling allows the government to designate anyone whose normal work activities, in the government's own view, concern the safety and security of the public. Three sets of negotiations have occurred since this decision, which permit an assessment of the government's future intentions. In two cases, the percentage of workers designated was increased by half—to over 40 per cent of all workers in the Program Managers category of the federal public service, and to over 90 per cent of heating and power workers. In the other case, Library Sciences, the number of designations remained insignificant.[18] It would appear that this difference reflects an implicit criterion of basing designations on the bargaining strength of a group of workers.

The use of back-to-work legislation and of designations primarily concern public sector workers. The statutory incomes policy of the Anti-Inflation Programme of 1975–78 suspended free collective bargaining for all workers. It was initiated by the government and upheld by the courts on the basis of an elastic definition of economic emergency. Once again, the rules of the game established in the post-war settlement were set aside through special legislation, which empowered the Anti-Inflation Board to examine newly negotiated agreements and roll back wage increases exceeding the government's guidelines. The act created an 'Administrator' to enforce a Board report or Cabinet order through the onerous penalties of unlimited fines and five years imprisonment. The new spirit of the era was adequately expressed by Prime Minister Trudeau when he cynically told a radio interviewer immediately after the initiation of the Anti-Inflation Programme that 'We'll put a few union leaders in jail for three years and others will get the message' (Panitch, 1976).

It is now virtually universally conceded that despite the government's rhetoric about equivalent price, dividend, and profit restraint under the Anti-Inflation Programme, the substantive aspect of the policy entailed only wage controls. Prime Minister Trudeau, in his October 1982 broadcast, referred to a comprehensive but temporary statutory prices and incomes policy of the 1975–78 type as follows: '. . .what controls are for [is] to place the coercive use of Government power between Canadians, like a referee who pushes boxers apart and forces them to their corners to rest up so that they can hit each other again' (qtd in *Globe and Mail*, 21 October 1982). A more appropriate metaphor for the 1975–78 case would have the referee holding the arms of one of the boxers while the other flailed away.

The New Era

As indicated in the introduction, the events of 1982 which combined the silence of the new constitution on bargaining and strike rights with the particularly draconian, 'temporary' suspension of those rights for a very large number of Canadian workers, signal a new era in labour relations. It inaugurates a new era, however, only in the sense that it makes explicit what was implicit in the developments of the last decade. What has been made explicit is that the *ad hoc*, selective, 'temporary' use of coercion is not merely directed at the particular groups of workers affected or at the particular issue or emergency at hand, but rather is designed to set an example for what is appropriate behaviour throughout the industrial relations system. The suspension in 1982 of public sector workers' rights was not proclaimed or defended in terms of what it would directly accomplish to stem inflation and reinvigorate Canadian capitalism. It was offered as an example of what other workers must voluntarily do if these objectives are to be attained.

What characterizes the new era is not only a series of *ad hoc* coercive measures by the state, but also the construction of a new ideology to extend the state's new coercive role to the working class as a whole. Because this new ideology is not legally codified in the manner of the post-war settlement—because it does not universally remove the right to strike and free collective bargaining—the new state coercion is paradoxically capable of being ideologically portrayed as 'voluntary'. Thus the Prime Minister's October 1982 broadcasts to the nation emphatically declared that the government had explicitly rejected the option of the 'coercive use of Government power':

> Controls could not create the trust in each other and belief in our country that alone would serve our future. Controls would declare, with the force of law, that Canadians cannot trust Canadians. . . . To choose to fight inflation, as a free people acting together—that is the course we chose. (qtd in *Globe and Mail*, 21 October 1982)

The successful presentation of increased use of state coercion in this obfuscatory way is conditional upon three elements. The first is a form of ideological excommunication regarding the rights of public sector workers *qua* Canadian citizens.

The draconian controls established over them in 1982 became hidden amidst careful phrases which asserted that only '*comprehensive* controls' were coercive and contrary to the principle of a 'free people acting together'. They were rather 'examples' for other workers' 'voluntarism'. That this sleight-of-hand can even be attempted rests upon a decade of denigration of state employees as parasites and a decade of denigration of state services, not long ago understood as essential to the community and social justice, as wasteful and unproductive.

The second element is that the specific acts of coercion—back-to-work legislation, designation, statutory incomes policies—be continually portrayed as temporary, exceptional, and emergency-related, regardless of how frequently they occur, and the increasing numbers of workers who fall within their scope or are threatened by their 'example'. In so far as the terminology of emergency and crisis can be made elastic enough to cover a whole era rather than specific events, months or even years, measures presented as temporary can come to characterize an entire historical period.

Finally, and perhaps most importantly, the voluntary ideological veneer of the new era rests upon the construction of a new set of norms to justify labour's subordinate role within capitalism. The post-war settlement sought to maintain capital's dominant position by establishing legal rights for organized labour to protect the workers' immediate material interests in a capitalist system. The new era's ideology reverses this earlier logic. It places the onus on labour to maintain capitalism as a viable economic system by acquiescing to capital's demand for the restriction or suspension of labour's previously recognized rights and freedoms, as well as sacrificing its immediate material interests. Whereas the 'question of social justice' was the key phrase in the construction of the hegemony of the 1940s, Trudeau's 'question of trust and belief' becomes the key phrase in the effort to reconstitute it in the 1980s.

It must be stressed that Trudeau and his government do not stand alone in effecting the construction of the 'trust and belief' element of the new ideology. They are aided not least by a bevy of industrial relations experts, many of whom are recognized publicly for their 'pro-labour' sentiments. A good example is provided by Paul Weiler. At one level, his book displays with refreshing candour the dilemmas of a liberal reformer in its attempt to combine a spirited defence of the right to strike with a model of state intervention which will ensure that this right will not be disruptive to capital. At another level, Weiler's study makes an unwitting contribution to the construction of the new ideology when he attempts to justify statutory incomes policies as being in labour's interests, Weiler acknowledges that the 1973–78 Anti-Inflation Programme only involved effective wage restraint, adding that for economic (the 'openness' of Canada's economy) and political (capitalist objections, the evils of bureaucracy) reasons, such programmes cannot do more than restrain incomes. Nor does he view wage increases as the sole cause of inflation. Nonetheless, he commends controls, if not the government's lack of candour, to labour, arguing that it is in labour's interests to acquiesce to such policies. The uncertainty that inflation creates 'interferes with rational business planning and investment', reduces the rate of job creation, and makes Canadian products less competitive internationally, all of which threaten to create 'unemployment in our plants and factories'. Controls in this context '*facilitate* an orderly winding down of inflation . . . with a minimum of disruption and unemployment' (Weiler, 1980: 254). In other words, labour should eschew efforts to defend its economic interests directly and entrust its future to capital.

The 'trust and belief' required of labour in this new era may sound reasonable, but it is not. It requires labour to trust that capital will use workers' forgone wages and social benefits to invest in Canada rather than abroad, without any guarantees that they will in fact do so. It requires labour to trust that capital will not speculate in land, currency, or commodity markets nor use re-established profit margins to reward executives lavishly. Indeed, if trust and belief in capital are the requirements of the day for workers, what, one might ask, is the use of unions at all? Perhaps they are useful only if they can be induced to contribute to spreading the new ideology and to policing their members; adherence to the new coercive interventions and their 'voluntary' by-products? One is reminded of an earlier Pierre Elliott Trudeau writing after the 1949 Asbestos Strike:

> In the present state of society, in fact, it is the possibility of the strike which enables workers to negotiate with their employers on terms of approximate equality. It is wrong to think that the unions are in themselves able to secure this equality. If the right to strike is suppressed, or seriously limited, the trade union movement becomes nothing more than one institution among many in the service of capitalism: a convenient organization for disciplining the workers, occupying their leisure time, and ensuring their profitability for business. (Trudeau, 1974: 334)

Towards the Future

What will be the labour movement's response to the new era? It cannot be assumed that Canadian labour will lie down and play dead. The CLC's national one-day general strike against the Anti-Inflation Programme, known as the Day of Protest

of 14 October 1976, was an early instance not only of Canadian labour's unwillingness to succumb to the first salvos in the new era of coercion, but also of a certain preparedness even among the top leadership, to respond with industrial action. Moreover, as the economic crisis deepened, some Canadian unions, such as the United Auto Workers, were much less cowed by their employers than their American counterparts and managed to obtain significantly better contract terms. Similarly, Canadian public employees appear to have been less frightened by threats of public expenditure cutbacks than have their American counterparts as evidenced by a number of public sector strikes, most notably by nurses in Alberta, hospital workers in Ontario, and federal clerical workers. But these facts may only explain why the state acted to restrict significantly the rights of the Canadian working class in 1982. They tell little about how workers will respond in the longer term.

There is little reason to expect that the Canadian labour movement will be capable of mounting any meaningful or sustained counter-offensive in the immediate future. The leaderships' commitment to the existing legal framework, even when new legislation has abrogated previous laws enshrining workers' rights, has been remarkable. This was graphically illustrated by the CLC's abandonment of the postal workers in 1978 and CLC President Denis McDermot's explicit attack on the union. It was seen again in 1983 when the CLC's initial public response to the BC government's evisceration of trade union rights, along with tenant and civil liberties protections, was to counsel the workers affected against taking strike action.

The union movement has been clearly unprepared for each successive coercive blow struck by the state over the past decade. The 1976 Day of Protest, while in itself a successful and unprecedented mobilization by the CLC, came ultimately to represent the climax of real opposition to the Anti-Inflation Programme rather than the onset of a campaign of sustained mass mobilization. Despite the repeated attacks on the right to strike, the CLC, virtually alone among large interest groups in Canada, remained aloof from the constitutional debate. It did not even make representation to the parliamentary hearings regarding inclusion of the right to strike, or free collective bargaining, or full employment in the Charter of Rights and Freedoms. Other liberal democratic constitutions contain such rights. Although the practical effects of such declarations may not be great, inclusion of such rights at least helps to legitimate union struggles around these issues. Even an unsuccessful campaign for including such rights in the constitution would have put the issue before their members and the broader public.

For various reasons, including the federal NDP's alliance with the Liberals and the reluctance of the Quebec Federation of Labour to be seen improving a constitution which the Quebec government unalterably opposed, the CLC did not act. Ironically, on the very day (12 January 1981) that the Justice Minister appeared before the special parliamentary committee to present the government's amendments to the Charter of Rights and Freedoms in response to the submissions received from about 100 groups across Canada, the National Union of Provincial Government Employees announced plans to seek action from the federal Labour Minister in the wake of an ILO ruling that the Alberta government had violated international labour conventions (ratified by Canada in 1972) by denying the right to strike to its own employees (*Globe and Mail*, 13 January 1982). Would the CLC have been less complacent about the constitution if it had known that but two months after its proclamation, the right to strike would be 'temporarily' removed from federal employees as well?

To be sure, the defence of the right to strike does not ultimately lie in representations to parliamentary committees on constitutional rights. But is it any less evident that the Canadian labour movement neither at the top nor the bottom is capable of undertaking a sustained coordinated defence—industrially, politically, ideologically—of the right to strike? In advance of the federal government's '6 and 5' legislation, a resolution calling for action up to and including a general strike in the event that the government abrogated the right to strike was carried by a huge majority at the CLC convention. The CLC leadership is not wrong in recognizing that such resolutions from the left contain a large measure of rhetorical flourish and lack mass support. Years of neglect of the mobilizing aspects of trade unionism and years of practice of legalism have taken their toll on the fighting capacity of union organizations. This of course neither excuses, nor more importantly explains, the failure of the union leadership seriously to attempt to build such support. The nature of the problem, which goes well beyond facile charges that the leadership lacks the will to fight, was cogently expressed by J.C. Parrot in a recent interview. Responding to the question of why resistance by the union leadership to the new coercion has been so weak, he noted:

Well, it starts with a feeling of being powerless. So why do they feel powerless? Well, first of all, the big thing is that we are fighting the government and fighting against the law. So you get the feeling, how can I do something? If you meet with lawyers two or three times in a week, they are not going to tell you that you have to fight on the streets. They are going to tell you what the legal avenues are, and so you get directed to that. And then, in addition, many leaders have no control over the unions. When I say control, I mean that it's not even controlled by the members either. The structure is made in such a way that in order for the leaders to get to the membership, they have to go through a structure, and never get to the membership, which is a serious problem. Especially at a time when you have to work with other unions, as in fighting Bill C-124, the structure of the labour movement is unbelievable. People don't seem to know what to do. It's like the leadership has never gotten involved in a struggle before. It seems you have to go through all the ABCs of what a struggle is in order to be able to get organized. (Parrot, 1983: 61)

Of course, one must not overestimate the dominance of capital and state in this crisis nor the permanence of the present union paralysis. The contradictions to be contained by the new ideology are not easily managed. The ideology of the era of free collective bargaining was rooted in a material basis of consent permitted by the expansion of post-war capitalism. It should be recalled, moreover, that the west's moral superiority in the Cold War was in part sustained precisely by the post-war settlement's legal proclamation of workers' democratic rights amidst the refrain of 'social justice'. Today, however, the material basis of consent can less easily be summoned up. And fighting the new Cold War entails defending Polish workers' rights at the same time as Canadian workers' rights are being denied.

The following *Globe and Mail* editorial refers to Poland but it could just as easily apply to Canada:

For this so-called 'rebirth of the trade union movement' to be genuine, however, it would have to include independent unions administered and led by officials who were nominated freely and elected by secret ballot. They must

also have the rights normally associated with labour unions, including the strike weapon. . . . The trade union movement, as envisioned by the bill, would not be so much a movement as an aggregation of individual unions. . . The right to strike would technically exist, but would be severely cramped by complex regulations. There would be a requirement of seven days notice preceding a strike. Any strike 'of a political character' would be prohibited, with the government having discretion to decide what is politically motivated. The bill would provide arbitration procedures for labour disputes and forbid any strike over an issue that could be arbitrated. . . . (*Globe and Mail*, 8 October 1982)

The conditions are obviously not propitious for selling the new coercion in terms of voluntarism and freedom. It is surely not by accident, after all, that the massive and broad-based opposition to the repressive measures imposed by the Bennett government in BC has rallied under the name Operation Solidarity. Moreover, one's assessment of the combative potential of the union movement should not be restricted to what the CLC or the union leadership accomplishes in its opposition to the new coercion. It is one of the paradoxes of depressions that they make workers acutely aware of the benefits of collective action and solidarity, precisely because their employers are less wary of asserting managerial authority in a period of high unemployment. There will certainly be a struggle on the ground, as there was in the 1930s, to change the character of the union movement in Canada. The era of 'free collective bargaining' induced legalism and complacency regarding union organization and officialdom. The era of discretionary coercion may be expected to induce a rather different, more combative labour movement in turn.

Notes

1. Immediate post-war reforms were often presented as 'down payments' towards more comprehensive measures. For example, federal assistance to the provinces for extending health facilities, particularly hospitals, was presented as a step towards health insurance—a Liberal Party 'promise' since 1919.

2. It is well recognized that the working conditions, including pay and managerial practices, of public employees were inferior to those of private sector workers employed by major corporations. It should be noted here that in 1944 the CCF government in Saskatchewan granted bargaining rights to provincial employees.

3. The unionized proportion of the work force did 'jump' from 30 to 33 per cent between 1952–53, and then slowly declined to just below 30 per cent in the mid-1960s. The 1952–53 increase was due primarily to a contraction of 100,000 in the labour force. In BC new restrictions were imposed on the right to strike generally, while in Alberta, what were deemed 'public interest disputes' were subject to more sweeping restrictions.

4. This position was common on the 'left' as well as in mainstream thinking. For example, see H. Marcuse, *One Dimensional Man* (Boston: Beacon, 1964), and J. O'Conner, *The Fiscal Crisis of the State* (New York: St Martin's Press, 1973).

5. A broadly similar argument is made by Jamieson, *Industrial Relations*.

6. For a good overview, see K. McRoberts and D. Posgate, *Quebec: Social Change and Political Crisis*, rev. ed. (Toronto: McClelland and Stewart, 1980).

7. There has been some suggestion that Jean Marchand, the former President of the CNTU and the most sought after of the 'three wise men', made granting the right to strike a condition for remaining in the government. (Personal communication from E. Swimmer.)

8. A useful, if somewhat dated, overview of provincial labour legislation is Goldenberg, 1973.

9. For a brilliant elaboration of this argument in the context of the US, see K. Klare, 'Juridical Deradicalization of the Wagner Act and the Origins of Modern Legal Consciousness 1937–1974', *Minnesota Law Review* 62 (1978): 265–339. R. Warskett, 'Trade Unions in the Canadian State: A Case Study of Bank Worker Unionization 1976–1980', MA thesis, Carleton University, 1981, develops a similar argument in her timely and insightful study of efforts to organize bank workers in Canada.

10. For a graphic illustration see J. Deverell, 'The

Ontario Hospital Dispute 1980–1981', *Studies in Political Economy: A Socialist Review* 9 (1982).

11. This boom was in fact the product of a historically specific set of conditions which existed at the end of World War II: the unchallenged dominance of the US *vis à vis* the major capitalist countries which allowed it to order the international financial system; the extensive task of post-war reconstruction in Europe; huge discoveries of cheap resources; the colonial or neo-colonial dependency of most of the Third World, and the moderation of the labour movement in the west, not least due to the Cold War. While signs of their passing were already dimly visible by the mid-sixties, the 'formal announcement' came in 1971, when US President Nixon renounced the Bretton Woods agreement on which the post-war international financial order was based. See, for example, I. Gough, 'State Expenditure in Advanced Capitalism', *New Left Review* 92 (1975).

12. See for example, D. Wolfe, 'The State and Economic Policy in Canada, 1968–1975', in L. Panitch, ed., *The Canadian State: Political Economy and Political Power* (Toronto: University of Toronto Press, 1977), 251–88, and I. Gillespie, 'On the Redistribution of Income in Canada', *Canadian Tax Journal* 24 (1976): 419–50.

13. See L. Panitch, 'The Development of Corporatism in Liberal Democracies', *Comparative Political Studies* 10 (1977).

14. A discussion of these attempts in Canada and the reasons for their failure is found in L. Panitch, 'Corporatism in Canada?', *Studies in Political Economy: A Socialist Review* 1 (1979): 43–92. See also A. Maslove and E. Swimmer, *Wage Controls in Canada 1975–1978: A Study of Public Decision Making* (Montreal: IRPP, 1980).

15. Based upon a detailed examination of these legislative orders by the federal and Ontario governments, Price concludes that seldom, if ever, was there such a threat. Rather, government intervention was designed to prevent serious disruption of immediate concern to a relatively small segment of society, or to prevent broad public inconvenience (Price, 1980: 90).

16. The 'designation' of the Governor General's gardener during the 1974 strike by the General Labour and Trades group illustrates the willingness of the government to exploit this provision.

17. See the Canadian Air Traffic Control Association vs the Treasury Board, Judgement dated 31 May 1982.

18. Information supplied by an official of PSAC.

References

Arthurs, H. 1971. *Collective Bargaining by Public Employees in Canada: The Five Models*. Ann Arbor: Institute of Labor and Industrial Relations.

Glasbeek, H.J., and M. Mandel. 1979. 'The Crime and Punishment of Jean-Claude Parrot', *Canadian Forum* (August 1979).

Globe and Mail. 1982. 13 January.

Globe and Mail. 1982. 'Editorial', 8 October.

Globe and Mail. 1982. 21 October.

Goldenberg, S. 1973. 'Collective Bargaining in the Provincial Public Services', *The Institute of Public Administration of Canada Collective Bargaining in the Public Service*. Toronto: IPAC.

Jamieson, S. 1973. *Industrial Relations in Canada*. Toronto: Macmillan.

'J.C. Parrot: An Interview'. 1983. *Studies in Political Economy: A Socialist Review* 11.

Lewis, David. 1981. *The Good Fight: Political Memoirs 1909–1958*. Toronto: Macmillan.

Logan, H.A. 1956. *State Intervention and Assistance in Collective Bargaining: The Canadian Experience, 1943–1956*. Toronto: University of Toronto Press.

Miliband, R. 1969. *The State in Capitalist Society*. New York: Quartet Books.

Offe, C., and Wiesenthal, H. 1979. 'Two Logics of Collective Action', *Political Power and Social Theory* 1.

Panitch, L. 1976. *Workers, Wages, and Controls: The Anti-Inflation Programme and its Implications for Canadian Workers*. Toronto: Hogtown Press.

Price, A. 1980. 'Back to Work Legislation: An Analysis of the Federal and Ontario Governments' Increased Propensity to End Strikes by Ad Hoc Laws 1950–1978', MA thesis, Queen's University.

Swartz, D. 1977. 'The Politics of Reform: Conflict and Accommodation in Canadian Health Policy', in L. Panitch, ed., *The Canadian State: Political Economy and Political Power*. Toronto: University of Toronto Press.

Swimmer, E. 1984. 'Militancy and Public Sector Unions', in M. Thompson and E. Swimmer, eds, *Conflict or Compromise: Public Sector Industrial Relations in Canada*. Toronto: IRPP.

Trudeau, P.E. 1974. *The Asbestos Strike*. Toronto: James Lewis and Sameul.

Weiler, Paul. 1980. *Reconcilable Differences: New Directions in Canadian Labour Law*. Toronto: Carswell.

CHAPTER 27

Neoliberalism and Working-Class Resistance in British Columbia: The Hospital Employees' Union Struggle, 2002–2004

David Camfield

Public sector workers and the services they deliver have been dramatically affected by the development and generalization of neoliberalism as a response to capitalist crisis since the end of the post-war economic boom in the mid-1970s. This has certainly been true in Canada, where workers employed by governments and government-funded organizations in the broader public sector have for three decades experienced an onslaught of attacks, including wage controls, layoffs, demands for concessions, back-to-work legislation, privatization, contracting-out, and imposed collective agreements. Some Canadian public sector workers have responded with angry defiance—consider the illegal nurses' strikes in Saskatchewan and Quebec in 1999, the Calgary laundry workers' wildcat of 1995, the willingness of some leaders of the Canadian Union of Postal Workers [CUPW] to spurn the law's dictates and face time in jail, and the resolute strike by teaching assistants, research assistants, and contract faculty at York University. More often workers have put up minimal resistance or simply acquiesced, believing that, to use Margaret Thatcher's phrase that has come to be emblematic of neoliberalism's *pensée unique*, 'There is no alternative.'[1]

The strike by over 40,000 hospital and long-term care facility workers in British Columbia in the spring of 2004 could be seen as simply one more instance of public sector unionists struggling to defend themselves and the services they deliver from employers and a government intent on re-organizing the public sector on neoliberal lines. However, this strike was distinguished from many others in a number of ways. This workforce was overwhelmingly made up of women, including many women of colour, and organized in the Hospital Employees Union [HEU], which has one of the more left-wing leaderships in the Canadian labour movement. The workers displayed a remarkable degree of determination in the face of the BC government's attempt to end their strike by legislative order. Their resistance evoked an unusual degree of support that took the form of active solidarity rather than just passive sympathy. Some BC workers saw in HEU's struggle an opportunity to hit back at a provincial government that had done much to earn their ire. So strong was the desire to act in support of HEU that it pushed top leaders of the BC labour movement towards the kind of confrontation with state power and employers that the existing regime of industrial legality was designed to prevent. How and why a strike with such uncommon features ended with a concessionary settlement and the cancellation of the province-wide mass strike set for the following day, leaving many strikers and supporters furious at the BC labour leadership and calling to mind the experience of BC's Solidarity movement of 1983, are questions with important implications for the future of the working-class movement. This article demonstrates the systemic causes of the BC health care strike, explores its background and trajectory, and explains and assesses its outcome. The analysis developed here highlights the significance of the character of the contemporary labour officialdom as a social layer whose conditions of existence lead it to usually oppose forms of collective action outside the bounds of industrial legality.[2]

Leaning Health Care: The Neoliberal Prescription in British Columbia

The restructuring of health care in BC is no isolated development, and needs to be understood as an integral part of processes unfolding on a global scale. . . . It is commonly observed that the central thrust of this reorganization of the broader public sector is a shift from the welfare state to a new kind of public administration whose 'primary objective [is] the fostering of a globally competitive economy' (Nolan, 2001: 185). . . . Critics have argued that the 'reform' of the public sector that often occurs under the banner of the New Public Management is a neoliberal project that involves a fundamental shift from the Keynesian welfare state to a state whose focus is the promotion of 'flexibility' and corporate profit (Jessop, 1994; McBride and Shields, 1997; Shields and Evans, 1998; Smith, 2000; Teeple, 2000, Duménil and Lévy, 2004). . . .

A more concrete conceptualization of contemporary public sector restructuring that is compatible with this understanding has been proposed by Alan Sears, who analyzes neoliberal 'reform' as a move from the broad welfare state built in the era of the post-war boom to the 'lean' state. Avoiding the mistake of treating this reorganization of the state in functionalist fashion, as a reflex response to capital's needs, it is understood as a contested process developed over time through trial and error by governments and public sector managers in various countries. The project of lean states is to restructure social reproduction in ways that facilitate the spread and consolidation of lean production methods in paid workplaces. This involves a new mode of the political administration of civil society by state power, a host of legal and administrative measures designed to generate 'flexible' workers and 'lean' persons. Within the public sector, building the lean state involves shrinking the number of workers employed by governments and public sector organizations and expanding the ranks of lower paid, less secure employees, including workfare recipients, working for nonprofit 'community' agencies, and private firms that move in to take advantage of new opportunities to profit from contracting-out and other kinds of corporate involvement (Sears, 1999).[3]

This analysis allows us to see how the restructuring of health care in BC since the election of the Liberal Party under Gordon Campbell in Victoria in 2001 has systemic causes and is part of a much broader class project for reshaping state and society. . . . In 2002, the BC Liberal government moved to reduce medical services through the elimination of coverage for physiotherapy, chiropractic, massage and other therapies, making cuts to the Pharmacare programme, closing hospitals and long-term care facilities, cutting services and beds in others, and removing housekeeping work from the home care provided to disabled and elderly people. At the same time, the Campbell government encouraged more corporate involvement in health care, including the building of a P3 [Public Private Partnership] ambulatory care centre in Vancouver and a P3 hospital in Abbotsford (*The Report of the Commission. . .*, 2002; Armstrong and Armstrong, 2003; Fuller, Fuller, and Cohen, 2003).

Another important piece of the Campbell government's restructuring of health care was Bill 29, The Health and Social Services Delivery Act. Thanks to the Liberals' overwhelming majority, this piece of legislation was passed in the middle of the night on 28 January 2002 after only a few hours of debate in the legislature. Bill 29 allowed for extensive privatization and the elimination or transfer of services without consultation. It also made it illegal for health care workers to discuss alternatives to privatization with their employers and enabled the closure of hospitals with two months notice. In a direct attack on unionized workers, it stripped key provisions from the Health Services and Support Facilities Subsector collective agreement that covers members of HEU along with members of nine other unions that have a small presence in hospitals and long-term care facilities, and also added new provisions. Workers lost their strong 'no contracting-out' protection as well as successor rights and bumping language that had helped higher seniority workers avoid unemployment. Retraining and job placement rights were cut, along with the Health Labour Adjustment Agency, a body responsible for assisting laid-off workers that had been established as part of the Health Accord signed under the previous New Democratic Party [NDP] provincial government. Employers were given the power to move workers between hospitals and to temporary assignments at distant workplaces. This bill, blatantly favourable to health care managers and private sector contractors and 'arguably . . . the most severe government intrusion into collective agreements in Canadian history', was in perfect conformity with the lean state project. It also contradicted Campbell's commitment in a pre-election interview with HEU's newspaper *Guardian*: 'I am not tearing up any agreements.' Little wonder, then, that health care workers who had actually believed the Liberal leader's promises were especially furious.[4]

In the Crosshairs: Workers and the HEU

Most of the workers at the centre of BC health care restructuring were members of HEU, which represents over 90 per cent of health support workers in hospitals and long-term care facilities. HEU members include a broad range of clerical, food services, housekeeping, laundry, maintenance, technical, trades, and patient care workers, including Licensed Practical Nurses [LPNs].[5] This workforce is overwhelmingly made up of women, who were 85 per cent of HEU's membership in 2002 at the time of the most recent union membership survey. At that time, approximately three in ten HEU members were workers of colour. Fully 32 per cent of HEU members were born outside Canada, notably in the Philippines, the UK or Ireland, and India, compared to the 20 per cent of the population of BC born in these countries. HEU workers were, on average, significantly older than those in other parts of the labour force, with 57 per cent of HEU members aged 45 or more. Many were also long-service workers: on average, HEU members had belonged to the union for 13.6 years. Only 20 per cent had been members for five years or less. Not surprisingly for a workforce many of whose members were mature women, 46 per cent of HEU members had at least one dependent child living with them and 26 per cent had at least one adult dependent in the home. Two-thirds were full-time employees; among the part-time employees, the average weekly hours worked, 25.6, represented much more than a marginal job. In addition, 15 per cent held another paid job in addition to their HEU work. In short, this was a mature and predominantly female workforce, including many women of colour, whose jobs were very important to them and the other members of their households. . . .

The attachment of HEU members to their jobs and their belief in the difficulty of finding comparable work in another part of the work force were in part founded on HEU's successful track record in raising workers' wages and benefits, including fighting for pay equity. Since the 1970s, HEU has been able to make considerable progress in

achieving pay equity through negotiated contract provisions, arbitrated settlements, complaints to the BC Human Rights Commission, political pressure, and a 1992 strike that won pay equity increases for over 90 per cent of HEU members. . . . This was a union whose leaders took seriously the proclamation in the preamble to its constitution that it is 'the right of those who toil to enjoy to the fullest extent the highest standard of living compatible with life within Canada.' It was also a union that from the late 1960s onwards was pushed by women members and staff to combat gendered inequalities among health care workers (Webb, 1994; *HEU Constitution and Bylaws*, 2002; Cohen and Cohen, 2004).[6]

. . . Difficult bargaining with Social Credit provincial governments during the years of the post-war Long Boom, the disappointment of seeing the Barrett NDP government change the Labour Code in 1975 to remove the newly gained right to strike from health care workers designated 'essential', major hospital strikes in 1976, 1989, and 1992, sometimes bitter strikes against smaller employers, involvement in the 1983 Solidarity movement, and women's activism produced a union that at the close of the century was distinguished by a higher level of militancy and political consciousness than most Canadian unions (Hebb, 1994).[7]

That said, the entire Canadian labour movement has been shaped in important ways by the practice of routinized and tightly regulated collective bargaining and contract administration within the regime of industrial legality instituted in the mid-1940s, and HEU is no exception. Two intimately interconnected effects stand out here. First, the fostering of bureaucracy, understood in Richard Hyman's sense as 'a corrosive pattern of *internal social relations* manifest in a differential distribution of expertise and activism; in a dependence of the mass of union members on the initiative and experience of a relatively small group of leaders—both official *and* "unofficial".' Second, the strengthening of the union officialdom as a social layer within the working-class movement whose existence at the heart of highly state-regulated relations between labour and capital confers on it interests distinct from those of the workers they legally and politically represent. Perhaps the most visible embodiment of these phenomena in HEU is the central role of a full-time hired staffer, the Secretary-Business Manager, who serves as a full member of the (otherwise elected) Provincial Executive [PE], in the style of some British unions. . . .

From Bill 29 to the Strike of 2004

The quick passage of Bill 29 at the end of January 2002—during a special weekend sitting of the legislature called to order striking teachers back to work—came as a shock to everyone in HEU. . . . Shortly thereafter HEU received a leaked cabinet minister's briefing book which revealed that the provincial government's plans for health care cuts included the elimination of 14,000 Full-Time Equivalents [FTEs][8] in the 2003–04 fiscal year and an additional 3,530 the next year. Soon the contracting-out of HEU work began. Women of colour were hit especially hard, as many were employed in the housekeeping, dietary, and laundry jobs targeted for contracting-out.[9]

The enactment of Bill 29 opened up a period that one staffer described as 'devastating' for HEU members; another called it 'stressful to say the least, and . . . a feeling growing . . . that the union was becoming ineffective in a lot of ways. I think that's how Joe member on the floor was feeling, that the employer just started unilaterally doing stuff that they would have never done before Bill 29.'[10] Bolstered by government actions, many employers adopted a hard-line stance around

workplace issues. . . . The 'unrelenting assault' from different health care sector employers, in the context of other attacks from the provincial government, 'created a lot of chaos'.[11]

The winter and spring of 2002 saw the BC Federation of Labour [BCFL] and a number of community coalitions organize large anti-cuts demonstrations in Victoria and Vancouver while smaller protests took place around the province. Activists like those of Vancouver's Prepare the General Strike Committee agitated for a general strike (Cariou, 2002; Harrison, 2002).[12] Within HEU, the PE directed efforts to explain the attacks to members and mobilize them for action. The union ran several public campaigns designed to counter the government's claims about cost savings and media reports which suggested that HEU members facing contracting-out were overpaid and undeserving. . . .

In the spring of 2003, shortly after a well-attended HEU fight-back conference that galvanized members around opposition to privatization and concessions and encouraged them to mobilize their coworkers for action, members were surprised at the announcement of a tentative agreement. 'Where did this come from'? A week and a half ago I thought we were gonna fight to the death' is how a staffer described the reaction of some activists.[13] The manner in which this deal had been reached disturbed some HEU members, accustomed as they were to being kept informed about negotiations. 'These negotiations were clearly backroom,'[14] noted another staffer, and they produced a three-year tentative agreement that capped job losses through contracting-out to 3,500 FTEs and contained $65 million in severance funds. It also made concessions on wages and vacation time and increased the workweek from 36 to 37.5 hours without an increase in pay.[15] . . .

The tentative agreement was rejected by a vote of 57 per cent. Some members voted against the deal because they distrusted the government that had stripped key provisions out of HEU's collective agreement by legislation (and changed the BCNU [BC Nurses' Union] twice in the span of a year) and therefore saw no reason to give concessions in exchange for a cap on the number of jobs to be lost through contracting-out. Others saw the cap as too high. In regions where few jobs had been contracted out, some workers did not truly believe their jobs were threatened. . . . In sum, top HEU officials, relieved to have negotiated some restriction on the contracting-out of jobs (inherently also a limit on the reduction of the union's dues base and therefore protection for HEU's institutional stability), rushed for a ratification vote, only to be stymied by an unexpected level of opposition. . . . With the rejection of the deal, HEU and the other unionized workers in the Health Services and Support Facilities Subsector Bargaining Association [HSSFSBA] were clearly heading for a confrontation with their employers. But the situation soon became even more difficult when it became known in July 2003 that Local I-3567 of the Industrial, Wood and Allied Workers [IWA] had signed 'partnership agreements' with three major multinational service provider corporations that were getting ready to take on the contracted-out work of HEU members. The companies had earlier approached seven other unions, all of which had refused to become involved in such agreements. Only IWA I-3567 had agreed to be the compliant collaborationist partner the companies sought (Cohen and Cohen, 2004).[16]

The highly unusual collective agreements signed by this IWA local gave it voluntary recognition before any of the corporations, Sodhexo, Compass, and Aramark, had even signed contracts with health managers, let alone hired any of the workers the IWA was to represent. Prospective employees—none of whom were to be laid-off HEU members—were required by the employers to sign IWA cards at job fairs before they were officially hired. The provisions of the 'partnership agreements' set wages for the new workforce, mostly women, at levels far below those won by HEU and below what the IWA's traditional membership base of men in the forestry sector enjoyed. . . . By entering into 'what can only be called . . . rat union contract[s]', in the words of Victoria activist Jim Herring (echoed by many other dismayed labour and community activists, including some outspoken IWA members), the IWA leadership 'adopted a strategy of accommodation with the New Era of privatization and low wages' (Herring, 2003) and made itself complicit in the government's and health management's assault on the pay, benefits, and working conditions of women health support workers and their union. It would now be much more difficult for HEU to attempt to organize the people hired to do contracted-out work.[17]

With HEU under attack from employers, backed by the provincial government, and from a local of a major affiliate of the BCFL, efforts continued to negotiate a new agreement to replace the one expiring on 31 March 2004. Management was, however, intransigent and tabled demands for major concessions while the number of HEU members losing their jobs reached into the thousands.[18] Faced with employers whose commitment to large-scale privatization outweighed their interest in labour peace and cooperative labour relations, HEU conducted local and regional strike preparation workshops, incorporated strike preparation into its basic educational courses, mounted a public relations campaign linking the defence of its members' jobs and quality public health care, and tried to put pressure on employers and contractors. There was a small wildcat and occupation at Royal Jubilee Hospital in Victoria in February 2004 by workers about to lose their jobs to contracting-out, followed immediately by a sit-in at Nanaimo Regional Hospital.[19] At the end of February, the PE unanimously adopted a resolution 'That job action would be required to gain employment security and defeat the concessions,' and determined that this would take the form of a two-day province-wide strike 'followed by creative job actions on a regional basis' (*Provincial Executive Bulletin* 130, 2004). The strike vote in March was 89.57 per cent in favour (*Provincial Executive Bulletin* 131, 2004). Efforts were also made to strengthen alliances with other unions and community groups. What remained unclear was the HEU leadership's strategy for *winning* a strike. . . .

Stronger organized ties of solidarity with HEU were built on Vancouver Island than in the metropolis of Vancouver. Important here was Greater Victoria's Communities Solidarity Coalition [CSC]. Formed in January 2002, the CSC united senior citizens, students, and anti-poverty activists with unionists from HEU, CUPE, BCGEU, and others. Like militants in other regions of BC, CSC demanded a general strike to defeat the Liberals and organized local actions, including a Day of Defiance on 7 October 2002 that saw flying squads shut down the University of Victoria, Ministry of Health, and other smaller locations, followed by a snake march and rally. This Day of Defiance took place in spite of the BCFL, which 'wasn't really supporting people getting militant, and . . . in fact . . . tried to squash' it. . . .

Such local activism and HEU's strike preparation did not take place as part of a growing wave of anti-government protest. Despite the resolutions demanding a general strike passed by many union locals and labour councils, the mass demonstrations in BC's two largest cities in 2002 were not followed by an escalation of resistance by BC's official labour leadership. Instead, the BCFL executive pursued a strategy centred around preparing to reelect the NDP in the provincial election fixed by law for 2005. Within this strategy, direct action was to be eschewed and working-class anger

at the cuts toned down lest they damage voter support for the NDP.[20] . . . Nevertheless, one major BCFL affiliate, CUPE-BC, did not place all its eggs in the basket of electoralism. It implemented Local Action Plans for membership mobilization including the possibility of a day of protest work stoppages and 'positive activities for members' originally dubbed 'Democracy Day', soon renamed 'Community Action Day'.[21] It was in this seemingly inauspicious conjuncture that HEU and the rest of the HSSFSBA finally struck. After some debate, at March and April meetings HEU's PE had revised its plan for a two-day provincial strike followed by rotating regional actions. . . . As soon as picket lines went up it was obvious that hospital workers who had endured intense stress and anxiety since the passage of Bill 29 were united and committed to the strike. Workers were so eager to picket that many locals found it difficult to provide enough essential service staff. Many workers picketed more than the 20 hours per week required to receive strike pay; some brought family members with them to the lines. 'It was, I think, just the most amazing support that people had ever seen at HEU.'[22] . . . In some locations, workers who had lost their jobs came out to picket. Most health care workers who belonged to unions not in the HSSFSBA, chiefly BCNU and HSA, and who were not classified as essential, did not cross the picket lines, and many joined them. . . .

As predicted, the BC government soon moved to pass legislation to end the strike. What came as a shock was the severity of the bill introduced on the afternoon of Wednesday, 28 April. Bill 37 ordered an end to the strike, but rather than referring the dispute to binding arbitration it imposed a new collective agreement that cut wages by 11 per cent retroactive to 1 April, incorporated the employers' proposal to increase the work week for regular full-time employees from 36 to 37.5 hours with no increase in pay (amounting to an additional 4 per cent pay cut), contained no protection against contracting-out, and weakened language on filling vacancies and bumping. There could be no doubt as to where the government stood: its support for the lean state project in health care was unmistakable. On the morning of Thursday, 29 April, the bill was proclaimed law. At its meeting soon after the bill's passage, the PE decided to keep HEU picket lines (dubbed 'protest lines' now that the strike was illegal) up, call for other unions and community groups to join them, arrange an emergency meeting with BCFL leaders, ask for May Day rallies to support HEU lines, and develop a political action plan to defeat the provincial Liberals. In contrast, BCGEU and the International Union of Operating Engineers directed their members in the HSSFSBA to return to work. At around the same time BCNU and HSA officials directed their members, who had been respecting HEU's lines, to cross them. The strike had entered a new phase, in contravention of the law.[23] . . .

If most HEU members, trusting in particular in their local leaders, were determined to ignore the odious Bill 37 and continue the struggle into which they had been forced, they were not fighting alone. On their own initiative and at the request of HEU, members of CUPE and other unions began to flock to the picket lines at hospitals and long-term care facilities across BC, in some places intervening to prevent managers from intimidating HEU members. Even some IWA members performing contracted-out work refused to cross HEU lines.[24] The HEU strike became a subject of discussion across the province. . . . Many people who were hostile to the Campbell government for its actions over the previous three years began to see supporting HEU as a meaningful way to channel their opposition to the Liberals. The strike had become 'a lightning rod for people's feelings around Campbell'.[25]

On Friday, 30 April, the working-class power drawn to the strike flashed across BC, casting HEU's battle in a new light. In at least 27 CUPE locals, workers were off the job, in defiance of the hallowed legal prohibition of such solidarity action; many strikers joined HEU lines, and in Vancouver, Victoria, and many smaller centres picket lines went up at municipal government offices, libraries, and other public sector workplaces. Participation was notably strong in school-board locals, where workers had experienced significant cuts. In several Vancouver Island school districts, teachers refused to cross CUPE lines. Acting on requests from BCFMWU members, CSC flying squads caused the cancellation of early morning ferry sailings before both HEU and BCFL leaders, apparently fearful of the consequences of this economic disruption, ordered the pickets to fold. . . . Smaller numbers of members of other unions, including the Communication, Energy and Paperworkers [CEP], BCNU, OPEU, International Brotherhood of Electrical Workers, Pulp and Paper Workers, and IWA, also struck. Together, these stoppages represented the largest solidarity strike in the province since November 1983, when the BC Teachers' Federation [BCTF] had defied the law and the expectations of many onlookers by walking out as part of Operation Solidarity's planned escalation linked to support of the legally striking BCGEU. Unlike the BCTF action, though, the job action of 30 April was mobilized on extremely short notice, was in support of an illegal strike, and was not limited to one union.[26]

It is vital to appreciate the full significance of this collective action in support of HEU. Since the entrenchment of the pluralist regime of industrial legality in the late 1940s, class struggle in Canada has usually played out in the form of tightly regulated sectional economic conflicts that stay within narrow legal and administrative confines. These restrictions have generally been internalized in most unionized workers' understandings of what unions can and should do, and raised to the level of principle in the minds of much of the labour officialdom. On 30 April, thousands of BC workers engaged in action that was completely antithetical to 'responsible' unionism's ossified repertoire of legitimate behaviour in order to support workers, mostly women, who were themselves defying a law widely regarded as cruel and unfair. By so doing, they changed the sense of the possible for themselves and for many other workers who were sympathetically watching HEU's battle with the government. They also altered social-political temporality. The slow and apparently unchangeable pace of life in a stable capitalist society in which the level of social struggle is low and what Marx dubbed 'the dull compulsion of economic relations' weighs heavily on working-class existence can be abruptly sped up by an event which is 'a caesura in temporal uniformity', to use a phrase of the French Marxist theorist Daniel Bensaïd (2002: 88). . . .

It was not long before the self-activity of insurgent workers prompted responses from the provincial government, evidently in some disarray: by early afternoon, Premier Campbell floated the possibility of changes to the settlement imposed by Bill 37 if HEU returned to work, and said on television that HEU members could avoid pay cuts altogether by giving other concessions. . . . In an effort to take advantage of the situation, BC NDP leader Carole James issued an open letter to the premier. Criticizing Bill 37 as 'a blatant attack on working people . . . that can only create further tension and confrontation in an already poisonous labour relations climate,' she called on the government to immediately recall the legislature 'to put an end to the crisis . . . that threatens to further erode investor confidence in British Columbia and destabilize the BC economy.' The blend of liberal pluralist labour relations-speak and business rhetoric in James's letter said much about the ideological orientation of the contemporary BC NDP (*BC NDP Newswire*, 2004).[27]

The front page of Saturday's *Vancouver Sun* reported on a BCFL document that revealed plans for escalating actions in support of HEU. Beginning with a shut-down of the public sector on Monday, 3 May, action would spread to federal and provincial government offices, private sector industry, and transportation, and then later in the week to hotels, cruise ships, and retail stores. . . . Activists handed out over 2,000 'General Strike' flags with ease, and there was 'verbal sparring' between those calling for a general strike and BCFL officials, who led the chant 'We Won't Back Down' to regain control of the rally. Across the province, excited labour and community activists prepared for solidarity actions on Monday on a scale larger than Friday's. Even Vancouver's Compassion Club (medical marijuana society) was preparing to strike (Beatty, 2004).

Meanwhile, behind closed doors, top officials from HEU, CUPE-National, CUPE-BC, the BCFL, and major private sector BCFL affiliates, met again with government representatives. For some labour radicals familiar with the union officialdom's ways, there was reason for concern. Noting the leaked BCFL document and the many BCGEU staff at a May Day rally, one reported, 'I knew by Saturday that we were in serious trouble.'[28] One HEU staffer saw the document as 'just a fake' that no union leadership had agreed to, released to allow top BCFL officials to regain political initiative and leadership of the movement from below for solidarity strikes. Thus 'as everyone else got more and more excited all weekend long, I was getting more and more depressed, knowing how they worked.'[29]

These concerns proved astute. Talks to reach a settlement continued while BC Rail workers struck on Sunday in support of HEU, the BC Supreme Court ruled HEU in contempt of court for not ordering members back to work, and activists continued to prepare for the following day. When a deal came, it was in the form of a memorandum signed by the provincial government, Health

Employers' Association, BCFL, and the HSSFBA. It amounted to a modification of the terms of the contract imposed by Bill 37. . . . Reconvening late in the afternoon for a meeting described by one official as 'excruciating', the HEU PE voted 13–7 to accept the deal, which was announced publicly on Sunday evening.[30] Before the night was out, the NDP issued a statement celebrating the end of the strike. It made no criticism of the wage cuts and job losses ('NDP Welcomes. . .', 2004).

The precise details of how the HEU PE came to vote in favour of the memorandum and which labour leaders were involved are unclear, but the heart of the matter is not. As HEU third Vice-President Dan Hingley (2004) later wrote, 'labour [sic] pressured the HEU leadership, citing the fact that 600 members [sic] diminished the risk of total privatization.' Another PE member specified the source of the pressure as 'officers of the BC Fed', and an HEU staffer referred to what took place as 'intimidation'. After the vote, HEU's fourth Vice-President resigned in protest.[31]

As news of the settlement and directive to return to work spread, reactions were intense among many of the tens of thousands of HEU members who had walked the lines for a week to defend their jobs and public health care. 'People were really, really angry. People had no idea that that was the deal that was being contemplated, people were angry that they didn't get to vote on it, people didn't understand why the plug was pulled at this zenith of support . . . it was just rage,' said a staffer.[32] 'Just huge, huge disappointment,' was how another staffer described the sentiment.[33] Vancouver General Hospital HEU local executive member Doreen Plouffe expressed sentiments shared by many members: 'I don't know how they could even call it a victory for working people. We have been sold out.'[34] Having defied their employers, the government, and the courts, some HEU members and their allies resisted the return to

work. . . . A small number of HEU members picketed HEU offices in Burnaby and Victoria, some calling for the resignation of Secretary-Business Manager Chris Allnut. These were sporadic rear-guard gestures by intransigents. Still, even after they had fizzled out the slogan on the placard of HEU picketer Susan Hibbs captured the feelings of a significant number of strikers: 'HEU Screwed By Our Own Leaders.'[35]

Explaining the Strike and Its Outcome

An analysis of the strike that gripped BC for a week in the spring of 2004 must proceed from an appreciation that this was no accidental conflict or simply the product of a government fired by anti-union animus. Its causes were systemic. The attack on HEU by health sector employers and the provincial government was one specific manifestation of capital's multi-pronged restructuring agenda to build a lean state for the age of lean production. As such, it was not a 'Lotus Land' phenomenon peculiar to one Pacific province. Similar developments have occurred and can be expected to continue to occur in other provinces, as they have internationally.

There were, of course, local specificities at play. The determination and strength of the HEU membership in the face of employer and state power was notable. We can partially account for this by considering who these workers are and their labour market context. Overwhelmingly women, including a large minority of women of colour, and mostly over 45, these were mostly workers who grasped that being laid-off meant being hurled into labour markets structured by systemic sexism and racism in which they would be unlikely to ever find wages, benefits, and working conditions on a par with those they had as members of HEU. 'Theirs were atypical jobs for women wage-earners, especially women of colour, because they conformed to the model of the Standard Employment Relationship enshrined as a norm for white working-class men during the post-war boom but in decline for the past quarter-century. In addition, these workers belonged to a union whose efforts had succeeded over years in winning better wages, working conditions, and benefits. . . . As a result, many members identified strongly with HEU and were ready for collective struggle.

Another singular issue that needs to be accounted for is the depth of support for HEU and the eagerness of significant numbers of BC workers to act in solidarity with them. Both exceeded what has been seen in a number of other major struggles against neoliberal governments in recent years. Support for a general strike in BC appears to have been stronger than it was in Ontario in 1996–7 at the height of the Days of Action mobilizations against the Conservative government of Mike Harris even though the labour left in BC was no better organized than its Ontario counterpart. . . . Possible reasons for this support include submerged but not extinguished traditions of militancy in the BC working class, a linkage of HEU workers with valued public health care in the minds of many, and a gendered sympathy with women health care workers. On a smaller scale, HEU support for community struggles was also a factor.

The most contentious explanatory question is *why* did the strike end as it did? Here several rival answers have already been formulated. One, articulated by top HEU officials and some officers and staff of other unions, contends that the strike ended as the result of a grim political calculation by HEU leaders in an objective situation in which a better settlement simply could not have been achieved. The leaders of most of the affiliates of the BCFL, particularly private sector unions, were not supportive of solidarity strike action beyond 3

May. The provincial government would have likely responded to a rejection of the memorandum by HEU by withdrawing the offer, painting the union as unreasonable in the media, and asking, in a top HEU official's words, 'who's actually running the province, is it the unions or the elected government?'[36] . . . According to former PE member Mike Barker, HEU's top leaders believed that rejecting the deal would have led to 'the full weight of the law' falling on HEU, and 'a crushing defeat' (2004: 3). On the question of union democracy, *Canadian Dimension's* regular labour commentator made explicit what few others did: 'With fines and lawsuits worth hundreds of thousands of dollars piling up daily, it was not practical to continue a strike for several days to take a membership vote' (Bickerton, 2004: 7). In other words, the strike ended as it did because HEU leaders made a wise but difficult decision which, in the given circumstances, was the best one.[37]

An alternative explanation popular among critics of the outcome of the strike emphasizes the politics of the labour officialdom, in particular its commitment to social democratic electoralism. More specifically, it has been argued that the belief of the vast majority of the BC labour officialdom that electing the NDP in 2005 was the only way to defeat the Campbell government produced a fear that mass strikes in support of HEU would allow the Liberals to portray labour as out of control and challenging constitutional authority, thereby damaging the NDP's chances of winning the 2005 provincial election (Cariou, 2004). . . .

Some militants in HEU, while sharing this view, have also advanced another line of explanation that goes beyond a critique of the ideology of top union leaders. They have suggested that the thinking of the union's leadership was shaped by where it was structurally located: the PE was isolated in meeting rooms and out of touch with the rapidly developing situation on the ground. As a result, they misread the level of support for escalating action: 'based on the experience that we're all having out on the line . . . the impetus was coming from the grassroots, it wasn't coming from the union leaders who were in that room saying, "Our members won't support you, we won't keep our members out".'[38] . . . They have also argued that the official labour leadership was frightened by the desire of so many workers to strike in support of HEU: 'It was never their plan to begin with, it was a swelling of the grassroots organizing themselves, so I think that there was a lot of fear that they'd have no control,' said one staffer.[39] . . .

In my view, both the explanation produced from within the labour officialdom itself and that which makes social democratic electoralism the key factor suffer from inadequate understandings of the contemporary Canadian labour officialdom. Both treat it as simply a collection of individuals without considering the conditions of existence and positioning within class relations of officials as a social layer. The thinking of some HEU militants is more probing. Their insights move in the direction of the kind of historical materialist analysis of the US labour officialdom developed by Robert Brenner, which also applies in the Canadian context. In brief, full-time union officials do not share the same conditions as members and are only indirectly affected by attacks on workers' wages and working conditions. The union institution provides officials with their livelihood and also 'constitutes for them a whole way of life—their day to day function, formative social relationships with peers and superiors on the organizational ladder, a potential career, and, on many occasions, a social meaning, a *raison d'être*'. . . . Its social-material existence also sheds light on why, as Mark Leier has suggested, the officialdom believes that workers 'cannot determine their own struggles' and must be managed (Brenner, 1985: 44–51; Leier, 1995: 34).[40]

Similarly, the concerns of top officials about fines and the legal prosecution of HEU appear in a different light when the interests of full-time union officials are not uncritically assumed to be the same as those of members. This kind of theoretical conceptualization also allows us to better understand the role that the belief that escalating solidarity strikes would hurt the NDP's prospects (and that support for the NDP is *the* political strategy for labour) played in informing the actions of key BCFL leaders, because it explains their support for the NDP as not simply an ideological choice but an expression of the distinct interests of the labour officialdom. . . . What this analysis does not directly answer is the challenge of those who argue that the HEU PE majority voted to accept the memorandum and end the strike because to do so was the best possible option in the circumstances. Evaluating this claim requires a broader evaluation of the strike.

Assessing the Strike and Its Implications

. . . Whether one draws the conclusion that the HEU strike was a victory or defeat for workers hinges on two key issues. First, what does the settlement objectively represent? Second, in the actual circumstances of early May 2004, could there have been an outcome more favourable for workers? The question of the settlement is relatively straightforward: a 15 per cent wage cut starting from 1 May rather than 1 April, longer hours of work, and enhanced severance. The cap that limits the loss of FTEs 'as a direct result of contracting out' to 600 over two years is more contentious. Dulmage has pointed out that 'the so-called cap on contracting-out does not include jobs lost to closures, restructuring, or privatization,' only contracting-out narrowly defined (qtd in Camfield, 2004: 6). Major concessions on wages, longer hours, some limitation on the loss of jobs through contracting-out, and severance funds do not amount to a convincing case for calling the strike a victory of any kind. . . .

Could a shut-down of the public sector and at least some strike action in the private sector have won the repeal of Bill 37 and a contract that protected health care workers' jobs against privatization, thereby ensuring that hospital and long-term care support services remained public and dealing an aggressive neoliberal government a stinging political defeat? While there is no way of definitively answering a question about events which did not take place, in my judgment the solidarity strikes that occurred on 30 April, the widespread popular support for HEU, and the willingness of a surprising number of workers to defy the law and strike in solidarity with HEU are sufficient to answer this in the affirmative. On this basis, then, the strike can be judged an avoidable defeat (though not as severe a defeat as it would have been if HEU had gone back to work as soon as Bill 37 was passed), a missed opportunity. The reasons why a strike in which over 40,000 strikers showed such resolve and received remarkable support ended as it did have already been outlined. In light of these, one can conclude that a necessary but missing condition for an outcome more favourable to workers was the existence of self-organized activists within the BC labour movement, or at least in HEU, capable of providing an alternative leadership in a conjuncture that was truly, to use Bensaïd's phrase, 'pregnant with events'. That such an organized presence did not exist is apparent: 'what people have talked about here is that there wasn't strong enough grassroots connections for people to have carried it off doing it in defiance of the leadership . . . connections between workplaces, and between towns and cities.'[41]

To conclude, what are the implications of this analysis of two years of difficult struggle for HEU?

Bills 29 and 37 are further reminders that neoliberal governments are prepared to dispense with the rights to collectively bargain and strike and with provisions in the contracts of public sector workers that hinder the implementation of capital's agenda.[42] Like strikes by nurses and other public sector workers in recent years, HEU's strike of 2004 demonstrates the unity and resolve with which a multiracial and mostly female workforce not traditionally seen as militant can act, given adequate workplace organization and leadership. The level of popular sympathy and active solidarity the strike sparked suggest that, contrary to the counsel of those who believe that public sector strikes are bound to meet with indifference or hostility from other working people, such strikes are capable of serving as effective rallying points for popular resistance to neoliberalism.[43] If the exceptional willingness to strike in support of HEU and in defiance of both labour law and ingrained assumptions in contemporary Canadian unionism reflected particular traditions in the BC working class, its sources are not reducible to this militant inheritance alone. They likely also included the association of health care workers with an eroding medicare system that still enjoys deep popular support and a certain gendered sympathy with women wage-earners, who in the Canadian working class today are increasingly seen to be as entitled to good jobs as men.[44] That HEU's confrontation with employers and the provincial government ultimately ended in defeat is best explained not simply by the politics of labour's official leadership but by the character of the contemporary labour officialdom as a distinct social layer which generally eschews forms of struggle that could threaten union institutions and established bargaining relationships. These analytical conclusions deserve serious consideration by all who are concerned about the future of the Canadian working-class movement.

Notes

1. On the Alberta examples mentioned, see Yonatan Reshef and Sandra Rastin, *Unions in the Time of Revolution: Government Restructuring in Alberta and Ontario* (Toronto: University of Toronto Press, 2003), 10–11, 156–61. On the Saskatchewan nurses, see Larry Haiven, 'Saskatchewan: Social Experimentation, Economic Development and the Test of Time', in Mark Thompson, Joseph B. Rose, and Anthony E. Smith, eds, *Beyond the National Divide: Regional Dimensions of Industrial Relations* (Montreal and Kingston: McGill-Queen's University Press, 2003), 188–9, and Saskatchewan Union of Nurses, 'The Strike of 1999', available at http://www.sun-nurses.sk.ca/about_history/1999_strike.html. On CUPW, see Bryan D. Palmer, *Working-Class Experience: Rethinking the History of Canadian Labour* (Toronto: McClelland and Stewart, 1992), 345, and Leo Panitch and Donald Swartz, *From Consent to Coercion: The Assault on Trade Union Freedoms* (Aurora: Garamond Press, 2003), 167–8. The York University strike of 2001 is assessed in Clarice Kuhling, 'How CUPE 3903 Struck and Won', *Just Labour: A Canadian Journal of Work and Society* 1 (2002): 77–85, available at http://www.yorku.ca/julabour/volume1/jl_kuhling.pdf. Many instances of public sector union quiescence and muted opposition in the face of neoliberalism in the 1990s are visible in Gene Swimmer, ed., *Public Sector Labour Relations in an Era of Restraint and Restructuring* (Don Mills: Oxford University Press, 2001). Two noteworthy studies of public sector strikes are Jerry P. White, *Hospital Strike: Women, Unions and Public Sector Conflict* (Toronto: Thomson Educational Publishing, 1990) and David Rapaport, *No Justice, No Peace: The 1996 OPSEU Strike Against the Harris Government in Ontario* (Montreal and Kingston: McGill-Queen's University Press, 1999).

2. As part of my research I conducted and recorded confidential semi-structured interviews with six key informants in the Hospital Employees Union [HEU] and the Canadian Union of Public Employees [CUPE]. All reference to interviews and correspondents in the endnotes are anonymous, identified by union affiliation and a letter-number code, with members holding union office (whether as stewards, local officials, or officials above the local level) given the suffix O, other members M, and staff S.

3. On lean production and related aspects of contemporary work reorganization and economic restructuring, see Kim Moody, *Workers in a Lean World: Unions in the International Economy* (London and New York: Verso, 1997), 41–113; Tony Smith, *Technology and Capital in the Age of Lean Production: A Marxian Critique of the 'New Economy'* (Albany: SUNY Press, 2000); Isa Bakker, ed., *Rethinking Restructuring: Gender and Change in Canada* (Toronto: University of Toronto Press, 1996); Leah F. Vosko, *Temporary Work: The Gendered Rise of a Precarious Employment Relationship* (Toronto: University of Toronto Press, 2000); Jamie Peck, *Work-Place: The Social Regulation of Labor Markets* (New York and London: Guilford Press, 1996).

4. 'Bill 29 Strips Rights, Paves Way for Closures, Cuts and Privatization', *Backgrounders* 3 (March 2002), available at http://www.heu.org/cgi-bin/pi.cgi?t:../pubs/past_article3_7.html; *2001–2004 Health Services and Support Facilities Collective Agreement between Association of Unions and Health Employers Association of British Columbia*; Mark Thompson and Brian Bemmels, 'British Columbia: The Parties Match the Mountains', in Thompson, Rose, Smith, eds, *Beyond the National Divide*, 108; 'Gordon Campbell Interview: Moving to the Middle', *Guardian* 18 (November–December 2000), available at http://www.heu.org/cgi-bin/pi.cgi?t:../pubs/past_article3_4.html.

5. Similar workers in a few facilities belonged to the BC Government and Service Employees Union [BCGEU]. Many professional employees are represented by the Health Sciences Association of BC [HSA]. Registered Nurses belong to the BC Nurses' Union [BCNU]. Some skilled tradespeople in health care are members of craft unions.

6. Working-class women's labour activism in the 1970s is surveyed in Meg Luxton, 'Feminism as a Class Act: Working-Class Feminism and the Women's Movement in Canada', *Labour/Le Travail* 48 (2001): 63–88.

7. HEU educational material included the IWW's 'How to Sack Your Boss: A Workers' Guide to Direct Action' and [Jody Hartmann], 'Some Examples of Direct Action in BC and HEU History' (n.d.). On postwar BC labour, see Thompson and Bemmels, 'British Columbia' and Bryan D. Palmer, *Solidarity: The Rise and Fall of an Opposition in British Columbia* (Vancouver: New Star Books, 1987).

8. Because a significant minority of HEU members are part-time employees, the actual number of workers who lose their jobs is greater than the number of FTEs cut, by approximately 50 per cent.

9. Interview with HEU O-3; *Draft Briefing Material for Minister of Health Services*, 16 February 2002; 'Women and Workers of Colour Hit Hardest By

Sellout' [Interview with Gretchen Dulmage], *New Socialist* 47 (May–June 2004): 27–8.

10. Interview with HEU S-1; Interview with HEU S-2.

11. Interview with HEU S-1.

12. In his pamphlet *Labour, the NDP, and Our Communities* (Victoria, 2003), Victoria activist Jim Herring pointedly describes the large demonstrations in Victoria (23 February) and Vancouver (25 May) as 'characterized mainly by . . . controlled, non-participation . . . and a slavish obedience to the demands of police and municipal authorities' (9–10).

13. Interview with HEU S-1.

14. Interview with HEU S-2.

15. 'Key Elements in the Framework Agreement Union Members Will Vote on Between April 28 and May 15', *Backgrounders* 4 (April 2003), available at http://www.heu.org/cgi-bin/pi.cgi?t:../pubs/past_article3_10.html.

16. See also Gary Steeves, Affidavit, 2 May 2002; Transcript of telephone conversation recorded 1 May 2002 between Jaynie Clark, Coordinator, Advocacy, BCGEU and Luciano Anjos, Management Consultant; Transcript of telephone conversation recorded 1 May 2002 between Gary Steeves, Director, Organizing and Field Services, BCGEU and Spencer Green, Regional Operations Director, Sodexho.

17. Pressure from members on the CUPE leadership led to CUPE pushing the CLC to appoint an umpire, who found that IWA I-3567's actions did indeed violate the CLC constitution. However, the local ignored a CLC executive council directive to sign no more voluntary recognition deals. Initial sanctions to the IWA were applied in March 2004. Beginning in May 2004, rulings by the BC Labour Relations Board began to remove IWA certifications on the grounds that the 'partnership agreements' had not been properly ratified and that a majority of workers had not freely chosen to be represented by the IWA, clearing the way for HEU efforts to organize workers hired by the contractors. The first ruling was B173/2004, 20 May 2004, Aramark Canada Facility Services Ltd. And Hospital Employees' Union and Industrial Wood and Allied Workers of Canada [IWA Canada], CLC, Local Union, Local No. I-3567.

18. The number of HEU members (full-time, part-time, and casual employees) who had lost their jobs through contracting-out in acute care and long-term care was estimated in early August 2004 as 7,917. Email from HEU S-3 to author, 9 August 2004.

19. Interview with HEU O-3; Bob Wilson, 'British Columbia Hospital Workers Stage Wildcat Strike Over Impending Job Losses', *Labor Notes*, 301 (April 2004), 6.

20. Herring, *Labour, the NDP, and Our Communities*, reports that BCFL President Jim Sinclair's presentation to the January 2003 meeting of the All Islands Coalition in Nanaimo 'amazed some activists with its utter disregard for the effects the cuts are having on people and infuriated many with the condescending, categorical imperative that was its main theme: there is no other option than waiting it out until we can re-elect the NDP' (9) and that Sinclair recommended that a planned day of action instead became 'a "celebration" of having survived two years of Liberal rule' (9), to the dismay of coalition members.

21. Interview with CUPE O-1; *CUPE BC Workplan* (September 2003); *CUPE Community Action Day Draft Speaking Notes* (22 March 2004). One CUPE activist described CUPE-BC's day of action plan as 'throwing a bone to the militant elements in CUPE' who had been demanding a general strike for two years (Interview with CUPE M-1).

22. Interview with HEU S-1.

23. See Bill 37—2004, Health Sector (Facilities Subsector) Collective Agreement Act; [HEU] *Provincial Executive Bulletin* 134, 1; 'Government Proclaims Back to Work Law', *CBC British Columbia*, 29 April 2004, available at http://vancouver.cbc.ca/regional/servlet/View?filename=bc_law20040429 (29 April 2004); Interview with HEU S-2.

24. Interview with HEU O-3.

25. Interview with HEU S-1.

26. Interview with CUPE O-1; Interview with HEU O-3; Fred Muzin, Speech to CUPE Ontario Divisional Convention, 29 May 2004 (tape recording); 'Protest Walkouts Spread', *CBC British Columbia*, 30 April 2004, available at http://vancouver.cbc.ca/regional/servlet/View?filename=bc_protest20040430 (1 May 2004); 'Nurses Walk Out in Several Communities', *CBC British Columbia*, 30 April 2004, available at http://vancouver.cbc.ca/regional/servlet/View?filename=bc_protest20040430 (1 May 2004); Norman Gidney, 'Labour Crisis Deepens', *Times Columnist* (Victoria), 1 May 2004, A1; William Boei and Jeff Lee, 'HEU Defies Board, Continues Strike With New Public Service Allies', *Vancouver Sun*, 1 May 2004: A1; E-mail from anonymous [a CUPE BC official or staffer], 'Re: Friday Protest Action updated 10:10 a.m.', 30 April 2004; Palmer, *Solidarity*, 65–8. The BC Labour Relations Board officially declared the HEU strike illegal on Friday morning.

27. As this NDP statement reports, NDP MLAs had attempted to amend (not block) Bill 37.

28. Interview with CUPE M-1.

29. Interview with HEU S-2.

30. Interview with HEU O-3; [HEU] *Provincial Executive Bulletin* 135, 1.
31. E-mail from HEU O-4 to author; Interview with HEU S-1.
32. Interview with HEU S-1.
33. Interview with HEU S-2.
34. Plouffe is quoted in 'Some Hospital Workers Remain Defiant', *CBC British Columbia*, 3 May 2004, available at http://vancouver.cbc.ca/regional/servlet/View?filename=bc_heu20040503.
35. Interview with CUPE M-1; Cindy E. Harnett, Doug Ward, and Frances Bula, 'Health Workers Feel "Sold Out" By Their Union Leaders', *Vancouver Sun*, 4 May 2004: A1; Jack Knox, 'Deal Leaves Picketers Angry, Fate of Mass Protest in Doubt', *Times Columnist* (Victoria), 3 May 2004: A1. A photograph of Hibbs appeared on the front page of the Vancouver edition of the *Globe and Mail*, 4 May 2004.
36. Interview with HEU O-3.
37. According to HEU S-1, in the aftermath of the strike top HEU leaders actively argued for this explanation within the union: 'there's a lot of effort being made to sell people on what the right version of history is here.'
38. Interview with HEU O-1.
39. Interview with HEU S-1.
40. Leier does not claim that *every* official shares this view, but that this belief is a characteristic feature of the outlook common to this social layer.
41. Interview with HEU S-1. My conclusion about HEU's struggle is similar to Palmer's conclusion about the solidarity movement in BC in 1983: a different outcome would have required at least 'serious organized opposition within the ranks that it [the top leadership] necessarily had to pay some attention to' (*Solidarity*, 89).
42. Thus they are but two more additions to the long list of similar pieces of legislation chronicled in Panitch and Swartz, *From Consent to Coercion*.
43. This is consistent with the international experience that public sector unions have been at the forefront of resistance to neoliberalism, as Moody points out in *Workers in a Lean World*, 272–3.
44. This is suggested by such studies as Meg Luxton and June Corman, *Getting By in Hard Times: Gendered Labour at Home and on the Job* (Toronto: University of Toronto Press, 2001), but this research also shows that working-class women continue to face many barriers to participation and equality in paid work.

References

Armstrong, Pat, and Hugh Armstrong. 2003. *Wasting Away: The Undermining of Canadian Health Care*. Don Mills, ON: Oxford University Press.

Barker, Mike. 2004. 'The HEU Strike: What Did We Gain, Could More Have Been Won?' Vancouver: n.p.

BC NDP Newswire. 2004. 'James Calls on Premier to Recall the Legislature to Resolve Crisis', 30 April.

Beatty, Jim. 2004. 'Union Document Reveals Plan for More Disruption', *Vancouver Sun*, 1 May: A1.

Bensaïd, Daniel. 2002. *Marx for Our Times: Adventures and Misadventures of a Critique*. London and New York: Verso.

Bickerton, Geoff. 2004. 'Public Sector Struggles Continue', *Canadian Dimension* 38 (May–June).

Brenner, Robert. 1985. 'The Paradox of Social Democracy: The American Case', in Mike Davis, Fred Pfeil, and Michael Sprinker, eds, *The Year Left: An American Socialist Yearbook*. London and New York: Verso.

Camfield, David. 2004. 'British Columbia Union Leaders Call Off Province-Wide Strike: Workers Unhappy with Settlement', *Labor Notes* 303 (June 2004): 6.

Cariou, Kimball. 2002. 'BC's Fightback', *Canadian Dimension* 36 (March–April 2002).

———. 2004. 'What Happened to British Columbia?', *Canadian Dimension* 38 (July–August): 8–9.

Cohen, Marjorie Griffin, and Marcy Cohen. 2004. *A Return to Wage Discrimination: Pay Equity Losses Through the Privatization of Health Care*. Vancouver: Canadian Centre for Policy Alternatives.

Duménil, Gérard, and Dominique Lévy. 2004. *Capital Resurgent: Roots of the Neoliberal Revolution*. Cambridge, MA and London: Harvard University Press.

Fuller, Sylvia, Colleen Fuller, and Marcy Cohen. 2003. *Health Care Restructuring in BC*. Vancouver: UBC Press.

Harrison, Donna. 2002. 'BC's Protracted Class War', *Canadian Dimension* 36 (July–August).

Herring, Jim. 2003. *Labour, the NDP, and Our Communities*. Victoria.

Hingley, Dan. 2004. 'An Explanation From One HEU Negotiator Dan Hingley', 25 May. Available at http://www.generalstrikenews.ca/Articles/2004-MAY-12_AN_EXPLANATION_FROM_.stm.

Jessop, Bob. 1994. 'Post-Fordism and the State', in Ash Amin, ed., *Post-Fordism: A Reader*. Oxford and Cambridge, MA: Blackwell.

Leier, Mark. 1995. *Red Flags and Red Tape: The Making of a Labour Bureaucracy*. Toronto: University of Toronto Press.

McBride, Stephen, and John Shields. 1997. *Dismantling a Nation: The Transition to Corporate Rule in Canada*. Halifax: Fernwood.

'NDP Welcomes Resolution of Crisis'. 2004. *News Detail*, 2 May. Available at http://nid-625.newsdetail.bc.ndp.ca.

Nolan, Brendan. 2001. 'Conclusion: Themes and Future Directions for Public Sector Reform', in Brendan C. Nolan, ed., *Public Sector Reform: An International Perspective*. Basingstoke and New York: Macmillan.

Provincial Executive Bulletin [HEU] 130. 2004. Meetings of 22–25 February and 4 March.

Provincial Executive Bulletin [HEU] 131. 2004. Meeting of 27 March 2004.

Sears, Alan. 1999. 'The "Lean" State and Capitalist Restructuring: Towards a Theoretical Account', *Studies in Political Economy* 59: 91–114.

Shields, John, and B. Mitchell Evans. 1998. *Shrinking the State: Globalization and Public Administration 'Reform'*. Halifax: Fernwood.

Smith, Murray E.G. 2000. 'Political Economy and the Canadian Working Class: Marxism or Nationalist Reformism?', *Labour/Le Travail* 46: 343–68.

Teeple, Gary. 2000. *Globalization and the Decline of Social Reform: Into the Twenty-First Century*. Toronto: Garamond Press.

The Report of the Commission on the Future of Health Care in Canada (The Romanow Commission): A Summary and Assessment. 2002. Ottawa: Public Works and Government Services.

Webb, Patricia G. 1994. *The Heart of Health Care: The Story of the Hospital Employees' Union*. Vancouver: Hospital Employee's Union.

CHAPTER 28

Race, Class, Gender, and the Making of Difference: The Social Organization of 'Migrant Workers'[1] in Canada

Nandita Rani Sharma

Introduction

Over the last two decades or so, as the current period of globalization has shifted social relations within the North and between the North and the South, renewed attention has been given to the fight for 'citizens' rights' by feminists concerned about the dismantling of 'their' Northern welfare states (Hagen and Jenson, 1988; Bakker, 1996; Brodie, 1996a, 1996b). We need, however, to recognize and account for the fact that the establishment of welfare states was largely a Northern development, a feature of restructured global relations of the ongoing privileging of Northern peoples following World War Two. Yet since this time, and before, the establishment of citizens' rights and entitlements has resulted in simultaneous *dis*-entitlement

for women and men identified as non-citizens. This development has been particularly harmful to women of colour attempting to enter and reside as permanent residents in Northern countries. In this paper, I investigate the contemporary meaning of Canadian citizenship and question the usefulness of using 'citizenship rights' as the banner under which feminists fight for women's equality.

A key part of my argument is that the exclusions organized by the concepts of 'citizenship' and citizens' rights are not merely a coincidence, nor can they be remedied by trying to expand the groups of people recognized as citizens. Rather, the notion of 'citizen' needs to be understood as the dominant, oppressive half of a binary code of negative dualities. The construction and reproduction of the category Canadian citizen thus activates the category of 'non-citizen.' The Self as the 'insider' and the 'foreigner' as Other/'outsider' that the nation-state system and nationalist practices organize brings about a particular material reality as well as a particular ideological understanding of our relationships with people. The existence of national borders, then, shapes both the organization of social relations and people's consciousness of our world.

In this accounting of the practices of citizenship, the citizen-Self has been intentionally created (and re-produced) in privileged relation to the Other. In Canada, it has been Indigenous women and women of colour who have been relegated as the archetypal Other through dominant beliefs about the legitimacy of national borders and national state practices concerning citizenship. This understanding clarifies that notions of citizenship are not a philosophical absolute. They are the mark of a particular kind of unequal relationship. Borders define not only spatial but ideological ground. Nationalized boundaries affect people's legal, political, and social position as well as the process of identity-formation.

I argue that instead of accepting the socially organized category of citizen, an examination of how 'citizenship' helps to legitimize the domination of those who are socially, as well as legally (although the two do not always neatly coincide), classified as non-citizens is necessary. This project involves an account of the ways in which nationalist discourses work as ideological practices within processes of globalization to organize differences between citizens and non-citizens inside the boundaries organized by (and for) the Self. This exercise should lead to an uncovering of the ideological and material processes that make some people—and not Others—'Canadian'.

During the last two decades, a growing number of people have crossed into Canadian territory,

but most of them have been denied permanent resident status and been classified instead as temporary, migrant workers. Those so classified are, arguably, the quintessential non-citizens within Canadian society. Understanding the daily processes by which groups become racialized and gendered through placement in differential state categories can help us to identify the demarcation of social spaces that separate people in Canada into discrete, hierarchically-organized groups. For this reason, I place the Canadian state's category of 'non-immigrants' (or the more popularly used term: 'migrant workers') at the centre of my inquiry.

To date, scholars have focused on select groups of people recruited as migrant workers (see Bakan and Stasiulis, 1996, on women domestic workers; and Wall, 1992, on farm workers). Here, I will focus on how the category itself has been socially organized. To understand the development of the category of migrant workers, I examine the ways in which the ideological practices of citizenship organize government actions that many 'Canadians' regard as perfectly legitimate. That is, instead of examining the daily lived experiences of groups of migrant workers in Canada, I examine how existing social relations in Canada help to organize the very normalcy of the category.

An investigation into ideological practices, it is argued, helps us to make good (as opposed to 'common') sense of the contrast between the growing number of restrictions placed by the state upon people entering Canada in search of a livelihood and the greater mobility rights of 'national treatment' (that is, citizenship) that the state has given to the capital of investors. I argue that these two developments are not at all contradictory but are integrally related. The existence of highly differentiated labour markets organized through the nation-state system continues to serve capitalists well in this period of restructuring.

Citizenship and (Im)migration in Canada: The Social Organization of Migrant Workers

The discourse on citizenship and immigration policy refracts issues of racialized, gendered, and nationalized inclusions/exclusions and their relationship to entitlements/dis-entitlements within Canadian society. This is because regulations governing the movement of people into Canada, as well as the legislation on citizenship, have historically shaped both the territorial boundaries of the Canadian nation and people's consciousness about 'being Canadian'. Consequently, the discourse on (im)migration has been one of the paramount arenas through which questions about the 'nation' have continued to surface and be challenged.

A key part of the contemporary process of Canadian 'nation'-building[2] is the state's active participation in this discourse and its espousing of the rhetoric of 'protecting Our borders', especially from 'Third World' women and men who, since the late 1960s, have often been represented as a major threat to Canadians. The exclusionary discursive practices of 'Canadian-ness' are of particular importance to the organization of the Canadian labour market, as is graphically displayed by the experiences of those categorized as migrant workers. They are made to work in unfree employment relationships as a condition of entering, residing, and working in Canada.

People so categorized enter through Canada's Non-Immigrant Employment Authorization Program (NIEAP) established in 1973. The Canadian system for migrant workers reveals different elements of nationalist projects that render some people as non-citizens. Stipulations regarding the criteria for entering under the NIEAP include an identified employer, location of employment, type of employment, condition of employment, and length of employment pre-arranged and stated on the person's temporary employment authorization prior to arrival in Canada. Once in the country, the affected person is bound to 'work at a specific job for a specific period of time for a specific employer' (Citizenship and Immigration Canada [CIC], 1994). Migrant workers cannot change any of their conditions of entry or employment without written permission from an immigration officer. If they leave the stipulated employer or change occupations without this approval they are subject to deportation.

The NIEAP operates as a forced *rotational* system of employment. People admitted through this program cannot exceed the length of time (maximum one year) stated in their temporary work visa. They are, however, able to renew their work visa if the *employer* agrees. Yet, even for those whose visas are renewed, a migrant worker's status in Canada is considered to be permanently 'temporary'. People so classified are not eligible to remain as permanent residents. Different people are brought in to work, removed, and replaced by Others. In this sense, migrant workers are caught in a 'revolving door of exploitation' (Ramirez, 1982).

Importantly, the government's increasing use of the NIEAP has resulted in a substantial repositioning of the balance between immigrant and 'non-immigrant' people recruited to work in Canada. For instance, in 1973, 57 per cent of all people classified as workers entering Canada arrived as 'landed immigrants' with permanent resident status—the first necessary step in becoming a Canadian citizen (Sharma, 1995). By 1993, however, of the total number of workers admitted to Canada, only 30 per cent received this status while 70 per cent came in under the NIEAP as migrant workers on temporary employment authorizations (Sharma, 1995).

I maintain that it was not sheer coincidence that the NIEAP was introduced amidst a highly racialized discourse about the changing 'character' of the

Canadian 'nation'. Such a discourse was centred on the fact that since 1967, people of colour from the South were for the first time able to enter Canada as permanent residents. Nor was it a coincidence that the NIEAP was introduced at a time when major re-alignments were underway within global capitalism. Following the pattern of 'guest worker' programs elsewhere, the Canadian government has successfully shifted its immigration policy away from one of permanent (im)migrant settlement towards a policy that increasingly relies on unfree, temporary labour.

The labour market into which migrant workers are inserted in Canada is highly racialized and gendered. The ideological processes of constructing 'race' and gender within Canada are most evident in the types of work that differentiated groups of migrant workers perform in Canada. Approximately 75 per cent of all people entering through the NIEAP are employed in non-professional employment, mostly in service sector jobs such as retail and clerical work and manufacturing (especially low skilled garment industry jobs), and primary sector jobs (especially farm workers). A comparatively small number of people employed in professional occupations are admitted under the NIEAP. Many of these professionals help to manage and administer the operations of corporations (CIC, 1995).[3]

Significantly, almost 90 per cent of professionals admitted under the NIEAP, especially managers and administrators, are from other capitalist countries in the North—mainly from the US or Japan—where the vast majority of transnational corporations remain headquartered (CIC, 1995). Overwhelmingly, most are men. On the other hand, 92 per cent of all people coming from the less economically advanced capitalist countries in the South work within non-'professional' occupations.

Through the NIEAP, the Canadian state is also able to reproduce and further entrench a gendered division of labour in Canada. The majority of women entering through the NIEAP are employed within non-professional occupations. Women remain segregated in the service sector (where 89 per cent of the workers are women), particularly in personal service jobs such as live-in domestic, child-care, or elder-care work (95 per cent), and clerical work (65 per cent) (Employment and Immigration Canada [EIC], 1992). For those jobs that 'Canadian' citizens find the least attractive, a racialized and gendered process articulates with notions of who 'naturally' should carry out this work. Thus, we find that the vast majority (70 per cent) of live-in domestic workers entering as migrant workers are women of colour from Asia and the Caribbean (Cornish, 1992).

Migrant workers are expressly recruited to serve the Canadian labour market, but permanent resident and citizenship status is formally denied them. They comprise a significant part of Canadian society but are simultaneously constructed as being outside of that society. Governmental practices categorize them as being part of a *foreign* labour force. The dual construction of a 'domestic' and a 'foreign' labour market within the space occupied by 'Canada' is accomplished through the category migrant worker. By controlling the scale, structure, and course of labour migration into Canada, the Canadian government has helped to create a highly 'flexible' (that is, precarious) labour force. What allows migrant workers to be used as a 'cheap' and largely unprotected labour power are not any inherent qualities of the people so categorized but, rather, state regulations that render them powerless.

Because they have been categorized as 'non-immigrants,' people entering as migrant workers do not possess many of the social or political rights that come with Canadian citizenship. For instance, migrant workers cannot stay in the country unless they work for a pre-specified employer, and they do not have access to the wide array of social programs and services associated with the 'entitlements' of citizenship in the Northern welfare-states. In effect, they work as unfree labour in the Canadian labour market; they are denied access to the social welfare programs and services that would provide them with an alternative to selling their labour power. Migrant workers are thus unable to decommodify themselves. Furthermore, they are denied basic political rights (voting) and so cannot hope to make changes in Canada's political system. At the same time, these workers are placed in a highly vulnerable situation that makes it difficult for them to speak out for themselves. That the employer or state officials have the power to find the worker 'unsuitable' and thereby subject to deportation severely limits what migrant workers are able or willing to say and do.

The NIEAP has allowed the government to continue to enjoy the support of employers demanding relatively unrestricted access to a supply of cheapened workers while also making migrant workers virtually invisible to those Canadians calling for the state to 'protect Our borders' and decrease immigration, especially from the 'Third World'. The migrant worker category also operates so as to enhance the Canadian government's capacity to attract and/or retain capital investment in 'its' territory by permitting employers in the country (whether 'domestic' or 'foreign' capitalists) to carry out a 'cheap labour strategy' of global competition.

Indeed, during the current period of capitalist restructuring, the Canadian government has been deeply concerned with both material and ideological processes of 'nation'-building. A major emphasis has been to enact policies to increase capital investment. Note, for instance, the following excerpt from the throne speech of Pierre Elliott Trudeau's Liberal government, delivered only a few days after the introduction of NIEAP.

It laid down the following: 'The Government will introduce legislation establishing a competition policy to preserve and strengthen the market system upon which our economy is based. The new policy will be in harmony with industrial policies in general and foreign investment policy in particular' (*Hansard*, 4 January 1973: 5).

The migrant workers recruitment program reflects the government's stated desire to 'strengthen the market system' in Canada and its willingness to (re)organize the labour market in Canada in order to attract 'foreign' investment. . . .

In response to the heightened mobility of capital, the Canadian government has fundamentally reshaped the working class in Canada through the migrant workers recruitment program. With the NIEAP, the Canadian government has produced a group of non-citizens who are largely exempted from laws that guarantee minimum employment standards, collective bargaining, and the provision of social services and programs such as unemployment insurance, social assistance, old-age pensions. This, in turn, cheapens and weakens the position of these workers. Citizenship, then, has become an important 'tool' in re-organizing the labour market in Canada to the benefit of capital investors.

The exploitation of migrant workers is concealed and reproduced through the notion that citizens can expect certain rights and entitlements that non-citizens cannot and that this expectation is 'normal'. As a result, it appears perfectly ordinary, or 'natural', that those categorized as non-citizens would be denied the same protections and rights to which 'Canadian citizens' are 'entitled'. Why should migrant workers get the same rights as citizens? They are, after all, migrant workers. This circular argument ensnares migrant workers in a particularly vicious way. In a world where capital is increasingly being granted 'national treatment' (that is, citizenship) rights, the denial of exactly this status to people who are categorized as migrant workers suggests how modern notions of 'citizenship' are derived from the ideological structure of a nation-state system in which ruling interests enjoy considerable power and influence.

The Sovereignty Story: The Project of Canadian 'Nation'-building

There is little attention paid to questioning the social organization of national states or to concepts of citizenship and how these serve to facilitate the very inequalities which capital investors find so profitable in this latest period of globalization (Bakker, 1996; Brodie, 1996a, 1996b). By leaving the concept of citizenship unchallenged, we are left instead with the notion that citizens, *and not people*, are being threatened by the forces of globalization, and that in order to achieve social justice, we must fight for a re-invigorated citizenship (Brodie, 1996a).

Such a view ignores the fact that 'nations' and, therefore, its citizens, are very much configured through struggles over the means of production and reproduction over time (including, but not exclusively, competition over particular pieces of land) and shaped by the convergence of various historical realities. 'Nations' are far from natural beings; they are materially and ideologically organized collectivities of people who exist in a particular time and space. They are very much 'imagined communities' (Anderson, 1991). The imagining of nations is understood to be a distinct and historically enduring 'style' of community formation, closely associated with the rise and proliferation of white, patriarchal, capitalist social relations. . . .

Notwithstanding the liberal rhetoric that claims equality between 'sovereign nations', the organization of national boundaries, both literally and figuratively, has historically been part of the process of (re)producing asymmetrical global social relations of 'race', gender, and class. The coherence of the nation-state system has, in fact, relied greatly upon the 'sovereignty story'. This story is based on the notion that there exists within nation-states a coincidence of identity, territory, and authority (Pettman, 1997). In the crafting of this story, people working within the apparatus of the nation-state (in Canada: parliamentarians, immigration and customs officials, and the security forces, for example) are seen to be legitimate in acting as gate-keepers to the entry of people into the state's territory as well as controlling membership criteria for belonging to the 'Canadian nation'. . . .

Significantly, the fight for citizens' rights is also seen to be occurring within the supposedly Self-contained space of the nation-state rather than being part of a global system of inequalities. This allows for the notion that those people without much in the way of rights are victims of their own 'weak' states, rather than a global system of asymmetrical social relations. There is little room left for the recognition that certain rights and entitlements have been gained by (some) people in the North *as a result of* global relations of power and dominance controlled by Northern states as well as the concerns for legitimacy by capitalists who largely remain headquartered there. Such notions operate as ideological practices for they conceal the global relations of white, capitalist patriarchy that organize North/South inequalities and that shape *who* has the ability to realize their rights and entitlements within the world (and within the North itself). It obscures from view the fact that contemporary notions, particularly of citizen and non-citizen, substantially reproduce the colonizer/colonized binary code.

The status of migrant workers is maintained, in part, through the practices shaped by the discourses on citizenship and the rights of citizens. Such notions have been codified within Canadian law, including in the Charter of Rights and Freedoms, which explicitly excludes non-citizens from the rights of mobility enjoyed by citizens (for example, the right *not* to be told where and who to work for). Such legislation exploits the existence of massive inequalities within the world capitalist system while taking advantage of the fact that nation-states are still seen as legitimately controlling 'their own' borders *vis à vis* 'foreigners'. This, in turn, positions migrant workers in particular ways within the social relations of production and reproduction in the country (and in the world market for labour power).

'Difference' and the Making of Canada

It is the social organization of 'difference' in Canada and continued adherence to the notion that *only* citizens have any legitimate claims for entitlements within the nation-state system that has helped to cheapen and weaken the labour power of those rendered non-citizen-Others. Throughout the initial project of Canadian 'nation'-building, the Other has existed not only outside the borders of the state (that is, in anOther nation). Rather, many people, including the original inhabitants, *within* Canada have been rendered as Other. The space that 'Canada' has historically occupied is not only territorial but also ideological. As a result, part of the ongoing nation-building project of 'Canada' has been the ideological construction of notions of Canadian-ness that rely on racist, sexist, and nationalist ideological criteria of 'belonging'. . . .

Through the continuing process of constructing differences between women and men who are white settlers, Aboriginal, and people of colour, the racialized and gendered meanings of 'being Canadian' has been concretized. Explicit reference to Aboriginal people and those from outside Northwestern Europe, especially people of colour

from the 'Third World', as the Other has secured the ideological construction of 'Canada' as a 'white settler colony' and an extension of the English and French nations (Abele and Stasiulis, 1989). . . .

The articulation of racism with the ideologies of sexism and nationalism has profoundly shaped the material realities of these women. Women rendered as the Other are seen as embodying the very differences between nations. Seen as belonging to Other nations, Indigenous women and other women of colour in Canada, for instance, have historically been portrayed as part of the process of establishing the permanent presence of the Other and therefore particularly disruptive of the 'character' of the Canadian nation (Thobani, 1998). Through the negative racializing of their gendered position, these women are made vulnerable to greater degrees of exploitation and they experience a consequent cheapening of their labour power and curtailment of any real alternatives to entering the waged labour market. Furthermore, difference has been sutured into the very (white) skin of the Canadian nation, but this 'difference' has been anything but a 'natural' process. Rather, differences have been explicitly organized and structured within Canadian society in order to privilege those recognized as Canadians within the relations shaped by global capitalism.

Those recognized as Canadians have been seen to be *entitled to* certain things ('good' jobs, political power, capital, etc.) that Others have not. This sense of special entitlement has been 'naturalized' through a harking back to the imagined community of the Canadian 'nation', when, it is argued, 'community' is responsible only for its own members—and not for Others who are expected to rely on 'their own people' as ideologically embodied in their 'weak' states. As a result, the ideological practices organized through binary concepts of gender, 'race', and nation have become synonymous with 'being Canadian' for many and a

Canadian identity has been continuously (re)imagined in opposition to those racialized, gendered, and classed as the Other (Miles, 1993: 102).

The existence of racialized and gendered relations of production is not simply an aberration from the 'normal' way of doing things in Canada. The introduction and increasing popularity of the NIEAP suggests otherwise. Employers benefit enormously from how this migrant workers' program organizes 'difference' within the world and within Canadian labour markets. The NIEAP, and the exclusionary practices of citizenship that are operationalized through it are an integral connecting piece between the material reality of global capitalism and the ideological configuration of 'Canadian-ness.'

Conclusion

By categorizing people as migrant workers, rather than citizens (or permanent residents), the Canadian government is able to force certain people to work within unfree employment relations as a condition of their entry, residence, and work in Canada. People categorized as migrant workers are often cheaper for employers to hire and less able to resist employers' demands not because of any inherent characteristics they are said to possess, but because their very categorization as migrant workers by the Canadian state offers them little recourse to being heavily exploited. The creation and daily reproduction of inequalities within the global capitalist system ensures a continuous source of people who seek to work in Canada under such restrictive conditions. The social underpinning of this strategy to provide 'cheap labour' to employers is greatly obscured, however, because ideological concepts—those that work to conceal the *social* organization of our relationships, such as 'race,' gender, or citizenship—are mystified through the ideological practices of racism, sexism, and

nationalism that help to naturalize structures of domination. The labour market in which migrant workers are inserted in Canada is highly racialized and gendered.

It is in the renewed attention to notions of 'Canadian-ness' evident since the 1970s that I locate the legitimacy given to the introduction of a migrant workers' program. As in earlier periods of Canadian nation-state building, there has been a profound articulation between the (re)organization of capitalist social relations and the ideological imaginings of Canadian-ness. Yet, it is crucial that we recognize that the existence, indeed the growing pervasiveness, of a discourse of Canadian-ness, of 'protecting Our borders', of 'protecting Canadians', has *not* resulted in a lessened mobility of people or a lessening of (im)migration to Canada. Globally, the number of people migrating has doubled in the last decade (United Nations, 1993). (Im)migration to Canada has actually increased during the last ten years. However, most people recruited to work in the country now enter as unfree, indentured 'migrant labour' rather than as permanent residents.

Thus, the discourse on Canadian-ness has not served to curtail migration, but rather, it has operated as an *ideological practice of differentiation* that has served to legitimize the denial of citizenship status to people migrating in search of work. The result is a further cheapened and weakened labour force that capital investors in search of profits can exploit. In this way, citizenship can be said to function as an 'architect of social inequality' (Fraser and Gordon, 1992: 49). How useful, then, is the concept of citizenship in feminist struggles for justice? Simply put, my answer is that it is not useful at all. Rather, it is extremely harmful to women in general and Indigenous women and women of colour in particular. The narrative of nation-as-community from which the concept of citizenship borrows hides from view the fact that the very construction of some people as citizens makes possible the creation of Others as non-citizens who are excluded from the 'imagined community' of the 'nation'. While this exclusion is not always a physical one, it nonetheless renders non-citizens highly vulnerable within the same society in which citizens enjoy certain rights. Indeed, my examination of the NIEAP shows that Canadian state practices have used their legitimized ability to construct differential categories of (im)migrants to socially organize 'difference' within Canadian society and within the labour market in particular.

A continued struggle to defend the rights of citizens at a time when capital has become increasingly transnational in its operations will not lead to a profound transformation in the global capitalist system. Instead it will serve to heighten and intensify existing unequal social relations between and within people living in separated nation-states along global fissures of North and South. . . .

An important challenge to this system is the demand for two related conditions of self-determination. First, people must have the power to 'stay'. That is, people must have the power to prevent their displacement. Currently, the overwhelming majority of those who are forced to become international (im)migrants have had to leave due to war, poverty, economic restructuring focused on trade liberalization and world disparities in income, and various opportunities that make some places more 'attractive' than others. But without the power to challenge such conditions, people's ability to 'stay' is meaningless.

Secondly, people must have the power to ensure that they are able to 'move'. Free and autonomous movement is necessary to ensure that local sites do not become holding cells for people who can be exploited because they are denied the option of leaving. We must also challenge the power of extra-local sites that are able to discriminate against people who are denied membership in these communities. Citizenship rights do not allow for the free, autonomous, and self-determinant movement of people. Instead, the current national state system is designed precisely to limit the mobility of people across nationalized borders. Finally, a call for *people's* sovereignty and not 'national sovereignty' requires a complete questioning and reworking of existing ruling relations. To achieve the related demands of staying and moving we have to accept the possibility of radical transformation of our relationships to each other and the planet. We cannot timidly accept changes that only reform the game of domination.

Notes

1. In this paper, readers should note that 'migrant workers' is a value loaded term and readers should assume quotation marks around them.
2. An example of a recent call for the Canadian government to 'protect Our border' can be found in a November, 1999 Angus Reid Group survey which said that for 60 per cent of those surveyed, the number one priority for Canadian immigration policy should be to stop 'illegal immigrants' (*Globe and Mail*, 22 November 1999: A5). It should be noted that such calls have been commonplace since the arrival of 599 refugee claimants from the Fujian province in China. These refugees have often been labelled as 'illegal immigrants' and held up as an example of the vulnerability of Canadian borders.
3. The bringing in of people to manage and administer the operations of corporations is one of the effects of the NIEAP. While this is a highly important aspect of the study of the NIEAP, I concentrate here on examining the effects of the NIEAP in producing the cheapened and weakened workforce within the Canadian labour market.

References

Abele, F., and D. Stasiulis. 1989. 'Canada as a "White Settler Colony": What about Indigenous and Immigrants?', in W. Clement and G. Williams, eds, *The New Canadian Political Economy*. Montreal and Kingston: McGill-Queen's University Press.

Anderson, Benedict. 1991. *Imagined Communities*. London: Verso.

Bakan, Abigail B., and Daiva K. Stasiulis. 1996. 'Structural Adjustment, Citizenship, and Foreign Domestic Labour: The Canadian Case', in I. Bakker, ed., *Rethinking Restructuring: Gender and Change in Canada*. Toronto: University of Toronto Press.

Bakker, Isabella. 1996. *Rethinking Restructuring: Gender and Change in Canada*. Toronto: University of Toronto Press.

Brodie, Janine, ed. 1996a. *Women and Canadian Public Policy*. Toronto: Harcourt Brace and Co.

———. 1996b. 'Restructuring and the New Citizenship', in I. Bakker, ed., *Rethinking Restructuring: Gender and Change in Canada*. Toronto: University of Toronto Press.

Citizenship and Immigration Canada (CIC). 1994. *Hiring Foreign Workers: Facts For Canadian Employers*. Ottawa: Minister of Supply and Services, 1994.

———. 1995. Unclassified information provided on request by the Electronic Information Management Office. Hull. Quebec.

Cornish, Cynthia D. 1992. 'Unfree Wage Labour, Women and the State: Employment Visas and Foreign Domestic Workers in Canada'. MA thesis, University of Victoria.

Employment and Immigration Canada (EIC). 1992. *1991 Immigration Statistics—Canada*. Ottawa: Minister of Supply and Services.

Fraser, Nancy, and Linda Gordon. 1992. 'Contract Versus Charity: Why is There No Social Citizenship in the United States?', *Socialist Review* 22, 3.

Hagen, Elisabeth, and Jane Jenson. 1988. 'Paradoxes and Promises: Work and Politics in the Postwar Years', in J. Jenseon, E. Hagen, and C. Reddy, eds, *Feminization of the Labour Force: Paradoxes and Promises*. Cambridge: Polity Press.

Hansard. 1973. House of Commons Debates. Official Report. First Session—Twenty Ninth Parliament, vol. V, 1973 (June 11 to July 18). Ottawa: Queen's Printer for Canada, Ottawa.

Miles, Robert. 1993. *Racism After 'Race Relations'*. London and NY: Routledge.

Pettman, Jan Jindy. 1997. 'Transcending National Identity: The Global Political Economy of Gender and Class'. Paper presented at the International Studies Association Conference, Toronto, March.

Ramirez, J. 1982. 'Domestic Workers Organize!', *Canadian Woman Studies* 4, 2.

Sharma, Nandita. 1995. 'The True North Strong and Unfree: Capitalist Restructuring and Non-Immigrant Employment in Canada, 1973–1993'. MA thesis, Simon Fraser University, Burnaby, BC.

———. 1996. 'Cheap Myths and Bonded Lives: Freedom and Citizenship in Canadian Society', *Beyond Law* 5, 17.

Smith, Dorothy. 1990. *The Conceptual Practices of Power: A Feminist Sociology of Knowledge*. Toronto: University of Toronto Press.

———. 1995. 'About Botanizing'. Handout. Graduate Seminar: The Social Organization of Knowledge, Ontario Institute for Studies in Education, September.

Thobani, Sunera. 1998. 'Nationalizing Citizens, Bordering Immigrant Women: Globalization and the Racialization of Women's Citizenship in Late 20th Century Canada'. PhD dissertation, Simon Fraser University, Burnaby, BC.

United Nations. 1993. *The State of World Population*. New York: United Nations Population Fund.

Wall, Ellen. 1992. 'Personal Labour Relations and Ethnicity in Ontario Agriculture', in V. Satzewich, ed., *Deconstructing a Nation: Immigration, Multiculturalism and Racism in '90s Canada*. Halifax: Fernwood Publishing.

Acknowledgements

Sedef Arat-Koç, 'From "Mothers of the Nation" to Migrant Workers', in Abigail Bakan and Daiva K. Stasiulis, eds, *Not One of the Family: Foreign Domestic Workers in Canada* (Toronto: University of Toronto Press, 1997), 53–80. Reprinted by permission of the publisher.

Denyse Baillargeon, 'Working for Pay and Managing the Household Finances', in Denyse Baillargeon, *Making Do: Women, Family, and Home in Montreal During the Great Depression* (Waterloo: Wilfrid Laurier University Press, 1999), 113–140. Reprinted by permission of the publisher.

Ruth Bleasdale, 'Class Conflict on the Canals of Upper Canada in the 1840s', *Labour/Le Travailleur* 7 (Spring 1981): 9–39. Reprinted by permission of the publisher.

Bettina Bradbury, 'Gender at Work at Home: Family Decisions, the Labour Market, and Girls' Contributions to the Family Economy', in Gregory S. Kealey and Greg Patmore, eds, *Canadian and Australian Labour History: Towards a Comparative Perspective* (St John's, Newfoundland: CCLH Publications, 1990), 119–139. Reprinted by permission of the publisher.

Christina Burr, '"The Other Side": The Rhetoric of Labour Reform', in Christina Burr, *Spreading the Light: Work and Labour Reform in Late Nineteenth-Century Toronto* (Toronto: University of Toronto Press, 1999), 14–31. Reprinted by permission of the publisher.

David Camfield, 'Neoliberalism and Working-Class Resistance in British Columbia: The Hospital Employees' Union Struggle, 2002–2004', *Labour/Le Travail* 57 (Spring 2006): 9–41. Reprinted by permission of the publisher.

Robert A. Campbell, 'Managing the Marginal: Regulating and Negotiating Decency in Vancouver's Beer Parlours, 1925–1954', *Labour/Le Travail* 44 (Fall 1999): 109–27. Reprinted by permission of the publisher.

Magdalena Fahrni, 'Parents, Pupils, and the Montreal Teachers' Strike of 1949', in Magdalena Fahrni, *Household Politics: Montreal Families and Postwar Reconstruction* (Toronto: University of Toronto Press, 2005), 133–43. Reprinted by permission of the publisher.

Alvin Finkel, 'Trade Unions and the Welfare State in Canada, 1945–1990', in Cy Gonick, Paul Phillips, and Jesse Vorst, eds, *Labour Gains, Labour Pains: Fifty Years of PC 1003* (Winnipeg: Society for Socialist Studies, 1995), 59–75. Copyright Society for Socialist Studies (Canada).

Ralph P. Güntzel, '"Rapprocher les lieux du pouvoir": The Québec Labour Movement and Québec Sovereigntism, 1960–2000', *Labour/Le Travail* 46 (Fall 2000): 369–95. Reprinted by permission of the publisher.

Craig Heron, 'The Workers' Revolt, 1917–1925', in Craig Heron, ed., 'National Contours: Solidarity and Fragmentation', *The Workers' Revolt in Canada, 1917–1925* (Toronto: University of Toronto Press, 1998), 268–304. Reprinted by permission of the publisher.

Bonnie Huskins, 'From *Haute Cuisine* to Ox Roasts: Public Feasting and the Negotiation of Class in Mid-Nineteenth-Century Saint John and Halifax', *Labour/Le Travail* 37 (Spring 1996): 9–36. Reprinted by permission of the publisher.

Gregory S. Kealey and Bryan D. Palmer, 'The Bonds of Unity: The Knights of Labor in Ontario, 1880–1900', *Histoire Sociale/Social History* 28 (November 1981): 369–412. Reprinted by permission of the publisher.

Mark Leier, 'Monopoly Capitalism' and 'Rallying Round the Standard in British Columbia', in Mark Leier, *Where the Fraser River Flows: The Industrial Workers of the World in British Columbia* (Vancouver: New Star Books, 1990), 1–5, 33–56. Reprinted by permission of the publisher.

John Lutz, 'After the Fur Trade: The Aboriginal Labouring Class of British Columbia, 1849–1890', *Journal of the Canadian Historical Association*, New Series 3 (1992): 69–94. Reprinted by permission of the publisher.

Peter S. McInnis, 'Teamwork for Harmony: Labour–Management Production Committees and the Post-War Settlement in Canada', *Canadian Historical Review* 77 (September 1996): 317–52. Reprinted by permission of University of Toronto Press Incorporated (www.utpjournals. com).

John Manley, '"Starve, Be Damned!": Communists and Canada's Urban Unemployed, 1929–1939', *Canadian Historical Review* 79 (September 1998): 466–91. Reprinted by permission of University of Toronto Press Incorporated (www.utpjournals.com).

Sarah-Jane (Saje) Mathieu, 'North of the Colour Line: Sleeping Car Porters and the Battle Against Jim Crow on Canadian Rails, 1880–1920', *Labour/Le Travail* 47 (Spring 2001): 9–41. Reprinted by permission of the publisher.

Janice Newton, 'The Plight of the Working Girl', in Janice Newton, *The Feminist Challenge to the Canadian Left, 1900–1918* (Montreal and Kingston: McGill-Queen's University Press, 1995): 78–109. Reprinted by permission of the publisher.

Bryan D. Palmer, 'Wildcat Workers in the 1960s: The Unruly Face of Class Struggle'. Reprinted by permission of the author.

Leo Panitch and Donald Swartz, 'Towards Permanent Exceptionalism: Coercion and Consent in Canadian Industrial Relations', *Labour/Le Travail* 13 (Spring 1984): 133–57. Reprinted by permission of the publisher.

Andrew Parnaby, '"The best men that ever worked the lumber": Aboriginal Longshoremen on Burrard Inlet, BC, 1863–1939', *Canadian Historical Review* 87 (March 2006): 53–78. Reprinted by permission of University of Toronto Press Incorporated (www.utpjournals. com).

Carmela Patrias, 'Race, Employment Discrimination, and State Complicity in Wartime Canada, 1939–1945', *Labour/Le Travail* 59 (Spring 2007): 9–42. Reprinted by permission of the publisher.

Carolyn Podruchny, 'Unfair Masters and Rascally Servants? Relations Among Bourgeois, Clerks, and Voyageurs in the Montreal Fur Trade, 1780–1821', *Labour/Le Travail* 43 (Spring 1999): 43–70. Reprinted by permission of the publisher.

Becki L. Ross, 'Bumping and Grinding on the Line: Making Nudity Pay', *Labour/Le Travail* 46 (Fall 2000): 221–50. Reprinted by permission of the publisher.

Joan Sangster, 'The Softball Solution: Female Workers, Male Managers, and the Operation of Paternalism at Westclox, 1923–1960', *Labour/Le Travail* 32 (Fall 1993): 167–99. Reprinted by permission of the publisher.

Nandita Rani Sharma, 'Race, Class, Gender, and the Making of Difference: The Social Organization of "Migrant Workers" in Canada', *Atlantis* 24 (Spring 2000): 5–15. Reprinted by permission of the publisher (www.msvu/ca/atlantis).

Pamela Sugiman, 'Becoming "Union-Wise", 1950–1963', in Pamela Sugiman, *Labour's Dilemma: The Gender Politics of Auto Workers in Canada, 1937–1979* (Toronto: University of Toronto Press, 1994), 98–136. Reprinted by permission of the publisher.